*A child-centered, literature based approach to literacy for preschool, kindergarten and first grade teachers and parents.*

WITHDRAWN

## Marjorie R. Nelsen

The author received her B.A. degree in Elementary Education from Wheaton College, Illinois, with post graduate work in Early Childhood. For nineteen years, Marjorie has been a primary teacher with thirteen years in the kindergarten classroom. She has taught Parent-Child Seminars for ten years. In 1987, Marjorie Nelsen was chosen Teacher of the Year for Seminole County, Florida, representing 2400 teachers. That same year she received a National Christa McAuliffe Fellowship for Educators to pilot and direct an early childhood parent education program that resulted in Partners in Learning, Inc. Marjorie is a third generation kindergarten teacher and the mother of four children.

## Jan L. Nelsen

Co-author, Jan Nelsen, is a Whole Language kindergarten teacher and a National Early Childhood Consultant for The Wright Group. Jan received her B.A. degree in Elementary Education from Wheaton College, Illinois, and a M.Ed. in Early Childhood from the University of Central Florida. Jan, a fourth generation kindergarten teacher, is a national speaker and trainer in Whole Language for primary educators.

## Nadine M. LaLonde • Graphic Design and Illustration

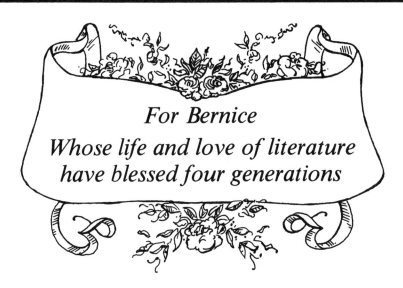

*For Bernice*
*Whose life and love of literature*
*have blessed four generations*

Contributing author, **Mary M. Cornelius**, received a B.S. degree in Early Childhood and Elementary Education from Florida Southern College. Mary has shared her love of books with her three sons, in kindergarten classrooms, and in preschool storytimes *extraordinaire*. Six of Mary's original finger plays appear in **Peak With Books.**

Contributing author, **Nancy S. Rolfs**, received her B.A. degree in Elementary Education from the University of Miami and her M.Ed. in Early Childhood Administration from The University of Cincinnati. Nancy, the mother of two, has been a whole language preschool teacher and administrator for eight years.

State and National Music Clinician, **Artie Almeida**, is a public school music teacher and an Adjunct Music Instructor at the University of Central Florida. Artie's focus on integrating music and classroom curriculum led to the music selections in **Peak With Books.**

## Acknowledgments

Grateful acknowledgment is made to the following for permission to reprint copyrighted material.

Adaptation of THE NAPPING HOUSE and feltboard activity from THE NAPPING HOUSE, Copyright © 1984 by Audrey Wood, by permission of Harcourt Brace Jovanovich, Inc. Adaptation of AND RAIN MAKES APPLESAUCE. Copyright © 1964 by Julian Scheer, with permission of Holiday House Publishers. *Gingerbread Boy* bulletin board by Barbara Gratsch, Broward County Public Schools.

"But I Wonder" and "Moonstruck" by Aileen Fisher from OUT IN THE DARK AND DAYLIGHT POEMS by Aileen Fisher. Copy right © 1980 by Aileen Fisher. Reprinted by permission of the author. "A House" by Charlotte Zolotow. Printed in SIDE BY SIDE by Lee Bennett Hopkins. Used by permission of the author who controls all rights. "Moon Boat" from ALL ASLEEP by Charlotte Pomerantz. Copyright © 1984 by Charlotte Pomerantz. Reprinted by permission of the author. "Pretending" by Bobbi Katz from UPSIDE DOWN AND INSIDE OUT: POEMS FOR ALL YOUR POCKETS by Bobbi Katz. Copyright © 1973 by Bobbi Katz. Used by permission of the author who controls all rights. "Two Sad" by William Cole. Copyright © 1977. Used by permission of the author who controls all rights. "Hide-and-Seek Shadow" from FARTHER THAN FAR by Margaret Hillert. Copyright © 1969 by Margaret Hillert. Used by permission of the author who controls all rights. "Brother" from HELLO AND GOOD-BY by Mary Ann Hoberman. Little, Brown and Co. Copyright © 1959, renewed 1987 by Mary Ann Hoberman. Reprinted by permission of the Gina Maccoby Literary Agency. "A Modern Dragon" and "When You Talk to A Monkey" by Rowena Bennett printed in READ ALOUD RHYMES FOR THE VERY YOUNG by Jack Prelutsky. Reprinted by permission of Plays, Inc. "Baby Bird" reprinted from WEE SING by Pamela Conn Beall and Susan Hagen Nipp. Copyright © 1977, 1979. By permission of Price Stern Sloan, Inc. "Yellow" from ONE AT A TIME by David McCord. Copyright © 1974 by David McCord. By permission of Little, Brown and Co. "Mice" from FIFTY-ONE NEW NURSERY RHYMES by Rose Fyleman. Copyright 1931, 1932 by Doubleday, a division of Bantam, Doubleday, Dell Publishing Group, Inc. By permission of Doubleday, a division of Bantam Doubleday Dell Publishing Group, Inc. "Munching Peaches" by Lee Bennett Hopkins from SIDE BY SIDE POEMS TO READ TOGETHER. Copyright © 1984 by Lee Bennett Hopkins. By permission of Curtis Brown, Ltd. "Jump or Jiggle" by Evelyn Beyer from ANOTHER HERE AND NOW STORYBOOK by Lucy Sprague Mitchell. Copyright © 1937 by E. P. Dutton, Inc. renewed 1965 by Lucy Sprague Mitchell. By permission of E.P. Dutton, Inc./Penguin USA. "The Nothing-Doings" from THE NEW KID ON THE BLOCK by Jack Prelutsky. Copyright © 1984 Jack Prelutsky. By permission of Greenwillow Books. "Something is There" by Lilian Moore from the book SPOOKY RHYMES AND RIDDLES. Copyright © 1972 by Lilian Moore. By permission of Scholastic Inc. "Sally and Manda" by Alice B. Campbell from CHILD LIFE Magazine, Copyright © 1934, 1962 by Rand McNally & Co. By permission of Rand McNally & Co. "So Many Monkeys" from OPEN THE DOOR by Marion Edey. Ills. by Dorothy Grider. NY: Charles Scribner's Sons, 1949. By permission of Charles Scribner's Sons. "Sun After Rain" from SMALL WONDERS by Norma Farber, is reprinted by permission of Coward, McCann & Geoghegan. Copyright © 1964, 1968, 1969 by Norma Farber. "Ducks in the Rain" from CRICKETY CRICKET THE BEST-LOVED POEMS OF JAMES S. TIPPETT. Copyright © 1973 by Martha K. Tippett. "Peter and Wendy" from BREAD AN' JAM by Wymond Garthwaite. Copyright © 1928 by Harper & Row, renewed 1956 by Merle M. Garthwaite. "Tommy" from BRONZEVILLE BOYS AND GIRLS by Gwendolyn Brooks. Copyright © 1956 by Gwendolyn Brooks Blakely. "A Frog and a Flea" from HALLOWEEN HECATE AND OTHER RHYMES TO SKIP TO by Cynthia Mitchell. Copyright© 1978 by Cynthia Mitchell. All printed by permission of Harper & Row Publishers Inc. "Wanted" by Rose Fyleman. Reprinted by permission of The Society of Authors, literary representative of the Estate of Rose Fyleman. "Night Comes" from A BUNCH OF POEMS AND VERSES by Beatrice Schenk deRegniers. Copyright © 1977 by Beatrice Schenk deRegniers. By permission of Marian Reiner for the author. "In the Rain" from A POSY OF LITTLE VERSES by Rene Cloke. By permission of The Hamlyn Publishing Group Ltd. "On Our Way" from CATCH A LITTLE RHYME by Eve Merriam. Copyright © 1966 by Eve Merriam. "It Fell in the City" from BLACKBERRY INK by Eve Merriam. Copyright © 1985 by Eve Merriam. Both reprinted by permission of Marian Reiner for the author. "The Mare" from PILLICOCK HILL by Herbert Asquith published by Macmillan. Copyright © 1926. By permission of William Heinemann Ltd.

References: *Florida Reading Quarterly*, March 1991, "Going in Circles," Sherry Crum, *Your Baby and Child*, Penelope Leach, 1990, Knopf, p. 427.

Partners In Learning, Inc. • 1417 Noble Street • Longwood, Florida 32750

ISBN 0-9630495-1-8

# Table of Contents

# A Theme Centered Approach

**ANIMAL HABITATS**
Brown Bear, Brown Bear, What
    Do You See?
Have You Seen My Duckling?
Make Way for Ducklings
Very Hungry Caterpillar, The

**BEAR HUGS**
Ask Mr. Bear
Bedtime for Frances
Blueberries for Sal
Brown Bear, Brown Bear, What Do
    You See?
Each Peach Pear Plum
Little Mouse, the Red Ripe Strawberry
    and the Big Hungry Bear, The

**BUGS**
Grouchy Ladybug, The
Have You Seen My Duckling?
Very Hungry Caterpillar, The

**CAPS AND HATS**
Caps for Sale
Whistle for Willie
Who Took the Farmer's Hat?

**CHICKS, DUCKS AND BUNNIES**
Good Morning, Chick
Have You Seen My Duckling?
Make Way for Ducklings
Mr. Rabbit and the Lovely Present
Rosie's Walk
Runaway Bunny, The
Tale of Peter Rabbit, The

**CIRCLE STORIES**
Chicka Chicka Boom Boom
Grouchy Ladybug, The
If You Give A Mouse A Cookie
Rosie's Walk
Runaway Bunny, The
Skip to My Lou
Where the Wild Things Are

**DAYTIME AND NIGHTTIME**
Bedtime for Frances
Freight Train
Goodnight Moon
Grouchy Ladybug, The
Napping House, The
Noah's Ark
Peter Spier's Rain
Snowy Day, The
Ten, Nine, Eight
Where the Wild Things Are

**FAMILY AND FRIENDS**
Ask Mr. Bear
Bedtime for Frances
Blueberries for Sal
Good Morning, Chick
May I Bring A Friend?
Mr. Rabbit and the Lovely Present
Peter's Chair
Runaway Bunny, The
Tale of Peter Rabbit, The
Ten, Nine, Eight
Whistle for Willie

**FARMYARD**
Good Morning, Chick
Little Red Hen, The
Rosie's Walk
Skip to My Lou
Who Took the Farmer's Hat?

**FOLKLORE AND FAIRY TALES**
Gingerbread Boy, The
Little Red Hen, The
Oh, A-Hunting We Will Go
Skip to My Lou
Three Billy Goats Gruff, The

**GIVING AND SHARING**
Ask Mr. Bear
If You Give A Mouse A Cookie
Little Mouse, the Red Ripe Strawberry,
    and the Big Hungry Bear, The
Mr. Rabbit and the Lovely Present
Peter's Chair

**MANNERS**
Grouchy Ladybug, The
If You Give A Mouse A Cookie
Little Red Hen, The
May I Bring A Friend?
Mr. Rabbit and the Lovely Present
Where the Wild Things Are

**PUDDLES, PONDS AND OCEANS**
Have You Seen My Duckling?
Make Way for Ducklings
Noah's Ark
Peter Spier's Rain
Three Billy Goats Gruff, The

**TIME**
Bedtime for Frances
Caps for Sale
Grouchy Ladybug, The
May I Bring A Friend?
Skip to My Lou
Very Hungry Caterpillar
Where the Wild Things Are

**WALKING**
Ask Mr. Bear
Blueberries for Sal
Brown Bear, Brown Bear, What Do
    You See?
Caps for Sale
Mr. Rabbit and the Lovely Present
On Market Street
Peter Spier's Rain
Rosie's Walk
Snowy Day, The
Three Billy Goats Gruff, The

**WIND AND WEATHER**
Bedtime for Frances
Napping House, The
Noah's Ark
Peter Spier's Rain
Snowy Day, The
Who Took the Farmer's Hat?

# Introduction

Dr. Burton L. White, author of *The First Three Years* and one of America's leading child development experts, maintains that for more than half a century psychologists focused on "sick" people and wondered, "What went wrong in their lives?" It is only recently that we've begun to focus on "well" individuals and wonder, "What went right?"

The same thing could be said for child development. For years, Dr. White notes, we studied children who behaved in a way that set them apart from their peers, children who were slower, less curious, less coordinated, and less prepared for school experiences. What went wrong, we wondered. But recently, experts like Dr. White have begun to focus on "well" children, to study their early childhood years to find out "what went right" in those formative years. And with that knowledge in hand, the next step would be to help unknowing parents put those "right" things into the lives of all children and not just some.

In numerous studies, certain things quickly became evident in the lives of children who achieved early school success with ease. These were children who had frequent conversations with adults. That is, they were talked to AND listened to. Their opinions and feelings were solicited in conversations with their care givers.

These successful children were the ones whose experiential background included more than just watching television adventures. Instead, they had their OWN adventures—bus rides, car trips, planes, visits to the zoo, museum, post office, fire station, and library. Through all of these experiences, language flowed between child and parent as the child built understanding with the blocks of experience.

Some of the most dramatic results were seen in studies of children whose parents or care givers read to them on a regular basis. Indeed, when the national Commission on Reading issued its 1985 report, Becoming a Nation of Readers, reading aloud to children was singled out as the single most important activity to insure future classroom success for the child.

In light of that finding, Marge Nelsen, a nationally acclaimed educator, has provided parents and teachers with a simple, hands-on guide to the experience of reading to young children. In **Peak With Books**, Marge and her co-author, Jan Nelsen, outline three dozen of the best books for reading aloud and provide follow-up activities that clarify or expand the child's understanding of the story.

It is these activities that separate this book from others in the market place. The authors' parent and classroom experiences convinced them of one thing above all others: The prime purpose of becoming a reader is to ENJOY reading. With that in mind, their activities avoid the drill and skill approach some would impose on youngsters. The questions, conversations, and activities are failure free and fun-filled.

Here are the simple, easy-to-do things that every parent or teacher can share with children to make a child's entry into the world of the formal classroom not only stress-free but a time of joy as well. Imagine the difference it makes when a child sits down to the learning table with all the tools a student needs: words for questions and answers, curiosity, attention span, confidence, and background knowledge. That difference, quite simply, is what **Peak With Books** is all about.

—Jim Trelease    author    *The New Read-Aloud Handbook*

## ☙ About the Format ❧

To **Peak With Books** simply means to reach the *highest point attainable* in emergent literacy through the warmth and friendship of books. Each of the thirty-six lessons is a self-contained literature-based lesson with its own distinct emphasis and appeal. Within each lesson, the interdisciplinary learning activities have been carefully planned for emergent readers and writers. From preschooler to first grader, you will find a progression of appropriate activities in every lesson.

## ☙ About the Style ❧

In our many years of teaching, we confess to a little resentment towards guides that told us what to say to children. That is not our intention in **Peak With Books**. Of course you will use your own words, ideas and style of teaching because you know your children better than anyone. The purpose of the chatty, conversational style is to keep us all focused on our mutual objective, teaching children through the excitement and pleasure of shared stories and shared love.

## ☙ About the Illustrations ❧

We can hear you now. "My children don't draw like that!" We know, and so does our talented graphic artist who is the mother of a kindergartener. We wanted you to smile and enjoy the charming illustrations of the ideas in the text as you motivate your children to be creative. You know the adage . . . a picture is worth a thousand words, or is it ten thousand?

## ☙ About the Music ❧

Children love music! The songs suggested in this book are thematic *springboards* into learning. They are lively, singable, participatory, and often humorous. Self-expression and body movement create a marvelous mood for positive learning. Don't plan your day without a happy song, or two, or three!

## ☙ About the Poetry ❧

Children will always love the rhythm and repetition, the silliness and seriousness of poetry. The language of poetry invites children into the endless learning of attentive listening. When poems become familiar, children create their own word pictures and illustrations. We took great pleasure in finding both humorous and beautiful poems we could *marry* to the themes of the lessons.

## ☙ About Parent Involvement ❧

No guide to early childhood learning is complete without family involvement. Because home and school must work together, the last page of every lesson offers creative suggestions for nurturing parenting and for literature-based, everyday learning activities. This page is a resource for classroom activities as well. (A parenting component for parents of preschool and kindergarten children is available in blackline reproducible form.)

## About Involvement/Interaction

The first reading of a story is intended to capture a child's attention and allow him to be immersed in the text and the illustrations. The interactive involvement that follows is a crucial link between input, the story's content, and output, the *meaning-making* process of comprehension. The numerous choral reading and dramatization activities will help children make sense out of what they hear and read before skills and vocabulary are emphasized.

## About Reproductions & Retellings

The reproductions of stories in the form of art, drama and music allow children to make the language come to life as they interact with the original text. In a retelling, the teacher takes dictation as the children retell the story's main idea and sequence of events in their own words.

## About Innovations & Caption Books*

Innovations follow reproductions. In an innovation, children create a new text by using the predictable, rhythmic pattern of a story. They may change the words, the characters, or the setting as they introduce new vocabulary in meaningful context. A caption book is an innovation with a repeated caption on each page. Blackline reproducibles of the patterned writing are available for each activity marked with an asterisk.*

## About Attribution

When your children innovate a story or poem, *always* give credit to the original work on the cover or the title page of their adaptation.

## About a Print-Rich Environment

Children learn to read by reading. Surround children with their own words written down . . . their class books, wall murals, journals, and language experience charts. Add print to your art activities and bulletin boards. Fill every learning center with independent reading activities. Create a poetry center, a pocket chart center, a listening center, an ABC Center, a story sequencing center, a theme library, a nonfiction library, art, writing, math, and science centers filled with literacy props, a read-the-room center with backscratchers and feathers and paint sticks as pointers. Surrounding children with print is a key to motivating readers. A literacy-rich environment offers repeated reading successes.

## About the Writing Process

Emergent Writing is a term that describes a child's developmental process in learning to write just as he learned to talk, through explorations and approximations. The *process*, not the product, is paramount, as the young child writes from his own experience without correction or constraint. Journals offer children the opportunity to give meaning to what they have heard as they record their thoughts and insights. Process writing is an invaluable part of a child's independent learning.

# Reinforcing Skills

| | Colors/Shapes | Number Concepts, Graphing | Time/Size | Rhyming Words | Perceptual Motor | Visual Discrimination | Recognizing Letters and Sounds | Language Development | Recognizing Parts of a Book | Story Participation | Story Comprehension | Sequencing | Memory | Classifying | Feelings and Emotions | Family Relationships |
|---|---|---|---|---|---|---|---|---|---|---|---|---|---|---|---|---|
| Ask Mr. Bear | | | | | • | | | • | | • | • | • | | • | • | • |
| Bedtime for Frances | | | • | | | • | • | • | • | • | • | | | | • | • |
| Blueberries for Sal | | • | | | • | | | • | | • | • | | | • | | • |
| Brown Bear, Brown Bear | • | | | | • | | | • | | • | • | | • | | | |
| Caps for Sale | • | • | | | • | • | • | • | | • | • | | | • | • | |
| Chicka Chicka Boom Boom | | | | • | | • | • | • | | • | • | • | | | | |
| Each Peach Pear Plum | | • | | • | • | • | | • | • | • | • | • | • | • | | |
| Freight Train | • | • | | | • | • | • | • | | • | • | • | • | • | | |
| Gingerbread Boy, The | | | | • | | | | • | | • | • | • | | | • | |
| Good Morning Chick | • | | • | | • | • | | • | | • | • | • | • | | | • |
| Goodnight Moon | • | • | • | • | | • | | • | | | • | | • | | • | • |
| Grouchy Ladybug, The | • | • | • | | | | | • | • | • | • | | | • | • | |
| Have You Seen My Duckling? | | • | | | • | • | | • | • | • | • | | | | • | • |
| If You Give A Mouse A Cookie | • | • | • | | | • | | | • | • | • | • | | • | | |
| Little Mouse, The Red Ripe Strawberry and the Big Hungry Bear | | • | • | | | • | | • | | • | • | | • | • | | |
| Little Red Hen, The | | | | | • | | | • | | • | • | • | • | | | |
| Make Way for Ducklings | | • | | • | • | • | • | • | | • | • | • | | | | |
| May I Bring A Friend? | | | • | • | | | | • | | • | • | | | • | • | |
| Mr. Rabbit and the Lovely Present | • | | | | | | | • | | • | • | | • | • | • | • |
| Napping House, The | | | • | | | • | | • | | • | • | • | | | | |
| Noah's Ark | | • | | | | • | • | | | | | | | • | | |
| Oh, A-Hunting We Will Go | | • | | • | • | • | | • | • | • | • | | • | • | | |
| On Market Street | • | • | | | | • | • | • | | • | • | | • | • | | • |
| Peter Spier's Rain | • | | • | | | • | | • | • | • | • | • | • | • | | • |
| Peter's Chair | • | | • | | | | | • | • | • | • | | | | • | • |
| Rosie's Walk | | | | | • | • | | • | • | • | • | • | | • | | |
| Runaway Bunny, The | • | | | | | • | | • | | • | • | | • | | | |
| Skip to My Lou | • | | • | • | • | • | | | | • | • | | | | | |
| Snowy Day, The | • | • | | | | | | • | | • | • | • | | • | • | |
| Tale of Peter Rabbit, The | | | | | | | • | • | • | • | • | | • | | • | • |
| Ten, Nine, Eight | | • | | • | | | | • | | • | • | • | • | • | • | • |
| Three Billy Goats Gruff, The | | • | • | | • | | | • | | • | • | • | | • | • | • |
| Very Hungry Caterpillar, The | • | • | • | | | | | • | | • | • | • | | • | • | • |
| Where the Wild Things Are | | • | | | | | | • | | • | • | • | | | • | • |
| Whistle for Willie | | | | • | • | | | • | | • | • | | | | • | • |
| Who Took the Farmer's Hat? | • | • | | | • | • | | • | | • | • | | | • | | |

# Ask Mr. Bear

## by Marjorie Flack

**TEACHING FOCUS**
- Animals and their products
- Sequencing
- Motor skills
- Giving

**SETTING THE STAGE**

Instantly singable songs and the appealing rhyme and rhythm of finger plays will encourage children to be involved in storytime.

**ON THE MOVE** by Greg and Steve, *On the Move*
 (An excellent musical game about motor skills)

**SHOO FLY** by Greg and Steve, *On the Move*
 (A calypso version of the original with movement activities)

**LITTLE COW**

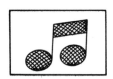

One little cow, all brown and saying "moo,"      *(lift fingers as rhyme*
Sat beside another one. Then there were two.     *indicates)*
Two little cows, happy as can be,
Another came to join them. Then there were three.
Along came another cow. Then there were four.
Four little cows, glad to be alive,
Found a lonely friend. Then there were five.
Five little cows, just happy as can be,
Five little cows, friends for you and me.

**CAN YOU WALK ON TIPTOE**

Can you walk on tiptoe                *(follow action as*
 As softly as a cat?                  *rhyme indicates)*
Can you stamp along the road
 Stamp, stamp, just like that?
Can you take some great big strides
 Just like a giant can?
Or walk along so slowly,
 Like a bent old man?

**FIRST READING**

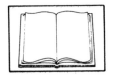

When you have a question about something, who do you usually ask? In our story today a little boy named Danny had a question, but he couldn't ask his mother because the question was about her! Who do you think he asked? Can you tell from the cover of the story? Danny asked some of his animal friends and one of them had just the right answer. The name of the story is **Ask Mr. Bear.** It was written by Marjorie Flack and she drew the pictures, too.

*Encourage the children to join in the predictable pattern of Danny's question and the animals' answers as anticipation builds to the surprise ending.*

**GETTING INVOLVED**

Every time a new animal joined Danny, they walked along together until they met another animal. Let's see if we can remember how they moved. First, Danny and the hen *skipped* along. When the goose joined them, how did they move? *(They hopped)* Next, Danny, the hen, the goose and the goat all *galloped* along. Last of all, when the sheep joined them, how did they move? *(They trotted.)* We can pretend to be the animals and move just like they did. I'll show you how. All we need are our legs. We won't need our voices. At the very end we can give ourselves a big, bear hug and sit down!

**A CLOSER LOOK**

With each rereading of a story, children gain new understanding. Pause often for a spontaneous flow of oral language as the children share their feelings and observations. Extend the learning process with your own questions in repeated readings of the story.

- What is Danny thinking in the little round picture after the title page? *(reasoning)*

- Every time I come to the words *until they met,* tell me the next animal before I turn the page. *(sequencing)*

- Why was an egg a good present for the hen to give Danny for his mother? *(association)*

- Why was a pillow a good gift for the goose to give? *(association)*

- How can a goat give a gift of cheese? *(association)*

- How can a sheep give a blanket for a gift? *(association)*

- Why didn't the animals want to go with Danny to find Mr. Bear? *(interpretation)*

- What did the bear whisper in Danny's ear? *(interpretation)*

- Did Danny's present for his mother cost him any money? *(interpretation)*

- Do we have to wait for birthdays to give special gifts? *(reasoning)*

**ROUNDING OUT STORYTIME**

**The Bear's Toothache**   by David McPhail

**The Surprise Party**   by Pat Hutchins

**Jiggle Wiggle Prance**   by Sally Noll

**In the Forest**   by Marie Hall Ets

**Who is the Beast?**   by Keith Baker

# Integrated Whole Language Activities

**ON OUR WAY**

What kind of walk shall we take today?
Leap like a frog? Creep like a snail?
Scamper like a squirrel with a furry tail?

Flutter like a butterfly? Chicken peck?
Stretch like a turtle with a poking-out neck?

Trot like a pony, clip clop clop?
Swing like a monkey in a treetop?

Scuttle like a crab? Kangaroo jump?
Plod like a camel with an up-and-down hump?

We could even try a brand-new way —
Walking down the street
On our own two feet.
*Eve Merriam*

**INVOLVEMENT**

**CREATIVE DRAMA**

The familiar, predictable pattern of **Ask Mr. Bear** invites children to join in spontaneously as you read. The words also set the stage for the children to pantomime the story characters as they move along the path with Danny. Add a variety of materials to your art center and encourage the children to make literacy props. They could make animal headbands with ears or beaks, paper plate stick puppets, or tagboard cards with pictures and names. Help the children create the story setting in your room by finding a step for Danny to sit on, a circle path to walk on, a hill to climb, and some woods for Mr. Bear to hide in.

Have the children form a circle. As you narrate the story, Danny can walk around inside the circle, stopping in front of the Hen to ask, *"Good morning, Mrs. Hen. Can you give me something for my mother's birthday?"* After the hen replies, the two children can skip around the circle. Continue dramatizing the story with the children moving as the animals moved. The special Big Birthday Bear Hug is a perfect ending!

Keep copies of **Ask Mr. Bear**, a tape of the children dramatizing the story and the literacy props in your drama center for an ongoing literacy activity!

**INTEGRATION**

**THE BIG BIRTHDAY BEAR HUG**

Pencil in the outline of a simple, outdoor scene on a large piece of bulletin board paper. Using small paint sponges or colored chalk for a subdued background effect, have the children illustrate the house, the path, the hill and the woods where Danny walked. Then have them paint the story characters on strong doubled paper. After they have cut out and stuffed the characters, staple them to the bulletin board for a colorful, three dimensional effect. Ask the children how they can make Danny into a stick puppet to move through the story.

Together, write short sentences such as *The hen skipped. The goose hopped. The goat galloped.* Have the children place them under the right animals. Print the story title, **Ask Mr. Bear** by Marjorie Flack, across the top of the mural. On the bottom, print the words, *Danny gave his mother a Big Birthday Bear Hug!* The mural will become an inviting reading experience as the children *walk* Danny through the story they have told.

## ASK MR. OWL*

Involve the children in a discussion of an animal they would like to substitute for Mr. Bear in an innovation of the story. Then brainstorm about the chosen animal's environment, such as Mr. Owl in the forest. Talk about other animals that also live there and what they could each give Danny for his mother. Encourage the children to think of words to describe the gifts, such as *a smooth skin from the snake, pointed antlers from the deer, bright feathers from the parrot,* and *tiny acorns from the squirrel.* Decide on Mr. Owl's gift which will be the surprise ending, such as *Danny gave his mother a wink and a hoot, I love yoooooo!*

When every child has an idea to draw, give each one a large piece of paper with the words printed on the bottom, *"I can give you my _____ _____ ," said the _____ .* Act as recorder and write down the words each child dictates. (You are teaching adjectives and quotation marks in meaningful context!) Choose pairs of children to illustrate the cover and the title page which will give credit to the author and the original story, **Ask Mr. Bear.** Bind the illustrated pages together in a class book titled **Ask Mr. Owl.** It will be a favorite in your reading center. Children return again and again to the books they have authored.

"I can give you my smooth skin."    "I can give you my bright feathers."    "I can give you my tiny acorns."    "I can give you a wink and a hoot, I love yoooo."

## PRESENTS FOR DANNY'S MOTHER

Because finding the perfect birthday present for Danny's mother wasn't easy, encourage the children to bring something from home that they would have offered Danny. Each morning, have a child hide his present inside a gift-wrapped box. The other children have a total of **Twenty Questions** to guess what is inside the box. The questions must be answered by *yes* or *no*. Have a child *tally* the questions asked in sets of five. Point out to the children how effective *concept-type* questions are in directing their thinking, such as, *"Is it round?"* or *"Is it made out of wood?"* The children will see how the information learned from all the *yes* answers helps them to reason and deduct what is inside the box.

Every time they are able to guess an object before the **Twenty Questions** are used up, list that gift on a class chart, **Presents for Danny's Mother.** Have the children illustrate the chart, sign all their names, and think of ways to deliver their *perfect* presents to Danny's mother. If you involve your children in theme cycle choices, you may find your next emphasis will be on writing letters to Danny or planning a trip to the post office!

## ON OUR WAY

Print the delightful poem on chart paper. Have the children highlight with yellow marker all the action words that depict how the animals moved. How can they turn those words into a reading and writing experience?

**EVERYDAY LEARNING ACTIVITIES**

Positive parenting, developmental learning activities and a warm, nurturing environment are major factors in a child's academic success and lifetime learning.

**Ask Mr. Bear** is the story of a little boy who went for a walk, looking for a present for his mother. His walk turned into an adventure with a very happy ending. Years ago, families had an advantage. They walked everywhere together. While they were walking, they probably talked about all the little things that parents and children like to share. You can do the same with your children. Even a short walk in your own neighborhood can be an adventure and a real learning experience for your child. Talk about traffic and things that move. Compare what goes fast with what moves slowly. Look at houses and buildings; compare their sizes and their structures. Teach your child to look up and tell you everything he sees, or to look down and do the same. Walk backwards and sideways and notice if things look different. Count dogs or bicycles, smiling faces or crying children. You are not only spending time together but also teaching your child to look around and notice his world. His vocabulary will increase continually. A child loves big words. If he hears them often enough, the words will become a natural part of his vocabulary. At bedtime ask your child to name everything he remembers from your walk, a great memory-builder. Your child will never have a better teacher than yourself. *(parenting skill)*

- New words are all around us. One short pleasure walk in your own neighborhood could teach your child the meaning of concrete, curb, gutter, property, hedge and foliage. Make a book with the same words on the bottom of each page . . . *I went for a walk and I saw* _____ . Fill in one word on each page with a simple illustration for a successful reading experience! *(vocabulary)*

- Walking together is a great time to practice the motor skills of hopping and skipping as the animals did in **Ask Mr. Bear.** Ask your child to hop to the next driveway on one foot, then change to the other. When she has mastered that with good balance, suggest alternate hopping, which means changing her feet with every hop. Skipping is one of the hardest motor skills to master. The easiest way to teach your child to skip is to take her hand and say, "Right foot, step and hop, left foot, step and hop," over and over again. When she can do it fast, she will be skipping! *(motor skills)*

- If your child is not ready for jumping rope the traditional way, have two people hold a rope close to the ground. Wiggle it as a snake. Have her jump over. Raise it a little for your child to *jump the river. (eye-foot coordination)*

- Suspend a child's plastic inner tube or a hula hoop (remember them?) from a porch ceiling or a tree limb. Give your child a beanbag to throw underhanded through the bulls-eye! As her skill increases, move her farther away from the target. Add to the learning by teaching addition! A bulls-eye is two points. Take turns throwing and catching. Children love catching beanbags because their fingers always manage to grab a corner! How about two more points for a catch? *(motor skills, math)*

# Bedtime
## for
# Frances

*by Russell Hoban*

**TEACHING FOCUS**
- Letter-sound association
- Recognizing fears
- Interpreting story events
- Concept of time

**SETTING THE STAGE**

Instantly singable songs and the appealing rhyme and rhythm of finger plays will encourage children to be involved in storytime.

**SLEEP, SLEEP** by Rosenshontz, *Share It*
(A hilarious song about children's excuses for not going to bed)

**A, YOU'RE ADORABLE** by Sharon, Lois & Bram, *Smorgasbord*

**THIS LITTLE GIRL**

| | |
|---|---|
| This little girl is ready for bed, | *(finger in other palm)* |
| Down on the pillow she lays her head; | *(thumb as a pillow)* |
| Wraps herself in covers so tight, | *(wrap fingers around)* |
| And this is the way she sleeps all night. | *(close eyes)* |
| | |
| Morning comes, she opens her eyes; | *(open eyes)* |
| Back with a toss the cover flies; | *(open fingers)* |
| Up she jumps, is dressed and away, | *(index finger up)* |
| Ready for frolic and play all day. | *(hops away)* |

**TEDDY BEAR**

| | |
|---|---|
| Teddy Bear, Teddy Bear, turn around. | *(follow action as rhyme indicates)* |
| Teddy Bear, Teddy Bear, touch the ground. | |
| Teddy Bear, Teddy Bear, show your shoe. | |
| Teddy Bear, Teddy Bear, that will do. | |

Teddy Bear, Teddy Bear, run upstairs.
Teddy Bear, Teddy Bear, say your prayers.
Teddy Bear, Teddy Bear, turn off the light.
Teddy Bear, Teddy Bear, say good night.

**FIRST READING**

Do you know what kind of an animal this is on the cover of our book? It *looks* like a little bear but it's really a badger and it belongs to the weasel family. Badgers get their name from the badge or marking on their faces. Can you see one on this little badger's face? Her name is Frances. The man who wrote the story, Russell Hoban, likes Frances so much he has written seven stories about her.

What do you think would be a good title for this story? Mr. Hoban has called it **Bedtime for Frances.** Let's find the words on the cover. Can you find them again on the title page? Do you think Frances wants us to come into her house? I'll just turn the pages and let you tell the story.

**GETTING INVOLVED**

When Frances couldn't fall asleep, she made up an alphabet song. We can turn her song into a game but let's be careful not to wake her up! Stand up in your place and say the words with me.

A is for apple pie. *(Pretend to smell the delicious pie.)*
B is for bear. *(Hunch over and shake your tail.)*
C is for crocodile combing his hair. *(Pretend to comb hair.)*
D is for dumplings. *(Rub your tummy and smile!)*
S is for sailboat. *(Move your hands through space.)*
T is for tiger. *(Make a low, growling sound)*
U is for underwear, down in the drier. *(Make spinning motion.)*

Why did Frances stop singing? What did she look for in her room? I am glad we don't have to worry about tigers in here! Let's sit down and look at the pictures again.

**A CLOSER LOOK**

With each rereading of a story, children gain new understanding. Pause often for a spontaneous flow of oral language as the children share their feelings and observations. Extend the learning process with your own questions in repeated readings of the story.

• How did Frances' mother know it was her bedtime? *(time recognition)*

• What did Frances want to do before she said "good night"? *(recall)*

• Why did France start to sing? *(comprehension)*

• Why did the letter "T" make Frances afraid? Do you remember why Frances' father thought it was a friendly tiger? *(interpretation)*

• Why did the crack in the ceiling frighten Frances? Who helped her watch the crack? *(memory)*

• What did Father say was the wind's job? Father's job? Frances' job? *(memory)*

• Who helped Frances watch the crack in the ceiling? *(memory)*

• Why did Frances finally decide to go to sleep? *(interpretation)*

• Have you ever had trouble going to sleep like Frances did? *(sharing)*

**ROUNDING OUT STORYTIME**

**Albert's Toothache**   by Barbara Williams

**Sloppy Kisses**   by Elizabeth Winthrop

**The Quilt Story**   by Tony Johnson

**Q is for Duck**   by Mary Elting

**The Quilt**   by Ann Jonas

17

# Integrated Whole Language Activities

**POETRY**

**NIGHT COMES...**

Night comes
leaking
out of the sky.

Stars come
peeking.

Moon comes
sneaking,
silvery-sly.

Who is
shaking,
shivery-
quaking?

Who is afraid
of the night?

Not I.

*Beatrice Schenk de Regniers*

**IN THE NIGHT**
by Marchette Chute
from *The Merry-Go-Round Book*
by Nancy Larrick

**INVOLVEMENT**

**AN ALPHABET SONG**

In the story, **Bedtime for Frances**, the little badger sang an alphabet song to put herself to sleep. Pretend you are singing to Frances and introduce your boys and girls to *A You're Adorable*, an alphabet song with a cheery melody that children love to sing. (See p. 16 ) With the music playing and the children sitting in a circle, tap one child to stand for each letter of the alphabet. Continue around the circle until all the children are standing. Play the song again and, this time, tap each child to sit down. (Just wait for the giggles when you get to *"K, You're so kissable"!*) It won't be many *sing-alongs* before the children have the words memorized.

*Extension:* Make alphabet cards by giving each child a letter of the alphabet to illustrate, with the words of the song printed under the letter. Keep a pointer, the alphabet cards, and a tape of the children singing *A You're Adorable* in a learning center. (Variation: Bind the alphabet cards into a book.)

**UNPACK YOUR PILLOW CASE!**

Review with the children all the things Frances wanted before she could go to sleep . . . a glass of milk, a piggyback ride, kisses, her teddy bear, a doll, and an open door. Because children are fascinated with little incidents from a teacher's own life, sit on the floor with a brightly colored pillow case on your lap. As you pull out one object at a time, tell the children a story about all the little things *you* do to get yourself ready for sleep. Then everyday pull a child's name out of your pillow case. That child will come to school the next day with her own pillow case full of little things that will describe her bedtime routine as she plays **Unpack Your Pillow Case.** The oral language will easily lead to a writing experience as each child draws, writes, or dictates a sentence about bedtime at her house.

*Extension:* The children could bring old, white pillow cases to decorate with permanent markers in your art center. The pillow cases will be nightly reminders of their little friend, Frances, whom they met in a story!

**INTEGRATION**

## GO TO SLEEP, FRANCES

The wooden bed, bench and window in Frances' bedroom are all made of simple shapes. Help the children cut out large rectangles to create a bed for Frances on a bulletin board. Small groups of children can put smaller shapes together to add a pillow, a window and curtains, and the bench. Have a child draw Frances to tuck into bed. After brainstorming together, have each child draw and cut out something to put in Frances' bed to help her go to sleep.

Together, write a letter to Frances telling her what the class has done. Print the children's words on chart paper, modeling the writing process for them as you think out loud about letters and sounds, spacing and capitalization. The children will want to illustrate the letter and sign all their names. They will read it again and again!

## A QUILT FOR FRANCES

Just as lullabies and bedtime go together, so do quilts and memories. Bring a quilt to class and tell the children why it is special to you. Introduce stories about quilts, including the charming books, **The Quilt** by Ann Jonas, **The Quilt Story** by Tony Johnston, and **The Keeping Quilt** by Patricia Polacco. After you have reread the stories, ask the children to tell you everything they discovered about the patterns, colors and pictures in the quilts. Print a list of their observations on a chart.

Involve the children in a discussion of what kind of quilt Frances might have enjoyed having on her bed. Then give the children an endless supply of brightly colored, precut shapes to create their own quilt designs on large white squares. Mount their quilt pieces on vivid background squares and paste them on a large piece of colored bulletin board paper. Your quilters will be proud of their color-splashed **Quilt for Frances!**

## THE WIND'S JOB

When the wind blew the curtains and frightened Frances, her daddy told her that the wind was just doing its job. What a springboard to learning about the many ways air, water, and wind work for us. Read the appealing nonfiction book, **Feel the Wind** by Arthur Dorros.

The children will especially enjoy the beautiful language and delightful ending of **Gilberto and the Wind** by Marie Hall Ets and the rhyme and cumulative text of **The Wind Blew** by Pat Hutchins. Then give the children the opportunity to decide what their next reading and writing experience will be.

**EVERYDAY LEARNING ACTIVITIES**

Positive parenting, developmental learning activities and a warm, nurturing environment are major factors in a child's academic success and lifetime learning.

Your child probably loved identifying with the little badger who just couldn't go to sleep in **Bedtime For Frances**. At some time or other, bedtime becomes a scary time for almost every child. Fears and anxieties often intensify in the dark when a child is separated from his family. Respect those feelngs. Your child needs to know you understand. Let him have the comfort of a night light, a stuffed animal or soft music. Leave the door open and tell him exactly where you will be. A frightened child usually needs a response from you, and only *you* can decide just how much reassurance he needs. Remember that putting himself to sleep is a skill every child must learn. Being able to deal with separation is one of many steps towards independence and self-sufficiency. *(parenting skill)*

- Help your child *talk through* his fears at bedtime. Make a very simple book by just folding some plain paper. On the bottom of each page, write the same sentence . . . *I'll talk to a _____ and I'll say _____.* Have your child tell you the word for whatever might frighten him . . . a monster, a robber, etc. End the little book with *I'll talk to my teddy bear and I'll say good night.* Let your child read his book to you at bedtime. *(words in print, identifying fears)*

- When Frances couldn't sleep in the story, **Bedtime For Frances**, she made up an alphabet song. Make a simple bedtime alphabet book with your child. Put one letter on each page and have your child think of a word that begins with that letter. Write complete sentences such as *A is for alligator.* Use the book as a part of your bedtime routine every night. The last page could say, *Good night, Frances! (letter-sound association, words in print)*

- Understanding the concepts of before and after, yesterday and tomorrow, and morning, afternoon and evening, are all part of a child's grasp of time. Refer often to the hours on a clock. They will begin to have meaning when they are connected to the activities of your child's day. *(concept of time)*

- It is helpful to have a quieting down activity at bedtime rather than a loud or busy activity that will *rev* a child's motor! Puzzles are an excellent activity and also are wonderful skill builders. The eyes and hands must work together. Often when a puzzle has been mastered, it can be made more challenging by mixing the pieces of two or three puzzles together and completing all three at the same time. Another variation is to do the puzzle upside down. Puzzles can be easily made by gluing a magazine picture to a piece of cardboard and cutting it up. *(visual discrimination)*

# Blueberries
## for
# *Sal*

### by Robert McCloskey

**TEACHING FOCUS**
- Comparative thinking
- Language development
- Counting and grouping
- Creative play

**SETTING THE STAGE**

Instantly singable songs and the appealing rhyme and rhythm of finger plays will encourage children to be involved in storytime.

**PEANUT BUTTER AND JELLY** by Sharon, Lois & Bram, *Smorgasbord*
  (Digging peanuts and picking berries)

**PAW PAW PATCH** by Hap Palmer, *Simplified Folk Songs*
  ( A game song about "picking")

**MY FACE**

| | |
|---|---|
| Two little eyes to look around, | *(point to body parts as rhyme* |
| Two little ears to hear each sound, | *indicates)* |
| One little nose to smell what's sweet, | |
| One little mouth that likes to eat! | |

**THE BEAR WENT OVER THE MOUNTAIN**

| | |
|---|---|
| The bear went over the mountain, | *(walk in place, then fingertips* |
| The bear went over the mountain, | *together)* |
| The bear went over the mountain, | |
| To see what he could see! | *(hand over eyes)* |
| To see what he could see! | |
| To see what he could see! | |
| The other side of the mountain, | *(walk in place, then fingertips* |
| The other side of the mountain, | *together)* |
| The other side of the mountain, | |
| Was all that he could see! | *(hands out, palms up)* |

**FIRST READING**

Look at the picture on the cover of our book today. Where do you think the little girl is? What do you think she is picking? Let me give you some clues! They are small and blue. They are round and smooth. They grow in clusters on bushes and are simply delicious. The name of our book is **Blueberries for Sal.** Now do you know what she is picking?

Can you find Sal and her mother and the blueberries in the very first picture in the book? What do you think they are doing with the blueberries? Does their kitchen look like the kitchen in your house? Let's find Sal on the title page and look for the author's name, too.

**GETTING
INVOLVED**

Let's go blueberry picking together. First we'll pretend we are Little Sal. Stretch your arm out straight; now curl it into your body to make a pail. You can pick blueberries with your other hand while you're tramping along behind mother. Kuplink, kuplank, kuplunk! Reach for the blueberries to the right of you, now to the left, and down by your feet. Be careful not to squish any blueberries!

Now let's walk like Little Bear and hustle along to catch up with mother. When you find her, give her a big hug and sit down to rest right in the middle of the blueberries.

**A CLOSER LOOK**

With each rereading of a story, children gain new understanding. Pause often for a spontaneous flow of oral language as the children share their feelings and observations. Extend the learning process with your own questions in repeated readings of the story.

- How was Little Sal's mother getting ready for winter? *(interpretation)*

- Why is Little Sal smiling as she picks berries? *(inferential)*

- Why didn't the blueberries sound "kuplink" in mother's pail? *(interpretation)*

- Why were there more blueberries in mother's pail than in Little Sal's pail? *(interpretation)*

- Why did Little Bear and his mother come to eat berries? Are they getting ready for winter the same way as Little Sal's mother? *(reasoning)*

- Were any other animals eating berries on Blueberry Hill? *(memory)*

- Tell me how Little Bear and Little Sal and their mothers got all mixed up on Blueberry Hill? *(reasoning)*

- What made Little Sal's mother turn around? Little Bear's mother? *(interpretation)*

- What do you think Little Bear and his mother did when they got home? What did Little Sal and her mother do? Have you seen the last picture before? *(opinion, memory)*

**ROUNDING OUT
STORYTIME**

**Peanut Butter and Jelly**   by Nadine Bernard Westcott

**Good Morning, Granny Rose**   by Warren Ludwig

**The Biggest Bear**   by Lynd Ward

**Jamberry**   by Bruce Degen

**Lost!**   by David McPhail

# Integrated Whole Language Activities

POETRY

### LEAP AND DANCE

The lion walks on padded paws,
The squirrel leaps from limb to limb,
While flies can crawl straight up a wall,
And seals can dive and swim.
The worm, it wiggles all around,
The monkey swings by its tail,
And birds may hop upon the ground,
Or spread their wings and sail.
But boys and girls have much more fun;
They leap and dance
And walk
And *run*.

*Anonymous*

### YELLOW BUTTER
by Mary Ann Hoberman
from *Read Aloud Rhymes
for The Very Young*
by Jack Prelutsky

INVOLVEMENT

### ON BLUEBERRY HILL

Because there is action in almost every sentence in **Blueberries for Sal**, the story is an easy one for creative dramatics. Set up your room for a dramatization of the story by deciding on an area for Blueberry Hill, a clump of bushes on one side for Little Sal, and a clump (children will love the word!) of bushes on the other side for Little Bear. Find a place for the rock from which Little Sal heard a noise.

In your art center, help the children create two pails, two sets of headband bear ears, and signs to label Blueberry Hill, the rock and the bushes. Because children often feel more confident dramatizing a story when they act in pairs, print two sets of name cards for Little Sal, Mother, Little Bear, and Little Bear's Mother. As you narrate the story, the children will listen intently for cues as they role play the characters. Have the other children join in on *kuplink, kuplank, kuplunk*.

INTEGRATION

### THE BEAR WENT OVER THE MOUNTAIN

As with many traditional favorites, *The Bear Went Over the Mountain* has a simple, singable melody that children enjoy. It will not be long before they have the text memorized. Write the words on chart paper, modeling the writing process for the children as you *think out loud* about letters and sounds and spacing. Print with the same color the words that are repeated, i.e., *The bear went* in brown, the word *over* in blue, and the phrase, *the mountain*, in green. Write the sentence, *To see what he could see,* in black. Repeat a color pattern in the last verse also. The children will want to illustrate the chart with bears and mountains for colorful reading.

*Extension:* Using the same colors, print the text on sentence strips for children to arrange in sequence or match to the chart poem. For an additional reading activity, print one sentence on each page of a book for the children to illustrate. Bind the mounted pages into a class big book to add to your listening center, along with a tape of the children singing.

## A SEMANTIC WEB

Make a semantic map of **Blueberries for Sal** by having the children identify the characters and main objects in the story. Write their words around the story title. In a retelling, children reproduce a story by using their own language to tell the story. Guide the children's retelling of **Blueberries for Sal** by asking them questions about the beginning, middle and end of the story they have already dramatized. Encourage them to use words from the semantic web. Cross out each word as it is used. Print the children's retelling on a language experience chart for paired or individual reading.

## A LETTER TO LITTLE BEAR

Little Sal and Little Bear didn't even meet each other when they were picking berries! Have Little Sal write a letter to Little Bear, inviting him to come to her house to play and eat blueberries. As the children dictate the sentences, write the letter on a language experience chart to which they will surely want to add some pictures and sign their names.

## BLUEBERRIES, BLUEBERRIES

After talking about all the ways we enjoy eating blueberries, give each child a long, narrow piece of paper with the words, *Blueberries, Blueberries,* printed on the left. On the folded flap on the right print the words, *I like them . . . .* Under the flap have each child draw and write his favorite way to eat blueberries, i.e., *on my pancakes, in my muffins,* etc. Bind the illustrated pages into a new reading book for your reading center.

## MY BERRY, YOUR BERRY

Author Bruce Degen has written a special message on the last page of his visually delightful book, **Jamberry.** His message is a wonderful introduction to the rhyming, rollicking adventure of a bear and a little boy on a berry hunt. List on a four-column wall graph the kinds of berries the child and the bear found. Have each child draw a picture of his favorite berry to paste to the graph. Write a summary of the graph results. Which berry was the least favorite? The most? How many more? How many less?

## LET'S LOOK AT BEARS

What kind of a bear was Little Bear? How do bears stay warm in the winter? Write the children's questions on a chart titled, *What Do We Want to Know About Bears?* Introduce nonfiction books such as the appealing **Let's Look At Bears** by Malcolm Penny, **How Do Bears Sleep** by E. J. Bird, and **Animals in Winter** by Susanne Riha. Have each child draw a picture and write a sentence about one thing she has learned. Then, as a class, write a second class chart, *What We Know About Bears!*

**EVERYDAY LEARNING ACTIVITIES**

Positive parenting, developmental learning activities and a warm, nurturing environment are major factors in a child's academic success and lifetime learning.

Your child is already developing eating habits and food likes and dislikes that he will probably carry with him for the rest of his life. If your child craves sugar and sweets now, he will most likely crave them twenty years from now. Don't give sweets as a source of comfort and don't withhold them as a punishment. That makes them twice as desirable. When sweets are used as snacks, they rob a child of his appetite at mealtime. Most children are happy with fruit, raw vegetables, cheese or peanut butter which make far better nutritious snacks. Offer the best variety of foods at the meal which your child eats best. Be relaxed and nonchalant about the amount of food your child eats. Power plays result when a child gets too much negative reinforcement about eating. An uptight mom sets the stage. We also influence a child's eating habits by our casual conversation, often talking to others about a reluctant eater when he is present. Every time he hears that he doesn't eat well, he will prove you are right. The principle that a child will repeat the behavior for which he gets attention can work for you in encouraging good eating habits. *(parenting skill)*

- Is it blueberry season? Find a pick-your-own commercial blueberry patch and pick blueberries for a wonderful, hands-on learning experience. Guaranteed to fill the tummy! Look for blueberries at the grocery store. Since there are no blueberry bushes in the store, how did the blueberries get there? Study the packaging. Decide if the berries are the same as the ones in **Blueberries for Sal.** *(sensory experience)*

- Count your blueberries. Make piles of ten. Then group your blueberries into piles of dark and light blue, or big and small, or stem and no stem. Let your child think of new ways to group. *(counting and grouping)*

- Have your child make up his own recipe for blueberry jam. Write the ingredients and the steps for cooking exactly as he dictates! Tape the recipe inside **Blueberries for Sal** and read it often, together. *(language)*

- Ask your child to name all the real berries she can think of. Make a list. Then have fun writing a list of fanciful berries (hayberries, pinkberries, etc.) Paint a picture for each list. *(language)*

- Using blocks or Legos, make a pattern on the floor by simply repeating two colors . . . red, blue, red, blue, etc. Ask your child what color will come next in the pattern. When she can extend a two-color pattern, add a third color, then a fourth. Vary the object sizes as well. Tell your child to think up the hardest pattern she can possibly think of for you to complete. Make a pattern with Cheerios, raisins, grapes, etc. and end the game with a party! *(visual skills)*

# Brown Bear, Brown Bear, What Do You See?

by Bill Martin, Jr.

**TEACHING FOCUS**
- Color Recognition
- Classification
- Sequencing
- Visual Memory

**SETTING THE STAGE**

Instantly singable songs and the appealing rhyme and rhythm of finger plays will encourage children to be involved in storytime.

**MARY WORE HER RED DRESS** by Raffi, *Everything Grows*
  (A musical *fashion show* using colors)

**THE BEAR WENT OVER THE MOUNTAIN**, Traditional

**COLORS**

| | |
|---|---|
| Colors, colors, what do I see? | *(hand shade eyes)* |
| I see colors all around me! | *(look all around)* |
| I see the blue sky | *(point up)* |
| Where the birds go. | |
| I see the green grass | *(point down)* |
| Tickle my toe. | |
| Colors, colors, what do I see? | *(hand shade eyes)* |
| I see colors all around me. | *(look all around)* |
| I see flowers just for you, | *(pick flowers)* |
| Red and yellow and purple, too! | |
| Colors, colors, what do I see? | *(hand shade eyes)* |
| I see colors all around me! | *(look all around)* |

            *Mary Cornelius*

**SPECKLED RED**

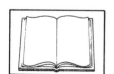

| | |
|---|---|
| Chook, chook, chook, chook, chook, | *(curtsy or bow)* |
| Good morning, Mrs. Hen. | |
| How many chickens have you got? | |
| Madam, I've got ten. | *(hold up ten fingers)* |
| Four of them are yellow, | *(close all but four)* |
| And four of them are brown, | *(four on other hand)* |
| And two of them are speckled red, | *(wiggle two thumbs)* |
| The nicest in the town. | |

**FIRST READING**

What do you see on the cover? What is that bear doing? The title of the book tells us the bear is looking at something . . . **Brown Bear, Brown Bear, What Do You See?** The book was written by Bill Martin and the colorful pictures were done by Eric Carle, the man who wrote **The Very Hungry Caterpillar.**

Are you ready for a look inside the cover? Why are all those pretty colors there? What else do you see? What words do you see on the title page? Now I will just quietly turn the pages and let you tell me everything you see.

Do we know the story yet? Sometimes the whole story isn't found in the beautiful illustrations. We must also hear the words printed on each page. Some stories, like **Brown Bear, Brown Bear, What Do You See?** are meant to be read aloud! This book is especially fun because of the pattern of words. See if you can hear what the pattern is. Then you can help me read.

**GETTING
INVOLVED**

Do you think Brown Bear was sitting down when he saw the animals? How does a bear move? Tell me how a bird moves? A duck? A horse? Would a cat, a dog, and a sheep all move the same way? How? Tell me how a frog moves, a goldfish, a teacher? Now it's your turn to move! I'll name the animals and you show me how you think each one was moving when Brown Bear saw it.

Now let's sing the words of Brown Bear. *(Sing to the tune of Row, Row, Row Your Boat.)* I will sing all the questions and you sing all the answers. Watch my book. I'll turn up the corner of the page to help you remember the next animal!

**A CLOSER LOOK**

With each rereading of a story, children gain new understanding. Pause often for a spontaneous flow of oral language as the children share their feelings and observations. Extend the learning process with your own questions in repeated readings of the story.

- Tell me the name of a color. What animal was that color in the story? *(association)*

- Of the colors you usually find in your crayon box, what color did Brown Bear not see? What color did he see instead? *(deductive thinking)*

- This time when we read the story, tell me what Brown Bear will see next *before* I turn the page. *(predicting)*

- Which two animals did the illustrator color with fanciful colors, just for fun? *(interpretation)*

- Look at the feet of all the animals. Can we group the animals by their different kinds of feet? *(classifying)*

- Which animals live in water? In the air? On land? How else can we group the animals? *(classifying)*

- Count the children and the animals. Which set has more? Less? *(math concepts)*

- If you could have one animal for a pet, which one would you choose? *(opinion)*

**ROUNDING OUT
STORYTIME**

**But Where Is the Green Parrot?**   by Thomas Zacharias

**The Mixed-Up Chameleon**   by Eric Carle

**A Children's Zoo**   by Tana Hoban

**I Went Walking**   by Sue Williams

**Color Zoo**   by Lois Ehlert

# *Integrated Whole Language Activities*

**POETRY**

**THE ANIMAL FAIR**

I went to the animal fair,
The birds and beasts were there.
The big baboon, by the light of the moon,
Was combing his auburn hair.
The funniest was the monk.
He climbed up the elephant's trunk.
The elephant sneezed and fell on his knees,
And what became of the monk, the monk?

*Anonymous*

**IN THE SUMMER WE EAT**
by Zhenya Gay
from *Read Aloud Rhymes for The Very Young* by Jack Prelutsky

**INVOLVEMENT**

**CREATIVE DRAMA**

The repetitive chant and bright, appealing characters of **Brown Bear, Brown Bear, What Do You See?** lend themselves beautifully to expression through drama. Have each child choose a favorite character to draw and color. Be sure someone draws the teacher and the group of children! Mount the children's drawings on paper plates to make face masks or on tagboard to hang around the children's necks. The children may prefer to add popsicle sticks to create stick puppets! Separate the children into groups of redbirds, yellow ducks, etc. as they hold their props. Read **Brown Bear, Brown Bear** again with each group joining in on their character's part and then asking the next question.

**INTEGRATION**

**BROWN BEAR'S WALK**

Involve the children in a discussion about all the places Brown Bear must have walked to see his animal friends. Using small paint sponges or colored chalk, create a simple outdoor scene on a large piece of bulletin board paper. Label the path of Brown Bear's walk with directionality phrases such as *under a nest, around a pond, across a pasture, beside a farm, over a stream, and in front of a house.* Have the children paint and cut out the story characters to add to the appropriate places on the wall mural. The scene will become an independent or paired reading experience as the children walk a puppet Brown Bear through the story!

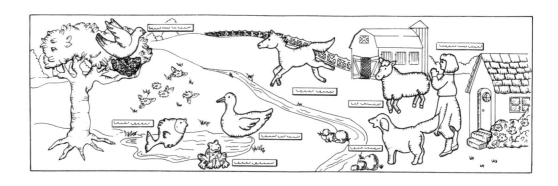

## CHILDREN, CHILDREN, WHO DO YOU SEE? *

Because authoring often begins with oral language, have fun with an oral innovation of the story by substituting the children's names in the repetitive pattern. *"Jeremy, Jeremy, Who do you see?"* and Jeremy answers, "I see Nathan looking at me." After every child has participated, decide on a sequence of names. Give each child a piece of paper with the words of the question, " _____ , _____ , *Who do you see?"* printed at the top and the answer printed at the bottom, *"I see _____ looking at me."* The children will probably think of copying name cards as they write names in the spaces on their pages. Bind the illustrated pages in a class book titled, **Children, Children, Who Do You See?** Because children return to their own books again and again, this one will soon be a well-read favorite in your Reading Center!

*Extension:* Have each child bring an individual photo of himself to class. Use the same text as above, but print the question on the top left of each child's paper. A child's picture and the answer to the question will be hidden under a folded flap on the right side of each page. The children must lift the flaps to read the story. Be sure to include the teacher's picture and a class picture of all the children on the last two pages.

## MY BROWN BEAR BOOK

The rhythm and predictability of **Brown Bear, Brown Bear** is a constant delight to children. It presents a wonderful opportunity for them to write independently. To help the children imagine Brown Bear in a different plot and setting, introduce them to the magnificent illustrations and rich vocabulary of **Imagine** by Alison Lester. This beautiful book really celebrates the imagination of children as it takes them into the jungle, under the sea, and even to Australia! Give each child a blank book to draw and tell his own Brown Bear adventure. You will need a sign-up sheet by the Author's Chair for children who will be eager to read their innovations to the class!

## WHERE ARE YOU GOING NEXT, BROWN BEAR?*

For a fascinating nonfiction unit that will probably take you into next month(!), build on the curiosity and language inspired by Alison Lester's **Imagine**. Fill your library corner with other extraordinary nonfiction books, i.e., the clever, wordless **In the Pond** by Ermanno Cristini, the superbly illustrated **Junglewalk** by Nancy Tafuri, the appealing and informative **All About Farm Animals** by Brenda Cook, and the beautifully laid out **When We Went to the Zoo** by Jan Ormerod.

Ask the children to name different animal habitats (they will love the big word!) that Brown Bear might have visited. Print the habitats on a classroom chart. List the animals the children suggest for each category. Have them decide on a habitat and a sequence of animals and their colors, such as *Red parrot, Red parrot, What do you see?* Don't forget an all-important surprise ending as you plan a class adaptation of Brown Bear, Brown Bear.

**EVERYDAY LEARNING ACTIVITIES**

Positive parenting, developmental learning activities and a warm, nurturing environment are major factors in a child's academic success and lifetime learning.

The appealing, repetitive text of **Brown Bear, Brown Bear, What Do You See?** is simply the result of asking the same question to a group of endearing animals. A wise parent stimulates his child's learning by asking skillful, open-ended questions. Effective questions require your child to organize his thoughts and process the information in his mind. *What does that mean? What would happen if . . . ? Which would you choose? Will it fit? Why won't it float?* Asking questions is a game that can be played anywhere, anytime. Questioning leads to logical thinking and sequencing and problem-solving. Your questions also say, "I am listening. Your thoughts are important. I really do want to know what you are thinking!" Such approval adds something to a child's inner stature. Even more important than teaching your child's eager mind, you are building his confidence in himself. Your *voice* will always be your greatest teaching tool because you are conveying feelings as well as words. The emotional well-being of your child is perhaps your single most important task as a parent. *(parenting skill)*

- Have your child draw simple outlines of the animals from **Brown Bear** on large index cards, color them, and glue dried beans on the outlines. Line them up for an animal parade with Brown Bear leading the way and the other animals following in sequence. The same activity on a simple flannelboard (just flannel or felt laid over cardboard) is fascinating to a child. You could lay thin paper over each animal on the last page of the book. Then lay the traced outline on a piece of felt or pellon and cut out the animals. *(Allowing a child to trace can make him dissatisfied with his own art work.) (sequencing)*

- *Concept* development is easy in the context of play. Using the same animal cutouts, arrange them in different ways to have fun with smaller and bigger, in the middle, on the left or right, above, under, next to, between, before and after. On succeeding days, add the concept of ordering from smallest to largest, or learning first, second, third, few and many, more or less, every other one, adding or taking away, or grouping by sets. Be sure to let your child have the fun of being the teacher and giving you directions to follow! *(directionality, math concepts)*

- *Predict* how many candies, colored marshmallows or pieces of cereal are in a handful. Then predict how many there will be of each color before you separate the colors. Which color has the most? The least? Make a simple graph. Then have a party and eat the graph! *(colors, math concepts)*

- Have a *color* day at home. Pick a favorite color like red. Everyone in the family could wear something red, eat a red food, build with red blocks and paint with red paint. *(colors)*

# Caps
### for
# Sale

## by Esphyr Slobodkina

**TEACHING FOCUS**
- Color recognition
- Directionality
- Auditory discrimination
- Story participation

**SETTING THE STAGE**

Instantly singable songs and the appealing rhyme and rhythm of finger plays will encourage children to be involved in storytime.

**COPYCAT** by Greg and Steve, *Kidding Around*

**JUST LIKE ME** by Greg and Steve, *We All Live Together, Vol. 4*
   (a mirror movement musical game)

**MONKEY SEE, AND MONKEY DO**

| | |
|---|---|
| A little monkey likes to do | |
| Just the same as you and you. | *(point)* |
| When you sit up very tall | *(straighten back)* |
| Monkey sits up very tall. | |
| When you pretend to throw a ball | *(stand)* |
| Monkey pretends to throw a ball. | *(act out)* |
| When you move your arms up and down | *(move arms)* |
| Monkey moves his arms up and down. | |
| When you sit down on the ground, | *(sit down)* |
| Monkey sits down on the ground. | |

**QUIET BE**

| | |
|---|---|
| Let your hands clap, clap, clap; | *(clap hands three times)* |
| Let your fingers tap, tap, tap, | *(tap fingers three times)* |
| Fold your arms and quiet be, | *(fold arms)* |
| Roll your hands so wide awake. | *(roll hands)* |
| Let your fingers shake, shake, shake. | *(shake fingers)* |
| Climb the ladder; do not fall, | *(climb hands up, up)* |
| Till we reach the steeple tall. | *(hands make steeple)* |
| Fold your hands and quiet be. | *(fold hands)* |

**FIRST READING**

Tell me all the things on the cover of this book that make you smile. What do you think is happening? Is it strange to see a man in the tree and the monkeys on the ground?

The name of the story is **Caps For Sale**, A Tale of A Peddler, Some Monkeys and Their Monkey Business. Do you know what a peddler is? He is someone who sells things but he does not have a store. Instead, he brings what he is selling right to you. Can you find the peddler on the cover? What do you think the words *monkey business* mean? Let's read about the trouble a peddler had with some mischievous monkeys!

*The children will naturally begin to speak along with the peddler and the monkeys. Their participation is part of the fun of the story.*

**GETTING INVOLVED**

Let's talk about some of the new words we heard in **Caps for Sale.** The peddler carried his *wares* on his head. Tell me what that word means. Then the peddler walked slowly so as not to *upset* his caps. What does *upset* mean? Next he leaned against the tree so he wouldn't *disturb* the caps. I'm wondering what the word *disturb* means. And last, did the story tell you what the words *monkey-business* mean?

Stand up tall in your very own space and we'll act out those new words. Reach up and stack your *wares* on your head, first your own checked cap, next the gray caps, then the brown, the blue, and last, the red ones. Walk slowly, slowly. Don't *upset* your caps! Now sit down ever so carefully. Don't *disturb* your caps while you take a nap. Oh, those silly monkeys are up to their *monkey-business*. Shake your finger at them! Pretend to throw down your cap! It worked! Pile all the caps back on your head and walk ever so slowly back to your place.

**A CLOSER LOOK**

With each rereading of a story, children gain new understanding. Pause often for a spontaneous flow of oral language as the children share their feelings and observations. Extend the learning process with your own questions in repeated readings of the story.

- How many caps are there of each color? How many caps altogether? *(counting)*

- Why did the peddler hold himself very straight? *(comprehension)*

- Where did the peddler sell his wares? *(observation)*

- Why did the peddler call out, "Caps for sale?" *(interpretation)*

- Why didn't the peddler have any lunch? *(memory)*

- What clever thing did the peddler do to get his caps back? Why did it work? *(interpretation)*

- What color cap would you have bought from the peddler? *(opinion)*

- Look again at the cover. Why is the peddler in the tree? *(opinion)*

**ROUNDING OUT STORYTIME**

**What Do You Do with a Kangaroo?**   by Mercer Mayer

**The Monkey and the Crocodile**   by Paul Galdone

**The Turtle and the Monkey**   by Paul Galdone

**Barn Dance**   by Bill Martin Jr.

**Curious George**   by H. A. Rey

# *Integrated Whole Language Activities*

**POETRY**

**WHEN YOU TALK TO A MONKEY**

When you talk to a monkey
  He seems very wise.
He scratches his head,
  And he blinks both his eyes;
But he won't say a word.
  He just swings on a rail
And makes a big question mark
  Out of his tail.
          *Rowena Bennett*

**BEFORE THE MONKEY'S CAGE**
by Edna Becker
from *Read Aloud Rhymes for The Very Young* by Jack Prelutsky

**INVOLVEMENT**

**DRAMATIZATION**

**Caps for Sale** offers an ideal setting for creative dramatics. To make the language come to life, have the children freely pantomime the movement of all the story characters. Add a variety of colors of fabric, felt and wallpaper to your art center and encourage the children to make the peddler's checked hat and a bunch of gray, brown, blue and red caps. Just plain circles may stack best on the peddler's head. With one child role-playing the peddler and the other children acting as monkeys (and loving it!), the caps are the only literacy props you will need for a hilarious dramatization!

**INTEGRATION**

**A TREEFUL OF MONKEYS**

Pencil in a simple outline on a large piece of bulletin board paper for the children to paint. Include a road, a large tree with many branches, and some hills and houses in the background. Painting with small sponges or drawing with chalk will create a pleasant, subdued mural. Have the children draw or paint the peddler, the monkeys and the caps to add to the scene. Print the words **Caps for Sale** by Esphyr Slobodkina on your wall mural or bulletin board. Can't you just see that treeful of smiling, scolding monkeys!

**A HAT ON MY HEAD!**

Have each child bring one hat of any size, shape, or color to school. Ask the children how the hats could be sorted, i.e. by colors, shapes, feathers, rims, sports, careers or seasons. Make a multi-column picture graph by having each child draw a picture of her favorite hat to place on the graph. As a group, tally the results and write summary sentences next to the graph. Which column of hats has the most? The least? How many more? How many less?

*Extension:* Introduce the clever, informative book, **Whose Hat?** by Margaret Miller, in Shared Reading. The colorful pictures identify hats associated with various careers and then depict a child role-playing the career and wearing the hat. Have each child draw a picture of herself wearing a hat. Act as scribe as she dictates a sentence about her picture. The children can take turns reading their sentences and talking about their pictures as they sit in the Author's Chair. Reading from memory is a literacy activity!

**THE PEDDLER LOOKED!**\*

With the story illustrations as a guide, brainstorm with the children about other places the peddler might have looked to find his caps. Emphasize position words. Choose a small group of children to illustrate a cover, a title page, and a surprise ending for your story. Then give each child a piece of paper with the words, *He looked* _____ ., written at the top, and the phrase, *No caps!*, printed at the bottom. After each child has illustrated a page, have her write or dictate the words she has chosen to finish the sentence. Bind the mounted pictures in a big book or hang them on the wall for paired or independent reading.

He looked under a rock. No caps!

He looked in the sand. No caps!

He looked behind a church. No caps!

Then he looked _____. And what do you think he saw?

**THE PEDDLER'S WARES** \*

The idea of someone walking up and down the street selling something is a new concept to children. Discuss the word *wares* and brainstorm about other items that could be sold by a peddler. Talk about the prices he might charge. Give each child a blank book with the sentence. *A* _____ *for* _____ *cents.* printed on each page. Each day have the children draw something new, decide on a price, and dictate the words to finish the sentence. Miss Slobodkina updated an old folk tale when she wrote **Caps for Sale.** Your authors will be doing the same!

*Extension:* Make a class book, **The Peddler's Wares ABC Book**, by deciding on *wares* beginning with every letter of the alphabet.

**MONKEY TAILS**

The poem, **When You Talk To A Monkey**, gives us a word picture of monkeys turning their tails into question marks. Lead the children in a discussion of what questions monkeys would ask if they could talk! Have each child draw and cut out a monkey with a big question mark tail. Act as recorder and write the monkey's question on a sentence strip to tuck under his tail. You have taught questions and question marks in meaningful context, decorated the walls, and provided another fascinating reading experience!

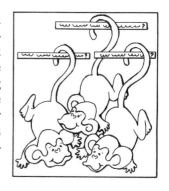

**A THREE HAT DAY**

Laura Geringer's warm, comical story about a lonely man and his extraordinary collection of hats offers a wealth of language, drama, art, and writing possibilities. **A Three Hat Day**, with charming illustrations by Arnold Lobel, will be a favorite!

**EVERYDAY
LEARNING
ACTIVITIES**

Positive parenting, developmental learning activities and a warm, nurturing environment are major factors in a child's academic success and lifetime learning.

There is nothing so appealing, at any age, as good manners. How often we wish our little ones would simply inhale good manners overnight! Being respectful is a composite of all good manners. Because children are imitators, parents do their best teaching when they are modeling the right behaviors themselves. That means saying *please* and *thank you* to your child, not interrupting her, honoring her feelings and so on. A child who has been treated with respect can be expected to treat others the same. Parents and children should be more polite to each other than they are to anyone else. Parents must insist on manners and allow plenty of time for practice, over and over again. Praise is a better motivator than punishment. A child with good manners is welcome anywhere and a pleasure to have around. *(parenting skill)*

- Listening for unusual sounds, like those the monkeys made in **Caps for Sale**, will help your child's auditory discrimination. Help her stay tuned to the sounds in her environment. Listen together for sounds and rhythms around you: your heart, a dripping faucet, rain, a tree branch scraping, popcorn popping. Listen for sounds outside and inside, and compare daytime and nighttime sounds. *(auditory perception)*

- Have some family fun with music, a wonderful mood-changer. Teach your child some of the songs you learned as a child. Clap out rhythms and let your child echo you. Clap the rhythm of a familiar song for her to guess. Reverse roles, too! You are sharpening your child's listening skills. *(auditory perception)*

- Learning left and right is an ongoing process. Encourage learning the skill in relaxed everyday situations. Mimic the peddler's actions in **Caps for Sale**. He looked for his caps *to the right* and *to the left*, in *back* of him and *behind* the tree. Reinforce the left/right concept by putting a drop of lotion or cologne on your child's right wrist every morning. Always identify each hand but only the right one gets the lotion. After several days in a row, your child will automatically hold out his right hand. Encourage your child to identify his right and left hand or foot as he dresses, washes, eats or plays, but give reminders freely and don't expect mastery. It is a continuing learning process. *(laterality)*

- Recycling broken or stubby crayons will peak your child's interest in the colors of his world. As he identifies a crayon color, ask him to name all the things he can think of that match that color. Put the broken, mixed pieces of crayons in a lightly greased muffin tin. Heat them in a slow oven (250° - 300°) until the crayons are melted together. Don't stir. Allow them to harden away from little hands. When the recycled crayons are cool, encourage your child to describe what happened and then color a rainbow picture. *(color recognition)*

# Chicka Chicka Boom Boom

## by Bill Martin, Jr. and John Archambault

| | |
|---|---|
| **TEACHING FOCUS** | • Rhyming words<br>• Letter recognition<br>• Story participation<br>• Letter-sound association |

**SETTING THE STAGE**

Instantly singable songs and the appealing rhyme and rhythm of finger plays will encourage children to be involved in storytime.

**ALPHABET SONG/ABC JIG**
by Sharon, Lois & Bram, *Sing A-Z*
(An appealing alphabet jig that includes nursery rhymes)

**L-O-L-L-I-P-O-P/S-M-I-L-E-/W-A-L-K/B-I-N-G-O**
by Sharon, Lois & Bram, *Sing A-Z*
(A spelling medley)

**CLAP, CLAP, CLAP YOUR HANDS**

Clap, clap, clap your hands
As slowly as you can.
Clap, clap, clap your hands
As quickly as you can.

Shake, shake, shake your hands
As slowly as you can.
Shake, shake, shake your hands
As quickly as you can.

*(follow actions as rhyme indicates)*

Repeat the verse with roll, rub, wiggle, and pound.

**DID YOU EVER GO FISHING**

Did you ever go fishing on a bright sunny day—
Sit on a fence and have the fence give way?
Slide off the fence and rip your pants,
And see the little fishes do the hootchy-kootchy dance.
*Anonymous*

*(follow action as rhyme indicates)*

**FIRST READING**

Can you tell from the cover what this story will be about? Let me read the title for you, **Chicka Chicka Boom Boom.** Do you know yet? Let's look inside the cover. Now do you have an idea? What do you think about the colors the artist has used for the alphabet letters?

Now look at the title page. Does it look like the cover of the book? Read the words with me. Look for the same words on the next page.

One of the authors, Bill Martin, Jr., wrote **Brown Bear, Brown Bear, What Do You See?** That rhyming story was about animals. This story is about the letters of the alphabet trying to climb a coconut tree.

**GETTING INVOLVED**

Here are all the lower case letters of the alphabet lined up so you can see them. When I tap you, pick out any letter you want and sit down with that letter.

Now let's look at the cards on the floor in the middle of the circle. They are the matching capital letters turned over so you can't see them. This time when I tap you, turn over two letters on the floor and see if you can find the capital letter that matches your letter. Watch closely because someone else may turn over the very letter you need and you will want to remember exactly where it is.

Whatever alphabet letter you are holding is the letter you will be in the story. This time as I read, listen for your letter. Stand up when you hear it. After the whole alphabet is up the tree, **Chicka Chicka Boom,** everyone falls and we will start all over again.

**A CLOSER LOOK**

With each rereading of a story, children gain new understanding. Pause often for a spontaneous flow of oral language as the children share their feelings and observations. Extend the learning process with your own questions in repeated readings of the story.

- Did all the alphabet letters rhyme with the word *tree*? *(auditory discrimination)*

- Who followed the letter D up the tree? *(letter identification)*

- Why was the letter K called *tag-along*? *(vocabulary)*

- Did the tree change when the letter T climbed to the top? *(visual detail)*

- What happened when W, X, Y, and Z joined the race? *(visual detail)*

- Why are the capital letters Z, R, and N wrapped around the lower case letters? *(comprehension)*

- How do we know D, E, and F were hurt in the fall from the tree? *(reasoning)*

- What was different about M, N, and O after the fall? *(vocabulary)*

- How can you tell that P has a black eye and T has a loose tooth? *(visual detail)*

- Do you think the letters climbed the tree again? *(opinion)*

**ROUNDING OUT STORYTIME**

**Polar Bear, Polar Bear, What Do You Hear?**   by Bill Martin, Jr.

**All Aboard ABC**   by Doug Magee and Robert Newman

**A, My Name is Alice**   by Jane E. Boyer

**The Alphabet Tale**   by Jan Garten

**Alphabatics**   by Suse MacDonald

# Integrated Whole Language Activities

## POETRY

### SO MANY MONKEYS

Monkey Monkey Moo!
Shall we buy a few?
Yellow monkeys,
Purple monkeys,
Monkeys red and blue.
Be a monkey, do!
Who's a monkey, who?
He's a monkey,
She's a monkey,
You're a monkey, too!
>     *Marion Edey and Dorothy Grider*

### HAND-CLAPPING RHYME

Did you eever iver ever
In your long-legged life,
See a long-legged sailor
Kiss his long-legged wife?
No, I neever niver never
In my long-legged life,
Saw a long-legged sailor
Kiss his long-legged wife!
>     *Traditional*

## INVOLVEMENT

### CHORAL READING

What a story for joining in! The lively rhythm, rhyme, and steady beat of **Chicka Chicka Boom Boom** are an instant invitation to children to join in the fun. Have them suggest a movement to accompany the phrase, *chicka, chicka, boom, boom* every time it appears in the story, i.e. jumping up, moving shoulders up and down, playing instruments, etc. Then have the children start a steady beat by slapping their knees. As the children keep the beat, begin reading the story again . . . and again!

### THE COCONUT TREE DRAMA

Choose a child to stand on a small chair with a sign around his neck that says *coconut tree*. (Can't you see it now?) Give each of the children sitting in a circle a yarn-tied letter card with a single letter on it to put around their necks. (QRS can be on one card and XYZ on another.) As you slowly read the story, have each child go to the coconut tree as his letter is called, pretend to climb and then stand by the tree. When you read, *Oh, no! Chicka Chicka . . . BOOM! BOOM!* the coconut tree sways and the letters fall, with the remaining children running to the tree to help the letters. As you continue reading, the letters get up one by one, until . . . letter A starts the Coconut Tree Drama all over again.

## INTEGRATION

### MEET YOU AT THE COCONUT TREE!

Repeat the bold colors of **Chicka Chicka Boom Boom** on a bulletin board that will brighten your room for days. Draw a pencil outline of a large coconut tree. Have the children paint and stuff with newspaper the bending tree trunk, leaves, coconuts, and cheery sun. Give each child a square with a black letter in the middle. The children will surround the black letters with bright crayon colors and then *paint-wash* over the *crayon resist*. The colorful alphabet squares will climb up, hang from, and fall off the swaying tree! Add the book title and author's name to your appealing bulletin board.

*Extension:* Involve the children in a discussion of the overloaded coconut tree. Did the tree like the alphabet letters racing to the top? How did that feel? Write a letter from the coconut tree to the alphabet, an idea the children can also use when writing in their journals.

### SIDEWAYS AND UPSIDE DOWN *

In her fascinating book, **Alphabatics**, illustrator Suse MacDonald turns alphabet letters into objects. Children can do the same. Hold up a letter and slowly turn it sideways and upside down. Ask your children to picture something the letter could be turned into. Do the same with additional letters.

Make a caption book with the sentence, *I turned my _____ into _____* printed on every page. With black crayon, print a different lower case letter in the middle of each page. Encourage the children to draw in and around the letters as they create something. Finish each child's sentence as she dictates, for example, *I turned my a into an owl.* Give each child the opportunity to show her picture and talk about what she has made.

### A WEB OF WORDS

To teach letter-sound association in meaningful context, choose a letter from the coconut tree to put in the center of a web. Then have the children look at the print around the room to find words that contain that letter. Print the words around the letter as you talk about the sound the letter makes. Ask the children if the letter appears in any of their names. Print those on the web, too. Add new words as children discover them in their reading and writing.

### AWAY THEY SWAM TO THE BOTTOM OF THE SEA*

Brainstorm ideas with the children about where else the alphabet letters could have met . . . at the zoo, in space, at the bottom of the sea! With the children clapping and with alphabet cards in view, create your own rhythmic chant, such as:

*A chased B, B chased C, Away they swam to the bottom of the sea!*
*C chased D, D chased E, Away they swam to the bottom of the sea!*

Keep chanting the letters. Every time you come to a letter that rhymes (G, P, T, V, and Z), chant the words, *Away they swam to the bottom of the sea!* Together, decide on a surprise ending.

Add to the fun by writing your chant. On every page print the pattern, _____ *chased* _____ . (Give each child a small piece of paper showing the letters he will be writing.) You will need seven pages that say, *Away they swam to the bottom of the sea!* Display your mounted illustrations for fun reading.

Away They Swam
by _____

Adapted from
Chicka Chicka Boom Boom

A chased B,

B chased C,

Away they swam to the bottom of the sea!

### A CELEBRATION

Celebrate your ABC theme by having the children plan an alphabet day.

- Bring alphabet games to school to play in small groups.
- Make alphabet letters out of play dough or craft dough.
- Decorate cupcake treats with alphabet letters on the frosting.
- Dramatize **Chicka Chicka Boom Boom**, read alphabet books, and sing alphabet songs such as *A You're Adorable* to invited guests.

**EVERYDAY LEARNING ACTIVITIES**

Positive parenting, developmental learning activities and a warm, nurturing environment are major factors in a child's academic success and lifetime learning.

When asked in an interview how her family heritage had contributed to her success, a famous author answered that her father had given her the *habit of happiness*. What a gift! Although satisfying relationships probably have the most to do with a child's inner sense of well-being, we can guide a child into a *habit of happiness*. Encourage your child to be resourceful in creating play from what he has. Nurture him with your own laughter, with happy music, and with cheery, mood-setting stories like **Chicka Chicka Boom Boom**. The infectious chant is irresistible. Who could read the story and not smile? Introduce your child to the authors and illustrators who are especially talented in creating fun with words and pictures. Always begin a story by pointing out the author's name and the illustrator's name. They will become real people to your child and soon he will be looking for more books by his favorite authors. A child who loves books will want to learn to read himself, an accomplishment that can bring many hours of happiness. *(parenting skill)*

- Draw a simple coconut tree like the one in **Chicka Chicka Boom Boom.** Put it on your refrigerator or breakfast table. Every morning, hang a simple message on the tree for your child to find. She will be learning that the silly letters that raced up the coconut tree can be put together to make words. Children love to receive messages. They soon understand that learning to read means receiving a message. *(understanding words in print)*

- Letters are everywhere in a child's world, in alphabet books like **Chicka Chicka Boom Boom**, on stores and signs, on toys and games. Have fun pointing them out everywhere. Collect some colorful, familiar labels from cereal boxes, toothpaste, soup cans, etc. and put them in an attractive Reading Basket. Put the basket close to your child's books or blocks or dolls, to use in her play. It doesn't matter if she points to the wrong word when she reads the label. What does matter is that words have meaning for her. *(word meaning)*

- Children are also learning about letters as they watch you write. Surround your child with words written down. Label things in her bedroom. Write names and words on photos in your family photo albums. Let your child dictate a simple story to you about anything she wants. As she watches, write one short sentence on the bottom of each page of a book you have made by stapling pieces of white paper together. Have your child draw a picture on each page. Read her book with her often until she has memorized the words. Reading from memory is a beginning step in reading. *(reading readiness)*

- Make an *alphabet basket* for your child by using any little basket he will enjoy carrying around. Put just one letter inside, both capital and lower case. Walk through your house together, looking for little objects that begin with the sound of that letter, such as a marble, marshmallow and marker for the letter M. Find that letter in **Chicka Chicka Boom Boom.** Have fun with the same letter for a week, adding objects and words to the basket. Encourage your child to take his *alphabet basket* with him in the car or to bed at night so he will feel that letters and words are very special. *(letter-sound association)*

# Each Peach Pear Plum

by Janet and Allan Ahlberg

**TEACHING FOCUS**
- Rhyming words
- Directional vocabulary
- Visual discrimination
- Recognizing nursery rhymes

**SETTING THE STAGE**

Instantly singable songs and the appealing rhyme and rhythm of finger plays will encourage children to be involved in storytime.

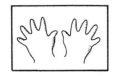

**RHYME TIME** by Greg and Steve, *Kidding Around*
(A game song in which children call out rhyming words)

**GOIN' ON A PICNIC** by Raffi, *Corner Grocery Store*

**LITTLE BO PEEP**

| | |
|---|---|
| Little Bo Peep has lost her sheep, | |
| And can't tell where to find them. | *(hands over eyes, looking)* |
| Leave them alone and they'll come home, | *(beckoning motion)* |
| Wagging their tails behind them. | *(hands behind back)* |

**JACK AND JILL**

| | |
|---|---|
| Jack and Jill went up the hill | *(thumbs "climb" hill)* |
| To fetch a pail of water. | *(grasp pail)* |
| Jack fell down, | *(one thumb fall to lap)* |
| And broke his crown | *(hands on head)* |
| And Jill came tumbling after. | *(roll hands)* |

**FIRST READING**

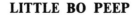

Our story today is really a hide and seek book. There are many tiny things hidden all over the front and back covers. *(Open the book so children can see the front and back simultaneously.)* You must look ever so carefully to find them. Do you see any little animals that fly in the air? Swim in the water? Walk or crawl on land? Can you find any kinds of food? What else do you see? That's the way it is in the story, too. There are little animals and people hidden on every page so we can play a hide and seek game called *I spy with my eye.* What do you think that means? The name of the book is **Each Peach Pear Plum**. It was written by Janet and Allan Ahlberg.

You read the title with me on the next page. What is the little mouse doing? I wonder if we will see that plum pie again in the story? Listen to the words of the poem. Now let's turn to the title page and you read the title with me one more time. Do you think this story takes place in the city or the country? Do you *spy* anything that was on the cover? Let's see what we can *spy* in the story.

*Because finding the characters in the pictures is the fun part of this story, encourage the children to join in. Point out to them that the first time they spy a character they can see only part of him. All of the character is shown in the very next picture.*

46

**GETTING
INVOLVED**

Let's play our own hide and seek game. If you are chosen to hide, make sure that some tiny part of you is still showing so we can *spy* you. I'm looking for someone to be the first little person who was hidden in the story. Who was that? *(Role-play the characters in sequence, giving the children quick glances at the story for reminders of who was spied next.)*

*Another time have the children stay seated and use just their eyes to find colors, shapes, or objects in the room. Give at least two visual clues. Encourage the children to answer, "I spy with my eye," when they have located the object described. And be sure to give them the opportunity to choose the objects and give the clues!*

**CLOSER LOOK**

With each rereading of a story, children gain new understanding. Pause often for a spontaneous flow of oral language as the children share their feelings and observations. Extend the learning process with your own questions in repeated readings of the story.

- What is growing on the trees? Why is Tom Thumb a good name for the little boy? *(observation)*

- Are Tom Thumb and Old Mother Hubbard *inside* the same house we saw on the title page? *(interpretation)*

- What do you spy in Mother Hubbard's cellar that you would not find anywhere in *your* house? *(association)*

- What does the word *bunting* mean? Where is Baby Bunting? What happened to Little Bear's gun? *(interpretation)*

- Tell me when you see a picture of the two nursery rhymes we said before our story. *(association)*

- How many things can you spy in Robin Hood's den? *(visual detail)*

- How did Baby Bunting get to the bridge? *(comprehension)*

- Do you spy any story characters hiding at the picnic? What will happen to the plum pie? *(visual memory, predicting)*

- Can you name everyone who came to that wonderful picnic? *(memory)*

**ROUNDING OUT
STORYTIME**

**Old Mother Hubbard**   by Alice and Martin Provensen

**Have You Seen the Crocodile?**  by Colin West

**Are You There, Bear?**   by Ron Maris

**The Three Bears**   by Paul Galdone

**Little Bo-Peep**   by Paul Galdone

# *Integrated Whole Language Activities*

**POETRY**

### TWO SAD

It's such a shock, I almost screech,
   When I find a worm inside my peach!
But then, what *really* makes me blue
   Is to find a worm who's bit in two!
          *William Cole*

### MUNCHING PEACHES

Munching peaches in the summer,
Munching peaches cool and sweet,
Munching peaches morn to midnight,
Munching peaches. Such a treat.
Munching peaches. Munching peaches.
What a way to spend the time.

While munching,
    munching,
        munching peaches,

I had time to write this rhyme.
         *Lee Bennett Hopkins*

**INVOLVEMENT**

### CHORAL READING

The simple text of **Each Peach Pear Plum** is ideal for a choral reading activity. Divide the children into two groups, with each group alternating phrases. Choose a child to direct the choral reading with a pointer!

### RHYME TIME

An oral *cloze* activity will help the children identify the rhyming word pairs in the story. Pause as you read, giving the children time to fill in the rhyming words. When they are familiar with the word pairs, write the words on color coded word cards. Pass out the word cards and let each child find her rhyming word partner. As you read **Each Peach Pear Plum** again, pause and let each child answer when you come to her word in the story. Keep the rhyming word pairs, a tape of the choral reading, and the storybook available for an independent or paired reading activity.

### READING GLASSES!

Involve the children in a discussion of which story characters were from Mother Goose rhymes and which were from fairy tales or folklore. Make two lists to put up in your library corner. Start a collection of Mother Goose books in one basket and fairy tales in another. Perhaps the children will want to bring their own books from home. Keep an assortment of reading glasses (no lens, of course!) nearby. A child's desire is to read like an adult! Have the children play their own version of *I SPY* as they read the books and look for the characters from **Each Peach Pear Plum.**

**INTEGRATION**

### THE LETTER P

As you write the words Peach, Pear, and Plum in the middle of a semantic web, ask the children how the words are similar. Have them look at the print around the room for other words that contain the letter P. Write them on the web. Add new words as the children discover them in their reading, writing, and listening experiences.

**INTEGRATION**
(continued)

## I SPY *

Write the poem that appears on the title page of **Each Peach Pear Plum** on the first page of a class retelling of the story. Write the words *I Spy* _____ on the bottom of each child's page. Offer a choice of art materials and let every child choose a story character to hide somewhere in her drawing. Choose pairs of children to illustrate the cover, the title page (which will give credit to the author and the original story), and all the story characters on the last page. Bind the brightly mounted pages into a class big book for your reading center.

## FAVORITE CHARACTERS

Write the names of the story characters on a wall graph. Give each child a small white square on which to draw his favorite character, and a choice of background colors for mounting his square. As the children make observations about the graph, talk about sets, more and less, equal and zero. Write their summarizing sentences on a chart.

## FAIRY TALES

That children do not weary of classic folktales is shown by the multiple versions of the timeless stories that continue to satisfy children. Look for unusual retellings of fairy tales for your library corner. Compare **Deep in the Forest**, the story of **The Three Bears** from Goldilocks' viewpoint by Brinton Turkle, with the traditional story by Paul Galdone. Compare **Little Red Riding Hood** as told in verse by Trina Schart Hyman with the humorous retelling by James Marshall or the lovely traditional version by Beatrice Schenk de Regniers. The contrasting art styles are a study in themselves.

## A PICNIC CELEBRATION

The charming scene at the end of **Each Peach Pear Plum** is an irresistible invitation to have a picnic! Bring a picnic basket to school full of wonderful stories about picnics, such as **Ernest and Celestine's Picnic** by Gabrielle Vincent, **The School Picnic** by Jan Steffy, **In The Forest** by Marie Hall Ets, and **The Teddy Bears' Picnic** by Jimmy Kennedy. Arrange the classroom for an indoor picnic storytime, complete with a checkered cloth, food, and utensils.

Plan a picnic for guests. Let the children decide the time, place, food, and invitations. Make charts . . . *What do we need?* and *What will we make?* During the actual picnic, have someone jot down comments the children make as they enjoy the festivities. Read the comments to the children the next day. Then write them in a book, *A Picnic Celebration*, for the children to illustrate.

**EVERYDAY LEARNING ACTIVITIES**

Positive parenting, developmental learning activities and a warm, nurturing environment are major factors in a child's academic success and lifetime learning.

Children who have already been introduced to Mother Goose will enjoy **Each Peach Pear Plum** because they will recognize the characters from the nursery rhymes hidden on the pages. One of the reasons Mother Goose has been a favorite for so long is the rhythm and rhyme of the language, which is a constant delight to the ears of little children. They simply love the musical flow of the sounds, and in many homes, Mother Goose was one of their first listening experiences. Even though the rhymes were written years ago in another country, many of them still match a child's every day activities today. You will build wonderful associations and happy memories if you begin repeating a specific rhyme for the same activity every day. Your child will love to hear *One, Two, Buckle My Shoe* while he is getting dressed, *Little Jack Horner* while he is eating, *Rub-a-Dub-Dub* for bathtime, and *Deedle, Deedle, Dumpling* for bedtime. Even better, sing the words. Music stimulates early learning in a child. Every child should have a well-illustrated Mother Goose book of his very own. He just won't tire of it! *(parenting skill)*

- Play fill in the missing word with nursery rhymes that your child already knows. Leave out a rhyming word and wait for him to supply it. Your child will love it when you switch roles, letting him say the rhyme and waiting for you to fill in the missing word. *(auditory memory)*

- Many Mother Goose Rhymes are full of direction or position words. Stop every time you come to one and have your child act it out for you, such as *over* the moon or *up* the hill. When your child is able to act out a concept with his body, it is far easier for him to understand it on paper. *(position)*

- Talk about the delightful picnic in the story, **Each Peach Pear Plum**. Let your child plan the menu and invite his stuffed animals to your own picnic. Write down the menu and the *guest* list. Hide each animal so only a tiny part is showing for your own game of *I spy with my eye*. Encourage your child to describe where he found each hidden *guest . . . under* the tablecloth, *behind* the teapot or *next to* the basket. *(directionality)*

- Play *I Spy* in your kitchen, the back yard, driving in a car, shopping in a store, anywhere! Include clues that will help your child organize information in his mind such as *I spy a fruit and it is red* or *I spy something with two wheels and it is smaller than a car*. Be sure to let your child do the spying and give you clues. *(classifying)*

- Exercising together can be a great family time. Be sure to include balancing with one foot off the floor, eyes open and then closed; hopping on one foot and then alternating feet; jumping with two feet together as though they were tied with an imaginary rope; and walking backwards, eyes open and then closed. *(gross motor skills)*

# Freight Train

*by Donald Crews*

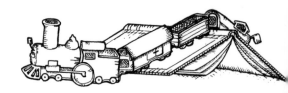

**TEACHING FOCUS**

- Left to right progression
- Building vocabulary
- Color recognition
- Introduction to trains

**SETTING THE STAGE**

Instantly singable songs and the appealing rhyme and rhythm of finger plays will encourage children to be involved in storytime.

**WORKIN' ON THE RAILROAD**
by Raffi, *More Singable Songs for the Very Young*

**CLICKETY CLACK** by Hap Palmer, *Witches Brew*
(A super song about what a freight train carries)

**THE TRAIN**

| | |
|---|---|
| I ride in the train | *(point to self)* |
| The whistle I blow | *(pull cord)* |
| I can do all the things | *(wheel motions with* |
| That will make the train go. | *hands)* |
| Whoo, whoo, goes the whistle, | *(hands to mouth)* |
| Clickety-clack go the wheels. | *(arms in wheel motions)* |
| I'm the chief engineer | *(pat chest)* |
| Til I'm called in for meals. | *(pretend to eat)* |

**TOOT! TOOT!**

| | |
|---|---|
| A peanut sat on a railroad track, | *(point to floor)* |
| His heart was all a-flutter; | *(hand over heart)* |
| The five-fifteen came rushing by— | *(point to wrist)* |
| Toot! toot! peanut butter! | *(pull cord)* |

| | |
|---|---|
| A second peanut sat on a railroad track, | *(same motions)* |
| His heart was all a-flutter; | |
| The five-fifteen came rushing by— | |
| Toot! toot! more peanut butter! | |

**FIRST READING**

*Flannelboards are like magic to young children. Without saying a word, put colored felt shapes on the flannelboard until you have created a colorful train. Ask . . .*

What did I make? Where do you think the train is going? Does it look like the train on the cover of our story? There are many different kinds of trains. This one is a freight train. I know, because that is the title of the book, **Freight Train.** It was written and illustrated by Donald Crews. He has his name on the cover, too, right under the title. See if you can find out what the word *freight* means. We have a lot to learn about trains. All aboard. Here we go!

**GETTING INVOLVED**

Let's make our own **Freight Train.** What shapes will we need? Here are eight different colored rectangles *(felt or construction paper)* for the train cars. What color do we need first? Let's put the *red* rectangle way over here on the *left* for the caboose. Keep telling me what color comes next until all the train cars are lined up. Why do we have two black rectangles?

Now let's be readers and match these color words to the colors of the train cars. Look at the first letter. Listen to the beginning sound. What color do you think that is? Let's put the color word *red* right under the red caboose. *(Match all the color words to the train cars.)* Where do you think our freight train is going? Will it make any stops along the way?

Do we have more words to add? Do the cars on the train have names? Let's begin on the *left* again. Right next to the word *red* we will add the word *caboose.* Read that with me, *red caboose.* Next to the word *orange*, let's add the words *tank car. (Add the remaining word cards and read all the phrases together!)*

**A CLOSER LOOK**

With each rereading of a story, children gain new understanding. Pause often for a spontaneous flow of oral language as the children share their feelings and observations. Extend the learning process with your own questions in repeated readings of the story.

- Where do the railroad tracks begin in the book? *(visual perception)*

- Name the colors and train cars with me. *(colors, vocabulary)*

- Find the words *freight train* on the page. What do they mean? What do you think each train car is carrying? *(interpretation)*

- Why are the colors blurred? *(comprehension)*

- What did the train go through? Go by? Go across? *(visual perception)*

- What is a tunnel? A trestle? Are they alike? *(vocabulary)*

- How does a train travel in darkness? *(critical thinking)*

- Would you rather travel in the daytime or nighttime? Why? *(reasoning)*

- Tell me your favorite car on the **Freight Train.** *(making choices)*

**ROUNDING OUT STORYTIME**

**Hey! Get Off Our Train**   by John Burningham

**Choo Choo**   by Virginia Lee Burton

**The Train**   by David McPhail

**Round Trip**   by Ann Jonas

**Trains**   by Anne Rockwell

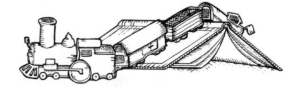

# Integrated Whole Language Activities

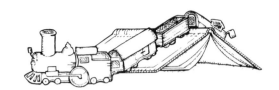

**POETRY**

**A MODERN DRAGON**

A train is a dragon that roars through the dark.
He wriggles his tail as he sends up a spark.
He pierces the night with his one yellow eye,
And all the earth trembles when he rushes by.
*Rowena Bennett*

**OUNCE and BOUNCE**
by Jack Prelutsky
from *The New Kid on the Block* by J. Prelutsky

**INVOLVEMENT**

**CHORAL READING**

The bold colors and visual clues invite children to spontaneously join in and read chorally with the teacher, again and again!

**MOVING RIGHT ALONG!**

Have the children identify things in the room that can become a train station, train tracks, a tunnel, a city, and trestles (the supports for the bridge). Hang a sign around each child's neck showing the name and color of each train car. Choose an engineer to hook up the eight cars in sequence and direct the train to chug, speed up, slow down or refuel as it goes over, under, through, and around objects in the room.

**INTEGRATION**

**GOING, GOING, CHUG, CHUG, CHUG, GONE!!**

Write a class innovation of **The Freight Train**. On sentence strips or chart paper, print open-ended phrases about *moving*, like the phrase *Going through* _____ . As the children suggest things a train could move through such as the countryside, the snow or a thunderstorm, record each of their answers on separate post-its and add them to the end of the phrase. After taking dictation for four or five phrases, have the children decide which post-it to keep for each phrase in their story. Print the words they have chosen in the blanks. Then have the children decide on an action for each phrase, similar to the familiar **We're Going on a Bear Hunt** story by Michael Rosen. Your new train story might look something like this . . .

Going through a thunderstorm *(slap thighs with alternating hands)*
Going by a highway *(pretend to honk horn)*
Crossing a river *(hands swish, swish)*
Moving in a fog *(hands shading eyes)*
Going, going, chug, chug, gone! *(circular wheel motions by sides)*

*Extension:* Using the text the class has written, print one sentence on each page of a class book for the children to illustrate.

**INTEGRATION**
(continued)

## A WALL MURAL

Pencil in a simple background outline on a large piece of bulletin board paper for the children to paint. Include railroad tracks, a tunnel, a city skyline and trestles. Have the children paint and cut out eight big (!) train cars. Be sure to cut out the windows in the caboose and steam engine before placing the cars on the tracks. Print the name and color of each car on word cards and place the cards under the train. Add the words **The Freight Train** by Donald Crews to your colorful mural. It will become an independent or paired reading experience as your children *read the walls*!

## LOADING THE CARS

Involve the children in a discussion of the purpose and the contents of each of the freight train cars. Brainstorming will give them time to think and to prepare. After each child has an idea of something he can load into one of the cars, give the children drawing paper and construction paper scraps to create and cut out their ideas. Then gather the children around the wall mural. One by one, have them add their *freight* or *people* to the appropriate train car. Discuss the results. How many objects in each car? Which car has the most? The least?

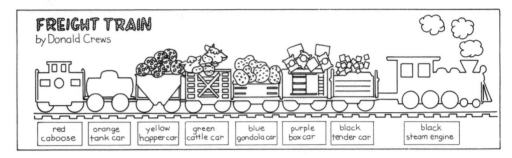

*Exension:* Graph the results on an eight column graph with the name and color of each train car printed at the top. Have each child make a small picture of his *freight* or *person* to add to the graph. As a group, write a summary statement to hang beside the graph for more print to read.

## ALL ABOARD!

Use a nonfiction book such as **Trains** by Anne Rockwell to expand your thematic unit. Have each child draw a picture of something he has learned. You act as recorder as he dictates a sentence about his picture. Make a *train* on your wall of all the mounted illustrations or bind them in a class big book, **All Aboard!**

Add appropriate train props and signs in your dramatic play area. Keep literacy related materials visible, i.e. pencils and crayons, various colors and sizes of paper, blank books and magazines. Participate in the children's play as you guide them in literacy activities. For example, on a passenger train the children could write tickets and schedules, number the seats, make *no smoking* and *exit* signs, write messages for passengers, and label the parts of the train. Have the children create their own costumes in the art center and dress up as the ticket taker, conductor, porter, engineer and passengers. Write name cards. Locate destinations on a map. Make a large clock to show departures and arrivals. You are setting the stage for successful role-playing and writing experiences. **All aboard!**

## HEY! GET OFF OUR TRAIN

Consider the marvelous drama, art, and writing possibilities of **Hey! Get Off Our Train**, John Burningham's appealing story with a timely message.

**EVERYDAY LEARNING ACTIVITIES**

Positive parenting, developmental learning activities and a warm, nurturing environment are major factors in a child's academic success and lifetime learning.

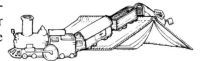

In the crucial early learning years, children master new words and meanings faster than at any other time of life. Children need to be surrounded with language and that makes you the most important language teacher they will ever have! This is the perfect opportunity to build vocabulary. Don't be afraid to use unfamiliar words as you talk. Children love big words like *gondola* and *trestle* in **Freight Train.** Try cutting your child's sandwich in a *diagonal,* or offering *privacy* in the bathroom, or giving her a *compliment* on good behavior. When she is learning to read and comes across a new word such as *garage,* she will remember the word if she has a mental picture in her head of what a garage is. So the more words a child understands, the more successful she will be in reading. Think of a new word and use it often, even in silly ways, and your child will love it! *(parenting skill)*

- Teach your child the magic of color in your own kitchen. Fill three large clear glasses with water. Add red food coloring to one glass, blue to the second and yellow to the third. Now set out three empty glasses. Pour some yellow water and some blue water into the same empty glass and talk about what is happening. The new color you have made, green, is the most dramatic mixture. Next pour some red and yellow into an empty glass to make orange. The last combination is red and blue to make purple. Purple is the hardest to see so be sure to hold it up to the light. Line up all six glasses of colors. Label them and name them. *(color recognition)*

- Simple thinking games can be wonderful memory builders. Ask your child to tell you all the things she can remember that she saw today . . . at the store or in the yard or in a storybook. The more you praise her, the longer the list will grow! Ask her to remember things from yesterday like what she was wearing or what she had to eat. Try *anticipating (she will love the big word)* what you will see tomorrow. Make a list so she can see her words in print. Don't be surprised if your child starts asking you to list what you remember! *(memory, categorizing)*

- It is important for a child to both recognize shapes and name them. Shapes help a child see how things are alike and different. Introduce only one shape at a time and focus on that shape in conversation and in simple activities for a number of days before introducing another. For example, together find all the circle shapes in the kitchen like a clock, dinner plates, bottom of pots, pizza pan, etc. After a child can recognize and name circles, squares, and triangles, play matching games. Sort objects or shapes cut from paper into several piles—a circle pile, a square pile, etc. Mix them up again and build a train from circles or a train from squares. *(identifying shapes)*

# The Gingerbread Boy

## by Paul Galdone

**TEACHING FOCUS**
- Sequencing
- Vocabulary
- Story participation
- Creative play

**SETTING THE STAGE**

Instantly singable songs and the appealing rhyme and rhythm of finger plays will encourage children to be involved in storytime.

**BISCUITS IN THE OVEN** by Raffi, *Baby Beluga* (Watch 'em rise!)

**SOMETHING IN MY SHOE** by Raffi, *Rise and Shine*
(a cumulative song about funny things a boy finds in his shoe)

**RIGHT HAND, LEFT HAND**

| | |
|---|---|
| This is my right hand, I'll raise it way up high. | *(right hand up)* |
| This is my left hand, I'll touch the sky. | *(left hand up)* |
| Right hand, left hand | *(show palms)* |
| Whirl them round and round, | *(twirl hands)* |
| Right hand, left hand | *(show palms)* |
| Pound, pound, pound. | *(pound fists together)* |

**I SEE YOU**

| | |
|---|---|
| I have two eyes to see with, | *(touch eyes)* |
| I have two feet to run with, | *(tap feet)* |
| I have two hands to clap with, | *(clap hands)* |
| And nose I have but one, | *(touch nose)* |
| I have two ears to hear with, | *(touch ears)* |
| And a tongue to click each day, | *(click tongue)* |
| And two red cheeks for you to kiss, | *(touch cheek)* |
| And now I'll run away. | |

**FIRST READING**

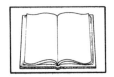

Our story today is one that has been around for a very long time. Your grandmas probably heard this story when they were little. Paul Galdone is a man who decided to draw the pictures and tell the story one more time, for children like you to enjoy.

Tell me about the little boy on the cover. What do you think he is made of? Have you ever tasted gingerbread? The title of our book is **The Gingerbread Boy** and it is the story of a gingerbread cookie that popped right out of the oven and ran away!

*Point out the gingerbread letters on the title page. Encourage the children to join you on the repetitive phrases.*

**GETTING INVOLVED**

Let's pretend we are bakers just like the old woman in the story. We are ready to make a whole batch of gingerbread boys. What ingredients do you think we will need? Let's list them on a chart. Now we're ready to mix. Put a big bowl right in front of you. Measure some shortening into your measuring cup and dump it in. Next comes the brown sugar and a little molasses and now some eggs. Better crack them first on the edge of your bowl! Now let's sift some flour and some ginger spice to make it smell good in the oven. Time to stir and stir. Now roll out your dough with your rolling pin. Next use your fingers to shape every part of his body. Looking good! Don't forget raisins for his eyes and mouth and buttons. How about a cinnamon drop for his nose? Now you are ready to slip your gingerbread boy into the oven and close the door very carefully. Sit down right in front of the oven so he doesn't run away!

**A CLOSER LOOK**

With each rereading of a story, children gain new understanding. Pause often for a spontaneous flow of oral language as the children share their feelings and observations. Extend the learning process with your own questions in repeated readings of the story.

- Why did the little old woman decide to make a Gingerbread Boy? *(comprehension)*

- What did the little old woman smell? *(memory)*

- What surprised the little old woman when she opened the oven door? *(comprehension)*

- What happened when the little Gingerbread Boy met a cow? A horse? *(memory)*

- What does *threshing* wheat mean? Why are the threshers holding sticks? *(vocabulary)*

- What were the mowers doing? What are they holding? Did they frighten the little Gingerbread Boy? *(comprehension)*

- Why was the little Gingerbread Boy proud of himself? What does it mean to *strut* and *prance*? *(vocabulary)*

- How did the fox trick the gingerbread boy? *(interpretation)*

- Did you like the ending of the story? How would you change the ending? *(opinion)*

- Do you think you could have caught the Gingerbread Boy? *(opinion)*

**ROUNDING OUT STORYTIME**

**King Rooster, Queen Hen**   by Anita Lobel

**Three Blind Mice**   by John W. Ivimey

**Mike's Kite**   by Elizabeth MacDonald

**One Fine Day**   by Nonny Hogrogian

**Henny Penny**   by Paul Galdone

# *Integrated Whole Language Activities*

**POETRY**

**THE GINGERBREAD MAN**

Smiling girls, rosy boys,
Come and buy my little toys;
Monkeys made of gingerbread,
And sugar horses painted red.
*Anonymous*

**JUST WATCH**

by Myra Cohn Livingston
from *Read Aloud Rhymes for the Very Young* by Jack Prelutsky

**THE GINGERBREAD MAN**
by Rowena Bennett
from *Sing a Song of Popcorn* selected by Beatrice Schenk de Regniers

**INVOLVEMENT**

- The repetitive phrases and predictability of **The Gingerbread Boy** are an invitation to children to join in the story. They also offer an ideal setting for creative dramatics. Have the children create drama props in your art center or look in your dress-up box for hats or costumes. The tools for the threshers and mowers could be rulers or dowels with foil covered cardboard blades. The children who are not playing the part of the characters can join in on the chant.

- Draw simple pictures of the story characters on small pieces of paper. Give a picture to each of fourteen children. Give clues to the children, such as, *I am thinking of a story character that had two legs and wore a bonnet.* The child who is holding the picture of the little old woman would come sit by you. After the children have matched their pictures to your clues, have the child who was the Gingerbread Boy line them up in the order they ran after him in the story.

**INTEGRATION**

**AN ABC COLLAGE OF GINGERBREAD BOYS**

In collage art, every finished product is an expression of the child who created it. There are no losers, just as there are no two alike. To make collage art gingerbread boys, let each child choose any two of an assortment of colors. The first color will be the body of his gingerbread boy. The second will be the collage color. Have every child tear out a head, body, arms and legs for a gingerbread boy, gluing them down on a piece of white paper. Then have him tear small pieces from his second color to arrange and rearrange on his gingerbread boy until he is satisfied with the design and ready to glue the pieces in place. Offer scraps of bright accent colors to tear for eyes, nose, mouth and buttons.

Print an upper and lower case letter on the top of each page. Write the words, *I ran away from an _____ . Run! Run! Run! Catch me if you can!* on the bottom. The child can dictate to you what his gingerbread boy ran away from. (Have all the children help with ideas for the difficult letters, perhaps suggesting a (porcupine) quill for Q or a railroad crossing for X.) Choose a group of children to create a cover, a title page and the last page of your caption book . . . *And I can run away from you, I can! I can!*

60

## CATCH ME IF YOU CAN!

Tell the story of **The Gingerbread Boy** on a wall or bulletin board in your room. Have the children create large faces of the fourteen characters in the story. Offer a variety of art materials . . . tempera paint, watercolor paint, collage, tear art, construction paper, felt and fabric scraps, and water-based markers.

Put the face of the Gingerbread Boy on the far left with the faces of the other characters sequenced across the mural. Across the top of your scene, print the words, *"Run! Run! Run! Catch me if you can!"* Under each face, put the sentence, *"Stop," said the* _____ . The familiar words of the story will offer one more opportunity for emergent reading.

Run! Run! Run! Catch me if you can!

"Stop," said the woman. "Stop," said the man. "Stop," said the cow. "Stop," said the horse. "Stop," said the thresher. "Stop," said the mower.

## THE EMPTY OVEN

Children's ideas of recipe ingredients and proportions are hilarious! Have the children name the ingredients you will need to make a gingerbread boy, the amount needed of each item, the directions for mixing and baking and the oven temperature. Write their recipe on chart paper for the children to read and illustrate.

Show the children an actual gingerbread recipe you have written on separate paper. Have fun comparing the two recipes and deciding which one to follow! On a cookie sheet, shape the batter into a large gingerbread boy, add raisins for the features and bake.

Return to the oven *after* someone has had a chance to hide the Gingerbread Boy. Have the children find a hot, empty oven with a note on the oven door saying, *"You can't catch me! I'm the Gingerbread Boy, I am! Meet me in the office."* When the children go to the office, they will find another note. The clues will send the children to various places in the school . . . the clinic, the custodian's room, etc. until the last clue directs them back to their own classroom, where the Gingerbread Boy is waiting!

## THE KITCHEN

Create a simulation of a kitchen in your room. Arrange a collection of cook books in a basket to invite readers. Provide a supply of pencils, paper, and small blank books for children to write or copy recipes, including your own Gingerbread Boy recipe. Put out food coupons, a small message board, a calendar, a note pad, food cartons, mixing bowls, measuring cups, table settings, and whatever the children suggest for their imaginative role-playing. Add a tub of colored dry rice with funnels, spoons and a variety of containers. Keep individual chalkboards and chalk nearby. As the children work in pairs, they can estimate and tally the spoonsful of rice it will take to fill each container.

**EVERYDAY LEARNING ACTIVITIES**

Positive parenting, developmental learning activities and a warm, nurturing environment are major factors in a child's academic success and lifetime learning.

**The Gingerbread Boy** is an example of a traditional tale that probably gave each of you a warm feeling when you heard the words again. Perhaps the story is a memory of your mother reading to you. When you think of your mother's voice, you are really thinking of her as a person, because the voice and person are inseparable in your mind. That means you can use your own voice to create a wonderful association in your child's mind, just by reading to him often. Books and the memory of your voice can be an exciting part of your child's heritage. Some of the happiest memories we have of our own childhood focus on the things our family did together . . . the things that gave continuity and a "oneness" to our family living. They were the experiences we could count on every year, the traditions that were expressions of love that kept on repeating themselves. By creating the tradition of reading in your home, you are giving your child a lifetime of memories. *(parenting skill)*

- Baking is always a learning experience in measuring, sequencing and following directions. Bake **The Gingerbread Boy** with your child, but let her find an empty oven when the timer goes off. Plan a trail of simple messages from the gingerbread boy . . . brief clues on little pieces of paper that will eventually lead your child to his hiding place. Party time! *(words in print)*

- Drawing, cutting and pasting are all fine motor skills. Draw part of a gingerbread boy and let your child finish the drawing. Let her draw more, all shapes and sizes, and then cut, paste, and decorate them with markers and buttons and bits of colored paper. Have your child paste the gingerbread people in a book and dictate a sentence for you to write on each page. *(fine motor)*

- Make jello together. As you add a variety of tidbits (celery, nuts, apple and banana slices, mini-marshmallows, etc.), ask your child to predict which will sink and which will float. Make a different color jello every week. Encourage your child to identify that color wherever he sees it, inside, outside, shopping, in the car, in books, everywhere! *(predicting, colors)*

- Encourage your child to copy shapes. Put big, bold dots on a piece of paper and show your child how to connect them to make a shape. Show him that circles begin at the top and are drawn counter-clockwise. To make a triangle, also begin at the top and count out loud, 1, 2, 3, as you draw the three sides. Count 1, 2, 3, 4 as you draw a square. Praise all of a child's efforts and don't expect the end result to be perfect. *(copying shapes)*

- You can expand your child's vocabulary by teaching him the purpose or the function of many objects that he can already name. Make up "What Am I?" riddles for your child to guess, such as, "I am made of wood. I have an eraser on top. What am I?" You can make the game harder by asking, "I am a pencil. What do I do?" Use common household and classroom objects, and when your child is really good at solving the riddles, remember to reverse roles and let him make up some for you to solve. *(language)*

# Good Morning, Chick

## by Mirra Ginsburg

**TEACHING FOCUS**
- Identifying farm animals
- Visual/Auditory Discrimination
- Color recognition
- Shape recognition

**SETTING THE STAGE**

Instantly singable songs and the appealing rhyme and rhythm of finger plays will encourage children to be involved in storytime.

**RISE AND SHINE** by Raffi, *Rise and Shine*

**ROCKIN' ROUND THE MULBERRY BUSH**
by Greg and Steve, *We All Live Together, Vol. 3*

**THE FLUFFY CHICKENS**

| | |
|---|---|
| Five eggs and five eggs | *(hold up two hands)* |
| That makes ten. | |
| Sitting on the top is the Mother Hen | *(one hand covers* |
| Crackle, crackle, crackle, | *other fist)* |
| What do I see? | *(move hand that was* |
| Ten fluffy chickens | *the fist)* |
| As yellow as can be! | *(hold up two hands again)* |

**BUSY MORNING**

| | |
|---|---|
| I am busy in the morning, | *(hand open, palm up)* |
| I have many things to do. | *(other hand same)* |
| I like to get all ready | |
| When the day is bright and new. | *(hands open, by face)* |
| | |
| I wash my face, I comb my hair, | *(imitate action)* |
| I eat my breakfast in my chair. | *(imitate action)* |
| And then it's time to go and play, | *(thumb over shoulder)* |
| And that is how I spend my day. | *(hands in lap)* |
|       *Mary Cornelius* | |

**FIRST READING**

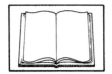

Tell me a story about the picture on the cover of this book. How did you know the animals were on a farm? Can you see the animal that usually wakes up first on a farm? Look at the two little animals watching the mother hen from a distance. I wonder if we will see them again in the story.

What do you think the mother hen and the little chick are saying? Perhaps the mother hen has just said *good morning* to the baby chick. Those are the exact words of the title. Read the words on the cover with me, **Good Morning, Chick**, by Mirra Ginsburg, pictures by Byron Barton.

*The repetitive phrase, like this, invites the children to join in spontaneously.*

**GETTING INVOLVED**

Did we see a farmer in the story, **Good Morning, Chick**? Do you think there was one? Pretend to be the farmer waking up in the yellow farmhouse. Wake up *(stretch arms)*, get dressed *(act out)*, eat breakfast *(hand to mouth)* and walk out the front door *(clap hands for the door closing)*.

Tell me the sounds the farmer heard in his barnyard that morning. Let's put those sounds in order. First, the farmer heard the chick breaking out of it's shell, *tap-tap, crack.* Next he heard Speckled Hen teaching the chick to eat, *peck-peck, peck-peck.* Then the farmer heard the black cat *hissing* and the mother hen scolding him, *cluck-cluck-cluck.* The rooster started crowing, *cock-a-doodle-do!* but the little chick could only say *peep-peep.* Then the farmer heard the chick fall into the water, *plop*, and the frog laughed, *qua-ha, qua-ha.* The last sound the farmer heard was the mother hen and the happy chick looking for worms and seeds, *peck-peck, peck-peck.*

*Another time, let the children volunteer other animal sounds that a farmer might hear on a farm.*

**A CLOSER LOOK**

With each rereading of a story, children gain new understanding. Pause often for a spontaneous flow of oral language as the children share their feelings and observations. Extend the learning process with your own questions in repeated readings of the story.

- What do you remember that was the color *red* in the story? *Yellow? Blue? (color recognition)*

- What did the hen's house look like? The chick's house? *(visual perception)*

- How did the baby chick get out of his house? *(comprehension)*

- Did the little chick look like his mother? *(comparison)*

- Was Speckled Hen a good name for the mother? *(reason)*

- How did the chick learn to do things in the barnyard? *(interpretation)*

- Who is the black cat watching? What will she do? *(predicting)*

- How did the Speckled Hen protect her chick? *(recall)*

- Why did the frog laugh at the chick? *(comprehension)*

- Was Speckled Hen a good mother? Why? *(reasoning)*

**ROUNDING OUT STORYTIME**

**The Box with Red Wheels**   by Maud Petersham

**Across the Stream**   by Mirra Ginsburg

**The Chicken Book**   by Garth Williams

**Benjamin's Barn**   by Reeve Lindbergh

**Color Farm**   by Lois Ehlert

# *Integrated Whole Language Activities*

**POETRY**

**BABY BIRD**

Watch the baby bird.
   He's hatching from his shell!
Out comes his head,
   And then comes his tail.
Now his legs he stretches,
   His wings he gives a flap.
Then he flies and flies and flies.
   Now what do you think of that?
Down, down, down, down, down, down, down, OUCH
*Pamela Conn Beall*

**INVOLVEMENT**

**BABY BIRD**

The poem, **Baby Bird**, is a scale song that can be sung easily with no accompaniment. With the children crouched low to the floor, begin singing the song on a low note on the scale. Sing all the words of the first phrase on that same note. Move up one note on the scale as you sing each phrase and have the children stand a little taller with each note. After singing *"Now what do you think of that?"* you are ready to come back down the scale again. Repeat the word *down* on each descending note. With the last word *"OUCH!"* the children will be laughing on the floor and asking to sing the song again!

**CHICKENS CAN, CHICKENS CAN'T**

Cut a large chick from doubled, sturdy paper. The children can paint and stuff it. Talk about all the parts of the chick's body. To encourage children to think in details, have them suggest words that describe each part of the chick. Print their descriptive phrases on word cards as you label the parts.

Talk about all the things the little chick could already do in the story, **Good Morning, Chick.** He could split open his egg, look around, peck, eat worms, etc. Write the action words on word cards. Then individually, in pairs, or in groups, have the children pantomime the sentence, *Chickens can _____ like this!* Those watching must guess the missing action word, find it, and put it in the sentence.

Add to the fun by orally extending the sentence to: *Chickens can _____ like this but can't _____ like this.* Ask the children to think of and pantomime both actions. For example, Chickens can *peck* like this but can't *smile* like this. The children will enjoy the silly ones best!

**INTEGRATION**

**LIKE THIS! \***

The predictable text of **Good Morning, Chick** makes it easy for children to write a simplified innovation of the story. Review the children's ideas about what chicks can do. Refer to the illustrations in the book until every child has an idea to draw. Give each child a piece of paper with the words, *Chickens can _____* printed at the top. Print the phrase, *like this,* on the bottom.

**INTEGRATION**
(continued)

Have each child dictate to you the word(s) he has chosen to finish his sentence. Choose children to draw a cover and a title page. Mount the illustrated pages on colorful background paper and bind them in a class book to add to your library corner.

*Extension:* Make a caption book using the same sentence on every page, *Chickens can* _____ *like this but can't* _____ . Give each child the opportunity to share his page with the class. The humor of this book will certainly make it a favorite!*

### A BARNYARD IN THE MORNING

The bold colors of **Good Morning, Chick** will create a beautiful story on the wall. Have the children create a simple background of grass and sky on a large piece of bulletin board paper. Talk about all the things Mirra Ginsburg put in her pictures to tell the story, such as the trees, house, barn, fence, pond, etc. Let the children decide on the characters and objects they want in their story. (This activity would adapt well to *tear art*, using brightly colored construction paper.) Staple or glue everything the children have made to the background. Your colorful mural will look like an original book cover! Add the story title and the author's name.

*Variation:* A simpler activity would be to have each child draw and cut out a chick, hen, or rooster. Group the animals on the farm scene mural. Add a bright sun and smile at your *waking up* barnyard family!

### WHEN I AM BIGGER! *

Involve the children in a discussion about things older children and grownups can do that they can't. Talk about how they feel when they want to do something and are told to wait until they are bigger. After every child has had a chance to think of something, have him draw his idea on a large piece of paper. Act as recorder and write the sentence he dictates on his drawing. Then give everyone a second piece of paper with the words printed on the bottom, *Oh, well! I'll wait 'til I am bigger!* On those pages the wishes come true!

I want to mow the lawn.

Oh, well I'll wait til I am bigger.

I want to wear make up.

Oh, well I'll wait til I am bigger.

### CHICKENS AREN'T THE ONLY ONES

The children's curiosity about the little chick pecking its way out of its shell can lead to an interest in other animals that lay eggs. **Chickens Aren't The Only Ones** by Ruth Heller is an outstanding, nonfiction book with appealing, rhyming text and lovely pictures! Just charting the variety of animals that lay eggs offers an opportunity for emergent reading and writing. Have each child draw a picture of something he has learned and then invent his spellings as he writes a sentence about his picture. The children will be eager to read their sentences. **Chickens Aren't The Only Ones** will fascinate your beginning readers for a long time. Who knows what theme the book will lead to?

67

**EVERYDAY LEARNING ACTIVITIES**

Positive parenting, developmental learning activities and a warm, nurturing environment are major factors in a child's academic success and lifetime learning.

In the story, **Good Morning, Chick**, the baby chick learned everything about the world around him by imitating his mother. Children are born imitators, too. They never stop learning by imitation. Children imitate friends and siblings, television and videos. And they imitate parents. . . your tone of voice, your language, your actions, the way you problem solve or spend your time. That means *who* you are, the person you are, speaks louder than what you say. Children are very likely to imitate in their own lives the values that you live out in front of them. That can be a very positive teaching tool. Children will spontaneously imitate the good behaviors you model day after day. *(parenting skill)*

- Give your child step by step directions for a simple activity like putting on her socks and shoes, or washing her hands. Let her repeat the words *like this* as she follows your directions. Include activities she might really need to practice such as cutting and pasting. *(following directions)*

- A child usually *matches* shapes before she identifies them by name. Read **Good Morning, Chick** again, looking for a specific shape such as *triangles* to match the hen's beak. Another time, look for *circles* to match the chick's eyes or *squares* to match the henhouse door. (Watch out for the perception change!) When your child has mastered those shapes, add *rectangles* like the fenceposts or *ovals* to match the chick's egg. Activities that have meaning for a child provide far more effective learning than flash cards or workbooks. *(shape recognition)*

- Imitating can become a memory game. Tell your child to watch you as you make two different motions. Then slowly count to five before you ask her to repeat the two motions in sequence. When she is consistently successful, increase the number to three actions, then four. Change the activity to a listening skill by simply *saying* the directions. Watch to see how well she listens. It adds to the fun and the learning if you reverse roles, too! *(perceptual skills)*

- Pretend to be the animals in **Good Morning, Chick** and act out the story. Another time, make up your own game by choosing one child to be Speckled Hen with everyone else pretending to be chicks. When Speckled Hen closes her eyes, the chicks find hiding places and make quiet peeping noises. Mother Hen must find her chicks by listening for the peeps and probably a few giggles as well! *(auditory skills)*

# Goodnight Moon

## by Margaret Wise Brown

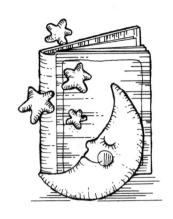

**TEACHING FOCUS**
- Visual discrimination
- Night and day, light and dark
- Rhyming words
- Colors

**SETTING THE STAGE**

Instantly singable songs and the appealing rhyme and rhythm of finger plays will encourage children to be involved in storytime.

**GOODNIGHT** by Hap Palmer, *Witches Brew*
(Describes where all the creatures go to sleep)

**STARLIGHT/BYE 'N BYE/TWINKLE** by Sharon, Lois & Bram
*One Elephant, Deux Elephants*, (Three old favorites!)

**WEE WILLIE WINKIE**

| Wee Willie Winkie | |
| runs through the town, | *(run in place)* |
| Upstairs and downstairs | *(stepping motion)* |
| in his nightgown, | |
| Rapping at the window, | *(knocking motion)* |
| Crying through the lock, | *(hands to mouth)* |
| "Are the children in their beds? | |
| For now it's eight o'clock." | *(eight fingers up)* |

**HEY DIDDLE, DIDDLE**

| Hey diddle, diddle; The cat in the fiddle; | *(play fiddle under chin)* |
| The cow jumped over the moon. | *(hands make jumping motion)* |
| The little dog laughed to see such a sport; | *(hand to mouth, laughing)* |
| And the dish ran away with the spoon | *(two fingers run up arm)* |

**FIRST READING**

Before I even tell you the title of today's story, I'm going to just silently turn the pages. You be the storytellers. Use your eyes very carefully and tell me everything you see. What do you think is happening?

I think Margaret Wise Brown would have loved your story. I know *I* did! In her story, the little bunny is already tucked into bed. Before he goes to sleep, he says good night to everything he can see in his room . . . good night to the clocks and his socks, good night to the mittens and the kittens, and even good night to the moon he can see through his bedroom window. And that's the name of the story, **Goodnight Moon.**

**GETTING INVOLVED**

When the little bunny said good night to everything in his room, he was relaxing before he went to sleep. I'm sure he would love to be here right now to do some relaxing exercises with us. Stand up and spread out your arms carefully so you have some space all your own. First, let's bend over and hang our arms down like a rag doll. Now pretend you are a puppet and there is a string on the top of your head. Pull the string to pull yourself up straight. Pretend you are a balloon and take three deep breaths to fill yourself up with air. Gently float around in a circle, moving your arms slowly up and down. Float down, down, down to the ground. Now pretend you are taking a trip on a magic carpet. You are flying right through the clouds, over the trees, into your own room and right into your cozy bed. Before you go to sleep, let's say good night to the cow jumping over the moon. *(Say Hey Diddle, Diddle together.)*

**A CLOSER LOOK**

With each rereading of a story, children gain new understanding. Pause often for a spontaneous flow of oral language as the children share their feelings and observations. Extend the learning process with your own questions in repeated readings of the story.

- Tell me all the things you remember that the bunny said good night to. *(memory)*

- Every time I pause in the story, you say the rhyming word. *(auditory discrimination)*

- Did you see a picture of a bunny fishing? It is from another book by Margaret Wise Brown called **The Runaway Bunny.** *(visual perception)*

- Who is the quiet old lady? What is she doing? *(association)*

- Why are the colors changing in the bunny's room? *(comprehension)*

- Why is there no picture on one page? *(comprehension)*

- Did you find the little mouse in every colored picture? *(visual perception)*

- Let's look for other things in the pictures to say good night to. Can you think of rhyming words? *(fire, lamp, rug, book, stars, spoon, bed, etc.)* *(auditory skills)*

**ROUNDING OUT STORYTIME**

**Squawk to the Moon, Little Goose**   by Edna Mitchell Preston

**Where Does the Sun Go at Night?**   by Mirra Ginsburg

**Hush Little Baby**   by Aliki

**Owl Moon**   by Jane Yolen

**Moongame**   by Frank Asch

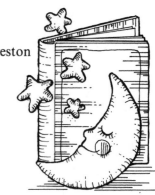

# Integrated Whole Language Activities

**POETRY**

### MOON BOAT

Moon Boat, little, brave and bright,
Tossed upon the seas of night,
One day when I'm free to roam,
I'll climb aboard and steer you home.
*Charlotte Pomerantz*

### KEEP A POEM IN YOUR POCKET

by Beatrice Schenk de Regniers
from *The Random House Book of Poetry*

### SILVERLY

by Dennis Lee
from *Read Aloud Rhymes for the Very Young* by Jack Prelutsky

**INVOLVEMENT**

- Play quiet lullaby music as a background setting for a choral reading of **Goodnight Moon.** Keep turning the volume of the music softer as the pictures of the bunny's room gradually darken.

- Make a cassette tape of the music and the choral reading for a listening center.

- Encourage the children to read the illustrations for clues as you wait for them to add the rhyming words of the text in an oral cloze activity.

**INTEGRATION**

### WHISPER GOODNIGHT

Guide the children in recalling the many things the bunny said good night to in the story. Have each child decide on one thing to draw on his square of white paper. Add the words, *Goodnight* _____ under each child's drawing. (It won't matter if some objects from the story are duplicated or some are omitted.) Mount them on larger squares of green construction paper if you want to group them later in a *great green room* collage.

Have the children bring their finished pictures to the circle as you play quiet music and turn off the lights. Be *the quiet old lady who whispered "hush"* as each child whispers good night to whatever he has drawn. End the game by whispering, *Goodnight noises everywhere*, as the children get ready for rest time or a quiet activity.

### MOON BOAT

The poem, **Moon Boat**, creates a wonderful word image of children steering moon boats across the sky. Create a night scene on your bulletin board by covering it with dark blue paper. Let every child cut (or tear) a moon boat and an oval from construction paper. Have him draw his face on the oval and paste it in the crescent moon to steer it across the dark sky. Add some glitter stars to the night scene. Place the mounted chart poem, **Moon Boat**, on one side of your bulletin board. Children will be drawn to their own art work and the poetry as they *read the walls!*

## GOODNIGHT RHYMES

Have the children study the story illustrations in **Goodnight Moon** to find other things the bunny could have said *goodnight* to in the green room. Write the words GOODNIGHT TO . . . on the top of your chart paper. Then list the children's suggestions, such as fire, lamp, rug, book, stars, spoon, bed, etc. Ask the children to think of words that rhyme with each word on their list. Write the rhyming words also. You are really creating an oral innovation of the story.

To make a class big book, give each child a piece of paper with the words, *Goodnight _____ and goodnight _____* written on the bottom. Each child can choose a pair of rhyming words from your chart or from the story to illustrate on his page. Write the words he dictates to finish his sentence. Choose children to make a cover, a first page that says, *The bunny in the bed closed his eyes and said*, and a last page that says, *Goodnight moon.*

## OUR GOODNIGHT JOURNAL

When you occasionally initiate a project that involves families, you are building a bridge from home to school. Make a class big book with a night scene drawn by the children on the cover. Laminate it for protection. Prepare a page for every child in your room with these words printed on the bottom:

*This is _____ 's room.*
*Goodnight _____ and goodnight _____*

Provide a very special bookbag or canvas bag to hold the Goodnight Journal, crayons, pencils, markers, rulers, and a laminated note explaining the project to parents.

One at a time, let the children take the Goodnight Journal home, draw their bedrooms and the things they say goodnight to every night. Parents can help complete the sentences. Let every child read his sentences and talk about his picture when he brings the book back. When your Goodnight Journal is complete, put it inside the canvas bag and keep it in your reading center for all to enjoy.

## A GRAPHING TUB

From time to time add something to a graphing tub in your room, explaining to the children that when it is full you will all decide how to graph what is inside. Empty the contents on the floor in the middle of a circle with the children sitting around you. Have them name and talk about all the objects, such as a balloon, slipper, teddy bear, toothbrush, comb, soap, socks, etc. until they have decided on two categories for grouping.

The categories might be objects that were in the bunny's great green room or not in the great green room, objects that are part of bedtime or not part of bedtime, objects found in a bathroom or found in a bedroom. Another day their choices might be the qualities of the objects such as hard or soft, cloth or not cloth, or colors. Graph the actual objects on a two-column floor graph as you make conclusions about more than, less than, equal sets and unequal sets.

**EVERYDAY LEARNING ACTIVITIES**

Positive parenting, developmental learning activities and a warm, nurturing environment are major factors in a child's academic success and lifetime learning.

**Goodnight Moon** is probably the best-loved bedtime book ever written. Your child will want to hear it over and over again because children don't tire of repetition as we do. Familiar stories become warm friends and are especially comforting at night. A predictable bedtime routine provides loving security to a child, both in repetition and in knowing limits. Allowing your child to make some choices in the sequencing of the routine is a great way to get her cooperation. Start early enough to allow time in the evening for yourself. Most children go to bed far too late, so remember the choice should not be theirs. Focus on quieting down activities and be sure to include a bedtime book. Quiet music is soothing also, and children love the familiarity of the same bedtime music. When your routine is over, be quietly firm. Set limits and mean it when you say, "Our time is over. Good night and sweet dreams!" Put your child to sleep every night with a good thought about herself. . . something she has said or done that day that has pleased you. Over the years, that adds up to a powerful package of what a child can believe about herself. *(parenting skill)*

- The gradually darkening pictures and the stars and moon showing through the window are a perfect ending to this gentle story, **Goodnight Moon.** Plan a night for you and your child to star gaze. Allow her to stay up until the stars are visible. Take a large blanket and two pillows outside and lie side by side looking at the stars. Try to count twenty stars and encourage your child to choose a favorite. Say the nursery rhymes "Twinkle, Twinkle, Little Star" and "Star Light, Star Bright" together. Be sure to say good night to the stars and moon when you're ready to come in. *(night and day, Mother Goose)*

- Just before bedtime, sit in a chair together in your child's room. Let him name all of his favorite things in the room. Suggest he add describing words, including colors. Then turn off the light, and see how many things he can remember. Encourage him to picture everything in his mind and say good night to each special thing, one by one. Since children are often afraid of the dark, it can be reassuring to remember all the familiar, friendly things in a room that don't change when the lights go off. *(visual memory)*

- Make up bedtime stories in which your child is the heroine, making all the right choices that you will want her to make some day in real life. She will feel more important and special with each new *chapter* you tell, and at the same time you will be subtly conveying all the values that you want her to learn. You'll probably surprise yourself with the stories you can create! *(self-esteem)*

74

# The Grouchy Ladybug

*by Eric Carle*

**TEACHING FOCUS**
- Comparing sizes
- Concept of time
- Animal defenses
- Identifying emotions

**SETTING THE STAGE**

Instantly singable songs and the appealing rhyme and rhythm of finger plays will encourage children to be involved in storytime.

**ROCK AROUND THE CLOCK**, Sharon, Lois & Bram, *Stay Tuned*
  (A lively children's version from 1 - 12 o'clock)

**BABY BELUGA**, by Raffi, *Baby Beluga,* (A little whale on the move)

**BYE-BYE, BEE!**

| | |
|---|---|
| What do you suppose? | *(cock head to side)* |
| A bee sat on my nose! | *(put finger on nose)* |
| And what do you think? | *(cock head to side)* |
| She gave me a wink! | *(wink or blink)* |
| Then she said, "I beg your pardon, | |
| I thought you were the garden." | |
| Bye-bye, bee! | *(move finger through the air)* |

**CLAP YOUR HANDS**

| | |
|---|---|
| Clap your hands, clap your hands, | *(do each motion)* |
| Clap them just like me. | |
| Touch your shoulders, touch your shoulders, | |
| Touch them just like me. | |
| Tap your knees, tap your knees, | |
| Tap them just like me. | |
| Shake your head, shake your head, | |
| Shake it just like me. | |
| Clap your hands, clap your hands, | |
| Now let them quiet be. | *(fold hands in lap)* |

**FIRST READING**

What kind of bug is on the cover of our story today? Would you want to hold one? What do you know about ladybugs? Sometimes ladybugs are red and sometimes they are yellow, but they always have big dots on their backs. Those big dots are often black. Ladybugs are our good friends because they eat tiny insects called aphids that chew on our trees. Usually ladybugs are friendly, quiet, little bugs. But look at the face on this ladybug. How do you think she is feeling? You are right . . . she is so very cross that the name of our story is **The Grouchy Ladybug**. It was written by Eric Carle. Perhaps you have seen his name before on **The Very Hungry Caterpillar.** Mr. Carle wrote us a special message about aphids and ladybugs right across from the title page. Let's read it together.

*Read* **The Grouchy Ladybug** *through completely, remembering that the first reading is for enjoying the story, and discussion will come later. Begin with a soft, small voice for the yellow jacket and get a little louder with each page until the whale is the loudest of all.*

**GETTING INVOLVED**

Have you ever felt like the grouchy ladybug? Have you stayed cross for a long time? A whole day went by in the story, **The Grouchy Ladybug.** The story started in the morning with breakfast and it was nighttime before the two ladybugs ate all the aphids. Let's *pretend* our way through a whole day. It is morning and you are just waking up. Stretch one arm high, now the other. Time to get out of bed and stand in your very own spot for this game. Now wash your face before breakfast. Can you eat standing up? Do you want aphids for breakfast? What will you choose? Of course you will put your clothes on before you go outside. Show me how you get dressed. Are you going to climb a tree or look for ladybugs in your yard? Now, you tell me all the things you want to do for the rest of the day, right up til bedtime when the fireflies will come out to dance around the moon.

**A CLOSER LOOK**

With each rereading of a story, children gain new understanding. Pause often for a spontaneous flow of oral language as the children share their feelings and observations. Extend the learning process with your own questions in repeated readings of the story.

- What kind of painting do you see inside the cover? Will it match the leaf or the whale? *(inferential)*

- What do the words *if you insist* mean? *(vocabulary)*

- Are the animals on each page getting larger or smaller? Are the pages changing size? What about the words on each page? *(comparing sizes)*

- Why is the sun going *higher* on each page? When does it start going *lower*? *(concept of time)*

- How does the snake say the words *if you insist*? *(association)*

- What protection does each animal have? *(association)*

- Which animal would frighten you the most? *(opinion)*

- Why can't we see all of the whale on one page? *(comparing sizes)*

- How does the friendly ladybug greet the grouchy ladybug? *(identifying emotions)*

- Why did the leaf say *thank you* to the two ladybugs? *(interpretation)*

**ROUNDING OUT STORYTIME**

**A Firefly Named Torchy**   by Bernard Waber

**The Very Quiet Cricket**   by Eric Carle

**Ladybug, Ladybug**   by Ruth Brown

**Time To . . .**   by Bruce McMillan

**Millions of Cats**   Wanda Gag

77

# Integrated Whole Language Activities

## POETRY

### BUT I WONDER

But I wonder . . .
The crickets in the thickets,
and the katydids in trees,
and ants on plants, and butterflies,
and ladybugs and bees
don't smell with little noses
but with *feelers*, if you please.
They get along quite nicely,
but I wonder how they *sneeze*.

*by Aileen Fisher*

### THE BIG CLOCK

Slowly ticks the big clock;
## Tick-Tock, Tick-Tock!
But Cuckoo clock ticks double quick;
Tick-a-tock-a, tick-a-tock-a,
Tick-a-tock,-a, tick!

*author unknown*

## INVOLVEMENT

### DRAMATIZATION

The dramatic words of **The Grouchy Ladybug's** encounters just beg children to join in the dialog of the story. Simple props add to the drama. Provide a variety of art materials in your art center and encourage the children to create headbands or stick puppets for the story characters. *(The emphasis is on the creative process, not the product!)* Be sure to include a friendly ladybug, the whale's flippers, fins and tail, and some fireflies.

Have the children wear or carry the props as they sequence themselves in a line or a circle. As you narrate the story, encourage each child to dramatize the action and answer with an appropriate voice. Shakespeare couldn't have asked for a better *in the round* drama!

Add to the fun with a large clock made from the side of an appliance box. Write large numbers on the face of the clock and attach the hands with big brads. Have two children stand beside the clock and rotate the hands for each time change in the story.

Keep the props available in a drama center for individual play. What child can resist the line, *"Hey you, want to fight?"*

## INTEGRATION

### LADYBUG AND FRIENDS

Fingerpaint red ladybugs. Add black spots and scowling eyes with black paint, markers, or felt circles. Staple pipe cleaner *feelers* and *legs* to the ladybugs. Fingerpaint leaves and cover them with sponge-painted aphids. Paint fireflies and add sponge-painted *taillights*. Cut out the ladybugs, leaves and fireflies to paste on an outdoor scene mural of **Ladybug and Friends.** Create a variety of insects to illustrate the chart poems, **But I Wonder** and **Firefly**. Children return often to read the print that they have illustrated!

**THE GROUCHY LADYBUG'S JOURNEY** *

To write an adaptation of the original story, begin with a class brainstorming session about other animals the grouchy ladybug might have met on her journey. Talk about the size, habitat and protection of each new animal. Sequence the animals according to size and create your own ladybug journey big book! Cut the cover and all the pages of your book in the shape of a ladybug. At the top of the pages of text, print the words, *The grouchy ladybug saw a* _____ . At the bottom of each page print, *It was too* _____ *to fight.* The text on the last page could be, *The grouchy ladybug saw a lady bug. Who wants to fight anyway?* After the children have illustrated the pages and dictated the words for the sentences, bind the pages into a class book for your library corner. (As with any innovation, give credit to the original story and author on the title page.)

**THE GROUCHY BOOK**

Discuss feelings and the things that happen to children that make them feel grouchy. Then talk about ways children can handle their grouchy feelings without fighting. List the ways on a class chart, **When I Am Grouchy**, such as, *I will say I am grouchy. I will stamp my feet. I will jump up and down. I will go to Australia!* The children can illustrate an original sentence to share in the Author's Chair or illustrate one chart sentence per page to make a class big book, **The Grouchy Book.**

**A NATURE STUDY**

Introduce a variety of nonfiction books such as **My Ladybug** by Herbert H. Wong in Shared Reading. Chart the facts learned such as *My ladybug can fly. My ladybug has six legs.* Hang the chart up in the room and read it together often. The children may want to choose a sentence to copy under their own fun drawings of those wonderful little bugs!

**LADYBUG MATH**

*Estimate* the total number of feelers, legs, wings and black spots on your class mural or chart poems.

Glue sets of black dots on tagboard ladybugs. *Match* sets and numerals, *sequence* numbers, and *add* or *subtract* number families.

**LADYBUG SNACKS**

Write the old-time favorite Rice Krispie cookie recipe together, modeling the writing process for the children as you think out loud about letters and sounds. Shape the no-bake, red-tinted ingredients into cookie ladybugs. Add raisin *spots* and apple slice *legs* and *feelers.*

Make red jello or pudding in small paper cups. Decorate with raisins and colored toothpicks for a Friendly Ladybug Party!

**EVERYDAY LEARNING ACTIVITIES**

Positive parenting, developmental learning activities and a warm, nurturing environment are major factors in a child's academic success and lifetime learning.

Sometimes children are just like the ladybug in **Grouchy Ladybug**, acting tough or in very inappropriate ways, simply because they are children. They are just learning what behavior is acceptable in the adult world. The word discipline is really a very positive word. It means the process of teaching that goes on all the time that quietly trains a child to use desirable behavior and avoid undesirable behavior. Remember the basic principle, your child will repeat whatever behavior gets the *payoff* of your attention. You want to "catch him doin' good" and respond with attention and praise. Your child is so desirous of your approval that he will repeat the behavior you noticed and responded to. In fact, if his choice is between the negative attention of a scolding or a spanking, or no attention at all, he will choose the negative. If your child is being as stubborn as **The Grouchy Ladybug**, step in early. Take control and stop the undesirable behavior calmly and firmly. Have him sit on a *time-out* chair until the timer on the stove goes off. Don't say, "Now the next time . . ." because that just challenges a child to misbehave again. Expect obedience. Never make a request that you don't intend to follow through on. Your child will soon learn if you are a person of empty words or of action. It is the overall atmosphere of quiet firmness that conveys the message, "You are safe. I won't let you go too far." That's what good discipline is all about! *(parenting skill)*

- In the story, **The Grouchy Ladybug**, every animal had its own form of protection. Read the story again and discuss why animals need protection. Talk about the skunk's *defense,* the yellow jacket's stinger, the lobster's claws, etc. Go out in the yard and look for aphids on the underside of leaves. Decide if they have any form of protection. *(science concepts)*

- Have your child arrange all of her stuffed animals according to size, from smallest to largest. Another day, arrange them from largest to smallest. Group them according to colors or buttons or ribbons. *(comparing)*

- Teach your child to identify her feelings and work through them without hurting others. You may want to say, "The rule in our house is there will be no hitting" or "no unkind words." Sometimes a whole family needs to find ways to respect the feelings of others. *(identifying feelings)*

- Using old magazines and construction paper, let your child cut and paste an animal collage. Have her dictate a title and a sentence for you to write on her picture. *(classifying, print)*

- A child must understand the concept of morning, afternoon and evening before he is able to tell time. Talk about what you do each part of the day. Point out the hands of the clock at different times during the day. When your child is ready for the skill of telling time, you will enjoy **The Grouchy Ladybug** all over again. It is a good example of a book that offers continuous learning as a child grows. *(concept of time)*

# Have You Seen My Duckling?

## by Nancy Tafuri

**TEACHING FOCUS**
- Visual discrimination
- Counting sets
- Interpreting a wordless book
- Safety awareness

**SETTING THE STAGE**

Instantly singable songs and the appealing rhyme and rhythm of finger plays will encourage children to be involved in storytime.

**FIVE LITTLE DUCKS** by Raffi, *Rise and Shine*

**SIX LITTLE DUCKS** by Raffi, *More Singable Songs for the Very Young*

**FIVE LITTLE DUCKS**

| | |
|---|---|
| Five little ducks went in for a swim; | *(hold up hand, extend fingers)* |
| The first little duck put his head in. | |
| The second little duck put his head back; | *(point to each finger in turn)* |
| The third little duck said, "Quack, quack, quack." | |
| The fourth little duck with his tiny brother, | *("walk" fingers up opposite arm)* |
| Went for a walk with his father and mother. | |

**I CAN**

I can tie my shoe lace,
I can brush my hair,
I can wash my hands and face
And dry myself with care.

I can clean my teeth too,
And fasten up my frocks.
I can say "How do you do"
And pull up both my socks.

(lead the children through appropriate motions with each phrase)

**FIRST READING**

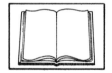

*Wordless books have a valuable place in children's literature. The joyful process of reading pictures is the earliest stage of reading. Wordless books encourage children to notice the details of beautiful illustrations, to make discoveries for themselves, and to anticipate what is going to happen next. Because the plot is supplied through the illustrations, children concentrate on telling the story in their own words. You are just a skillful guide. The children are the real story tellers. They will feel a sense of accomplishment in their ability to read a complete book.*

The title of this book, **Have You Seen My Duckling?**, is a question that a mother duck asks her friends who live nearby in the pond. Count the ducklings on the cover. How many are sleeping? Are any turned backwards? What do you think will happen?

If you begin with the title page and then look carefully at every picture, you will be able to tell the story in your very own words. Be sure to always count the ducklings. Watch the butterfly and see if you can spot the wandering duckling in every picture.

**GETTING INVOLVED**

Play *Find the Missing Duckling* with a mama duck and her ducklings. While everyone's eyes are covered, select one duckling to wander away from the nest. First have the children identify which duckling is missing. *(visual memory)* Then act out the story with the missing duckling quacking softly as his family searches for him. Celebrate with hugs and soft quacks when he is discovered.

Have the children name, in sequence, the pond animals that Mother Duck talked to as she swam around the pond. Write the names of the animals on name cards to hang around the children's necks. Because children love dramatizing, let them role-play the story with the mother duck asking the crane, turtle, beaver, catfish, and duck if they have seen her duckling.

**A CLOSER LOOK**

With each rereading of a story, children gain new understanding. Pause often for a spontaneous flow of oral language as the children share their feelings and observations. Extend the learning process with your own questions in repeated readings of the story.

- Why did the duckling leave the nest? Did he see the butterfly again? *(observation)*

- Who noticed the duckling leaving? What are they saying to him? *(opinion)*

- What are the ducklings saying to mother duck? *(interpretation)*

- What animals did mother duck meet? Were they friends? *(opinion)*

- Why was the pond a good place for the animals to live? *(interpretation)*

- Did the other duck and ducklings look the same as mother duck? *(observation)*

- Who found the duckling? Was he ever very far away? Was he lost? *(opinion)*

- What is the little duckling saying to the turtle and butterfly? (opinion)

- Why does the last picture look peaceful? Where do you think the butterfly is? *(opinion)*

**ROUNDING OUT STORYTIME**

**Fish Eyes: A Book You Can Count On**   by Lois Ehlert

**Six Little Ducks**   retold by Chris Conover

**Across the Stream**   by Mirra Ginsburg

**The Story of Ping**   by Marjorie Flack

**Jump, Frog, Jump!**   by Robert Kalan

# Integrated Whole Language Activities

### SALLY AND MANDA

Sally and Manda are two little lizards
Who gobble up flies
   in their two little gizzards.
They live by a toadstool
   near two little hummocks
And crawl all around
   on their two little stomachs.
     *Alice B. Campbell*

### DUCKS IN THE RAIN

Ducks are dabbling in the rain,
Dibbling, dabbling in the rain.
Drops of water from each back
Scatter as ducks flap and quack.

I can only stand and look
From my window at the brook,
For I cannot flap and quack
And scatter raindrops from my back.
     *James S. Tippett*

**INVOLVEMENT**

### QUACK, QUACK, QUACK

Children enjoy singing the catchy melody of the song, **Six Little Ducks.** (See p. 82 ) Each time you sing, choose a child to hold a feather and sing the words, *"Quack, quack, quack"* all alone. After the children have memorized the words, ask them to suggest other actions to substitute for *quack, quack, quack,* such as *"He led the others with a waddle, waddle, waddle"* or *"a flap, flap, flap."* The children won't need much encouragement to move as the ducks moved!

*Extension:* Print the words of **Six Little Ducks** on the pages of a book for the children to illustrate. Put the book and a tape of the children singing in a listening center for independent or paired reading.

**INTEGRATION**

### IN A POND

Compare the pond where the duckling lived in **Have You Seen My Duckling?** to a river, a lake, and an ocean. As the children read the pictures and retell the story, ask them to look for other animals that lived in the pond. Print the animals they identify (bird, beaver, turtle, catfish, salamander, etc.) on chart paper. Another time, have the children look for characteristics of a pond habitat, such as cattails, reeds, lily pads, etc. Print the words on a second list. Add a variety of nonfiction books to your reading center, such as the short and simple **Busy Beavers** by Lydia Dabcovich or the more factual **Animals Large and Small** by Annette Tison and Talus Taylor. As the children discover new animals or new characteristics of a pond habitat, add them to your lists. (Don't forget lizards like Sally and Manda!)

Now you are ready to show off a little and create a pond habitat on a large piece of bulletin board paper. Decide on a daytime scene with butterflies or a nighttime scene with fireflies. Pencil in a simple background for the children to paint, encouraging them to add all the things unique to a pond setting that you have listed. Have each child draw, tear or cut out something that lives in the pond, again referring to your list. Hopefully, you will have room to add Mother Duck and the eight ducklings swimming right through the middle of your pond.

**INTEGRATION**
(continued)

### AUTHOR'S CHAIR

The simple plot and familiar setting of **Have You Seen My Duckling** offers a perfect opportunity for independent writing. Provide an individual blank book for each child to retell the story or create an original story based on the book's pattern. It can be a wordless book, one written with developmental spelling, or with the child's language dictated to the teacher. Then, sitting in the Author's Chair, let each child role-play the teacher as she leads the children through her story. Children read their own language best!

### NO, I HAVE BEEN BUSY! *

The animals in the story did not respond when Mother Duck asked if they had seen her duckling. Involve the children in a discussion of what each animal might have said. Perhaps the beaver was too busy chewing, the frog was busy croaking, the salamander was busy laying eggs! Refer to your list of pond animals until every child has an animal to draw. Each child will have two pages to illustrate. The first page will have the words *"Have you seen my duckling?"* printed at the top. The second page will say, *"No, I have been _____ . "* Mount and sequence the pages in a class book that your emergent readers will return to again and again.

### HAVE YOU SEEN MY BABY BEAVER? *

Every time children write an innovation they are reprocessing a familiar story and making it their own. Create an original story based on **Have You Seen My Duckling?**'s format, pattern and setting. As a group, decide on a different mother animal, where she will look for her missing baby and who she will ask. For example, a mother beaver with seven little beavers behind her could swim under and above water, asking a fish, snake, frog, turtle, etc., *"Have you seen my baby beaver?"* Have children illustrate the pages individually or in pairs with the same sentence repeated on each page. Of course the hidden baby beaver will reappear on the last page for a happy reunion.

*Extension:* This activity would adapt well to small group learning, with each group of three or four children deciding on a different animal for their story. Mount the illustrated pages and bind them in class books or display them on the walls. By now, your room will probably resemble a pond!

### SALLY AND MANDA

Because of the funny words in **Sally and Manda**, it will not be long before the children have memorized the poem. Model the writing process as you write the text on chart paper, *thinking out loud* about letters and sounds. The language will come to life when the children illustrate the words. Then write the lines on sentence strips for the children to sequence or match to the chart poem in your Poetry Corner.

85

**EVERY DAY
LEARNING
ACTIVITIES**

Positive parenting, developmental learning activities and a warm, nurturing environment are major factors in a child's academic success and lifetime learning.

In the story, **Have You Seen My Duckling?**, the little duckling was safe even though it was out of sight. Sadly, in today's world, children are no longer safe. It is the parents' responsibility to protect them. No longer can children be out of sight, even for a minute. . . in grocery stores, parking lots, malls, schoolyards and playgrounds. Set boundaries and make consistent rules for your child. In her book, **Your Baby and Child**, Dr. Penelope Leach encourages parents to establish the absolute rule that a child "must never go anywhere with anybody without coming to tell you, or whoever is looking after him, first." She states that the message is easy for this age to understand and to remember because it can be practiced every day. Rather than create fears, always assure your child that it is your job to keep him safe. *(parenting skill)*

- Every child needs to be able to identify himself and where he lives. Sometimes we use a child's full name only when we are upset with him! Instead, we should make a child feel special when we use his first, middle and last name. After all, he is probably the only person in the world with that exact name. Talk to him often about the day he was born and of everyone's happiness at his birth. Teach him his birthdate and also his full address. A child needs to know the name of his town or city, as well as the street he lives on. He can easily learn his phone number as well, for a child learns simply by repetition. *(safety, self-esteem)*

- A fun way to practice gross motor skills, using the large muscles of arms and legs, is to pretend to be different animals. Running like a horse, hopping like a frog, jumping like kangaroos are all ways to practice these skills outside. *(motor skills)*

- To increase visual memory skills, place four different items on a tabletop. Have your child close her eyes while you remove one item. When she guesses, switch roles. Gradually build up the number of items until she can spot one item removed from ten. *(visual memory)*

- Encourage your child to look, really look, at something the way a scientist would. Choose a different object to observe each day . . . a ray of sunshine on the floor, an animal, clouds, ants, insects. Be clever. Keep drawing out observations about how things look, move, make noise, have color, shape, legs, wings, and protection. *(visual discrimination, science)*

- Every time a child looks at a storybook, she should be able to see something new she has not seen before. Reading pictures is a beginning step in reading. *(visual discrimination)*

# *If You Give a Mouse a Cookie*

## *by Laura Joffe Numeroff*

**TEACHING FOCUS**
- Predicting skills
- Comparing Sizes
- Sharing
- Feelings

**SETTING THE STAGE**

Instantly singable songs and the appealing rhyme and rhythm of finger plays will encourage children to be involved in storytime.

**FRIENDS** by Greg and Steve, *On the Move*

**BE MY FRIEND** by Hap Palmer, *Getting to Know Myself*

**THE BABY MICE**

| | |
|---|---|
| Where are the baby mice? Squeak, squeak, squeak. | *(one hand behind back)* |
| I cannot see them. Peek, peek, peek. | *(one hand over eyes)* |
| Here they come from the hole in the wall. | *(bring one hand around)* |
| One, two, three, four, five—that's all! | *(count fingers)* |

**I RAISED A GREAT HULLABALOO**

| | |
|---|---|
| I raised a great hullabaloo | *(arms waving overhead)* |
| When I found a large mouse in my stew, | *(hold up mouse)* |
| Said the waiter, "Don't shout | *(finger to lips)* |
| And wave it about, | *(waving motion)* |
| Or the rest will be wanting one, too!" | *(pointing all around)* |

**FIRST READING**

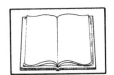

Why does the picture on the cover of this book make you smile? What do you think is happening? Have you ever shared a cookie with a mouse? The name of our story is **If You Give a Mouse a Cookie.** It was written by Laura Numeroff and the pictures were drawn by Felicia Bond. She must really like little mice. You are going to smile when you see her wonderful pictures! Look for the mouse on every page. Sometimes he is very tiny, but he is there!

*Turn to the first title page.* Where do you think the little mouse is walking? What does he have on his back? Can you read the words on the page?

Where do you think the little boy is on the next *title page*? What is he doing? Do you see the mouse? We have already seen the words **If You Give a Mouse a Cookie** three times. Can you read them? I'll turn the pages silently. You tell me the story.

**GETTING INVOLVED**

Make yourself as tiny as a mouse. Tell me how that feels. Why would you have to be very careful? How would you move? Do you think mice make any noise when they scurry about? What about when they talk to each other?

I think you know enough about those tiny animals that you could pretend to be little mice yourselves! Stand up and curl your hands up in front of your bodies. Remember, we can tiptoe, make chattering sounds and move softly around the room. When I clap my hands one time, stop wherever you are and curl up without a sound, for the clap is a warning that someone may be coming into our house. When I clap three times, tiptoe back to your very own mouse hole!

**A CLOSER LOOK**

With each rereading of a story, children gain new understanding. Pause often for a spontaneous flow of oral language as the children share their feelings and observations. Extend the learning process with your own questions in repeated readings of the story.

- Why did the little boy invite the mouse to come inside his house? *(comprehension)*

- Why did the mouse need a straw? *(comprehension)*

- What is a milk mustache? *(vocabulary)*

- Was the little mouse a hard worker? *(interpretation)*

- What did the little boy use for a mouse bed? *(visual detail)*

- What are the words on the crayons? *(recognizing print)*

- Who did the little mouse draw in his picture? Is he there? *(reasoning)*

- How did the mouse get his picture so far up on the refrigerator? *(picture clues)*

- What will happen if the boy gives the mouse another glass of milk? *(comprehension)*

- Will that be the end of the story? *(reasoning)*

**ROUNDING OUT STORYTIME**

**Alexander and the Wind up Mouse**   by Leo Lionni

**Nicholas, where have you been?**   by Leo Lionni

**Ernest and Celestine**   by Gabrielle Vincent

**Who Sank the Boat?**   by Pamela Allen

**Fat Mouse**   by Harry Stevens

# Integrated Whole Language Activities

## POETRY

**MICE**

I think mice
Are rather nice.

> Their tails are long,
> Their faces small,
> They haven't any
> Chins at all.
> Their ears are pink,
> Their teeth are white,
> They run about
> The house at night.
> They nibble things
> They shouldn't touch
> And no one seems
> To like them much.

But I think mice
Are nice.
> *Rose Fyleman*

**THE OLD WOMAN**
by Beatrix Potter

**GOOD NEIGHBORS**
by May Justus

from *The Read Aloud Rhymes for The Very Young* by Jack Prelutsky

## INVOLVEMENT

**COOKIES AND MICE**

What an irresistible combination . . . a charming mouse and a child's favorite cookie! No wonder children never tire of listening to **If You Give A Mouse A Cookie.** Add to the fun with a mouse puppet turning the pages as the children listen and share cookies. (See Cookie Math!) Pause often for a *cloze* activity with familiar nouns in the story, i.e. *When he's finished giving himself a trim, he'll want a _____ to sweep up.*

Another time, have the children sit in a circle with all the objects from the story (a cookie, glass of milk, straw, napkin, mirror, etc.) in the middle. As you read, ask the children to sequence the objects in a circular pattern. They will discover the story begins and ends with the cookie.

## INTEGRATION

**A CIRCLE STORY MAP**

Create a circle story map by drawing a large circle on chart paper and dividing it into twelve equal sections. Place a cookie above the circle to identify the beginning and ending point of the story. Moving clockwise, with the circle story map on the floor, have the children add one object to each section of the circle as you read the story.

## A CIRCLE STORY MAP (continued)

Replace the objects with child-drawn pictures. Paste them on the story map and hang it up in the room. Create a mouse corner with the chart, some stuffed animals and a rocking chair. The predictable sequence will invite the children to become the storytellers.

*Extension:* Print the names of the objects for children to match to the pictures. Keep the word cards and the mouse puppet available in a Reading Basket. Smiles and reading guaranteed!

## A MOUSE ACCORDION BOOK

Make a class accordion book of the twelve objects in the story, **If You Give A Mouse A Cookie.** The children can work individually or in pairs as they draw or paint a cover, a title page, one page for each object with the word printed under the picture, and a last page that says, *"And chances are . . ."* Mount the pages on poster board, tape them together with clear tape, and your colorful accordion book will tell its own story.

## OUR MOUSE STORY

Your children can create an innovation of the original story by dictating new content to the familiar pattern. As a class, begin with the mouse and cookie and brainstorm what the mouse might want next. For example, "If you give a mouse a cookie, he's going to ask for a glass of milk. When you give him milk, he'll probably ask you for some cereal." Continue innovating the text, using the children's ideas. Print their new text, cover, and title page on white pages. Bind the illustrated, mounted pages into a class book. The circle story map and accordion book ideas could also be adapted to your new story.

## MOUSE BEDS

Have the children bring in very small boxes of varying sizes and shapes. Let each child decorate a box to create a mouse bed for the little mouse he has made out of modeling clay. Provide fabric, tissue paper and cotton to add pillows and blankets to each labeled mouse bed. To display the mouse beds, have the children group them into families of mice.

Alana's mouse bed

## COOKIE MATH

As the class looks at a large chocolate chip cookie, have each child *estimate* the number of chocolate chips in the cookie. Record their estimates on a chart. Then break apart the cookie, count the chocolate chips and compare that number with their estimates. How many children estimated too few chocolate chips? Too many?

Tell your children something special about your favorite chocolate chip cookie recipe. As the children watch, print on a chart the list of ingredients needed for your recipe. Print the directions for making the cookies on a second chart. Plan when you can make the cookies together, an interactive experience at its best!

After baking the cookies, *sort* them by appearance. Talk about all the differences you have discovered! Then make a list of all the ways the children can think of to eat the cookies, i.e., alone, with others, one chip at a time, nibbles, eyes closed, etc.! At last, it's time to invite the mice and have a party!

**EVERYDAY LEARNING ACTIVITIES**

Positive parenting, developmental learning activities and a warm, nurturing environment are major factors in a child's academic success and lifetime learning.

In the safety of play, a child can be the boss, make up the rules, and try on any role for size. He can experiment with the power of words as he says, "I am the mother and you must drink your milk." Play is a safe place for a child to express his feelings as he learns that it is the adults in his life who set up the rules for acceptable behavior. It is adults who must quietly insist on a child taking responsibility for his own actions. And it is adults who must show a child that all his little ploys and promises won't change the rules for acceptable behavior. A child who is a cryer must learn that tears won't make you change your mind. A child who is a manipulator must learn that it simply will not work to promise, "I won't do it again if you let me play just this once." The pouting child must learn that you won't change your mind when he is giving you the message, "See, I'm not having any fun and it's all your fault." The child who blames someone else when he was the one who misbehaved must learn it's simply unacceptable to say, "George did it!" The retaliator, who *accidentally* knocks down someone else's blocks must learn the rules of fair play. You simply won't accept unacceptable behavior! That's all a part of preparing your child to live life skillfully. *(parenting skill)*

- Make a tape of a family member reading **If You Give A Mouse A Cookie.** Begin with the title, author and illustrator. Your child can point to the words as he listens for a particular sound that tells him when to turn the pages. *(prereading skill)*

- Have your child draw or paint his own mouse family picture to hang on your refrigerator. Add yarn or pipe cleaner whiskers and tails. Write each mouse's name under his picture and make up a story about the little mouse sharing his cookie with his family. *(art, language)*

- Read the words of a cookie recipe together. There are so many skills to learn about measuring ingredients (he will love the big word!) and following directions. After the cookies are baked, encourage your child to divide them onto two plates, teaching full, empty, more, less, equal, and sets. Be sure to end your fun by sharing with a friend! *(math readiness)*

- In the story **If You Give A Mouse A Cookie**, we see the mouse only in the daytime. Encourage your child to think about where the mouse might be at night. Where do other animals sleep at night? Do they like the dark? Are they protected? Talk about people at night and the jobs that some people do while others sleep. Compare nighttime sounds with daytime sounds. Night and day are a good introduction to the concept of opposites. *(comparisons)*

# The Little Mouse, The Red Ripe Strawberry

## and

# The Big Hungry Bear

*by Don and Audrey Wood*

**TEACHING FOCUS**
- Sharing
- Concept of half
- Comprehension
- Comparing size

**SETTING THE STAGE**

Instantly singable songs and the appealing rhyme and rhythm of finger plays will encourage children to be involved in storytime.

**SHARE IT** by Rosenshontz, *Share It*
   (Share with a friend and feel good about yourself)

**THE SHARING SONG** by Raffi, *Singable Songs for the Very Young*

**ME**

| | |
|---|---|
| This is my nose, | *(point to body parts)* |
| These are my ears, | |
| These are my eyes | |
| That make the tears. | |
| This is my mouth, | |
| It smiles when I say. | *(big smile!)* |
| I think I like myself | *(pat on the back)* |
| Just this way! | |

**ONE LITTLE BODY**

| | |
|---|---|
| Two little hands go clap, clap, clap. | *(act out each line)* |
| Two little feet go tap, tap, tap. | |
| Two little hands go thump, thump, thump. | |
| Two little feet go jump, jump, jump. | |
| One little body turns around. | |
| One little body sits quietly down. | |

**FIRST READING**

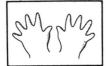

The name of our story today is one of the longest book titles I have ever read! It's **The Little Mouse, The Red Ripe Strawberry, and THE BIG HUNGRY BEAR.** *(Move your hand from left to right under the words of the title.)* I can see a little mouse and that enormous, red, ripe strawberry, but can you find a big hungry bear on the cover? Do you think the mouse has his finger up to his mouth because the bear is close by? Is that why he is on a ladder? I wonder where that big, hungry bear is!

Perhaps he will appear on the *title page.* No, he is not there either! Why do you think the letters of his name, THE BIG HUNGRY BEAR, are larger than the other letters in the title? Why is that little door open with a ladder sticking out? Let's read and find out!

**GETTING INVOLVED**

Now let's have some fun with our story. Stand up and stretch out your arms so you have some space of your own. Pretend that you are the little mouse. Watch me and I will show you everything the little mouse did:

First walk in place with the ladder under your arm.
Now stand the ladder against the bush and start climbing.
Pull hard on the strawberry until it falls to the ground.
Carry it to your little house and put chains around it.
Time to disguise the strawberry with some glasses and a funny nose and a mustache.
Uh, oh! You can hear the big, hungry bear!
Better get a knife fast and cut the strawberry in half.
Will you share half with me? Thank you for sharing!
Now settle down into your little hammock and close your eyes.

**A CLOSER LOOK**

With each rereading of a story, children gain new understanding. Pause often for a spontaneous flow of oral language as the children share their feelings and observations. Extend the learning process with your own questions in repeated readings of the story.

- Where does the little mouse live? *(deduction)*

- Why does the mouse need a ladder? *(deduction)*

- Does his face tell you what he is thinking? *(interpretation)*

- Why are the vine, the strawberry and the mouse all shaking? *(interpretation)*

- How does the mouse hide the strawberry? Will it work? *(predicting)*

- Why are there chains on the strawberry? *(comprehension)*

- What does it mean to tromp? To guard? To disguise? *(vocabulary)*

- How does the mouse solve his problem? *(comprehension)*

- Notice the mouse's face, his front paw, and his *hat* in the hammock. *(interpretation)*

- Do you think there really is a big, hungry bear? *(opinion)*

**ROUNDING OUT STORYTIME**

**How Joe the Bear and Sam the Mouse Got Together**
   by Beatrice de Regniers

**Where Are You Going, Little Mouse?**   by Robert Kraus

**Bravo, Ernest and Celestine**   by Gabrielle Vincent

**The Giant Jam Sandwich**   by John Vernon Lord

**The Doorbell Rang**   by Pat Hutchins

# Integrated Whole Language Activities

**POETRY**

**WANTED**

I'm looking for a house
Said the little brown mouse,
        with
One room for breakfast,
One room for tea,
One room for supper,
And that makes three.
One room to dance in,
When I give a ball,
A kitchen and a bedroom,
Six rooms in all.
     *Rose Fyleman*

**THE HOUSE OF THE MOUSE**
by Lucy Sprague Mitchell
from *A New Treasury of Children's Poetry* by Joanna Cole

**INVOLVEMENT**

- **The Little Mouse, The Red Ripe Strawberry, and The Big Hungry Bear** has all the qualities of a children's story that makes it endearing . . . a story that teaches, entertains, has a simple text, and is beautifully illustrated. Oh, the face of that dear little mouse! In your next rereading, focus the children's attention on the changing expressions of the mouse. Has the artist told the story on the mouse's face?

- With the lights off in your room, give each child a strawberry to hold (or a red felt one if it isn't strawberry season). Pretend a bear is stalking the room, waiting to have a feast. Brainstorm ways to save the strawberries they are holding from the hungry bear. The children can think of reasons why their ideas may not save the berries. Continue the discussion until a child comes up with the idea that the only way to outsmart the bear is to eat the strawberries . . . now! Then turn the lights on and have the children find paw prints and a message from the bear, "Oh how I wanted those strawberries!"

- Plan a sharing day. Have each child bring something edible to school that has already been cut in half. After rereading the story with the children sitting in a circle, suggest each child share half of what he has brought with the child on his left. Each child will have half of his own treat and half of his neighbor's to enjoy.

**INTEGRATION**

**SIX ROOMS IN ALL**

How do the children picture the six rooms in the little mouse's house in the poem, **Wanted**? Do they picture a whole family of mice living there? Would the rooms look like the mouse's home in **The Big Hungry Bear**? Using six large pieces of paper, with one phrase of the poem printed on the bottom of each page, have the children illustrate the story of the brown mouse's house in a wall story format.

*Extension:* Have the children decide on a room in their own home to draw. Encourage them to visualize everything in that room to draw in their picture. Each child can use his own inventive spelling to label everything in the room and then create a frame and a roof for his house with painted popsicle sticks.

## THE RED RIPE STRAWBERRY

Ask the children to think of all the things the little mouse did with the red ripe strawberry. *He picked it. He carried it. He hid it in the dirt*, and so on. As the children retell the story in their own words, write one sentence on the bottom of each page of a big book for a child to illustrate. Cut the cover and the pages in the shape of a strawberry.

Keep strawberry-shaped books available in your writing center for children to draw and write their own stories.

## WHERE ARE YOU, BEAR?

The children will have their own ideas of why the bear never appeared in the story. Was he nearby? Was he hiding? Have fun hunting for the big hungry bear by acting out the chant, **We're Going On a Bear Hunt**, now beautifully illustrated in a book by Michael Rosen. The language is exceptional as a father and his four children splash, splosh, and stumble through a field, a deep river, swampy mud, a dark forest, a whirling snowstorm and a gloomy cave, looking for a bear.

## JOURNAL OF A TRAVELING MOUSE

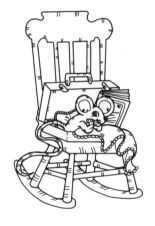

There is probably no animal more appealing to children than a little mouse. Think of ways to include a lovable, stuffed mouse or a soft mouse puppet in your daily teaching until the children consider it a real part of your class. When they arrive one morning, have a little suitcase waiting in your chair. Explain that each child will have a turn to take the suitcase home. Have the children guess what is inside before you open the suitcase and show the little mouse, a blanket, a small journal, and a note to parents asking them to write a few sentences about what the lovable mouse did with their child before it came back to school. At the end of the year, you will have a marvelous story to share about each of your children and a traveling mouse.

## A TASTING PARTY

Prepare four small containers with the hidden tastes of *sweet, sour, salty* and *spicy*. Working with small groups of children on a number of successive days, have each child dip a popsicle stick or coffee stirrer into the four containers. Guide them into categorizing and labeling the tastes. Print the headings *sweet, sour, salty* and *spicy* on a four-column wall graph.

Have the children each bring something from home, talk about its taste, and then draw a small square picture to add to the right column on the chart.

Write sentences about what the children bring in your daily class news or encourage the children to write in their journals.

**EVERYDAY LEARNING ACTIVITIES**

Positive parenting, developmental learning activities and a warm, nurturing environment are major factors in a child's academic success and lifetime learning.

In the story, **The Big Hungry Bear**, the little mouse had several plans to protect the strawberry. Being able to think of a plan of action and to problem-solve is a skill that even a young child can learn. It will encourage your child to organize her thoughts and build her verbal skills. Ask her often for suggestions. For example, if her pants get torn, ask her, "What can we do about it?" She might suggest sewing them or buying a new pair of pants or wearing them torn. By repeating your child's choices, you are telling her you like her thinking! "Good, we have three choices. We can sew your pants or buy new ones or let you wear them torn. Which plan should we use? You decide." The more opportunities your child has to think, to plan, to make choices and to follow through, the more confident and self-directed she will become. *(parenting skill)*

- If sharing always means giving up something that is very special, it isn't appealing to a child. We make it so hard on a child at birthday parties and holidays when we want her to be excited about a gift we have chosen just for her, and then in the next breath, expect her to share it with someone else! Help her make up a "sharing basket" of games and toys she feels good about sharing with anyone, and let her keep a few treasures of her own in a special place. Or sometimes it works to set the timer on the stove. When the buzzer goes off, it's time to share, and no one gets cross with mommy! *(social development)*

- Enjoy ripe, red strawberries (or any fruit) with your child. Using a dull table knife, let your child slice the strawberry in half. Talk about how two halves make a whole. Next put two strawberries on a plate and let your child decide how to divide them. If she figures that out easily, try four strawberries on a plate to be shared. Suggest "One for you and one for me." Everyday activities are rich learning experiences because a child learns best by doing. *(concept of half)*

- Tiny animals and animal homes fascinate children. That is why the character of the little mouse in **The Big Hungry Bear** is so appealing. Start observing insects and little animals in your yard and in your child's storybooks. How do they travel? Do they make noise? Where do they sleep? How do they protect themselves? What do they eat? Add to the learning by creating a shoebox *home* for little animals. Every day put in a new set of written or picture clues for your child to guess the name of the imaginary little critter inside. Estimate how many tiny animals could fit in the shoebox *home*. *(science, observation)*

- Whether at the kitchen sink or in a large plastic tub on the floor, pouring rice involves the eyes and hands working together as well as the ability to make judgments. To make pouring more challenging, place rubber bands around clear plastic containers, perhaps at the halfway mark. Tell your child to pour to the rubber band. Add scoops, funnels and measuring cups. Ask her to estimate how many scoops of rice it will take to fill each cup. Add some small plastic animals and little people to the tub for creative fun. *(coordination, math concepts)*

# The Little Red Hen

by Paul Galdone

| TEACHING FOCUS | • Teaching responsiblity<br>• Building vocabulary<br>• Story participation<br>• Motor skills |

**SETTING THE STAGE**   Instantly singable songs and the appealing rhyme and rhythm of finger plays will encourage children to be involved in storytime.

**IN MY GARDEN** by Raffi, *One Light, One Sun*

**OATS, PEAS, BEANS** by Raffi, *Baby Beluga*

### DIG A LITTLE HOLE

| Dig a little hole, | *(dig)* |
| Plant a little seed, | *(drop seed)* |
| Pour a little water, | *(pour)* |
| Pull a little weed. | *(pull up and throw away)* |

| Chase a little bug, | *(chasing motions with hands)* |
| Heigh-ho, there he goes! | *(shade eyes)* |
| Give a little sunshine, | *(cup hands, lift to the sun)* |
| Grow a little rose. | *(smell flower, eyes closed, smiling)* |

### MAKING BISCUITS

| I am making biscuit dough, | |
| Round and round the beaters go. | *(demonstrate the motions for* |
| Add some flour from a cup, | *each phrase)* |
| Stir and stir the batter up. | |
| Roll them, cut them nice and neat. | |
| Put them on a cookie sheet. | |
| Bake them, count them: one, two, three, | |
| Serve them to my friends and me. | |

**FIRST READING**

Tell me about the hen on the cover of our book today. Do you think she has a job to do? Does she have any tools to work with? I wonder if she will need help with her job. The name of the story is **The Little Red Hen.** It was illustrated by Paul Galdone and he is a man who loves to draw animal pictures. I know they will make you smile. Let's turn to his first picture on the title page. What do you see?

*Encourage the children to join in every time an animal answers, "Not I!" and every time the little red hen replies, "Then I will."*

**GETTING INVOLVED**

Let's talk about some of the new words in **The Little Red Hen.** The story said the little red hen's house was *cozy.* What does *cozy* mean? Show me what the little mouse did when she *snoozed* all day. The little red hen also *tended* the wheat. Was that important? How did she *hoe* the garden? The story said the wheat was *ripe.* What does that mean? Show me how the cat moved when she *strolled.* How did the mouse move when she *scampered?*

Now let's have some fun with this story? I'll pretend to be the little red hen and you pretend to be her helpers, not lazy at all like the cat and dog and mouse in the story. Ready? Who will help me plant this wheat? *(Lead the children through the actions as they pretend to plant the wheat in the ground.)* Now the wheat is tall and yellow. Who will help me cut this wheat? *(Lead the children through the cutting motions.)* At last it's all cut! Who will help me take this wheat to the mill? *(Pretend to sling the wheat over your shoulder and walk in place to the mill.)* And now my last question, "Who will help me make this wheat into a cake?" You deserve to eat the cake! We didn't have a lazy cat or dog or mouse in the room.

**A CLOSER LOOK**

With each rereading of a story, children gain new understanding. Pause often for a spontaneous flow of oral language as the children share their feelings and observations. Extend the learning process with your own questions in repeated readings of the story.

- Why are there four mailboxes by the cozy house? *(reasoning)*

- What is the cat dreaming of? The dog? The mouse? *(observation)*

- What chores did the little red hen do inside the house? How did she get water? *(interpretation)*

- What chores did the little red hen do outside? *(memory)*

- Why did she take the wheat to the mill? *(comprehension)*

- Did you spy any little animals in the pictures? (ladybug, fly, worm, caterpillar, spider, ant) *(visual detail)*

- What made the cat, dog, and mouse wake up? *(memory)*

- Was the hen selfish? What lesson did the animals learn? *(comprehension)*

**ROUNDING OUT STORYTIME**

**Miss Poppy and the Honey Cake**   by Elizabeth McDonald

**I Will Not Go To Market Today**   by Harry Allard

**Pancakes for Breakfast**   by Tomie dePaola

**Another Mouse to Feed**   by Robert Kraus

**A Treeful of Pigs** by Arnold Lobel

# Integrated Whole Language Activities

**POETRY**

**THE NOTHING-DOINGS**

Meet the lazy Nothing-Doings,
all they do is stand around,
when it's time for doing nothing,
Nothing-Doings can be found,
when it's time for doing something,
you won't find a single one,
for the Nothing-Doings vanish
when there's work that must be done.
*Jack Prelutsky*

**I WENT UPSTAIRS**

I went upstairs to make my bed.
I made a mistake and bumped my head.
I went downstairs to milk my cow.
I made a mistake and milked the sow.
I went in the kitchen to bake a pie.
I made a mistake and baked a fly.
*Traditional*

**INVOLVEMENT**

- The predictable pattern of the words, "Not I" and "Then I will," encourages children to enter into the story with the very first reading of **The Little Red Hen.** To vary their participation and to keep them listening intently, divide the children into four groups. As you narrate the story, have one group join you on the little red hen's words and the other groups join in for the dog, the cat and the mouse.

- Help the children create drama props in your art center, making hats, headbands or ears for each animal. Paper bags also make good props. Cut large holes in the front of the bags for the children's faces and slit the sides to fit over the children's shoulders. They can draw feathers, fur, ears, or whiskers around the holes to create their story characters.

- Add to the fun by making word cards to hang around the necks of the children who are playing the part of the dogs, cats, and mice. On one side print, "Not I," and on the other side print, "I will!" Have the children turn the cards at just the right moment in the drama.

- Read and dramatize other versions of **The Little Red Hen.** Have the children decide which drama they would like to perform (with props, of course!) for their parents or another class.

**INTEGRATION**

**"NOT I!" \***

As the children retell **The Little Red Hen** in their own words, write their sentences on a language experience chart. The obvious pattern of the little red hen's questions and the *"Not I"* answers will be appealing to emergent readers because of the repetition. Draw the faces of the hen, dog, cat, and mouse on the chart.

Create a class big book using the children's retelling as your text. Print one sentence on each page for the children to illustrate. Mount the pages on colorful paper and bind them into a class book to add to your collection of different versions of the story. The child-authored version will probably be the favorite in your library corner.

102

## A WALL STORY

Have the children imagine that the little red hen asked other animals for help and they all said, "Not I." But the dog, cat, and mouse answered "I will." Tell the story of the lesson they learned on a wall mural in your room for all to read.

## THE NOTHING-DOINGS

Ask the children if they think Jack Prelutsky had the story of **The Little Red Hen** in mind when he wrote the poem, *The Nothing-Doings*. As you read the story again, have the children listen for the *other* jobs the little red hen had to do by herself . . . she cooked the meals, washed the dishes, made the beds, and so on. There's quite a list! Could the dog and cat and mouse be called *Nothing-Doings?*

For contrast, read **Mrs. Huggins and Her Hen Hannah** by Lydia Dabcovich, a touching story about a dear old lady and her pet hen who were inseparable as they worked. Could they be called a *Nothing-Doing?* Compare the stories orally and decide which animals were responsible helpers, a theme you can introduce in your classroom.

## RESPONSIBLE HELPERS

- Brainstorm with the children about all the jobs around your room that need to be done every day. Make a Responsible Helpers chart for the classroom, listing the jobs and the names of the children who will be the helpers that week. Make Responsible Helper badges for the children to wear.

- Talk about ways the children can be responsible helpers at home as well. Have every child decide on something she can do to help at home. Each child can draw her idea and dictate a sentence on a page in your class book, Responsible Helpers.

- Take a walk around school . . . down the halls, in the cafeteria, on the sidewalks and out on the playground. Decide on ways to be responsible helpers for your whole school. Could your plan include recycling?

- Enjoy the nonfiction Start to Finish book, **From Grain to Bread.** Demonstrate what you have learned about being helpers by copying a recipe and baking a loaf of bread together. The children can help in the preparation. Read your class version of **The Little Red Hen** one more time as you enjoy the bread.

- Have the dog, cat, and mouse write a letter of apology to the little red hen, explaining that they are now responsible helpers. Include some ways they can help the hen from now on.

**EVERYDAY LEARNING ACTIVITIES**

Positive parenting, developmental learning activities and a warm, nurturing environment are major factors in a child's academic success and lifetime learning.

**The Little Red Hen** teaches a meaningful lesson in a delightful way. One of the biggest tasks a parent has is to teach a child to be responsible for his own actions. A child who blames others or makes excuses, or can't follow through on a job he has been given, is not ready for success in school. Begin by giving your child at least one job to do every day. Insist it be done before play or television begins. He needs to know that he has no choice in whether or not he must do his chores. It is time for your child to be responsible in other ways like picking up his toys or putting his clothes in the hamper. Work on one thing at a time. Take whatever responsibility is most lacking in your child. Be clever and creative and come up with a way to make it his concern and not yours. Make a simple star chart and let him put up a star or a sticker every time he follows through on his responsibility. Or let him put a penny in a jar, or stay up ten minutes longer at bedtime. You are rewarding the very behavior you want repeated. That's teaching responsibility! *(parenting skill)*

- Watch the miracle of the growth of a seed. Fill a clear plastic cup with wet paper towels. Gently slide three or four fast growing seeds, like lima bean seeds, down the inside of the cup, between the cup and the paper towel. Keep the towels moist each day . . . a good responsibility for your child. Soon you will see the seed, roots, stems and leaves through the cup. It is especially fun to plant more of the same seeds in dirt outside so you *know* what's happening under the ground before you see a plant growing. *(science concept)*

- Soft balls of all sizes are wonderful for developing motor skills. Have fun creating your own bowling alley, especially on a rainy day. Gather up some non-breakable containers like a plastic water jug, empty milk cartons, oatmeal boxes, or soda bottles. Line them up across a hallway. From the other end of the *bowling alley,* see how many *pins* your child can knock down by rolling a soft ball. Make it even more fun by putting the number one or two or three on each *pin* and show your child how to add up his score. Try to guard against winners and losers in games! *(gross motor skills)*

- Cutting with scissors is an often-forgotten skill that requires a lot of practice. It helps develop a child's fine motor coordination. Scissors can be dangerous and destructive so always supervise. Children like to *fringe* paper by snipping all around the edges. They enjoy cutting pictures from junk mail or catalogs. This skill can be frustrating and your child may want to give up before he has mastered it. Give short periods of practice with lots of praise and encouragement. You'll be glad *you* didn't give up! *(fine motor skills)*

# Make Way
## for
# Ducklings

## by Robert McCloskey

**TEACHING FOCUS**

- Family relationships
- Rhyming Words
- Interpreting a story through pictures
- Importance of safety

**SETTING THE STAGE**

Instantly singable songs and the appealing rhyme and rhythm of finger plays will encourage children to be involved in storytime.

**SAFETY BREAK** by Greg and Steve, *Kidding Around*
   (An upbeat song about crossing the street safely)

**LITTLE WHITE DUCK** by Raffi, *Ever Grows*

**SIX LITTLE DUCKS**

| | |
|---|---|
| Six little ducks that I once knew | *(six fingers up)* |
| Short ones, fat ones, skinny ones, too | |
| But the one little duck | *(one finger up)* |
| With the feather on his back | *(finger feathers on back)* |
| He ruled the others | |
| With his quack, quack, quack. | *(hands hinged, open, shut)* |
| | |
| Down to the river they would go, | |
| Wibble, wobble, wibble wobble to and fro | *(hands on hips)* |
| But the one little duck | *(one finger up)* |
| With the feather on his back | *(finger feathers backside)* |
| He ruled the others | |
| With his quack, quack, quack. | *(hands hinged, open, shut)* |

**TEN LITTLE DUCKLINGS**

Ten little ducklings; dash, dash, dash!
Jumped in the duck pond; splash, splash, splash!
When the mother called them; quack, quack, quack!
Ten little ducklings came swimming right back.

**FIRST READING**

Tell me what you see on the cover of our story. Where do you think the ducklings are? Is that a strange place for ducks? What do you think the story will be about?

The name of the story is **Make Way for Ducklings** and it was written by Robert McCloskey. When Mr. McCloskey was writing this story, he visited a family of eight ducklings on a pond close to his house. Mr. McCloskey enjoyed watching them so much that he decided to tell children all about the ducklings' adventures.

**GETTING INVOLVED**

Mr. and Mrs. Mallard could move about and get from place to place three different ways. How did they move? Which way shall we move first?

Tell me all the things you can see around you as you are flying. Are you safe? What are you looking for down below?

When the ducklings followed Mr. and Mrs. Mallard by walking or swimming, how did they stay safe? Get in a line behind me and we'll move about together. *(Lead children in different motions . . . swimming, diving for fish, pecking at peanuts, waddling, quacking at cars, marching across the street.)* Now it's time to swim back to our nest on the island and go to sleep for the night.

*Another time, print the names of the eight ducklings on name cards for the children to read and wear as they line up in sequence.*

**A CLOSER LOOK**

With each rereading of a story, children gain new understanding. Pause often for a spontaneous flow of oral language as the children share their feelings and observations. Extend the learning process with your own questions in repeated readings of the story.

- What were Mr. and Mrs. Mallard looking for? *(comprehension)*

- What do ducks fish with? *(interpretation)*

- How did the mallards get a second breakfast? *(comprehension)*

- Why did Mrs. Mallard want to raise her ducklings on the pond? Why did she change her mind? *(reasoning)*

- Do Mr. and Mrs. Mallard look the same? *(visual discrimination)*

- What does it mean to molt? *(comprehension)*

- How was Mrs. Mallard a good mother? What did she teach her ducklings? *(memory)*

- What is unusual about the names of the ducklings? Do you have a favorite? *(auditory discrimination)*

- How was Michael a good friend? Would the ducks have been safe in the city without Michael? *(reasoning)*

- Why did Mrs. Mallard take the ducklings to the Public Garden? *(comprehension)*

**ROUNDING OUT STORYTIME**

**The Wildlife 1-2-3: A Nature Counting Book**   by Jan Thornhill

**Dibble and Dabble**   by Dave and Julie Saunders

**Three Ducks Went Wandering**   by Ron Roy

**Follow the River**   by Lydia Dabcovich

**Ducks Can Fly**   by Lydia Dabcovich

107

# Integrated Whole Language Activities

## PETER AND WENDY

My ducks are so funny, I think.
    They peck at the bugs in the ground,
And always wherever they go
    They follow each other around.

They like to play Follow the Leader.
    Just watch them awhile and you'll find
There's one of them always in front,
    The other one always behind.
                    *Wymond Garthwaite*

**INVOLVEMENT**

## CREATIVE DRAMA

The illustrations in **Make Way for Ducklings** are so detailed and visually rich that the children will enjoy just talking about them in rereadings of the story. Creative drama will also help them to develop story comprehension. Set up your room for a dramatization by deciding on an area for the Public Garden, the Charles River and the island, the buildings and the highway. Identify the places with signs. Make name cards for Mr. and Mrs. Mallard and the eight ducklings. See if the children can use the alphabetical order of the ducklings' names to decide how they should line up for *follow the leader* in the story. That will be the fun part as the children pantomime the drama.

**INTEGRATION**

## A SAFE PLACE IN THE CITY

Review with the children the many hazards that faced the ducks as they tried to nest and live in the city. Then see if they can think of at least eight reasons why the island was an ideal, safe place . . . no foxes, turtles, bikes and cars, but a quiet place to swim, dive, catch fish and eat peanuts, with Michael nearby. List their answers on a chart for another reading experience in your room.

Have the children create their own colorful wall mural of **A Safe Place in the City**. Pencil sketch a simple outline of the river and island for the children to paint, leaving plenty of room for Mr. and Mrs. Mallard and the eight ducklings! Have some fun orally matching the phrases on the chart to the ducklings, imagining what each one might have said. Then have the children print the phrases as words coming from the ducklings' beaks. They will be telling their own story as they swim across the mural!

*Extension:* Involve the children in a discussion of all the things Mrs. Mallard had to teach the ducklings to keep them safe. Compare that list with the many things children must learn in order to be safe in and around school.

## A LETTER TO MICHAEL

Undoubtedly the children listed Michael, the policeman, as one of the reasons why Mr. and Mrs. Mallard found the perfect spot to raise their family. Have each child draw a picture and write a sentence with invented spelling about Michael helping the ducks.

Follow that activity by involving all the children in writing a letter to Michael *from the ducklings*. What would the ducks thank Michael for? As the children dictate the sentences, write them on a language experience chart. Choose a small group of children to illustrate the letter and sign the ducklings' names. Surrounding children with print is a key to motivating readers.

## THE SWAN BOAT

The beautiful swan boat in the story would capture any child's (or any duckling's) imagination! Have the children create a boat out of blocks or boxes with rows of small chairs for the passengers. Add literacy props to the center, encouraging children to think of all the things that could be written on the swan boat . . . numbers on the seats, tickets, a name card for the tour guide, peanuts for the ducks, sights to see, and departure times (big words are fascinating!) Be sure to include a sign-up sheet for tourists in the Public Garden.

## BUILDING THE SETTING

Because children of all ages learn best by *doing*, give them the hands-on experience of creating the story setting for **Make Way for Ducklings.** Cover a large rectangular table with white bulletin board paper, taped down at the corners. Draw a simple outline of the river banks, island, and city roads. Small groups of children can complete the details on the table top setting with markers or crayons. Let the children decide what to add next, perhaps a bridge, buildings, and cars all made with Legos, or ducks, policemen and a swan boat made from clay. Keep a copy of the book nearby as children manipulate the characters and retell the story.

## ALIKE BUT DIFFERENT

Even in the book's lithographed drawings, it is evident that Mr. Mallard was more vividly marked than Mrs. Mallard. Using books such as **The Wildlife 1-2-3; A Nature Counting Book** by Jan Thornhill, have the children find other animals where the male is larger or more colorful than the female. Make a list of the children's discoveries and conclude if that is usual or unusual in the animal kingdom.

## COMPARING ADVENTURES

**Ducks Fly** is the engaging story of a young duck's first flight, with simple text and lively illustrations by Lydia Dabcovich. In **Follow the River** by the same author, a duck family swims from the mountains to the sea. Let the children compare the adventures of the duck families in the joyful stories.

**EVERY DAY LEARNING ACTIVITIES**

Positive parenting, developmental learning activities and a warm, nurturing environment are major factors in a child's academic success and lifetime learning.

**Make Way for Ducklings** is a delightful story of a family taking care of each other and keeping the little ones safe. Your child's world is rather small. A child loves the "familiar," and finds security in everything staying the same. That means changes, moves, new experiences, and even going to school can be scary to a child because they are all unknown. The family is the safety zone for a child who continually moves in and out of new developmental stages and new experiences. She will never be loved or protected by the world as she is by her family. Be sure to create a sense of family in your home . . . that your family is special, and your family is a team with everyone working together to take care of each other. Some children are so busy vying for acceptance and approval that they can't feel love for a brother or a sister. Start a family box which is simply a little box containing the name of every member of your family, including mom and dad. Each person draws a name from the box and finds all the ways he can take care of that person . . . being kind, helping, looking out for him, doing things without being asked. You might have more fun keeping the names secret. Draw new names every week until every one has had a chance to take care of all the others. *(parenting skill)*

- Protecting your child will always be your responsibility, so teaching safety outside the home is essential. Teach your child relentlessly about looking before crossing the street and watching traffic lights. If your child will be walking to school, walk the route with her many times. Point out landmarks and hazards along the way. Insist that she walk or play with other children and that she knows exactly what to do if she ever needs help. *(safety)*

- Have your child draw the ducklings and Mr. and Mrs. Mallard from **Make Way for Ducklings.** Count and name the ducklings. Cover each duck with thin white glue and let your child add cereal, rice, dry pasta, or bits of colored paper for a collage. *(creative learning)*

- Write one of the ducklings' rhyming names on each page of a little book. Point out that the names sound alike because they end the same. Talk about each beginning letter and the sound it makes. Have your child illustrate her book and read it to you! *(rhyming words)*

- Look around the house for sets of eight objects. Collect them. Make a little book and have your child draw or glue a set of eight objects on each page. Label the sets. *(counting sets)*

- A child loves to make up nonsense words to rhyme with his own name. Be ready for the sillies! *(rhyming words)*

# May I Bring a Friend?

## by Beatrice de Regniers

**TEACHING FOCUS**
- Days of the Week
- Language Development
- Sequencing
- Rhyming Words

**SETTING THE STAGE**

Instantly singable songs and the appealing rhyme and rhythm of finger plays will encourage children to be involved in storytime.

**THE MORE WE GET TOGETHER**, by Raffi, *Singable Songs for the Very Young*

**GOING TO THE ZOO**, by Raffi, *Singable Songs for the Very Young*

**THE ELEPHANT**

| | |
|---|---|
| The elephant has a trunk for a nose, | *(arms out, hands clasped* |
| And up and down is the way it goes; | *(move arms up, down)* |
| He has such a saggy, baggy hide! | *(flop arms and chest)* |
| Do you think two elephants would fit inside? | *(hold up two fingers)* |

**HERE'S A CUP OF TEA**

| | |
|---|---|
| Here's a cup, and here's a cup, | *(make two fists)* |
| And here's a pot of tea; | *("pop" thumb out of fists)* |
| Pour a cup and pour a cup | *(pour into left, then right)* |
| And have a cup with me! | *(extend cup to neighbor and pretend to drink)* |

**FIRST READING**

Tell me all the things you see on the cover of our story. How are the king and queen dressed? Where do you think they are? What do you think the small boy is saying? I will just turn the pages without saying a word. You be the storytellers. Tell me everything you see and what you imagine is happening.

Beatrice de Regniers would have loved your story. I know I did! In her story, the little boy received a very special invitation to have tea in the king and queen's castle. The child asked one question, **May I Bring A Friend?** That is the title of our story. The illustrator, Beni Montresor, was given a very important award, the Caldecott Medal, for his beautiful pictures.

As I read, listen for the words, "So I brought my friend . . . ." You tell me who the friend was before I turn the page!

**GETTING INVOLVED**

Here are name cards of the days of the week and here are picture cards with the names of all the animal guests who came to the castle. What can we do with them? Where shall we begin? (The children may suggest putting the days of the week name cards around their necks, lining up sequentially, and then matching the animal pictures.)

The first day of the week is always Sunday, so we will begin there. Who came to tea on Sunday? Who ate everything at the dinner on Monday? Which friends played at lunch on Tuesday? Who did the king and queen sit on during Wednesday's breakfast? Which friends wore masks for Halloween on Thursday? On Friday, Apple Pie Day, who played the horn? Which friends enjoyed tea at the zoo on Saturday?

The king and queen entertained themselves each time they waited for the small boy and his friends to arrive. Show me how you think the king and queen looked as they sat on their royal thrones, picked flowers, danced together, went fishing, caught butterflies, went swinging, and wound yarn into a ball.

**A CLOSER LOOK**

With each rereading of a story, children gain new understanding. Pause often for a spontaneous flow of oral language as the children share their feelings and observations. Extend the learning process with your own questions in repeated readings of the story.

- What was inside the little boy's letter? *(auditory memory)*

- How many animal guests do you remember? Which one surprised you the most? Why? *(reasoning)*

- Did the animals all come for tea? *(auditory memory)*

- What was the problem with the elephant? How did the king and queen solve the problem? *(comprehension)*

- Why did the lions wear masks? Why did they roar? *(comprehension)*

- Did the king and queen and little boy have good manners? Did the guests? *(opinion)*

- Why did the king and queen have tea at the City Zoo? *(comprehension)*

- What do the banners say over the zoo? *(language)*

- Did you like the ending? Can you think of a new ending? *(creativity)*

**ROUNDING OUT STORYTIME**

**The Trouble With Elephants**   by Chris Riddell

**Do You Want to be My Friend?**   by Eric Carle

**Is Your Mama A Llama?**   by Deborah Guarino

**Can I Keep Him?**   by Steven Kellogg

**Cookie's Week**   by Cindy Ward

113

# *Integrated Whole Language Activities*

**POETRY**

### WAY DOWN SOUTH

Way down south
   where bananas grow,
A grasshopper stepped
   on an elephant's toe.
The elephant said,
   with tears in his eyes,
"Why don't you pick
   on someone your size?"
           *Anonymous*

### TABLE MANNERS
by Gelett Burgess
from *The Random House Book of Poetry*
by Jack Prelutsky

**INVOLVEMENT**

### MAY I BRING A FRIEND?

A king, a queen, an invitation to the castle, tea, and animal friends that just won't sit still . . . what a setting for creative dramatics. Have the children find a place in your room for the throne and a table for tea. Provide gold and glitter in the art center for crowns, a scepter, and a horn. Look in the dress-up box for royal robes. Hang a yarn-tied picture name card around each child's neck, showing the king, the queen, the invited child, and the animal guests. Group the monkeys and the lions. With you as narrator, have the children freely pantomime the movement of the story characters. Perhaps you can precede the drama with a discussion about manners in the castle!

**INTEGRATION**

### RHYME TIME

The rhyming words that add so much to the listening pleasure of **May I Bring A Friend** are simple, familiar words for which children can easily create rhyming word families. Each day write one rhyming word from the story, such as *boy*, in the center of a semantic web. As the children discover words in their reading, writing and listening experiences that rhyme with the key word, add them to the web. Continue choosing new words from the story, i.e., *king, queen, tea, may* or *bring*, to create new webs.

Graph the results on a multi-column wall graph with the semantic web key words at the top of each column. Graph the words the children have discovered. Add small pictures on the words, if needed. Which word family was the largest? The smallest? The favorite?

### A NEW CHAPTER

What happened on Saturday at half-past two after having tea at the City Zoo? Did the little boy continue to visit the king and queen? Did he bring other friends? Involve the children in a discussion of what might have happened next in the story. Have each child draw a picture and write a sentence for a new ending to **May I Bring A Friend?** Give each child the opportunity to share in the Author's Chair (now we're rhyming, too!)

114

**SUNDAY, MONDAY**

Review with the children the guests that came on each day of the week. Choose a small group to illustrate a page for each day. At the top left of each page print the day of the week and the phrase, *I brought my friend(s), the . . .* On the right, under a flap, have the children draw the animals guest(s) that came that day. Change the print on the last page to read, *On Saturday, we had tea at the zoo.* Under that flap, the children will draw all the animals having tea at the zoo. Your pages will tell a colorful story on the wall, out in the hall, or bound into a class big book.

**MORE FRIENDS FOR TEA**

Imagine what the story would have been like if the little boy had invited friends from the jungle, the ocean, an animal store, or his own neighborhood. Read **What Do You Do At A Petting Zoo**, a charming nonfiction book by Hana Machotka with a simple text and beautiful, close-up photographs of animals. Try to imagine the petting zoo inside the castle! Or read **Maggie and the Pirates**, a touching story about a child and his pet cricket. Imagine Maggie and the cricket's insect friends visiting the king and queen.

To introduce another innovation idea, read the children's favorite stories about friends, such as **Ernest and Celestine** or **Elizabeth and Larry** or **Mrs. Huggins and Her Hen Hannah.** Have the children decide on a new group of friends to invite to have tea with the king and queen. On what days of the week will they visit? Will they have good manners in the castle? Your innovation will be a new story about friends to add to your library corner.

**YOU ARE INVITED TO A TEA PARTY!**

Plan a tea party in your room. Will you invite stuffed animals? Moms, Dads, Grandmas, Grandpas? Another class? Make lists of things you need to do to prepare and what you want to do for your guests. Your lists might include:

- Write and decorate invitations shaped like teacups.
- Make placemats and paste paper doilies where the teacups will go.
- Mix lemonade tea.
- Cut out tea sandwiches with cookie cutters.
- Make streamers for the room and a welcome banner for the door.
- Decorate the pages of a guest book for guests to sign.
- Invite someone special from your school to be the king and queen and read **May I Bring A Friend?** to the guests.
- Sing the songs, *Will You Be My Friend, The More We Get Together,* and *Going to the Zoo.*
- Share the class stories you have written before you say good-bye.

**EVERYDAY LEARNING ACTIVITIES**

Positive parenting, developmental learning activities and a warm, nurturing environment are major factors in a child's academic success and lifetime learning.

Much of the appeal of **May I Bring A Friend?** is the poetry of the rhyming words. Children and poetry go together. Your child's first poetry was the rhythmic heartbeat he heard in the womb. His next poetic experience was probably the delightful rhyme of nursery rhymes and folk songs. Because of the repetition, your child memorized the patterns of the sounds without even trying. Poems are good memory-builders. They fit easily into the shared moments of busy days. A child loves poetry that relates to all the little things he experiences each day . . . smiles and tears, friends and animals, rain and sunshine. The nonsense and appeal of silly rhymes nudges open the door of imagination in a child's mind. Poems are also the perfect beginning to the read-aloud habit and a marvelous addition to any child's bedtime routine. Your child will be captivated by the poetry and charming illustrations of *Read-Aloud Rhymes for the Very Young* by Jack Prelutsky or *The Random House Book of Mother Goose* by Lobel. No child should be without his very own treasured book of poetry. *(parenting skill)*

- Create a calendar by dividing a large strip of paper into seven blocks. Write each day of the week across the top and read the words with your child. Every morning ask your child to invite a guest for tea, i.e., a real or imaginary friend, a stuffed animal, or a character from **May I Bring A Friend?** Together, set the table for a special tea party. Use a cookie cutter to cut bread or cheese or meat tea sandwiches. Talk about how the food looks, tastes and feels! Have fun role-playing good and bad manners. At the end of the week decide which guest had manners fit for a king and queen! *(days of week, social skills))*

- Write colorful little invitations or messages, such as, "Time to read a story," or "You are invited to a tea party," or "You have just earned three hugs and a big kiss!" Hide the messages in obvious places during the day. When your child finds one, have him describe where he found it, i.e. under his plate or beside his teddy bear or on the car seat. Then read the message! Surrounding your child with print, or words written down, is one of the first steps of reading. *(language)*

- A ladder can provide endless practice in gross motor skills. Your child will have twice the fun if he can invite a friend to join the activity. Begin with a simple skill like walking between the rungs of a ladder that is lying flat on the ground. Next have him crawl between the rungs of a ladder held on its side, or climb up an inclined ladder. Make the skills progressively more difficult. Lay the ladder flat on the ground and hold the child's hand as he walks on top of the rungs of the ladder, jumps over the rungs one at a time, walks sideways along a side beam, walks on hands and feet between the rungs, or walks with one foot on a rung and one foot on a side beam. Laughter and silliness guaranteed! *(gross motor skills)*

- Think of rhyming word families for some of the words in **May I Bring A Friend?** (i.e. boy, king, queen, tea, may, and bring). Write them down. Which list is longest, shortest? *(rhyming, words in print, counting sets)*

116

# Mr. Rabbit
## and the
# Lovely Present

## by Charlotte Zolotow

**TEACHING FOCUS**
- Classifying
- Self-esteem
- Color recognition
- Family relationships

**SETTING THE STAGE**

Instantly singable songs and the appealing rhyme and rhythm of finger plays will encourage children to be involved in storytime.

**APPLES AND BANANAS** by Raffi, *One Light, One Sun*
   (A hilarious game song with vowels.)

**JENNY JENKINS** by Sharon, Lois & Bram, *Smorgasbord*
   (Rhyming song using colors)

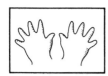

**THE VERY NICEST HOUSE**

| | |
|---|---|
| The fish lives in a brook, | *(hands wiggle)* |
| The bird lives in a tree, | *(hands fly)* |
| But home's the very nicest place | *(hands make roof)* |
| For a little child like me. | *(arms hug self)* |

**WHAT COLORS DO I SEE?**

| | |
|---|---|
| See, see, see | |
| What colors do I see? | |
| Purple plums | *(point to thumb)* |
| Red tomatoes | *(point to first finger)* |
| Yellow corn | *(point to second finger)* |
| Brown potatoes | *(point to third finger)* |
| Green lettuce | *(point to fourth finger)* |
| Yum, yum, yum, good! | |
| I learn so many colors | |
| When I eat my food! | |

**FIRST READING**

Look at the cover of this book and tell me what you see. Where do you think the little girl and the rabbit are? What do you think their conversation is about? Would you like to *predict* what will happen? Let's write down your predictions and see if they happen in the story.

The name of the story is **Mr. Rabbit and the Lovely Present.** It was written by Charlotte Zolotow and the pictures were done by Maurice Sendak. He also illustrated the book, **Where the Wild Things Are.** See if you think these illustrations are different. Now let's read about the rabbit and the lovely present.

**GETTING**
**INVOLVED**

What were the four colors the little girl's mother liked? Let's list them one at a time and name all the gifts that Mr. Rabbit suggested. We'll circle the gift the little girl chose for each color.

Now look at these little drawings of the presents Mr. Rabbit suggested for the color *red*. Name them as I spread them out . . .   red underwear, red roofs, red cardinals, red fire engines, and red apples. Help me *match* the pictures to the words we have listed under *red* on our color chart. *(Do the same for each color group.)*

*Colored markers and 3x5 cards are a fast way to prepare this activity. A piece of rolled tape on the back of each card will hold it up on a flannelboard or chart for an eye-catching way to classify. Another time, ask the children to name new categories you could use for grouping, such as jewels, time, birds, things you can eat and things that have an engine.*

**A CLOSER LOOK**

With each rereading of a story, children gain new understanding. Pause often for a spontaneous flow of oral language as the children share their feelings and observations. Extend the learning process with your own questions in repeated readings of the story.

- Where are Mr. Rabbit and the little girl having their conversation? *(interpretation)*

- What time of day is it at the beginning of the story? The end? *(observation)*

- Why did the little girl need help? *(reasoning)*

- Why did Mr. Rabbit say you can't give your mother the color red? *(reasoning)*

- Where did the little girl's mother like the birds to be? Why? *(reasoning)*

- What are emeralds and sapphires? Why couldn't the little girl afford them? *(reasoning)*

- Where do you think the rabbit went when he said goodbye? *(opinion)*

- If the little girl's mother had liked the color orange, what things do you think that Mr. Rabbit would have suggested? *(association)*

- Do you think the little girl's mother liked her present? Would your mother have liked it? *(opinion)*

**ROUNDING OUT**
**STORYTIME**

**A Chair for My Mother**   by Vera B. Williams

**Mary Wore Her Red Dress**   by Merle Peek

**Happy Birthday, Moon**   by Frank Asch

**Planting A Rainbow**   by Lois Ehlert

**Feathers for Lunch**   by Lois Ehlert

# Integrated Whole Language Activities

**POETRY**

**YELLOW**

Green is go,
and red is stop,
and yellow is peaches
with cream on top.

Earth is brown,
and blue is sky;
yellow looks well
on a butterfly.

Clouds are white,
black, pink, or mocha;
yellow's a dish of
tapioca.

*David McCord*

**A TASTE OF PURPLE**
by Leland B. Jacobs

**WHAT IS PINK?**
by Christina Rossetti

from *The Random House Book of Poetry*
by Jack Prelutsky

**INVOLVEMENT**

**A LOVELY PRESENT**

To help your children appreciate the gentle warmth of **Mr. Rabbit and the Lovely Present**, choose a new focus each time you read the story. First, listen for the phrase, *"She likes,"* as the little girl identifies the colors her mother likes. Next, listen for the phrase as it relates to birds, and finally, to the lovely present of fruit.

Write a sentence on a felt backed sentence strip for each color and each fruit the mother likes. Have the children draw small, labeled pictures of the four birds and four fruits; a tree, and a basket. Display all the sentences and pictures in front of the children. As you read the story again, pause every time a child should put a sentence on the feltboard or put a bird in the tree. The fruit pictures will go in the basket at the end of the story. Keep the pictures, sentences, and a tape of the story in their own pretty little basket for an independent or paired reading experience!

**INTEGRATION**

**OBSERVATIONS, PLEASE!**

Put all kinds and colors of fruit on a table in your science center. Provide a magnifying glass, a balance scale, a measuring tape, and a ruler for children to independently explore, make observations, and compare. Add literacy props to your table for children to draw or write their observations.

**OUR BOOK OF COLORS** *

To make a class book of a rainbow of colors, give every child a page with the sentence, *What is* _____ *?*, printed at the top. Let each child choose a color word as well as the objects she will draw and label on her page, such as a fire truck, a stoplight, and a rose for the color red. Mount each child's picture on a background that matches the color she has chosen. Bind the pages into a colorful, easily read class book.

*Extension:* With one line printed on the top of each page, the illustrated phrases of the poem, **Yellow**, would make a beautiful wall display or class big book.

**PRESENTS ARE EVERYWHERE** *

Unwrap three gift-wrapped boxes as you introduce the theme that presents are everywhere in our world. Discuss the idea until the children conclude that the *acorn is a present from a tree, the rainbow is a present from the rain, and the smile is a present from a baby.* When every child has an idea to illustrate, give him a page with the sentence, *A* _____ *is a present from a* _____ , printed on the bottom. Record the words the children dictate to finish their sentences, brightly mount the pages, and display them so children can *read the walls!*

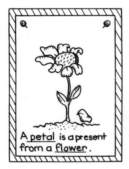   

A petal is a present from a flower.  A raindrop is a present from a cloud.  A skin is a present from a snake.  A bone is a present from a dinosaur.

**A BASKET IS A PRESENT FROM A FRIEND**

Have each child bring a piece of fruit to school. Using a floor graph, have the children suggest different ways to sort the fruit. Record your observations on a language experience chart for another emergent reading and writing experience. Then line several baskets with pretty tissue paper and fill them with the fruit. As a group, decide who will receive your *lovely presents.*

**A CELEBRATION OF PRESENTS**

*Presents* can be a delightful theme celebration with mommies, daddies, and caregivers as guests! Create the invitations in the shape of little presents. Make decorations for a bright, festive room and decide on refreshments the children can serve. Plan a program for the guests, perhaps incorporating the following activities:

- Sing **Apples and Bananas** and **Jenny Jenkins**, perfect choices for guests to join in the fun!

- With you as narrator, have the children tell the story of **Mr. Rabbit and the Lovely Present** on the flannelboard.

- Show the colorful **Fruit Baskets** and explain who will receive them.

- Have each child read her illustrated page from **A Petal is A Present From A Flower** and give it as a present to her guest!

**EVERYDAY LEARNING ACTIVITIES**

Positive parenting, developmental learning activities and a warm, nurturing environment are major factors in a child's academic success and lifetime learning.

The softness and warmth of the story, **Mr. Rabbit and the Lovely Present**, makes you think the little girl must have had a very special relationship with her mother. It is during the all-important early years that a child learns to think of himself as a special person. Usually the way a child feels about himself when he enters kindergarten is the way he will feel about himself as an adult. Self-esteem is determined so early. A child has to believe what adults say about him for he has no other basis on which to form a concept of who he is. If you label your child lazy or dumb, he will live up to that label because he believes you. If you label your child friendly or happy or helpful, he will see himself as all of those things. Usually a child becomes exactly what adults tell him he is. Give your child a wonderful image to live up to! Let him overhear you praising him as you talk to friends. The mistakes or problems need not be mentioned again. Remember praise is a great motivator! There isn't a human being alive who doesn't need more affirmation than ciriticism. *(parenting skill)*

- Children love to feel generous and to give gifts to those who are special to them. Put a little box or tiny basket in a corner of your child's drawer. Give him special jobs to do and a weekly allowance of nickles or dimes. Then when it is time to buy a birthday or holiday present for someone in the family, your child will have his own supply of money to use. The size or cost of the gift doesn't matter. Learning to give is a wonderful lesson, along with the fun of shopping and making a choice. *(social skill)*

- Children can experience the feeling of generosity without any money being spent. The best kind of present is the one the child makes himself. Give him a little box of odds and ends like yarn bits, cookie crinkly paper, straws, buttons, fabric pieces, colored paper and crayons. Encourage your child to create his own gifts and cards. The praise and attention he will get for his creations will be a wonderful esteem builder. *(creativity, self-esteem)*

- Have your child go through a catalog and cut out *gifts* he would give to Grandma or some other special person. Have him paste his choices on a piece of paper and label them. Write down your child's words as he dictates a simple letter of love to give or mail to Grandma. Words have a purpose! *(readiness)*

- Create a Color Basket. First just put in pairs of color cards for your child to match. Next add *color words* to match to the colors. Last, play *Concentration* with pairs of color words for your child to turn over and match. *(color and word recognition)*

- Make *a coupon book* for your child to give a loved one. Each page will have one gift that the child decides to give. Have your child draw a picture and dictate a sentence for each coupon, i.e. *I will give you a hug. I will sing you a song. I will tell you a story. I will bring you the newspaper.* *(giving, print)*

# The Napping House

## by Audrey Wood

**TEACHING FOCUS**
- Cumulative Rhyme
- Sequencing
- Visual Perception
- Cause and Effect

**SETTING THE STAGE**

Instantly singable songs and the appealing rhyme and rhythm of finger plays will encourage children to be involved in storytime.

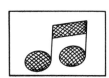

**THE RATTLIN' BOG**, by Sharon, Lois & Bram, *In the Schoolyard* (a fun, cumulative song)

**FIVE LITTLE MONKEYS**, by Sharon, Lois & Bram, *One Elephant, Deux Elephants*

### GRANNY'S SPECTACLES

| | |
|---|---|
| Here are Granny's spectacles | *(fingers around eyes)* |
| Here is Granny's Hat | *(hands on head)* |
| Here's the way she folds her arms | *(arms folded)* |
| And sits like that! | |
| Here are Grandpa's spectacles | *(bigger glasses)* |
| Here's the way he folds his arms | *(bigger hat)* |
| And sits like that! | *(arms folded)* |

### FIVE LITTLE MONKEYS

| | |
|---|---|
| Five little monkeys | *(five fingers up)* |
| Jumping on the bed, | *(jump to other hand)* |
| One fell off | *(one finger up)* |
| And bumped his head. | *(hold head)* |
| Momma called the doctor | *(phone to ear)* |
| And the doctor said, | |
| "No more monkeys jumping on the bed!" | *(shake finger)* |

Repeat with four monkeys, etc.
until no more monkeys remain.

**FIRST READING**

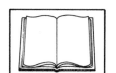

Why does the cover of this book make you smile? You be the storytellers and tell me what you think is happening? The name of the story is **The Napping House.** It was written by Audrey Wood, and her husband, Don Wood, added the beautiful illustrations.

What is happening on the title page? Why do you think the fence and lovely flowers are there? Look! There they are again on the next page. Can you guess what words are on the mailbox? Why is the gate open? *(Turn the page.)* Oh, now we know! The fence and flowers and mailbox and gate are all inviting us into **The Napping House.**

*The charming, cumulative text will have the children joining in long before the delightful surprise ending!*

**GETTING INVOLVED**

**The Napping House** would not have been nearly as much fun to read if the words had said *a flea on a house on a cat on a dog.* Let's act out all the wonderful words the author used to describe the characters in the story . . . *snoring* granny, *dreaming* child, *dozing* dog, *snoozing* cat, *slumbering* mouse and *wakeful* flea.

Now lie down on the floor and pretend you are a dreaming child on a snoring granny on your own cozy bed. Pile on the dog, next the snoozing cat, then the slumbering mouse and last . . . oh-oh! Here comes the wakeful flea. Look out! Crash! No one now is sleeping!

**A CLOSER LOOK**

With each rereading of a story, children gain new understanding. Pause often for a spontaneous flow of oral language as the children share their feelings and observations. Extend the learning process with your own questions in repeated readings of the story.

- Does the first picture suggest there might be children inside the house? *(interpretation)*

- When did it start raining? When did it stop? *(visual perception)*

- Where was the dog before it climbed on the bed? The cat? The mouse? *(visual perception)*

- Was the flea in the room before it bit the mouse? How did the artist make the flea easy to find in every picture? *(visual perception)*

- How did one little flea bite cause such a commotion? *(cause and effect)*

- Do you see any circles in the pictures? Ovals? Squares? *(shape recognition)*

- How does the bed change in the story? Do the pitcher and basin change? *(visual discrimination)*

- Does the house look the same at the end of the story? What invites you inside? *(interpretation)*

**ROUNDING OUT STORYTIME**

**The House That Jack Built**   by David Cutts

**Many Luscious Lollipops**   by Ruth Heller

**No Jumping on the Bed**   by Tedd Arnold

**Teeny Tiny**   by Jill Bennett

**Five Little Monkeys Jumping on the Bed**   by Eileen Christelow

# *Integrated Whole Language Activities*

## A FROG AND A FLEA

A frog and a flea
And a kangaroo
Once jumped for a prize
In a pot of glue:
The kangaroo stuck
And so did the flea,
And the frog limped home
With a fractured knee.

*by Cynthia Mitchell*

## A FLY AND A FLEA IN A FLUE

A fly and a flea in a flue
Were imprisoned, so what could they do?
  Said the fly, "Let us flee!"
  "Let us fly!" said the flea,
And they flew through a flaw in the flue.

*Anonymous*

## INVOLVEMENT

## CHORAL READING

Children love familiar, predictable reading patterns. The strong rhythm and compelling sequence of words in **The Napping House** will have the children reading with you, over and over again! It will be impossible for them to stay quiet!

## A FLANNELBOARD NAPPING HOUSE STORY

Print the story title and the eight phrases . . . *a cozy bed, a snoring granny, a dreaming child, a dozing dog, a snoozing cat, a slumbering mouse, a wakeful flea,* and *the napping house where no one now is sleeping,* on pellon or flannel-backed sentence strips.

Have the children draw small pictures for each phrase. As you read **The Napping House**, encourage the children to read each phrase as you place it on the flannelboard, building the sequence from the bottom up. Ask a child to add each matching picture. After the flea causes everything to tumble, read the last phrase together . . . *in the napping house where no one now is sleeping.* Keep the phrases and pictures available for paired or individual sequencing and reading during center time. *(Variation: Use chart paper or a sentence strip holder.)*

## A SLUMBER PARTY

Have each child bring a teddy bear to school for storytime. Before each child leaves for the day, have him place his teddy bear somewhere in the room to spend the night at a slumber party in the **The Napping House.** After the children have gone, rearrange and group the teddy bears in play centers in the room. In the morning, have each child look for his teddy bear, describe where he found it and what he imagined his teddy bear did during the slumber party in **The Napping House.**

**INTEGRATION**

## INDIVIDUAL ACCORDION BOOKS

As a class, discuss new characters to pile on top of granny on the cozy bed. Talk about the all important words that will describe each character. Then orally sequence the characters by size, saving the tiniest one for last. To make individual accordion books, cut a 12″ x 14″ piece of paper in half lengthwise. Put the two pieces together to make one long rectangle, now 6″ x 28″. Fold the rectangle into eight pages, accordion style. (Make one as a sample. It really is <u>not</u> complicated!) Print the title, then *the cozy bed*, and the new characters' names on the bottom of each page for the children to illustrate.

## THE NAPPING CLASSROOM*

Lead the children in a discussion of the colorful describing words Audrey Wood has used so skillfully, in **The Napping House.** For emphasis, read the story again, deleting all the adjectives! What a difference! Then brainstorm with the children about words that could describe them as they are napping, ideally words that begin with the initial sounds of their names. *(Extend your teaching by reading* **Many Luscious Lollipops: A Book About Adjectives**, *a delightful book by Ruth Heller that makes language come to life.)*

Choose a small group of children to illustrate the cover and title page of your class book, **The Napping Classroom.** These three pages would come next.

| Page One: | Page Two: | Page Three: |
|---|---|---|
| There is a classroom | And in that classroom | And on that rug |
| A napping classroom | There is a rug, | There is a . . . |
| Where everyone is sleeping | A cozy rug in a napping classroom | |
| | Where everyone is sleeping | |

Then give each child his own page to illustrate, adding a cozy rug cut from fabric, felt or wallpaper before he draws himself napping. The last page could read, *In a napping classroom where everyone is snoring!* Children love to select their own reading material. They will return to this book again and again!

dozing David,

snoozing Susan,

cheerful Chad,

in a napping classroom where everyone is snoring!

**EVERYDAY LEARNING ACTIVITIES**

Positive parenting, developmental learning activities, and a warm, nurturing environment are major factors in a child's academic success and lifetime learning.

In his first few years of life, your child will learn more at a faster rate than any other time. That means you are the most important *teacher* your child will ever have. You can do nothing better for your child than to introduce him at an early age to the joy and excitement of books. Reading together will create a loving, close bond between you and your child. It will plant within him the desire to learn to read himself. He will be hooked on the pleasure and delight of books long before he meets vowel sounds and dittos and tests in school. In a fun, natural way, you will be teaching your child the skills he will need for school success. Books will train his ears to listen to the sounds of letters and rhyming words, to pay attention and to stay on task. Books will train your child's eyes to follow from left to right and to recognize colors and shapes, letters and numbers. Books will stretch both his imagination and his vocabulary. A child who loves books will want to read! He will be ready and you will have made it happen. Remember, a child learns most from the people he loves. *(parenting skill)*

- A child's own **Napping House** bedtime routine will be a delightful ending to his day. What will he choose to pile on top of himself on his cozy bed? What tiny thing will start everything falling? Be sure to add interesting describing words and action words. (Don't hesitate to call them *adjectives* and *verbs* . . . The words will fascinate!) Tell the whole story together every night in your own napping house. Bedtime and laughter should go together! *(vocabulary, sequencing)*

- The story, **The Napping House**, ends with the phrase, *Where no one now is sleeping.* What an ideal way to introduce the *concept of zero!* Not even one snoring granny means zero snoring grannies, and so on through the characters of the story. Another time, because children love a touch of the ridiculous, ask your child how many wakeful animals are eating at her table! Zero fleas, elephants or baboons are sure to bring giggles. Find new ways to teach zero while driving in the car or after snacks are gone. Have fun! *(math concepts)*

- A child's mastery of *gross motor skills* precedes her mastery of *fine motor skills.* Practice is essential! Show your child how to jump forward, then backward over an object, her feet tied together with an imaginary rope! Have her practice rhythmic jumping by swinging her arms, first a quarter turn, then a half turn, then a full turn around, smiles guaranteed! Have her hold a beanbag between her knees and jump, tumbles guaranteed! Jump into a tire or circle and out again, fun guaranteed! *(motor skills)*

- The characters in **The Napping House** . . . the flea, mouse, dog and cat, are easy words to rhyme. Create rhyming word *families* as your child learns to hear the final sound in each word. *Predict* (your child will love the word) how many words you will think of for each *family* before you begin. *(auditory discrimination)*

# Noah's Ark

## by Peter Spier

**TEACHING FOCUS**
- Interpreting pictures
- Left - right progression
- Sequencing
- Classifying

**SETTING THE STAGE**

Instantly singable songs and the appealing rhyme and rhythm of finger plays will encourage children to be involved in storytime.

**NOAH'S OLD ARK** by Sharon, Lois & Bram, *Elephant Show Record*

**WHO BUILT THE ARK** by Raffi, *More Singable Songs*

### PITTER PATTER

| | |
|---|---|
| Pitter patter, pitter patter, Rain is coming down | *(fingers raining down)* |
| Pitter patter, pitter patter, Wind is blowing round. | *(hands side to side)* |
| Pitter patter, pitter patter, Rain is here and there | *(fingers left and right)* |
| Pitter patter, pitter patter, Rain is everywhere! | *(fingers in wide circles)* |

### TWO MOTHER PIGS

| | |
|---|---|
| Two mother pigs lived in a pen, | *(show thumbs)* |
| Each had four babies and that made ten. | *(fingers up)* |
| These four babies were black as night, | *(one hand up, thumb bent)* |
| These four babies were black and white. | *(other hand, thumb bent)* |
| But all eight babies loved to play, | |
| And they rolled and rolled in the pen all day, | *(roll hands)* |
| At night, with their mothers, they curled up in a heap | *(make fists)* |
| And squealed and squealed till they went to sleep. | |

**FIRST READING**

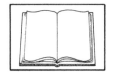

*Wordless books have a valuable place in children's literature. The joyful process of reading pictures is the earliest stage of reading. Wordless books encourage children to notice the details of beautiful illustrations, to make discoveries for themselves and to anticipate what is going to happen next. Because the plot is supplied through the illustrations, children concentrate on telling the story in their own words. You are just a skillful guide. The children are the real storytellers. They will feel a sense of accomplishment in their ability to read a complete book.*

Most of the stories we have read have been make-believe stories. The authors used their imaginations as they wrote. But today's story comes from the Bible. It is the story of Noah and the flood and it is called **Noah's Ark**. Peter Spier, the man who painted the pictures, received a very special award for this book called the Caldecott Medal. Every time you look at the pictures you will see something new you didn't see before.

Look at the cover of **Noah's Ark.** What do you see? What do you think is happening? The story begins just inside the cover. Can you find Noah? The title page shows us the very large boat he built because he knew a flood was coming. Did Noah work alone? The author, Peter Spier, wants *you* to tell the story as you *read* the pictures.

**GETTING INVOLVED**

Would you have liked being on the ark with Noah? Tell me all the animals you can remember that had two legs. Let me show you a picture again. Now tell me all the animals you can remember that had four legs. Were there any animals that had no legs at all? *(List the answers on a chart for another experience with words in print.)*

Do you think it was a big job to feed all the animals? Do you think Noah had any help? Stand up in your very own space. Even animals don't like to get bumped. Let's pretend it is feeding time on the ark. You name the animals and we'll all help feed them.

Now that we are finished, let's sit down with Noah and have our own dinner. What do you think it will be?

**A CLOSER LOOK**

With each rereading of a story, children gain new understanding. Pause often for a spontaneous flow of oral language as the children share their feelings and observations. Extend the learning process with your own questions in repeated readings of the story.

- What jobs did Noah have to do before he moved the animals into the ark? *(visual memory)*

- What do you think Noah is saying to the different animals as they move up the gangplank into the ark? *(imagination)*

- Why did Noah close the door? *(reasoning)*

- How did it sound inside the ark? *(reasoning)*

- Do you know what the word conversation means? Is Noah having a conversation with the lions? Are the mice having a conversation with the elephant? *(vocabulary, imagination)*

- Why didn't Noah put the fish and dolphins and turtles inside the ark? *(reasoning)*

- How did the ark rise high enough to get stuck on a mountain? *(comprehension)*

- Why was it a happy day when the dove returned with a leaf? *(comprehension)*

- Did the story have a happy ending? What do you think happened to the ark? *(opinion)*

**ROUNDING OUT STORYTIME**

**Oh, Were They Ever Happy!**  by Peter Spier

**Mr. Gumpy's Outing**  by John Burningham

**Aardvarks, Disembark!**  by Ann Jonas

**Come a Tide**  by George Ella Lyon

**Follow Me Cried Bee**  by Jan Wahl

# *Integrated Whole Language Activities*

**POETRY**

**SUN AFTER RAIN**

Rain, rain,
went away.
Sun came out
with pipe of clay,
blew a bubble
whole-world-wide,
stuck a rainbow
on one side.
*Norma Farber*

**ANCHORED**
by Shel Silverstein
from *Light in the Attic* by Shel Silverstein

**OLD NOAH'S ARK**
Folk rhyme from *Side by Side*
by Lee Bennett Hopkins

**INVOLVEMENT**

**PICTURE WALKS**

Because Peter Spier's detailed illustrations are so visually rich and humorous, the children will delight in repeated *picture walks* through **Noah's Ark.** To help them make new discoveries, choose a new focus each time you *read the pictures*, such as, the variety of birds, the number of water animals, or finding the tiniest animals on board the ark.

**MICE IN THE CORNER**

Lead the children in a discussion of the dangers of being a very small animal on the crowded ark. Look for the little mice that are shown in every picture inside the ark. The children will surely have a story to tell about the elephant standing on the mouse's tail!

Pretend the children are all mice on **Noah's Ark.** Designate four corners of your room as hiding places from the larger animals on the boat. Hang the numbers 1, 2, 3, and 4 above the corners. Choose a child to be Noah who closes his eyes and says, "Mice in the corner." As he slowly counts to ten, all the other children quietly tiptoe to the four corners of the room. Noah then calls out the number of one corner before he opens his eyes. The mice hiding in that corner must go back to their seats. Noah closes his eyes again and says, "Mice in the corner." All the remaining mice scatter to *any* of the four corners. Noah calls out another number and the mice in that corner must sit down, and so on. (Anytime Noah calls the number of an empty corner, a new Noah is chosen.) The suspense builds as the number of mice gets fewer and fewer until none is left.

**OLD NOAH SAID, "COME ON IN!"**

Enjoy another *picture walk* through the ark. This time have the children name all the animals they can find. Make a list of their answers on chart paper. The children will be amazed at the length of the list!

To play *Old Noah Said, "Come On In"* find a place in the room for the ark, perhaps a boat the children have made from blocks or cardboard boxes. Using the chart list, prepare two printed name cards for each animal. Add little picture clues next to the words. Make enough cards for each child to hold the name of an animal.

With the children sitting in a circle, begin the chant, *Old Noah said, "Come on in." So the* _____ *went in, two by two*. Repeat the chant using animal names while the children clap and get the beat! To incorporate the name cards in the game, have the children continue the chant while you call out the name of an animal. The two children holding the cards for that animal get up, walk up the ramp and into the ark as the others continue just clapping to the beat. Then start the chant again, calling out the name of another animal, and so on, until all the animals are inside the ark! As a conclusion, let each child match his animal name to the list on the chart before placing his card in *Noah's Basket* for independent reading on the ark!

**INTEGRATION**

### AN ARK FULL OF ANIMALS

Turn your bulletin board or a wall into a huge ark! Draw a simple outline of the ark for a small group of children to paint. Have each child draw a pair of animals or someone from Noah's family to cut out and add to the scene. Print the book title and author's name on your colorful mural which will look like an original book cover even Peter Spier would be proud of!

### NOAH'S ABC BOOK OF ANIMALS *

Make an ABC book for the alphabet center in your room. Print the upper and lower case letter on pages cut in the shape of an ark. Then decide on an animal that lived on the ark for every letter of the alphabet. Bind the cover, title page, and illustrated pages in your ark shaped book.

### TWO BY TWO BY TWO!*

Make a class book using the caption, *Old Noah said, "Come on in." So the* _____ *went in, two by two*. Let each child decide what pair of animals he will draw on his paper. He can copy the name of his animal from the class chart to finish the caption already printed on his page. Spread the finished pages on the floor and ask the children how they could classify the animals ... those that fly, that swim, that walk on two legs, four legs, or no legs? Sequence the pictures according to the groups the children have suggested and make a class book of Noah's friends.

### THERE'S WORK TO BE DONE *

Ask the children if Noah's work was done when he finished the huge job of building the ark. In another *picture walk* through the story, find all the other jobs Noah had to do, from milking the cows to planting a vineyard! Print the children's sentences on a chart. Have the children find and highlight with yellow marker the action word in each sentence. Then cut the impressive list apart, giving each sentence to a pair of children to illustrate and paste on a page cut  in the shape of the ark. Choose children to create a cover, a title page, and an ending to your story (chances are it will be a rainbow!) The book will be a clever retelling of the story, and surely a favorite in your library corner.

### SUN AFTER RAIN

Each phrase of the poem, **Sun After Rain,** creates a wonderful word image for children to interpret. With four large pictures illustrating the four phrases, the language of the poem will come to life in your room.

**EVERYDAY LEARNING ACTIVITIES**

Positive parenting, developmental learning activities and a warm, nurturing environment are major factors in a child's academic success and lifetime learning.

Imagine the variety of sounds on **Noah's Ark** from the driving rain to the relentless animal noises, each carrying its own message to Noah's ears. Training a child's ears to listen to sounds everywhere will prepare him to hear the differences in letter sounds and rhyming words. This week, focus on all that your child can learn through his sense of hearing. The experiences are endless if he has been encouraged to listen, really listen, to the sounds around him — wind, birds, water, sirens, animals, insects, cooking, bells, laughter, music. Compare sounds that are high and low, loud and soft, pleasant and unpleasant. Compare daytime and nighttime sounds. Lie down in the grass outside, on your child's bed or anywhere, and just listen! Have your child close his eyes while you make sounds for him to guess, like bouncing a ball, tearing a paper, tapping your finger, or clicking your tongue. Soon your child will be pointing out sounds for *you* to hear! *(parenting skill)*

- Give your child something specific to listen for. When he is watching television, ask him to listen for a person's name and to tell you when he hears it. When he is listening to a record or tape, direct his attention to something specific, such as, "I wonder if you will hear an animal sound." *(auditory perception)*

- Give your child the opportunity to follow two-step directions in sequence, an important auditory skill. "Put your pajamas in the hamper, then find your teddy." "Touch your toes and then sit on the kitchen floor." The actions must be done in sequence, first action first, second action second. Build up to three actions. Have fun, laugh often, and praise continually. Be sure to turn the tables and let your child give you a set of directions to follow. Watch out! *(sequencing)*

- Repeating words in sequence is another readiness skill that can be learned anywhere . . . in the car, waiting in line, or while you are fixing dinner and your child is finding it impossible to wait! Repeat silly words in sequence, like MacDuff, Pouf-pouf, and Lilac. Try sentence building, always beginning with a complete sentence, but making it increasingly longer each time your child can successfully repeat it. "The kangaroo is playing." "The kangaroo is playing outside." "The kangaroo is playing outside in the rain." "The kangaroo is playing outside in the rain at the zoo." *(sequencing)*

- Balloons are good skill-builders. Blow up a balloon and gently toss it back and forth to your child. Chant a nursery rhyme together as you are tossing. *(gross motor skills)*

134

# Oh, A-Hunting We Will Go

## by John Langstaff

**TEACHING FOCUS**

- Story participation
- Reading pictures
- Recognizing rhyming words
- Understanding that print carries a message

**SETTING THE STAGE**

Instantly singable songs and the appealing rhyme and rhythm of finger plays will encourage children to be involved in storytime.

**WILLOUGHBY WALLABY WOO**
by Raffi, *Singable Songs for the Very Young*

**DOWN BY THE BAY** by Raffi, *Singable Songs for the Very Young*

**LITTLE RABBIT**

| | |
|---|---|
| Little rabbit in the wood, | *(two fingers up for ears)* |
| Little man by the window stood, | *(hands like glasses over eyes)* |
| Saw a rabbit hopping by, | |
| Knocking at his door. | *(knocking motion)* |
| Help me! Help me! | *(arms up and down, fast)* |
| Or the hunter will shoot me dead! | *(gun motion)* |
| Little rabbit, come inside. | *(beckoning motion)* |
| Safe with me abide. | *(stroking rabbit ears)* |

**HANDS ON SHOULDERS**

| | |
|---|---|
| Hands on shoulders, hands on knees, | *(follow action as rhyme indicates)* |
| Hands behind you, if you please. | |
| Touch your shoulders, now your nose, | |
| Now your chin and now your toes. | |
| Hands up high in the air, | |
| Down at your sides; then touch your hair. | |
| Hands up high as before, | |
| Now clap your hands, | |
| One, two, three, four. | |

**FIRST READING**

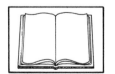

Oh, a-hunting we will go, a-hunting we will go; we'll catch a fox and put him in a box, and then we'll let him go! *(Softly sing or say the words as you hold up the opened book so both the front and back covers are visible to the children.)* The title of our story says, **Oh, A-Hunting We Will Go**, but I don't see any guns or bows and arrows. What do you see? Do the animals and people on the cover look like they are friends? This must be a different kind of hunting. Let's join them and go a-hunting, too!

*This book is a marvelous example of all that we want children's books to be . . . a book that entertains, delights the ear, and teaches, all at the same time. Don't move too quickly through the pages. The wonderful illustrations catch all the humor and absurdity of the words. Ask your children to join in on the repetitive phrase, "And then we'll let him go."*

**GETTING INVOLVED**

Quietly stand and I will help you make a circle by holding hands. After we make a big, round circle, we'll drop hands and stay standing. Let's sing every verse of the song together. When we name the animal to be caught, I will point to a child to be that animal and stand in the middle of our circle. I wonder if our circle will disappear! Sing with me . . . **Oh, A-Hunting We Will Go.** *(The traditional melody is printed on the last page of the book.)*

*Another activity could focus on just the rhyming word pairs. With the children still sitting, name an animal in the story and ask the children to say the rhyming word. Extend the learning by asking them to think of an animal not included in the story and pair it with a rhyming word. Pretend animals or nonsense words will just add to the fun and creativity!*

**A CLOSER LOOK**

**Oh, A-Hunting We Will Go** is so rich in humor and visual detail that a few questions can't begin to capture the playfulness of the delightful text and illustrations. The children will enjoy the story again and again.

- For each hunting adventure, ask the children to point out *where* the people were hunting, how they were *dressed*, and what specific *tools* or *food* they used to capture each animal. Encourage the children to point out all the humorous things in each picture. *(visual perception)*

- Do you know what a pair of words are called when they sound the same? *(vocabulary)*

- Why do you think the author named this book, **Oh, A-Hunting We Will Go?** *(logical thinking)*

- What does it mean to pretend? *(vocabulary)*

- Let's read all the words on every page together. When we come to a rhyming word, I will listen for you to say the word that rhymes. *(understanding that print carries a message)*

- What did the friends do with all the animals they caught? How did that make you feel? Would you change the ending of the story? *(feelings)*

- The *dedication* page in the book tells us that children helped Mr. Langstaff make up some of the verses. Let's make up our own new verses. *(parts of a book)*

**ROUNDING OUT STORYTIME**

**I Was Walking Down the Road**   by Sarah E. Barchas

**the day the goose got loose**   by Reeve Lindberg

**The Hunter and the Animals**   by Tomie dePaola

**Hunter and his Dog**   by Brian Wildsmith

**Sheep in a Jeep**   by Nancy Shaw

# Integrated Whole Language Activities

## POETRY

### IF YOU EVER MEET A WHALE

If you ever, ever, ever, ever,
    ever meet a whale,
You must never, never,
    never, never
grab him by his tail.

If you ever, ever, ever, ever,
    grab him by his tail—
You will never, never,
    never, never
meet another whale.

*Author unknown*

## INVOLVEMENT

- The strong rhythm and predictable pattern of **Oh, A-Hunting We Will Go** just begs children to join in and read with you. If ever a book was written for the pleasure of participation, this one was! After reading the story together a few times, divide the children into two groups. The groups can alternate reading the pages, with both groups joining in on the last page. The playful words are also fun to sing and the melody is printed on the last page of the book.

- To dramatize the story, make name cards for each of the twelve animals and the four hunters. Hang the yarn-tied cards around the children's necks. As everyone sings the words, have the hunters find each animal and pretend to put the animal in its *cage* as the child mimes the part. The goat could jump into the boat and steady his sea legs! The snake could slither into a cake. The pig could flip his head to show off his extraordinary wig, and so on. The children will know what to do, especially when it is the skunk's turn!

## INTEGRATION

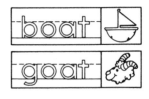

### RHYME TIME

It is the rhyming word pairs in the story that create the fun. See how many word pairs the children can name from memory. Print each animal's name on a card. Print the *cage* the animal was put into on another card. Draw small pictures clues (or have the children draw them) on both the animal and *cage* cards. Display all the words in front of the story. As you read the story again, call on children to find the right rhyming word pairs and place them in a pocket chart or on the chalkboard with magnets. (This activity could also be adapted to a feltboard by making the words and pictures on sturdy pellon.)

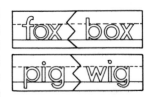

*Extension:* Put each rhyming word pair, such as fox and box, on a sentence strip. Cut a jagged line between the words fox and box, making two puzzle pieces that will fit together when a child finds the right match. (For an additional self-checking cue, make the jagged line with a colored marker.) Keep the puzzle word pairs, a copy of **Oh, A-Hunting We Will Go**, and a tape of the children singing the song in a listening center for an independent reading activity.

138

**WHICH IS YOUR FAVORITE?**

Make a large horizontal wall graph with the heading, What was your favorite animal in **Oh, A-Hunting We Will Go?** List the names of the animals down the left hand side of the graph. Give each child a square of white paper on which to draw and write the name of her favorite animal. Mount the squares on colored paper and place them on the graph. As the children make conclusions, write their sentences on chart paper next to the graph. Which animal had the most pictures? The least? How many more chose the brontosaurus than the armadillo?

**OH, A-HUNTING WE WILL GO, TOO!**[*]

John Langstaff dedicated his book to *"all the children who helped me make up extra verses for this folk song."* Even today as he travels, he inspires children to make up verses of their own. Brainstorm with your children about what it would be like to have John Langstaff in your room. What verses would the children write? What equipment would the four hunters need? Make a list of the animals and the clever rhyming *places* where the children would put them.

Print the *verse* of the folk song on every child's page, leaving a blank for the name of his new animal. Under a folded flap on the right, print the *refrain* with a blank for his new rhyming word. Print the last verse of the song on the last page, with a picture under the flap showing all the animals running away. Bind the pages into a class big book for your reading center. Lifting the flap will be part of the fun as the children read their book!

**THREE JOVIAL HUNTSMEN**

Susan Jeffers has adapted and illustrated **Three Jovial Huntsmen**, an old Mother Goose rhyme, with muted colors overlaying pen and ink drawings. The result is a visually rich book with animals hidden in the woods on every page. This delightful book is another *hunting* experience for eager readers.

**IT'S GETTING CROWDED IN HERE!**

In the charming story, **The Mitten**, woodland animals wiggle into a child's mitten they find in the snow. The warm, cozy mitten becomes very crowded as each new animal squeezes in! After reading the story, have the children decided which one of their *cages* from **Oh, A-Hunting We Will Go, Too** could hold *all* their animals. Write the children's story on a language experience chart. Repeat the phrase, *It's getting crowded in here,* after every third animal moves in! (For example: *A snail rolled in. A frog hopped in. A hippo sloshed in. It's getting crowded in here!*) Your illustrated innovation will become an independent reading experience as your children *read the walls.*

**EVERYDAY LEARNING ACTIVITIES**

Positive parenting, developmental learning activities and a warm, nurturing environment are major factors in a child's academic success and lifetime learning.

It is parents who can best introduce a young child to the pleasures of books. Reading aloud to a child is the best way to plant within him the desire to learn to read himself, long before he meets vowel sounds and dittos and tests in school. The special attention and loving bond of a parent and child reading together can result in a child's lifelong enthusiasm for reading. The rewards are too great to pass up, even in the hectic pace of every day living. The best way to teach your child the value of books is to be sure he has many of his very own. Buy him book plates to identify his own. Books are wonderful to touch. They are warm friends, not cold and impersonal like television. Books can be a private world or they can be shared, but they are always friends. *(parenting skill)*

- In the story, **Oh, A-Hunting We Will Go**, each animal was caught and put into a make-believe *house*. Talk about all the kinds of houses animals really live in, whether they are in your yard or in the park or just in your imagination. For example, a tree is a house for a woodpecker, dirt is a house for ants, a hole is a house for a squirrel, a log is a house for a worm! The book, **A House is a House for Me**, by Mary Ann Hoberman is a delightful learning experience. *(creative thinking)*

- Plan your own hunting trip around the house and hunt for something different each time. Let your child decide what's fair game. . . a certain shape, a color, anything that is breakable, things that grow, objects that begin with the same sound as the first letter in your child's name. You will be surprised at the endless possibilities. *(recognizing and classifying)*

- Make up your own hunting game with a box of animal crackers. Whatever animal your child pulls out of the box, he must think of a word to rhyme with it before he can eat the evidence. *(auditory discrimination)*

- You will have instant attention if you begin with your child's own name when you talk about rhyming words. Make up silly words to rhyme with her name. She will soon hear that rhymes simply end with the same sound. Make up nonsense words to rhyme with Superman or spaghetti or pizza. Careful, the giggles are contagious. *(auditory discrimination)*

- Make texture rubbings by putting paper over textured surfaces and rubbing a peeled crayon over the paper. Like magic the texture will show through. With a marker, have your child create animals or animal houses from the drawings. *(texture art)*

# *On Market Street*

## *by Arnold Lobel*

**TEACHING FOCUS**
- Letter-sound Association
- Visual discrimination
- Vocabulary
- Classifying

**SETTING THE STAGE**

Instantly singable songs and the appealing rhyme and rhythm of finger plays will encourage children to be involved in storytime.

**ABC ROCK,** by Greg and Steve, *We all Live Together, Vol. 1*
   (A bright, singable tune with letter echoes)

**SOUNDS FROM A-Z,** Rosenshontz, *Share It*
   (Clever sounds for each letter of the alphabet with an easy refrain)

**ALPHABET LETTERS**

| | |
|---|---|
| Alphabet letters here and there, | *(point left and right)* |
| Twenty-six letters everywhere, | *(point all over)* |
| Mix them up and move them around, | *(roll hands)* |
| And you'll find words all over town. | *(hands open, palms up)* |
| | |
| Letters are short, and letters are tall. | *(hand low, hand high)* |
| And some have the silliest shape of all. | |
| But put them all together and you will see | *(roll hands)* |
| How helpful alphabet letters can be. | *(hands open, palms up)* |

                     *Mary Cornelius*

**JACK-IN-THE-BOX**

| | |
|---|---|
| Jack-in-the-box all shut up tight. | *(Fingers wrapped around thumb)* |
| Not a breath of air, not a ray of light. | *(Other hand covers fist)* |
| How tired we must be all down in a heap. | *(Lift off)* |
| I'll open the lid and up you will leap. | *(Thumb pops up)* |

**FIRST READING**

Tell me everything you see on the interesting cover of this book. Do you wonder how one little boy can carry all those things? The name of the book is **On Market Street.** It was given a special award called the Caldecott Award because of the very beautiful pictures. The artist's name is Anita Lobel and the words were written by Arnold Lobel. The story is about a little boy who went shopping **On Market Street.** He bought something for every letter of the alphabet.

Just inside the cover you will see the boy putting on his shoes. Are his clothes different from yours? What is on the floor by his chair? Perhaps that pouch will hold the coins the boy will need to buy things **On Market Street.** Listen to the poem that begins our story.

**GETTING INVOLVED**

Let's go on our own shopping trip on Market Street. Stand up tall in your very own space and pretend you have a shopping cart in front of you. Look all around to see what the merchants have. Tell me when you see something you would like to buy. We'll all reach way up high or way down low to find it on the shelves. We can shop until our carts just won't hold any more.

There are many ways to group the things the little boy bought **On Market Street.** How would you like to group them? How many categories shall we have? *(They will love the big word!)* We will make a list of objects for each category. *(One day you might divide the purchases into things to eat, things to wear, things to play with. Another day you might categorize by the stores where the objects could be bought.)*

**A CLOSER LOOK**

With each rereading of a story, children gain new understanding. Pause often for a spontaneous flow of oral language as the children share their feelings and observations. Extend the learning process with your own questions in repeated readings of the story.

- *This book is an extraordinary visual experience from beginning to end. Point out fascinating details and something humorous or special on each page. For example, on the letter E page, notice the rooster faces, the eggcup knees, the cooked eggs and the decorated egg on a ribbon.*

- Let's talk about the words in the poem. Who is a *merchant*? What is a *market*? What do the words mean *to catch my eye, I strolled the length,* and *darkness fell*? *(vocabulary)*

- This time through the book, you be the teacher. I will say the letter for each page and you tell me all the wonderful things your eyes can find. Let's begin with A and go all the way to the letter Z. *(participation, interpretation, visual discrimination, vocabulary)*

- Did it surprise you that the little boy was buying presents for a friend? Who was his friend? *(interpretation)*

- If you could give away everything in the story, who would you give the apples to? The books? The clocks?, etc. Why? *(association)*

- Did you see the cover picture anywhere in the story? *(visual memory)*

- Find a present for every letter of the alphabet in the picture with the cat. What was your favorite? *(visual memory, opinion)*

- Would you enjoy this book as a bedtime story? *(reasoning)*

**ROUNDING OUT STORYTIME**

**A is For Angry: An Animal & Adjective Alphabet**   by Sandra Boynton

**From Letter to Letter**   by Teri Sloat

**The Guinea Pig ABC**   by Kate Duke

**Animal Capers**   by Kerry Argent

**Alison's Zinnias**   by Anita Lobel

# Integrated Whole Language Activities

**POETRY**

### I HAD A NICKEL

I had a nickel and I walked around the block.
I walked right into a baker shop.
I took two doughnuts right out of the grease;
I handed the lady my five-cent piece.
She looked at the nickel and she looked at me,
And said, "This money's no good to me.
There's a hole in the nickel, and it goes right through"
Says I, "There's a hole in the doughnut, too."
*Folklore*

**INVOLVEMENT**

• The opening verse in **On Market Street** sets the stage and gives a purpose to all the pages that follow. The closing verse brings everything to a satisfying conclusion. It is the poetry that tells the heartwarming story. Emphasize something different in the words each time you read. Stop often for a *cloze* activity, perhaps pausing for the children to provide the action word in each sentence. Another time as you read, omit the nouns. The children will soon memorize the familiar words.

• Gather the actual objects Anita Lobel has drawn for each letter. Add small pictures for the few things you can't bring to class. Put all the objects together in the middle of your circle. As you read, call on a child to find the object that was purchased **On Market Street** for each alphabet letter.

• Write word cards to replace the objects. The next time you *stop at all the stores* **On Market Street**, have the children match the word cards to the alphabet letters.

• Continue the activity suggested in A Closer Look on the preceding page and have the children give away all the beautiful things in the story. To whom would they give the apples? Why? The books? Why?

• Compare the detailed, visually rich illustrations of this story with the art styles of other alphabet books in your room, such as the lively, bold pictures in **Chicka Chicka Boom Boom.**

**INTEGRATION**

### A POUCH OF PENNIES *

The child carried the coins he spent **On Market Street** in a little pouch. Fill a pouch with twenty-six pennies. Brainstorm with the children about spending the pouch of pennies in just one store . . . a toy store, a pet store, a food store, etc. What could they buy for each letter of the alphabet? When the children have decided where they will go shopping, create a store-shaped caption book. On each page, print the words, *A penny for _____ .* Add a letter of the alphabet to each page before you give them to the children to illustrate. Choose a small group of children to draw a story cover, **A Pouch of Pennies**, a title page, and a final page, *We spent them all on Market Street!*

Hh

A penny for
a hamster .

## I STOPPED AT ALL THE STORES

Take an imaginary walk down a Market Street your children have created in the room. Name the kinds of stores you find there and the goods sold in each store. Divide the children into small groups, with each group deciding which store they will draw on a large section of white paper. Label the storefronts and tape the sections together into one long mural. Hang your mural on the wall, in the hall, or on a clothesline so everyone *can stroll the length of Market Street to see what they might buy.*

## F IS FOR FAMILY!

Activities that involve a child's family build a bridge from home to school. To create your own class alphabet book, give each child an alphabet letter to take home with a note explaining the activity is to be a family project. Together, the family will decide what to draw for the child's letter and how to decorate the page, using scraps and odds and ends at home. (Of course you will arrange for any child to do his page at school, if necessary.) As the illustrated pages are brought back to school, mount them on pieces of colorful poster board. Tape the pages together to make an unusual accordion alphabet book that will stretch across your room.

## A LETTER GRAPH

To have some fun with letter-sound association, make letter cards or create letter boxes from cut-off milk cartons for each letter of the alphabet. Write an upper and lower case letter on each one and line them up around your room. Have the children bring two small items from home (another good family activity) and line them up in front of the appropriate letter on the floor. You have created a floor graph! Which letter has the most objects? The least? The same as another letter? How many more objects in B than Z?

*Extension:* Have each child draw pictures of his objects on small pieces of paper. Glue the children's pictures on a picture graph to hang in the room.

## A CORNER STORE

Create a simulation of an old-time corner store in your classroom. Provide shelves, a counter, a cash register, play money, paper and pencils and markers, plastic fruit and vegetables, shopping baskets, food bins, paper bags, dress-up clothes, and perhaps a pouch of pennies. Have the children help supply the props as well as canned goods, empty food boxes, and little baskets. Add a sign-up sheet for store clerks to take turns at the cash register. Create a store sign or a banner to hang over your store. Let the children decide how they want to write about their Corner Store.

**EVERYDAY LEARNING ACTIVITIES**

Positive parenting, developmental learning activities and a warm, nurturing environment are major factors in a child's academic success and lifetime learning.

**On Market Street** is a magnificent example of the importance of quality art in children's books. Pictures invite a child into a book and create the excitement that makes him turn each page. Pictures give information that would take chapters to describe. Parents can encourage a child to look, really look, until he is immersed in the illustrations. Every time he opens the book, he will see things he didn't notice before. Look for beautiful art work. Know the names of some skillful, gifted illustrators of children's books. *(parenting skill)*

- Encourage your child to be free to give answers and opinions without fear of correction. Play "Let's Window Shop" when you have extra time at the mall. Stand in front of any store window and ask your child what gift he would choose to buy for grandma. Whatever the choice, assure him that she would just love it! Then you pick out something for a friend. Just do one or two people per window and keep the game fun. You are trying to reinforce the fact that the child's ideas are good. You can do the same activity with catalogs or just pretending, to develop imagination. *(self-confidence)*

- When it is time to do some real shopping, have your child help you make a list. Circle the beginning letter of every item on the list and see if she can name them. When you are in the store, find the right section for an item on your list and see if your child can find it by recognizing the first letter. *(letter identification)*

- When your child is interested in learning to write his name, help him make letters out of clay or pipe cleaners, in sand or rice, or by tracing over your letters on a magic slate. Always have his name in front of him while he is learning, with one capital letter and the other letters lower case. When your child is ready for paper, a green dot on the left side is a signal to begin here! Show your child how to make each letter, always starting at the top and coming down, always large and on paper that has no lines. Make a colorful card with his name on it. Let him take it to bed, put it on his cereal bowl, tape it on his door or tie it on his teddy bear. Pride's the name of the game! *(name recognition)*

- Turn your home into an **On Market Street** shopping adventure. Give your child a pouch of twenty-six pennies "to see what she might buy." Every time she finds something for a letter of the alphabet, she gives a penny to the merchant . . . mom, dad, whoever! (Variation: pretend to visit a pet store or the zoo. Buy an animal for each letter of the alphabet.) *(letter-sound association)*

# Peter Spier's
# Rain

## by Peter Spier

**TEACHING FOCUS**
- Interpreting pictures
- Sequencing
- Left to right progression
- Language skills

**SETTING THE STAGE**

Instantly singable songs and the appealing rhyme and rhythm of finger plays will encourage children to be involved in storytime.

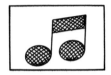

**IT'S RAINING, IT'S POURING MEDLEY,** by Sharon, Lois & Bram, *Mainly Mother Goose*

**MISTER SUN,** by Raffi, *Singable Songs for the Very Young*

**MY STORYBOOK**

I love my little storybook.
I read it every day.
I cannot read the the words just yet,
But I know another way.

I look at all the pictures,
They tell me what to say.
So now I read to Mommy
'Cause that's the game we play!
*Mary Cornelius*

**FIRST READING**

*Wordless books have a valuable place in children's literature. The joyful process of reading pictures is the earliest stage of reading. Wordless books encourage children to notice the details of beautiful illustrations, to make discoveries for themselves, and to anticipate what is going to happen next. Because the plot is supplied through the illustrations, children concentrate on telling the story in their own words. You are just a skillful guide. The children are the real storytellers. They will feel a sense of accomplishment in their ability to read a complete book.*

*Peter Spier's Rain is an extraordinary example of an illustrator skillfully beginning a story before the title page. After encouraging the children to discuss the cover and the title, lead them through the marvelous story-telling details of the opening pages.*

Our story about rain begins on the very first page inside the cover. Where are the children playing? Tell me what animals you see. Can you name everything that is growing? Tell me about the little houses in the picture. How many times do you see water? Do you see any shapes? Anything made out of metal? Of wood? Of rubber? Of cloth? Do you spy any garden tools? Would you like to be playing there, too?

Look at the changes in the picture on the first title page. Why is the little girl holding out her hand? Why is the cat running? Do you see any more little houses?

Now look at the changes on the next title page. Why is mother beckoning? What is happening? Do you see any more houses for insects or animals or make-believe? (A hutch is a house for rabbits, a beehive for bees, a rain barrel is a house for rain, a sunflower is a house for seeds, etc.)

**GETTING INVOLVED**

Let's think about all the things you like to do in the rain, like stomping or splashing or sliding. You add some words to the list. Now listen very quietly to my humming voice and see if you know the song I am humming. *(Hum the tune of The Farmer in the Dell.)* This time you hum along with me. Now we're ready to sing some words . . . "We're stomping in the rain; We're stomping in the rain; Hi-ho the derry-o; We're stomping in the rain." *(Children stomp with you as the whole group sings.)* Every verse we will change to a new word you gave me, *(such as clapping, marching, dancing, sailing, jumping, etc.)* until it is time to go inside out of the rain.

**A CLOSER LOOK**

With each rereading of a story, children gain new understanding. Pause often for a spontaneous flow of oral language as the children share their feelings and observations. Extend the learning process with your own questions in repeated readings of the story.

- *Point out some specific things you want the children to see . . . water reflections, drainpipes, footprints in the mud, animals hiding, a spider web shining with raindrops, a driving rain, scavenger raccoons and mice, etc. Every page in this book is rich in visual detail and in language. (reading pictures)*

- What did the children put on before they went out in the rain? *(vocabulary)*

- Do you think they are very far from home? *(deduction)*

- Why does rain pour out of gutters? *(interpretation)*

- Do birds get wet when it rains? *(interpretation)*

- Tell me when you see an animal hiding. Do ducks need to hide? *(picture reading)*

- Why did little brother's umbrella turn inside out? *(reasoning)*

- Did the children's fun end when they went inside? *(interpretation)*

- How can you tell it is nighttime? How can you tell it's morning? *(interpreting pictures)*

- Tell me about the animals in the morning picture. *(comparing)*

**ROUNDING OUT STORYTIME**

**Better Not Get Wet, Jesse Bear**   by Nancy White Carlstrom

**The Magic Schoolbus at the Waterworks**   by Joanna Cole

**Ernest and Celestine's Picnic**   by Gabrielle Vincent

**Mushroom in the Rain**   by Mirra Ginsburg

**Rain Talk**   by Mary Serfozo

149

# *Integrated Whole Language Activities*

**POETRY**

**IN THE RAIN**

There is no color in the rain
It's only water, wet and plain.
It makes damp spots upon my book
And splashes on my new dress, look!
But puddles, in the rainy weather,
Glisten like a peacock's feather.
*René Cloke*

**MUD**
by Polly Chase Boyden
from *Read-Aloud Rhymes for the Very Young* by Jack Prelutsky

**INVOLVEMENT**

- Rain is so much a part of our everyday lives that children already know and enjoy many songs about rain. Every time you are ready to take another *picture walk* through **Peter Spier's Rain**, hum the melody of a familiar rain song. Encourage the children to join in as soon as they recognize the melody. Sharon, Lois, and Bram have a fun medley of rain songs beginning with *It's Raining, It's Pouring* and B.J. Thomas uses children's voices in a catchy rendition of *Raindrops Keep Falling On My Head.*

- Each illustration in **Peter Spier's Rain** is full of extraordinary story-telling details. Guide the children through many rereadings of the story by focusing on something different each time you read the pictures.

- Name everything the children in the story wore in their adventure in the rain.

- Find all the things that caught the rain as it fell . . . the bird bath, swimming pool, puddles, a wheelbarrow, the children's boots, and many more.

- Look for animals in the pictures. Decide which ones were happy to be in the rain.

- Find compound words in the illustrations. Drainpipe, swingset, footprint, clothesline, woodpile and doghouse are just a beginning.

- Decide which of the above activities you want to list on a chart. Each one is a springboard into a reading and writing experience. If the children decide to write the words of a song, have them make an illustrated big book of the text. Put the book and a tape of the children singing the song in a listening station.

**INTEGRATION**

**RAIN, RAIN, RAIN! ***

A wordless book always presents an opportunity for children to tell the story in their own words. Brainstorm together about all the things the rain fell on in the story until every child has an idea of something to draw. Give each child a page with the words, *Rain on the _____* printed at the top. Act as scribe and finish each child's sentence with the words he has illustrated. Create a cover for your caption book, **Peter Spier's Rain**, a retelling by . . . .

**RAINCOATS, PLEASE!**

Have children bring various kinds of rainwear to class. Compare your collection to what the children wore in the story. Then dress up one child in all the articles of rain gear. Have him stretch out on the floor on a large piece of bulletin board paper. Trace around his body and cut it out for the children to paint. Label everything the child is wearing and center it on a bulletin board. Incorporate one of the above activities and have each child decide what he wants to add from the story. Paint the stormy sky with a light blue *paint wash* and add a few raindrops made from small pieces of aluminum foil for a bulletin board that tells the story of **Rain.**

**AND RAIN MAKES APPLESAUCE \***

Talk about the silly things that happened in the imaginative storybook, **And Rain Makes Applesauce** by Julian Scheer. Ask the children to think of other silly things that could happen in their own story. Talking and laughing together as you share ideas will give everyone a chance to think of an idea to draw on his apple-shaped page. Print the sentence each child dictates. Make some additional pages with only the words, *And rain makes applesauce*, to add as every fourth page of the book. Mount the precut pages on red paper and bind them into a class big book for your reading center.

**MUD AND MORE MUD! \***

• Mud is always fascinating to children. Perhaps that is why there are so many lovable picture books about mud, such as **Mudpies** by Judith Grey, the **Marvelous Mud Washing Machine** by Patty Wolcott, and **Mud for Sale** by Brenda Nelson.

• Using the same format as the caption book, **Rain**, write the words *Mud on the* _____ on each page. Have each child paint his idea with light water colors, adding the mud with large splotches of brown paint.

• After enjoying a story about mud, show the children a jar of mud and water and ask them if they think the two can mix. Without coming to a conclusion, simply put the jar in a writing center. As the children go to the center during the week, have them shake the jar and write and illustrate sentences about what they discovered.

**THE READING CORNER**

Consider the drama, art, and writing possibilities of **Mushroom in the Rain**, a heartwarming story of a mushroom sheltering animals from the rain, and **Rain Talk**, the story of a little girl enjoying the sounds and pleasures of a rainy day. Also enjoy **Let's Look At Rain**, a colorful nonfiction book by Jacqueline Dineen.

**EVERYDAY LEARNING ACTIVITIES**

Positive parenting, developmental learning activities and a warm, nurturing environment are major factors in a child's academic success and lifetime learning.

A child learns by watching, but mostly by doing. It is the first-hand, real-life experiences that create learning. Think about the word *water*. It is usually among a child's first words because he actually experiences the word in so many ways . . . he drinks it, bathes in it, swims in it. That's a key to the way any child learns best, by actually experiencing something. It is the sensory experiences that are the most important of all. Take a ride in a truck, a boat or a train. Show your child a waterfall, a pond, a river. Visit a petting zoo. Let her talk to a policeman and visit the fire station. Visit daddy or mommy's workplace. Go to a music store and have someone demonstrate the instruments. Take her fishing. A child is acquiring knowledge all the time through her five senses, and that knowledge becomes the basis for thinking skills. *(parenting skills)*

- Let your child have her own wonderful adventure in the rain, just like the storybook **Peter Spier's Rain**, if you are sure there is no danger of lightning. You could create your own rain by shooting a hose into the air in your yard, or an old shower curtain can be turned into a quick slip and slide. *(sensory experience)*

- Water play is a natural tranquilizer. Squeezing soap bubbles out of a sponge or just playing in soapy water can calm an overstimulated child. Let your child handwash some dishes, pouring water back and forth from cups to containers, or whip up a soapy froth with an eggbeater. *(sensory experience)*

- Every age loves the water. Provide a bucket of water and an old paint brush or sponge. Let your child wash the car *(you won't have to worry about soap drying)*, or "paint" the side of the house, a wood fence, tree trunks, sidewalks, rocks, the driveway, whatever! *(sensory experience)*

- Water does many fascinating things. It can turn to ice, melt, or create hot steam. Water can clean the dirt from your hands or turn dirt into mud. It can make seeds grow, turn soap into bubbles, cook food, or make popsicles. Try them all and see. *(science concepts)*

- Will they sink or float? Fill a pan full of water. Put it on a folded towel on the floor or in the bathtub or play outside with the pan! Collect some objects . . . a cork, spoon, pebble, sponge, marble. Explain you are doing an experiment to see what will sink and what will float. Ask your child to predict (a word that will fascinate) after you have tried a few objects. Use the same group of objects a number of days in a row. See if she can pre-sort into sink or float piles. *(classifying)*

- More fun with a sponge . . . and water, of course. Add a small amount of liquid detergent to the water and let your child squeeze out some bubbles. Or add a drop of red food coloring to one bowl and blue to the other. Mix the colors and watch them turn purple. *(sensory experience)*

# Peter's Chair

## by Ezra Jack Keats

**TEACHING FOCUS**

- Labeling emotions
- Sibling relationships
- Recognizing title and author
- Colors and shapes

**SETTING THE STAGE**

Instantly singable songs and the appealing rhyme and rhythm of finger plays will encourage children to be involved in storytime.

**I WONDER IF I'M GROWING UP?** by Raffi
*Singable Songs for the Very Young*

**SING A HAPPY SONG** by Greg and Steve, *We All Live Together, Vol. 3*
(How to get your smile back when things go wrong)

**THE LITTLE RED BOX**

| | |
|---|---|
| Oh, I wish I had a little red box | *(make shape with hands)* |
| To put my mommy in. | *(hands lift into box)* |
| I'd take her out and kiss, kiss, kiss | *(lift to mouth and kiss)* |
| And put her right back again. | *(place back in box)* |
| | |
| Oh, I wish I had a little red box | *(make shape with hands)* |
| To put my daddy in. | *(hands lift into box)* |
| I'd take him out and hug, hug, hug | *(wrap arms around self)* |
| And put him right back again. | *(place back in box)* |

Repeat, changing to brother and jump, jump, jump
Repeat, changing to sister and tickle, tickle, tickle
Repeat, changing to baby and rock, rock, rock

**GUESS WHAT I SEE**

| | |
|---|---|
| If I look in the mirror, | |
| Guess what I see? | *(fingers circle eyes)* |
| Someone who looks just like me! | *(point to self)* |
| And if you stand beside me, | |
| It is also true, | *(fingers circle eyes)* |
| I can see someone who looks just like you! | *(point away)* |

**FIRST READING**

Do you remember these stories by Ezra Jack Keats? *(Hold up* **Whistle for Willie** *and* **The Snowy Day**.*)* Do you recognize the little boy on the cover of this book? What else do you see? Where do you think Peter is? What is Peter looking at? That little blue chair is so special that the name of this story is **Peter's Chair**. Read the title with me. Can you read the author's name, too?

Let's turn to the title page for a surprise. Look, there's Willie! Read that page with me, too. Now we are ready for the story about Peter, Willie, and the blue chair.

154

**GETTING INVOLVED**

Look at all the different kinds of shoes in this pile! When I hold up a pair, tell me who you think would wear the shoes . . . an infant or someone your size or a teen-ager or a mommy?

Now I am going to mix them all up and see if you can sort them into pairs. Then we can line them up in a row, from smallest to largest.

What do we do with shoes when they are too small for our feet?

Now let's see who has the quietest shoes in the room. When we look at our book again, we'll find Peter's shoes in a strange place!

**A CLOSER LOOK**

With each rereading of a story, children gain new understanding. Pause often for a spontaneous flow of oral language as the children share their feelings and observations. Extend the learning process with your own questions in repeated readings of the story.

- Why did Peter stretch? *(visual detail)*

- What colors do you see? What shapes? *(observation)*

- What made the building fall? What shapes went flying? Why did the noise bother Peter's mother? *(interpretation)*

- What was painted pink? Why pink? How did Peter feel? Have you ever felt that way? *(identifying feelings)*

- Why did Peter run to his room with his chair? *(identifying feelings)*

- Why is Willie licking Peter's face? *(comprehension)*

- What did they decide to take with them? Why did Peter take his baby picture? *(identifying feelings)*

- Where did Peter and Willie go? Was that far? What shapes do you see? What colors? *(observation)*

- Why couldn't Peter fit in his chair? *(comprehension)*

- How did Peter's mother know he was home? *(observation)*

- Why did Peter help his father paint the chair pink? *(identifying feelings)*

**ROUNDING OUT STORYTIME**

**Do You Know What I'll Do?**   by Charlotte Zolotow

**Whose Mouse Are You?**   by Robert Kraus

**Happy Birthday, Sam**   by Pat Hutchins

**Pig Pig Grows Up**   by David McPhail

**William's Doll**   by Charlotte Zolotow

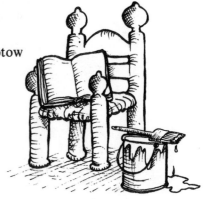

# Integrated Whole Language Activities

**POETRY**

**BROTHER**

I had a little brother
And brought him to my mother
And I said I want another
Little brother for a change.
But she said don't be a bother
So I took him to my father
And I said this little bother
Of a brother's very strange.

But he said one little brother
Is exactly like another
And every little brother
Misbehaves a bit he said.
So I took the little bother
From my mother and my father
And put the little bother
Of a brother back to bed.

*Mary Ann Hoberman*

**INVOLVEMENT**

**A SPECIAL CHAIR**

Ezra Jack Keats didn't give us any particular reasons why **Peter's Chair** was special, other than Peter wanted to save it from being painted pink like all his other baby things! Put a chair in the middle of the circle. Ask the children to think of describing words to tell you all about that chair. Then ask them to think of reasons why that chair was special to Peter.

Choose a child to sit in Peter's chair. Surround him with the other items from the story: blocks, a stuffed dog, a cradle and high chair (hopefully from a nearby housekeeping center!), a cookie and a dog bone, a shopping bag, a picture of a baby, a picture of an alligator, a pair of shoes, and a paint brush. As you read the story, go around the circle and have each child pick up an item to give to Peter. (Can you see the juggling act?) At the end of the story, let Peter decide what things he will share and what things he will keep.

**INTEGRATION**

**WE ARE SPECIAL, TOO!**

Children never tire of a dress-up box! Have them bring dress-up items and fun accessories from home until your box is overflowing. Pair up the children and let them help each other dress. (Obviously, two at a time will be just right for this activity!) Then give each child a large piece of butcher block or bulletin board paper to draw his dressed-up friend. To add print, have each child dictate a sentence to add to the cut-out drawing. Arrange the cut outs of the children on a large bulletin board titled, **We Are Special, Too!** Reading and smiles guaranteed!

**A TREASURE SHELF**

Think of something special from your childhood, such as an old quilt. Bring the quilt to class, hidden in a bag. Give describing words as clues to help the children guess what is in the bag. Then print a phrase, such as *Miss Lane's patchy quilt*, and put it with the quilt in a special place in your room. Have the children take turns bringing in things that are special to them. Encourage them to use descriptive words as clues as they play the same guessing game. Display all the objects in your special place, with a describing phrase in front of each treasure.

## UNPACK YOUR PERSONALITY!

Gather the children around you as you sit with a brightly decorated bag on your lap. As you slowly pull things out of the bag, explain that each item tells something special about you. You have included a book because reading is still an adventure for you. You put in a tennis ball because you are proud you are always learning something new. You included a little tree branch because you like to be outside to jog or hike whenever you can. When you have emptied your bag, explain that you have just unpacked your personality . . . all the different things that make you who you are.

Everyday pull a child's name from the bag. It is her turn to take the bag home, fill it with her personality and bring it back to class. Write a brief note to parents emphasizing it is the child's responsibility to choose the items for the bag. (It helps to keep two bags going so someone is always ready to share!) When a child has had a turn, have her draw a picture and write emergently about all the things she brought when she unpacked her personality.

## THE IMPORTANT THING ABOUT PETER

In the classic nonfiction book, **The Important Book**, Margaret Wise Brown writes about a variety of topics. Although the author lists many facts about each topic, she begins and ends with the most important thing, such as, *The most important thing about rain is that it is wet.*

Brainstorm with the children about all the things that made Peter special. Decide on the most important thing. For example, *The most important thing about Peter was that he shared.* Write the children's sentence at the beginning of your chart story. Then write a few more sentences that describe Peter and end your story with the same statement, *The most important thing about Peter was that he shared.*

## THE IMPORTANT THING ABOUT ME!

The last page of **The Important Book** is a message from Margaret Wise Brown to each child who reads her story, *The most important thing about you is that you are you!* Lead the children in a discussion about what makes each one of them special and different from anyone else in the room.

Give each child a piece of 12″ by 18″ white paper on which is printed, *The most important thing about me is* _____ . After each child has drawn a big picture of himself, act as scribe and complete the sentence with the words he dictates. Frame the pictures, just as Peter's baby picture was framed. Cut large rectangles from the center of brightly colored 12″ by 18″ construction paper, leaving a two inch border all the way around for the frame. Let each child decorate his frame before pasting it on top of his picture. Display the pictures in your room as a gallery of very important little people!

## A CELEBRATION

Have a baby day! Invite moms to bring their babies to class and share with the children about baby care, routines and schedules. The moms can show baby clothes, lotions, baby food, and toys, and talk about the purpose of each. Most importantly, have the moms share what is special about each baby and each big brother or sister who is proudly watching in the room!

**EVERYDAY
LEARNING
ACTIVITIES**

Positive parenting, developmental learning activities and a warm, nurturing environment are major factors in a child's academic success and lifetime learning.

The story, **Peter's Chair**, may open the door for your children to be honest about their own feelings . . . that someone else in the family seems more important right now. A child needs to be understood and to be able to say, "Today I feel like Peter!" Each child needs to hear that no one can ever take his place. Show your children there is enough love to go around. Give some special little attention every day. It is natural for brothers and sisters to want your undivided attention. Siblings can be best friends but it takes skillful parenting to make each child feel good about himself. Don't compare your children! Comparing just says someone is "not measuring up." It causes resentment and destroys a child's self-esteem. Remember, no two children are alike and each one came with his own set of "blueprints." When they are getting along, praise, praise, praise them for taking care of each other. *(parenting skill)*

- Play Peter's game of *hiding*. Remind your child to leave her shoes sticking out from under the curtains or the bed or the couch. Be sure to hide your shoes for her to find! List all the hiding places for some fun with words in print. *(creative play)*

- Get a plain, cardboard box so your child can act out the song *"Oh, I Wish I Had a Little Red Box."* There are so many concepts you can teach with a box. You may be busy in the kitchen but all you need is your voice to keep your child thinking. Is the box full or empty, heavy or light, rough or smooth, round or rectangle, old or new, big or small? Will it fit under your bed, on the chair, inside the cabinet? *(classifying, critical thinking)*

- Children need to be taught over and over that they are special and have a very special first and last name. Encourage your children to *introduce* themselves by using both first and last names. Let them print a name, including their own last name, to hang on every teddy bear, doll, or animal in the house. Ask them to give Peter a last name . . . it will probably be their own! *(self-esteem)*

- Copying simple shapes prepares your child for the more exacting task of copying letters. Give her unlined paper, a green dot for a starting point, an example to look at, and lots of praise! *(fine motor)*

- Make each child in your family feel special by being the Child of the Week. Just rotate the weeks and mark the calendar. The Child of the Week makes all the little decisions that are so important to children . . . where to sit in the car or at the dinner table, what cereal to buy, what bedtime books to choose, what special friend to invite over. Add an unusual table setting at the Child of the Week's place at the table. Just one more way to make a child feel special! *(self-esteem)*

# Rosie's Walk

## by Pat Hutchins

**TEACHING FOCUS**
- Directionality
- Predicting
- Visual Perception
- Gross Motor Skills

**SETTING THE STAGE**

Instantly singable songs and the appealing rhyme and rhythm of finger plays will encourage children to be involved in storytime.

**WALK OUTSIDE** by Raffi, *One Light, One Sun*
(A bouncy, happy song about what a child finds on a walk)

**WALKIN'** by Sharon, Lois & Bram, *Stay Tuned*

### LITTLE BOY BLUE

| | |
|---|---|
| Little boy blue, | *(beckon)* |
| Come blow your horn, | *(blow horn)* |
| The sheep's in the meadow, | *(point to right)* |
| The cow's in the corn! | *(point to left)* |
| Where is the boy who looks after the sheep? | *(raise arms questioningly)* |
| He's under the haystack fast asleep. | *(sleep)* |

### HERE IS THE BEEHIVE

| | |
|---|---|
| Here is the beehive. Where are the bees? | *(left hand fisted)* |
| Hidden away where nobody sees. | *(cover with right hand)* |
| Watch and you'll see them come out of the hive, | *(uncover beehive)* |
| One, two, three, four, five. | *(fingers up)* |
| Bzzzzzzzz. . . all fly away! | *(fingers fly away)* |

**FIRST READING**

Today we are going to read a funny little story about Rosie, the hen. The name of the book is **Rosie's Walk.** It was written and illustrated by Pat Hutchins and she did a very clever thing in her book. She used very few words because she wanted the pictures to tell the story and make you smile.

What do you see on the cover? Does that little house have a name? Does Rosie know she is being followed? What do you think will happen? Let's turn to the *title page* for a bigger picture of where Rosie lives. If you look very closely, your eyes will find many different things on Rosie's farm. What do you see? Tell me how the colors make you feel!

Now let's read. Before I turn each page, tell me what you think is going to happen.

**GETTING INVOLVED**

It's time now to have some fun with the story. Let's pretend that you are Rosie, out for a walk in the barnyard. Look around the room and see what we can use for the rake *on* the ground, the pond that Rosie walked *around*, and the haystack she climbed *over*. Next, we need something for the mill, and then the fence that Rosie walked *through*, and last, the beehive she walked *under*. Better not forget her henhouse. That's where the story begins and ends! There! We have the barnyard all set. Listen carefully to my directions. I know where the fox is hiding and I will be sure to keep you safe. Here we go, hens!

*Another time, give different directions to individual children and create new paths for Rosie's walk around the barnyard.*

**A CLOSER LOOK**

With each rereading of a story, children gain new understanding. Pause often for a spontaneous flow of oral language as the children share their feelings and observations. Extend the learning process with your own questions in repeated readings of the story.

- How did Rosie get out of her henhouse? *(visual comprehension)*

- Why do we call a fox *sly*? Why is he crouching? *(interpretation)*

- Why didn't the fox see the rake when he pounced on Rosie? *(comprehension)*

- Did Rosie know she was being followed? Did the frogs know? The goat? The beaver? *(opinion)*

- Did Rosie know the string was around her foot when she walked past the mill? *(interpretation)*

- What do you think the string will do? *(predicting)*

- What was the funniest thing that happened to the fox? *(opinion)*

- Did Rosie ever know she was in danger? *(comprehension)*

- Do you think the fox will come back? *(opinion)*

**ROUNDING OUT STORYTIME**

**The Fox Went Out on a Chilly Night**   by Peter Spier

**Flossie and the Fox**   by Patricia McKissock

**Guinea Pigs Far and Near**   by Kate Duke

**Watch Where You Go**   by Sally Noll

**Hattie and the Fox**   by Mem Fox

# Integrated Whole Language Activities

**POETRY**

### A LITTLE TALK

The big brown hen and Mrs. Duck
Went walking out together;
They talked about all sorts of things—
The farmyard, and the weather.
But all I heard was:
"Cluck! Cluck! Cluck!"
And "Quack! Quack! Quack!"
from Mrs. Duck.

*Anonymous*

### JUMP OR JIGGLE

Frogs jump
Caterpillars hump

Worms wiggle
Bugs jiggle

Rabbits hop
Horses clop

Snakes slide
Sea gulls glide

Mice creep
Deer leap

Puppies bounce
Kittens pounce

Lions stalk—
But—
I walk!

*Evelyn Beyer*

**INVOLVEMENT**

### CHORAL READING

The humor and bold colors of **Rosie's Walk** will easily lead emergent readers through the thirty-two words of the simple text. Even the youngest of children will be ready to join you in your initial rereadings of **Rosie's Walk.**

**INTEGRATION**

### A WALL MURAL

Children can *retell* the story of Rosie and the fox with one big barnyard scene much like the title page of the book. Using colored chalk or small paint sponges, have the children create a simple ground and sky backdrop on large bulletin board paper. Let each child paint and cut out something from construction paper to add to the background, such as the henhouse, barn, trees, pond, haystack, etc. Add the story title and the author's name. Label the mural with the story phrases *across the yard, around the pond,* etc. for independent, paired, or choral reading. Children will return again and again to *read the walls!*

### AUTHOR'S CHAIR

Before encouraging authoring, brainstorm with the children about other things that could have happened to Rosie and the fox in the barnyard. Then give *each* child an individual blank book to create his own story. If the child wants a text, you can act as scribe and write the words or phrases that he dictates. Then, sitting in the Author's Chair, let each child *role-play* the teacher as he leads the children through his own story. Children love the success of reading their own language!

### A CIRCLE STORY MAP

There are six major events in **Rosie's Walk** which begins and ends at the henhouse. Diagram the events on a large circle story map divided into six sections. Tell the story with pictures, beginning with a picture of Rosie's henhouse placed over the top of the circle. As you read **Rosie's Walk,** have a child place a simple child-drawn picture of each event in one section of the circle, i.e. the *barnyard, pond, haystack, mill, fence and beehives.*

Print the *directionality phrases* on sentence strips for children to *match* to the pictures as they *retell* the story in independent or paired reading. Keep **Rosie's Walk**, the pictures and the phrase cards available to the children, perhaps in a Reading Basket or in your dramatic play center, for repeated reading successes!

### PREDATOR AND PREY

Select *nonfiction* natural science books about predators and their prey in the animal world. Feature the books during read-aloud time and keep them available in your science center. Classify and chart the facts you are learning on a three-column wall chart with the headings, *PREDATOR, PREY* and *BOTH*. Then brainstorm with the children to give them time to prepare and think about an innovation of **Rosie's Walk**. Decide on two new animal characters such as a bird and worm, an octopus and fish, or a mouse and hawk. Discuss the *setting* and the *plot* for your story, i.e. a mouse in the desert going *over a rock, around a cactus, through a tumbleweed, across a snake's back*, unaware that it is being followed by a hawk! Have the children dictate new *directionality phrases* and illustrate the pages individually or in pairs. The very last page could read *and got back in time for dinner*. Authoring a story motivates children to practice reading it again and again! Be sure to bind your new class book and add it to your reading center.

### JUMP OR JIGGLE

Make the rich vocabulary and strong rhythm of **Jump or Jiggle** come alive by pantomiming the action words. Write the poem in a class *accordion book*. Have the children illustrate a cover, a title page, (be sure to give credit to Evelyn Beyer), and thirteen pages with a different phrase such as *frogs jump* written at the top of each page. Encourage the children to depict the action of each animal as well as where the animal might be. Provide an additional **But I walk** . . . page for the remaining children to illustrate and add every third page of the book. Can't you just see the action? Because the children have already memorized the text with oral repetition, they will delight in reading their book!

### WATCH WHERE YOU GO

Sally Noll's charming story of a little mouse being warned of danger by a clever dragonfly presents an irresistible whole language learning opportunity. A painted jungle landscape could be a perfect backdrop for the hidden animals and the *directionality phrases* of the mouse's adventure!

**EVERYDAY LEARNING ACTIVITIES**

Positive parenting, developmental learning activities, and a warm, nurturing environment are major factors in a child's academic success and lifetime learning.

The delightful hen in **Rosie's Walk** was alone on her walk and made all her own choices. She was an independent little hen. One of the best ways parents can help young children is to give them opportunities to make choices, to make small decisions on their own, to begin to reason and to think for themselves. Giving choices is also a positive discipline tool. So often you can avoid a power play or a head-on collision in getting your child to do something by simply giving him a choice. With your help and with safe boundaries, a young child is able to make choices—a wonderful step towards independence! Start out by giving your child two well thought-out options, such as "Would you like to have a friend over or do you want to play outside with your brother?" "Do you want me to read you a story now or when you are ready for bed?" Allowing a child to make decisions is teaching him early to be a problem-solver and an independent person. Right after your child has made a choice, he needs immediate acceptance. Don't crush the self you are trying to encourage! *(parenting skill)*

- Have fun with the *directionality* concepts in **Rosie's Walk.** Set up a simple path for your child, saying the words with her as she goes *around* a chair, *over* a pillow on the floor, *under* a table, and *through* an open-ended box. Add new words: *next to, in front of, behind, beside, above, between, on the top, middle,* and *bottom.* When children understand *directional* words with their bodies first, it is much easier for them to understand such words in print. *(perceptual motor)*

- Blocks and Legos are excellent, creative toys that allow your child to use her imagination. Blocks can be anything she decides in her mind they will be, such as the henhouse, silo, windmill, tractor, beehives, fence or milk cans from **Rosie's Walk.** Your child will discover new ways to stack, build, and balance blocks as she learns by trial and error. *(creative play)*

- Ask your child to *think of details* as she describes a character or an object you name from **Rosie's Walk.** To develop *visual memory,* ask her to describe what her friend looks like, or her room, a bird, a flower, etc. *(visual perception)*

- Walking on a *balance beam* is great for coordination, muscle control and balance. Balance beams are everywhere . . . they are on landscaping timbers in front yards, concrete strips that mark off parking spaces in parking lots, cracks in sidewalks, low walls, a ladder flat on the ground, a yardstick put down on the floor, or even a strip of masking tape on the carpet. Begin with a *beam* that is on the ground so your child will be at ease as she practices. After she masters walking in a straight line, try walking sideways or even backwards! *(gross motor coordination)*

# The Runaway Bunny

## by Margaret Wise Brown

**TEACHING FOCUS**
- Visual memory
- Family relationships
- Vocabulary
- Identifying emotions

**SETTING THE STAGE**

Instantly singable songs and the appealing rhyme and rhythm of finger plays will encourage children to be involved in storytime.

**SKINNAMARINK** by Sharon, Lois & Bram, *Elephant Show Record*

**A BUSHEL AND A PECK** by Sharon, Lois & Bram, *In the Schoolyard*

### LITTLE BUNNY

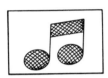

| | |
|---|---|
| There was a little bunny who lived in the wood. | |
| He wiggled his ears as a good bunny should. | *(fingers over ears)* |
| He hopped by a squirrel. | *(jump fingers up arm)* |
| He wiggled by a tree. | *(wiggle hands)* |
| He hopped by a duck. | *(jump fingers up arm)* |
| And he wiggled by me. | *(point to self)* |
| He stared at the squirrel. | *(circles around eyes)* |
| He peeked round the tree. | *(peek through hands)* |
| He stared at the duck. | *(circles around eyes)* |
| But he winked at me! | *(wink!)* |

### LITTLE ELEPHANTS

| | |
|---|---|
| One, two, three, four, five, | *(count fingers)* |
| Five little elephants standing in a row. | |
| This little elephant stubbed his toe. | *(point to each finger)* |
| This little elephant said, "Oh, oh, oh," | |
| This little elephant laughed and was glad, | |
| This little elephant so thoughtful and good, | |
| He ran for the doctor as fast as he could. | |

**FIRST READING**

Do you remember the story **Goodnight Moon?** The same author, Margaret Wise Brown, wrote this story, too. It is called **The Runaway Bunny.** In fact, the man who drew the illustrations hid one of the pictures from **The Runaway Bunny** on one of the pages in **Goodnight Moon.** Let me show you. *(Show the picture of the bunny fishing from The Runaway Bunny and also the page from Goodnight Moon where the same picture is hanging on the bedroom wall.)* Then Margaret Wise Brown put a picture from Goodnight Moon in this book. *(Show Hey Diddle Diddle.)* Finding the same picture in another book is like finding a secret message from the author! This story is about a little bunny who tells his mother how he will run away. She answers by telling him how she will catch him every time and bring him back, because she loves him so much.

**GETTING INVOLVED**

Let's talk about some of the new words we just heard in the story. There were always some clues to help us understand the words. When the bunny wanted to be a fish, he used the word *trout*. What does that mean? When the bunny talked about a garden, he said he would be a *crocus*. What's a crocus? When the bunny decided to join a circus, he used the words *trapeze* and *tightrope*. Did you find them in the circus picture? Now that we have learned the new words, let's stand up and pretend to be the mother rabbit. Every time the bunny runs away, we will bring him back.

| When the bunny decides to: | We will: |
|---|---|
| ... swim in the trout stream | ... cast out our fishing lines |
| ... be a rock | ... climb the mountain to find him |
| ... hide as a crocus | ... be gardeners with hoes to find him |
| ... fly as a bird | ... be tall trees for him to fly to |
| ... sail as a boat | ... blow gently and bring him back |
| ... swing on a trapeze | ... walk the tightrope carefully |
| ... run back home | ... give him a big hug and climb into our hole in the ground. |

**A CLOSER LOOK**

With each rereading of a story, children gain new understanding. Pause often for a spontaneous flow of oral language as the children share their feelings and observations. Extend the learning process with your own questions in repeated readings of the story.

- Did the little bunny ever tell his mother why he was running away? Do you have any ideas? *(comprehension)*

- Why is mother rabbit fishing with a carrot instead of a worm? *(association)*

- What equipment did mother rabbit need to be a mountain climber? *(visual memory)*

- Where in the garden did the little bunny hide? *(visual memory)*

- Why is mother rabbit in the clouds? *(comprehension)*

- Why did the little bunny decide to stay the way he was? *(comprehension)*

- Which picture was your favorite? Why? *(opinion)*

- Wherever the bunny decided to go, his mother was always there. Why? *(comprehension)*

**ROUNDING OUT STORYTIME**

**Sylvester and the Magic Pebble**   by William Steig

**What Game Shall We Play?**   by Pat Hutchins

**Bye Bye Baby**   by Janet and Allan Ahlberg

**Where Are You Going, Little Mouse?**   by Robert Kraus

**Noisy Nora**   by Rosemary Wells

167

# Integrated Whole Language Activities

**POETRY**

### A HOUSE

Everyone has a house,
      a house,
everyone has a house.
The bear has a cave,
the bird a nest,
the mole a hole,
but what is best
is a house like ours
      with windows and doors
      and rugs and floors.
Everyone has a house,
      a house,
everyone has a house.
      *Charlotte Zolotow*

### MOONSTRUCK

I'd like to see rabbits
under the moon,
dancing in winter,
dancing in June,
dancing around
while twilight lingers
and blinkey-eyed stars
look down through their fingers.
I'd like to see rabbits
under the moon,
but I always,
*always*
have to go to bed too soon.
      *Aileen Fisher*

**INVOLVEMENT**

- After each rereading of **The Runaway Bunny**, celebrate the mother's love for the little bunny by singing *Skinnamarink* or *A Bushel and A Peck*, cheerful songs about love.

- After dramatizing all the ways the bunny will run away and how his mother will find him, have the children think of new things the bunny might become. How will the mother bunny find him and bring him back?

- Make pairs of word cards showing what the bunny will be and what the mother will become to find him, i.e. a fish and a fisherman, a crocus and a gardener, etc. Include the new ideas the children have suggested. Draw picture clues next to the words. Give every child a word card to hang around his neck as he looks for the child who has the other card in his pair. The bunny with the fish picture will look for the mother bunny with the fisherman picture and so on. The children will sit in pairs, ready to stand and dramatize their part as the story is read again.

- Turn all the word cards face down on the floor. The children can play a memory game, turning the cards over one at a time, trying to make matches.

**INTEGRATION**

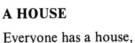

### THE RUNAWAY BUNNY

To write a class innovation of **The Runaway Bunny** use the patterned text, *I will be a* _____ on the bottom of every page. The children can work in pairs and refer to the word cards used in the dramatization of the story. On the first page, a child will draw the runaway bunny as a *fish*. He can copy the word *fish* from the word card to finish his sentence. On the second page, a child will draw the mother bunny as a *fisherman* and finish the sentence by copying the word from his word card. Include the new ideas the children suggested in the dramatization. Decide what the picture and the text will be on the last page. Bind the mounted pages in a class book for independent reading.

**INTEGRATION**
(continued)

## I WILL BE A CROCUS

The warm colors in the illustration of the runaway bunny in the garden are much like the bold, bright pictures of Lois Ehlert's beautiful story, **Planting A Rainbow.** Her cheery book is also the story of a mother and a child as they plant flowers (including crocuses!) in the family garden every year. A rainbow garden would surely brighten your room for days!

Divide your children into small groups, each group deciding on the color they will use to create flowers for the garden . . . red, orange, yellow, green, blue, and purple. Offer each group a choice of art materials, i.e. bright tempera paint, construction paper, tissue paper, water-based markers, etc. to mix and match as they create the flowers for their part of your wall mural garden. Cluster the same colored flowers together as Lois Ehlert did in her vivid garden pictures. Let the children decide what art medium to use to make the runaway bunny and his mother and where to put them in your colorful rainbow garden.

*Extension:* Read the simply written text of **The Reason For A Flower**, an excellent nonfiction book by Ruth Heller, and **The Tiny Seed**, Eric Carle's colorful story of a seed that becomes a flower.

## A HOUSE

When the children have memorized the text of the poem, *A House*, write the words on chart paper. Talk out loud as you write to help children develop letter-sound awareness. Make a list of everything the children discover about the poem . . . the repetition of the phrase *everyone has a house*, the arrangement of the words, the sounds they hear, the different houses, etc.

Tell the children what is important about your own house, encouraging them to think and share about their homes, too. Read entertaining books about animal houses such as the imaginative **A House is A House For Me** by Mary Ann Hoberman. Keep nonfiction books that show animal habitats such as **Water** by Su Swallow in your library center. Then give the children the opportunity to choose any of the following activities:

- Create an animal and its house from clay. Have the children decide how to group and label their animal houses, perhaps by habitats.

- Paint or draw an animal house and write a sentence about it.

- Draw, paint, or tear from construction paper the child's home, perhaps labeling the windows and doors, rugs and floors.

- Print the text of the poem, *A House*, on four large pieces of paper. Create a wall mural for the children to illustrate and read.

**EVERYDAY LEARNING ACTIVITIES**

Positive parenting, developmental learning activities and a warm, nurturing environment are major factors in a child's academic success and lifetime learning.

In the story, **The Runaway Bunny**, a little bunny tells his mother all the ways he will run away. She reassuringly tells him all the ways she will find him and bring him back. It is a comforting story of warmth and security and love. Perhaps it carries the message that every child is looking for when he has been naughty or has threatened to run away. He wants to know, especially after he has been disciplined, that he is still loved. Of course he is! Love is a very real part of discipline. The two terms do not have to contradict each other. The only time they will is when a parent belittles a child and destroys his self-esteem by making statements such as, "You are bad," or "You never do anything right," or "You never learn! How many times do I have to tell you?" Harsh words condemn the child as a person and destroy his sense of being loved. In contrast, loving discipline conveys the message "I love you too much to let you go too far. What you did was wrong, but I still love you as a person." Good discipline leaves the *door* open for a time of reattachment that says, "I love you." A child needs to hear the words over and over again. Touching your child when you tell him that you love him just reinforces the message. A child needs to know that there is nothing he can ever do or say that you will stop loving him. He doesn't have to earn your love by being good. He has it by being born, just like the little bunny in **The Runaway Bunny.** *(parenting skill)*

- A picnic is a simple family activity that is a real favorite with children. Give your child the responsibility of planning your next picnic . . . a wonderful lesson in making choices. Let her decide where it will be *(even the backyard is an option!)* Write lists of what food you will have and who will come, including a special guest she gets to invite herself. *(making decisions)*

- In the story, **The Runaway Bunny**, the little bunny seemed to be a gentle, quiet bunny. Sometimes we call a gentle, quiet child a shy child, as though something is wrong! Every time we repeat that label in her presence, we cause her to become more shy. She will prove we are right because she believes us. If you feel your child is unusually shy, don't label her. Instead, appreciate your child's temperament. Build her confidence. Encourage her to look into your eyes when she is speaking. Teach her to give eye contact to others as well. The more you encourage your child, the more relaxed she will be. *(social development)*

- Give your child the opportunity to be a gardener like the mother rabbit in **The Runaway Bunny.** Show her how to prepare the soil and plant real seeds. Plant a wooden stick in the garden, also. Give your child the responsibility of watering both the seeds and the stick. Chart your observations daily! *(observation)*

- Put three small, familiar objects, *i.e. button, marble, bottle cap,* in front of your child. Have her turn around while you hide one object in your hand and ask, "What do I have?" Make the game more difficult by increasing the number of objects you put out or by choosing unfamiliar objects. Name them and talk about them. You are increasing her vocabulary while having fun. Be sure to give your child some turns at choosing and hiding. Some day make the items all edible and end the game with party time! *(concentration)*

# Skip to
# My Lou

## by Nadine Bernard Westcott

**TEACHING FOCUS**

- Rhyming words
- Visual discrimination
- Sequencing
- Parts of a book

**SETTING THE STAGE**

Instantly singable songs and the appealing rhyme and rhythm of finger plays will encourage children to be involved in storytime.

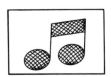

**SKIP TO MY LOU,** by Greg & Steve, *We All Live Together*

**GRANDPA'S FARM,** by Sharon, Lois & Bram, *Sing A-Z*

### STEPPING OVER STEPPING STONES

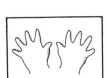

| | |
|---|---|
| Stepping over stepping stones, | *(walk in place)* |
| One, two, three, | *(clap three times)* |
| Stepping over stepping stones, | *(walk in place)* |
| Come with me. | *(beckon)* |
| The river's very fast, | *(roll hands)* |
| And the river's very wide, | *(arms out wide)* |
| And we'll step across on stepping stones, | *(walk in place)* |
| And reach the other side. | *(jump with two feet)* |

### FIVE FAT SAUSAGES

| | |
|---|---|
| Five fat sausages frying in a pan, | *(hold up five fingers)* |
| All of a sudden one went 'BANG' | *(clap hands loudly)* |
| Four fat sausages frying in a pan, | *(hold up four fingers)* |
| All of a sudden one went 'BANG' | *(clap hands loudly)* |
| Three fat sausages frying in a pan, | *(hold up three fingers)* |
| All of sudden one went 'BANG' | *(clap hands loudly)* |
| Two fat sausages frying in a pan, | *(hold up two fingers)* |
| All of a sudden one went 'BANG' | *(clap hands loudly)* |
| One fat sausage frying in a pan, | *(hold up one finger)* |
| All of a sudden it went 'BANG!' | *(clap hands loudly)* |
| and there were NO sausages left! | *(no fingers left)* |

**FIRST READING**

Does the cover of this book make you smile? Tell me a story about what you think is happening. There is a word in the title that tells us the animals and the little boy are skipping. The title of the story is **Skip to My Lou.** Some of the words of the story are from an old, old American folk song. Nadine Bernard Westcott knew all about that song when she wrote and illustrated this book. When you name the animals and the people in the picture on the title page, you have already found most of the characters in the story.

The next page shows us that Ms. Westcott dedicated the book to her mother and father. Why do you think she drew a picture of a kitchen table under those words? On the page next to the dedication page you can see the musical notes for the song. Look on the shelf above the song. The fun has started!

**GETTING INVOLVED**

Many years ago, a fiddler played the music of **Skip to My Lou** on his fiddle while children and old people clapped their hands and danced to the beat of the happy music. Let's pretend there is a fiddler sitting right here in the middle of our circle. We'll clap and sing the words to the chorus while he plays his fiddle . . . *Lou, Lou, skip to my Lou, (sing three times), Skip to my Lou, my darling.* Then the children all got partners and skipped around the circle while they sang the words. Each one of you can get a partner and we'll skip and sing just as they did.

Maybe the children skipped too fast because the next verse tells us they lost their partners! The words are, *Lost my partner, what'll I do? (sing three times), Skip to my Lou, my darling.* Let's stand in our places in the circle and sing that verse, too.

I know the children started the singing game all over again because the next verse says, *I'll get another prettier than you, (sing three times), Skip to my Lou, my darling.* Let's get new partners and skip around the circle one more time. Then we can sit down in our places and look at the story again.

**A CLOSER LOOK**

Skip to My Lou is so rich in humor and visual detail that a few questions can't begin to capture the playfulness of the delightful text and illustrations. The children will want to study the pictures again and again.

- What do the words mean, *The farm's all in order? (comprehension)*

- How did the flies discover the sugarbowl? *(reasoning)*

- How did the cats discover the buttermilk? *(visual detail)*

- What's a parlor? How did the pigs get the pancakes? *(interpretation)*

- Did each cow have a different job to do in the kitchen? *(picture reading)*

- What is a pantry? What did the roosters get into? *(picture reading)*

- How did the little boy and the dog end up in the bathtub? *(visual detail)*

- Which room do you think was the messiest? *(opinion)*

- Why was the boy worried when he looked at the clock? *(comprehension)*

- Did the fun stop when the animals helped clean up? *(picture reading)*

**ROUNDING OUT STORYTIME**

**The Lady with the Alligator Purse**   by Nadine Bernard Westcott

**I Know An Old Lady**   by Nadine Bernard Westcott

**Down By The Bay**   by Raffi

**Teddy Bears' Picnic**   by Jimmy Kennedy

**There's A Hole in the Bucket**   by Nadine Bernard Westcott

# Integrated Whole Language Activities

## POETRY

### JELLY ON THE PLATE

Jelly on the plate,
Jelly on the plate,
*Wibble wobble, wibble wobble,*
Jelly on the plate.

Paper on the floor,
Paper on the floor,
Pick it up, pick it up,
Paper on the floor.

Piggy in the house,
Piggy in the house,
Kick him out, kick him out,
Piggy in the house.

*Traditional*

## INVOLVEMENT

- The foot-tapping, infectious melody of **Skip to My Lou** makes it impossible for children to stay quiet. No wonder it has been around for so long. For a different rereading, have the children hum the tune and read the pictures as you turn the pages. Another time, sing every word of the text to the melody of the chorus. The children will spontaneously join in singing or clapping.

- Make name cards for the animal characters: the flies, cats, pigs, cows, roosters and sheep. Add picture clues by drawing the faces of the animals on the word cards. Give each child a yarn-tied name card to put around his neck. Group the pigs together, the roosters together, etc. as the children sit in a circle. As you reread the story, have the children join in only on the words their animals say. For example only the flies will say *Shoo fly shoo*, only the cats will say *two by two*, only the roosters will say, *Cock-a-doodle-do*, and so on.

- Turn the name cards over and write the names of the animals without any picture clues. Spread them out in front of the children. Let each one point to an animal name he can read and put that word card around his neck for the dramatization.

- Put the word cards, a tape of the children singing, and a copy of **Skip to My Lou** in your listening center for a rollicking good time in independent reading!

- Have the children stand in a circle with one child in the middle. As you begin singing the chorus of the song, the child in the middle closes her eyes and twirls around with her arm extended. Whoever she is pointing to when you finish the chorus joins her in the middle. The two join hands and skip around the circle as the children sing the name of the child just chosen:

> Lisa, Lisa, skip tomy Lisa,
> Lisa, Lisa, skip to my Lisa,
> Lisa, Lisa, skip to my Lisa,
> Skip to my Lisa, my darling!

Then Lisa becomes the child in the middle, repeating the game and choosing a new child the same way. Everyone sings that child's name as the two skip around the circle.

174

## SKIP TO MY LISA, MY DARLING*

Children are always pleased to see their names in print. Give each child a page with the words of the game they have just played printed on the bottom. Leave blank spaces for the child to write in her own name. Encourage her to decide what to draw on her page, the art materials she would like to use, and the color background for mounting her picture. Then have the children return to the circle with the finished pages and help you sequence them in a class caption book.

## QUARTER TO THREE

A book as rich in humor and visual detail as this one will surely spark the imaginations of children. What might the little boy have found next if mom and dad hadn't returned until three o'clock? Have everyone draw or paint a picture of an animal creating a new distrubance on the farm. Encourage each child to put herself in the picture and then write or dictate a sentence about what she has drawn. Plan time for sharing!

*Extension:* Group your children into small groups of four. Have each group decide where the animals in their pictures might have caused a disturbance. Expect a lot of conversation as the children share ideas! One kindergarten group decided to put *fleas in the haystack, birds in the popcorn*, and *goats in the closet*. They illustrated one phrase on each page and the fourth page was just the text, *Skip to my Lou, my darling*. Have each group decide on a background color for their four pages. The different colors will become natural dividers as you bind the various stanzas into a class big book.

fleas in the haystack,     birds in the popcorn,     goats in the closet,     Skip to my Lou, my darling!

## OUR FAVORITE CHARACTERS

Have the children recall the mischievous characters as they appeared in the story. Write the name of each animal at the top of a six column wall graph. Then give each child a small square of paper on which to draw her favorite character. Let her choose a background from a variety of colored squares and mount her picture.

Before you place the pictures on the graph, have the children estimate how many drawings will be tallied in each column. Record their estimates. With the children sitting in front of the graph, add each child's picture to the appropriate column.

Encourage the children to make observations of the columns as you talk about more than, less than, how many more, how many less, equal and zero. Have the children dictate summarizing sentences. Write them on a chart which the children can illustrate. They will read the graph and the sentences often because the silliness of the animal characters is so appealing.

**EVERYDAY LEARNING ACTIVITIES**

Positive parenting, developmental learning activities and a warm, nurturing environment are major factors in a child's academic success and lifetime learning.

Evenings for today's busy families can be extra hectic when parents are oh, so tired, and children are oh, so desirous of the spotlight. Stop a minute as you arrive home, or even if you have been there all day long. Gather everyone close—perhaps all on your lap at the same time, all talking at once, all needing hugs and attention. Give it, and you will find it will be so much easier to move on to the next thing on the schedule. Sometimes we let television take over because it keeps children quiet. Remember that television doesn't challenge your child's mind or her body, and it robs her of time spent with you. Sometimes only fifteen minutes together will change the whole mood of an evening. Use those minutes to sing silly songs or read a story. That's what reading is all about, sharing happy moments together. If you merely looked at the words to **Skip to My Lou** on the pages of the story book, something would be missing. In order to convey the rhythm and the absurdity of the story, the words must be read aloud or sung. In just those few minutes of reading or singing together, you can create an infectious, happy mood in your home. *(parenting skill)*

- **Skip to My Lou** is an example of a book that will last a child through many years of learning. There is always something new to discover in the extraordinary illustrations. Each time you read the story, have your child point out new things he has discovered on the pages. He will be creating a lens for himself through which he will always view the book. *(visual discrimination)*

- The child and the animals in **Skip to My Lou** started to straighten up the house at quarter to two, getting everything done in fifteen minutes. Talk about what your child is usually doing around that hour. Play a game of cleaning up your child's room or some part of the house. See how much you can do before the clock says two o'clock! Make your child conscious of the many numbers in his world. Have him look for other numbers inside the house, on the telephone and the oven, on storybook pages and the television. Look for numbers outside, such as speed limits and house numbers. *(numeral concepts)*

- Make up some directions in everyday activities that will help your child learn the concept of left and right. Ask her to wash her right arm first, dry her left leg first, open the car door with her right hand, etc. Remember to be helpful. Your child will work on left and right a long time before mastering the skill. *(left and right)*

- Make each child in your family feel special by being the Child of the Week. Just rotate the weeks and mark the calendar. The Child of the Week makes all the little decisions that are so important to children . . . where to sit in the car or at the dinner table, what cereal to buy, what bedtime books to choose, what special friend to invite over. Add an unusual table setting at the Child of the Week's place for one more way to make a child feel special! *(self-esteem)*

# The Snowy Day

## by Ezra Jack Keats

**TEACHING FOCUS**
- Identifying seasons
- Sequencing first, next, last
- Author recognition
- Story comprehension

**SETTING THE STAGE**

Instantly singable songs and the appealing rhyme and rhythm of finger plays will encourage children to be involved in storytime.

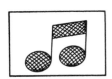

**GOOD MORNING MR. WEATHERMAN**, by Hap Palmer, *Patriotic and Morning Time Songs*

**OH, WHAT A MIRACLE**, by Hap Palmer, *Walter the Waltzing Worm*
(I am something special. Look what my body can do!)

**THE SNOWMAN**

Roll him and roll him until he is big.          *(follow action as rhyme*
Roll him until he is fat as a pig.              *indicates)*
He has two eyes and a hat on his head.
He'll stand there all night,
While we go to bed.

**SNOW MEN**

Five little snow men                 *(one hand open)*
Standing in a row.
Each with a hat                      *(hand over head)*
And a big red bow.                   *(hand under chin)*
Five little snow men                 *(one hand open)*
Dressed for a show,                  *(move hands head to toe)*
Now they are ready,
Where will they go?
Wait 'til the sun shines,            *(circle arms over head)*
Soon they will go
Down through the fields              *(arms down to lap)*
With the melting snow.               *(curl up as you melt)*

**FIRST READING**

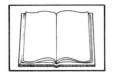

Look at the cover of our story today. What kind of a day is it? Those are the very words the author chose for the title of the story, **The Snowy Day.** Does the little boy look familiar? Do you know his name? Ezra Jack Keats wrote two other stories about Peter and his dog, Willie. (**Whistle for Willie** and **Peter's Chair**) I will turn the pages without saying a word. You be the storytellers. Tell me everything you see and what you imagine is happening.

Let's look at the pages inside the cover. You will see each of those pictures again somewhere in the story. Now let's read about Peter and **The Snowy Day.**

*By reading three books by the same author, children will feel they know Peter and will recognize the author's name. They will understand that Ezra Jack Keats' work is writing and illustrating books.*

**GETTING INVOLVED**

Let's share Peter's delightful adventure in the snow! First, better put on your warm snowsuit, next pull on your rubber boots, then your hood and scarf, and last, your mittens. Now we are ready to join Peter outside! Pretend your feet are sinking into the crunchy snow. Point your toes out. Point your toes in. Smack that snow-covered tree with a stick. Uh-oh, brush the snow off your head! Now lie down in the snow and gently move your arms and legs to make a snow angel. Make a snowball and carefully put it in your pocket before you go inside. Now let your mother help you take off all that heavy clothing and get ready for bed. Oh dear, where is your snowball now? Climb into your warm bed, pull up the covers, and dream of more snow gently falling everywhere.

*Another time, have a mitten match. Each child will match his mitten (real or paper) to one hanging on a clothesline or lined up on the floor. Sort the mittens by size or by color. Then make a mitten floor graph.*

**A CLOSER LOOK**

With each rereading of a story, children gain new understanding. Pause often for a spontaneous flow of oral language as the children share their feelings and observations. Extend the learning process with your own questions in repeated readings of the story.

- Was it a winter or summer morning when Peter woke up? *(association)*

- What did the snow cover? *(visual memory)*

- Did the traffic light look like the light in **Whistle for Willie**? *(comparison)*

- Name all the things Peter did with his feet; his hands. *(visual memory)*

- What made the *three* tracks in the snow? *(comprehension)*

- Why didn't Peter join the snowball fight? Was he big enough to do other things? *(feelings)*

- How could Peter have saved his snowball? *(problem solving)*

- Where did Peter live if his friend was *across the hall*? *(interpretation)*

- What do you think they did together in the deep snow? *(reasoning)*

**ROUNDING OUT STORYTIME**

**The Jacket I Wear in the Snow**   by Shirley Neitzel

**Katy and the Big Snow**   by Virginia Lee Burton

**Henrietta's First Winter**   by Rob Lewis

**Thomas' Snowsuit**   by Robert Munsch

**The Mitten**   adapted by Jan Brett

# Integrated Whole Language Activities

**POETRY**

**IT FELL IN THE CITY**

It fell in the city,
It fell through the night,
And the black rooftops
All turned white.

Red fire hydrants
All turned white.
Blue police cars
All turned white.

Green garbage cans
All turned white.
Gray sidewalks
All turned white.

Yellow NO PARKING signs
All turned white
When it fell in the city
All through the night.

*Eve Merriam*

**INVOLVEMENT**

**A CELEBRATION OF SNOW**

• The song, *Oh, What A Miracle*, invites children to delight in moving their bodies. Music is a great accompaniment to body expression and pantomime. After rereading **A Snowy Day**, play music softly and encourage children to move as Peter moved . . . whirling, skipping, sliding down a hill, making a snowman, packing round, firm snowballs, and making angels in the snow.

• The last sentence of **A Snowy Day** says, *After breakfast Peter called to his friend from across the hall, and they went out together into the deep, deep snow.* Ask the children to think about where Peter lived, who his friend might be, and what new adventures they had together in the snow. They will be creating new endings to the story and sharing ideas for journal writing.

• Enjoy a family's anticipation of the arrival of snow in Charlotte Zolotow's marvelous story, **Something Is Going to Happen.** Let the children celebrate with the story characters by turning their bodies into a single snowflake, a blizzard, an icicle, a snowman, a snow-covered tree, or any way they would like to move to interpret the happiness of the story.

**INTEGRATION**

**WHEN WINTER COMES**

Explore the fascinating world of snow and how it protects plants and animals. **Snow Is Falling** is a clearly written and appealing nonfiction book by Franklyn M. Branley. **When Winter Comes**, a nonfiction book by Russell Freedman, describes how animals prepare for and survive the winter season in the woods. Have each child write one fact she has learned. As a group, decide what sentences to write on a class chart, *What We Know About Snow*.

*Extension:* **The Snowy Day** can introduce a weather theme, culminating with the children writing original stories about Peter on *The Rainy Day* or *The Windy Day.* The above study could also lead to an interest in what happens to plants and animals on stormy, foggy, windy, or very hot days. Encourage the children to decide the next topic of study.

## SNOW ON THE ROOFTOPS *

In Eve Merriam's poem, *It Fell In The City*, the simple text paints a lovely word picture of colors turning white in a silent snowfall. Print the poem on chart paper. Encourage the children to make observations about the repetition of phrases, the arrangement of the words, the sounds they hear, and the meaning of the poem. Have them suggest a way to identify the color words and the words *turned* and *white* every time they appear in the poem.

Decide how you can tell the story of snow falling in the city on a wall mural in your room. With a variety of art mediums available, i.e. tempera paint, construction paper, fabric scraps, water-based markers, etc. let each child choose what he will make to add to the scene. Then have the children decide how to transform your colorful city into a blanket of snow.

*Extension:* Read the story, **Snow**, a lovely wordless picture book by Isao Sasaki about a little train station *outside the city* almost buried by snow. Have the children write their own poem about snow falling everywhere. Print the phrase, *Snow on the _____* , on each page of a caption book. Every child can decide what things snow will fall on in her picture.

## THE SNOWMAN PARTY

What child hasn't dreamed about a snowman as a friend? **The Snowman**, a charming wordless book by Raymond Briggs, **Midnight Snowman** by Caroline Feller Bauer (which begins with a teacher reading the story, **The Snowy Day!**), **Our Snowman** by M.B. Goffstein, and **The Snowman Who Went For A Walk** by Mira Lobe are all adventures with snowmen on wonderfully snowy nights.

Imagine what would happen if the snowmen came to life after the children went to bed? How would they move? Would they celebrate by having a party? Who would come to the party? Let the children create a wall mural using whatever art medium and sentences they choose to tell their story.

## THE CLASS SNOWMAN

Put a large snowman outline on a bulletin board. Ask the children to estimate how many cotton balls it will take to cover each of the three circles in the snowman's body. Record their estimates. Have the children count out sets of ten cottonballs and tally the sets as they use them to fill each circle. Contrast the number of sets needed for the small, medium and large circles. Compare the numbers with their estimates.

Then have the children add features, clothing, a name, and labels for all the parts of their snowman. Together, write a language experience story using the labels already on the snowman, such as *"Hi! My name is Sparkles. I have a red hat, a carrot nose, stretchy suspenders, black boots,"* and so on! Would Peter enjoy receiving a letter from the class snowman?

**EVERYDAY LEARNING ACTIVITIES**

Positive parenting, developmental learning activities and a warm, nurturing environment are major factors in a child's academic success and lifetime learning.

In the book, **The Snowy Day,** Peter was curious about the snowball when he put it in his pocket. A child's curiosity is enormous! It is the most powerful tool she has for learning. Your child is programmed to learn about the world around her through her five senses. She needs to feel, to smell, to taste, to watch and listen, and to learn by doing. Parents can encourage this wonderful curiosity. Ask your child questions that cause her to think and predict and problem solve. Accept all her answers, right or wrong, and praise her thinking so she will keep on trying. And when she asks you questions, take the time to answer. You really want your child to wonder about things and ask "why!" A curious child will never stop learning. *(parenting skill)*

- Children have a natural curiosity about animals. How do they stay warm? Where do they sleep? How do they find food in the winter? Look for nonfiction library books such as **Up North in Winter** by Deborah Hartley. As a family, string cheerios on pipe cleaners to put out for the birds. Spread peanut butter and bird seed on pine cones or bread. Watch from a window and tally the number of birds who come daily for a snack! *(science, math concepts)*

- Put out a bowl of crushed ice. Let your child feel the ice, with and without mittens. *(sensory learning)*

- For a summer activity, suggest that your child place an ice cube on a hot sidewalk. As she watches it melt, ask *thinking* type questions such as why our earth is warm. When all signs of the water are gone, explain the word evaporation. . . that the sun lifts tiny drops of water high into the air and they form rain clouds. When the clouds get heavy with water drops, it will rain. Almost everything we do with a child, inside and outside, can become an impromptu learning experience! *(logical thinking)*

- Enjoy reading **The Snowy Day** again. Have your child draw or cut out her own *smiling snowman* and add cotton balls, a hat, pipe, buttons, scarf, nose, arms, and feet. Then encourage her to think of a short, simple story about her *smiling snowman*. Write down the story that she dictates. Read the story with her over and over as you move your fingers under each line. Your child will recognize that letters become words written down, one of the first steps of understanding print on a page. *(pre-reading)*

- Whatever the season, encourage your child to observe and describe what her ears hear, how the sky and plants look, how the air smells, and how the wind and ground feel. *(sensory learning, language skills)*

# The Tale
## of
# Peter Rabbit

*by Beatrix Potter*

**TEACHING FOCUS**
- Recognizing a title and author
- Bulding vocabulary
- Story comprehension
- Gross and fine motor skills

**SETTING THE STAGE**

Instantly singable songs and the appealing rhyme and rhythm of finger plays will encourage children to be involved in storytime.

**LITTLE RABBIT FOO-FOO**, by Sharon, Lois & Bram, *Mainly Mother Goose*
(Children love this song about a naughty bunny and the consequences of his actions)

**ALL I REALLY NEED**, by Raffi, *Baby Beluga*
(All I really need is a song in my heart and a loving family)

**LITTLE RABBIT**

Run, little rabbit; climb right up here.        *(make fingers of hand run up*
He is so hungry he nibbles my ear.              *arm, take hold of ear)*

**LITTLE PETER RABBIT**

Little Peter Rabbit                             *(follow action as rhyme indicates)*
had a fly upon his nose.
Little Peter Rabbit
had a fly upon his nose.
Little Peter Rabbit
had a fly upon his nose
And he flicked it till it flew away.

**FIRST READING**

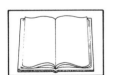

Today's story is called **The Tale of Peter Rabbit.** Another way to say it would be **The *Story* of Peter Rabbit**, because the word *tale* means a story. Peter is really a dear, friendly little rabbit but he's standing all alone. Do you have any idea where he might be? He was a very curious rabbbit, and that got him into trouble. Do you know what the word curious means? I'm sorry to say Peter also was naughty and that got him into trouble, too.

Beatrix Potter is the lady who wrote the story about Peter, many years ago. She was lonely when she was growing up so she made friends with all the little animals around her house and wrote stories about them to cheer up a sick neighbor boy who lived up the lane. Beatrix Potter also drew the beautiful pictures. Now I'm curious to take a look!

The inflection and feeling in your voice will help the children understand the wonderful new words Beatrix Potter uses, like *implored, exerted himself, trembling* and *scuttered.*

**GETTING INVOLVED**

Now it's your turn to be just a little bit naughty and get into mischief! You can be Peter Rabbit. Watch me and I'll show you just what to do, but we must be very quiet so cross old Mr. McGregor doesn't catch us in his garden. First, let's squeeze under the gate. *(Get down low, but stay in your place.)* We better rush all over the garden because Mr. McGregor discovered us and we forgot the way back to the gate. *(Run silently in place.)* Oh-oh, our jackets are caught in the gooseberry net and we better wriggle free. *(Wriggle from head to toe.)* There's the watering can in the tool shed. Jump in and hide. *(Make one jumping motion in place.)* Uh-oh, water! Better jump out without a sound! Let's start running *(run in place)* and not stop 'til we are safely home underneath the big fir tree.

*Another time, have the children interpret the marvelous, descriptive words in the story . . . implored, exert, trembling, puzzled, lippity-lippity and scuttered.*

**A CLOSER LOOK**

With each rereading of a story, children gain new understanding. Pause often for a spontaneous flow of oral language as the children share their feelings and observations. Extend the learning process with your own questions in repeated readings of the story.

- What happened to Peter Rabbit's father? *(deduction)*

- Why do you think Mrs. Rabbit bought five currant buns? *(opinion)*

- Why did Peter Rabbit look for some parsley? *(comprehension)*

- What is a gooseberry net? How did it trap Peter? *(visual detail)*

- Was the watering can a good hiding place? *(comprehension)*

- Why couldn't the mouse give Peter directions? *(memory)*

- How did Peter Rabbit know the cat was a real cat? *(memory)*

- What do you think cousin Benjamin Bunny told Peter Rabbit about cats? *(opinion)*

- Did Mr. McGregor return Peter Rabbit's jacket and shoes? *(comprehension)*

- Do you think the camomile tea was medicine? *(opinion)*

- Do you think Peter Rabbit ever visited Mr. McGregor's garden again? *(opinion)*

**ROUNDING OUT STORYTIME**

**Even That Moose Won't Listen to Me**   by Martha Alexander

**Little Penguin's Tale**   by Audrey Wood

**Two Bad Ants**   by Chris Van Allsburg

**Seven Little Rabbits**   by John Becker

**Littlest Rabbit**   by Robert Kraus

# Integrated Whole Language Activities

## POETRY

**TOMMY**

I put a seed into the ground
And said, "I'll watch it grow."
I watered it and cared for it
As well as I could know.
One day I walked in my back yard,
And oh, what did I see!
My seed had popped itself right out
Without consulting me.
*Gwendolyn Brooks*

**THE TOAD AND THE RABBIT**

by John Martin
from *Read Aloud Rhymes for the Very Young* by Jack Prelutsky

## INVOLVEMENT

- Beatrix Potter was a master at using beautiful language to convey the meaning of her text to children. Can you imagine what would happen to her wonderful word picture of the friendly sparrows, *who flew to Peter in great excitement and implored him to exert himself*, if the story was using a controlled vocabulary? The inflection of your voice and the context of the words will give meaning to the rich vocabulary in **The Tale of Peter Rabbit.** Talk with the children about the many new words they have heard in the story . . . *mischief, frame, implored, exert, sieve, lippity-lippity, trembling, puzzled, scuttered, fortnight, and camomile.*

- Add to the children's understanding by dramatizing the story. Have them find places in the room for the fir tree, the baker, the gate to Mr. McGregor's garden, his tool shed, and the pond. Mark the places with signs. Make name cards with the story characters' names and pictures to hang around the children's necks. As you read the story again, the children can mime their parts with expression and movement.

- As an oral language experience, guide the children in a discussion of the parts of the story they thought were sad, funny, or suspenseful. Talk about the beginning, middle, and end of the story and give the children the opportunity to think of a new ending for **The Tale of Peter Rabbit.**

- Begin each day with another of Beatrix Potter's many stories about Peter Rabbit and his animal friends. Keep a collection in your library corner.

## INTEGRATION

**PETER RABBIT'S ABC BOOK**

Print one letter of the alphabet on each line of a class chart. Let the children decide on characters from the Peter Rabbit stories for each letter of the alphabet, adding imaginary rabbit names for the difficult letters such as Q, Y, and Z. When the chart is complete, give each child a page with an upper and lower case letter printed on it. Write the name of the story character each child has drawn under his picture. Choose children to make a cover, **Peter Rabbit's ABC Book**, and a title page. Mount the pages on colorful construction paper and add your class book to your collection of Beatrix Potter stories.

## A NEW ADVENTURE

To make a semantic map of the story, draw Peter in the center of a large piece of unlined paper. Then beginning at the top and moving clockwise, write the names of the story characters sequentially as the children name them. Make a story web by drawing lines from Peter Rabbit to the names of the characters, including the sparrows, the old mouse, and the white cat. The children can add small pictures by the names.

Ask the children if they think **The Tale of Peter Rabbit** was the only adventure in Peter's life or if we can assume there were more. With the children sitting in front of the story web, begin another tale about Peter. For example, *One dark stormy night little Peter Rabbit scuttered out of his home in the fir tree. He hurried lippity-lippity across the meadow to a large circus tent.* Have the children continue the story with their own ideas, including the characters they added to the semantic web. Storytelling is a form of authoring that provides a valuable oral language experience.

## A SIMULATION: THE GARDEN

- As you talk about the things that grew in Mr. McGregor's garden, the children will discover that everything was a vegetable except the black-currants. Continue the theme of gardening by reading **Rabbit Seeds** by Bijou LeTord, the story of a little rabbit gardener who carefully tends his garden, and the brightly colored **Growing Vegetable Soup** by Lois Ehlert.

- Make a list of everything the children will need to plant a garden. Recall the tools used in the stories and look for more in **Who Uses This?**, a nonfiction picture-book by Margaret Miller. List all the work jobs the children will be responsible for. Decide together on the best place in the room to plant your garden.

- Because lima bean seeds germinate quickly with the stem, roots, and leaves easily visible, have the children plant their seeds in clear plastic cups or baggies. Plant additional seeds close by in a container filled with soil. The children will understand the growing process that is taking place under the soil before the leaves appear.

- Invite moms and dads to school to talk about their gardens, help plant additional seeds, contribute gardening gloves and tools and seedlings, and make simple graphs for the children to record daily observations.

- Keep paper, pencil and rulers in your garden for the children to make signs, label the seeds and the rows of plants, print schedules for watering and write messages to Peter Rabbit about their garden!

- Have the children make a class scarecrow from old clothing, with a stuffed paper bag head and painted face, an old hat, and some straw. Prop it up on a broomstick. Add a watering can and a child-size wheelbarrow full of books about rabbits, seeds, and gardens to your inviting gardener's corner.

**EVERYDAY LEARNING ACTIVITIES**

Positive parenting, developmental learning activities and a warm, nurturing environment are major factors in a child's academic success and lifetime learning.

In **The Tale of Peter Rabbit**, mother rabbit quietly stated her limits to her children, "You may go into the fields or down the lane, but don't go into Mr. McGregor's garden." When Peter disobeyed and lost his clothes for the second time, mother rabbit quietly put him to bed.

You are probably doing your best parenting when your voice is softest. A quiet voice usually conveys kindness and love and understanding. A quiet voice says you are in control of yourself and the situation, and when a parent is speaking softly, children must quiet down to hear what is being said. In contrast, yelling is probably the poorest kind of discipline there is. The child is actually in control because he has caused *you* to lose your control! When speaking quietly, it is far easier to train your child to listen and do what you ask. Your voice can convey a great deal of love and respect, and expect the same in return. When your child is grown, however he remembers your voice is probably the way he remembers you. *(parenting skill)*

- Reading aloud to your child is the single most important way to plant within him the desire to learn to read himself. Even more important, your child will associate reading with something wonderful . . . your attention and your quiet voice. Make a list of each year's favorite read-aloud book titles for your child to keep. What a pleasant memory for a child! *(reading readiness)*

- As your child's vocabulary continues to grow, encourage him to see the connection between *opposite* words. Begin with obvious pairs such as big and little, and happy and sad. Encourage your child to find opposites for open, out, over, rough, tiny, sick, long and broken. This is a good game to play if you are busy in the kitchen, riding in the car, or waiting somewhere away from home. Also let your child give a word to you and you supply the opposite. *(language development)*

- Wrap a piece of tape on one end of a piece of yarn, stiffening it so it can act as a needle. Tie a small section of straw to the other end of the yarn. Help your child cut straws into one inch sections. You have already taught three new words: stiffening, inch, and sections! Stringing the straw pieces will develop small muscles. *(eye-hand coordination, language)*

- Using masking tape on the floor, make a *hopping path* for your child and **Peter Rabbit.** Have her hop forward along the tape, first on one foot, then the other. With toes parallel to the tape, have your child hop over and back again on one foot. With practice, add hopping backwards, hopping with alternate feet, and, finally, with eyes closed! *(gross motor skills)*

# Ten, Nine, Eight

## by Molly Bang

**TEACHING FOCUS**
- Matching numerals to sets
- Concept of one less
- Rhyming words
- Bedtime routines

**SETTING THE STAGE**

Instantly singable songs and the appealing rhyme and rhythm of finger plays will encourage children to be involved in storytime.

**TEN IN THE BED** by Sharon, Lois & Bram, *Elephant Show Record*
    (A very funny version with many *surprises*)

**GO TO SLEEP/WHERE'S MY PAJAMAS?**
    by Sharon, Lois & Bram, *Elephant Show Record*

**ONE, TWO, BUCKLE MY SHOE**

One, two, buckle my shoe;            *(follow actions as rhyme indicates)*
Three, four, knock at the door;
Five, six, pick up sticks;
Seven, eight, lay them straight;
Nine, ten a big fat hen.

**I HAVE TEN LITTLE FINGERS**

I have ten little fingers and they all belong to me.    *(follow action as
I can make them do things, would you like to see?       rhyme indicates)*
I can shut them up tight. I can open them wide.
I can put them together . . . or make them hide!
I can make them jump high, I can make them jump low.
I can put them together, and hold them just so.

**FIRST READING**

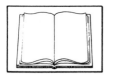

Tell me a story about the little girl in yellow on the cover. There is only one other person in this story. Let's look at the *title page*. Who do you think that person is? Now let's look on the next page. Tell me what you think they are doing. Could they be counting the little girl's toes?

When you count, do you begin with the number ten or the number one? The little girl in our story always begins with the number ten because she likes to count backwards. That's because she and her daddy have a special little routine every night when it is bedtime. The name of our story is **Ten, Nine, Eight** and it was written by Molly Bang.

**GETTING INVOLVED**

*Put a mystery bag on the floor in front of the children. Ask a child to reach into the bag and describe an item by feeling it before he pulls it out. Then ask him what the item is used for and if he saw one like it in the story,* **Ten, Nine, Eight.** *Include ordinary bedtime things like a toothbrush, pajamas, a teddy bear, soap, a water glass, and a story book. Also include some items that have nothing to do with going to bed, like a ball or a pencil.*

*Group the items into two piles. Have ten things in the bedtime group. Then count down from ten to zero as you remove one object at a time from the group.*

**A CLOSER LOOK**

With each rereading of a story, children gain new understanding. Pause often for a spontaneous flow of oral language as the children share their feelings and observations. Extend the learning process with your own questions in repeated readings of the story.

- Whose ten little toes are these? *(story interpretation)*

- How many of the nine soft friends are stuffed animals? Which would be the lightest to carry? The heaviest? *(reasoning)*

- Are there more windowpanes than toys in the picture? *(comparing sets)*

- Do you think the shoes are all the same size? What happened to the missing shoe? *(visual perception)*

- Why is the cat looking at the shells? *(opinion)*

- Can you find something the color of every button on the yellow gown? Did you find the missing shoe? *(visual perception)*

- Tell me when you see pairs of things as we finish the story. *(association)*

- Let's turn the pages again and look for *stripes (or shapes, patterns, colors)* in the pictures. *(visual perception)*

- Which stuffed animal would you take to bed? *(opinion)*

- How did the story make you feel? Would you change anything? *(feelings)*

**ROUNDING OUT STORYTIME**

**The Right Number of Elephants**   by Jeff Sheppard

**The Midnight Farm**   by Reeve Lindbergh

**10 Bears in My Bed**   by Stan Mack

**Ten Little Mice**   by Joyce Dunbar

**Gorilla**   by Anthony Browne

191

# Integrated Whole Language Activities

## POETRY

### PRETENDING

When you are in bed and it's cold outside,
do you ever pretend that you have to hide?
Do you curl up your toes?
Do you wrinkle your nose?
Do you make yourself little so none of you shows?

Do you pull the sheet over the whole of your face
and pretend you are in some faraway place?
Mother thinks you are sleeping,
but she does not know
that all tucked in your bed, you have places to go.

*Bobbi Katz*

### HUSHABYE MY DARLING

by Clyde Watson
from *Read Aloud Rhymes for the Very Young*
by Jack Prelutsky

## INVOLVEMENT

- A loving book, warm pictures, bedtime, and music just go together. Don't overlook the Sharon, Lois & Bram songs mentioned on a preceding page. *Ten in the Bed* and *Go to Sleep/Where's My Pajamas*, a lullaby that turns into a rollicking, hoedown-style hunt for bedtime items, are too much fun to miss.

- Include a variety of songs in your rereadings of **Ten, Nine, Eight**. The traditional song, *Ten Little Indians*, reinforces the emphasis on sets that is found in the story. The music to the familiar folk song, *Roll Over! A Counting Song* is included in the storybook. If you are feeling really adventurous, sing the words of **Ten, Nine, Eight** to the tune of *This Old Man*. Just keep turning the pages as you sing the melody. The text for the numbers ten through seven will make up the first verse, the numbers six through three will be the second verse, the numbers two and one and then singing the numbers ten through one backwards will finish out the last verse. It is surprising how easily the words fit the tune. Make a tape of the children singing their favorite song. Put it in a listening center along with a copy of the book.

- Most children know and enjoy the game, *Doggie, Doggie, Where's Your Bone?* Adapt it to the story by putting a shoe under a chair and changing the words to *Ten, nine, eight; Where's your shoe? Somebody took it; I know who!*

## INTEGRATION

### FOCUSING ON WORDS

- The simple rhythm of **Ten, Nine, Eight** makes it a natural for rereadings. When focusing on language rather than number sets, have the children listen for rhyming words. Write the rhyming word pairs on a chart. Copy each pair of words on a sentence strip. Draw a boldly-colored, jagged line down the middle of the strip to separate the words. Cut them apart. Let the children find the rhyming word pairs by matching the colored jagged edges.

- Another time, listen for describing words. Make a book of adjectives by printing one phrase, such as *round* buttons, on each page for the children to illustrate.

## MY BEDTIME COUNTING BOOK

Young children are fascinated with the concept of homework. Why not give them the assignment of creating their own bedtime counting books? Prepare a small blank book for each child to take home along with a brief note to parents. Each child will study her bedroom and decide what she would like to say good night to, drawing a set of ten objects on the first page, nine on the second, and so on until she reaches the number one and says *Good night* on the last page. Parents can label the sets on the bottom of each page. Have the children bring their **Ten, Nine, Eight** books to school to share before making them a part of their bedtime routines.

## A COUNTING SONG

In **Roll Over! A Counting Song**, Merle Peek has illustrated the old American folk song, *Roll Over*. Mordecai Gerstein uses amusing animals and adjectives in his delightful version of this bedtime favorite.

After singing and dramatizing the words, have the children write a class innovation. Using water color paints, crayons, or a collage of colored scraps, have them make a quilt on a bed for each page, with the faces of the children (or animals or teddy bears) just above the quilt. Print the verse or the words *Roll Over, Roll Over!* on the left side of each page. Under a folded flap on the right, print the words, *And one fell out*. The number of children's faces above the quilt will decrease from ten to one on succeeding pages, with the last child saying *Good night!* on the last page.

Stan Mack's **Ten Bears In My Bed** can be adapted to the same countdown innovation, as can Joyce Dunbar's **Ten Little Mice**, a beautifully illustrated story of mice leaving one by one to find a safe mouse hole. Your children will also enjoy **Ten Little Animals**, a delightful story by Laura Jane Coats. She has used ten different animals and a rhyming text to expand the well-known favorite, *Five little monkeys jumping on the bed; One fell off and bumped his head*. In **One Bear All Alone**, Caroline Bucknall has combined cuddly teddy bears, bedtime, counting, and a rhyming text. Each book offers integrated learning at its best!

## A SORTING TUB

Fill a colorful plastic tub with small objects. Have the children sort the objects, making a set for each numeral, i.e. ten legos, nine buttons, eight crayons, etc. Add laminated numeral cards, including zero, to the tub. Ask the children what they found in the tub to match to the zero. Were there any elephants? Then there were zero elephants! Any chocolate cakes? Then there were zero chocolate cakes! As the children take turns sorting the sets, they will be eager to tell you what they found in the tub for the set of zero.

**EVERYDAY LEARNING ACTIVITIES**

Positive parenting, developmental learning activities and a warm, nurturing environment are major factors in a child's academic success and lifetime learning.

Try not to compare your days, or your parenting, to other mothers or fathers who appear to never have a bad day! Remember that children have different temperaments, and parents have different frustration levels and problems. There are no perfect parents or perfect children anywhere. Sometimes we just have to tell our children that we are sorry we yelled or made a poor decision, but that doesn't mean we stopped loving them. Smile at the bad days and tell the world about the good ones! Mornings are always new beginnings. *(parenting skill)*

- Draw simple stick figures of each part of your child's bedtime routine, like brushing his teeth, taking a bath, getting a drink (one drink!), putting on his pajamas, and reading a book. Print the phrase at the bottom of each page. You could be really clever and take photos of your child, or cut pictures of a toothbrush, soap, pajamas, etc, out of magazines and paste them on paper or index cards. Put your child's name on the front and call it his very own bedtime book. Have your child sequence the pictures in just the order he wants to get ready for bed, with the understanding that when you have finished the last picture, it is time to say good night! It simply takes the power play out of getting into bed. The pictures say we are done! Why not make the last picture of your child in bed with his favorite stuffed animal? *(sequencing)*

- Review all the positive and fun things that happened during your day, perhaps as your child is in bed and you are quietly talking. Begin with morning, then afternoon, then evening. Ask questions like, "Do you remember what you ate for breakfast?" or "What did we do after your lunch today?" This will encourage your child to think in sequence as well as end the day on a happy note. By always following the morning, afternoon, and evening pattern, your child will be practicing first, middle, and last. *(memory)*

- Make your own **Ten, Nine, Eight** bedtime book. Staple the pages together, decide on your routine and write the numerals and phrases on the pages, such as:

  | | | |
  |---|---|---|
  | 10 - brush teeth | 6 - a bedtime story | 3 - lights out |
  | 9 - wash face and hands | 5 - a hug | 2 - count down 10-1 |
  | 8 - pajamas | 4 - a kiss | 1 - good night! |
  | 7 - drink of water | | |

- Mix a small amount of desired food coloring and milk together. With a small paintbrush, paint a numeral on a slice of bread. Then toast and butter it for a nice surprise! Have your child count out a matching set of carrot curls or cheerios to enjoy eating with the magic number toast. *(numerals and sets)*

# The Three Billy Goats Gruff

## by Paul Galdone

**TEACHING FOCUS**

- Comparative Sizes
- Directionality
- Story Participation
- Sequencing

**SETTING THE STAGE**

Instantly singable songs and the appealing rhyme and rhythm of finger plays will encourage children to be involved in storytime.

**ONCE I SAW THREE GOATS** by Sharon, Lois & Bram, *Singin' and Swingin'*

**3 MONKEYS** by Sharon, Lois & Bram, *Smorgasbord*
(A delightful, rhythmic chant)

**OVER THE HILLS**

| | |
|---|---|
| Over the hills and far away | *(bounce hands)* |
| We skip and run and laugh and play. | *(clap hands)* |
| Smell the flowers | *(sniff a flower)* |
| and fish the streams, | *(cast a fishing line)* |
| Lie in the sunshine | *(sleep, cheek resting on hand)* |
| and dream sweet dreams. | |

**THE ANT HILL**

| | |
|---|---|
| Once I saw an ant hill | |
| With no ants about. | *(closed fist)* |
| So I said, "Dear little ants, | |
| Won't you please come out?" | *(hands cupped to mouth)* |
| Then, as if they'd heard me call, | |
| One, two, three, four, five | *(bring fingers out)* |
| Came out—and that was all! | *(big shrug)* |

**FIRST READING**

The name of our story today is . . . why don't I let you guess? What animal do you see on the cover? How many are there? You've already guessed two of the words in the title. Another word is Billy and the goats' last name is Gruff. Can you put those words together to make a title? Let's read it . . . **Three Billy Goats Gruff.**

This story has been a favorite story for many years. Your grandma and grandpa probably read this book when they were children. I think you will like it as much as they did. The three goats have a problem. Let's see how they solve it in **The Three Billy Goats Gruff.**

**GETTING INVOLVED**

In the story, the three Billy Goats all trip-trapped over the bridge to get to the other side. Which Billy Goat Gruff went first? What sound did his hooves make on the bridge? Show me what his voice sounded like when he answered the ugly troll. Which Billy Goat Gruff went next? How did his hooves sound on the bridge? Show me what his voice sounded like. Did the troll's voice change, too? Tell me all about the largest Billy Goat Gruff.

I will pretend to be the troll under the bridge and you be the three Billy Goats. All you will need are your voices, your stomping feet and horns on your heads. Think of how your hands could change to make little horns, middle sized and then great big horns for the three goats. What could be a bridge? Where's the meadow full of flowers? I know you can't wait to get there!

Now, let's get ready to look at **The Three Billy Goats Gruff** one more time. Everyone take a big breath, now a bigger one, now the biggest breath you can take. Do it one more time, but don't let me hear a sound.

**A CLOSER LOOK**

With each rereading of a story, children gain new understanding. Pause often for a spontaneous flow of oral language as the children share their feelings and observations. Extend the learning process with your own questions in repeated readings of the story.

- Tell me all the ways the goats were different.  *(observation)*

- Where do you think the Three Billy Goats Gruff were going when they crossed over the bridge? *(reasoning)*

- Who lived under the bridge? Is troll a good name for him? *(vocabulary)*

- What did he look like? *(descriptive words)*

- What did the troll roar at the billy goats when they crossed the bridge? *(story recall)*

- Why did the first two goats tell the troll to wait for their brother? *(interpretation)*

- How did the billy goats solve their problem? *(interpretation)*

- Did they trick the troll? *(logical thinking)*

- Was the meadow a good place for the Billy Goats to live? *(opinion)*

**ROUNDING OUT STORYTIME**

**Quack, Said the Billy Goat**   by Charles Causley and Barbara Firth

**Anno's Counting Book**   by Mitsumasa Anno

**Over in the Meadow**   by Ezra Jack Keats

**Three by the Sea**   by James Marshall

**Goat's Trail**   by Brian Wildsmith

# *Integrated Whole Language Activities*

**POETRY**

**OVER IN A MEADOW**

Over in a meadow, in the sand, in the sun,
Lived an old mother frog and her little froggie one.
"Croak!" said the mother; "I croak," said the one,
So they croaked and they were glad in the sand, in the sun.

Over in a meadow, in a stream so blue,
Lived an old mother fish and her little fishies two.
"Swim!" said the mother; "We swim," said the two,
So they swam and were glad in the stream so blue.

*Folk Rhyme*

**INVOLVEMENT**

**DRAMATIZATION**

- With the familiar, predictable pattern of **The Three Billy Goats Gruff**, choral reading will be spontaneous. The children are probably already joining you in the rhythmic repetition of *trip, trap, trip, trap* and the voice of the troll saying, *"Who's that tramping over my bridge?" Add to the fun and keep children listening intently by dividing the children into five groups, one group to be the voice of the bridge saying trip trap*, a group to respond for each of the three goats, and one group to be the angry voice of the troll.

- **The Three Billy Goats Gruff** presents an ideal setting for creative dramatics. The language will come to life as the children role play the characters. Have the children find a place in your room for a meadow, a river, and a bridge made from blocks, boxes, or a table. Provide materials in your art center for children to create hats or headband goat ears, and a wild hat or an ugly nose for the troll. Because children often gain confidence dramatizing parts in pairs, create two props for each character. Leave the props in your dramatic play center. Add paper and pencil to the center to encourage children to use written language in their play.

**INTEGRATION**

**ON THE WAY TO THE MEADOW**

To tell the story on your bulletin board, pencil sketch on white paper a simple outline of hills, a meadow, and a bridge for children to paint. Use the medium of tear art to make the troll, goats, flowers, trees, fish and rocks to add to the scene. (You probably won't lack for volunteers to make the snaggle-tooth troll!) Have the children recall position words used in the story . . . *in the valley, up the hillside, over a river,* and so on. Print the phrases on sentence strips for the children to add to the mural. Be sure to keep some pointers nearby for paired or independent reading.

**A RETELLING**

The lovable story illustrations of the three goats makes them appear to walk off the pages and into your room. Have the children think about first names for the goats and an appropriate name for the unhappy troll before retelling the story in their own words. Model the writing process as you write their story on a language experience chart.

### LET ME READ YOU A STORY

Copy the children's language experience story, one line at a time, on large pieces of paper. Choose pairs of children to illustrate the print on each page. Mount their drawings, cover, and title page. Let the children decide if their retelling should be a wall story or a big book. In independent reading, child-authored stories are often chosen over the originals because of the simple, familiar text.

### FLIP, FLOP, FLIP, FLOP

To write an innovation of **The Three Billy Goats Gruff**, brainstorm with the children about other animals that could be the main characters in the story. Talk about changing the setting and the noisy sounds of the characters, for example, three wandering seals flip-flopping over a bridge to an island on the other side. After allowing plenty of time for oral language (children often talk in *paragraphs!*), help them develop the plot, one sentence at a time, as you record the story on a chart. After many rereadings, let the children decide how to reproduce the story.

### MESSAGES

Children love to receive messages, anywhere, anytime. Start every day with a message for your class on a message board. Encourage them to also write messages, perhaps in their daily journal writing.

Dear Troll,
Let's be friends. We need a guard at the gate to the meadow. Will you please come?

The Three Billy Goats Gruff

Surprise your children one morning with an exciting message that there is a special-delivery letter for them in the office. You won't want to leave anyone behind as you pick up your letter . . . a scroll-like, ribbon-tied message from the three billy goats gruff to the troll. Read the letter slowly, waiting for the children to read as many words as they can. Then, as a class, write an answer from the surprised troll to his new friends, the three goats. What activities will the letter lead to in your open-ended thematic approach?

### THREE BY THREE

The number three is the most often used number in fairy tales and nursery rhymes . . . three little kittens, three blind mice, three little pigs, and many more. Have fun with the number three in the context of stories and poetry in your shared reading. Introduce your children to the fascinating water color art of **Anno's Counting Book.** Anno, who says every child is a natural mathematician, has interwoven sets of numbers into a countryside scene that changes with the seasons. See how many sets of threes your children can discover in Anno's interesting picture. Keep the book in a center so children can study the many details.

Have each child bring from home a set of three objects to talk about and to draw. Print the caption, *Three* _____ , on each child's page to make a simple, easily read caption book to add to your collection of books about the number three.

**EVERYDAY LEARNING ACTIVITIES**

Positive parenting, developmental learning activities and a warm, nurturing environment are major factors in a child's academic success and lifetime learning.

Staying on task is a skill every child must develop for successful learning. Encourage your child to practice that skill at home by allowing her to do more and more things by herself. Expect her to finish a job you give her to do. Require her to put toys away before bedtime. She will learn to stay on task if you begin with small jobs you know she can succeed in. Then build up to larger tasks. The more you praise a child, the harder she will try, and the better she will feel about herself. By participating in family chores, your child will know she is a valuable member of the family. It's nice to be counted on! Encourage her to also stay on task when eating, or playing, or looking at a book. Reading requires a child to attend to the end! *(parenting skill)*

- Build bridges out of blocks, pillows, chairs or bodies. Have fun acting out **The Three Billy Goats Gruff** with the whole family. *(creative play)*

- Make an obstacle course using furniture. Children can jump over a pillow, crawl under a table, hop around a stool, walk backwards to a chair, etc. Play Follow the Leader. (Include only those activities you normally allow in your home!) *(perceptual motor)*

- Make cookies together. Place different sizes of dough on the cookie sheet. Talk about size when eating the cookies, or group them according to big, bigger, biggest. *(comparative sizes)*

- Blow bubbles together. Talk about big, bigger and biggest, or first, second and third, or small, middle and large. Watch the bubbles float over and under things. Do bubbles move differently when a fan is on or when you blow them outside? *(comparative sizes)*

- Make a collection of balls. Have your child sort them according to weight and size. Ask her to predict how the balls will move down a simple ramp made of cardboard, books, or a piece of wood. *(comparisons)*

- Make a tape of you and your child reading **The Three Billy Goats Gruff** together. By pointing to the familiar, repetitious words on the page as she listens to the tape, your child will understand that print carries a message and that reading is fun! *(prereading skills)*

- Encourage your child to retell **The Three Billy Goats Gruff** in her own words. She will learn to organize her thoughts, put things in proper order, and speak in complete sentences. Even the troll would be proud! *(sequencing)*

# The Very Hungry Caterpillar

## by Eric Carle

**TEACHING FOCUS**
- Days of the week
- Counting sets
- Classifying
- Color recognition

**SETTING THE STAGE**

Instantly singable songs and the appealing rhyme and rhythm of finger plays will encourage children to be involved in storytime.

**DAYS OF THE WEEK** by Greg and Steve, *We All Love Together, Vol. 4*

**EVERYBODY HAPPY** by Sharon, Lois & Bram, *Elephant Show Record*
  (A cumulative song that names chores for each day of the week)

**SLEEPY CATERPILLARS**

| | |
|---|---|
| Let's go to sleep the little caterpillars said | *(wiggle fingers)* |
| As they tucked themselves into their beds. | *(fold into hand)* |
| They will awaken by and by | *(open hands slowly)* |
| And each will be a lovely butterfly! | *(fly fingers)* |

**WIGGLE WORM**

| | |
|---|---|
| Do you always have to wiggle? | *(wiggle in chair)* |
| Do you always have to squirm? | |
| You wiggle and you jiggle, | *(wiggle and jiggle)* |
| Like a little wiggle worm. | *(wiggle hands)* |
| You wiggle in your chair, | *(wiggle in chair)* |
| And you wiggle in your bed. | |
| You wiggle with your legs, | *(wiggle legs)* |
| And you wiggle with your head. | *(shake head)* |
| You wiggle with your hands, | *(shake hands)* |
| And you wiggle with your feet. | *(move feet)* |
| You wiggle when you're playing, | |
| And you wiggle when you eat. | *(pretend to eat)* |
| I guess you're made to wiggle | *(wiggle all over)* |
| And I guess you're made to squirm, | |
| So I'll like the wiggle-jiggle, | |
| And I'll love my wiggle worm. | *(hugging motion)* |

**FIRST READING**

Tell me about the little creature on the cover of this book. What colors do you see? What are the little lines on his body? What do you think the story will be about?

The name of the story is **The Very Hungry Caterpillar.** It is the only book I know of that has little round holes in it! Eric Carle drew the colorful pictures and he also wrote the words. The story is about a little caterpillar and a very special home he built for himself. But I don't want to spoil the surprise. Let's read!

*The compelling sequence and color-splashed pictures will encourage the children to join in on the repetitive phrase, "But he was still hungry."*

**GETTING INVOLVED**

Are you ready for a really big word . . . a really, really big word? It is *metamorphosis*. Say that slowly with me. That big word means everything that happened to the caterpillar from the day of his birth until he became a beautiful butterfly.

Let's pretend you are all tiny caterpillars. First, *pop* out of your tiny eggs. Now *stretch* out on your leaves and *rub* your tummies because you are hungry. *Nibble* through one apple, then two pears, *(name all the foods in sequence)*. Oh dear, now you all have stomachaches! Better *nibble* some green leaves and then build cocoons all around yourselves. *Lie* very still and sleep awhile. Now it's time to *chew* a little hole to get out. Look at you! You are beautiful butterflies! *Fly* away and find green leaves to land on. *(Model every action as you lead the children through the body movements.)*

**A CLOSER LOOK**

With each rereading of a story, children gain new understanding. Pause often for a spontaneous flow of oral language as the children share their feelings and observations. Extend the learning process with your own questions in repeated readings of the story.

- What was growing inside the tiny egg? *(comprehension)*

- Did the caterpillar eat more or less fruit each day? *(comparing sets)*

- How did the pages change when the caterpillar ate through the fruit? *(comparing sizes)*

- Does a caterpillar have a big appetite? Why? *(reasoning)*

- What colors and shapes did he see on Saturday? *(visual detail)*

- Why did eating a leaf make the caterpillar feel better? *(reasoning)*

- Is two weeks a long time? *(understanding time)*

- What do you think happened inside the cocoon? *(reasoning)*

- What do you know about butterfly wings? *(comprehension)*

- What will happen all over again? *(comprehension)*

**ROUNDING OUT STORYTIME**

**What Comes in 2's, 3's, & 4's?**  by Suzanne Aker

**The Biggest House in the World**  by Leo Lionni

**one bright Monday morning**  by Arline Baum

**Rooster's Off to See the World**  by Eric Carle

**Charlie the Caterpillar**  by Dom DeLuise

# Integrated Whole Language Activities

**POETRY**

**LITTLE ARA BELLA MILLER**

Little Ara Bella Miller
Had a fuzzy caterpillar.
First it crawled upon her mother,
Then upon her baby brother.
      They said to
      Ara Bella Miller,
      "Put away
      Your caterpillar!"
        *Anonymous*

**FUZZY WUZZY, CREEPY CRAWLY**

by Lilian Schulz
    from *Real Aloud Rhymes for the Very Young* by Jack Prelutsky

**ONLY MY OPINION**
    BY Monica Shannon
    from *Read Aloud Rhymes for the Very Young* by Jack Prelutsky

**INVOLVEMENT**

**A FLANNELBOARD STORY**

Put all your little artists to work making the thirty-two objects in **The Very Hungry Caterpillar**, including the moon, two leaves, the egg, the sun, a small and a large caterpillar, a cocoon and a butterfly. Provide tagboard, fabric scraps, tissue paper, markers and a very important paper punch! Back each item with a piece of felt. Involve the children in sequencing the story on a flannelboard.

Write name cards for the days of the week, modeling the writing process for the children as you *think out loud* about letters and sounds. Have the children match objects to the correct day of the week. Start them off with Sunday, the sun, the egg and the tiny caterpillar! Keep the pictures and words available for a colorful, *reading for fun* learning center activity. Who can resist telling this irresistible story?

**CATERPILLAR SNACKS**

Plan fruit snacks for each day of the week, showing how the sets *increase* as the caterpillar grows.

**INTEGRATION**

**FEED THE HUNGRY CATERPILLAR!**

Using a large piece of bulletin board paper, have the children paint a huge caterpillar with twelve body segments. Be sure to put his smiling face on the left! Add to the learning by researching how many feet and eyespots a caterpillar has. Print the story title and the author's name on your bulletin board.

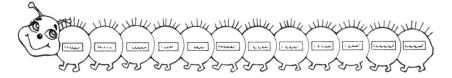

On tagboard, print sets of word cards for the days of the week, the months of the year, and number words, again verbalizing about sound-symbol relationships as you write. The children can independently choose a set of cards to read and sequence right on the segments of **The Very Hungry Caterpillar!**

## MY HUNGRY CATERPILLAR *

Have a small group of children create a cover and a title page for a class caption book. Give each child a piece of white construction paper with the same sentence printed on the bottom, *"My hungry caterpillar _____ ."* After brainstorming about all the things busy little caterpillars do, have each child choose one action word to finish his sentence. Encourage him to depict the hunching or inching or chewing or slithering as he illustrates his sentence. Tear art or sponge paint would make wonderfully bright caterpillars, dressed up with yarn *spines* or pipe cleaner antennae. Books that children write themselves are the most popular ones in the room!

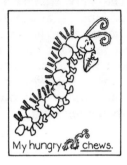
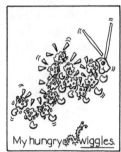

## STOMACHACHE STORIES *

After discussing why the caterpillar got a stomachache, brainstorm different food combinations the children might eat that would give them stomachaches. Choose a small group of children to create a cover and a title page for your book of **Stomachache Stories.** Give each child a piece of paper with the same sentence written at the top, *"Child's name ate _____ , _____ , and _____ ."* At the bottom of each page write, *"That night (he, she) had a stomachache!"* Have each child draw three food items on his paper and write his words emergently or dictate them to the teacher. On the last page, let the class decide on three healthful foods to write above the words, *"That night we all had a good night's sleep!"* What a winning combination for a class book . . . wacky food, a shared story and a cure for stomachaches!

## NUTRITION

Using real food or the flannelbacked pieces from **The Very Hungry Caterpillar,** p. 204 , have the children sort the food the caterpillar ate into healthful and not healthful groups. Using a floor graph with two columns, graph the healthful and not healthful food. Discover which has more, which has less, how many more, how many less. The children can also make a picture graph to hang up by drawing the food items on small squares of paper and charting them on a large piece of bulletin board paper. Brainstorm additional categories for graphing . . . hot and cold, shapes, colors, taste, or food sections in the supermarket.

## A LIFE CYCLE

Introduce nonfiction books such as the fascinating **Backyard Insects** by Millicent E. Selsam or **From Egg to Butterfly** by Marlene Reidel. Write brief, factual sentences together on chart paper, the overhead or the chalkboard. Chart the metamorphosis of a butterfly on a large paper circle, including the egg, caterpillar, chrysalis and butterfly. Let pairs of children draw above the text of each stage. They will probably want to add colorful, hungry caterpillars somewhere! Be sure to hang up the chart for paired or independent reading.

**EVERYDAY
LEARNING
ACTIVITIES**

Positive parenting, developmental learning activities and a warm, nurturing environment are major factors in a child's academic success and lifetime learning.

In the story, **The Very Hungry Caterpillar**, the caterpillar's home was a very special place for him. . . a safe and protected place where he could grow and change. To children also, home is a haven and a safety zone. Our children need to hear us say, "Our home is special and different from any other. You are safe here and we will take care of you. You don't have to be like anyone else. You can make mistakes and no one will laugh at you. You are always loved. When you walk in that door you are safe because our home is a very special place." *(parenting skill)*

- On trips to the grocery store, have your child look for foods the caterpillar ate in **The Very Hungry Caterpillar.** *(recall)*

- Make up your own counting songs. Children will love them. Practice counting in everyday activities: putting on shoes, setting the table, cracks in the sidewalk, cars on the street. *(counting sets)*

- Sketch four simple pictures on index cards: an egg, a caterpillar, a chrysalis and a butterfly. Write the words on the bottom. Have your child sequence them, beginning on the left. *(sequencing)*

- Write the days of the week on the top of seven index cards. On each card, have your child draw what **The Very Hungry Caterpillar** ate that day. Write the numeral that matches each set. (Let your child choose what he wants on Saturday's card!) Put a ring through *caterpillar* holes in the upper left corner of the cards and make your own book. *(days of week and sets)*

- Every day choose a different way to *classify* food: hot or cold, healthful or not healthful, finger food or silverware food, smooth or rough texture. You could also *group* by colors, fruit, vegetables, dairy products or desserts. Remember your child enjoys sensory learning so let her touch, taste and smell as she groups. *(classification)*

- Draw, color and cut out a paper butterfly. Eric Carle made his from a tissue paper collage! Staple the butterfly's body to a narrow strip of paper you have already made into a circle by stapling the ends together. The paper circle slips over your child's hand and the butterfly moves as he waves his hand. *(fine motor skills)*

- Find foods in the pantry or in the store to match every color in the beautiful butterfly. *(color recognition)*

# Where the Wild Things Are

### by Maurice Sendak

**TEACHING FOCUS**
- Identifying feelings
- Story comprehension
- Building vocabulary
- Family relationships

**SETTING THE STAGE**

Instantly singable songs and the appealing rhyme and rhythm of finger plays will encourage children to be involved in storytime.

**SHAKE MY SILLIES OUT** by Raffi, *More Singable Songs for the Very Young*

**WHEN THINGS DON'T GO YOUR WAY** by Hap Palmer, *Backwards Land*

**WILD THINGS**

| | |
|---|---|
| I have five terrible wild things. | *(hold up one hand)* |
| I dreamed them in my head. | *(point to head)* |
| And if they try to scare me | *(two hands up, scary)* |
| I'll dream that they are dead! | *(fist closed)* |
| They'll run with me. | *(wiggle five fingers)* |
| They'll jump with me. | *(jump five fingers)* |
| But when I'm done with them, | *(five fingers still)* |
| I'll say 'good bye' | *(wave with left hand)* |
| and they will fly | *(fingers fly away)* |
| out of my life again! | *(hand behind back)* |

*Mary Cornelius*

**THREE GHOSTESSES**

| | |
|---|---|
| Three little ghostesses, | *(three fingers up)* |
| Sitting on postesses, | *(sitting motion)* |
| Eating buttered toastesses. | *(fingers to mouth)* |
| Greasing their fistesses, | *(rub hands together)* |
| Up to their wristesses, | *(touch wrists)* |
| Oh, what beastesses | *(shake finger)* |
| To make such feastesses! | *(palms up)* |

**FIRST READING**

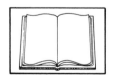

Tell me everything you see on the cover of this book. *(Show the front and back covers simultaneously.)* Why is the boat there? What do you think is happening?

The name of our story is **Where the Wild Things Are.** The man who wrote the story also drew all the wonderful pictures in the book. When Mr. Sendak finished his book, some people were concerned that little children would be frightened by the pictures. But they were wrong! Children loved both the story and the illustrations and they were not frightened at all. In fact, Mr. Sendak received a very important award called the Caldecott Award for his wonderful make-believe wild things. You can see one of the wild things right here on the cover. **Where the Wild Things Are** is about a little boy named Max having an adventure with some pretend wild things who become his friends.

**GETTING
INVOLVED**

Tell me some of the words you heard in Max's adventure with the wild things. What words do you remember? Let's talk about some of the words that might be new words.

The story said that Max made *mischief.* Tell me what that word means. Next it said the vines were hanging from the *ceiling.* Where would that be? Our story said the ocean *tumbled.* What does *tumble* mean? Max sailed off in a *private* boat. I'm wondering what the word *private* means. Our story said the wild things *gnashed* their teeth. Was that something good? And last of all, what did Max mean when he wanted the wild *rumpus* to start?

To help us remember the new words, I'll say them all one more time. We can act out the meaning of each one of them right here in our places. When we are finished, we will wave good-bye to Max and curl up quietly in our places while we wait for supper!

**A CLOSER LOOK**

With each rereading of a story, children gain new understanding. Pause often for a spontaneous flow of oral language as the children share their feelings and observations. Extend the learning process with your own questions in repeated readings of the story.

- Tell me about the problem Max had in the beginning of the story. *(comprehension)*

- Have you ever made mischief? *(opinion)*

- What happened in Max's imagination? *(comprehension)*

- How did Max's bedroom change? *(visual memory)*

- Tell me all the words you can think of to describe the wild things. *(vocabulary)*

- Do you think the wild things had families? *(opinion)*

- Why did the wild things make Max their king? *(comprehension)*

- How did Max punish the wild things like his mother had punished him? *(association)*

- Why do you think Max's supper was waiting for him? *(association)*

**ROUNDING OUT
STORYTIME**

**One Hungry Monster: A Counting Book in Rhyme**   by Susan O'Keefe

**There's An Alligator Under My Bed**   by Maurice Sendak

**There's A Nightmare in My Closet**   by Maurice Sendak

**Elbert's Bad Word**   by Audrey Wood

**Clyde Monster**   by Robert L. Crowe

# Integrated Whole Language Activities

**POETRY**

### SOMETHING IS THERE

Something is there
  there on the stair
    coming down
      coming down
        stepping with care
       Coming down
        coming down
         slinkety-sly.

Something is coming and wants to get by.
*Lilian Moore*

### IN A DARK WOOD

In a dark, dark wood
  there was a dark, dark house,
And in that dark, dark house
  there was a dark, dark room,
And in that dark, dark room
  there was a dark, dark cupboard,
And in that dark, dark cupboard
  there was a dark, dark shelf,
And on that dark, dark shelf
  there was a dark, dark box,
And in that dark, dark box
  there was . . .
    A MONSTER!
*Author Unknown*

**INVOLVEMENT**

- Children will delight in many rereadings of **Where the Wild Things Are.** To help them interpret and verbalize the story, choose a new *focus* each time you read. Discuss *feelings, imagination, problem-solving, predicting,* or the *meaning* of the wonderful vocabulary.

- **Where the Wild Things Are** offers an ideal setting for *creative dramatics.* To make the language come to life, have the children *pantomime* the movement of all the story characters. Another time, have them add sound effects.

- Create wild thing paper bag *hand puppets*, paper plate *face masks* or *stick puppets*. Have Max, the King, lead a Wild Thing Parade, ending with his marvelous magic trick as you return to the forest!

- Involve the children in making simple *literacy props,* i.e. headband wolf ears for Max, headband monster horns, yarn hair and tails, a cardboard box boat and paper tree branches. The children will want to *dramatize* the story again and again in their own dramatic play.

**INTEGRATION**

### CLAY WILD THINGS

Modeling clay is an excellent medium for creative expression. Give each child a clump of clay to create his own wild thing. Encourage verbal interaction between the children as they describe their wild things taking shape and having a rumpus! Give each child a sentence strip beginning with his name, i.e. *Jason's wild thing* _____ . Finish each child's sentence as he dictates. Display the clay wild things and sentences in a prominent place for independent reading, perhaps standing the clay figures on a table with the print on the wall behind each figure to make a wall story.

## A WALL MURAL

Using a large piece of bulletin board paper and small paint sponges or colored chalk, create a simple forest scene illustration of **Where the Wild Things Are.** Have each child paint and cut out his own wild thing to add to the background. The individuality and variety of wild things will tell a wonderful story! Add the book title and author's name to your wall mural.

## IN MY IMAGINATION *

Lead the children in a discussion of why Mom, Max, and the animals felt as they did and how Max problem-solved by using his imagination. Brainstorm ideas about the endless things we can do in our imaginations. Give each child a large piece of drawing paper with one sentence printed on the bottom . . . *In my imagination, I can _____ .* After each child has drawn his picture, have him write his words emergently or dictate them to you. Mount the pages and make an *accordion book* titled **In My Imagination.**

## A TREEFUL OF WILD THINGS

Introduce nonfiction books about trees in your Shared Reading. Involve the children in a discussion about why children, animals and wild things like to climb trees! Then have the children paint a large, seasonal tree you have outlined in pencil on bulletin board paper. Let them create their own wild things from construction paper and a variety of materials. *Hang* the creatures on the tree. Add a *conversation bubble* coming from each wild thing's mouth, *"I like to _____ ."* Your children will be *reading the walls* during play time!

## CAPTION BOOK IDEAS *

Choose *one* of the following sentences as the title and text of a *caption book:*

My wild thing _____ .
  *(You are teaching action words!)*

My wild thing is a _____ monster.
  *(You are teaching describing words!)*

My wild thing says, "_____ ."
  *(You are teaching quotation marks!)*

As a group, brainstorm all the ways you could finish the sentence. Print the sentence at the top of each page of the caption book, perhaps duplicated in the shape of a wild thing. Each child then draws his own wild thing and writes or dictates the word(s) he has chosen to complete his sentence.

## A CIRCLE STORY

Because the story begins and ends in Max's bedroom, **Where the Wild Things Are** can be retold as a *circle story map* to add to your writing-rich environment!

**EVERYDAY LEARNING ACTIVITIES**

Positive parenting, developmental learning activities, and a warm, nurturing environment are major factors in a child's academic success and lifetime learning.

In the story, **Where the Wild Things Are**, little Max got angry when his mother disciplined him. It is natural for a child to respond in anger to discipline. However, it is a parent's job to contain the emotions of a young child. A child out of control needs a parent who is calm and in control, offering the security of consistent limits that say, "You're safe. I won't let you go too far." That doesn't mean asking a child to deny his feelings. Instead, label his feelings for him and say in a calm, matter-of-fact voice, "You are angry because . . . but the rule in our house is, there will be no hitting." You can take so much emotion out of upsets when you have simple, unbendable rules. This is not an age for wishy-washy parenting. Are you wondering about a good starting point? Why not begin with, "The rule in our house is, I will speak to you only one time when I ask you to do something." Then follow through. Parents who repeat their requests and get louder and louder until they finally yell, just train their children to not respond until they hear parents yelling. That really makes children the winners and parents the losers. There is so much less anger in a situation when parents stay in control and quietly prevent a power play. Remember, "The rule in our house is . . . ." *(parenting skill)*

- Help your child create her own Wild Thing using a paper plate for a face and scrap items such as bits of yarn, rubberbands, bottle caps, string, twist tabs, buttons, markers, etc. Give her a large paper bag for storing her Wild Thing. Since she created it, she gets to control her Wild Thing and *send* it away whenever she wants. *(dramatic play)*

- Encourage your child to *sail away* in a cardboard box or a plastic laundry basket. Ask her questions about *where* she is going, *what* she will be seeing, and *who* will be traveling with her. If you encourage your child to use her imagination now, she will be far less apprehensive later about right or wrong answers. Build both her confidence and her language ability by praising all her answers and entering into the fun yourself. *(dramatic play)*

- Ask your child to make up a story about a magazine picture or perhaps just one page in an imaginative story like **Where the Wild Things Are.** Listen carefully. Perhaps you will *hear* her own feelings as she talks. Ask just the right questions to encourage her story telling. *(feelings)*

- Help your child make his very own good night book. Simply fold some pieces of plain, white paper and on the bottom of each page write the words, "Good night _____ ." Fill in the blanks with whatever words he chooses and have him draw or cut out a picture to go with each page. Your child will love *reading* his own book every night as he says good night to the people and things that are special to him. *(words in print)*

212

# Whistle
## for
# Willie

## by Ezra Jack Keats

**TEACHING FOCUS**
- Recognizing title and author
- Left to right progression
- Identifying feelings
- Dramatic play

**SETTING THE STAGE**

Instantly singable songs and the appealing rhyme and rhythm of finger plays will encourage children to be involved in storytime.

**I'M IN THE MOOD** by Raffi, *Rise and Shine*
(An upbeat song about whistling, singing, clapping)

**CANDY MAN, SALTY DOG**
by Sharon, Lois and Bran, *One Elephant, Deux Elephants*

**FIVE LITTLE PUPPIES**

| | |
|---|---|
| Five little puppies were playing in the sun; | *(left hand up)* |
| This one saw a rabbit and he began to run. | *(bend thumb)* |
| This one saw a butterfly and he began to race; | *(bend second finger)* |
| This one saw a pussy cat and he began to chase; | *(bend third finger)* |
| This one tried to catch his tail | |
| And he went round and round. | *(bend fourth finger)* |
| This one was so quiet; he never made a sound. | *(bend little finger)* |

**MY LOOSE TOOTH**

| | |
|---|---|
| I had a loose tooth, | *(follow action as rhyme* |
| A wiggly, jiggly loose tooth. | *indicates)* |
| I had a loose tooth, hanging by a thread. | |
| So I pulled my loose tooth, | |
| This wiggly, jiggly loose tooth, | |
| And put it 'neath my pillow, | |
| And then I went to bed! | |

**FIRST READING**

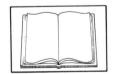

What is the boy doing on the cover of our story? Look at his pucker! Can you make your lips pucker like his? Now slowly say the word *whistle*. Did you hear a whistling sound? The word *whistle* is the first word in the title of the story. Who do you think the boy is whistling for? The dog's name is also in the title and it begins with a *W*, too. Can you guess his name? Let's read the title and the author's name together.

The first book Mr. Keats wrote about Peter and Willie was called **The Snowy Day.** Children enjoyed that book so much he decided to write another story about the little boy and his dog. In this story, **Whistle for Willie**, Peter wished he could whistle. Have you ever wished you could do something other children can do? Let's read the *title page* together.

*The uninterrupted initial reading of* **Whistle for Willie** *will immerse the children in the rich text and illustrations of the story as they anticipate the delightful ending.*

**GETTING
INVOLVED**

Let's move to the music and do all the things Peter did in the story. Whirl around on the sidewalk . . . whirl *to the left*, whirl *to the right*, whirl *faster and faster*, now *slower and slower*. Careful! You feel just like Peter did when he stopped whirling. Do you remember what Peter did next? Climb *inside* the empty carton and try to whistle. Now hold your chalk and draw a long line on the sidewalk. Go *around* the girls jumping rope and *around* the barber pole and right up to your front door. Pucker up again! Can you whistle yet? Put an old hat on your head and practice in front of the mirror. Now walk like Peter did *along* a crack in the sidewalk. Can you run away from your shadow? Jump *high*, jump *low*, jump *to the left*, jump *to the right*. Oh, Oh, here comes Willie! Scramble *under* the carton. Pucker up! Blow *up*, blow *down*, blow *to the left*, blow *to the right*. You did it! I hear your whistles and so does Willie. Here he comes! Give him a great big hug and carry him home to your mom and dad. Now whistle your way to the grocery store and whistle your way home again with the groceries.

*Another time, have the children pretend to blow up three balloons and act out the rhyme . . . "Here is a big balloon, here is a bigger balloon, here is the biggest balloon you can see. Can you help me count them? One, two, three." Direct the children to blow one balloon to the left, one to the right and one straight up in the air, blowing hard until all the balloons disappear!*

**A CLOSER LOOK**

With each rereading of a story, children gain new understanding. Pause often for a spontaneous flow of oral language as the children share their feelings and observations. Extend the learning process with your own questions in repeated readings of the story.

- Can you find the word *Whistle* on the title page? the word *Willie*? the author's name? What does *To Ann* mean? *(parts of a book)*

- How did Peter feel when he leaned against the streetlight? *(feelings)*

- Why did Peter want to learn to whistle? *(comprehension)*

- Why does it look like the lights are popping off the streetlight? *(interpretation)*

- What happened to Peter's chalk when he came to the girls' jumprope? The barber pole? *(visual detail)*

- Why did Peter pretend to be his father? *(interpretation)*

- Why couldn't Peter jump off his shadow? *(reasoning)*

- How did Peter learn to whistle? Was he proud of himself? Who else was proud? *(comprehension)*

**ROUNDING OUT
STORYTIME**

**Shadows and Reflections**   by Tana Hoban

**Leo the Late Bloomer**   by Robert Kraus

**Pulling My Leg**   by Jo Carson

**Lentil**   by Robert McCloskey

**Bear Shadow**   by Frank Asch

# Integrated Whole Language Activities

**POETRY**

### HIDE-AND-SEEK SHADOW

I walked with my shadow,
I ran with my shadow,
I danced with my shadow,
I did.
Then a cloud came over
And the sun went under
And my shadow stopped playing
And hid.

*Margaret Hillert*

### WHISTLING
by Jack Prelutsky
from *Read Aloud Rhymes for
the Very Young*
by Jack Prelutsky

**INVOLVEMENT**

### WHISTLING A TUNE

Music quickly captures a child's interest and creates a happy mood. Set the stage for rereading **Whistle for Willie** by enjoying *I'm in the Mood*, a Raffi song about whistling and singing, and *Candy Man, Salty Dog*, an engaging echo song that explores vocal sounds including whistling.

Play instrumental music with a varying beat to encourage the children to freely explore moving as Peter did, whirling, walking, running, and jumping off their shadows. Keep the music playing softly as the children sit down. Begin reading **Whistle for Willie.** Stop at just the right point to let the children interact with the text by moving as Peter did. Then begin reading again, following that pattern until Peter whistles his way to the store. The children will have choreographed their own musical version of the story.

**INTEGRATION**

### SHADOWS

- Margaret Hillert's poem, **Hide- and- Seek Shadow**, repeats all the movement of the story. The children will memorize the words quickly because of the catchy rhythm. After they have learned the text, print the words on chart paper as the children watch. Have them find the action words in the poem and highlight them with yellow marker. Ask the children how they could mark the words *shadow, cloud* and *sun* each time they appear in the text.

- Enjoy reading **Bear Shadow** by Frank Asch and Tana Hoban's fascinating **Shadows and Reflections.** Go outside on a sunny day and let the children try to catch their own shadows. Let them discover what happens to their shadows when they stand in a shaded place and when they come inside.

- Create your own bulletin board of shadows. If the children color houses and trees, have them decide where to add dark shadows. Then give each child a large piece of white construction paper to draw a colorful picture of himself. Have him tear a free-form shadow from black construction paper to attach to his own figure. The children will be walking, running and dancing with their shadows, right across your mural.

216

## WHISTLE JUST FOR FUN! *

Begin a discussion of all the reasons why people whistle by telling a story about when you heard someone whistling. When an adult tells a story, it sets the stage for children to tell stories. Begin writing on chart paper all the reasons why people whistle.

When each child has an idea to draw, give him a paper with the caption written on the bottom, *Whistle for* _____ . Have each child draw a picture of his own face and add whistling lips cut or torn from red construction paper. Finish each child's sentence as he dictates. Every fourth page print *WHISTLE JUST FOR FUN!* Have a small group of children decorate the cover with red whistling lips. Mount the pages on red construction paper and bind them into a class book for your reading center.

## SILLY WILLIES

Children look for the little dog, Willie, in Ezra Jack Keat's stories. The fact he is a daschund just adds to the appeal. With brown paint and skinny potato halves, let each child potato print Willie's long body, adding a pointed nose, dark eyes, floppy ears, short legs and a thin tail with brown or black markers. Surround the Silly Willie pictures on your wall with book covers from **The Snowy Day, Whistle for Willie**, and **Peter's Chair.**

Keep blank books available in your writing center for children to draw and write their own stories about Peter and Willie. Put a sign-up sheet by the Author's Chair for children to take turns sharing their stories with the class.

## WHAT PETER CAN DO!

As you read the story again, ask the children to listen for all the things Peter can do. List their answers on a class chart. Write the same sentences on sentence strips for children to match to the chart or sequence in a pocket chart. Keep plenty of pointers in your reading center for children who will read the chart as an independent learning center activity.

Have children copy and illustrate each sentence on large pieces of paper. Double mount the pictures and sequence them as a wall story. A bright combination of colors will draw children's eyes to the story again and again.

**EVERYDAY
LEARNING
ACTIVITIES**

Positive parenting, developmental learning activities and a warm, nurturing environment are major factors in a child's academic success and lifetime learning.

In **Whistle for Willie**, it took Willie awhile to be able to do what the older children could already do. In a child's imagination, he can do anything and become anyone he wants to be. Young children love the play world of fantasy and imagination where they can pretend to be big and powerful. Most children love a *dress-up* box of old shoes and hats and clothes. Every day they will think up something new to do or *be,* and thinking is a real part of creativity and imagination. It is so easy to increase a child's language skills when he is role-playing by asking where he is going, what tools he will need and who he will see along the way. The development of imagination also allows a child to play more by himself. Some children take comfort in imaginary friends who are always loyal, always loving, and always ready to play! *(parenting skill)*

- Expand your child's imaginary play to include the whole family. Collect props for a *prop box* to role play whatever your child or your family is interested in . . . a camping trip, a shoe store, a restaurant, a beauty salon (now who wouldn't smile at daddy with curlers in his hair?) It doesn't require many props to act out a heartwarming story like **Whistle for Willie!** *(dramatic play)*

- Look for everyday shapes and objects to sort according to size. In the kitchen, gather all kinds of spoons together and have your child sort them and place *like* sizes in piles. Use measuring spoons, soup spoons, teaspoons, serving spoons, mixing spoons and wooden spoons. Count the piles and compare sets. Teach *greater than* and *less than.* Another day, line up the spoons from smallest to largest. Teach *left and right, in the middle, next to, between, first, second* and *third. (size, directionality)*

- Be ready to play the Spoon Game more than once! Have your child count out ten spoons for you to hide anywhere in the house. The spoons should be partly visible. Set the timer on the stove and see how many spoons your child can find before the timer goes off. Beat the clock or beat the score! *(visual perception)*

- To help your child learn *left to right progression*, point out that we always read the left page of a storybook first, the right page next. (In writing, we always start at the left side of the page. Put a green dot for *go* in the left corner.) A fun way to reinforce this idea is to begin reading a well-loved book *upside down.* Your child will delight in correcting you! Then, with the book held the proper way, point to and read the *right* page first, then the *left.* Your child will recognize the mixed-up story and love the silliness! *(directionality)*

- Tape the voices of your family all taking parts reading a favorite story like **Whistle for Willie.** Play the tape in the car or as part of a bedtime routine. Use the familiar voices as a *security blanket* when someone in the family has to be away for awhile. *(family relationships)*

# Who Took
## the
# Farmer's Hat?

*by Joan L. Nodset*

**TEACHING FOCUS**

- Visual perception
- Repetitive joining-in
- Colors and shapes
- Classifying animals

**SETTING THE STAGE**

Instantly singable songs and the appealing rhyme and rhythm of finger plays will encourage children to be involved in storytime.

**DOWN ON GRANDPA'S FARM** by Raffi, *One Light, One Sun*

**GRANDMOTHER'S FARM** by Hap Palmer, *Witches Brew*

### THE FARMER'S TREE

| | |
|---|---|
| Here is the tree with leaves so green. | *(make tree with arms)* |
| Here are the apples that hang between. | *(clench fists)* |
| When the wind blows the apples fall. | *(fists fall)* |
| Here is a basket to gather them all. | *(hands make basket)* |

### SOLOMON GRUNDY

| | |
|---|---|
| Solomon Grundy, | *(raise one finger for each day of the week)* |
| Born on a Monday, | |
| Christened on Tuesday, | |
| Married on Wednesday, | |
| Took ill on Thursday, | |
| Worse on Friday, | |
| Died on Saturday, | |
| Buried on Sunday, | |
| This is the end | *(hand behind back)* |
| Of Solomon Grundy. | |

**FIRST READING**

There is a funny picture on the cover of our book today. Have you ever seen a hat walking along the grass? Who do you think is under that hat? I think it's a duck, too, because of the webbed feet. Do you have any idea who would wear a big hat like that? The answer is in the title, **Who Took The Farmer's Hat?**

What do you notice about the colors in the title? What does that squiggly mark mean after the word *Hat?* See if you can find the squiggly mark, the hat, the mouse, and the duck on the *title page*.

*Children love the predictable pattern in* **Who Took the Farmer's Hat.** *Encourage them to join in every time the farmer asks, "Did you see my old brown hat?"*

220

**GETTING INVOLVED**

Have any of you ever played the game, "Doggie, Doggie, Where's Your Bone?" Today we are going to play a game just like that only we are going to change the words and say, "Farmer, farmer, where's your hat? Somebody took it just like that!" I need a farmer to sit in this chair and I'm going to put this little hat under the chair. Now close your eyes and I'll choose a squirrel to come take the hat and hide it behind his tail! Shhh, move ever so quietly, squirrel. Don't let the farmer hear you. Everyone else say the words with me, "Farmer, farmer, where's your hat? Somebody took it just like that!" *(Let each child have a turn taking the farmer's hat. Use the animals in sequence as they appeared in the story.)*

**A CLOSER LOOK**

With each rereading of a story, children gain new understanding. Pause often for a spontaneous flow of oral language as the children share their feelings and observations. Extend the learning process with your own questions in repeated readings of the story.

- Before we open the book again, can you remember all the places the farmer looked for his hat? *(recall)*

- What animals in the pictures usually live on farms? *(classifying)*

- Did the hen like being lifted from her nest? *(interpretation)*

- Why were the words round and brown important? *(colors, shapes)*

- What did the squirrel think the farmer's hat was? The mouse? The fly? The duck? *(visual memory)*

- What moved the hat from place to place? *(comprehension)*

- Why did the farmer let the bird keep his hat? *(interpretation)*

- Did the mother bird lay more than one egg in her nest? *(association)*

- Did the story have a happy ending? Why? *(interpretation)*

**ROUNDING OUT STORYTIME**

**Gilberto and the Wind**   by Marie Hall Ets

**Chicken Little**   by Steven Kellogg

**The Wind Blew**   by Pat Hutchins

**Cock a Doodle Doo**   by Franz Brandenberg

**Old McDonald Had a Farm**   retold by Lorinda Cawley

221

# Integrated Whole Language Activities

**POETRY**

### THE MARE

Look at the mare of Farmer Giles!
She's brushing her hooves on the mat;

Look at the mare of Farmer Giles!
She's knocked on the door, rat-a-tat!

With a clack of her hoof and a wave of her head
She's tucked herself up in the four-post bed,

And she's wearing the Farmer's hat!
*by Herbert Asquith*

### THE SPRING WIND
by Charlotte Zolotow
from *Read-Aloud Rhymes for the Very Young* by Jack Prelutsky

**INVOLVEMENT**

### THE FARMER LOST HIS HAT

Play the music to the song, *The Farmer in the Dell*. First have the children walk to the rhythm; then clap to the rhythm. Next, have the children clap and sing as they play the familiar game, *The Farmer in the Dell*.

Brainstorm with the children about ways they could adapt the words of the song to the story, **Who Took the Farmer's Hat?** Their variation might be something like this, beginning with a farmer in the middle of the circle and adding one child with every verse:

> The farmer lost his hat, The farmer lost his hat,
> Heigh-ho, the derry-o, The farmer lost his hat.
>
> The farmer asked the Squirrel, The farmer asked the Squirrel,
> Heigh-ho, the derry-o, The farmer asked the Squirrel.
> *(Add verses for the Mouse, the Fly, the Goat, the Duck, and the Bird.)*
>
> The Bird found the hat; the Bird found the hat,
> Heigh-ho, the derry-o, The Bird found the hat.
> *(Sing the Bird stands alone for the final verse.)*

### THE FARMER AND HIS FRIENDS

Involve the children in a discussion of what they should include in a farmyard scene to tell the story of **Who Took the Farmer's Hat?** Pencil in a simple outline on a large piece of bulletin board paper to guide them as they paint. Then have the children paint the story characters, the farmer, and his hat on strong doubled paper. After they have cut out and stuffed the characters, staple them to the bulletin board for a colorful, three-dimensional mural. Label everything the children have painted and add the author's name and the story title. Across the bottom print the words, *The farmer had a hat, an old brown hat. Oh, how he liked that old brown hat!* You have added another fun experience with *words in print* to your room!

222

# DID YOU SEE MY OLD BROWN HAT? *

Bring an old brown hat to class. Talk about all the things that Squirrel, Mouse, Fly, Goat, Duck and Bird imagined the farmer's hat to be. As you twist and turn the hat into different shapes and positions, ask the children to describe what the hat looks like to them and where they might have found it.

Have each child tear a hat out of brown construction paper and paste it on a piece of white paper on which the words, *"Did you see my old brown hat?"* are printed on the top, and the words, *"No,"* said _____ , *"I saw a _____"* are printed on the bottom. Using crayons, markers or scraps of paper, encourage the children to turn their hats into something imaginary. Give each child the opportunity to read his sentence and talk about his picture. Then choose children to illustrate a cover, a title page, and a surprise ending to your new class book, **Did You See My Old Brown Hat?**

## HAT DAY

Send notes home on little paper hats, announcing the Hat Day when every child may wear *any* kind of a hat to class. Let the children wear the hats all day! Enjoy stories about hats such as **Jennie's Hat** by Ezra Jack Keats and **The 500 Hats of Bartholomew Cubbins** by Dr. Seuss. As each child models his hat, decide on something that makes that hat *unique*, such as, *Beth's hat has a scratchy feather.* Write a sentence about each child's hat. Model the writing process for the children as you verbalize about word spacing, punctuation, and sound-symbol relationships.

Have each child draw a picture of a friend wearing a hat. The child could copy the sentence about his friend's hat from the chart or write one of his own on his picture. (You have taught *possessives* and *adjectives* in a meaningful context!)

## THE HAT SHOPPE

Provide an endless assortment of supplies for the children to create their own original hats, i.e. paper plates, bowls and cups, feathers, felt and fabric pieces, pipe cleaners and straws, cotton, buttons, sparkles, ribbon and yarn, strawberry baskets and meat trays, crepe and tissue paper, etc. Surely you will want to show off just a little! Draw a parade route and mark the rooms and people you want to visit. Enjoy a class **Hat Parade** with you and the children wearing your original hats. Tally the compliments you received while parading!

After returning, have each child decide on a price tag for his hat. Staple the hats to your **Hat Shoppe** bulletin board, complete with price tags, names and sentences. Create a hat store in front of your bulletin board. Provide play money, a cash register, paper and pencils to write store hours, open and closed signs, receipts, a tally of sales, and a sign-up sheet for clerks and customers. Sale's on!

## HAT MATH

Graph the hats using a three-column floor graph. Let the children decide on the criteria such as Fun Hats, Fancy Hats and Work Hats. *Estimate* the circumference of each hat. Use yarn to measure. Hang the pieces of yarn vertically on a chart. Compare the lengths and arrange them from shortest to longest. *Estimate* how many cotton balls will fill the center of the smallest and largest hats. Then fill the hats. Count the cotton balls into sets of ten and compare the numbers.

Positive parenting, developmental learning activities and a warm, nurturing environment are major factors in a child's academic success and lifetime learning.

When the wind took the farmer's hat in the story, **Who Took The Farmer's Hat?**, he asked each of his animal friends the very same question, "Did you see my old brown hat?" Each animal answered by telling the farmer what it had actually seen. . . *the old brown pot* or *the old brown boat*. The animals were sharing the information they had gathered just by looking with their eyes. That's the way children learn, too, and that knowledge becomes the basis for thinking skills. This week concentrate on all that your child can learn through seeing. With a little guidance, your child can be taught to really *look and see*. Everything he notices visually will be getting him ready for the complex skill of reading where he must notice the many differences in letters and words. Try looking out the window together and naming everything you can see, both far and near. Compare what you can see at night, from the same window, with what you can see in the daytime. Sit in a favorite chair together and name everything you can see in the room. At night, in the dark, try to remember everything you saw in the daytime. Look out of the window of the car, or pretend you are looking out the window of a moving train. Whether in the park or in the schoolyard or in a store, encourage your child to observe everything, and to talk about what he sees. So much can be learned through the fun, casual experiences of everyday living! *(parenting skill)*

- Eye-hand coordination is essential to a child's fine motor development. The fingers are one of the last areas of the body to develop. Give a child many, many opportunities to cut and paste. Teach her to paste around the outside of things, which is a *tracking* skill in itself. Just putting a blob of paste in the middle of something doesn't give much practice in developing the skill. Give her paper or old catalogs to simply cut, cut, cut, which is another *tracking* skill. *(eye-hand coordination)*

- Another effective activity to strengthen finger muscles and develop coordination is to give a child spring-type clothespins to pinch open and put around the top of a container or a coffee can. Give her some objects, like fat uncooked beans, to pick up with the snapping motion of the clothespin and drop inside the container. When the game is over, everything can go inside the coffee can for a fast clean-up, waiting for the next time. *(fine motor skills)*

- The grocery store is an excellent place to reinforce many learning concepts. Look at a can of beans. What shape is the lid? Hold a pineapple. Does it feel rough or smooth? What size container of milk should we buy? Show me the largest box of laundry powder. Find a fruit that is yellow. Point to a box that is a square. Questions like these can keep your child occupied while he learns to really look and see. *(visual perception)*

- To encourage independence, your child should be making some choices and dressing herself. She should be able to take care of all her own personal needs . . . the bathroom, blowing her nose, and washing her hands. If putting on her own shoes is a problem, paint a happy face on her right big toe with some bright nail polish. Then paint a similar face on the inside of her right shoe! *(left and right)*

*10 Bears in My Bed* by Stan Mack, 1974 Pantheon, 191, 193.

*500 Hats of Bartholomew Cubbins, The* by Dr. Seuss, 1938 Vanguard, 223.

*A Chair for My Mother,* by Vera B. Williams, 1982, Greenwillow, 119

*A Children's Zoo* by Tana Hoban, 1985 Greenwillow, 29

*A Firefly Named Torchy* by Bernard Waber, 1970 Houghton Mifflin, 77

*A House is a House for Me* by Mary Ann Hoberman, 1978 Viking, 169

*A is For Angry: An Animal & Adjective Alphabet* by Sandra Boynton, 1987 Workman, 143

*A Three Hat Day* by Laura Geringer, 1985 Harper & Row, 37

*A Treeful of Pigs* by Arnold Lobel, 1979 Greenwillow, 101

*A, My Name is Alice* by Jane E. Bayer, 1984 Dial, 41

*Aardvarks, Disembark!* by Ann Jonas, 1990 Greenwillow, 131

*Across the Stream* by Mirra Ginsburg, 1982 Greenwillow, 65, 83

*Albert's Toothache* by Barbara Williams, 1974 Dutton, 17

*Alexander and the Wind Up Mouse* by Leo Lionni, 89

*Alison's Zinnia* by Anita Lobel, 1990 Greenwillow, 143

*All Aboard ABC* by Doug Magee, Robert Newman, 1990 Dutton, 41

*All About Farm Animals* by Brenda Cook, 1989 Doubleday, 31

*Alphabatics* by Suse MacDonald, 1986 Bradbury Press, 41, 43

*Alphabet Tale, The* by Jan Garten, 1964 Random House, 41

*And Rain Makes Applesauce* by Julian Scheer, Holiday House, 149

*Animal Capers* by Kerry Argent, 1986 Dial, 143

*Animals in Winter* by Susanne Riha, 1989 Carolrhoda, 25

*Animals Large and Small* by Annette Tison and Talus Taylor, 85

*Anno's Counting Book* by Mitsumasa Anno, 1975 Crowell, 197, 199

*Another Mouse to Feed* by Robert Kraus, 1980 Simon & Schuster, 101

*Are You There, Bear?* by Ron Maris, 1984 Greenwillow, 47

*Backyard Insects* by Millicent E. Selsam, 1981 Four Winds, 205

*Barn Dance* by Bill Martin, Jr. and J. Archambault, 1986 Rand, 35

*Bear Shadow* by Frank Asch, 1984 Prentice-Hall, 215, 216

*Bear's Toothache, The* by David McPhail, 1972 Little, Brown, 11

*Benjamin's Barn* by Reeve Lindbergh, 1990 Dial, 65

*Better Not Get Wet, Jesse Bear* by Nancy White Carlstrom, 1988 Macmillan, 149

*Biggest Bear, The* by Lynd Ward, 1952 Houghton Mifflin, 23

*Biggest House in the World, The* by Leo Lionni, 1968 Pantheon, 203

*Box with Red Wheels, The* by Maud Petersham, 1949 Macmillan, 65

*Bravo, Ernest and Celestine* by Gabrielle Vincent, 1982 Greenwillow, 95

*But Where is the Green Parrot?* by Thomas Zacharias, 1968 Delacorte, 29

*Bye Bye Baby* by Janet and Allan Ahlberg, 1989 Little, Broown, 167

*Can I Keep Him?* by Steven Kellogg, 1971 Dial, 113

*Charlie the Caterpillar* by Dom Deluise, 1990 Simon & Schuster, 203

*Chicken Book, The* by Garth Williams, 1970 Delacorte, 65

*Chicken Little* by Steven Kellogg, 1985 Morrow, 221

*Chickens Aren't the Only Ones* by Ruth Heller, 1981 Grosset, 67

*Choo Choo* by Virginia Lee Burton, 1937 Houghton Mifflin, 53

*Clyde Monster* by Robert Crowe, 1976 Dutton, 209

*Cock a Doodle Doo* by Franz Brandenberg, 1986 Greenwillow, 221

*Color Farm* by Lois Ehlert, 1990 Lippincott, 65

*Color Zoo* by Lois Ehlert, 1989 Lippincott, 29

*Come a Tide* by G.E. Lyon, 1990 Orchard, 131

*Cookie's Week* by Cindy Ward, 1989 G.P. Dutnam's Sons, 113

*Curious George* by H.A. Rey, 1941 Houghton Mifflin, 35

*day the goose got loose, the* by Reeve Lindberg, 1990 Dial, 137

*Deep in the Forest* by Brinton Turkle, 1976 Dutton, 49

*Do You Know What I'll Do?* by Charlotte Zolotow, 1958 Harper & Row, 155

*Do You Want to be My Friend?* by Eric Carle, 1987 Harper & Row, 113

*Doorbell Rang, The* by Pat Hutchins, 1986 Greenwillow, 95

*Down By The Bay* by Raffi, 1987 Crown, 173

*Ducks Fly* by Lydia Dabcovich, 1990 Dutton, 107, 109

*Elbert's Bad Word* by Audrey Wood, 1988 Harcourt, 209

*Elizabeth and Larry* by Marilyn Sadler, 1990 Simon & Schuster, 115

*Ernest and Celestine* by Gabrielle Vincent, 1982 Greenwillow, 115

*Ernest and Celestine's Picnic* by Gabrielle Vincent, 1982 Greenwillow, 47, 149

*Even That Moose Won't Listen to Me* by Martha Alexander, 1987 Dial, 185

*Fat Mouse* by Harry Stevens, 1987 Viking, 89

*Feathers for Lunch* by Lois Ehlert, 1990 Harcourt, 119

*Feel the Wind* by Arthur Dorros, 1989 Crowell, 19

*Fish Eyes: A Book You Can Count On* by Lois Ehlert, 1990 Harcourt, 83

*Five Little Monkeys Jumping on the Bed* by Eileen Christelow, 1989 Clarion, 125

*Flossie and the Fox* by Patricia McKissack, 1986 Dial, 161

*Follow Me Cried Bee* by Jan Wahl, 1976 Crown, 131

*Follow the River* by Lydia Dabcovich, 1980 Dutton, 107, 109

*Fox Went Out on a Chilly Night, The* by Peter Spier, 1961 Doubleday, 161

*From Egg to Butterfly* by Marlene Reidel, 1974 Carolrhoda, 205

*From Grain to Bread* by Ali Mitgutsch, 1981 Carolrhoda, 103

*From Letter to Letter* by Teri Sloat, 1989 Dutton, 143

*Giant Jam Sandwich, The* by John Vernon Lord, 1972 Houghton Mifflin, 95

*Gilberto and the Wind* by Marie Hall Ets, 1963 Viking, 221, 223

*Goat's Trail* by Brian Wildsmith, 1986 Knopf, 197

*Good Morning, Granny Rose* by Warren Ludwig, 1990 Putnam, 23

*Gorilla* by Anthony Browne, 1983 F. Watts, 191

*Growing Vegetable Soup* by Lois Ehlert, 1987 Harper, 187

*Guinea Pig ABC, The* by Kate Duke, 1983 Dutton, 143

*Guinea Pigs Far and Near* by Kate Duke, 1984 Dutton, 161

*Happy Birthday, Moon* by Frank Asch, 1982 Prentice-Hall, 119

*Happy Birthday, Sam* by Pat Hutchins, 1978 Greenwillow, 155

*Hattie and the Fox* by Mem Fox, 1988 Bradbury, 161

*Have You Seen the Crocodile?* by Colin West, 1986 Lippincott, 47

*Henny Penny* by Paul Galdone, 1968 Clarion, 59

*Henrietta's First Winter* by Rob Lewis, 1990 Farar, Straus, 181

*Hey! Get Off Our Train* by John Burningham, 1989 Crown, 53, 55

*House That Jack Built, The* by Paul Galdone, 1961 McGraw Hill, 125

*How Do Bears Sleep?* by B. J. Bird, 1990 Carolrhoda, 25

*Hunter and his Dog* by Brian Wildsmith, 1979 University, 137

*Hunter and the Animals, The* by Tomie dePaola, 1981 Holiday House, 137

*Hush Little Baby* by Aliki, 1968 Prentice-Hall, 71

*I Know An Old Lady* by Nadine Bernard Westcott, 1980 Little, Brown, 173

*I Was Walking Down the Road* by Sarah Barchas, 1975 Scholastic, 137

*I Went Walking* by Sue Williams, 1990 Harcourt, 29

*I Will Not Go To Market Today* by Harry Allard, 1979 Dial, 101

*Imagine* by Alison Lester, 1990 Houghton Mifflin, 31

*Important Book, The* by Margaret Wise Brown, 157

*In the Forest* by Marie Hall Ets, 1944 Viking, 11, 49

*In the Pond* by Ermanno Cristini, 1984 London, 31

*Is Your Mama A Llama?* by Deborah Guarino, 1989 Scholastic, 113

*Jacket I Wear in the Snow, The* by Shirley Neitzel, 1989 Greenwillow, 179

*Jamberry* by Bruce Degan, 1985 Harper, 23, 25

*Jennie's Hat* by Ezra Jack Keats, 1966 Harper & Row, 223

*Jiggle Wiggle Prance* by Sally Noll, 1987 Greenwillow, 11

*Jump, Frog, Jump!* by Robert Kalan, 1981 Greenwillow, 83

*Junglewalk* by Nancy Tafuri, 1988 Greenwillow, 31

*Katy and the Big Snow* by Virginia Lee Burton, 1943 Houghton Mifflin, 179

*Keeping Quilt, The* by Patricia Polacco, 1988 Simon & Schuster, 19

*Kids Are Baby Goats* by Janet Chiefari, 1984 Dodd Mead, 199

*King Rooster, Queen Hen* by Anita Lobel, 1975 Greenwillow, 59

*Lady with the Alligator Purse, The* by Nadine Bernard Westcott, 1988 Joystreet, 173

*Ladybug, Ladybug* by Ruth Brown, 1988 Dutton, 77

*Lentil* by Robert McCloskey, 1940 Viking, 215

*Leo the Late Bloomer* by Robert Kraus, 1971 Crowell, 215

*Let's Look at Bears* by Malcolm Penny, 1989 Bookwright, 25

*Let's Look at Rain* by Jacqueline Dineen, 151

*Little Bo Peep* by Paul Galdone, 1986 Houghton Mifflin, 47

*Little Penguin's Tale* by Audrey Wood, 1990 Harcourt, 185

*Little Red Riding Hood* by Beatrice Schenk deRegniers, 1972 Atheneum, 49

*Little Red Riding Hood* by James Marshall, 1987 Dial, 49

*Little Red Riding Hood* by Trina Schart Hyman, 1983 Holiday House, 49

*Lost!* by David McPhail, 1990 Little, Brown, 23

*Maggie and the Pirates* by Ezra Jack Keats, 1979 Scholastic, 115

*Magic Schoolbus at the Waterworks, The* by Joanna Cole, 1986 Scholastic, 149

*Many Luscious Lollipops; A Book About Adjectives* by Ruth Heller, 1989 Grossett & Dunlop, 125

*Marvelous Mud Washing Machine* by Patty Wolcott, 1974 Addision Wesley, 151

*Mary Wore Her Red Dress* by Merle Peek, 1985 Clarion, 119

*Midnight Farm, The* by Reeve Lindbergh, 1987 Dial, 191

*Midnight Snowman* by Caroline Feller Bauer, 1987 Atheneum, 181

*Mike's Kite* by Elizabeth MacDonald, 1990 Robert Kendall, 59

*Millions of Cats* by Wanda Gag, 1928 Coward McCann, 77

*Miss Poppy and the Honey Cake* by Elizabeth MacDonald, 1989 Claire Smith, 101

*Mitten, The* adapted by Jan Brett, 1989 Putnam, 139, 179

*Mixed-Up Chameleon, The* by Eric Carle, 1975 Scholastic, 29

*Monkey and the Crocodile, The* Paul Galdone, 1969 Seabury Press, 35

*Moongame* by Frank Asch, 1984 Prentice Hall, 71

*Mr. Gumpy's Outing* by John Burningham, 1970 Holt, 131

*Mrs. Huggins and Her Hen Hannah* by Lydia Dabcovich, 1985 Dutton, 115

*Mud for Sale* by Brenda Nelson, 1984 Houghton Mifflin, 151

*Mudpies* by Judith Grey, 1981 Troll, 151

*Mushroom In the Rain* by Mirra Ginsburg, 1974 Macmillan, 149, 151

*My Ladybug* by Herbert Wong, 1969 Addison, 79

*Nicolas, where have you been?* by Leo Lionni, 1987 Knopf, 89

*No Jumping on the Bed* by Ted Arnold, 1987 Dial, 125

*Noisy Nora* by Rosemary Wells, 1973 Dial, 167

*Oh, Were They Ever Happy!* by Peter Spier, 1978 Doubleday, 131

*Old McDonald Had a Farm* by Robert Quackenbush, 1972 Lippincott, 221

*Old Mother Hubbard* by Lisa Amorosa, 1987 Knopf, 47

*One Bear All Alone* by Caroline Bucknall, 1985 Dial, 193

*one bright Monday morning* by Arline and Joseph Baum, 1962 Random House, 203

*One Fine Day* by Nonny Hogrogian, 1971 Macmillan, 59

*One Hungry Monster: A Counting Book in Rhyme* by Susan O'Keefe, Little, Brown, 209

*Our Snowman* by M.B. Goffstein, 1986 Harper & Row, 181

*Over in the Meadow* by Ezra Jack Keats, 1971 Scholastic, 197

*Over in the Meadow* by Olive A. Wadsworth, 193

*Owl Moon* by Jane Yolen, 1987 Philomel, 71

*Pancakes for Breakfast* by Tomie dePaola, 1978 Holiday House, 101

*Peanut Butter and Jelly* by Nadine Bernard Westcott, 1987 Dutton, 23

*Pig Pig Grows Up* by David McPhail, 1980 Dutton, 155

*Planting A Rainbow* by Lois Ehlert, 1988 Harcourt, 119, 169

*Polar Bear, Polar Bear, What Do You Hear?* by Bill Martin, Jr., 1991 Holt, 41

*Pulling My Leg* by Jo Carson, 1990 Orchard Books, 215

*Q is for Duck* by Mary Elting, 1980 Houghton, 17

*Quack! Said the Billy Goat* by Charles Causley, 1986 Lippincott, 197

*Quilt Story, The* by Tony Johnston, 1985 Putnam, 17, 19

*Quilt, The* Ann Jonas, 1984 Greenwillow, 17, 19

*Rabbit Seeds* by Bijou LeTord, 1984 Four Winds, 187

*Rain Talk* by Mary Serfozo, 1990 McElderry, 149, 151

*Reason For A Flower, The* by Ruth Heller, 1983 Scholastic, 169

*Right Number of Elephants, The* by Jeff Sheppard, 1990 Harper & Row, 191

*Roll Over* by Mordicai Gerstein, 1984 Crown, 193

*Roll Over! A Counting Song* by Merle Peek, 1981 Houghton Mifflin, 193

*Rooster's Off to See the World* by Eric Carle, 1972 Scholastic, 203

*School Picnic, The* by Jan Steffy, 49

*Seven Little Rabbits* by John Becker, 1973 Walker, 185

*Shadows and Reflections* by Tana Hoban, 1990 Greenwillow, 216

*Sheep in a Jeep* by Nancy Shaw, 1986 Houghton Mifflin, 137

*Six Little Ducks* by Chris Conover, 1976 Crowell, 83

*Sloppy Kisses* by Elizabeth Winthrop, 1980 Collier, 17

*Snow* by Isao Sasaki, 1980 Viking, 181

*Snow is Falling* by Franklyn M. Branley, 1986 Crowell, 181

*Snowman Who Went For A Walk, The* by Mira Lobe, 1984 Morrow, 181

*Snowman, The* by Raymond Briggs, 1986 Random House, 181

*Something is Going to Happen* by Charlotte Zolotow, 1988 Harper & Row, 17

*Squawk to the Moon, Little Goose* by Edna Preston, 1974 Viking, 71

*Story of Ping, The* by Marjorie Flack, 1933 Viking, 83

*Surprise Party, The* by Pat Hutchins, 1969 Macmillan, 11

*Sylvester and the Magic Pebble* by William Steig, 1969 Windmill, 167

*Teddy Bears' Picnic, The* by Jimmy Kennedy, 1983 Green Tiger, 49, 175

*Teeny Tiny* by Jill Bennett, 1986 Putnam, 125

*Ten Little Animals* by Laura Jane Coats, 1990 Macmillan, 193

*Ten Little Mice* by Joyce Dunbar, 1990 Harcourt, 191, 193

*There's A Hole in the Bucket* by Nadine Bernard Westcott, 1990 Harper & Row, 173

*There's A Nightmare in My Closet* by Mercer Mayer, 1968 Dial, 209

*There's An Alligator Under My Bed* by Mercer Mayer, 1987 Dial, 209

*Three Bears, The* by Paul Galdone, 1972 Seabury Press, 47

*Three Blind Mice* by John W. Ivimey, 1987 Clarion, 61

*Three by the Sea* by James Marshall, 1981 Dial, 197

*Three Ducks Went Wandering* by Ron Roy, 1979 Seabury, 107

*Three Jovial Huntsmen* by Susan Jeffers, 1973 Bradbury, 139

*Time To . . .* by Bruce McMillan, 1989 Lee & Shepard, 77

*Tiny Seed, The* by Eric Carle, 1987 Scholastic, 169

*Train, The* by David McPhail, 1977 Little, Brown, 53

*Trains* by Anne Rockwell, 1988 Dutton, 55

*Trouble With Elephants, The* by Chris Riddell, 1988 Lippincott, 113

*Turtle and the Monkey, The* by Paul Galdone, 1982 Clarion, 35

*Two Bad Ants* by Chris Van Allsburg, 1988 Houghton Mifflin, 185

*Very Quiet Cricket, The* by Eric Carle, 1990 Philomel, 77

*Watch Where You Go* by Sally Noll, 1990 Greenwillow, 163

*Water* by Su Swallow, 1990 Watts, 169

*We're Going On A Bear Hunt* by Michael Rosen, 1989 McElderry, 54, 97

*What Comes in 2's, 3's, & 4;s?* by Suzanne Aker, 1990 Simon & Schuster, 203

*What Do You Do At A Petting Zoo?* by Hana Machotka, 1990 Morrow, 115

*What Do You Do with a Kangaroo?* by Mercer Mayer 1973 Scholastic, 35

*What Game Shall We Play?* by Pat Hutchins, 1990 Greenwillow, 167

*When We Went to the Zoo* by Jan Ormerod, 31

*When Winter Comes* by Russell Freedman, 1981 Dutton, 181

*Where Does the Sun Go At Night* by Mirra Ginsburg, 1981 Greenwillow, 71

*Where Are You Going, Little Mouse?* by Robert Kraus, 1986 Greenwillow, 95, 167

*Where Does the Sun Go At Night?* by Mirra Ginsburg, 1981 Greenwillow, 71

*Who is the Beast?* by Keith Baker, 1990 Harcourt, 11

*Who Sank the Boat?* by Pamela Allen, 1982 Coward McCann, 83

*Who Uses This?* by Margaret Miller, 1990 Greenwillow, 187

*Whose Hat?* by Margaret Miller, 1988 Greenwillow, 37

*Whose mouse are you?* by Robert Kraus, 1970 Macmillan, 155

*Wildlife 1-2-3: A Nature Counting Book, The* by Jan Thornhill, 1989 Simon & Schuster, 107

*William's Doll* by Charlotte Zolotow, 1972 Harper & Row, 155

*Wind Blew, The* by Pat Hutchins, 1974 Macmillan, 221, 223

*Z was Zapped, The* by Chris Van Allsburg, 1987 Houghton Mifflin, 41

## PEAK WITH BOOKS

*Ask Mr. Bear* by Marjorie Flack, 1932 Macmillan, 9

*Bedtime for Frances* by Russell Hoban, 1960 Harper & Row, 15

*Blueberries for Sal* by Robert McCloskey, 1948 Penguin, 21

*Brown Bear, Brown Bear, What Do You See?* by Bill Martin, Jr., 1971 Holt, 27

*Caps for Sale* by Esphyr Slobodkina, 1940 Addision Wesley, 33

*Chicka Chicka Boom Boom* by Bill Martin, Jr. & John Archambault, 1989 Simon & Schuster, 39

*Each Peach Pear Plum* by Janet & Allan Ahlberg, 1978 Penquin, 45

*Freight Train* by Donald Crews, 1978 Puffin, 51

*Gingerbread Boy, The* by Paul Galdone, 1975 Clarion, 57

*Good Morning, Chick* by Mirra Ginsburg, 1980 Mulberry, 63

*Goodnight Moon* by Margaret Wise Brown, 1947 Harper & Row, 69

*Grouchy Ladybug, The* by Eric Carle, 1977 Harper & Row, 75

*Have You Seen My Duckling?* by Nancy Tafuri, 1984 Penquin, 81

*If You Give A Mouse A Cookie* by Laura Joffe Numeroff, 1985 Harper & Row, 87

*Little Mouse, The Red Ripe Strawberry, and THE BIG HUNGRY BEAR, The* by Don & Audrey Wood, 1984 Child's Play, 93

*Little Red Hen, The* by Paul Galdone, 1973 Clarion, 99

*Make Way for Ducklings* by Robert McCloskey, 1941 Penguin, 105

*May I Bring A Friend?* by Beatrice Schenk de Regniers, 1964 Alladan, 111

*Mr. Rabbit and the Lovely Present* by Charlotte Zolotow, 1962 Harper & Row, 117

*Napping House, The* by Audrey Wood, 1984 Harcourt, 123

*Noah's Ark* by Peter Spier, 1977 Doubleday, 129

*Oh, A-Hunting We Will Go* by John Langstaff, 1974 Macmillan, 135

*On Market Street* by Arnold Lobel, 1981, Greenwillow, 141

*Peter Spier's Rain* by Peter Spier, 1982 Doubleday, 147

*Peter's Chair* by Ezra Jack Keats, 1967 Harper & Row, 153, 217

*Rosie's Walk* Pat Hutchins, 1968 Macmillan, 159

*Runaway Bunny, The* by Margaret Wise Brown, 1942 Harper & Row, 165

*Skip to My Lou* by Nadine Bernard Westcott, 1989 Little, Brown, 171

*Snowy Day, The* by Ezra Jack Keats, 1962 Penguin, 177, 217

*Tale of Peter Rabbit, The* by Beatrix Potter, 1893 London, 1986 Scholastic, 183

*Ten, Nine, Eight* by Molly Bang, 1983 Penguin, 189

*Three Billy Goats Gruff, The* by Paul Galdone, 1973 Clarion, 195

*Very Hungry Caterpillar, The* by Eric Carle, 1969 Collins World, 201

*Where the Wild Things Are* by Maurice Sendak, 1963 Harper Collins, 207

*Whistle for Willie* by Ezra Jack Keats, 1964 Viking, 213

*Who Took the Farmer's Hat?* Joan L. Nodset, 1963 Harper & Row, 219

# Index of Songs

# Index of Finger Plays

# ✿ Index of Poetry ✿

## POETRY BIBLIOGRAPHY

*Read-Aloud Rhymes for the Very Young* by Jack Prelutsky, Knopf 1986
*Merry-Go-Round Book, The* by Nancy Larrick, Delacorte 1989
*A New Treasury of Children's Poetry* by Joanna Cole, Doubleday 1984
*The New Kid on the Block* by Jack Prelutsky, Greenwillow 1984

*The Random House Book of Poetry for Children* by Jack Prelutsky, Random House 1983
*Sing a Song of Popcorn* by Beatrice Schenk de Regniers, Scholastic 1988
*Side by Side* by Lee Bennett Hopkins, Simon and Schuster 1988
*Cyndy Szekeres' Book of Poems* by Cyndy Szekeres, Western 1981, 1987

## DISCOGRAPHY

RAFFI: A&M Records, Inc., POB 118, Hollywood, CA 90028; Baby Beluga (SL-0210), Corner Grocery Store, Everything Grows, More Singable Songs for the Very Young (SL-0204), One Light, One Sun (SL-0228), Rise and Shine (SL-0223), Singable Songs for the Very Young (SL-0202)

SHARON, LOIS & BRAM: Elephant Records, POB 101, Station Z, Canada, M5N 2Z3; Elephant Show Record (LFN 8613), In the Schoolyard (LFN 8105), Mainly Mother Goose (LFN 8409-A), One Elephant, Deux Elephants (LFN 7801), Sing A-Z (25651-0310-2), Singin' and Swingin' (LFN 8004), Smorgasbord (LFN 7902), Stay Tuned (EF 0306)

GREG AND STEVE: Youngheart Records, POB 27784, Los Angeles, CA 90027; Kidding Around (YR-007R), On the Move (YR-005R), We All Live Together, Vol. 1-4; Vol 1 - (YMES-0001), Vol 2 - (YMES-0002), Vol 3 (YMES-0003), Vol 4 -(YMES-0004)

ROSENSHONTZ: RS Records, Box 651, Brattleboro, VT 05301; Share It (WRCI-2418)

HAP PALMER: Educational Activities, Box 392, Freeport, NY 11520; Backwards Land (HP100), Folk Song Carnival (AR 524), Getting to Know Myself, Patriotic and Morning Time Songs (AR 519), Simplified Folk Songs, Walter the Waltzing Worm (AR 555), Witches Brew (AR 576)

# Laboratory Safety: General Guidelines

1. Notify your instructor immediately if you are pregnant, color blind, allergic to any insects or chemicals, taking immunosuppressive drugs, or have any other medical condition (such as diabetes, immunologic defect) that may require special precautionary measures in the laboratory.

2. Upon entering the laboratory, place all books, coats, purses, backpacks, etc. in designated areas, not on the bench tops.

3. Locate and, when appropriate, learn to use exits, fire extinguisher, fire blanket, chemical shower, eyewash, first aid kit, broken glass container, and cleanup materials for spills.

4. In case of fire, evacuate the room and assemble outside the building.

5. Do not eat, drink, smoke, or apply cosmetics in the laboratory.

6. Confine long hair, loose clothing, and dangling jewelry.

7. Wear shoes at all times in the laboratory.

8. Cover any cuts or scrapes with a sterile, waterproof bandage before attending lab.

9. Wear eye protection when working with chemicals.

10. Never pipet by mouth. Use mechanical pipeting devices.

11. Wash skin immediately and thoroughly if contaminated by chemicals or microorganisms.

12. Do not perform unauthorized experiments.

13. Do not use equipment without instruction.

14. Report all spills and accidents to your instructor immediately.

15. Never leave heat sources unattended.

16. When using hot plates, note that there is no visible sign that they are hot (such as a red glow). Always assume that hot plates are hot.

17. Use an appropriate apparatus when handling hot glassware.

18. Keep chemicals away from direct heat or sunlight.

19. Keep containers of alcohol, acetone, and other flammable liquids away from flames.

20. Do not allow any liquid to come into contact with electrical cords. Handle electrical connectors with dry hands. Do not attempt to disconnect electrical equipment that crackles, snaps, or smokes.

21. Upon completion of laboratory exercises, place all materials in the disposal areas designated by your instructor.

22. Do not pick up broken glassware with your hands. Use a broom and dustpan and discard the glass in designated glass waste containers; never discard with paper waste.

23. Wear disposable gloves when working with blood, other body fluids, or mucous membranes. Change gloves after possible contamination and wash hands immediately after gloves are removed.

24. The disposal symbol indicates that items that may have come in contact with body fluids should be placed in your lab's designated container. It also refers to liquid wastes that should not be poured down the drain into the sewage system.

25. Leave the laboratory clean and organized for the next student.

26. Wash your hands with liquid or powdered soap prior to leaving the laboratory.

27. The biohazard symbol indicates procedures that may pose health concerns.

The caution symbol points out instruments, substances, and procedures that require special attention to safety. These symbols appear throughout this manual.

# Measurement Conversions

| Metric to American Standard | American Standard to Metric |
|---|---|

### Length

| | |
|---|---|
| 1 mm = 0.039 inches | 1 inch = 2.54 cm |
| 1 cm = 0.394 inches | 1 foot = 0.305 m |
| 1 m = 3.28 feet | 1 yard = 0.914 m |
| 1 m = 1.09 yards | 1 mile = 1.61 km |

### Volume

| | |
|---|---|
| 1 mL = 0.0338 fluid ounces | 1 fluid ounce = 29.6 mL |
| 1 L = 4.23 cups | 1 cup = 237 mL |
| 1 L = 2.11 pints | 1 pint = 0.474 L |
| 1 L = 1.06 quarts | 1 quart = 0.947 L |
| 1 L = 0.264 gallons | 1 gallon = 3.79 L |

### Mass

| | |
|---|---|
| 1 mg = 0.0000353 ounces | 1 ounce = 28.3 g |
| 1 g = 0.0353 ounces | 1 pound = 0.454 kg |
| 1 kg = 2.21 pounds | |

### Temperature

To convert temperature:

$$°C = \frac{5}{9}(F - 32) \qquad °F = \frac{9}{5} + 32$$

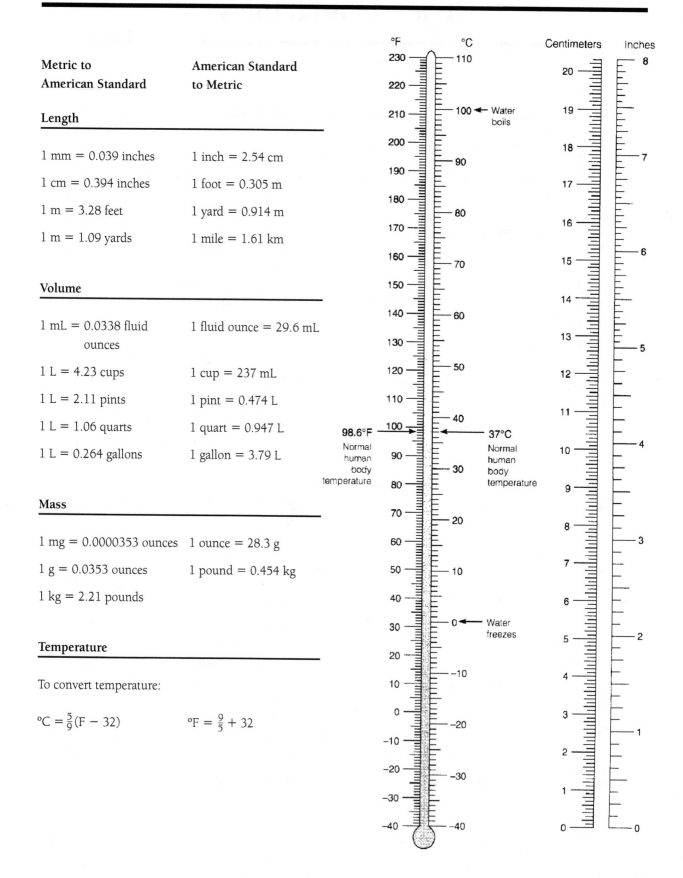

# Table of Contents

# The Language of Anatomy

**MATERIALS**

- ☐ Human torso model (dissectible)
- ☐ Human skeleton
- ☐ Demonstration: sectioned and labeled kidneys [three separate kidneys uncut or cut so that (a) entire, (b) transverse sectional, and (c) longitudinal sectional views are visible]
- ☐ Gelatin-spaghetti molds
- ☐ Scalpel

**OBJECTIVES**

1. Describe the anatomical position, and explain its importance.
2. Use proper anatomical terminology to describe body regions, orientation and direction, and body planes.
3. Name the body cavities and indicate the important organs in each.
4. Name and describe the serous membranes of the ventral body cavities.
5. Identify the abdominopelvic quadrants and regions on a torso model or image.

**PRE-LAB QUIZ**

1. Circle True or False. In anatomical position, the body is lying down.
2. Circle the correct underlined term. With regard to surface anatomy, abdominal / axial refers to the structures along the center line of the body.
3. The term *superficial* refers to a structure that is:
   a. attached near the trunk of the body
   b. toward or at the body surface
   c. toward the head
   d. toward the midline
4. The _____ plane runs longitudinally and divides the body into right and left sides.
   a. frontal        c. transverse
   b. sagittal       d. ventral
5. Circle the correct underlined terms. The dorsal body cavity can be divided into the cranial / thoracic cavity, which contains the brain, and the sural / vertebral cavity, which contains the spinal cord.

M ost of us are naturally curious about our bodies. This fact is demonstrated by infants, who are fascinated with their own waving hands or their mother's nose. Unlike the infant, however, the student of anatomy must learn to observe and identify the dissectible body structures formally.

A student new to any science is often overwhelmed at first by jargon used in that subject. The study of anatomy is no exception. But without this specialized terminology, confusion is inevitable. For example, what do *over, on top of, superficial to, above,* and *behind* mean in reference to the human body? Anatomists have an accepted set of reference terms that are universally understood. These allow body structures to be located and identified precisely with a minimum of words.

This exercise presents some of the most important anatomical terminology used to describe the body and introduces you to basic concepts of **gross anatomy,** the study of body structures visible to the naked eye.

From Exercise 1 of *Human Anatomy & Physiology Laboratory Manual,* Main Version, Tenth Edition. Elaine N. Marieb, Susan J. Mitchell, Lori A. Smith. Copyright © 2014 by Pearson Education, Inc. All rights reserved.

## Anatomical Position

When anatomists or doctors refer to specific areas of the human body, the picture they keep in mind is a universally accepted standard position called the **anatomical position.** It is essential to understand this position because much of the body terminology used in this text refers to this body positioning, regardless of the position the body happens to be in. In the anatomical position the human body is erect, with the feet only slightly apart, head and toes pointed forward, and arms hanging at the sides with palms facing forward **(Figure 1a).**

☐ Assume the anatomical position, and notice that it is not particularly comfortable. The hands are held unnaturally forward rather than hanging with palms toward the thighs.

Check the box when you have completed this task.

## Surface Anatomy

Body surfaces provide a wealth of visible landmarks for study. There are two major divisions of the body:

**Axial:** Relating to head, neck, and trunk, the axis of the body

**Appendicular:** Relating to limbs and their attachments to the axis

### Anterior Body Landmarks

Note the following regions (Figure 1a):

**Abdominal:** Anterior body trunk region inferior to the ribs

**Acromial:** Point of the shoulder

**Antebrachial:** Forearm

**Antecubital:** Anterior surface of the elbow

**Axillary:** Armpit

**Brachial:** Arm

**Buccal:** Cheek

**Carpal:** Wrist

**Cephalic:** Head

**Cervical:** Neck region

**Coxal:** Hip

**Crural:** Leg

**Digital:** Fingers or toes

**Femoral:** Thigh

**Fibular (peroneal):** Side of the leg

**Frontal:** Forehead

**Hallux:** Great toe

**Inguinal:** Groin area

**Mammary:** Breast region

**Manus:** Hand

**Mental:** Chin

**Nasal:** Nose

**Oral:** Mouth

**Orbital:** Bony eye socket (orbit)

**Palmar:** Palm of the hand

**Patellar:** Anterior knee (kneecap) region

**Pedal:** Foot

**Pelvic:** Pelvis region

**Pollex:** Thumb

**Pubic:** Genital region

**Sternal:** Region of the breastbone

**Tarsal:** Ankle

**Thoracic:** Chest

**Umbilical:** Navel

## Posterior Body Landmarks

Note the following body surface regions (Figure 1b):

**Acromial:** Point of the shoulder

**Brachial:** Arm

**Calcaneal:** Heel of the foot

**Cephalic:** Head

**Dorsum:** Back

**Femoral:** Thigh

**Gluteal:** Buttocks or rump

**Lumbar:** Area of the back between the ribs and hips; the ioin

**Manus:** Hand

**Occipital:** Posterior aspect of the head or base of the skull

**Olecranal:** Posterior aspect of the elbow

**Otic:** Ear

**Pedal:** Foot

**Perineal:** Region between the anus and external genitalia

**Plantar:** Sole of the foot

**Popliteal:** Back of the knee

**Sacral:** Region between the hips (overlying the sacrum)

**Scapular:** Scapula or shoulder blade area

**Sural:** Calf or posterior surface of the leg

**Vertebral:** Area of the spinal column

**ACTIVITY 1**

### Locating Body Regions

Locate the anterior and posterior body landmarks on yourself, your lab partner, and a human torso model before continuing. ■

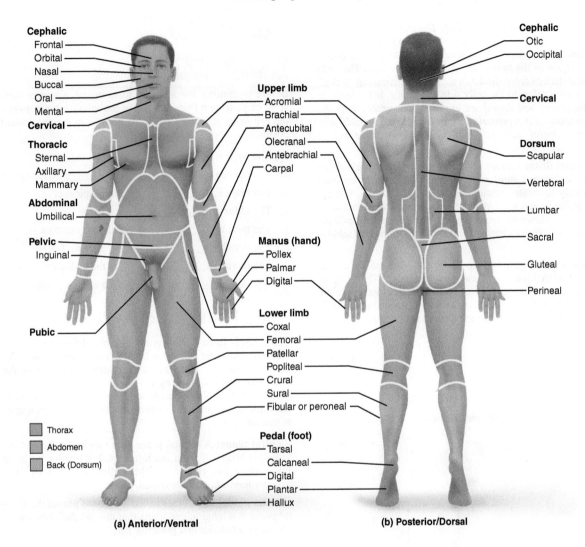

**Cephalic**
- Frontal
- Orbital
- Nasal
- Buccal
- Oral
- Mental

**Cervical**

**Thoracic**
- Sternal
- Axillary
- Mammary

**Abdominal**
- Umbilical

**Pelvic**
- Inguinal

**Pubic**

Thorax
Abdomen
Back (Dorsum)

**Upper limb**
- Acromial
- Brachial
- Antecubital
- Olecranal
- Antebrachial
- Carpal

**Manus (hand)**
- Pollex
- Palmar
- Digital

**Lower limb**
- Coxal
- Femoral
- Patellar
- Popliteal
- Crural
- Sural
- Fibular or peroneal

**Pedal (foot)**
- Tarsal
- Calcaneal
- Digital
- Plantar
- Hallux

**Cephalic**
- Otic
- Occipital

**Cervical**

**Dorsum**
- Scapular
- Vertebral
- Lumbar
- Sacral
- Gluteal
- Perineal

**(a) Anterior/Ventral**

**(b) Posterior/Dorsal**

**Figure 1 Surface anatomy. (a)** Anatomical position. **(b)** Heels are raised to illustrate the plantar surface of the foot.

# Body Orientation and Direction

Study the terms below (see **Figure 2** for a visual aid). Notice that certain terms have a different meaning for a four-legged animal (quadruped) than they do for a human (biped).

**Superior/inferior** *(above/below):* These terms refer to placement of a structure along the long axis of the body. Superior structures always appear above other structures, and inferior structures are always below other structures. For example, the nose is superior to the mouth, and the abdomen is inferior to the chest.

**Anterior/posterior** *(front/back):* In humans the most anterior structures are those that are most forward—the face, chest, and abdomen. Posterior structures are those toward the backside of the body. For instance, the spine is posterior to the heart.

**Medial/lateral** *(toward the midline/away from the midline or median plane):* The sternum (breastbone) is medial to the ribs; the ear is lateral to the nose.

The terms of position just described assume the person is in the anatomical position. The next four term pairs are more absolute. They apply in any body position, and they consistently have the same meaning in all vertebrate animals.

**Cephalad (cranial)/caudal** *(toward the head/toward the tail):* In humans these terms are used interchangeably with *superior* and *inferior,* but in four-legged animals they are synonymous with *anterior* and *posterior,* respectively.

**Dorsal/ventral** *(backside/belly side):* These terms are used chiefly in discussing the comparative anatomy of animals,

3

assuming the animal is standing. *Dorsum* is a Latin word meaning "back." Thus, *dorsal* refers to the animal's back or the *back* side of any other structures; for example, the posterior surface of the human leg is its dorsal surface. The term *ventral* derives from the Latin term *venter,* meaning "belly," and always refers to the belly side of animals. In humans the terms *ventral* and *dorsal* are used interchangeably with the terms *anterior* and *posterior,* but in four-legged animals *ventral* and *dorsal* are synonymous with *inferior* and *superior,* respectively.

**Proximal/distal** *(nearer the trunk or attached end/farther from the trunk or point of attachment):* These terms are used primarily to locate various areas of the body limbs. For example, the fingers are distal to the elbow; the knee is proximal to the toes. However, these terms may also be used to indicate regions (closer to or farther from the head) of internal tubular organs.

**Superficial (external)/deep (internal)** *(toward or at the body surface/away from the body surface):* These terms locate body organs according to their relative closeness to the body surface. For example, the skin is superficial to the skeletal muscles, and the lungs are deep to the rib cage.

**ACTIVITY 2**

## Practicing Using Correct Anatomical Terminology

Before continuing, use a human torso model, a human skeleton, or your own body to specify the relationship between the following structures when the body is in the anatomical position.

1. The wrist is _____ to the hand.
2. The trachea (windpipe) is _____ to the spine.
3. The brain is _____ to the spinal cord.
4. The kidneys are _____ to the liver.
5. The nose is _____ to the cheekbones.
6. The thumb is _____ to the ring finger.
7. The thorax is _____ to the abdomen.
8. The skin is _____ to the skeleton. ■

## Body Planes and Sections

The body is three-dimensional, and in order to observe its internal structures, it is often helpful and necessary to make use of a **section,** or cut. When the section is made through the body wall or through an organ, it is made along an imaginary surface or line called a **plane.** Anatomists commonly refer to three planes **(Figure 3),** or sections, that lie at right angles to one another.

**Sagittal plane:** A sagittal plane runs longitudinally and divides the body into right and left parts. If it divides the body into equal parts, right down the midline of the body, it is called a **median,** or **midsagittal, plane.**

**Frontal plane:** Sometimes called a **coronal plane,** the frontal plane is a longitudinal plane that divides the body (or an organ) into anterior and posterior parts.

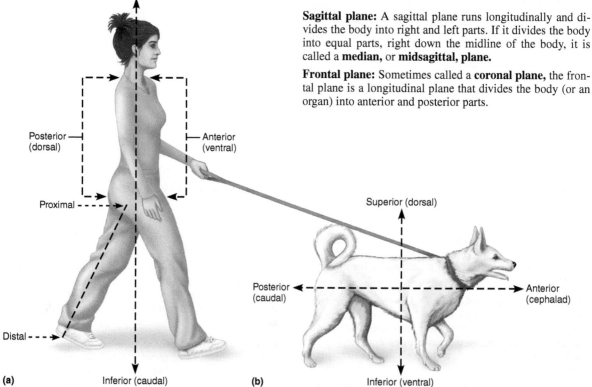

**Figure 2 Anatomical terminology describing body orientation and direction.**
**(a)** With reference to a human. **(b)** With reference to a four-legged animal.

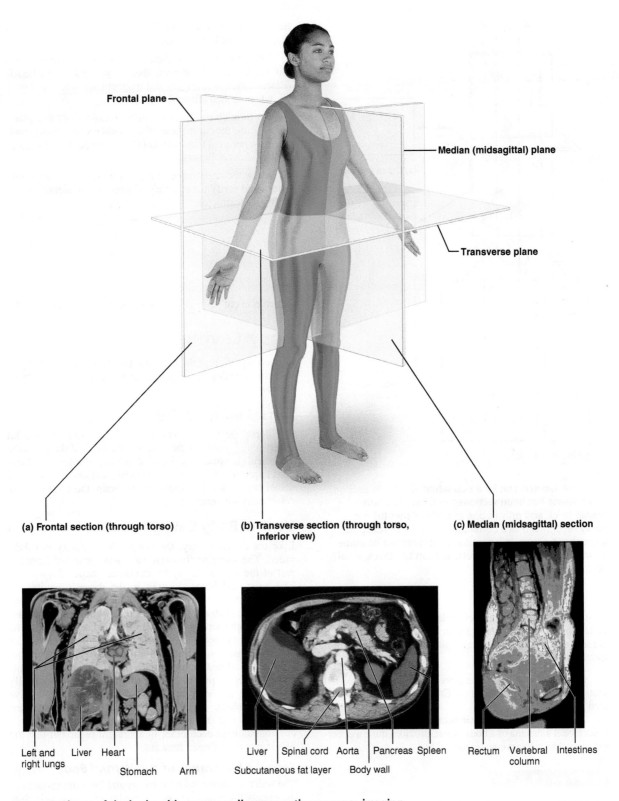

(a) Frontal section (through torso)

(b) Transverse section (through torso, inferior view)

(c) Median (midsagittal) section

Left and right lungs   Liver   Heart   Stomach   Arm

Liver   Spinal cord   Aorta   Pancreas   Spleen   Subcutaneous fat layer   Body wall

Rectum   Vertebral column   Intestines

**Figure 3** **Planes of the body with corresponding magnetic resonance imaging (MRI) scans.**

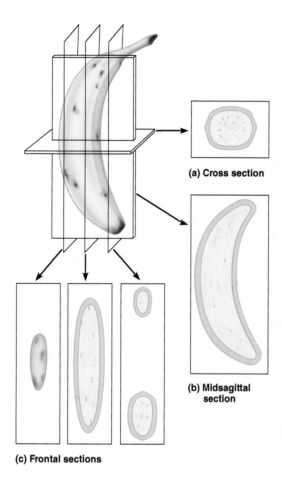

**(a) Cross section**

**(b) Midsagittal section**

**(c) Frontal sections**

**Figure 4 Objects can look odd when viewed in section.** This banana has been sectioned in three different planes **(a–c)**, and only in one of these planes **(b)** is it easily recognized as a banana. If one cannot recognize a sectioned organ, it is possible to reconstruct its shape from a series of successive cuts, as from the three serial sections in **(c)**.

**Transverse plane:** A transverse plane runs horizontally, dividing the body into superior and inferior parts. When organs are sectioned along the transverse plane, the sections are commonly called **cross sections.**

On microscope slides, the abbreviation for a longitudinal section (sagittal or frontal) is l.s. Cross sections are abbreviated x.s. or c.s.

A sagittal or frontal plane section of any nonspherical object, be it a banana or a body organ, provides quite a different view than a transverse section **(Figure 4).**

**ACTIVITY 3**

## Observing Sectioned Specimens

1. Go to the demonstration area and observe the transversely and longitudinally cut organ specimens (kidneys). Pay close attention to the different structural details in the samples because you will need to draw these views in the Review Sheet at the end of this exercise.

2. After completing instruction 1, obtain a gelatin-spaghetti mold and a scalpel and bring them to your laboratory bench. (Essentially, this is just cooked spaghetti added to warm gelatin, which is then allowed to gel.)

3. Cut through the gelatin-spaghetti mold along any plane, and examine the cut surfaces. You should see spaghetti strands that have been cut transversely (x.s.), some cut longitudinally, and some cut obliquely.

4. Draw the appearance of each of these spaghetti sections below, and verify the accuracy of your section identifications with your instructor.

Transverse cut        Longitudinal cut        Oblique cut ■

# Body Cavities

The axial portion of the body has two large cavities that provide different degrees of protection to the organs within them **(Figure 5)**.

## Dorsal Body Cavity

The dorsal body cavity can be subdivided into the **cranial cavity,** which contains the brain within the rigid skull, and the **vertebral** (or **spinal**) **cavity,** within which the delicate spinal cord is protected by the bony vertebral column. Because the spinal cord is a continuation of the brain, these cavities are continuous with each other.

## Ventral Body Cavity

Like the dorsal cavity, the ventral body cavity is subdivided. The superior **thoracic cavity** is separated from the rest of the ventral cavity by the dome-shaped diaphragm. The heart and lungs, located in the thoracic cavity, are protected by the bony rib cage. The cavity inferior to the diaphragm is often referred to as the **abdominopelvic cavity.** Although there is no further physical separation of the ventral cavity, some describe the abdominopelvic cavity as two areas: a superior **abdominal cavity,** the area that houses the stomach, intestines, liver, and other organs, and an inferior **pelvic cavity,** the region that is partially enclosed by the bony pelvis and contains the reproductive organs, bladder, and rectum. Notice in the lateral view (Figure 5a) that the abdominal and pelvic cavities are not continuous with each other in a straight plane but that the pelvic cavity is tipped forward.

### Serous Membranes of the Ventral Body Cavity

The walls of the ventral body cavity and the outer surfaces of the organs it contains are covered with an exceedingly thin, double-layered membrane called the **serosa,** or **serous membrane.** The part of the membrane lining the cavity walls is referred to as the **parietal serosa,** and it is continuous with a similar membrane, the **visceral serosa,** covering the external

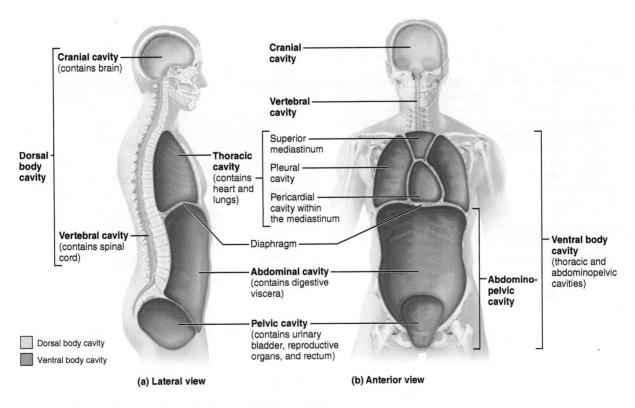

**Cranial cavity**
(contains brain)

**Cranial cavity**

**Vertebral cavity**

**Dorsal body cavity**

Superior mediastinum

Pleural cavity

Pericardial cavity within the mediastinum

**Thoracic cavity** (contains heart and lungs)

**Vertebral cavity** (contains spinal cord)

Diaphragm

**Abdominal cavity** (contains digestive viscera)

**Pelvic cavity** (contains urinary bladder, reproductive organs, and rectum)

**Ventral body cavity** (thoracic and abdominopelvic cavities)

**Abdomino-pelvic cavity**

☐ Dorsal body cavity
■ Ventral body cavity

**(a) Lateral view**

**(b) Anterior view**

**Figure 5  Dorsal and ventral body cavities and their subdivisions.**

surface of the organs within the cavity. These membranes produce a thin lubricating fluid that allows the visceral organs to slide over one another or to rub against the body wall with minimal friction. Serous membranes also compartmentalize

the various organs so that infection of one organ is prevented from spreading to others.

The specific names of the serous membranes depend on the structures they surround. The serosa lining the abdominal cavity and covering its organs is the **peritoneum,** that enclosing the lungs is the **pleura,** and that around the heart is the **pericardium (Figure 6)**.

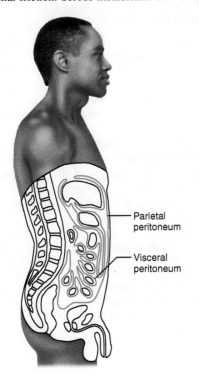

Parietal peritoneum

Visceral peritoneum

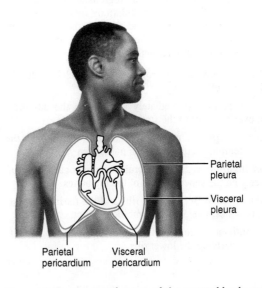

Parietal pleura

Visceral pleura

Parietal pericardium

Visceral pericardium

**Figure 6  Serous membranes of the ventral body cavities.**

### Abdominopelvic Quadrants and Regions

Because the abdominopelvic cavity is quite large and contains many organs, it is helpful to divide it up into smaller areas for discussion or study.

A scheme used by most physicians and nurses divides the abdominal surface and the abdominopelvic cavity into four approximately equal regions called **quadrants.** These quadrants are named according to their relative position—that is, *right upper quadrant, right lower quadrant, left upper quadrant,* and *left lower quadrant* (Figure 7). Note that the terms left and right refer to the left and right side of the body in the figure, not the left and right side of the art on the page. The left and right of the figure are referred to as **anatomical left and right.**

### ACTIVITY 4

## Identifying Organs in the Abdominopelvic Cavity

Examine the human torso model to respond to the following questions.

Name two organs found in the left upper quadrant.

_____ and _____

Name two organs found in the right lower quadrant.

_____ and _____

What organ (Figure 7) is divided into identical halves by

the median plane? _____ ▬

A different scheme commonly used by anatomists divides the abdominal surface and abdominopelvic cavity into nine separate regions by four planes (Figure 8). Although the names of these nine regions are unfamiliar to you now, with a little patience and study they will become easier to remember. As you read through the descriptions of these nine regions, locate them (Figure 8), and note the organs contained in each region.

**Umbilical region:** The centermost region, which includes the umbilicus (navel)

**Epigastric region:** Immediately superior to the umbilical region; overlies most of the stomach

**Hypogastric (pubic) region:** Immediately inferior to the umbilical region; encompasses the pubic area

**Iliac, or inguinal, regions:** Lateral to the hypogastric region and overlying the superior parts of the hip bones

**Lumbar regions:** Between the ribs and the flaring portions of the hip bones; lateral to the umbilical region

**Hypochondriac regions**: Flanking the epigastric region laterally and overlying the lower ribs

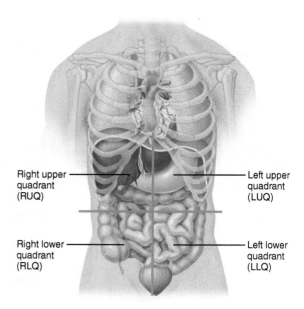

Figure 7 **Abdominopelvic quadrants.** Superficial organs all shown in each quadrant.

### ACTIVITY 5

## Locating Abdominal Surface Regions

Locate the regions of the abdominal surface on a human torso model and on yourself before continuing. ▬

## Other Body Cavities

Besides the large, closed body cavities, there are several types of smaller body cavities (Figure 9). Many of these are in the head, and most open to the body exterior.

**Oral cavity:** The oral cavity, commonly called the mouth, contains the tongue and teeth. It is continuous with the rest of the digestive tube, which opens to the exterior at the anus.

**Nasal cavity:** Located within and posterior to the nose, the nasal cavity is part of the passages of the respiratory system.

**Orbital cavities:** The orbital cavities (orbits) in the skull house the eyes and present them in an anterior position.

**Middle ear cavities:** Each middle ear cavity lies just medial to an eardrum and is carved into the bony skull. These cavities contain tiny bones that transmit sound vibrations to the hearing receptors in the inner ears.

**Synovial cavities:** Synovial cavities are joint cavities—they are enclosed within fibrous capsules that surround the freely movable joints of the body, such as those between the vertebrae and the knee and hip joints. Like the serous membranes of the ventral body cavity, membranes lining the synovial cavities secrete a lubricating fluid that reduces friction as the enclosed structures move across one another.

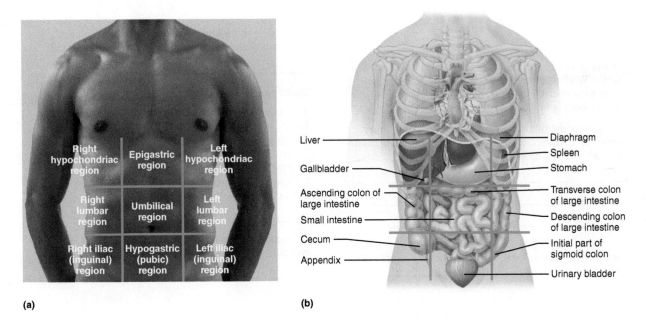

**(a)**

**(b)**

**Figure 8 Abdominopelvic regions.** Nine regions delineated by four planes.
**(a)** The superior horizontal plane is just inferior to the ribs; the inferior horizontal plane is at the superior aspect of the hip bones. The vertical planes are just medial to the nipples. **(b)** Superficial organs are shown in each region.

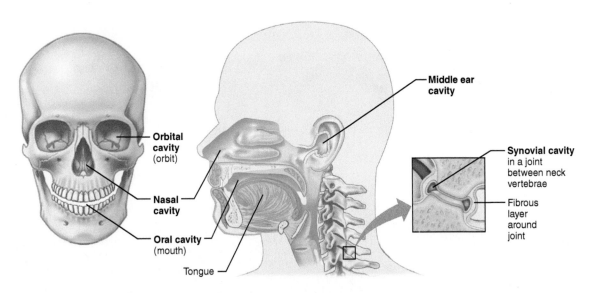

**Figure 9 Other body cavities.** The oral, nasal, orbital, and middle ear cavities are located in the head and open to the body exterior. Synovial cavities are found in joints between many bones such as the vertebrae of the spine, and at the knee, shoulder, and hip.

**GROUP CHALLENGE**

## The Language of Anatomy

Working in small groups, complete the tasks described below. Work together, but don't use a figure or other reference to answer the questions. As usual, assume that the human body is in the anatomical position.

1. Arrange the following terms from superior to inferior: cervical, coxal, crural, femoral, lumbar, mental, nasal, plantar, sternal, and tarsal. _____

_____

_____

_____

2. Arrange the following terms from proximal to distal: antebrachial, antecubital, brachial, carpal, digital, and palmar. _____

_____

3. Arrange the following terms from medial to lateral: acromial, axillary, buccal, otic, pollex, and umbilical.

_____

_____

4. Arrange the following terms from distal to proximal: calcaneal, femoral, hallux, plantar, popliteal, and sural.

_____

_____

5. Name a plane that you could use to section a four-legged chair and still be able to sit in the chair without falling over. _____

_____

6. Name the abdominopelvic region that is both medial and inferior to the right lumbar region.

_____

7. Name the type of inflammation (think "-itis") that is typically accompanied by pain in the lower right quadrant.

_____

Name _____

Lab Time/Date _____

# The Language of Anatomy

## Surface Anatomy

**1.** Match each of the numbered descriptions with the related term in the key, and record the key letter or term in front of the description.

*Key:* a. buccal       c. cephalic       e. patellar
      b. calcaneal      d. digital        f. scapular

___buccal___ 1. cheek

___digital___ 2. fingers

___scapula___ 3. shoulder blade region

___patellar___ 4. anterior aspect of knee

___calcaneal___ 5. heel of foot

___cephalic___ 6. head

**2.** Indicate the following body areas on the accompanying diagram by placing the correct key letter at the end of each line.

*Key:*

a. abdominal
b. antecubital
c. brachial
d. cervical
e. crural
f. femoral
g. fibular
h. gluteal
i. lumbar
j. occipital
k. oral
l. popliteal
m. pubic
n. sural
o. thoracic
p. umbilical

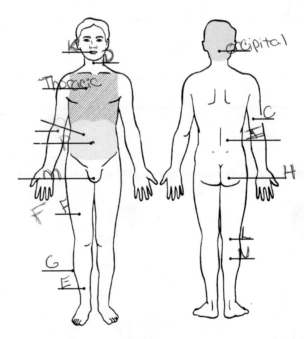

**3.** Classify each of the terms in the key of question 2 above into one of the large body regions indicated below. Insert the appropriate key letters on the answer blanks.

_____ 1. appendicular        _____ 2. axial

## Body Orientation, Direction, Planes, and Sections

**4.** Describe completely the standard human anatomical position. _____

_____

**5.** Define *section.* _____

**6.** Several incomplete statements are listed below. Correctly complete each statement by choosing the appropriate anatomical term from the key. Record the key letters and/or terms on the correspondingly numbered blanks below. Some terms are used more than once.

*Key:*
| | | | | | | | |
|---|---|---|---|---|---|---|---|
| a. | anterior | d. | inferior | g. | posterior | j. | superior |
| b. | distal | e. | lateral | h. | proximal | k. | transverse |
| c. | frontal | f. | medial | i. | sagittal | | |

In the anatomical position, the face and palms are on the _1_ body surface; the buttocks and shoulder blades are on the _2_ body surface; and the top of the head is the most _3_ part of the body. The ears are _4_ and _5_ to the shoulders and _6_ to the nose. The heart is _7_ to the vertebral column (spine) and _8_ to the lungs. The elbow is _9_ to the fingers but _10_ to the shoulder. The abdominopelvic cavity is _11_ to the thoracic cavity and _12_ to the spinal cavity. In humans, the dorsal surface can also be called the _13_ surface; however, in quadruped animals, the dorsal surface is the _14_ surface.

If an incision cuts the heart into right and left parts, the section is a _15_ section; but if the heart is cut so that superior and inferior portions result, the section is a _16_ section. You are told to cut a dissection animal along two planes so that both kidneys are observable in each section. The two sections that will always meet this requirement are the _17_ and _18_ sections. A section that demonstrates the continuity between the spinal and cranial cavities is a _19_ section.

1. _____    8. _____    14. _____

2. _____    9. _____    15. _____

3. _____    10. _____    16. _____

4. _____    11. _____    17. _____

5. _____    12. _____    18. _____

6. _____    13. _____    19. _____

7. _____

**7.** Correctly identify each of the body planes by inserting the appropriate term for each on the answer line below the drawing.

  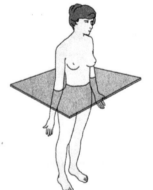

(a) Midsagetal    (b) Frontal    (c) transverse

**8.** Draw a kidney as it appears when sectioned in each of the three different planes.

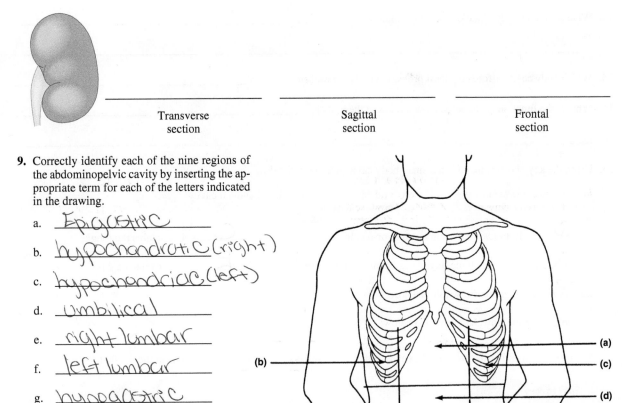

|  |  |  |
|---|---|---|
| Transverse section | Sagittal section | Frontal section |

**9.** Correctly identify each of the nine regions of the abdominopelvic cavity by inserting the appropriate term for each of the letters indicated in the drawing.

a. _Epigastric_

b. _hypochondrotic (right)_

c. _hypochondriac (left)_

d. _umbilical_

e. _right lumbar_

f. _left lumbar_

g. _hypogastric_

h. _right iliac_

i. _left iliac_

# Body Cavities

**10.** Which body cavity would have to be opened for the following types of surgery or procedures? (Insert letter of key choice in same-numbered blank. More than one choice may apply.)

*Key:* a. abdominopelvic   c. dorsal   e. thoracic
b. cranial   d. spinal   f. ventral

___E___ 1. surgery to remove a cancerous lung lobe   ___A___ 4. appendectomy

___A___ 2. removal of the uterus, or womb   ___A___ 5. stomach ulcer operation

___B___ 3. removal of a brain tumor   _____ 6. delivery of pre-operative "saddle" anesthesia

**11.** Name the muscle that subdivides the ventral body cavity. _____

**12.** What are the bony landmarks of the abdominopelvic cavity? _____

_____

**13.** Which body cavity affords the least protection to its internal structures? _____

**14.** What is the function of the serous membranes of the body? _____

_____

**15.** Using the key choices, identify the small body cavities described below.

*Key:* a.  middle ear cavity          c.  oral cavity          e.  synovial cavity
         b.  nasal cavity             d.  orbital cavity

____D____ 1. holds the eyes in an anterior-facing position          ____C____ 4. contains the tongue

____A____ 2. houses three tiny bones involved in hearing          ____E____ 5. surrounds a joint

____B____ 3. contained within the nose

**16.** On the incomplete flowchart provided below:

- Fill in the cavity names as appropriate to boxes 3–8.
- Then, using either the name of the cavity or the box numbers, identify the descriptions in the list that follows.

Body cavities

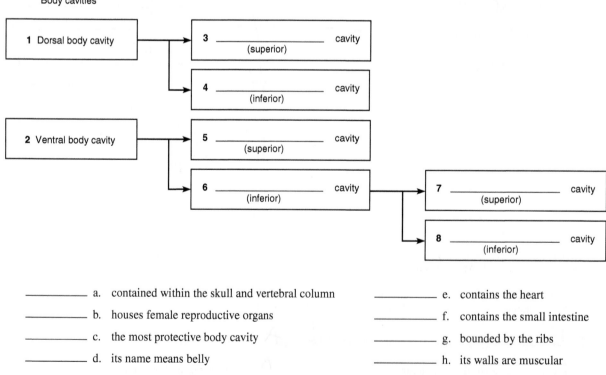

_____ a.  contained within the skull and vertebral column          _____ e.  contains the heart

_____ b.  houses female reproductive organs          _____ f.  contains the small intestine

_____ c.  the most protective body cavity          _____ g.  bounded by the ribs

_____ d.  its name means belly          _____ h.  its walls are muscular

## Photo Credits

**Credits are listed in order of appearance.**

3.1: Jenny Thomas, Pearson Education. 3a: Scott Camazine/Photo Researchers. 3b: James Cavallini/Photo Researchers. 3c: CNRI/Science Photo Library/Photo Researchers. 8a: John Wilson White, Pearson Education.

## Illustration Credits

**All illustrations are by Imagineering STA Media Services, except for Review Sheet art and as noted below.**

1: Imagineering STA Media Services/Precision Graphics. 2, 4: Precision Graphics. 9: Adapted from Marieb and Mallatt, *Human Anatomy,* 3e, F1.10, © Benjamin Cummings, 2003.

# Organ Systems Overview

## MATERIALS

- ☐ Freshly killed or preserved rat [predissected by instructor as a demonstration or for student dissection (one rat for every two to four students)] or predissected human cadaver
- ☐ Dissection trays
- ☐ Twine or large dissecting pins
- ☐ Scissors
- ☐ Probes
- ☐ Forceps
- ☐ Disposable gloves
- ☐ Human torso model (dissectible)

## OBJECTIVES

1. Name the human organ systems and indicate the major functions of each.
2. List several major organs of each system and identify them in a dissected rat, human cadaver or cadaver image, or in a dissectible human torso model.
3. Name the correct organ system for each organ when presented with a list of organs studied in the laboratory.

## PRE-LAB QUIZ

1. Name the structural and functional unit of all living things. _____
2. The small intestine is an example of a(n) _____, because it is composed of two or more tissue types that perform a particular function for the body.
   - a. epithelial tissue
   - b. muscular tissue
   - c. organ
   - d. organ system
3. The _____ system is responsible for maintaining homeostasis of the body via rapid transmission of electrical signals.
4. The kidneys are part of the _____ system.
5. The thin muscle that separates the thoracic and abdominal cavities is the _____.

The basic unit or building block of all living things is the **cell.** Cells fall into four different categories according to their structures and functions. Each of these corresponds to one of the four tissue types: epithelial, muscular, nervous, and connective. A **tissue** is a group of cells that are similar in structure and function. An **organ** is a structure composed of two or more tissue types that performs a specific function for the body. For example, the small intestine, which digests and absorbs nutrients, is made up of all four tissue types.

An **organ system** is a group of organs that act together to perform a particular body function. For example, the organs of the digestive system work together to break down foods and absorb the end products into the bloodstream to provide nutrients and fuel for all the body's cells. In all, there are 11 organ systems (described in **Table 1**). The lymphatic system also encompasses a *functional system* called the immune system, which is composed of an army of mobile *cells* that act to protect the body from foreign substances.

Read through this summary of the body's organ systems before beginning your rat dissection or examination of the predissected human cadaver. If a human cadaver is not available, the figures provided in this exercise (Figures 3–6), will serve as a partial replacement.

MasteringA&P® For related exercise study tools, go to the Study Area of MasteringA&P. There you will find:
- Practice Anatomy Lab PAL
- PhysioEx PEx
- A&PFlix *A&PFlix*
- Practice quizzes, Histology Atlas, eText, Videos, and more!

From Exercise 2 of *Human Anatomy & Physiology Laboratory Manual,* Main Version, Tenth Edition. Elaine N. Marieb, Susan J. Mitchell, Lori A. Smith. Copyright © 2014 by Pearson Education, Inc. All rights reserved.

| Table 1 | Overview of Organ Systems of the Body | |
|---|---|---|
| **Organ system** | **Major component organs** | **Function** |
| Integumentary (Skin) | Epidermal and dermal regions; cutaneous sense organs and glands | • Protects deeper organs from mechanical, chemical, and bacterial injury, and drying out<br>• Excretes salts and urea<br>• Aids in regulation of body temperature<br>• Produces vitamin D |
| Skeletal | Bones, cartilages, tendons, ligaments, and joints | • Body support and protection of internal organs<br>• Provides levers for muscular action<br>• Cavities provide a site for blood cell formation |
| Muscular | Muscles attached to the skeleton | • Primary function is to contract or shorten; in doing so, skeletal muscles allow locomotion (running, walking, etc.), grasping and manipulation of the environment, and facial expression<br>• Generates heat |
| Nervous | Brain, spinal cord, nerves, and sensory receptors | • Allows body to detect changes in its internal and external environment and to respond to such information by activating appropriate muscles or glands<br>• Helps maintain homeostasis of the body via rapid transmission of electrical signals |
| Endocrine | Pituitary, thymus, thyroid, parathyroid, adrenal, and pineal glands; ovaries, testes, and pancreas | • Helps maintain body homeostasis, promotes growth and development; produces chemical messengers called hormones that travel in the blood to exert their effect(s) on various target organs of the body |
| Cardiovascular | Heart, blood vessels, and blood | • Primarily a transport system that carries blood containing oxygen, carbon dioxide, nutrients, wastes, ions, hormones, and other substances to and from the tissue cells where exchanges are made; blood is propelled through the blood vessels by the pumping action of the heart<br>• Antibodies and other protein molecules in the blood protect the body |
| Lymphatic/ Immunity | Lymphatic vessels, lymph nodes, spleen, thymus, tonsils, and scattered collections of lymphoid tissue | • Picks up fluid leaked from the blood vessels and returns it to the blood<br>• Cleanses blood of pathogens and other debris<br>• Houses lymphocytes that act via the immune response to protect the body from foreign substances |
| Respiratory | Nasal passages, pharynx, larynx, trachea, bronchi, and lungs | • Keeps the blood continuously supplied with oxygen while removing carbon dioxide<br>• Contributes to the acid-base balance of the blood via its carbonic acid–bicarbonate buffer system |
| Digestive | Oral cavity, esophagus, stomach, small and large intestines, and accessory structures including teeth, salivary glands, liver, and pancreas | • Breaks down ingested foods to minute particles, which can be absorbed into the blood for delivery to the body cells<br>• Undigested residue removed from the body as feces |
| Urinary | Kidneys, ureters, bladder, and urethra | • Rids the body of nitrogen-containing wastes including urea, uric acid, and ammonia, which result from the breakdown of proteins and nucleic acids<br>• Maintains water, electrolyte, and acid-base balance of blood |
| Reproductive | Male: testes, prostate gland, scrotum, penis, and duct system, which carries sperm to the body exterior | • Provides germ cells called sperm for perpetuation of the species |
| | Female: ovaries, uterine tubes, uterus, mammary glands, and vagina | • Provides germ cells called eggs; the female uterus houses the developing fetus until birth; mammary glands provide nutrition for the infant |

### DISSECTION AND IDENTIFICATION: The Organ Systems of the Rat

Many of the external and internal structures of the rat are quite similar in structure and function to those of the human, so a study of the gross anatomy of the rat should help you understand our own physical structure. The following instructions include directions for dissecting and observing a rat. In addition, the descriptions for organ observations (Activity 4, "Examining the Ventral Body Cavity" page) also apply to superficial observations of a previously dissected human cadaver. The general instructions for observing external structures also apply to human cadaver observations. (The photographs in Figures 3 to 6 will provide visual aids.)

Note that four organ systems (integumentary, skeletal, muscular, and nervous) will not be studied at this time, as they require microscopic study or more detailed dissection. ■

18

**Figure 1 Rat dissection: Securing for dissection and the initial incision.**
**(a)** Securing the rat to the dissection tray with dissecting pins. **(b)** Using scissors to make the incision on the median line of the abdominal region.
**(c)** Completed incision from the pelvic region to the lower jaw.
**(d)** Reflection (folding back) of the skin to expose the underlying muscles.

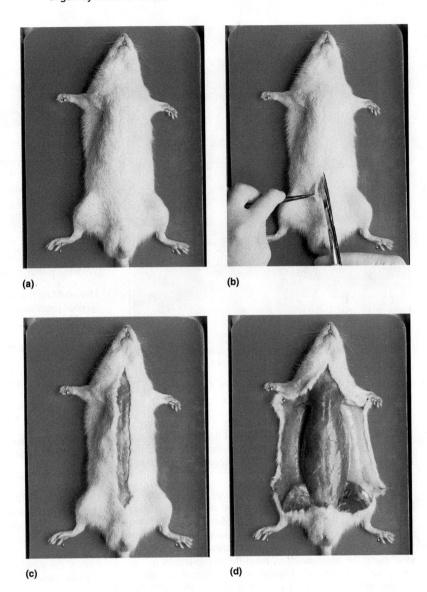

(a)

(b)

(c)

(d)

## Observing External Structures

1. If your instructor has provided a predissected rat, go to the demonstration area to make your observations. Alternatively, if you and/or members of your group will be dissecting the specimen, obtain a preserved or freshly killed rat, a dissecting tray, dissecting pins or twine, scissors, probe, forceps, and disposable gloves, and bring them to your laboratory bench.

If a predissected human cadaver is available, obtain a probe, forceps, and disposable gloves before going to the demonstration area.

2. Don the gloves before beginning your observations. This precaution is particularly important when handling freshly killed animals, which may harbor internal parasites.

3. Observe the major divisions of the body—head, trunk, and extremities. If you are examining a rat, compare these divisions to those of humans. ▬

## Examining the Oral Cavity

Examine the structures of the oral cavity. Identify the teeth and tongue. Observe the extent of the hard palate (the portion underlain by bone) and the soft palate (immediately posterior to the hard palate, with no bony support). Notice that the posterior end of the oral cavity leads into the throat, or pharynx, a passageway used by both the digestive and respiratory systems. ▬

## Opening the Ventral Body Cavity

1. Pin the animal to the wax of the dissecting tray by placing its dorsal side down and securing its extremities to the wax with large dissecting pins **(Figure 1a)**.

If the dissecting tray is not waxed, you will need to secure the animal with twine as follows. (Some may prefer

19

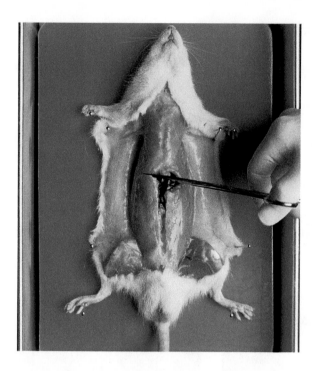

**Figure 2 Rat dissection:** Making lateral cuts at the base of the rib cage.

this method in any case.) Obtain the roll of twine. Make a loop knot around one upper limb, pass the twine under the tray, and secure the opposing limb. Repeat for the lower extremities.

2. Lift the abdominal skin with a forceps, and cut through it with the scissors (Figure 1b). Close the scissor blades and insert them flat under the cut skin. Moving in a cephalad direction, open and close the blades to loosen the skin from the underlying connective tissue and muscle. Now, cut the skin along the body midline, from the pubic region to the lower jaw (Figure 1c). Finally, make a lateral cut about halfway down the ventral surface of each limb. Complete the job of freeing the skin with the scissor tips, and pin the flaps to the tray (Figure 1d). The underlying tissue that is now exposed is the skeletal musculature of the body wall and limbs. It allows voluntary body movement. Notice that the muscles are packaged in sheets of pearly white connective tissue (fascia), which protect the muscles and bind them together.

3. Carefully cut through the muscles of the abdominal wall in the pubic region, avoiding the underlying organs. Remember, to *dissect* means "to separate"—not mutilate! Now, hold and lift the muscle layer with a forceps and cut through the muscle layer from the pubic region to the bottom of the rib cage. Make two lateral cuts at the base of the rib cage **(Figure 2).** A thin membrane attached to the inferior boundary of the rib cage should be obvious; this is the **diaphragm,** which separates the thoracic and abdominal

cavities. Cut the diaphragm where it attaches to the ventral ribs to loosen the rib cage. Cut through the rib cage on either side. You can now lift the ribs to view the contents of the thoracic cavity. Cut across the flap, at the level of the neck, and remove it. ▪

**ACTIVITY 4**

### Examining the Ventral Body Cavity

1. Starting with the most superficial structures and working deeper, examine the structures of the thoracic cavity. (Refer to **Figure 3**, which shows the superficial organs, as you work.) Choose the appropriate view depending on whether you are examining a rat (a) or a human cadaver (b).

**Thymus:** An irregular mass of glandular tissue overlying the heart (not illustrated in the human cadaver photograph).

With the probe, push the thymus to the side to view the heart.

**Heart:** Medial oval structure enclosed within the pericardium (serous membrane sac).

**Lungs:** Lateral to the heart on either side.

Now observe the throat region to identify the trachea.

**Trachea:** Tubelike "windpipe" running medially down the throat; part of the respiratory system.

Follow the trachea into the thoracic cavity; notice where it divides into two branches. These are the bronchi.

**Bronchi:** Two passageways that plunge laterally into the tissue of the two lungs.

To expose the esophagus, push the trachea to one side.

**Esophagus:** A food chute; the part of the digestive system that transports food from the pharynx (throat) to the stomach.

**Diaphragm:** A thin muscle attached to the inferior boundary of the rib cage; separates the thoracic and abdominal cavities.

Follow the esophagus through the diaphragm to its junction with the stomach.

**Stomach:** A curved organ important in food digestion and temporary food storage.

2. Examine the superficial structures of the abdominopelvic cavity. Lift the **greater omentum,** an extension of the peritoneum that covers the abdominal viscera. Continuing from the stomach, trace the rest of the digestive tract **(Figure 4).**

**Small intestine:** Connected to the stomach and ending just before the saclike cecum.

**Large intestine:** A large muscular tube connected to the small intestine and ending at the anus.

**Cecum:** The initial portion of the large intestine.

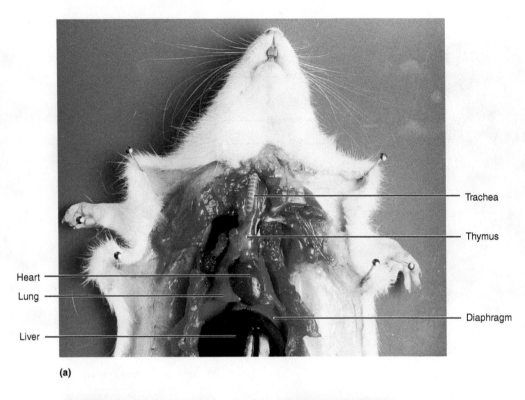

Trachea

Thymus

Heart

Lung

Diaphragm

Liver

**(a)**

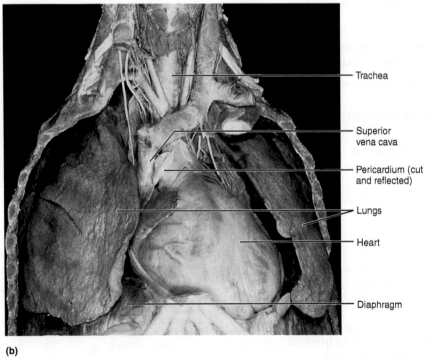

Trachea

Superior
vena cava

Pericardium (cut
and reflected)

Lungs

Heart

Diaphragm

**(b)**

**Figure 3 Superficial organs of the thoracic cavity. (a)** Dissected rat.
**(b)** Human cadaver.

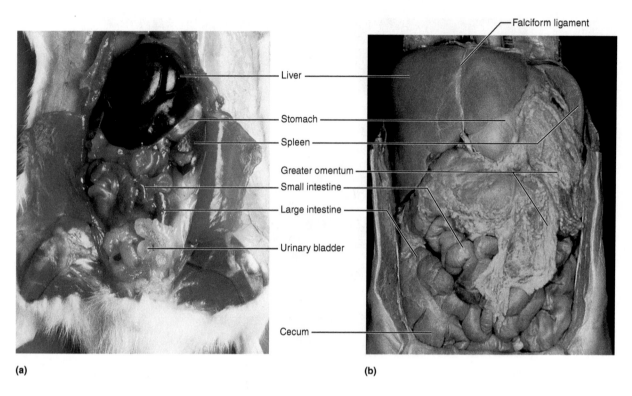

**Figure 4 Abdominal organs. (a)** Dissected rat, superficial view. **(b)** Human cadaver, superficial view.

Follow the course of the large intestine to the rectum, which is partially covered by the urinary bladder **(Figure 5)**.

**Rectum:** Terminal part of the large intestine; continuous with the anal canal.

**Anus:** The opening of the digestive tract (through the anal canal) to the exterior.

Now lift the small intestine with the forceps to view the mesentery.

**Mesentery:** An apronlike serous membrane; suspends many of the digestive organs in the abdominal cavity. Notice that it is heavily invested with blood vessels and, more likely than not, riddled with large fat deposits.

Locate the remaining abdominal structures.

**Pancreas:** A diffuse gland; rests dorsal to and in the mesentery between the first portion of the small intestine and the stomach. You will need to lift the stomach to view the pancreas.

**Spleen:** A dark red organ curving around the left lateral side of the stomach; considered part of the lymphatic system and often called the red blood cell graveyard.

**Liver:** Large and brownish red; the most superior organ in the abdominal cavity, directly beneath the diaphragm.

3. To locate the deeper structures of the abdominopelvic cavity, move the stomach and the intestines to one side with the probe.

Examine the posterior wall of the abdominal cavity to locate the two kidneys (Figure 5).

**Kidneys:** Bean-shaped organs; retroperitoneal (behind the peritoneum).

**Adrenal glands:** Large endocrine glands that sit on top of the superior margin of each kidney; considered part of the endocrine system.

Carefully strip away part of the peritoneum with forceps and attempt to follow the course of one of the ureters to the bladder.

**Ureter:** Tube running from the indented region of a kidney to the urinary bladder.

**Urinary bladder:** The sac that serves as a reservoir for urine.

4. In the midline of the body cavity lying between the kidneys are the two principal abdominal blood vessels. Identify each.

**Inferior vena cava:** The large vein that returns blood to the heart from the lower body regions.

**Descending aorta:** Deep to the inferior vena cava; the largest artery of the body; carries blood away from the heart down the midline of the body.

5. Only a brief examination of reproductive organs will be done. If you are working with a rat, first determine if the animal is a male or female. Observe the ventral body surface beneath the tail. If a saclike scrotum and an opening for the anus are visible, the animal is a male. If three body openings—urethral, vaginal, and anal—are present, it is a female.

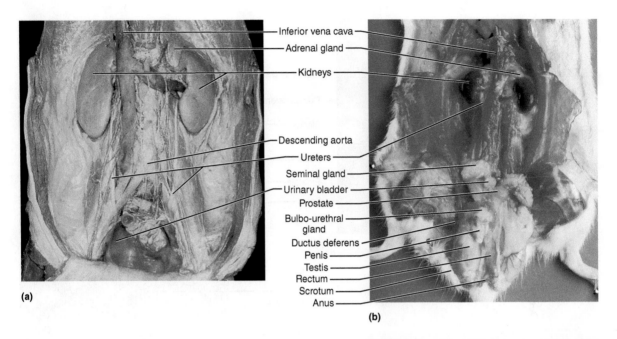

- Inferior vena cava
- Adrenal gland
- Kidneys
- Descending aorta
- Ureters
- Seminal gland
- Urinary bladder
- Prostate
- Bulbo-urethral gland
- Ductus deferens
- Penis
- Testis
- Rectum
- Scrotum
- Anus

**(a)**

**(b)**

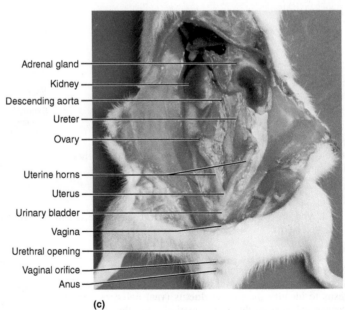

- Adrenal gland
- Kidney
- Descending aorta
- Ureter
- Ovary
- Uterine horns
- Uterus
- Urinary bladder
- Vagina
- Urethral opening
- Vaginal orifice
- Anus

**(c)**

**Figure 5 Deep structures of the abdominopelvic cavity. (a)** Human cadaver. **(b)** Dissected male rat. (Some reproductive structures also shown.) **(c)** Dissected female rat. (Some reproductive structures also shown.)

### Male Animal

Make a shallow incision into the **scrotum.** Loosen and lift out one oval **testis.** Exert a gentle pull on the testis to identify the slender **ductus deferens,** or **vas deferens,** which carries sperm from the testis superiorly into the abdominal cavity and joins with the urethra. The urethra runs through the penis and carries both urine and sperm out of the body. Identify the **penis,** extending from the bladder to the ventral body wall. (Figure 5b indicates other glands of the male rat's reproductive system, but they need not be identified at this time.)

### Female Animal

Inspect the pelvic cavity to identify the Y-shaped **uterus** lying against the dorsal body wall and superior to the bladder (Figure 5c). Follow one of the uterine horns superiorly to identify an **ovary,** a small oval structure at the end of the uterine horn. (The rat uterus is quite different from the uterus of a human female, which is a single-chambered organ about the size and shape of a pear.) The inferior undivided part of the rat uterus is continuous with the **vagina,** which leads to the body exterior. Identify the **vaginal orifice** (external vaginal opening).

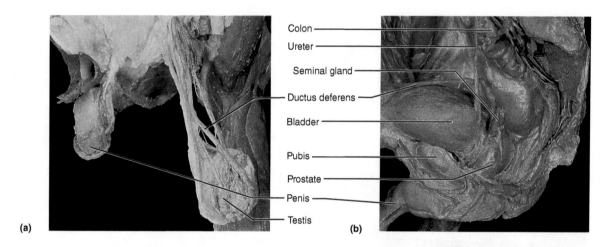

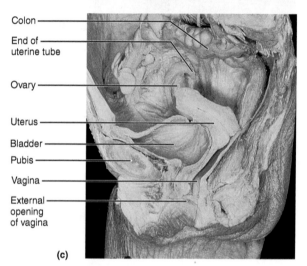

**Figure 6 Human reproductive organs. (a)** Male external genitalia. **(b)** Sagittal section of the male pelvis. **(c)** Sagittal section of the female pelvis.

If you are working with a human cadaver, proceed as indicated next.

### Male Cadaver

Make a shallow incision into the **scrotum (Figure 6a).** Loosen and lift out the oval **testis.** Exert a gentle pull on the testis to identify the slender **ductus (vas) deferens,** which carries sperm from the testis superiorly into the abdominal cavity and joins with the urethra (Figure 6b). The urethra runs through the penis and carries both urine and sperm out of the body. Identify the **penis,** extending from the bladder to the ventral body wall.

### Female Cadaver

Inspect the pelvic cavity to identify the pear-shaped **uterus** lying against the dorsal body wall and superior to the bladder. Follow one of the **uterine tubes** superiorly to identify an **ovary,** a small oval structure at the end of the uterine tube (Figure 6c). The inferior part of the uterus is continuous with the **vagina,** which leads to the body exterior. Identify the **vaginal orifice** (external vaginal opening).

6.  When you have finished your observations, rewrap or store the dissection animal or cadaver according to your instructor's directions. Wash the dissecting tools and equipment with laboratory detergent. Dispose of the gloves. Then wash and dry your hands before continuing with the examination of the human torso model. ▆

### ACTIVITY 5

## Examining the Human Torso Model

1.  Examine a human torso model to identify the organs listed. Some model organs will have to be removed to see the deeper organs. If a torso model is not available, the photograph of the human torso model **(Figure 7)** may be used for this part of the exercise.

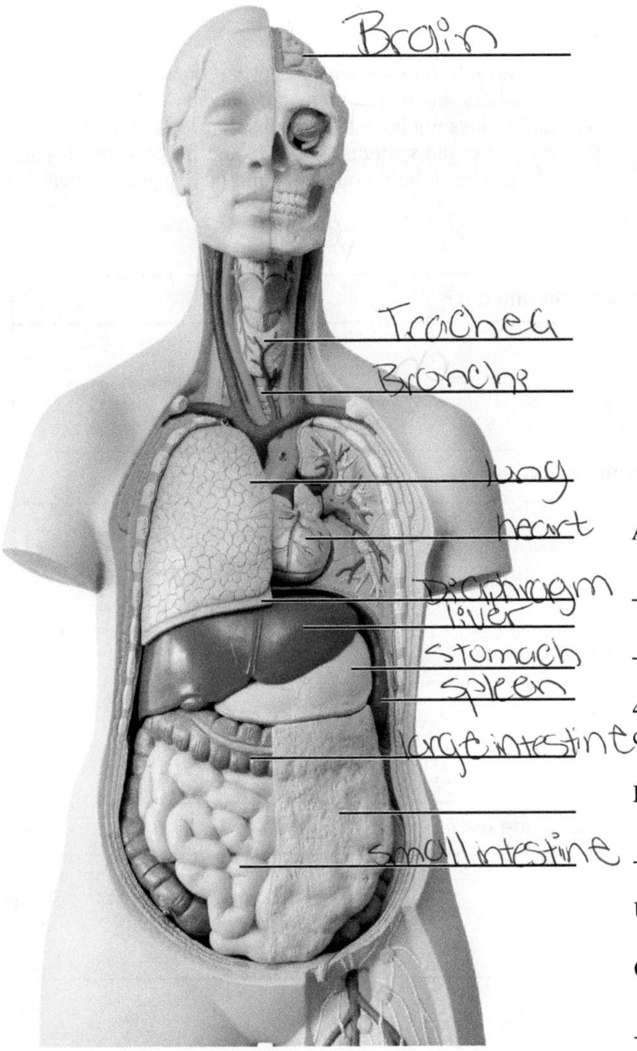

*Handwritten labels on torso model:* Brain, Trachea, Bronchi, lung, heart, Diaphragm, liver, stomach, spleen, large intestine, small intestine

Adrenal gland
Aortic arch
Brain
Bronchi
Descending aorta
Diaphragm
Esophagus
Greater omentum
Heart
Inferior vena cava
Kidneys
Large intestine
Liver

Lungs
Mesentery
Pancreas
Rectum
Small intestine
Spinal cord
Spleen
Stomach
Thyroid gland
Trachea
Ureters
Urinary bladder

Abdominopelvic cavity_____

_____

_____

4.  Now, assign each of the organs to one of the organ system categories listed below.

Digestive: _____

_____

Urinary: _____

Cardiovascular: _____

_____

Endocrine: _____

Reproductive: _____

Respiratory: _____

Lymphatic/Immunity: _____

Nervous: _____

**Figure 7  Human torso model.**

2.  Using the terms at the right of the torso model photo (Figure 7), label each organ supplied with a leader line in the photo.

3.  Place each of the listed organs in the correct body cavity or cavities. For organs found in the abdominopelvic cavity, also indicate which quadrant they occupy.

Dorsal body cavity_____

Thoracic cavity_____

_____

_____

_____

_____

## Odd Organ Out

Each of the following sets contains four organs. One of the listed organs in each case does not share a characteristic that the other three do. Circle the organ that doesn't belong with the others and explain why it is singled out. What characteristic is it missing? Sometimes there may be multiple reasons why the organ doesn't belong with the others. Include as many as you can think of but make sure it does not have the key characteristic. Use the overview of organ systems (Table 1) and the pictures in your lab manual to help you select and justify your answer.

| 1. Which is the "odd organ"? | Why is it the odd one out? |
|---|---|
| Stomach<br>Teeth<br>Small intestine<br>Oral cavity | |

| 2. Which is the "odd organ"? | Why is it the odd one out? |
|---|---|
| Thyroid gland<br>Thymus<br>Spleen<br>Lymph nodes | |

| 3. Which is the "odd organ"? | Why is it the odd one out? |
|---|---|
| Ovaries<br>Prostate gland<br>Uterus<br>Uterine tubes | |

| 4. Which is the "odd organ"? | Why is it the odd one out? |
|---|---|
| Stomach<br>Small intestine<br>Esophagus<br>Large intestine | |

Name _____

Lab Time/Date _____

# Organ Systems Overview

1. Use the key below to indicate the body systems that perform the following functions for the body; note that some body systems are used more than once. Then, circle the organ systems (in the key) that are present in all subdivisions of the ventral body cavity.

Key: a. cardiovascular    d. integumentary    g. nervous    j. skeletal
       b. digestive    e. lymphatic/immunity    h. reproductive    k. urinary
       c. endocrine    f. muscular    i. respiratory

_____urinary_____ 1. rids the body of nitrogen-containing wastes

_____ 2. is affected by removal of the thyroid gland

_____skeletal_____ 3. provides support and levers on which the muscular system acts

_cardiovascular_ 4. includes the heart

_reproductive_ 5. has a menstrual cycle in females

_____ 6. protects underlying organs from drying out and from mechanical damage

_lymphatic_ 7. protects the body; destroys bacteria and tumor cells

_digestive_ 8. breaks down ingested food into its building blocks

_respitory_ 9. removes carbon dioxide from the blood

_respitory_ 10. delivers oxygen and nutrients to the tissues

_muscular_ 11. moves the limbs; facilitates facial expression

_urinary_ 12. conserves body water or eliminates excesses

_____ and _____ 13. facilitate conception and childbearing

_Endocrine_ 14. controls the body by means of chemical molecules called hormones

_Integumentary_ 15. is damaged when you cut your finger or get a severe sunburn

2. Using the above key, choose the organ system to which each of the following sets of organs or body structures belongs.

_lymphatic_ 1. thymus, spleen, lymphatic vessels    _Integumentns_ 5. epidermis, dermis, and cutaneous sense organs

_____ 2. bones, cartilages, tendons

_Endocrine_ 3. pancreas, pituitary, adrenals    _reproductive_ 6. testis, ductus deferens, urethra

_respiratory_ 4. trachea, bronchi, lungs    _digestive_ 7. esophagus, large intestine, rectum

_muscular_ 8. muscles of the thigh, postural muscles

**3.** Using the key below, place the following organs in their proper body cavity.

*Key:* a. abdominopelvic     b. cranial     c. spinal       d. thoracic

*abdominopelvic* stomach    *abd/pelvic* 4. liver    *Thoracic* 7. heart

*Thoracic* 2. esophagus    *spinal* 5. spinal cord    *Thoracic* 8. trachea

*abd/pelvic* 3. large intestine    *abd/pelvic* 6. urinary bladder    *pelvic* 9. rectum

**4.** Using the organs listed in question 3 above, record, by number, which would be found in the abdominal regions listed below.

*urinary* ___ 1. hypogastric region       *Stomach* 4. epigastric region

_____ 2. right lumbar region       _____ 5. left iliac region

_____ 3. umbilical region       _____ 6. left hypochondriac region

**5.** The levels of organization of a living body are chemical, _____, _____,

_____, _____ , and organism.

**6.** Define *organ.* _____

_____

**7.** Using the terms provided, correctly identify all of the body organs provided with leader lines in the drawings shown below. Then name the organ systems by entering the name of each on the answer blank below each drawing.

*Key:* blood vessels     heart       nerves       spinal cord       urethra
       brain         kidney      sensory receptor    ureter       urinary bladder

a. _____     b. _____     c. _____

**8.** Why is it helpful to study the external and internal structures of the rat? _____

_____

## Photo Credits

**Credits are listed in order of appearance.**

1a–d, 2, 3a, 4a, 5b,c: Elena Dorfman, Pearson Education. 3b, 4b, 5a, 6a–c: From *A Stereoscopic Atlas of Human Anatomy* by David L. Bassett, M.D. 7: Shutterstock.com.

# The Microscope

## MATERIALS

- ☐ Compound microscope
- ☐ Millimeter ruler
- ☐ Prepared slides of the letter e or newsprint
- ☐ Immersion oil
- ☐ Lens paper
- ☐ Prepared slide of grid ruled in millimeters
- ☐ Prepared slide of three crossed colored threads
- ☐ Clean microscope slide and coverslip
- ☐ Toothpicks (flat-tipped)
- ☐ Physiological saline in a dropper bottle
- ☐ Iodine or dilute methylene blue stain in a dropper bottle
- ☐ Filter paper or paper towels
- ☐ Beaker containing fresh 10% household bleach solution for wet mount disposal
- ☐ Disposable autoclave bag
- ☐ Prepared slide of cheek epithelial cells

**Note to the Instructor:** The slides and coverslips used for viewing cheek cells are to be soaked for 2 hours (or longer) in 10% bleach solution and then drained. The slides and disposable autoclave bag containing coverslips, lens paper, and used toothpicks are to be autoclaved for 15 min at 121°C and 15 pounds pressure to ensure sterility. After autoclaving, the disposable autoclave bag may be discarded in any disposal facility, and the slides and glassware washed with laboratory detergent and prepared for use. These instructions apply as well to any bloodstained glassware or disposable items used in other experimental procedures.

## OBJECTIVES

1. Identify the parts of the microscope and list the function of each.
2. Describe and demonstrate the proper techniques for care of the microscope.
3. Demonstrate proper focusing technique.
4. Define *total magnification, resolution, parfocal, field, depth of field* and *working distance.*
5. Measure the field size for one objective lens, calculate it for all the other objective lenses, and estimate the size of objects in each field.
6. Discuss the general relationships between magnification, working distance, and field size.

## PRE-LAB QUIZ

1. The microscope slide rests on the _____ while being viewed.
   a. base
   b. condenser
   c. iris
   d. stage
2. Your lab microscope is *parfocal*. This means that:
   a. The specimen is clearly in focus at this depth.
   b. The slide should be almost in focus when changing to higher magnifications.
   c. You can easily discriminate two close objects as separate.
3. If the ocular lens magnifies a specimen 10×, and the objective lens used magnifies the specimen 35×, what is the total magnification being used to observe the specimen? _____
4. How do you clean the lenses of your microscope?
   a. with a paper towel
   b. with soap and water
   c. with special lens paper and cleaner
5. Circle True or False. You should always begin observation of specimens with the oil immersion lens.

MasteringA&P® For related exercise study tools, go to the Study Area of MasteringA&P. There you will find:
- Practice Anatomy Lab PAL
- PhysioEx PEx
- A&PFlix *A&P Flix*
- Practice quizzes, Histology Atlas, eText, Videos, and more!

With the invention of the microscope, biologists gained a valuable tool to observe and study structures like cells that are too small to be seen by the unaided eye. The information gained helped in establishing many of the theories basic to the understanding of biological sciences. This exercise will familiarize you with the workhorse of microscopes—the compound microscope—and provide you with the necessary instructions for its proper use.

From Exercise 3 of *Human Anatomy & Physiology Laboratory Manual,* Main Version, Tenth Edition. Elaine N. Marieb, Susan J. Mitchell, Lori A. Smith. Copyright © 2014 by Pearson Education, Inc. All rights reserved.

# Care and Structure of the Compound Microscope

The **compound microscope** is a precision instrument and should always be handled with care. *At all times you must observe the following rules for its transport, cleaning, use, and storage:*

• When transporting the microscope, hold it in an upright position with one hand on its arm and the other supporting its base. Avoid swinging the instrument during its transport and jarring the instrument when setting it down.

• Use only special grit-free lens paper to clean the lenses. Use a circular motion to wipe the lenses, and clean all lenses before and after use.

• Always begin the focusing process with the lowest-power objective lens in position, changing to the higher-power lenses as necessary.

• Use the coarse adjustment knob only with the lowest-power lens.

• Always use a coverslip with wet mount preparations.

• Before putting the microscope in the storage cabinet, remove the slide from the stage, rotate the lowest-power objective lens into position, wrap the cord neatly around the base, and replace the dust cover or return the microscope to the appropriate storage area.

• Never remove any parts from the microscope; inform your instructor of any mechanical problems that arise.

### ACTIVITY 1

## Identifying the Parts of a Microscope

1. Using the proper transport technique, obtain a microscope and bring it to the laboratory bench.

• Record the number of your microscope in the **Summary Chart**.

Compare your microscope with the photograph **(Figure 1)** and identify the following microscope parts:

**Base:** Supports the microscope. (*Note:* Some microscopes are provided with an inclination joint, which allows the instrument to be tilted backward for viewing dry preparations.)

**Substage light** or **mirror:** Located in the base. In microscopes with a substage light source, the light passes directly upward through the microscope: light controls are located on the microscope base. If a mirror is used, light must be reflected from a separate free-standing lamp.

**Stage:** The platform the slide rests on while being viewed. The stage has a hole in it to permit light to pass through both it and the specimen. Some microscopes have a stage equipped with *spring clips;* others have a clamp-type *mechanical stage* (as shown in Figure 1). Both hold the slide in position for viewing; in addition, the mechanical stage has two adjustable knobs that control precise movement of the specimen.

**Condenser:** Small substage lens that concentrates the light on the specimen. The condenser may have a *rack and pinion knob* that raises and lowers the condenser to vary light delivery. Generally, the best position for the condenser is close to the inferior surface of the stage.

**Iris diaphragm lever:** Arm attached to the base of the condenser that regulates the amount of light passing through the condenser. The iris diaphragm permits the best possible contrast when viewing the specimen.

**Coarse adjustment knob:** Used to focus on the specimen.

**Fine adjustment knob:** Used for precise focusing once coarse focusing has been completed.

**Head** or **body tube:** Supports the objective lens system, which is mounted on a movable nosepiece, and the ocular lens or lenses.

**Arm:** Vertical portion of the microscope connecting the base and head.

**Ocular** (or *eyepiece*): Depending on the microscope, there are one or two lenses at the superior end of the head or body tube. Observations are made through the ocular(s). An ocular lens has a magnification of 10×; it increases the apparent size of the object by ten times or ten diameters. If your microscope has a **pointer** to indicate a specific area of the viewed specimen, it is attached to one ocular and can be positioned by rotating the ocular lens.

**Nosepiece:** Rotating mechanism at the base of the head. Generally carries three or four objective lenses and permits sequential positioning of these lenses over the light beam passing through the hole in the stage. Use the nosepiece to change the objective lenses. Do not directly grab the lenses.

**Objective lenses:** Adjustable lens system that permits the use of a **scanning lens**, a **low-power lens**, a **high-power lens,** or an **oil immersion lens.** The objective lenses have different magnifying and resolving powers.

2. Examine the objective lenses carefully; note their relative lengths and the numbers inscribed on their sides. On many microscopes, the scanning lens, with a magnification between 4× and 5×, is the shortest lens. If there is no scanning lens, the low-power objective lens is the shortest and typically has a magnification of 10×. The high-power objective lens is of intermediate length and has a magnification range from 40× to 50×, depending on the microscope. The oil immersion objective lens is usually the longest of the objective lenses and has a magnifying power of 95× to 100×. Some microscopes lack the oil immersion lens.

• Record the magnification of each objective lens of your microscope in the first row of the Summary Chart. Also, cross out the column relating to a lens that your microscope does not have. Plan on using the same microscope for all microscopic studies.

3. Rotate the lowest-power objective lens until it clicks into position, and turn the coarse adjustment knob about 180 degrees. Notice how far the stage (or objective lens) travels during this adjustment. Move the fine adjustment knob 180 degrees, noting again the distance that the stage (or the objective lens) moves. ▪

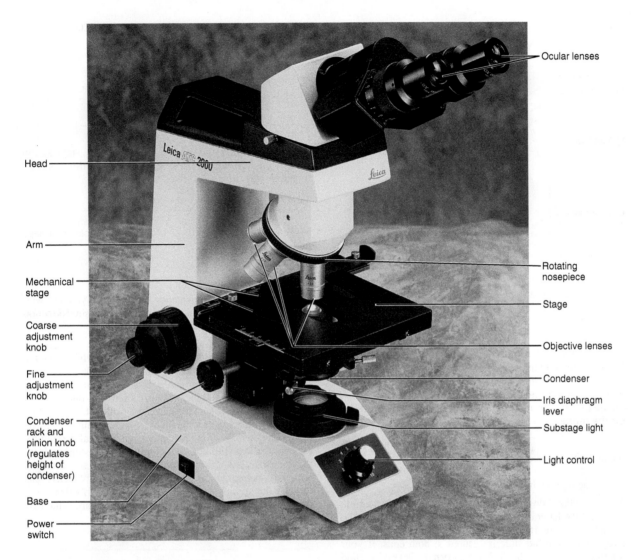

**Figure 1 Compound microscope and its parts.**

## Magnification and Resolution

The microscope is an instrument of magnification. In the compound microscope, magnification is achieved through the interplay of two lenses—the ocular lens and the objective lens. The objective lens magnifies the specimen to produce a **real image** that is projected to the ocular. This real image is magnified by the ocular lens to produce the **virtual image** seen by your eye **(Figure 2)**.

The **total magnification** (TM) of any specimen being viewed is equal to the power of the ocular lens multiplied by the power of the objective lens used. For example, if the ocular lens magnifies 10× and the objective lens being used magnifies 45×, the total magnification is 450× (or 10 × 45).

• Determine the total magnification you may achieve with each of the objectives on your microscope, and record the figures on the third row of the Summary Chart.

The compound light microscope has certain limitations. Although the level of magnification is almost limitless, the **resolution** (or resolving power), that is, the ability to discriminate two close objects as separate, is not. The human eye can resolve objects about 100 μm apart, but the compound microscope has a resolution of 0.2 μm under ideal conditions. Objects closer than 0.2 μm are seen as a single fused image.

*Resolving power* is determined by the amount and physical properties of the visible light that enters the microscope. In general, the more light delivered to the objective lens, the greater the resolution. The size of the objective lens aperture (opening) decreases with increasing magnification, allowing less light to enter the objective. Thus, you will probably find it necessary to increase the light intensity at the higher magnifications.

**ACTIVITY 2**

### Viewing Objects Through the Microscope

1. Obtain a millimeter ruler, a prepared slide of the letter *e* or newsprint, a dropper bottle of immersion oil, and some lens paper. Adjust the condenser to its highest position and switch

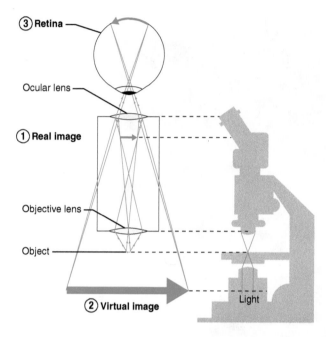

③ Retina

Ocular lens

① Real image

Objective lens

Object

② Virtual image

Light

**Figure 2  Image formation in light microscopy.**
**Step** ① The objective lens magnifies the object, forming
the real image. **Step** ② The ocular lens magnifies the real
image, forming the virtual image. **Step** ③ The virtual
image passes through the lens of the eye and is focused
on the retina.

on the light source of your microscope. If the light source is
not built into the base, use the curved surface of the mirror to
reflect the light up into the microscope.

2.   Secure the slide on the stage so that you can read the slide
label and the letter *e* is centered over the light beam passing
through the stage. If you are using a microscope with spring
clips, make sure the slide is secured at both ends. If your
microscope has a mechanical stage, open the jaws of its slide
holder by using the control lever, typically located at the rear
left corner of the mechanical stage. Insert the slide squarely
within the confines of the slide holder. Check that the slide
is resting on the stage, not on the mechanical stage frame,
before releasing the control lever.

3.   With your lowest-power (scanning or low-power) objective
lens in position over the stage, use the coarse adjustment knob to
bring the objective lens and stage as close together as possible.

4.   Look through the ocular lens and adjust the light for comfort using the iris diaphragm. Now use the coarse adjustment
knob to focus slowly away from the *e* until it is as clearly
focused as possible. Complete the focusing with the fine adjustment knob.

5.   Sketch the letter *e* in the circle on the Summary Chart
just as it appears in the **field**—the area you see through the
microscope.

How far is the bottom of the objective lens from the specimen? In other words, what is the **working distance**? Use a
millimeter ruler to make this measurement.

Record the working distance in the Summary Chart.

How has the apparent orientation of the *e* changed top to
bottom, right to left, and so on?

_____

_____

6.   Move the slide slowly away from you on the stage as you
view it through the ocular lens. In what direction does the
image move?

_____

Move the slide to the left. In what direction does the image
move?

_____

At first this change in orientation may confuse you, but with
practice you will learn to move the slide in the desired direction
with no problem.

7.   Today most good laboratory microscopes are **parfocal;**
that is, the slide should be in focus (or nearly so) at the
higher magnifications once you have properly focused. *Without touching the focusing knobs*, increase the magnification
by rotating the next higher magnification lens into position
over the stage. Make sure it clicks into position. Using the fine
adjustment only, sharpen the focus. If you are unable to focus
with a new lens, your microscope is not parfocal. Do not try
to force the lens into position. Consult your instructor. Note
the decrease in working distance. As you can see, focusing
with the coarse adjustment knob could drive the objective lens
through the slide, breaking the slide and possibly damaging
the lens. Sketch the letter *e* in the Summary Chart. What new
details become clear?

_____

_____

As best you can, measure the distance between the objective
and the slide.

Record the working distance in the Summary Chart.

Is the image larger or smaller? _____

Approximately how much of the letter *e* is visible now?

_____

Is the field larger or smaller? _____

Why is it necessary to center your object (or the portion of the
slide you wish to view) before changing to a higher power?

_____

| Summary Chart for Microscope # _____ | | | | | | | |
|---|---|---|---|---|---|---|---|
| | **Scanning** | | **Low power** | | **High power** | | **Oil immersion** |
| Magnification of objective lens | _____ × | | _____ × | | _____ × | | _____ × |
| Magnification of ocular lens | ____10____ × | | ____10____ × | | ____10____ × | | ____10____ × |
| Total magnification | _____ × | | _____ × | | _____ × | | _____ × |
| Working distance | _____ mm | | _____ mm | | _____ mm | | _____ mm |
| Detail observed Letter e | ◯ | | ◯ | | ◯ | | ◯ |
| Field size (diameter) | ____ mm ____ µm | | ____ mm ____ µm | | ____ mm ____ µm | | ____ mm ____ µm |

Move the iris diaphragm lever while observing the field. What happens?

_____

Is it better to increase *or* decrease the light when changing to a higher magnification?

_____ Why? _____

_____

8. If you have just been using the low-power objective, repeat the steps given in direction 7 using the high-power objective lens. What new details become clear?

_____

_____

Record the working distance in the Summary Chart.

9. Without touching the focusing knob, rotate the high-power lens out of position so that the area of the slide over the opening in the stage is unobstructed. Place a drop of immersion oil over the *e* on the slide and rotate the oil immersion lens into position. Set the condenser at its highest point (closest to the stage), and open the diaphragm fully. Adjust the fine focus and fine-tune the light for the best possible resolution.

**Note:** If for some reason the specimen does not come into view after adjusting the fine focus, do not go back to the 40× lens to recenter. You do not want oil from the oil immersion lens to cloud the 40× lens. Turn the revolving nosepiece in the other direction to the low-power lens and recenter and refocus the object. Then move the immersion lens back into position, again avoiding the 40× lens. Sketch the letter *e* in the Summary Chart, What new details become clear?

_____

_____

Is the field again decreased in size? _____

As best you can, estimate the working distance, and record it in the Summary Chart. Is the working distance less *or* greater than it was when the high-power lens was focused?

_____

Compare your observations on the relative working distances of the objective lenses with the illustration (Figure 3). Explain why it is desirable to begin the focusing process at the lowest power.

_____

_____

_____

10. Rotate the oil immersion lens slightly to the side and remove the slide. Clean the oil immersion lens carefully with lens paper, and then clean the slide in the same manner with a fresh piece of lens paper. ▬

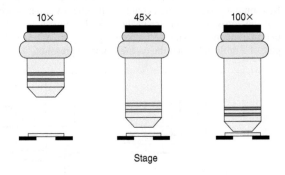

**Figure 3** **Relative working distances of the 10×, 45×, and 100× objectives.**

| Table 1 | Comparison of Metric Units of Length | |
|---|---|---|
| **Metric unit** | **Abbreviation** | **Equivalent** |
| Meter | m | (about 39.3 in.) |
| Centimeter | cm | $10^{-2}$ m |
| Millimeter | mm | $10^{-3}$ m |
| Micrometer (or micron) | μm (μ) | $10^{-6}$ m |
| Nanometer (or millimicrometer or millimicron) | nm (mμ) | $10^{-9}$ m |
| Ångstrom | Å | $10^{-10}$ m |

## The Microscope Field

By this time you should know that the size of the microscope field decreases with increasing magnification. For future microscope work, it will be useful to determine the diameter of each of the microscope fields. This information will allow you to make a fairly accurate estimate of the size of the objects you view in any field. For example, if you have calculated the field diameter to be 4 mm and the object being observed extends across half this diameter, you can estimate that the length of the object is approximately 2 mm.

Microscopic specimens are usually measured in micrometers and millimeters, both units of the metric system. (You can get an idea of the relationship and meaning of these units from **Table 1**.)

### ACTIVITY 3

### Estimating the Diameter of the Microscope Field

1. Obtain a grid slide, which is a slide prepared with graph paper ruled in millimeters. Each of the squares in the grid is 1 mm on each side. Use your lowest-power objective to bring the grid lines into focus.

2. Move the slide so that one grid line touches the edge of the field on one side, and then count the number of squares you can see across the diameter of the field. If you can see only part of a square, as in the accompanying diagram, estimate the part of a millimeter that the partial square represents.

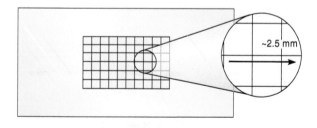

~2.5 mm

Record this figure in the appropriate space marked "field size" on the Summary Chart. (If you have been using the scanning lens, repeat the procedure with the low-power objective lens.)

Complete the chart by computing the approximate diameter of the high-power and oil immersion fields. The general formula for calculating the unknown field diameter is:

Diameter of field $A$ × total magnification of field $A$ = diameter of field $B$ × total magnification of field $B$

where $A$ represents the known or measured field and $B$ represents the unknown field. This can be simplified to

$$\text{Diameter of field } B = \frac{\text{diameter of field } A \times \text{total magnification of field } A}{\text{total magnification of field } B}$$

For example, if the diameter of the low-power field (field $A$) is 2 mm and the total magnification is 50×, you would compute the diameter of the high-power field (field $B$) with a total magnification of 100× as follows:

Field diameter $B$ = (2 mm × 50)/100
Field diameter $B$ = 1 mm

3. Estimate the length (longest dimension) of the following microscopic objects. *Base your calculations on the field sizes you have determined for your microscope.*

Object seen in low-power field:

approximate length:

_____ mm

Object seen in high-power field:

approximate length:

_____ mm

or _____ μm

Object seen in oil immersion field:

approximate length:

_____ μm

4. If an object viewed with the oil immersion lens looked as it does in the field depicted below, could you determine its approximate size from this view?

If not, then how could you determine it? _____

_____

_____

_____ ▬

## Perceiving Depth

Any microscopic specimen has depth as well as length and width; it is rare indeed to view a tissue slide with just one layer of cells. Normally you can see two or three cell thicknesses. Therefore, it is important to learn how to determine relative depth with your microscope. In microscope work the **depth of field** (the thickness of the plane that is clearly in focus) is greater at lower magnifications. As magnification increases, depth of field decreases.

**ACTIVITY 4**

### Perceiving Depth

1. Obtain a slide with colored crossed threads. Focusing at low magnification, locate the point where the three threads cross each other.

2. Use the iris diaphragm lever to greatly reduce the light, thus increasing the contrast. Focus down with the coarse adjustment until the threads are out of focus, then slowly focus upward again, noting which thread comes into clear focus first. (You will see two or even all three threads, so you must be very careful in determining which one first comes into clear focus.) Observe: As you rotate the adjustment knob forward (away from you), does the stage rise or fall? If the stage rises, then the first clearly focused thread is the top one; the last clearly focused thread is the bottom one.

If the stage descends, how is the order affected? _____

_____

Record your observations, relative to which color of thread is uppermost, middle, or lowest:

Top thread _____

Middle thread _____

Bottom thread _____ ▬

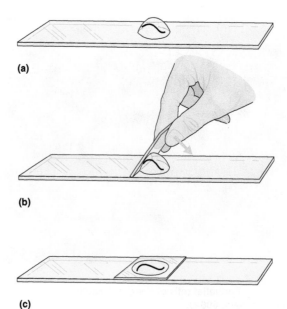

**(a)**

**(b)**

**(c)**

**Figure 4 Procedure for preparation of a wet mount.**
**(a)** The object is placed in a drop of water (or saline) on a clean slide, **(b)** a coverslip is held at a 45° angle with the fingertips, and **(c)** it is lowered carefully over the water and the object.

## Viewing Cells Under the Microscope

There are various ways to prepare cells for viewing under a microscope. Cells and tissues can look very different with different stains and preparation techniques. One method of preparation is to mix the cells in physiological saline (called a wet mount) and stain them with methylene blue stain.

If you are not instructed to prepare your own wet mount, obtain a prepared slide of epithelial cells to make the observations in step 10 of Activity 5.

**ACTIVITY 5**

### Preparing and Observing a Wet Mount

1. Obtain the following: a clean microscope slide and coverslip, two flat-tipped toothpicks, a dropper bottle of physiological saline, a dropper bottle of iodine or methylene blue stain, and filter paper (or paper towels). Handle only your own slides throughout the procedure.

2. Place a drop of physiological saline in the center of the slide. Using the flat end of the toothpick, *gently* scrape the inner lining of your cheek. Transfer your cheek scrapings to the slide by agitating the end of the toothpick in the drop of saline **(Figure 4a)**.

 *Immediately* discard the used toothpick in the disposable autoclave bag provided at the supplies area.

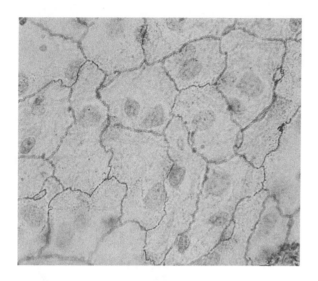

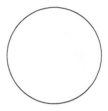

8. Make a sketch of the epithelial cells that you observe.

Use information on your Summary Chart to estimate the diameter of cheek epithelial cells.

_____ μm

Why do *your* cheek cells look different than those in the photomicrograph (Figure 5)? (Hint: What did you have to *do* to your cheek to obtain them?)

_____

_____

**Figure 5 Epithelial cells of the cheek cavity (surface view, 600×).**

3.   Add a tiny drop of the iodine or methylene blue stain to the preparation. (These epithelial cells are nearly transparent and thus difficult to see without the stain, which colors the nuclei of the cells and makes them look much darker than the cytoplasm.) Stir again.

 *Immediately* discard the used toothpick in the disposable autoclave bag provided at the supplies area.

4.   Hold the coverslip with your fingertips so that its bottom edge touches one side of the fluid drop (Figure 4b), then *carefully* lower the coverslip onto the preparation (Figure 4c). *Do not just drop the coverslip,* or you will trap large air bubbles under it, which will obscure the cells. *A coverslip should always be used with a wet mount* to prevent soiling the lens if you should misfocus.

5.   Examine your preparation carefully. The coverslip should be tight against the slide. If there is excess fluid around its edges, you will need to remove it. Obtain a piece of filter paper, fold it in half, and use the folded edge to absorb the excess fluid. You may use a twist of paper towel as an alternative.

 Before continuing, discard the filter paper or paper towel in the disposable autoclave bag.

6.   Place the slide on the stage, and locate the cells at the lowest power. You will probably want to dim the light with the iris diaphragm to provide more contrast for viewing the lightly stained cells. Furthermore, a wet mount will dry out quickly in bright light because a bright light source is hot.

7.   Cheek epithelial cells are very thin, six-sided cells. In the cheek, they provide a smooth, tilelike lining (Figure 5). Move to high power to examine the cells more closely.

9. When you complete your observations of the wet mount, dispose of your wet mount preparation in the beaker of bleach solution, and put the coverslips in an autoclave bag.

10. Obtain a prepared slide of cheek epithelial cells, and view them under the microscope.

Estimate the diameter of one of these cheek epithelial cells using information from the Summary Chart.

_____ μm

Why are these cells more similar to those in the photograph (Figure 5) and easier to measure than those of the wet mount?

_____

_____

_____

11. Before leaving the laboratory, make sure all other materials are properly discarded or returned to the appropriate laboratory station. Clean the microscope lenses and put the dust cover on the microscope before you return it to the storage cabinet. ■

Name ______________________________

Lab Time/Date ______________________

# The Microscope

## Care and Structure of the Compound Microscope

**1.** Label all indicated parts of the microscope.

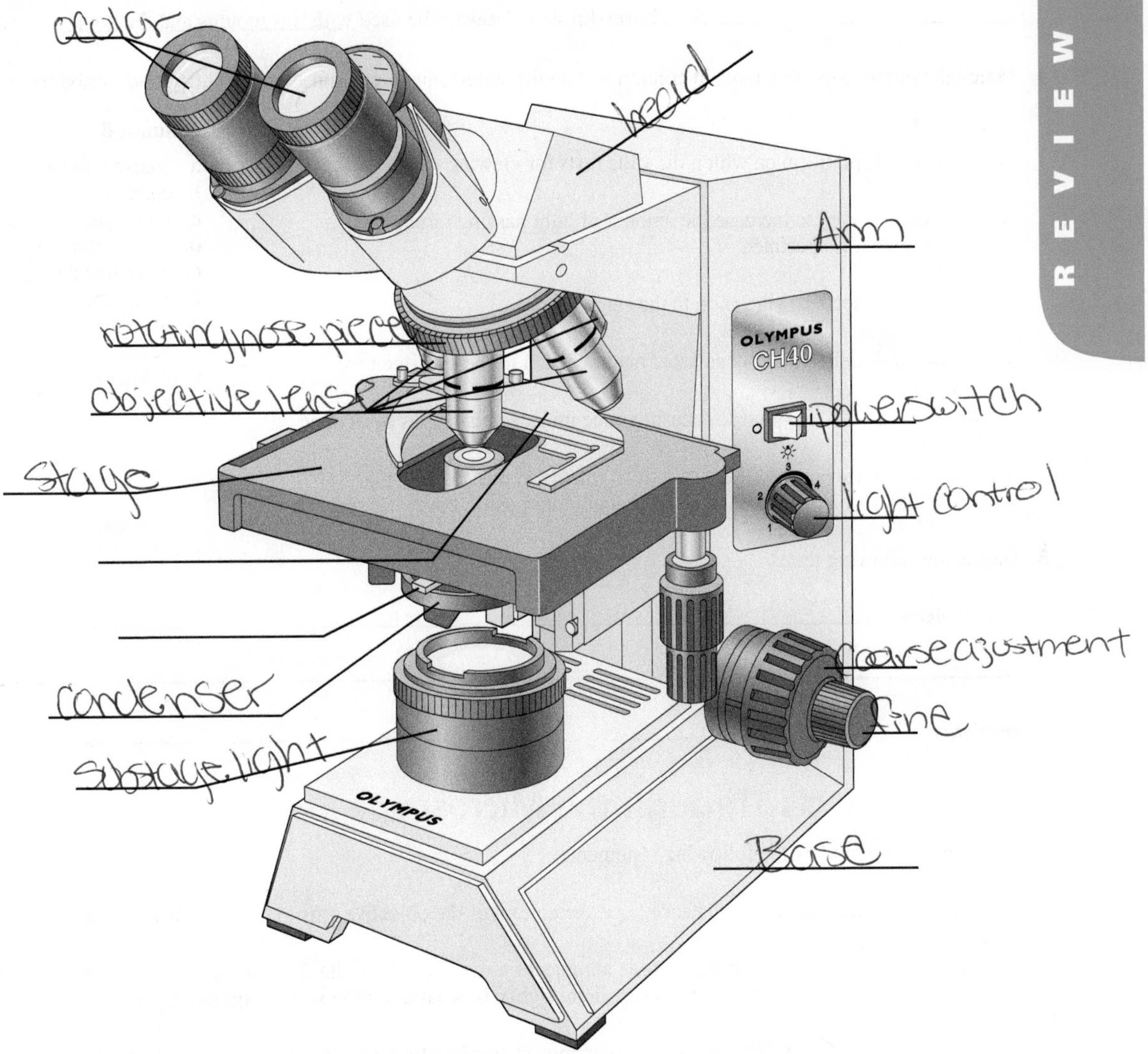
OLYMPUS
CH40
OLYMPUS
ocular
head
Arm
rotating nose piece
objective lense
power switch
Stage
light control
coarse ajustment
condenser
fine
substage light
Base

**2.** Explain the proper technique for transporting the microscope.

_______________________________________________________________

**3.** The following statements are true or false. If true, write *T* on the answer blank. If false, correct the statement by writing on the blank the proper word or phrase to replace the one that is underlined.

_____*False*_____ 1. The microscope lens may be cleaned <u>with any soft tissue</u>.

_____ 2. The microscope should be stored with the <u>oil immersion</u> lens in position over the stage.

_____ 3. When beginning to focus, use the <u>lowest-power</u> lens.

_____ 4. When focusing, always focus <u>toward</u> the specimen.

_____ 5. A coverslip should always be used <u>with wet mounts and the high-power and oil lenses</u>.

**4.** Match the microscope structures in column B with the statements in column A that identify or describe them.

**Column A**

_____ 1. platform on which the slide rests for viewing

_____ 2. used to increase the amount of light passing through the specimen

_____ 3. secure(s) the slide to the stage

_____ 4. delivers a concentrated beam of light to the specimen

_____ 5. used for precise focusing once initial focusing has been done

_____ 6. carries the objective lenses; rotates so that the different objective lenses can be brought into position over the specimen

**Column B**

a. coarse adjustment knob
b. condenser
c. fine adjustment knob
d. iris diaphragm
e. mechanical stage
f. nosepiece
g. objective lenses
h. ocular
i. spring clips
j. stage

**5.** Define the following terms.

*virtual image:* _____

_____

*resolution:* _____

# Viewing Objects Through the Microscope

**6.** Complete, or respond to, the following statements:

_____ 1. The distance from the bottom of the objective lens to the specimen is called the _____.

_____ 2. Assume there is an object on the left side of the field that you want to bring to the center (that is, toward the apparent right). In what direction would you move your slide? _____

_____ 3. The area of the specimen seen when looking through the microscope is the _____.

_____ 4. If a microscope has a 10× ocular and the total magnification at a particular time is 950×, the objective lens in use at that time is _____ ×.

_____ 5. Why should the light be dimmed when looking at living (nearly transparent) cells?

_____ 6. If, after focusing in low power, only the fine adjustment need be used to focus the specimen at the higher powers, the microscope is said to be _____.

_____ 7. If, when using a 10× ocular and a 15× objective, the field size is 1.5 mm, the approximate field size with a 30× objective is _____ mm.

_____ 8. If the size of the high-power field is 1.2 mm, an object that occupies approximately a third of that field has an estimated diameter of _____ mm.

**7.** You have been asked to prepare a slide with the letter *k* on it (as shown below). In the circle below, draw the *k* as seen in the low-power field.

| k |

**8.** Figure out the magnification of fields 1 and 3, and the field size of 2. (*Hint:* Use your ruler.) Note that the numbers for the field sizes below are too large to represent the typical compound microscope lens system, but the relationships depicted are accurate.

5 mm          _____ mm          0.5 mm

1. →○←          2. →○←          3. →o←

_____ ×          100 ×          _____ ×

**9.** Say you are observing an object in the low-power field. When you switch to high-power, it is no longer in your field of view.

Why might this occur? _____

_____

What should be done initially to prevent this from happening? _____

_____

**10.** Do the following factors increase or decrease as one moves to higher magnifications with the microscope?

resolution: _____          amount of light needed: _____

working distance: _____          depth of field: _____

**11.** A student has the high-dry lens in position and appears to be intently observing the specimen. The instructor, noting a working distance of about 1 cm, knows the student isn't actually seeing the specimen.

How so? _____

**12.** Describe the proper procedure for preparing a wet mount.

_____

_____

_____

**13.** Indicate the probable cause of the following situations arising during use of a microscope.

a. Only half of the field is illuminated: _____

_____

b. Field does not change as mechanical stage is moved: _____

_____

41

## Photo Credits

**Credits are listed in order of appearance.**

1: Leica Microsystems, Inc. 5: Victor P. Eroschenko, Pearson Education. 4.1b: Don Fawcett/Science Source/Photo Researchers. 4.4.1–6, 4.RS2.1–3: William Karkow, Pearson Education.

## Illustration Credits

**All illustrations are by Imagineering STA Media Services, except for Review Sheet art and as noted below.**

2–4, Activity 3: Precision Graphics.

# The Cell: Anatomy and Division

## MATERIALS

- ☐ Three-dimensional model of the "composite" animal cell or laboratory chart of cell anatomy
- ☐ Compound microscope
- ☐ Prepared slides of simple squamous epithelium, teased smooth muscle (l.s.), human blood cell smear, and sperm
- ☐ Animation/video of mitosis
- ☐ Three-dimensional models of mitotic stages
- ☐ Prepared slides of whitefish blastulas
- ☐ Chenille sticks (pipe cleaners), two different colors cut into 3-inch pieces, 8 pieces per group

**Note to the Instructor:** See directions for handling wet mount preparations and disposable supplies. For suggestions on the animation/video of mitosis, see the Instructor Guide.

MasteringA&P® For related exercise study tools, go to the Study Area of MasteringA&P. There you will find:

- Practice Anatomy Lab PAL
- PhysioEx PEx
- A&PFlix *A&P Flix*
- Practice quizzes, Histology Atlas, eText, Videos, and more!

## OBJECTIVES

1. Define *cell, organelle,* and *inclusion.*
2. Identify on a cell model or diagram the following cellular regions and list the major function of each: nucleus, cytoplasm, and plasma membrane.
3. Identify the cytoplasmic organelles and discuss their structure and function.
4. Compare and contrast specialized cells with the concept of the "generalized cell."
5. Define *interphase, mitosis,* and *cytokinesis.*
6. List the stages of mitosis and describe the key events of each stage.
7. Identify the mitotic phases on slides or appropriate diagrams.
8. Explain the importance of mitotic cell division and describe its product.

## PRE-LAB QUIZ

1. Define *cell.* _____
   _____

2. When a cell is not dividing, the DNA is loosely spread throughout the nucleus in a threadlike form called:
   a. chromatin          c. cytosol
   b. chromosomes        d. ribosomes

3. The plasma membrane not only provides a protective boundary for the cell but also determines which substances enter or exit the cell. We call this characteristic:
   a. diffusion          c. osmosis
   b. membrane potential d. selective permeability

4. Proteins are assembled on these organelles.
   _____

5. Because these organelles are responsible for providing most of the ATP needed by the cell, they are often referred to as the "powerhouses" of the cell. They are the:
   a. centrioles         c. mitochondria
   b. lysosomes          d. ribosomes

6. Circle the correct underlined term. During <u>cytokinesis</u> / <u>interphase</u> the cell grows and performs its usual activities.

7. Circle True or False. The end product of mitosis is four genetically identical daughter nuclei.

8. How many stages of mitosis are there? _____

9. DNA replication occurs during:
   a. cytokinesis        c. metaphase
   b. interphase         d. prophase

10. Circle True or False. All animal cells have a cell wall.

The **cell,** the structural and functional unit of all living things, is a complex entity. The cells of the human body are highly diverse, and their differences in size, shape, and internal composition reflect their specific roles in the body. Still, cells do have many common anatomical features, and all cells must carry out certain functions to sustain life. For example, all cells can maintain their boundaries, metabolize, digest nutrients and dispose of wastes, grow and reproduce, move, and respond to a stimulus. This exercise focuses on structural similarities found in many cells and illustrated by a "composite," or "generalized," cell (Figure 1a) and considers only the function of cell reproduction (cell division).

## Anatomy of the Composite Cell

In general, all animal cells have three major regions, or parts, that can readily be identified with a light microscope: the **nucleus,** the **plasma membrane,** and the **cytoplasm.** The nucleus is typically a round or oval structure near the center of the cell. It is surrounded by cytoplasm, which in turn is enclosed by the plasma membrane. Since the invention of the electron microscope, even smaller cell structures—organelles—have been identified. See the diagram (Figure 1a) representing the fine structure of the composite cell. An electron micrograph (Figure 1b) reveals the cellular structure, particularly of the nucleus.

### Nucleus

The nucleus contains the genetic material, DNA, sections of which are called genes. Often described as the control center of the cell, the nucleus is necessary for cell reproduction. A cell that has lost or ejected its nucleus is programmed to die.

When the cell is not dividing, the genetic material is loosely dispersed throughout the nucleus in a threadlike form called **chromatin.** When the cell is in the process of dividing to form daughter cells, the chromatin coils and condenses, forming dense, darkly staining rodlike bodies called **chromosomes**—much in the way a stretched spring becomes shorter and thicker when it is released. Carefully note the appearance of the nucleus—it is somewhat nondescript when a cell is healthy. A dark nucleus and clumped chromatin indicate that the cell is dying and undergoing degeneration.

The nucleus also contains one or more small round bodies, called **nucleoli,** composed primarily of proteins and ribonucleic acid (RNA). The nucleoli are assembly sites for ribosomal particles that are particularly abundant in the cytoplasm. Ribosomes are the actual protein-synthesizing "factories."

The nucleus is bound by a double-layered porous membrane, the **nuclear envelope.** The nuclear envelope is similar in composition to other cellular membranes, but it is distinguished by its large **nuclear pores.** They are spanned by protein complexes that regulate what passes through and permit easy passage of protein and RNA molecules.

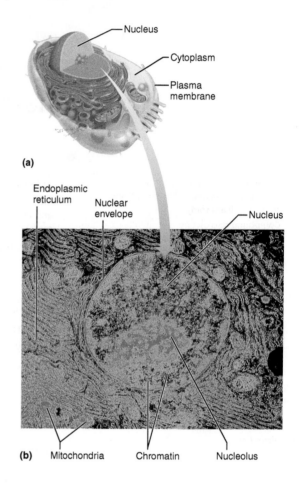

**(a)**

**(b)** Mitochondria    Chromatin    Nucleolus

**Figure 1 Anatomy of the composite animal cell.** **(a)** Diagram. **(b)** Transmission electron micrograph (5000×).

**ACTIVITY 1**

### Identifying Parts of a Cell

As able, identify the nuclear envelope, chromatin, nucleolus, and the nuclear pores (see Figure 1a and b and Figure 3.)

### Plasma Membrane

The **plasma membrane** separates cell contents from the surrounding environment. Its main structural building blocks are phospholipids (fats) and globular protein molecules. Some of the externally facing proteins and lipids have sugar (carbohydrate) side chains attached to them that are important in cellular interactions (Figure 2). Described by the fluid mosaic model, the membrane is a bilayer of phospholipid molecules in which the protein molecules float. Occasional cholesterol molecules dispersed in the bilayer help stabilize it.

Besides providing a protective barrier for the cell, the plasma membrane plays an active role in determining which substances may enter or leave the cell and in what quantity. Because of its molecular composition, the plasma membrane is selective about what passes through it. It allows

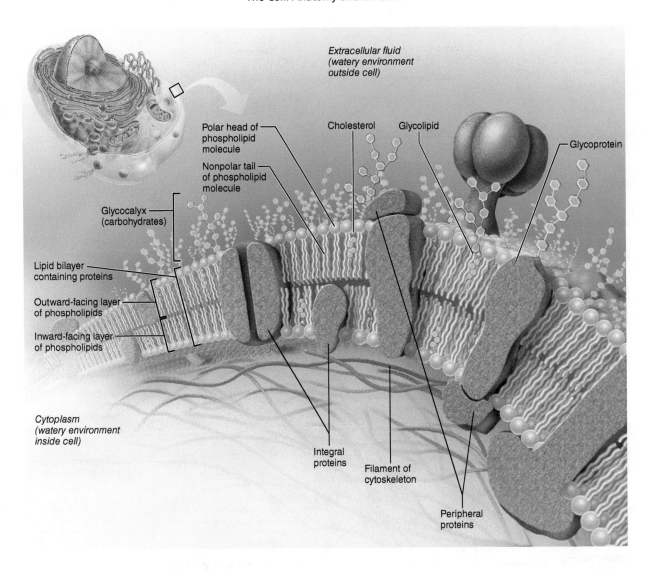

**Figure 2  Structural details of the plasma membrane.**

nutrients to enter the cell but keeps out undesirable substances. By the same token, valuable cell proteins and other substances are kept within the cell, and excreta, or wastes, pass to the exterior. This property is known as **selective permeability.** Transport through the plasma membrane occurs in two basic ways. In *active transport,* the cell must provide energy in the form of adenosine triphosphate, or ATP, to power the transport process. In *passive transport,* the transport process is driven by concentration or pressure differences.

Additionally, the plasma membrane maintains a resting potential that is essential to normal functioning of excitable cells, such as neurons and muscle cells, and plays a vital role in cell signaling and cell-to-cell interactions. In some cells the membrane is thrown into minute fingerlike projections or folds called **microvilli (Figure 3).** Microvilli greatly increase the surface area of the cell available for absorption or passage of materials and for the binding of signaling molecules.

**ACTIVITY 2**

## Identifying Components of a Plasma Membrane

Identify the phospholipid and protein portions of the plasma membrane in the figure (Figure 2). Also locate the sugar (*glyco* = carbohydrate) side chains and cholesterol molecules. Identify the microvilli in the generalized cell diagram (Figure 3). ■

## Cytoplasm and Organelles

The cytoplasm consists of the cell contents between the nucleus and plasma membrane. It is the major site of most activities carried out by the cell. Suspended in the **cytosol,** the fluid cytoplasmic material, are many small structures called **organelles** (literally, "small organs"). The organelles are the metabolic machinery of the cell, and they are highly organized to carry out specific functions for the cell as a

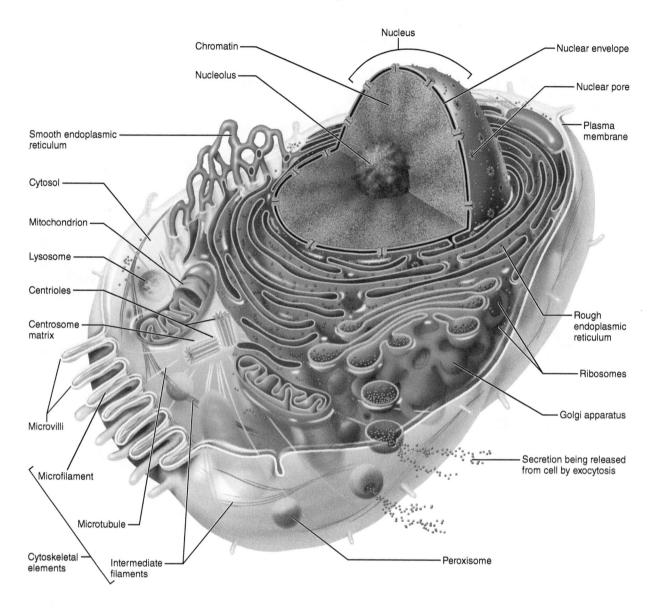

**Figure 3 Structure of the generalized cell.** No cell is exactly like this one, but this composite illustrates features common to many human cells. Not all organelles are drawn to the same scale in this illustration.

whole. The organelles include the ribosomes, endoplasmic reticulum, Golgi apparatus, lysosomes, peroxisomes, mitochondria, cytoskeletal elements, and centrioles.

### ACTIVITY 3

### Locating Organelles

Each organelle type is described in the following list (and summarized in **Table 1**). Read through the list and table and then, as best you can, locate the organelles in the illustrations (Figure 1b and 3). ▪

• **Ribosomes** are densely staining, roughly spherical bodies composed of RNA and protein. They are the actual sites

of protein synthesis. They are seen floating free in the cytoplasm or attached to a membranous structure. When they are attached, the whole ribosome-membrane complex is called the *rough endoplasmic reticulum.*

• The **endoplasmic reticulum (ER)** is a highly folded system of membranous tubules and cisterns (sacs) that extends throughout the cytoplasm. The ER is continuous with the nuclear envelope, forming a system of channels for the transport of cellular substances (primarily proteins) from one part of the cell to another. The ER exists in two forms, **rough ER** and **smooth ER.** A particular cell may have both or only one, depending on its specific functions. The rough ER is studded with ribosomes. Its cisterns modify and store the newly formed proteins and dispatch them to other areas of the cell. The external face of the rough ER is involved in phospholipid

Labels: Chromatin, Nucleolus, Smooth endoplasmic reticulum, Cytosol, Mitochondrion, Lysosome, Centrioles, Centrosome matrix, Microvilli, Microfilament, Microtubule, Cytoskeletal elements, Intermediate filaments, Nucleus, Nuclear envelope, Nuclear pore, Plasma membrane, Rough endoplasmic reticulum, Ribosomes, Golgi apparatus, Secretion being released from cell by exocytosis, Peroxisome

| Table 1 | Summary of Structure and Function of Cytoplasmic Organelles | |
|---|---|---|
| **Organelle** | | **Location and function** |
| Ribosomes |  | Tiny spherical bodies composed of RNA and protein; floating free or attached to a membranous structure (the rough ER) in the cytoplasm. Actual sites of protein synthesis. |
| Endoplasmic reticulum (ER) |  | Membranous system of tubules that extends throughout the cytoplasm; two varieties: rough and smooth. Rough ER is studded with ribosomes; tubules of the rough ER provide an area for storage and transport of the proteins made on the ribosomes to other cell areas; external face synthesizes phospholipids and cholesterol. Smooth ER, which has no function in protein synthesis, is a site of steroid and lipid synthesis, lipid metabolism, and drug detoxification. |
| Golgi apparatus |  | Stack of flattened sacs with bulbous ends and associated small vesicles; found close to the nucleus. Plays a role in packaging proteins or other substances for export from the cell or incorporation into the plasma membrane and in packaging lysosomal enzymes. |
| Lysosomes |  | Various-sized membranous sacs containing digestive enzymes including acid hydrolases; function to digest worn-out cell organelles and foreign substances that enter the cell. Have the capacity of total cell destruction if ruptured. |
| Peroxisomes |  | Small lysosome-like membranous sacs containing oxidase enzymes that detoxify alcohol, hydrogen peroxide, and other harmful chemicals. |
| Mitochondria |  | Generally rod-shaped bodies with a double-membrane wall; inner membrane is thrown into folds, or cristae; contain enzymes that oxidize foodstuffs to produce cellular energy (ATP); often referred to as "powerhouses of the cell." |
| Centrioles |  | Paired, cylindrical bodies lie at right angles to each other, close to the nucleus. As part of the centrosome, they direct the formation of the mitotic spindle during cell division; form the bases of cilia and flagella. |
| Cytoskeletal elements: microfilaments, intermediate filaments, and microtubules |  | Provide cellular support; function in intracellular transport. Microfilaments are formed largely of actin, a contractile protein, and thus are important in cell mobility, particularly in muscle cells. Intermediate filaments are stable elements composed of a variety of proteins and resist mechanical forces acting on cells. Microtubules form the internal structure of the centrioles and help determine cell shape. |

and cholesterol synthesis. The amount of rough ER is closely correlated with the amount of protein a cell manufactures and is especially abundant in cells that make protein products for export—for example, the pancreas cells that produce digestive enzymes destined for the small intestine.

The smooth ER does not participate in protein synthesis but is present in conspicuous amounts in cells that produce steroid-based hormones—for example, the interstitial endocrine cells of the testes, which produce testosterone. Smooth ER is also abundant in cells that are active in lipid metabolism and drug detoxification activities—liver cells, for instance.

• The **Golgi apparatus** is a stack of flattened sacs with bulbous ends and associated membranous vesicles that is generally found close to the nucleus. Within its cisterns, the proteins delivered to it by transport vesicles from the rough ER are modified, segregated, and packaged into membranous

vesicles that ultimately (1) are incorporated into the plasma membrane, (2) become secretory vesicles that release their contents from the cell, or (3) become lysosomes.

• **Lysosomes,** which appear in various sizes, are membrane-bound sacs containing an array of powerful digestive enzymes. A product of the packaging activities of the Golgi apparatus, the lysosomes contain *acid hydrolases,* enzymes capable of digesting worn-out cell structures and foreign substances that enter the cell via vesicle formation through phagocytosis or endocytosis. Because they have the capacity of total cell destruction, the lysosomes are often referred to as the "suicide sacs" of the cell.

• **Peroxisomes,** like lysosomes, are enzyme-containing sacs. However, their *oxidases* have a different task. Using oxygen, they detoxify a number of harmful substances, most importantly free radicals. Peroxisomes are particularly abundant in kidney and liver cells, cells that are actively involved in detoxification.

• **Mitochondria** are generally rod-shaped bodies with a double-membrane wall; the inner membrane is thrown into folds, or *cristae.* Oxidative enzymes on or within the mitochondria catalyze the reactions of the Krebs cycle and the electron transport chain (collectively called aerobic cellular respiration), in which end products of food digestion are broken down to produce energy. The released energy is captured in the bonds of ATP molecules, which are then transported out of the mitochondria to provide a ready energy supply to power the cell. Every living cell requires a constant supply of ATP for its many activities. Because the mitochondria provide the bulk of this ATP, they are referred to as the "powerhouses" of the cell.

• **Cytoskeletal elements** ramify throughout the cytoplasm, forming an internal scaffolding called the *cytoskeleton* that supports and moves substances within the cell. The **microtubules** are slender tubules formed of proteins called *tubulins.* Most microtubules radiate from a region of cytoplasm near the nucleus called the *centrosome,* and they have the ability to aggregate and then disaggregate spontaneously. Microtubules organize the cytoskeleton and form the spindle during cell division. They also transport substances down the length of elongated cells (such as neurons), suspend organelles, and help maintain cell shape by providing rigidity to the soft cellular substance. The stable **intermediate filaments** are proteinaceous cytoskeletal elements that act as internal guy wires to resist mechanical (pulling) forces acting on cells. **Microfilaments,** ribbon or cordlike elements, are formed of contractile proteins, primarily *actin.* Because of their ability to shorten and then relax to assume a more elongated form, these are important in cell mobility and are very conspicuous in muscle cells that are specialized to contract. A cross-linked network of microfilaments called the *terminal web* braces and strengthens the internal face of the plasma membrane.

The cytoskeletal structures are changeable and microscopic. With the exception of the microtubules of the mitotic spindle, which are very obvious during cell division, and the microfilaments of skeletal muscle cells, they are rarely seen, even in electron micrographs. (Note that they are not depicted in Figure 1b). However, special stains can reveal the plentiful supply of these important structures.

• The paired **centrioles** lie close to the nucleus within the centrosome in cells capable of reproducing themselves. They are rod-shaped bodies that lie at right angles to each other. Internally each centriole is composed of nine triplets of microtubules. During cell division, the centrosome complex that contains the centrioles directs the formation of the mitotic spindle. Centrioles also form the cell projections called cilia and flagella, and in that role are called basal bodies.

The cell cytoplasm contains various other substances and structures, including stored foods (glycogen granules and lipid droplets), pigment granules, crystals of various types, water vacuoles, and ingested foreign materials. However, these are not part of the active metabolic machinery of the cell and are therefore called **inclusions.**

## Examining the Cell Model

Once you have located all of these structures in the art (Figures 1b and 3), examine the cell model (or cell chart) to repeat and reinforce your identifications. ▬

# Differences and Similarities in Cell Structure

## Observing Various Cell Structures

1. Obtain a compound microscope and prepared slides of simple squamous epithelium, smooth muscle cells (teased), human blood, and sperm.

2. Observe each slide under the microscope, carefully noting similarities and differences in the cells. The oil immersion lens will be needed to observe blood and sperm. Distinguish the limits of the individual cells, and notice the shape and position of the nucleus in each case. When you look at the human blood smear, direct your attention to the red blood cells, the pink-stained cells that are most numerous. Sketch your observations in the circles provided.

3. Measure the length or diameter of each cell, and record below the appropriate sketch.

4. How do these four cell types differ in shape and size?

_____

_____

_____

_____

How might cell shape affect cell function?

_____

_____

_____

_____

_____

Which cells have visible projections? _____

_____

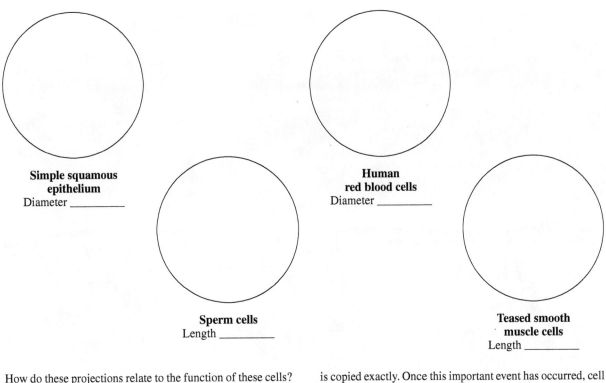

**Simple squamous epithelium**
Diameter _____

**Human red blood cells**
Diameter _____

**Sperm cells**
Length _____

**Teased smooth muscle cells**
Length _____

How do these projections relate to the function of these cells?

_____

_____

Do any of these cells lack a plasma membrane? _____

A nucleus? _____

In the cells with a nucleus, can you discern nucleoli?

_____

Were you able to observe any of the organelles in these cells?

_____ Why or why not? _____

_____

_____

_____

_____ ▬

# Cell Division: Mitosis and Cytokinesis

A cell's *life cycle* is the series of changes it goes through from the time it is formed until it reproduces itself. It consists of two stages—**interphase,** the longer period during which the cell grows and carries out its usual activities (Figure 4a), and **cell division,** when the cell reproduces itself by dividing. In an interphase cell about to divide, the genetic material (DNA) is copied exactly. Once this important event has occurred, cell division ensues.

Cell division in all cells other than bacteria consists of two events called mitosis and cytokinesis. **Mitosis** is the division of the copied DNA of the mother cell to two daughter cells. **Cytokinesis** is the division of the cytoplasm, which begins when mitosis is nearly complete. Although mitosis is usually accompanied by cytokinesis, in some instances cytoplasmic division does not occur, leading to the formation of binucleate or multinucleate cells. This is relatively common in the human liver.

The product of **mitosis** is two daughter nuclei that are genetically identical to the mother nucleus. This distinguishes mitosis from **meiosis,** a specialized type of nuclear division that occurs only in the reproductive organs (testes or ovaries). Meiosis, which yields four daughter nuclei that differ genetically in composition from the mother nucleus, is used only for the production of gametes (eggs and sperm) for sexual reproduction. The function of cell division, including mitosis and cytokinesis in the body, is to increase the number of cells for growth and repair while maintaining their genetic heritage.

The phases of mitosis include **prophase, metaphase, anaphase,** and **telophase.** (The detailed events of interphase, mitosis, and cytokinesis are described and illustrated in **Figure 4.**)

Mitosis is essentially the same in all animal cells, but depending on the tissue, it takes from 5 minutes to several hours to complete. In most cells, centriole replication occurs during interphase of the next cell cycle.

At the end of cell division, two daughter cells exist—each with a smaller cytoplasmic mass than the mother cell but genetically identical to it. The daughter cells grow and carry out the normal spectrum of metabolic processes until it is their turn to divide.

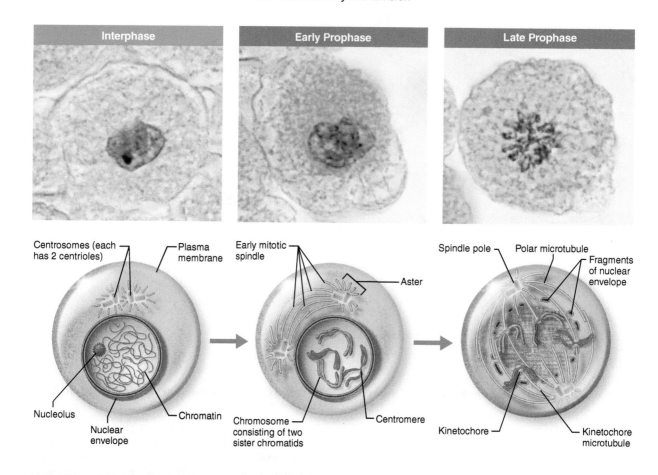

**Interphase**

Interphase is the period of a cell's life when it carries out its normal metabolic activities and grows. Interphase is not part of mitosis.

• During interphase, the DNA-containing material is in the form of chromatin. The nuclear envelope and one or more nucleoli are intact and visible.

• There are three distinct periods of interphase:
  $G_1$: The centrioles begin replicating.
  S:   DNA is replicated.
  $G_2$: Final preparations for mitosis are completed and centrioles finish replicating.

**Prophase—first phase of mitosis**

**Early Prophase**
• The chromatin condenses, forming barlike chromosomes.

• Each duplicated chromosome consists of two identical threads, called **sister chromatids**, held together at the **centromere**. (Later when the chromatids separate, each will be a new chromosome.)

• As the chromosomes appear, the nucleoli disappear, and the two centrosomes separate from one another.

• The centrosomes act as focal points for growth of a microtubule assembly called the **mitotic spindle**. As the microtubules lengthen, they propel the centrosomes toward opposite ends (poles) of the cell.

• Microtubule arrays called **asters** ("stars") extend from the centrosome matrix.

**Late Prophase**
• The nuclear envelope breaks up, allowing the spindle to interact with the chromosomes.

• Some of the growing spindle microtubules attach to **kinetochores**, special protein structures at each chromosome's centromere. Such microtubules are called **kinetochore microtubules**.

• The remaining spindle microtubules (not attached to any chromosomes) are called **polar microtubules**. The microtubules slide past each other, forcing the poles apart.

• The kinetochore microtubules pull on each chromosome from both poles in a tug-of-war that ultimately draws the chromosomes to the center, or equator, of the cell.

**Figure 4 The interphase cell and the events of cell division.** The cells shown are from an early embryo of a whitefish. Photomicrographs are above; corresponding diagrams are below. (Micrographs approximately 1600×.)

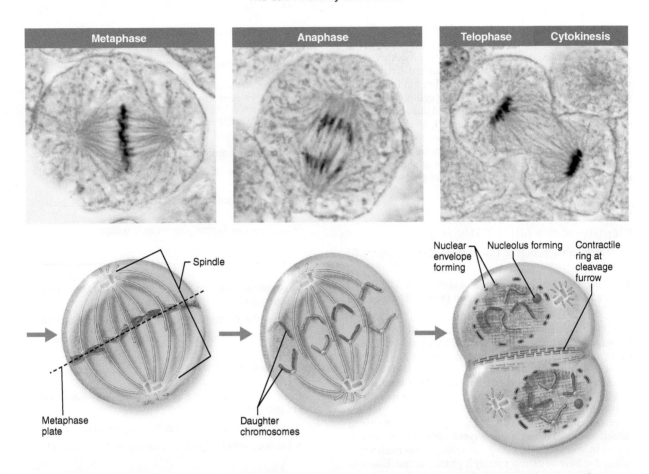

**Metaphase**

**Anaphase**

**Telophase    Cytokinesis**

Spindle

Metaphase plate

Daughter chromosomes

Nuclear envelope forming

Nucleolus forming

Contractile ring at cleavage furrow

### Metaphase—second phase of mitosis

• The two centrosomes are at opposite poles of the cell.

• The chromosomes cluster at the midline of the cell, with their centromeres precisely aligned at the **equator** of the spindle. This imaginary plane midway between the poles is called the **metaphase plate**.

• Enzymes act to separate the chromatids from each other.

### Anaphase—third phase of mitosis

The shortest phase of mitosis, anaphase begins abruptly as the centromeres of the chromosomes split simultaneously. Each chromatid now becomes a chromosome in its own right.

• The kinetochore microtubules, moved along by motor proteins in the kinetochores, gradually pull each chromosome toward the pole it faces.

• At the same time, the polar microtubules slide past each other, lengthen, and push the two poles of the cell apart.

• The moving chromosomes look V shaped. The centromeres lead the way, and the chromosomal "arms" dangle behind them.

• Moving and separating the chromosomes is helped by the fact that the chromosomes are short, compact bodies. Diffuse threads of chromatin would trail, tangle, and break, resulting in imprecise "parceling out" to the daughter cells.

### Telophase—final phase of mitosis

Telophase begins as soon as chromosomal movement stops. This final phase is like prophase in reverse.

• The identical sets of chromosomes at the opposite poles of the cell uncoil and resume their threadlike chromatin form.

• A new nuclear envelope forms around each chromatin mass, nucleoli reappear within the nuclei, and the spindle breaks down and disappears.

• Mitosis is now ended. The cell, for just a brief period, is binucleate (has two nuclei) and each new nucleus is identical to the original mother nucleus.

### Cytokinesis—division of cytoplasm

Cytokinesis begins during late anaphase and continues through and beyond telophase. A contractile ring of actin microfilaments forms the **cleavage furrow** and pinches the cell apart.

**Figure 4** *(continued)*

Cell division is extremely important during the body's growth period. Most cells divide until puberty, when normal body size is achieved and overall body growth ceases. After this time in life, only certain cells carry out cell division routinely—for example, cells subjected to abrasion (epithelium of the skin and lining of the gut). Other cell populations—such as liver cells—stop dividing but retain this ability should some of them be removed or damaged. Skeletal muscle, cardiac muscle, and most mature neurons almost completely lose this ability to divide and thus are severely handicapped by injury. Throughout life, the body retains its ability to repair cuts and wounds and to replace some of its aged cells.

### ACTIVITY 6

## Identifying the Mitotic Stages

1. Watch an animation or video presentation of mitosis (if available).

2. Using the three-dimensional models of dividing cells provided, identify each of the mitotic phases illustrated and described in the figure (Figure 4).

3. Obtain a prepared slide of whitefish blastulas to study the stages of mitosis. The cells of each *blastula* (a stage of embryonic development consisting of a hollow ball of cells) are at approximately the same mitotic stage, so it may be necessary to observe more than one blastula to view all the mitotic stages. A good analogy for a blastula is a soccer ball in which each leather piece making up the ball's surface represents an embryonic cell. The exceptionally high rate of mitosis observed in this tissue is typical of embryos, but if it occurs in specialized tissues it can indicate cancerous cells, which also have an extraordinarily high mitotic rate. Examine the slide carefully, identifying the four mitotic phases and the process of cytokinesis. Compare your observations with the photomicrographs (Figure 4), and verify your identifications with your instructor. ■■

### ACTIVITY 7

## "Chenille Stick" Mitosis

1. Obtain a total of eight 3-inch pieces of chenille, four of one color and four of another color (e.g., four green and four purple).

2. Assemble the chenille sticks into a total of four chromosomes (each with two sister chromatids) by twisting two sticks of the same color together at the center with a single twist.

What does the twist at the center represent? _____

_____

3. Arrange the chromosomes as they appear in early prophase.

Name the structure that assembles during this phase.

_____

Draw early prophase in the space provided in the Review Sheet (question 10).

4. Arrange the chromosomes as they appear in late prophase.

What structure on the chromosome centromere do the

growing spindle microtubules attach to? _____.

What structure is now present as fragments? _____

_____

Draw late prophase in the space provided on the Review Sheet (question 10).

5. Arrange the chromosomes as they appear in metaphase.

What is the name of the imaginary plane that the

chromosomes align along? _____.

Draw metaphase in the space provided on the Review Sheet (question 10).

6. Arrange the chromosomes as they appear in anaphase.

What does untwisting of the chenille sticks represent?

_____

_____

Each sister chromatid has now become a _____.

Draw anaphase in the space provided on the Review Sheet (question 10).

7. Arrange the chromosomes as they appear in telophase.

Briefly list four reasons why telophase is like the reverse of prophase.

_____

_____

_____

Draw telophase in the space provided on the Review Sheet (question 10).

# The Cell:
# Anatomy and Division

## Anatomy of the Composite Cell

**1.** Define the following terms:

*organelle:* _____

_____

*cell:* _____

**2.** Although cells have differences that reflect their specific functions in the body, what functions do they have in common?

_____

**3.** Identify the following cell parts:

_____   1. external boundary of cell; regulates flow of materials into and out of the cell; site of cell signaling

___lysomes___   2. contains digestive enzymes of many varieties; "suicide sac" of the cell

___Ribosomes___   3. scattered throughout the cell; major site of ATP synthesis

_____   4. slender extensions of the plasma membrane that increase its surface area

_____   5. stored glycogen granules, crystals, pigments, and so on

_____   6. membranous system consisting of flattened sacs and vesicles; packages proteins for export

_____   7. control center of the cell; necessary for cell division and cell life

___Mitochondria___   8. two rod-shaped bodies near the nucleus; associated with the formation of the mitotic spindle

___RER___   9. dense, darkly staining nuclear body; packaging site for ribosomes

_____   10. contractile elements of the cytoskeleton

_____   11. membranous system; involved in intracellular transport of proteins and synthesis of membrane lipids

_____   12. attached to membrane systems or scattered in the cytoplasm; site of protein synthesis

_____   13. threadlike structures in the nucleus; contain genetic material (DNA)

___peroxisomes___   14. site of free radical detoxification

**4.** In the following diagram, label all parts provided with a leader line.

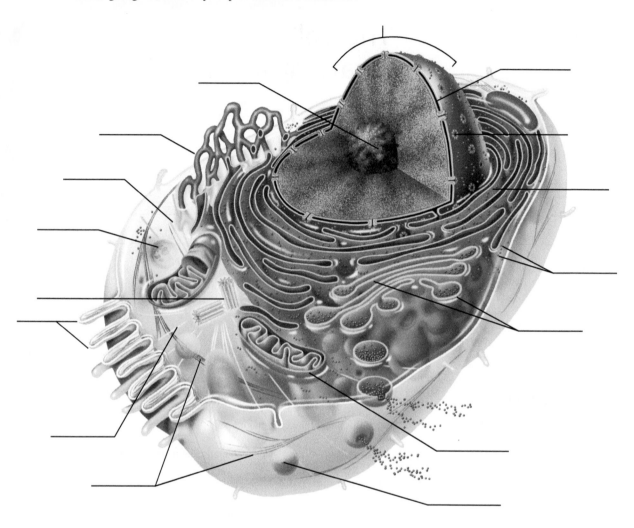

# Differences and Similarities in Cell Structure

**5.** For each of the following cell types, list (a) *one* important structural characteristic observed in the laboratory, and (b) the function that the structure complements or ensures.

squamous epithelium    a. _____

                            b. _____

sperm                   a. _____

                            b. _____

smooth muscle       a. _____

                            b. _____

red blood cells      a. _____

                            b. _____

**6.** What is the significance of the red blood cell being anucleate (without a nucleus)? _____

_____

Did it ever have a nucleus? (Use an appropriate reference.) _____ If so, when? _____

**7.** Of the four cells observed microscopically (squamous epithelial cells, red blood cells, smooth muscle cells, and sperm),

which has the smallest diameter? _____ Which is longest? _____

# Cell Division: Mitosis and Cytokinesis

**8.** Identify the three phases of mitosis in the following photomicrographs.

a. ___Metaphase___   b. ___Anaphase___   c. ___Late prophase___

**9.** What is the importance of mitotic cell division? _____

_____

**10.** Draw the phases of mitosis for a cell that contains four chromosomes as its diploid or 2*n* number.

**11.** Complete or respond to the following statements:

Division of the _1_ is referred to as mitosis. Cytokinesis is division of the _2_. The major structural difference between chromatin and chromosomes is that the latter are _3_. Chromosomes attach to the spindle fibers by undivided structures called _4_. If a cell undergoes mitosis but not cytokinesis, the product is _5_. The structure that acts as a scaffolding for chromosomal attachment and movement is called the _6_. _7_ is the period of cell life when the cell is not involved in division. Two cell populations in the body that do not routinely undergo cell division are _8_ and _9_.

1. _____

2. _____

3. _____

4. _____

5. _____

6. _____

7. _____

8. _____

9. _____

**12.** Using the key, categorize each of the events described below according to the phase in which it occurs.

*Key:*    a.  anaphase      b.  interphase      c.  metaphase      d.  prophase      e.  telophase

_____ 1. Chromatin coils and condenses, forming chromosomes.

_____ 2. The chromosomes are V shaped.

_____ 3. The nuclear envelope re-forms.

_____ 4. Chromosomes stop moving toward the poles.

_____ 5. Chromosomes line up in the center of the cell.

_____ 6. The nuclear envelope fragments.

_____ 7. The mitotic spindle forms.

_____ 8. DNA synthesis occurs.

_____ 9. Centrioles replicate.

_____ 10. Chromosomes first appear to be duplex structures.

_____ 11. Chromosomal centromeres are attached to the kinetochore fibers.

_____ 12. Cleavage furrow forms.

_____ and _____ 13. The nuclear envelope(s) is absent.

**13.** What is the physical advantage of the chromatin coiling and condensing to form short chromosomes at the onset of mitosis?

_____

_____

## Illustration Credits

All illustrations are by Imagineering STA Media Services, except for Review Sheet art and as noted below.

2: Imagineering STA Media Services/Precision Graphics. 3, 4.RS1: Tomo Narashima.

# The Cell: Transport Mechanisms and Cell Permeability

## MATERIALS

**Passive Processes**

*Diffusion of Dye Through Agar Gel*

☐ Petri dish containing 12 ml of 1.5% agar-agar

☐ Millimeter-ruled graph paper

☐ Wax marking pencil

☐ 3.5% methylene blue solution (approximately 0.1 *M*) in dropper bottles

☐ 1.6% potassium permanganate solution (approximately 0.1 *M*) in dropper bottles

☐ Medicine dropper

*Diffusion and Osmosis Through Nonliving Membranes*

☐ Four dialysis sacs or small Hefty® sandwich bags

☐ Small funnel

☐ 25-ml graduated cylinder

☐ Wax marking pencil

☐ Fine twine or dialysis tubing clamps

☐ 250-ml beakers

☐ Distilled water

☐ 40% glucose solution

☐ 10% sodium chloride (NaCl) solution

☐ 40% sucrose solution colored with Congo red dye

☐ Laboratory balance

☐ Paper towels

*(Text continues on next page.)*

MasteringA&P° For related exercise study tools, go to the Study Area of MasteringA&P. There you will find:

• Practice Anatomy Lab PAL

• PhysioEx PEx

• A&PFlix *A&PFlix*

• Practice quizzes, Histology Atlas, eText, Videos, and more!

## OBJECTIVES

1. Define *selective permeability* and explain the difference between active and passive transport processes.

2. Define *diffusion* and explain how simple diffusion and facilitated diffusion differ.

3. Define *osmosis*, and explain the difference between isotonic, hypotonic, and hypertonic solutions.

4. Define *filtration* and discuss where it occurs in the body.

5. Define *vesicular transport*, and describe phagocytosis, pinocytosis, receptor-mediated endocytosis, and exocytosis.

6. List the processes that account for the movement of substances across the plasma membrane and indicate the driving force for each.

7. Name one substance that uses each membrane transport process.

8. Determine which way substances will move passively through a selectively permeable membrane when given appropriate information about their concentration gradients.

## PRE-LAB QUIZ

1. Circle the correct underlined term. A passive process, <u>diffusion</u> / <u>osmosis</u> is the movement of solute molecules from an area of greater concentration to an area of lesser concentration.

2. A solution surrounding a cell is *hypertonic* if:
   a. it contains fewer nonpenetrating solute particles than the interior of the cell.
   b. it contains more nonpenetrating solute particles than the interior of the cell.
   c. it contains the same amount of nonpenetrating solute particles as the interior of the cell.

3. Which of the following would require an input of energy?
   a. diffusion
   b. filtration
   c. osmosis
   d. vesicular transport

4. Circle the correct underlined term. In <u>pinocytosis</u> / <u>phagocytosis</u>, parts of the plasma membrane and cytoplasm extend and engulf a relatively large or solid material.

5. Circle the correct underlined term. In <u>active</u> / <u>passive</u> processes, the cell provides energy in the form of ATP to power the transport process.

From Exercise 5 of *Human Anatomy & Physiology Laboratory Manual,* Main Version, Tenth Edition. Elaine N. Marieb, Susan J. Mitchell, Lori A. Smith. Copyright © 2014 by Pearson Education, Inc. All rights reserved.

*(Materials list continued.)*

- ☐ Hot plate and large beaker for hot water bath
- ☐ Benedict's solution in dropper bottle
- ☐ Silver nitrate ($AgNO_3$) in dropper bottle
- ☐ Test tubes in rack, test tube holder

*Experiment 1*

- ☐ Deshelled eggs
- ☐ 400-ml beakers
- ☐ Wax marking pencil
- ☐ Distilled water
- ☐ 30% sucrose solution
- ☐ Laboratory balance
- ☐ Paper towels
- ☐ Graph paper
- ☐ Weigh boat

*Experiment 2*

- ☐ Clean microscope slides and coverslips
- ☐ Medicine dropper
- ☐ Compound microscope
- ☐ Vials of animal (mammalian) blood obtained from a biological supply house or veterinarian—at option of instructor

- ☐ Freshly prepared physiological (mammalian) saline solution in dropper bottle
- ☐ 5% sodium chloride solution in dropper bottle
- ☐ Distilled water
- ☐ Filter paper
- ☐ Disposable gloves
- ☐ Basin and wash bottles containing 10% household bleach solution
- ☐ Disposable autoclave bag
- ☐ Paper towels

*Diffusion Demonstrations*

1. Diffusion of a dye through water

Prepared the morning of the laboratory session with setup time noted. Potassium permanganate crystals are placed in a 1000-ml graduated cylinder, and distilled water is added slowly and with as little turbulence as possible to fill to the 1000-ml mark.

2. Osmometer

Just before the laboratory begins, the broad end of a thistle tube is closed with a selectively permeable dialysis membrane, and the tube is secured to a ring stand. Molasses is added to approximately 5 cm above the thistle tube bulb, and the bulb is immersed in a beaker of distilled water. At the beginning of the lab session, the level of the molasses in the tube is marked with a wax pencil.

*Filtration*

- ☐ Ring stand, ring, clamp
- ☐ Filter paper, funnel
- ☐ Solution containing a mixture of uncooked starch, powdered charcoal, and copper sulfate ($CuSO_4$)
- ☐ 10-ml graduated cylinder
- ☐ 100-ml beaker
- ☐ Lugol's iodine in a dropper bottle

**Active Processes**

- ☐ Video showing phagocytosis (if available)
- ☐ Video viewing system

**Note to the Instructor:** See directions for handling wet mount preparations and disposable supplies.

PEx PhysioEx™ 9.0 Computer Simulation Ex.1 on p. PEx-3.

---

Because of its molecular composition, the plasma membrane is selective about what passes through it. It allows nutrients to enter the cell but keeps out undesirable substances. By the same token, valuable cell proteins and other substances are kept within the cell, and excreta or wastes pass to the exterior. This property is known as **selective,** or **differential, permeability.** Transport through the plasma membrane occurs in two basic ways. In **passive processes,** concentration or pressure differences drive the movement. In **active processes,** the cell provides energy (ATP) to power the transport process.

## Passive Processes

The two important passive processes of membrane transport are *diffusion* and *filtration*. Diffusion is an important transport process for every cell in the body. By contrast, filtration usually occurs only across capillary walls.

Molecules possess **kinetic energy** and are in constant motion. As molecules move about randomly at high speeds, they collide and ricochet off one another, changing direction with each collision (**Figure 1**). The driving force for diffusion is kinetic energy of the molecules themselves, and the speed of diffusion depends on molecular size and temperature. Smaller molecules move faster, and molecules move faster as temperature increases.

## Diffusion

When a **concentration gradient** (difference in concentration) exists, the net effect of this random molecular movement

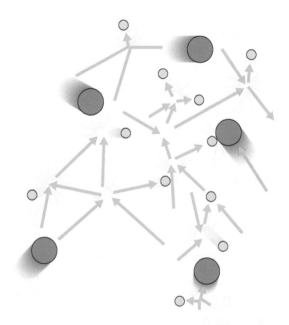

**Figure 1 Random movement and numerous collisions cause molecules to become evenly distributed.** The small spheres represent water molecules; the large spheres represent glucose molecules.

is that the molecules eventually become evenly distributed throughout the environment. **Diffusion** is the movement of molecules from a region of their higher concentration to a region of their lower concentration.

There are many examples of diffusion in nonliving systems. For example, if a bottle of ether was uncorked at the front of the laboratory, very shortly thereafter you would be nodding as the ether molecules became distributed throughout the room. The ability to smell a friend's cologne shortly after he or she has entered the room is another example.

The diffusion of particles into and out of cells is modified by the plasma membrane, which constitutes a physical barrier. In general, molecules diffuse passively through the plasma membrane if they can dissolve in the lipid portion of the membrane, as $CO_2$ and $O_2$ can. The unassisted diffusion of solutes (dissolved substances) through a selectively permeable membrane is called **simple diffusion.**

Certain molecules, for example glucose, are transported across the plasma membrane with the assistance of a protein carrier molecule. The glucose binds to the carrier and is ferried across the membrane. Small ions cross the membrane by moving through water-filled protein channels. In both cases, the substances move by a passive transport process called **facilitated diffusion.** As with simple diffusion, the substances move from an area of higher concentration to one of lower concentration, that is, down their concentration gradients.

## Osmosis

The flow of water across a selectively permeable membrane is called **osmosis.** During osmosis, water moves down its concentration gradient. The concentration of water is inversely related to the concentration of solutes. If the solutes can diffuse across the membrane, both water and solutes will move down their concentration gradients through the membrane. If the particles in solution are nonpenetrating solutes (prevented from crossing the membrane), water alone will move by osmosis and in doing so will cause changes in the volume of the compartments on either side of the membrane.

### Diffusion of Dye Through Agar Gel and Water

The relationship between molecular weight and the rate of diffusion can be examined easily by observing the diffusion of two different types of dye molecules through an agar gel. The dyes used in this experiment are methylene blue, which has a molecular weight of 320 and is deep blue in color, and potassium permanganate, a purple dye with a molecular weight of 158. Although the agar gel appears quite solid, it is primarily (98.5%) water and allows free movement of the dye molecules through it.

### ACTIVITY 1

### Observing Diffusion of Dye Through Agar Gel

1. Work with members of your group to formulate a hypothesis about the rates of diffusion of methylene blue and potassium permanganate through the agar gel. Justify your hypothesis.

2. Obtain a petri dish containing agar gel, a piece of millimeter-ruled graph paper, a wax marking pencil, dropper

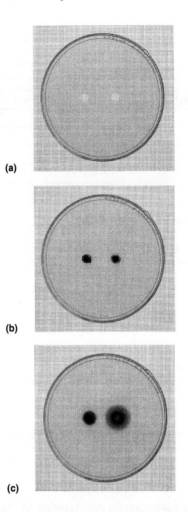

(a)

(b)

(c)

**Figure 2 Comparing diffusion rates.** Agar-plated petri dish as it appears after the diffusion of 0.1 *M* methylene blue placed in one well and 0.1 *M* potassium permanganate placed in another.

bottles of methylene blue and potassium permanganate, and a medicine dropper.

3. Using the wax marking pencil, draw a line on the bottom of the petri dish dividing it into two sections. Place the petri dish on the ruled graph paper.

4. Create a well in the center of each section using the medicine dropper. To do this, squeeze the bulb of the medicine dropper, and push it down into the agar. Release the bulb as you slowly pull the dropper vertically out of the agar. This should remove an agar plug, leaving a well in the agar. (See **Figure 2a.**)

5. Carefully fill one well with the methylene blue solution and the other well with the potassium permanganate solution.

Record the time. _____

6. At 15-minute intervals, measure the distance the dye has diffused from each well. Continue these observations for 1 hour, and record the results in the **Activity 1 chart.**

| Activity 1: Dye Diffusion Results | | |
|---|---|---|
| Time (min) | Diffusion of methylene blue (mm) | Diffusion of potassium permanganate (mm) |
| 15 | | |
| 30 | | |
| 45 | | |
| 60 | | |

Which dye diffused more rapidly? _____

What is the relationship between molecular weight and rate of molecular movement (diffusion)?

_____

Why did the dye molecules move? _____

_____

Compute the rate of diffusion of the potassium permanganate molecules in millimeters per minute (mm/min) and record.

_____ mm/min

Compute the rate of diffusion of the methylene blue molecules in mm/min and record.

_____ mm/min

7.  Prepare a lab report for these experiments. ▄

Make a mental note to yourself to go to demonstration area 1 at the end of the laboratory session to observe the extent of diffusion of the potassium permanganate dye through water. At that time, follow the directions given next.

### ACTIVITY 2

## Observing Diffusion of Dye Through Water

1.  Go to diffusion demonstration area 1, and observe the cylinder containing dye crystals and water set up at the beginning of the lab.

2.  Measure the number of millimeters the dye has diffused from the bottom of the graduated cylinder and record.

_____ mm

3.  Record the time the demonstration was set up and the time of your observation. Then compute the rate of the dye's diffusion through water and record below.

Time of setup _____

Time of observation _____

Rate of diffusion _____ mm/min

4.  Does the potassium permanganate dye diffuse more rapidly through water or the agar gel? Explain your answer.

_____

_____ ▄

### ACTIVITY 3

## Investigating Diffusion and Osmosis Through Nonliving Membranes

The following experiment provides information on the movement of water and solutes through selectively permeable membranes called dialysis sacs. Dialysis sacs have pores of a particular size. The selectivity of living membranes depends on more than just pore size, but using the dialysis sacs will allow you to examine selectivity due to this factor.

1.  Read through the experiments in this activity, and develop a hypothesis for each part.

2.  Obtain four dialysis sacs, a small funnel, a 25-ml graduated cylinder, a wax marking pencil, fine twine or dialysis tubing clamps, and four beakers (250 ml). Number the beakers 1 to 4 with the wax marking pencil, and half fill all of them with distilled water except beaker 2, to which you should add 40% glucose solution.

3.  Prepare the dialysis sacs one at a time. Using the funnel, half fill each with 20 ml of the specified liquid (see below). Press out the air, fold over the open end of the sac, and tie it securely with fine twine or clamp it. Before proceeding to the next sac, rinse it under the tap, and quickly and carefully blot the sac dry by rolling it on a paper towel. Weigh it with a laboratory balance. Record the weight in the **Activity 3 data chart**, and then drop the sac into the corresponding beaker. Be sure the sac is completely covered by the beaker solution, adding more solution if necessary.

- Sac 1: 40% glucose solution
- Sac 2: 40% glucose solution
- Sac 3: 10% NaCl solution
- Sac 4: Congo red dye in 40% sucrose solution

Allow sacs to remain undisturbed in the beakers for 1 hour. Use this time to continue with other experiments.

4.  After an hour, boil a beaker of water on the hot plate. Obtain the supplies you will need to determine your experimental results: dropper bottles of Benedict's solution and silver nitrate solution, a test tube rack, four test tubes, and a test tube holder.

5.  Quickly and gently blot sac 1 dry and weigh it. (**Note:** Do not squeeze the sac during the blotting process.) Record the weight in the data chart.

Was there any change in weight? _____

| Beaker | Contents of sac | Initial weight | Final weight | Weight change | Tests—beaker fluid | Tests—sac fluid |
|---|---|---|---|---|---|---|
| Beaker 1 ½ filled with distilled water | Sac 1, 20 ml of 40% glucose solution | | | | Benedict's test: | Benedict's test: |
| Beaker 2 ½ filled with 40% glucose solution | Sac 2, 20 ml of 40% glucose solution | | | | | |
| Beaker 3 ½ filled with distilled water | Sac 3, 20 ml of 10% NaCl solution | | | | AgNO₃ test: | |
| Beaker 4 ½ filled with distilled water | Sac 4, 20 ml of 40% sucrose solution containing Congo red dye | | | | Benedict's test: | |

**Activity 3: Experimental Data on Diffusion and Osmosis Through Nonliving Membranes**

Conclusions: _____

_____

_____

Place 5 ml of Benedict's solution in each of two test tubes. Put 4 ml of the beaker fluid into one test tube and 4 ml of the sac fluid into the other. Mark the tubes for identification and then place them in a beaker containing boiling water. Boil 2 minutes. Cool slowly. If a green, yellow, or rusty red precipitate forms, the test is positive, meaning that glucose is present. If the solution remains the original blue color, the test is negative. Record results in the data chart.

Was glucose still present in the sac? _____

Was glucose present in the beaker? _____

Conclusions: _____

_____

_____

6. Blot gently and weigh sac 2. Record the weight in the data chart.

Was there an *increase* or *decrease* in weight? _____

With 40% glucose in the sac and 40% glucose in the beaker, would you expect to see any net movement of water (osmosis) or of glucose molecules (simple diffusion)?

_____ Why or why not? _____

_____

7. Blot gently and weigh sac 3. Record the weight in the data chart.

Was there any change in weight? _____

Conclusions: _____

_____

Take a 5-ml sample of beaker 3 solution and put it in a clean test tube. Add a drop of silver nitrate (AgNO₃). The appearance of a white precipitate or cloudiness indicates the presence of silver chloride (AgCl), which is formed by the reaction of AgNO₃ with NaCl (sodium chloride). Record results in the data chart.

Results: _____

Conclusions: _____

8. Blot gently and weigh sac 4. Record the weight in the data chart.

Was there any change in weight? _____

Did the beaker water turn pink? _____

Conclusions: _____

_____

Take a 1-ml sample of beaker 4 solution and put the test tube in boiling water in a hot water bath. Add 5 drops of Benedict's solution to the tube and boil for 5 minutes. The presence of glucose (one of the hydrolysis products of sucrose) in the test tube is indicated by the presence of a green, yellow, or rusty colored precipitate.

Did sucrose diffuse from the sac into the water in the small

beaker? _____

Conclusions: _____

_____

9. In which of the test situations did net osmosis occur?

_____

In which of the test situations did net simple diffusion occur?

_____

What conclusions can you make about the relative size of glucose, sucrose, Congo red dye, NaCl, and water molecules?

_____

_____

_____

With what cell structure can the dialysis sac be compared?

_____

10. Prepare a lab report for the experiment. Be sure to include in your discussion the answers to the questions proposed in this activity. ■■

## ACTIVITY 4

### Observing Osmometer Results

Before leaving the laboratory, observe demonstration 2, the *osmometer demonstration* set up before the laboratory session to follow the movement of water through a membrane (osmosis). Measure the distance the water column has moved during the laboratory period and record below. (The position of the meniscus [the surface of the water column] in the thistle tube at the beginning of the laboratory period is marked with wax pencil.)

Distance the meniscus has moved: _____ mm

Did net osmosis occur? Why or why not?

_____

_____

_____ ■

## ACTIVITY 5

### Investigating Diffusion and Osmosis Through Living Membranes

To examine permeability properties of plasma membranes, conduct the following experiments. As you read through the experiments in this activity, develop a hypothesis for each part.

### Experiment 1

1. Obtain two deshelled eggs and two 400-ml beakers. Note that the relative concentration of solutes in deshelled eggs is about 14%. Number the beakers 1 and 2 with the wax marking pencil. Half fill beaker 1 with distilled water and beaker 2 with 30% sucrose.

2. Carefully blot each egg by rolling it gently on a paper towel. Place a weigh boat on a laboratory balance and tare the balance (that is, make sure the scale reads 0.0 with the weigh boat on the scale). Weigh egg 1 in the weigh boat, record the initial weight in the **Activity 5 data chart,** and gently place it into beaker 1. Repeat for egg 2, placing it in beaker 2.

3. After 20 minutes, remove egg 1 and gently blot it and weigh it. Record the weight, and replace it into beaker 1. Repeat for egg 2, placing it into beaker 2. Repeat this procedure at 40 minutes and 60 minutes.

4. Calculate the change in weight of each egg at each time period, and enter that number in the data chart. Also calculate the percent change in weight for each time period and enter that number in the data chart.

How has the weight of each egg changed?

Egg 1 _____

Egg 2 _____

Make a graph of your data by plotting the percent change in weight for each egg versus time.

How has the appearance of each egg changed?

Egg 1 _____

Egg 2 _____

A solution surrounding a cell is **hypertonic** if it contains more nonpenetrating solute particles than the interior of the cell. Water moves from the interior of the cell into a surrounding

| Activity 5: Experiment 1 Data from Diffusion and Osmosis Through Living Membranes | | | | | | |
|---|---|---|---|---|---|---|
| Time | Egg 1 (in distilled H$_2$O) | Weight change | % Change | Egg 2 (in 30% sucrose) | Weight change | % Change |
| Initial weight (g) | | — | — | | — | — |
| 20 min. | | | | | | |
| 40 min. | | | | | | |
| 60 min. | | | | | | |

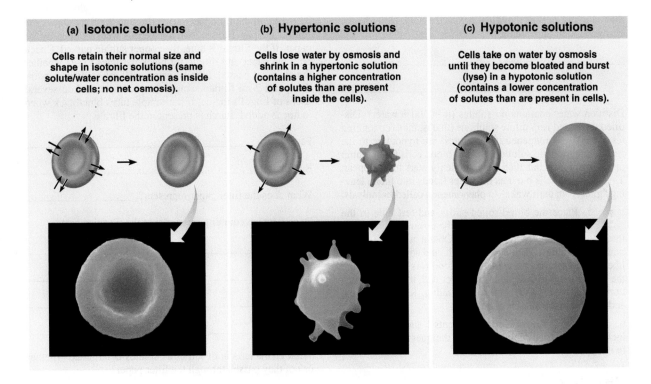

**Figure 3 Influence of isotonic, hypertonic, and hypotonic solutions on red blood cells.**

hypertonic solution by osmosis. A solution surrounding a cell is **hypotonic** if it contains fewer nonpenetrating solute particles than the interior of the cell. Water moves from a hypotonic solution into the cell by osmosis. In both cases, water moved down its concentration gradient. Indicate in your conclusions whether distilled water was a hypotonic or hypertonic solution and whether 30% sucrose was hypotonic or hypertonic.

Conclusions: _____

_____

_____

### Experiment 2

Now you will conduct a microscopic study of red blood cells suspended in solutions of varying tonicities. The objective is to determine if these solutions have any effect on cell shape by promoting net osmosis.

1. The following supplies should be available at your laboratory bench to conduct this experimental series: two clean slides and coverslips, a vial of animal blood, a medicine dropper, physiological saline, 5% sodium chloride solution, distilled water, filter paper, and disposable gloves.

 Wear disposable gloves at all times when handling blood (steps 2–5).

2. Place a very small drop of physiological saline on a slide. Using the medicine dropper, add a small drop of animal blood

to the saline on the slide. Tilt the slide to mix, cover with a coverslip, and immediately examine the preparation under the high-power lens. Notice that the red blood cells retain their normal smooth disclike shape (see **Figure 3a**). This is because the physiological saline is **isotonic** to the cells. That is, it contains a concentration of nonpenetrating solutes (e.g., proteins and some ions) equal to that in the cells (same solute/water concentration). Consequently, the cells neither gain nor lose water by osmosis. Set this slide aside.

3. Prepare another wet mount of animal blood, but this time use 5% sodium chloride (saline) solution as the suspending medium. Carefully observe the red blood cells under high power. What is happening to the normally smooth disc shape of the red blood cells?

_____

_____

_____

This crinkling-up process, called **crenation**, is due to the fact that the 5% sodium chloride solution is hypertonic to the cytosol of the red blood cell. Under these circumstances, water leaves the cells by osmosis. Compare your observations to the figure above (Figure 3b).

4. Add a drop of distilled water to the edge of the coverslip. Fold a piece of filter paper in half and place its folded edge at the opposite edge of the coverslip; it will absorb the saline solution and draw the distilled water across the cells. Watch

the red blood cells as they float across the field. Describe the change in their appearance.

_____

_____

Distilled water contains *no* solutes (it is 100% water). Distilled water and *very* dilute solutions (that is, those containing less than 0.9% nonpenetrating solutes) are hypotonic to the cell. In a hypotonic solution, the red blood cells first "plump up" (Figure 3c), but then they suddenly start to disappear. The red blood cells burst as the water floods into them, leaving "ghosts" in their wake—a phenomenon called **hemolysis.**

5. Place the blood-soiled slides and test tube in the bleach-containing basin. Put the coverslips you used into the disposable autoclave bag. Obtain a wash (squirt) bottle containing 10% bleach solution, and squirt the bleach liberally over the bench area where blood was handled. Wipe the bench down with a paper towel wet with the bleach solution and allow it to dry before continuing. Remove gloves, and discard in the autoclave bag.

6. Prepare a lab report for experiments 1 and 2. Be sure to include in the discussion answers to the questions proposed in this activity. ■

# Filtration

Filtration is a passive process in which water and solutes are forced through a membrane by hydrostatic (fluid) pressure. For example, fluids and solutes filter out of the capillaries in the kidneys and into the kidney tubules because the blood pressure in the capillaries is greater than the fluid pressure in the tubules. Filtration is not selective. The amount of filtrate (fluids and solutes) formed depends almost entirely on the pressure gradient (difference in pressure on the two sides of the membrane) and on the size of the membrane pores.

### ACTIVITY 6

### Observing the Process of Filtration

1. Obtain the following equipment: a ring stand, ring, and ring clamp; a funnel; a piece of filter paper; a beaker; a 10-ml graduated cylinder; a solution containing uncooked starch, powdered charcoal, and copper sulfate; and a dropper bottle of Lugol's iodine. Attach the ring to the ring stand with the clamp.

2. Fold the filter paper in half twice, open it into a cone, and place it in a funnel. Place the funnel in the ring of the ring stand and place a beaker under the funnel. Shake the starch solution, and fill the funnel with it to just below the top of the filter paper. When the steady stream of filtrate changes to countable filtrate drops, count the number of drops formed in 10 seconds and record.

_____ drops

When the funnel is half empty, again count the number of drops formed in 10 seconds and record the count.

_____ drops

3. After all the fluid has passed through the filter, check the filtrate and paper to see which materials were retained by the paper. If the filtrate is blue, the copper sulfate passed. Check both the paper and filtrate for black particles to see whether the charcoal passed. Finally, using a 10-ml graduated cylinder, put a 2-ml filtrate sample into a test tube. Add several drops of Lugol's iodine. If the sample turns blue/black when iodine is added, starch is present in the filtrate.

Passed: _____

Retained: _____

What does the filter paper represent? _____

During which counting interval was the filtration rate

greatest? _____

Explain: _____

_____

_____

What characteristic of the three solutes determined whether or not they passed through the filter paper?

_____ ■

# Active Processes

Whenever a cell uses the bond energy of ATP to move substances across its boundaries, the process is an *active process.* Substances moved by active means are generally unable to pass by diffusion. They may not be lipid soluble; they may be too large to pass through the membrane channels; or they may have to move against rather than with a concentration gradient. There are two types of active processes: *active transport* and *vesicular transport.*

## Active Transport

Like carrier-mediated facilitated diffusion, **active transport** requires carrier proteins that combine specifically with the transported substance. Active transport may be primary, driven directly by hydrolysis of ATP, or secondary, driven indirectly by energy stored in ionic gradients. In most cases the substances move against concentration or electrochemical gradients or both. Some of the substances that are moved into the cells by such carriers are amino acids and some sugars. Both solutes are insoluble in lipid and too large to pass through membrane channels but are necessary for cell life. Sodium ions ($Na^+$) are ejected from cells by active transport. Active transport is difficult to study in an A&P laboratory and will not be considered further here.

## Vesicular Transport

In **vesicular transport,** fluids containing large particles and macromolecules are transported across cellular membranes inside membranous sacs called *vesicles.* Like active

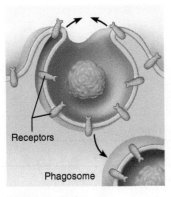

**(a) Phagocytosis**

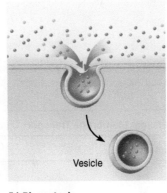

**(b) Pinocytosis**

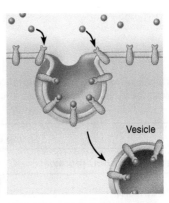

**(c) Receptor-mediated endocytosis**

**Figure 4 Three types of endocytosis. (a)** In phagocytosis, cellular extensions flow around the external particle and enclose it within a phagosome. **(b)** In pinocytosis, fluid and dissolved solutes enter the cell in a tiny vesicle. **(c)** In receptor-mediated endocytosis, specific substances attach to cell-surface receptors and enter the cell in protein-coated vesicles.

transport, vesicular transport moves substances into the cell **(endocytosis)** and out of the cell **(exocytosis)**. Vesicular transport can combine endocytosis and exocytosis by moving substances into, across, and out of cells as well as moving substances from one area or membranous organelle to another. Vesicular transport requires energy, usually in the form of ATP, and all forms of vesicular transport involve protein-coated vesicles to some extent.

There are three types of endocytosis: phagocytosis, pinocytosis, and receptor-mediated endocytosis. In **phagocytosis** ("cell eating"), the cell engulfs some relatively large or solid material such as a clump of bacteria, cell debris, or inanimate particles **(Figure 4a)**. When a particle binds to receptors on the cell's surface, cytoplasmic extensions called pseudopods form and flow around the particle. This produces an endocytotic vesicle called a *phagosome*. In most cases, the phagosome then fuses with a lysosome and its contents are digested. Indigestible contents are ejected from the cell by exocytosis. In the human body, only macrophages and certain other white blood cells perform phagocytosis. These cells help protect the body from disease-causing microorganisms and cancer cells.

In **pinocytosis** ("cell drinking"), also called **fluid-phase endocytosis,** the cell "gulps" a drop of extracellular fluid containing dissolved molecules (Figure 4b). Since no receptors are involved, the process is nonspecific. Unlike phagocytosis, pinocytosis is a routine activity of most cells, affording them a way of sampling the extracellular fluid. It is particularly important in cells that absorb nutrients, such as cells that line the intestines.

The main mechanism for *specific* endocytosis of most macromolecules is **receptor-mediated endocytosis** (Figure 4c). The receptors for this process are plasma membrane

proteins that bind only certain substances. This exquisitely selective mechanism allows cells to concentrate material that is present only in small amounts in the extracellular fluid. The ingested vesicle may fuse with a lysosome that either digests or releases its contents, or it may be transported across the cell to release its contents by exocytosis. The latter case is common in endothelial cells lining blood vessels because it provides a quick means to get substances from blood to extracellular fluid. Substances taken up by receptor-mediated endocytosis include enzymes, insulin and some other hormones, cholesterol (attached to a transport protein), and iron. Unfortunately, flu viruses, diphtheria, and cholera toxins also enter cells by this route.

**Exocytosis** is a vesicular transport process that ejects substances from the cell into the extracellular fluid. The substance to be removed from the cell is first enclosed in a protein-coated vesicle called a *secretory vesicle*. In most cases the vesicle migrates to the plasma membrane, fuses with it, and then ruptures, spilling its contents out of the cell. Exocytosis is used for hormone secretion, neurotransmitter release, mucus secretion, and ejection of wastes.

### ACTIVITY 7

### Observing Phagocytosis

Go to the video viewing area and watch the video demonstration of phagocytosis (if available). ■

**Note:** If you have not already done so, complete Activity 2 ("Observing Diffusion of Dye Through Water" page), and Activity 4 ("Observing Osmometer Results" page).

## Compare and Contrast Membrane Transport Processes

For each pair of membrane transport processes listed in the Group Challenge chart, describe ways in which they are similar and ways in which they differ.

| Group Challenge: Membrane Transport Comparison | | |
|---|---|---|
| **Membrane transport processes** | **Similarities** | **Differences** |
| Simple diffusion Osmosis | | |
| Simple diffusion Facilitated diffusion | | |
| Active transport Facilitated diffusion | | |
| Filtration Osmosis | | |
| Pinocytosis Receptor-mediated endocytosis | | |

Name _____

Lab Time/Date _____

# The Cell: Transport Mechanisms and Permeability

Choose all answers that apply to questions 1 and 2, and place their letters on the response blanks to the right.

1. Molecular motion _____.
   a. reflects the kinetic energy of molecules
   b. reflects the potential energy of molecules
   c. is ordered and predictable
   d. is random and erratic

2. Velocity of molecular movement _____.
   a. is higher in larger molecules
   b. is lower in larger molecules
   c. increases with increasing temperature
   d. decreases with increasing temperature
   e. reflects kinetic energy

3. Summarize the results of Activity 3, diffusion and osmosis through nonliving membranes, below. List and explain your observations relative to tests used to identify diffusing substances, and changes in sac weight observed.

   Sac 1 containing 40% glucose, suspended in distilled water

   _____

   _____

   Sac 2 containing 40% glucose, suspended in 40% glucose

   _____

   _____

   Sac 3 containing 10% NaCl, suspended in distilled water

   _____

   _____

   Sac 4 containing 40% sucrose and Congo red dye, suspended in distilled water

   _____

   _____

4. What single characteristic of the selectively permeable membranes *used in the laboratory* determines the substances that can

   pass through them? _____

   In addition to this characteristic, what other factors influence the passage of substances through living membranes?

   _____

   _____

5. A semipermeable sac containing 4% NaCl, 9% glucose, and 10% albumin is suspended in a solution with the following composition: 10% NaCl, 10% glucose, and 40% albumin. Assume that the sac is permeable to all substances except albumin. State whether each of the following will (a) move into the sac, (b) move out of the sac, or (c) not move.

glucose: ———————————————— albumin: ————————————————

water: ———————————————— NaCl: ————————————————

6. Summarize the results of Activity 5, Experiment 1 (diffusion and osmosis through living membranes—the egg), below. List and explain your observations.

Egg 1 in distilled water: ————————————————————————————————————

————————————————————————————————————————————

————————————————————————————————————————————

Egg 2 in 30% sucrose: ————————————————————————————————————

————————————————————————————————————————————

————————————————————————————————————————————

7. The diagrams below represent three microscope fields containing red blood cells. Arrows show the direction of net osmosis.

Which field contains a hypertonic solution? ——————— The cells in this field are said to be ———————. Which field

contains an isotonic bathing solution? ——————— Which field contains a hypotonic solution? ——————— What is

happening to the cells in this field? ————————————————————————————————

————————————————————————————————————————————

(a)          (b)          (c)

8. Assume you are conducting the experiment illustrated in the next figure. Both hydrochloric acid (HCl) with a molecular weight of about 36.5 and ammonium hydroxide (NH$_4$OH) with a molecular weight of 35 are volatile and easily enter the gaseous state. When they meet, the following reaction will occur:

$$HCl + NH_4OH \rightarrow H_2O + NH_4Cl$$

Ammonium chloride (NH$_4$Cl) will be deposited on the glass tubing as a smoky precipitate where the two gases meet. Predict which gas will diffuse more quickly and indicate to which end of the tube the smoky precipitate will be closer.

a. The faster-diffusing gas is ———————————————.

b. The precipitate forms closer to the ——————————————— end.

Rubber stopper     Cotton wad with HCl          Cotton wad with NH$_4$OH

Support

**9.** What determines whether a transport process is active or passive?

_____

**10.** Characterize membrane transport as fully as possible by choosing all the phrases that apply and inserting their letters on the answer blanks.

Passive processes: _____ Active processes: _____

    a.   account for the movement of fats and respiratory gases through the plasma membrane
    b.   explain solute pumping, phagocytosis, and pinocytosis
    c.   include osmosis, simple diffusion, and filtration
    d.   may occur against concentration and/or electrical gradients
    e.   use hydrostatic pressure or molecular energy as the driving force
    f.   move ions, amino acids, and some sugars across the plasma membrane

**11.** For the osmometer demonstration (Activity 4), explain why the level of the water column rose during the laboratory session.

_____

_____

**12.** Define the following terms.

_selective permeability:_ _____

_____

_diffusion:_ _____

_____

_simple diffusion:_ _____

_____

_facilitated diffusion:_ _____

_____

_osmosis:_ _____

_____

_filtration:_ _____

_____

_vesicular transport:_ _____

_____

_endocytosis:_ _____

_____

_exocytosis:_ _____

_____

## Photo Credits

**Credits are listed in order of appearance.**

2a–c: Richard Megna/Fundamental Photographs. 3a–c: David M. Philips/Photo Researchers.

## Illustration Credits

**All illustrations are by Imagineering STA Media Services, except for Review Sheet art and as noted below.**

1: Precision Graphics.

# Classification of Tissues

## MATERIALS

- ☐ Compound microscope
- ☐ Immersion oil
- ☐ Prepared slides of simple squamous, simple cuboidal, simple columnar, stratified squamous (nonkeratinized), stratified cuboidal, stratified columnar, pseudostratified ciliated columnar, and transitional epithelium
- ☐ Prepared slides of mesenchyme; of adipose, areolar, reticular, and dense (both regular and irregular connective tissues); of hyaline and elastic cartilage; of fibrocartilage; of bone (x.s.); and of blood
- ☐ Prepared slide of nervous tissue (spinal cord smear)
- ☐ Prepared slides of skeletal, cardiac, and smooth muscle (l.s.)
- ☐ Envelopes containing index cards with color photomicrographs of tissues

MasteringA&P® For related exercise study tools, go to the Study Area of MasteringA&P. There you will find:

- Practice Anatomy Lab PAL
- PhysioEx PEx
- A&PFlix *A&PFlix*
- Practice quizzes, Histology Atlas, eText, Videos, and more!

## OBJECTIVES

1. Name the four primary tissue types in the human body and state a general function of each.
2. Name the major subcategories of the primary tissue types and identify the tissues of each subcategory microscopically or in an appropriate image.
3. State the locations of the various tissues in the body.
4. List the general function and structural characteristics of each of the tissues studied.

## PRE-LAB QUIZ

1. Groups of cells that are anatomically similar and share a function are called:
   a. organ systems    c. organs
   b. organisms    d. tissues
2. How many primary tissue types are found in the human body?
   _____
3. Circle True or False. Endocrine and exocrine glands are classified as epithelium because they usually develop from epithelial membranes.
4. Epithelial tissues can be classified according to cell shape. _____ epithelial cells are scalelike and flattened.
   a. Columnar    c. Squamous
   b. Cuboidal    d. Transitional
5. All connective tissue is derived from an embryonic tissue known as:
   a. cartilage    c. mesenchyme
   b. ground substance    d. reticular
6. All the following are examples of connective tissue except:
   a. bones    c. neurons
   b. ligaments    d. tendons
7. Circle True or False. Blood is a type of connective tissue.
8. Circle the correct underlined term. Of the two major cell types found in nervous tissue, neurons / neuroglial cells are highly specialized to generate and conduct electrical signals.
9. How many basic types of muscle tissue are there? _____
10. This type of muscle tissue is found in the walls of hollow organs. It has no striations, and its cells are spindle shaped. It is:
   a. cardiac muscle
   b. skeletal muscle
   c. smooth muscle

From Exercise 6 of *Human Anatomy & Physiology Laboratory Manual*, Main Version, Tenth Edition. Elaine N. Marieb, Susan J. Mitchell, Lori A. Smith. Copyright © 2014 by Pearson Education, Inc. All rights reserved.

Cells are the building blocks of life and the all-inclusive functional units of unicellular organisms. However, in higher organisms, cells do not usually operate as isolated, independent entities. In humans and other multicellular organisms, cells depend on one another and cooperate to maintain homeostasis in the body.

With a few exceptions, even the most complex animal starts out as a single cell, the fertilized egg, which divides almost endlessly. The trillions of cells that result become specialized for a particular function; some become supportive bone, others the transparent lens of the eye, still others skin cells, and so on. Thus a division of labor exists, with certain groups of cells highly specialized to perform functions that benefit the organism as a whole. Cell specialization carries with it certain hazards, because when a small specific group of cells is indispensable, any inability to function on its part can paralyze or destroy the entire body.

Groups of cells that are similar in structure and function are called **tissues.** The four primary tissue types—epithelium, connective tissue, nervous tissue, and muscle—have distinctive structures, patterns, and functions. The four primary tissues are further divided into subcategories, as described shortly.

To perform specific body functions, the tissues are organized into **organs** such as the heart, kidneys, and lungs. Most organs contain several representatives of the primary tissues, and the arrangement of these tissues determines the organ's structure and function. Thus **histology,** the study of tissues, complements a study of gross anatomy and provides the structural basis for a study of organ physiology.

The main objective of this exercise is to familiarize you with the major similarities and differences of the primary tissues, so that when the tissue composition of an organ is described, you will be able to more easily understand (and perhaps even predict) the organ's major function. Because epithelial tissue and some types of connective tissue will not be considered again, they are emphasized more than muscle, nervous tissue, and bone (a connective tissue) in this exercise.

## Epithelial Tissue

**Epithelial tissue,** or an **epithelium,** is a sheet of cells that covers a body surface or lines a body cavity. It occurs in the body as (1) covering and lining epithelium and (2) glandular epithelium. Covering and lining epithelium forms the outer layer of the skin and lines body cavities that open to the outside. It covers the walls and organs of the closed ventral body cavity. Since glands almost invariably develop from epithelial sheets, glands are also classed as epithelium.

Epithelial functions include protection, absorption, filtration, excretion, secretion, and sensory reception. For example, the epithelium covering the body surface protects against bacterial invasion and chemical damage; that lining the respiratory tract is ciliated to sweep dust and other foreign particles away from the lungs. Epithelium specialized to absorb substances lines the stomach and small intestine. In the kidney tubules, the epithelium

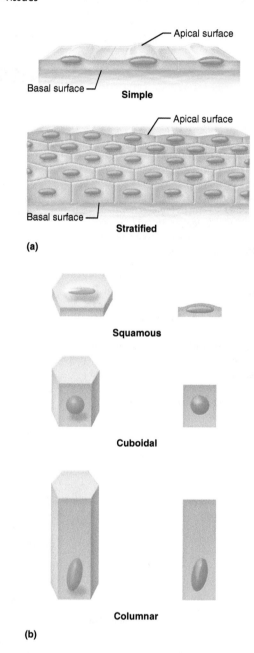

**(a)**

Simple — Apical surface, Basal surface

Stratified — Apical surface, Basal surface

**(b)**

Squamous

Cuboidal

Columnar

**Figure 1 Classification of epithelia. (a)** Classification based on number of cell layers. **(b)** Classification based on cell shape. For each category, a whole cell is shown on the left and a longitudinal section is shown on the right.

absorbs, secretes, and filters. Secretion is a specialty of the glands.

The following characteristics distinguish epithelial tissues from other types:

• Polarity. The membranes always have one free surface, called the *apical surface,* and typically that surface is significantly different from the *basal surface.*

• Specialized contacts. Cells fit closely together to form membranes, or sheets of cells, and are bound together by specialized junctions.

• Supported by connective tissue. The cells are attached to and supported by an adhesive **basement membrane,** which is an amorphous material secreted partly by the epithelial cells *(basal lamina)* and connective tissue cells *(reticular lamina)* that lie next to each other.

• Avascular but innervated. Epithelial tissues are supplied by nerves but have no blood supply of their own (are avascular). Instead they depend on diffusion of nutrients from the underlying connective tissue. Glandular epithelia, however, are very vascular.

• Regeneration. If well nourished, epithelial cells can easily divide to regenerate the tissue. This is an important characteristic because many epithelia are subjected to a good deal of friction.

The covering and lining epithelia are classified according to two criteria—arrangement or relative number of layers and cell shape **(Figure 1)**. On the basis of arrangement, there are **simple** epithelia, consisting of one layer of cells attached to the basement membrane, and **stratified** epithelia, consisting of two or more layers of cells. The general types based on shape are **squamous** (scalelike), **cuboidal** (cubelike), and **columnar** (column-shaped) epithelial cells. The terms denoting shape and arrangement of the epithelial cells are combined to describe the epithelium fully. *Stratified epithelia are named according to the cells at the apical surface of the epithelial sheet,* not those resting on the basement membrane.

There are, in addition, two less easily categorized types of epithelia. **Pseudostratified epithelium** is actually a simple columnar epithelium (one layer of cells), but because its cells vary in height and the nuclei lie at different levels above the basement membrane, it gives the false appearance of being stratified. This epithelium is often ciliated. **Transitional epithelium** is a rather peculiar stratified squamous epithelium formed of rounded, or "plump," cells with the ability to slide over one another to allow the organ to be stretched. Transitional epithelium is found only in urinary system organs subjected to periodic distension, such as the bladder. The superficial cells are flattened (like true squamous cells) when the organ is distended and rounded when the organ is empty.

Epithelial cells forming glands are highly specialized to remove materials from the blood and to manufacture them into new materials, which they then secrete. There are two types of glands, *endocrine* and *exocrine* **(Figure 2)**. **Endocrine glands** lose their surface connection (duct) as they develop; thus they are referred to as ductless glands. They secrete hormones into the extracellular fluid, and from there the hormones enter the blood or the lymphatic vessels that weave through the glands. **Exocrine glands** retain their ducts, and their secretions empty through these ducts either to the body surface or into body cavities. The exocrine glands include the sweat and oil glands, liver, and pancreas. Glands are discussed with the organ systems to which their products are functionally related.

The most common types of epithelia, their characteristic locations in the body, and their functions are described in the accompanying illustrations **(Figure 3)**.

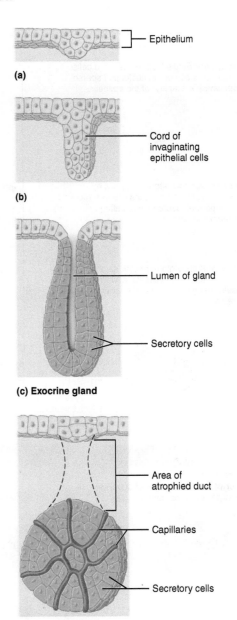

(a)

(b)

(c) Exocrine gland

(d) Endocrine gland

**Figure 2 Formation of endocrine and exocrine glands from epithelial sheets. (a)** Epithelial cells grow and push into the underlying tissue. **(b)** A cord of epithelial cells forms. **(c)** In an exocrine gland, a lumen (cavity) forms. The inner cells form the duct, the outer cells produce the secretion. **(d)** In a forming endocrine gland, the connecting duct cells atrophy, leaving the secretory cells with no connection to the epithelial surface. However, they do become heavily invested with blood and lymphatic vessels that receive the secretions.

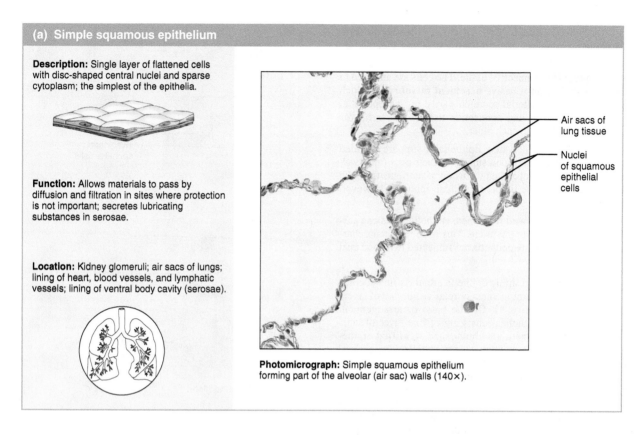

## (a) Simple squamous epithelium

**Description:** Single layer of flattened cells with disc-shaped central nuclei and sparse cytoplasm; the simplest of the epithelia.

**Function:** Allows materials to pass by diffusion and filtration in sites where protection is not important; secretes lubricating substances in serosae.

**Location:** Kidney glomeruli; air sacs of lungs; lining of heart, blood vessels, and lymphatic vessels; lining of ventral body cavity (serosae).

Air sacs of lung tissue

Nuclei of squamous epithelial cells

**Photomicrograph:** Simple squamous epithelium forming part of the alveolar (air sac) walls (140×).

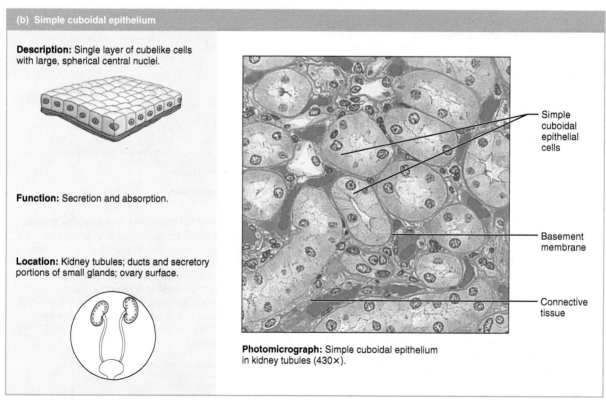

## (b) Simple cuboidal epithelium

**Description:** Single layer of cubelike cells with large, spherical central nuclei.

**Function:** Secretion and absorption.

**Location:** Kidney tubules; ducts and secretory portions of small glands; ovary surface.

Simple cuboidal epithelial cells

Basement membrane

Connective tissue

**Photomicrograph:** Simple cuboidal epithelium in kidney tubules (430×).

**Figure 3** **Epithelial tissues.** Simple epithelia **(a and b).**

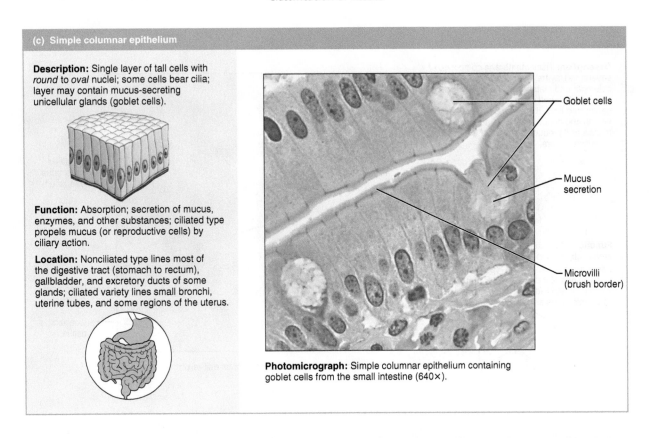

## (c) Simple columnar epithelium

**Description:** Single layer of tall cells with *round* to *oval* nuclei; some cells bear cilia; layer may contain mucus-secreting unicellular glands (goblet cells).

**Function:** Absorption; secretion of mucus, enzymes, and other substances; ciliated type propels mucus (or reproductive cells) by ciliary action.

**Location:** Nonciliated type lines most of the digestive tract (stomach to rectum), gallbladder, and excretory ducts of some glands; ciliated variety lines small bronchi, uterine tubes, and some regions of the uterus.

Goblet cells

Mucus secretion

Microvilli (brush border)

**Photomicrograph:** Simple columnar epithelium containing goblet cells from the small intestine (640×).

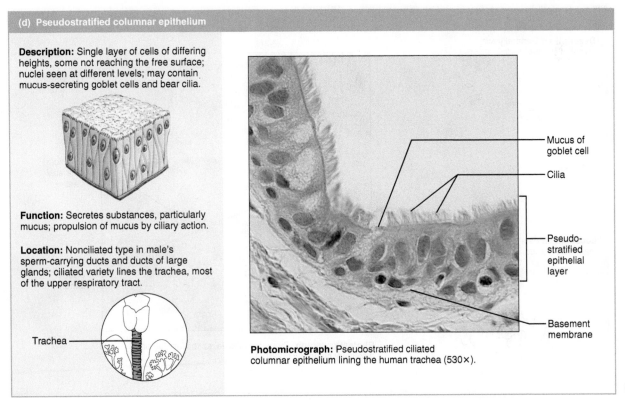

## (d) Pseudostratified columnar epithelium

**Description:** Single layer of cells of differing heights, some not reaching the free surface; nuclei seen at different levels; may contain mucus-secreting goblet cells and bear cilia.

**Function:** Secretes substances, particularly mucus; propulsion of mucus by ciliary action.

**Location:** Nonciliated type in male's sperm-carrying ducts and ducts of large glands; ciliated variety lines the trachea, most of the upper respiratory tract.

Trachea

Mucus of goblet cell

Cilia

Pseudo-stratified epithelial layer

Basement membrane

**Photomicrograph:** Pseudostratified ciliated columnar epithelium lining the human trachea (530×).

**Figure 3 *(continued)* Simple epithelia (c and d).**

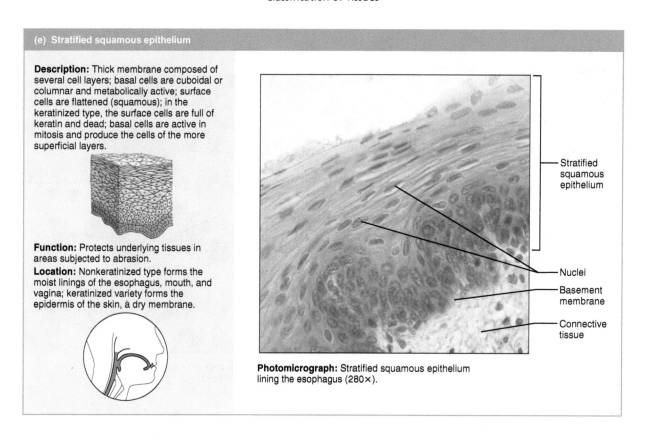

**(e) Stratified squamous epithelium**

**Description:** Thick membrane composed of several cell layers; basal cells are cuboidal or columnar and metabolically active; surface cells are flattened (squamous); in the keratinized type, the surface cells are full of keratin and dead; basal cells are active in mitosis and produce the cells of the more superficial layers.

**Function:** Protects underlying tissues in areas subjected to abrasion.

**Location:** Nonkeratinized type forms the moist linings of the esophagus, mouth, and vagina; keratinized variety forms the epidermis of the skin, a dry membrane.

Stratified squamous epithelium

Nuclei

Basement membrane

Connective tissue

**Photomicrograph:** Stratified squamous epithelium lining the esophagus (280×).

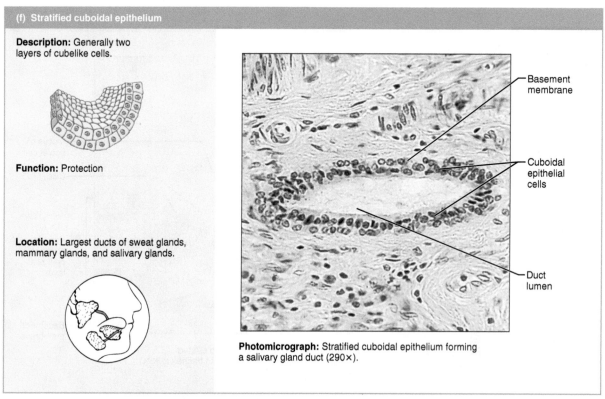

**(f) Stratified cuboidal epithelium**

**Description:** Generally two layers of cubelike cells.

**Function:** Protection

**Location:** Largest ducts of sweat glands, mammary glands, and salivary glands.

Basement membrane

Cuboidal epithelial cells

Duct lumen

**Photomicrograph:** Stratified cuboidal epithelium forming a salivary gland duct (290×).

**Figure 3** *(continued)* **Epithelial tissues.** Stratified epithelia (**e** and **f**).

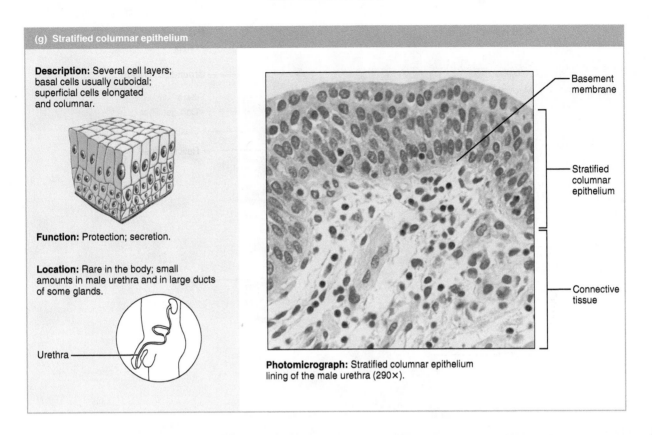

**(g) Stratified columnar epithelium**

**Description:** Several cell layers; basal cells usually cuboidal; superficial cells elongated and columnar.

**Function:** Protection; secretion.

**Location:** Rare in the body; small amounts in male urethra and in large ducts of some glands.

Urethra

Basement membrane

Stratified columnar epithelium

Connective tissue

**Photomicrograph:** Stratified columnar epithelium lining of the male urethra (290×).

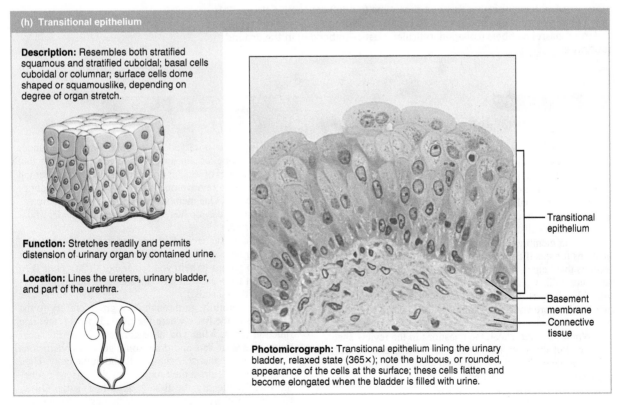

**(h) Transitional epithelium**

**Description:** Resembles both stratified squamous and stratified cuboidal; basal cells cuboidal or columnar; surface cells dome shaped or squamouslike, depending on degree of organ stretch.

**Function:** Stretches readily and permits distension of urinary organ by contained urine.

**Location:** Lines the ureters, urinary bladder, and part of the urethra.

Transitional epithelium

Basement membrane

Connective tissue

**Photomicrograph:** Transitional epithelium lining the urinary bladder, relaxed state (365×); note the bulbous, or rounded, appearance of the cells at the surface; these cells flatten and become elongated when the bladder is filled with urine.

**Figure 3** *(continued)* Stratified epithelia **(g** and **h).**

**Cell types**

**Extracellular matrix**

Macrophage

Fibroblast

Lymphocyte

Fat cell

Mast cell

Neutrophil

Ground substance

**Fibers**
- Collagen fiber
- Elastic fiber
- Reticular fiber

Capillary

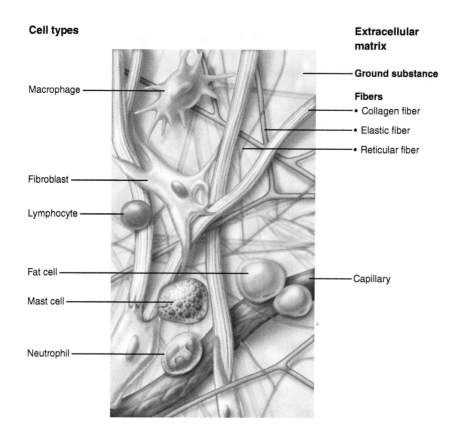

**Figure 4 Areolar connective tissue: A prototype (model) connective tissue.** This tissue underlies epithelia and surrounds capillaries. Note the various cell types and the three classes of fibers (collagen, reticular, elastic) embedded in the ground substance.

**ACTIVITY 1**

## Examining Epithelial Tissue Under the Microscope

Obtain slides of simple squamous, simple cuboidal, simple columnar, stratified squamous (nonkeratinized), pseudostratified ciliated columnar, stratified cuboidal, stratified columnar, and transitional epithelia. Examine each carefully, and notice how the epithelial cells fit closely together to form intact sheets of cells, a necessity for a tissue that forms linings or covering membranes. Scan each epithelial type for modifications for specific functions, such as cilia (motile cell projections that help to move substances along the cell surface), and microvilli, which increase the surface area for absorption. Also be alert for goblet cells, which secrete lubricating mucus. Compare your observations with the descriptions and photomicrographs (Figure 3.)

While working, check the questions in the review sheet at the end of this exercise. A number of the questions there refer to some of the observations you are asked to make during your microscopic study. ■

**GROUP CHALLENGE 1**

## Identifying Epithelial Tissues

Following your observations of epithelial tissues under the microscope, obtain an envelope for each group that contains images of various epithelial tissues. With your lab manual closed, remove one image at a time and identify the epithelium. One member of the group shall function as the verifier whose job it is to make sure that the identification is correct.

Remove the second image and repeat the process. After you have correctly identified all of the images, sort them into groups to help you remember them. (*Hint:* You could sort them according to cell shape, or number of layers of epithelial cells.)

Now, carefully go through each group and try to list one place in the body where the tissue is found, and one function for it. After you have correctly listed the locations, take your lists and draw some general conclusions about where epithelial tissues are found in the body. Then compare and contrast the functions of the various epithelia. Finally, identify the tissues described in the Group Challenge 1 chart and list several locations in the body.

| Group Challenge 1: Epithelial Tissue IDs | | |
|---|---|---|
| **Magnified appearance** | **Tissue type** | **Locations in the body** |
| • Apical surface has dome-shaped cells (flattened cells may also be mixed in)<br>• Multiple layers of cells are present | | |
| • Cells are mostly columnar<br>• Not all cells reach the apical surface<br>• Nuclei are located at different levels<br>• Cilia are located at the apical surface | | |
| • Apical surface has flattened cells with very little cytoplasm<br>• Cells are not layered | | |
| • Apical surface has square cells with a round nucleus<br>• Cells are not layered | | |

# Connective Tissue

**Connective tissue** is found in all parts of the body as discrete structures or as part of various body organs. It is the most abundant and widely distributed of the tissue types.

**Connective tissues** perform a variety of functions, but they primarily protect, support, and bind together other tissues of the body. For example, bones are composed of connective tissue (**bone,** or **osseous tissue**), and they protect and support other body tissues and organs. The ligaments and tendons (**dense connective tissue**) bind the bones together or bind skeletal muscles to bones.

**Areolar connective tissue** (Figure 4) is a soft packaging material that cushions and protects body organs. **Adipose** (fat) tissue provides insulation for the body tissues and a source of stored food. Blood-forming (**hematopoietic**) tissue replenishes the body's supply of red blood cells. Connective tissue also serves a vital function in the repair of all body tissues, since many wounds are repaired by connective tissue in the form of scar tissue.

The characteristics of connective tissue include the following:

• With a few exceptions (cartilages, tendons, and ligaments, which are poorly vascularized), connective tissues have a rich supply of blood vessels.

• Connective tissues are composed of many types of cells.

• There is a great deal of noncellular, nonliving material (matrix) between the cells of connective tissue.

The nonliving material between the cells—the **extracellular matrix**—deserves a bit more explanation because it distinguishes connective tissue from all other tissues. It is produced by the cells and then extruded. The matrix is primarily responsible for the strength associated with connective tissue, but there is variation. At one extreme, adipose tissue is composed mostly of cells. At the opposite extreme, bone and cartilage have few cells and large amounts of matrix.

The matrix has two components—ground substance and fibers. The **ground substance** is composed chiefly of interstitial fluid, cell adhesion proteins, and proteoglycans. Depending on its specific composition, the ground substance may be liquid, semisolid, gel-like, or very hard. When the matrix is firm, as in cartilage and bone, the connective tissue cells reside in cavities in the matrix called *lacunae*. The fibers, which provide support, include **collagen** (white) **fibers, elastic** (yellow) **fibers,** and **reticular** (fine collagen) **fibers.** Of these, the collagen fibers are most abundant.

Generally speaking, the ground substance functions as a molecular sieve, or medium, through which nutrients and other dissolved substances can diffuse between the blood capillaries and the cells. The fibers in the matrix hinder diffusion somewhat and make the ground substance less pliable. The properties of the connective tissue cells and the makeup and arrangement of their matrix elements vary tremendously, accounting for the amazing diversity of this tissue type. Nonetheless, the connective tissues have a common structural plan seen best in *areolar connective tissue* (Figure 4), a soft packing tissue that occurs throughout the body. Since all other connective tissues are variations of areolar, it is considered the model or prototype of the connective tissues. Notice that areolar tissue has all three varieties of fibers, but they are sparsely arranged in its transparent gel-like ground substance (Figure 4). The cell type that secretes its matrix is the *fibroblast,* but a wide variety of other cells (including phagocytic cells like macrophages and certain white blood cells and mast cells that act in the inflammatory response) are present as well. The more durable connective tissues, such as bone, cartilage, and the dense fibrous varieties, characteristically have a firm ground substance and many more fibers.

There are four main types of adult connective tissue, all of which typically have large amounts of matrix. These are **connective tissue proper** (which includes areolar, adipose, reticular, and dense [fibrous] connective tissues), **cartilage, bone,** and **blood.** All of these derive from an embryonic tissue called *mesenchyme.* The next set of illustrations (Figure 5) lists the general characteristics, location, and function of some of the connective tissues found in the body.

## (a) Embryonic connective tissue: Mesenchyme

**Description:** Embryonic connective tissue; gel-like ground substance containing fibers; star-shaped mesenchymal cells.

**Function:** Gives rise to all other connective tissue types.

**Location:** Primarily in embryo.

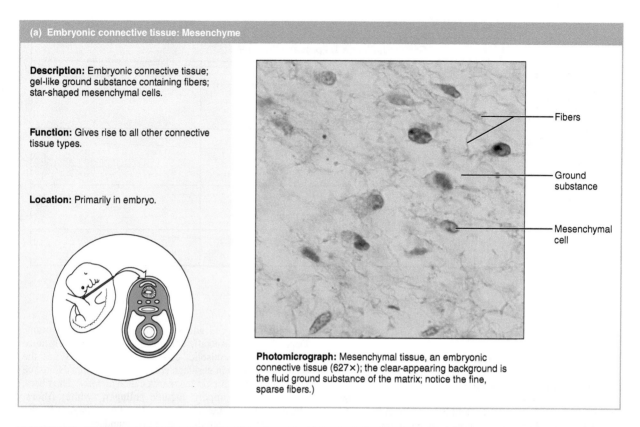

Fibers

Ground substance

Mesenchymal cell

**Photomicrograph:** Mesenchymal tissue, an embryonic connective tissue (627×); the clear-appearing background is the fluid ground substance of the matrix; notice the fine, sparse fibers.)

## (b) Connective tissue proper: loose connective tissue, areolar

**Description:** Gel-like matrix with all three fiber types; cells: fibroblasts, macrophages, mast cells, and some white blood cells.

**Function:** Wraps and cushions organs; its macrophages phagocytize bacteria; plays important role in inflammation; holds and conveys tissue fluid.

**Location:** Widely distributed under epithelia of body, e.g., forms lamina propria of mucous membranes; packages organs; surrounds capillaries.

Epithelium

Lamina propria

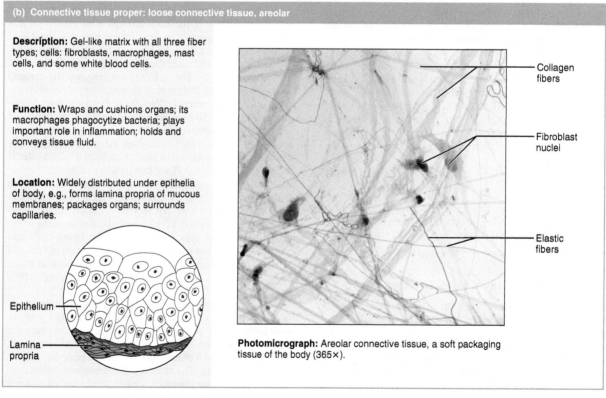

Collagen fibers

Fibroblast nuclei

Elastic fibers

**Photomicrograph:** Areolar connective tissue, a soft packaging tissue of the body (365×).

**Figure 5 Connective tissues.** Embryonic connective tissue **(a)** and Connective tissue proper **(b).**

**(c) Connective tissue proper: loose connective tissue, adipose**

**Description:** Matrix as in areolar, but very sparse; closely packed adipocytes, or fat cells, have nucleus pushed to the side by large fat droplet.

**Function:** Provides reserve fuel; insulates against heat loss; supports and protects organs.

**Location:** Under skin; around kidneys and eyeballs; within abdomen; in breasts.

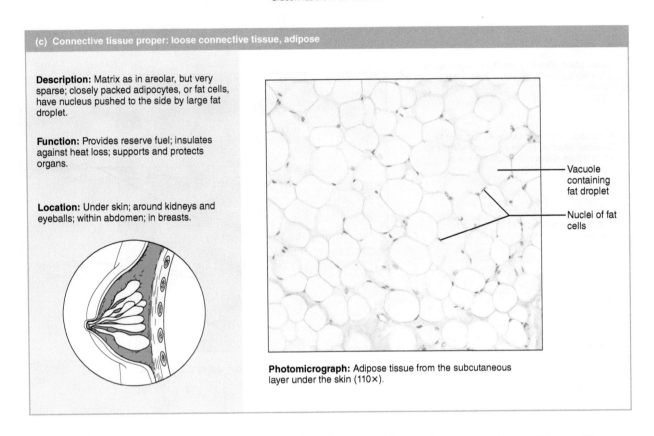

Vacuole containing fat droplet

Nuclei of fat cells

**Photomicrograph:** Adipose tissue from the subcutaneous layer under the skin (110×).

**(d) Connective tissue proper: loose connective tissue, reticular**

**Description:** Network of reticular fibers in a typical loose ground substance; reticular cells lie on the network.

**Function:** Fibers form a soft internal skeleton (stroma) that supports other cell types, including white blood cells, mast cells, and macrophages.

**Location:** Lymphoid organs (lymph nodes, bone marrow, and spleen).

Spleen

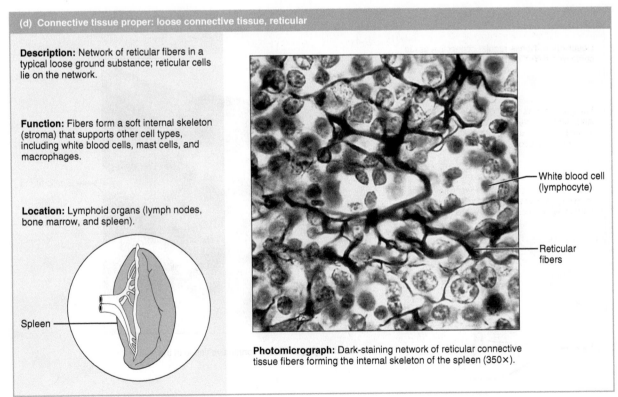

White blood cell (lymphocyte)

Reticular fibers

**Photomicrograph:** Dark-staining network of reticular connective tissue fibers forming the internal skeleton of the spleen (350×).

**Figure 5** *(continued)* Connective tissue proper **(c and d).**

**(e) Connective tissue proper: dense connective tissue, dense regular**

**Description:** Primarily parallel collagen fibers; a few elastic fibers; major cell type is the fibroblast.

**Function:** Attaches muscles to bones or to muscles; attaches bones to bones; withstands great tensile stress when pulling force is applied in one direction.

**Location:** Tendons, most ligaments, aponeuroses.

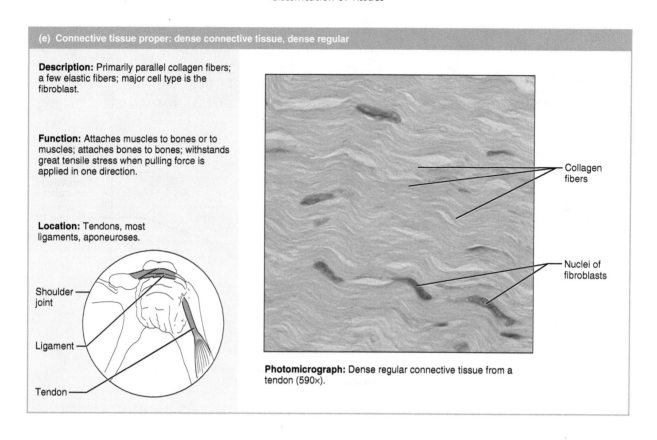

Shoulder joint

Ligament

Tendon

Collagen fibers

Nuclei of fibroblasts

**Photomicrograph:** Dense regular connective tissue from a tendon (590×).

**(f) Connective tissue proper: dense connective tissue, elastic**

**Description:** Dense regular connective tissue containing a high proportion of elastic fibers.

**Function:** Allows recoil of tissue following stretching; maintains pulsatile flow of blood through arteries; aids passive recoil of lungs following inspiration.

**Location:** Walls of large arteries; within certain ligaments associated with the vertebral column; within the walls of the bronchial tubes.

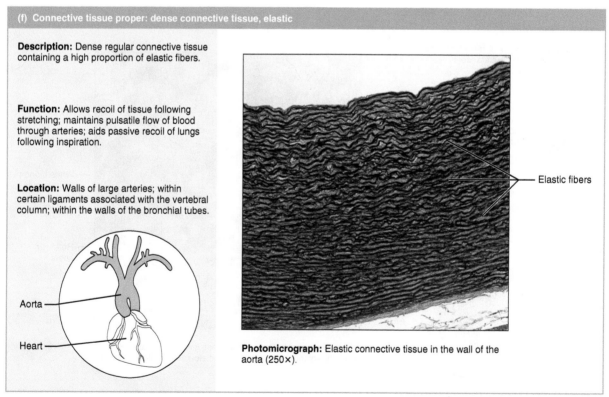

Aorta

Heart

Elastic fibers

**Photomicrograph:** Elastic connective tissue in the wall of the aorta (250×).

**Figure 5** *(continued)* **Connective tissues.** Connective tissue proper **(e)** and **(f)**.

**(g) Connective tissue proper: dense connective tissue, dense irregular**

**Description:** Primarily irregularly arranged collagen fibers; some elastic fibers; major cell type is the fibroblast.

**Function:** Able to withstand tension exerted in many directions; provides structural strength.

**Location:** Fibrous capsules of organs and of joints; dermis of the skin; submucosa of digestive tract.

Fibrous joint capsule

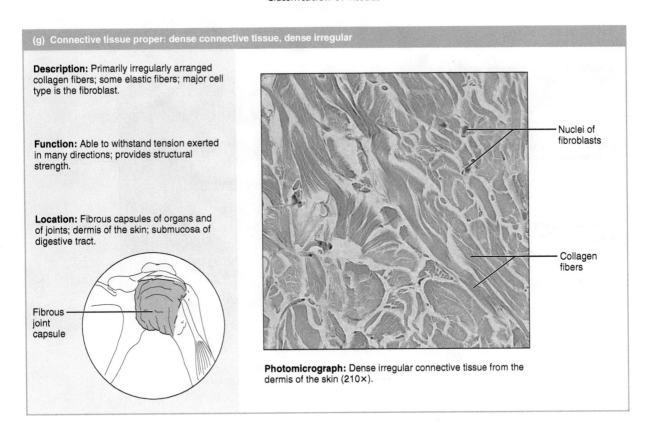

Nuclei of fibroblasts

Collagen fibers

**Photomicrograph:** Dense irregular connective tissue from the dermis of the skin (210×).

**(h) Cartilage: hyaline**

**Description:** Amorphous but firm matrix; collagen fibers form an imperceptible network; chondroblasts produce the matrix and when mature (chondrocytes) lie in lacunae.

**Function:** Supports and reinforces; serves as resilient cushion; resists compressive stress.

**Location:** Forms most of the embryonic skeleton; covers the ends of long bones in joint cavities; forms costal cartilages of the ribs; cartilages of the nose, trachea, and larynx.

Costal cartilages

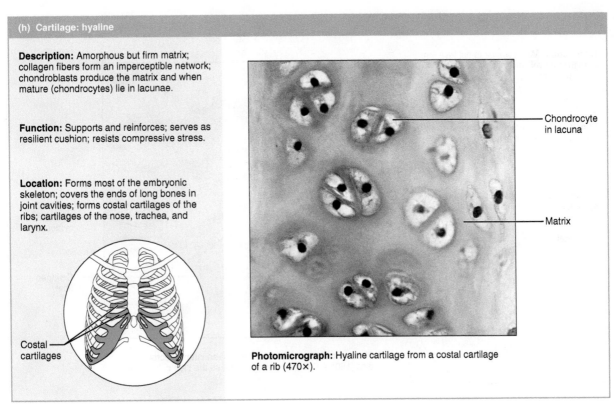

Chondrocyte in lacuna

Matrix

**Photomicrograph:** Hyaline cartilage from a costal cartilage of a rib (470×).

**Figure 5** *(continued)* Connective tissue proper **(g)** and Cartilage **(h).**

## (i) Cartilage: elastic

**Description:** Similar to hyaline cartilage, but more elastic fibers in matrix.

**Function:** Maintains the shape of a structure while allowing great flexibility.

**Location:** Supports the external ear (auricle); epiglottis.

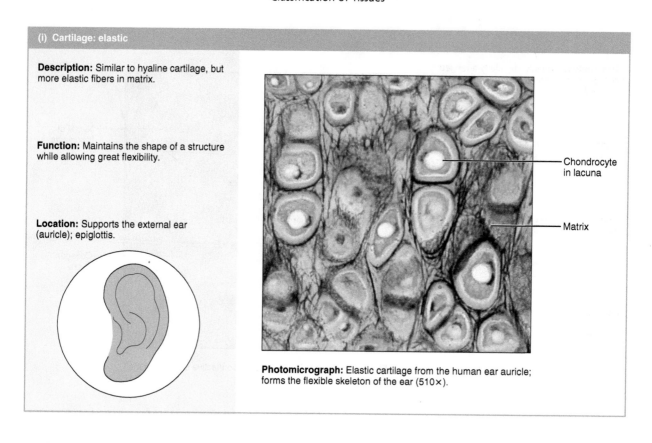

**Photomicrograph:** Elastic cartilage from the human ear auricle; forms the flexible skeleton of the ear (510×).

## (j) Cartilage: fibrocartilage

**Description:** Matrix similar to but less firm than that in hyaline cartilage; thick collagen fibers predominate.

**Function:** Tensile strength with the ability to absorb compressive shock.

**Location:** Intervertebral discs; pubic symphysis; discs of knee joint.

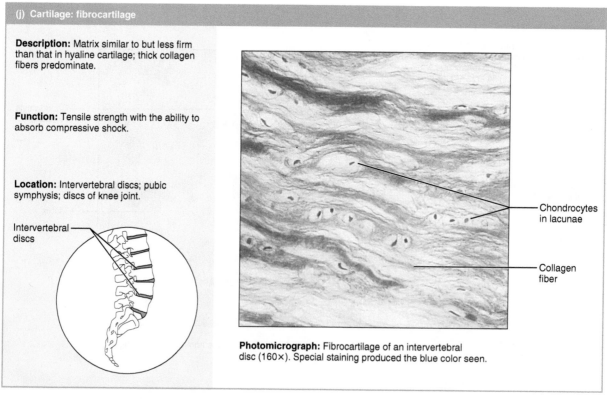

**Photomicrograph:** Fibrocartilage of an intervertebral disc (160×). Special staining produced the blue color seen.

**Figure 5** *(continued)* **Connective tissues.** Cartilage (**i** and **j**).

## (k) Bones (osseous tissue)

**Description:** Hard, calcified matrix containing many collagen fibers; osteocytes lie in lacunae. Very well vascularized.

**Function:** Bone supports and protects (by enclosing); provides levers for the muscles to act on; stores calcium and other minerals and fat; marrow inside bones is the site for blood cell formation (hematopoiesis).

**Location:** Bones

Central canal

Lacunae

Lamella

**Photomicrograph:** Cross-sectional view of bone (175×).

## (l) Blood

**Description:** Red and white blood cells in a fluid matrix (plasma).

**Function:** Transport of respiratory gases, nutrients, wastes, and other substances.

**Location:** Contained within blood vessels.

Plasma

Neutrophil

Red blood cells

Lymphocyte

**Photomicrograph:** Smear of human blood (1000×); two white blood cells (neutrophil and lymphocyte) are seen surrounded by red blood cells.

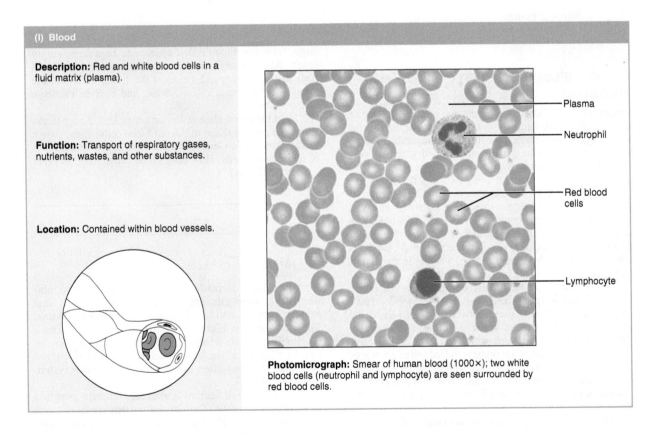

**Figure 5** *(continued)* Bone **(k)** and Blood **(l).**

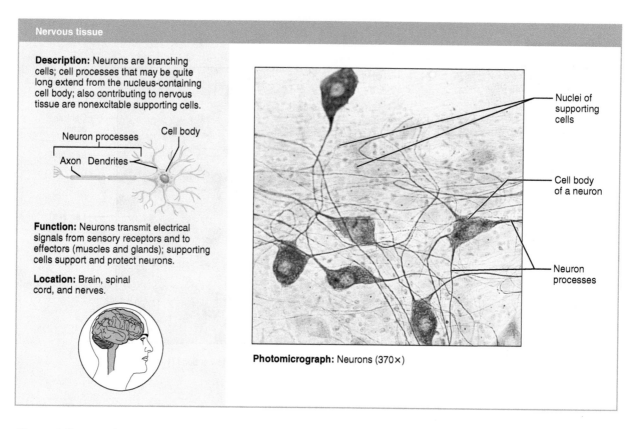

**Nervous tissue**

**Description:** Neurons are branching cells; cell processes that may be quite long extend from the nucleus-containing cell body; also contributing to nervous tissue are nonexcitable supporting cells.

Neuron processes

Axon Dendrites

Cell body

**Function:** Neurons transmit electrical signals from sensory receptors and to effectors (muscles and glands); supporting cells support and protect neurons.

**Location:** Brain, spinal cord, and nerves.

Nuclei of supporting cells

Cell body of a neuron

Neuron processes

**Photomicrograph:** Neurons (370×)

Figure 6 **Nervous tissue.**

### ACTIVITY 2

## Examining Connective Tissue Under the Microscope

Obtain prepared slides of mesenchyme; of adipose, areolar, reticular, dense regular, elastic, and irregular connective tissue; of hyaline and elastic cartilage and fibrocartilage; of osseous connective tissue (bone); and of blood. Compare your observations with the views illustrated (Figure 5).

Distinguish between the living cells and the matrix and pay particular attention to the denseness and arrangement of the matrix. For example, notice how the matrix of the dense regular and irregular connective tissues, respectively making up tendons and the dermis of the skin, is packed with collagen fibers. Note also that in the *regular* variety (tendon), the fibers are all running in the same direction, whereas in the dermis they appear to be running in many directions.

While examining the areolar connective tissue, notice how much empty space there appears to be (*areol* = small empty space), and distinguish between the collagen fibers and the coiled elastic fibers. Identify the starlike fibroblasts. Also, try to locate a **mast cell,** which has large, darkly staining granules in its cytoplasm (*mast* = stuffed full of granules). This cell type releases histamine, which makes capillaries more permeable during inflammatory reactions and allergies and thus is partially responsible for that "runny nose" of some allergies.

In adipose tissue, locate a "signet ring" cell, a fat cell in which the nucleus can be seen pushed to one side by the large, fat-filled vacuole that appears to be a large empty space. Also notice how little matrix there is in adipose (fat) tissue. Distinguish between the living cells and the matrix in the dense fibrous, bone, and hyaline cartilage preparations.

Scan the blood slide at low and then high power to examine the general shape of the red blood cells. Then, switch to the oil immersion lens for a closer look at the various types of white blood cells. How does blood differ from all other connective tissues?

## Nervous Tissue

**Nervous tissue** is made up of two major cell populations. The **neuroglia** are special supporting cells that protect, support, and insulate the more delicate neurons. The **neurons** are highly specialized to receive stimuli (excitability) and to generate electrical signals that may be sent to all parts of the body (conductivity). They are the cells that are most often associated with nervous system functioning.

The structure of neurons is markedly different from that of all other body cells. They have a nucleus-containing cell body, and their cytoplasm is drawn out into long extensions

## Identifying Connective Tissue

Following your observations of connective tissues under the microscope, obtain an envelope for each group that contains images of some of the tissues you have studied. With your lab manual closed, remove one image at a time and identify the tissue. One member of the group shall function as the verifier whose job it is to make sure that the identification is correct.

Remove the second image and repeat the process. After you have correctly identified all of the images, sort them into groups according to their primary tissue type and subcategory (if appropriate).

Now, carefully go through each group and try to list one place in the body where the tissue is found, and one function for it. After you have correctly listed locations take your lists and draw some general conclusions about where each primary tissue type is found in the body. Compare and contrast the functions of the primary tissue types, including epithelium. (If you have already completed Group Challenge 1 for epithelial tissues, you need not repeat that work here.)

Next, obtain an envelope from your instructor that contains an image of a section through an organ. Identify all of the tissues that you see in this section, and use it to review the relationship between the location and function of the tissue types that you have studied.

Finally, identify the tissues described in the Group Challenge 2 chart and list several locations in the body.

| Group Challenge 2: Connective Tissue IDs | | |
|---|---|---|
| **Magnified appearance** | **Tissue type** | **Locations in the body** |
| • Large, round cells are densely packed <br> • Nucleus is pushed to one side | | |
| • Lacunae (small cavities within the tissue) are present <br> • Lacunae are not arranged in a concentric circle <br> • No visible fibers in the matrix | | |
| • Fibers and cells are loosely packed with visible space between fibers <br> • Fibers overlap but do not form a network | | |
| • Extracellular fibers run parallel to each other <br> • Nuclei of fibroblasts are visible | | |
| • Lacunae are sparsely distributed <br> • Lacunae are not arranged in a concentric circle <br> • Fibers are visible and fairly organized | | |
| • Tapered cells with darkly stained nucleus centrally located <br> • No striations <br> • Cells layered to form a sheet | | |

(cell processes)—sometimes as long as 1 m (about 3 feet), which allows a single neuron to conduct an electrical signal over relatively long distances.

## Examining Nervous Tissue Under the Microscope

Obtain a prepared slide of a spinal cord smear. Locate a neuron and compare it to the photomicrograph (Figure 6). Keep the light dim—this will help you see the cellular extensions of the neurons. ▬

## Muscle Tissue

**Muscle tissue** (Figure 7) is highly specialized to contract and produces most types of body movement. As you might expect, muscle cells tend to be elongated, providing a long axis for contraction. The three basic types of muscle tissue are described briefly here.

**Skeletal muscle,** the "meat," or flesh, of the body, is attached to the skeleton. It is under voluntary control (consciously controlled), and its contraction moves the limbs and other external body parts. The cells of skeletal muscles are long, cylindrical, and multinucleate (several nuclei per cell), with the nuclei pushed to the periphery of the cells; they have obvious *striations* (stripes).

**Cardiac muscle** is found only in the heart. As it contracts, the heart acts as a pump, propelling the blood into the blood vessels. Cardiac muscle, like skeletal muscle, has striations, but cardiac cells are branching uninucleate cells that interdigitate (fit together) at junctions called **intercalated discs.** These structural modifications allow the cardiac muscle to act as a unit. Cardiac muscle is under involuntary control, which means that we cannot voluntarily or consciously control the operation of the heart.

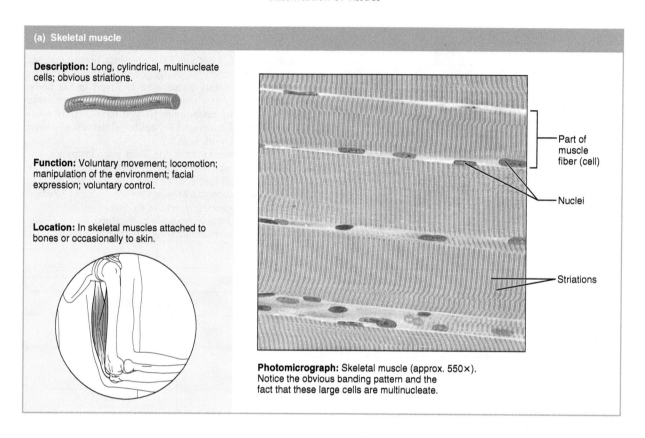

**(a) Skeletal muscle**

**Description:** Long, cylindrical, multinucleate cells; obvious striations.

**Function:** Voluntary movement; locomotion; manipulation of the environment; facial expression; voluntary control.

**Location:** In skeletal muscles attached to bones or occasionally to skin.

Part of muscle fiber (cell)

Nuclei

Striations

**Photomicrograph:** Skeletal muscle (approx. 550×). Notice the obvious banding pattern and the fact that these large cells are multinucleate.

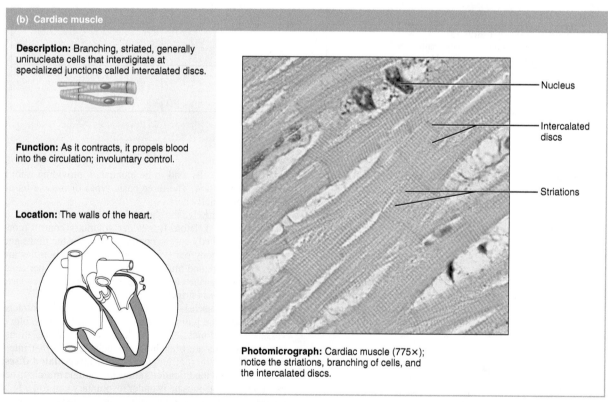

**(b) Cardiac muscle**

**Description:** Branching, striated, generally uninucleate cells that interdigitate at specialized junctions called intercalated discs.

**Function:** As it contracts, it propels blood into the circulation; involuntary control.

**Location:** The walls of the heart.

Nucleus

Intercalated discs

Striations

**Photomicrograph:** Cardiac muscle (775×); notice the striations, branching of cells, and the intercalated discs.

**Figure 7 Muscle tissues.** Skeletal muscle **(a)** and Cardiac muscle **(b).**

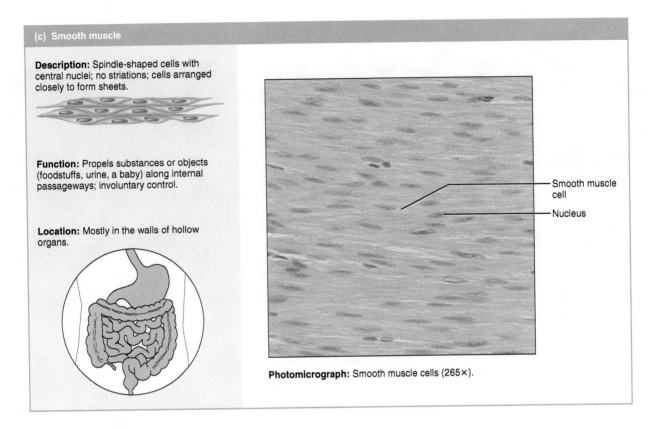

**(c) Smooth muscle**

**Description:** Spindle-shaped cells with central nuclei; no striations; cells arranged closely to form sheets.

**Function:** Propels substances or objects (foodstuffs, urine, a baby) along internal passageways; involuntary control.

**Location:** Mostly in the walls of hollow organs.

Smooth muscle cell

Nucleus

**Photomicrograph:** Smooth muscle cells (265×).

**Figure 7** *(continued)* Smooth muscle **(c).**

**Smooth muscle,** or *visceral muscle,* is found mainly in the walls of hollow organs (digestive and urinary tract organs, uterus, blood vessels). Typically it has two layers that run at right angles to each other; consequently its contraction can constrict or dilate the lumen (cavity) of an organ and propel substances along predetermined pathways. Smooth muscle cells are quite different in appearance from those of skeletal or cardiac muscle. No striations are visible, and the uninucleate smooth muscle cells are spindle-shaped. Like cardiac muscle, it is under involuntary control.

**ACTIVITY 4**

## Examining Muscle Tissue Under the Microscope

Obtain and examine prepared slides of skeletal, cardiac, and smooth muscle. Notice their similarities and dissimilarities in your observations and in the illustrations and photomicrographs (Figure 7). ■

# Classification of Tissues

## Tissue Structure and Function—General Review

1. Define *tissue*. _____

_____

2. Use the key choices to identify the major tissue types described below.

   *Key:* a.  connective tissue     b.  epithelium     c.  muscle     d.  nervous tissue

   _____ 1.  lines body cavities and covers the body's external surface

   _____ 2.  pumps blood, flushes urine out of the body, allows one to swing a bat

   _____ 3.  transmits electrical signals

   _____ 4.  anchors, packages, and supports body organs

   _____ 5.  cells may absorb, secrete, and filter

   _____ 6.  most involved in regulating and controlling body functions

   _____ 7.  major function is to contract

   _____ 8.  synthesizes hormones

   _____ 9.  the most durable tissue type

   _____ 10.  abundant nonliving extracellular matrix

   _____ 11.  most widespread tissue in the body

   _____ 12.  forms nerves and the brain

## Epithelial Tissue

3. Describe five general characteristics of epithelial tissue. _____

_____

_____

_____

4. On what basis are epithelial tissues classified? _____

**5.** List five major functions of epithelium in the body, and give examples of each.

Function 1: _____ Example: _____

Function 2: _____ Example: _____

Function 3: _____ Example: _____

Function 4: _____ Example: _____

Function 5: _____ Example: _____

**6.** How does the function of stratified epithelia differ from the function of simple epithelia? _____

_____

_____

**7.** Where is ciliated epithelium found? _____

_____

What role does it play? _____

_____

**8.** Transitional epithelium is actually stratified squamous epithelium with special characteristics.

How does it differ structurally from other stratified squamous epithelia? _____

_____

How does the structural difference support its function? _____

_____

_____

**9.** How do the endocrine and exocrine glands differ in structure and function? _____

_____

_____

_____

**10.** Respond to the following with the key choices. Some tissues are used more than once.

*Key:*  a.  simple squamous          c.  simple columnar                    e.  stratified squamous
        b.  simple cuboidal          d.  pseudostratified ciliated columnar  f.  transitional

_____ 1.  lining of the esophagus

_____ 2.  lining of the stomach

_____ 3.  alveolar sacs of lungs

_____ 4.  tubules of the kidney

_____ 5. epidermis of the skin

_____ 6. lining of bladder; peculiar cells that have the ability to slide over each other

_____ 7. forms the thin serous membranes; a single layer of flattened cells

## Connective Tissue

**11.** What are three general characteristics of connective tissues? _____

_____

_____

**12.** What functions are performed by connective tissue? _____

_____

**13.** How are the functions of connective tissue reflected in its structure? _____

_____

_____

**14.** Using the key, choose the best response to identify the connective tissues described below. Some tissues are used move than once.

_____ 1. attaches bones to bones and muscles to bones

_____ 2. insulates against heat loss

_____ 3. the dermis of the skin

_____ 4. makes up the intervertebral discs

_____ 5. forms the hip bone

_____ 6. composes basement membranes; a soft packaging tissue with a jellylike matrix

_____ 7. forms the larynx, the costal cartilages of the ribs, and the embryonic skeleton

_____ 8. provides a flexible framework for the external ear

_____ 9. firm, structurally amorphous matrix heavily invaded with fibers; appears glassy and smooth

_____ 10. matrix hard owing to calcium salts; provides levers for muscles to act on

_____ 11. acts as storage depot for fat

_____ 12. walls of large arteries

*Key:*
a. adipose connective tissue
b. areolar connective tissue
c. dense fibrous connective tissue
d. elastic cartilage
e. elastic connective tissue
f. fibrocartilage
g. hematopoietic tissue
h. hyaline cartilage
i. osseous tissue

**15.** Why do adipose cells remind people of a ring with a single jewel? _____

_____

# Nervous Tissue

16. What two physiological characteristics are highly developed in neurons (nerve cells)? _____

_____

17. In what ways are neurons similar to other cells? _____

_____

How are they different? _____

18. Describe how the unique structure of a neuron relates to its function in the body.

_____

_____

# Muscle Tissue

19. The three types of muscle tissue exhibit similarities as well as differences. Check the appropriate space in the chart to indicate which muscle types exhibit each characteristic.

| Characteristic | Skeletal | Cardiac | Smooth |
|---|---|---|---|
| Voluntarily controlled | | | |
| Involuntarily controlled | | | |
| Striated | | | |
| Has a single nucleus in each cell | | | |
| Has several nuclei per cell | | | |
| Found attached to bones | | | |
| Allows you to direct your eyeballs | | | |
| Found in the walls of the stomach, uterus, and arteries | | | |
| Contains spindle-shaped cells | | | |
| Contains branching cylindrical cells | | | |
| Contains long, nonbranching cylindrical cells | | | |
| Has intercalated discs | | | |
| Concerned with locomotion of the body as a whole | | | |
| Changes the internal volume of an organ as it contracts | | | |
| Tissue of the heart | | | |

# For Review

**20.** Label the tissue types illustrated here and on the next page, and identify all structures provided with leaders.

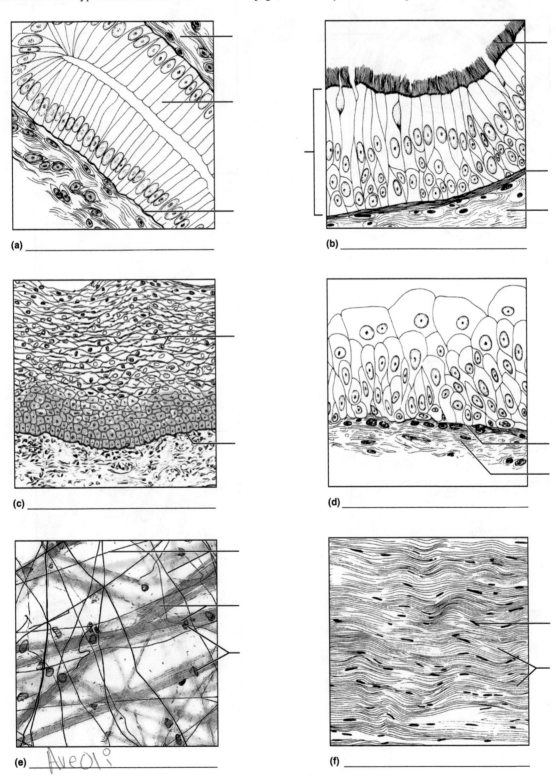

(a) _____

(b) _____

(c) _____

(d) _____

(e) _Aveoli_ _____

(f) _____

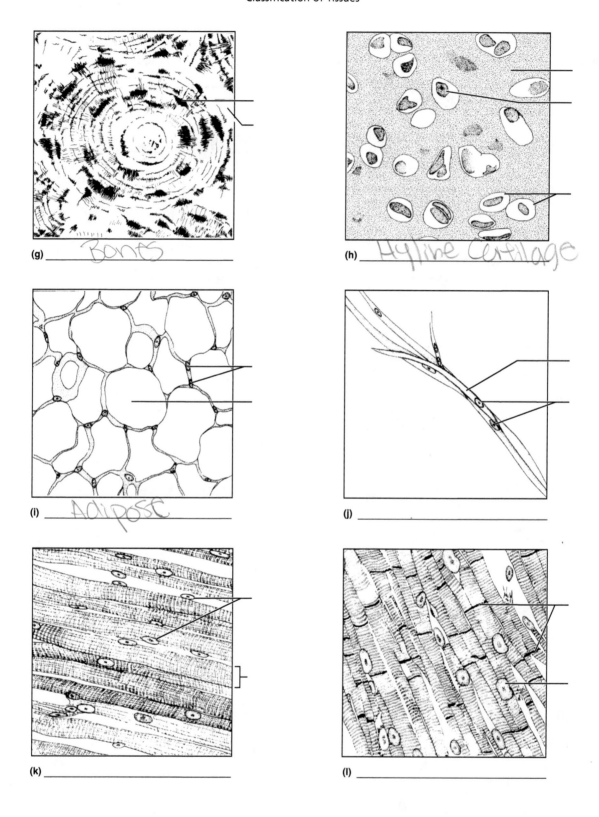

(g) _____Bones_____

(h) _____Hyline Cartilage_____

(i) _____Adipose_____

(j) _____

(k) _____

(l) _____

## Photo Credits

**Credits are listed in order of appearance.**

3a,d,g, 5a,b,e,g,l, 7b,c: William Karkow, Pearson Education. 3b,c,f,h, 5d,j,k: Allen Bell, Pearson Education. 3e, 5c,f,i, 7a: Nina Zanetti, Pearson Education. 5h: Steve Downing, PAL 2.0, Pearson Education. 6: Biophoto Associates/Photo Researchers.

## Illustration Credits

**All illustrations are by Imagineering STA Media Services, except for Review Sheet art and as noted below.**

2: Precision Graphics.

# The Integumentary System

## MATERIALS

- ☐ Skin model (three-dimensional, if available)
- ☐ Compound microscope
- ☐ Prepared slide of human scalp
- ☐ Prepared slide of skin of palm or sole
- ☐ Sheet of 20# bond paper ruled to mark off cm² areas
- ☐ Scissors
- ☐ Betadine® swabs, or Lugol's iodine and cotton swabs
- ☐ Adhesive tape
- ☐ Disposable gloves
- ☐ Data collection sheet for plotting distribution of sweat glands
- ☐ Porelon® fingerprint pad or portable inking foils
- ☐ Ink cleaner towelettes
- ☐ Index cards (4 in. × 6 in.)
- ☐ Magnifying glasses

MasteringA&P* For related exercise study tools, go to the Study Area of MasteringA&P. There you will find:
- Practice Anatomy Lab PAL
- PhysioEx PEx
- A&PFlix  A&PFlix
- Practice quizzes, Histology Atlas, eText, Videos, and more!

## OBJECTIVES

1. List several important functions of the skin, or integumentary system.
2. Identify the following skin structures on a model, image, or microscope slide: epidermis, dermis (papillary and reticular layers), hair follicles and hair, sebaceous glands, and sweat glands.
3. Name and describe the layers of the epidermis.
4. List the factors that determine skin color, and describe the function of melanin.
5. Identify the major regions of nails.
6. Describe the distribution and function of hairs, sebaceous glands, and sweat glands.
7. Discuss the difference between eccrine and apocrine sweat glands.
8. Compare and contrast the structure and functions of the epidermis and the dermis.

## PRE-LAB QUIZ

1. All the following are functions of the skin except:
   a. excretion of body wastes
   b. insulation
   c. protection from mechanical damage
   d. site of vitamin A synthesis
2. The skin has two distinct regions. The superficial layer is the _____ and the underlying connective tissue is the _____.
3. The most superficial layer of the epidermis is the:
   a. stratum basale          c. stratum granulosum
   b. stratum spinosum        d. stratum corneum
4. Thick skin of the epidermis contains _____ layers.
5. _____ is a yellow-orange pigment found in the stratum corneum and the hypodermis.
   a. Keratin                 c. Melanin
   b. Carotene                d. Hemoglobin
6. These cells produce a brown-to-black pigment that colors the skin and protects DNA from ultraviolet radiation damage. The cells are:
   a. dendritic cells         c. melanocytes
   b. keratinocytes           d. tactile cells
7. Circle True or False. Nails originate from the epidermis.
8. The portion of a hair that projects from the scalp surface is known as the:
   a. bulb                    c. root
   b. matrix                  d. shaft
9. Circle the correct underlined term. The ducts of sebaceous / sweat glands usually empty into a hair follicle but may also open directly on the skin surface.
10. Circle the correct underlined term. Eccrine / Apocrine glands are found primarily in the genital and axillary areas.

The **skin,** or **integument,** is considered an organ system because of its extent and complexity. It is much more than an external body covering; architecturally the skin is a marvel. It is tough yet pliable, a characteristic that enables it to withstand constant insult from outside agents.

The skin has many functions, most concerned with protection. It insulates and cushions the underlying body tissues and protects the entire body from abrasion, exposure to harmful chemicals, temperature extremes, and bacterial invasion. The hardened uppermost layer of the skin prevents water loss from the body surface. The skin's abundant capillary network (under the control of the nervous system) plays an important role in temperature regulation by regulating heat loss from the body surface.

The skin has other functions as well. For example, it acts as a mini-excretory system; urea, salts, and water are lost through the skin pores in sweat. The skin also has important metabolic duties. For example, like liver cells, it carries out some chemical conversions that activate or inactivate certain drugs and hormones, and it is the site of vitamin D synthesis for the body. Finally, the sense organs for touch, pressure, pain, and temperature are located here.

# Basic Structure of the Skin

The skin has two distinct regions—the superficial *epidermis* composed of epithelium and an underlying connective tissue, the *dermis* (Figure 1). These layers are firmly "cemented" together along a wavy border. But friction, such as the rubbing of a poorly fitting shoe, may cause them to separate, resulting in a blister. Immediately deep to the dermis is the **hypodermis,** or **superficial fascia,** which is not considered part of the skin. It consists primarily of adipose tissue. The main skin areas and structures are described below.

**ACTIVITY 1**

## Locating Structures on a Skin Model

As you read, locate the following structures in the diagram (Figure 1) and on a skin model. ◼

## Epidermis

Structurally, the avascular epidermis is a keratinized stratified squamous epithelium consisting of four distinct cell types and four or five distinct layers.

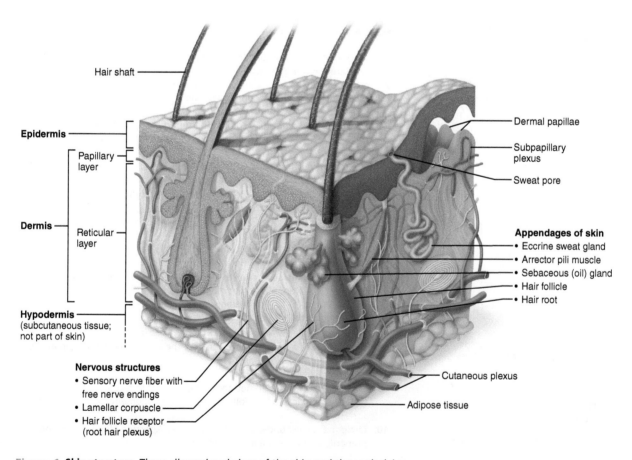

**Figure 1 Skin structure.** Three-dimensional view of the skin and the underlying hypodermis. The epidermis and dermis have been pulled apart at the right corner to reveal the dermal papillae.

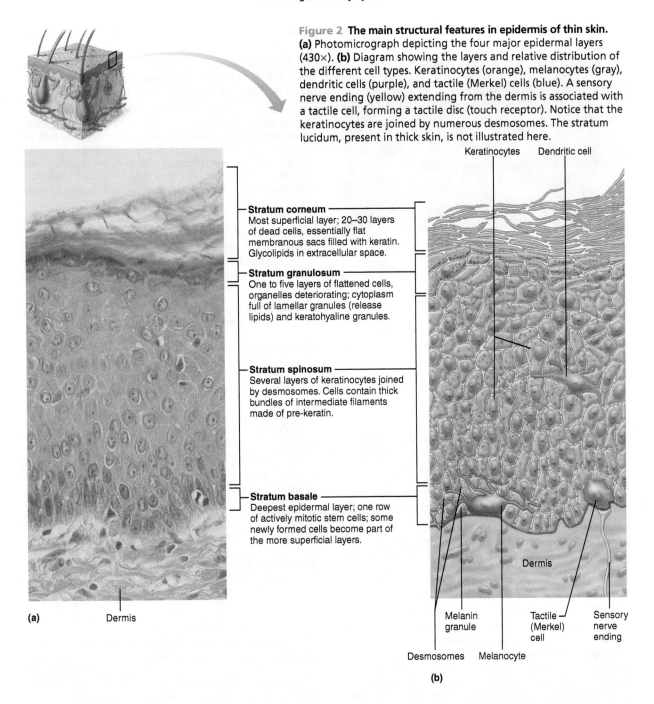

**Figure 2 The main structural features in epidermis of thin skin.**
**(a)** Photomicrograph depicting the four major epidermal layers
(430×). **(b)** Diagram showing the layers and relative distribution of
the different cell types. Keratinocytes (orange), melanocytes (gray),
dendritic cells (purple), and tactile (Merkel) cells (blue). A sensory
nerve ending (yellow) extending from the dermis is associated with
a tactile cell, forming a tactile disc (touch receptor). Notice that the
keratinocytes are joined by numerous desmosomes. The stratum
lucidum, present in thick skin, is not illustrated here.

Keratinocytes    Dendritic cell

**Stratum corneum**
Most superficial layer; 20–30 layers
of dead cells, essentially flat
membranous sacs filled with keratin.
Glycolipids in extracellular space.

**Stratum granulosum**
One to five layers of flattened cells,
organelles deteriorating; cytoplasm
full of lamellar granules (release
lipids) and keratohyaline granules.

**Stratum spinosum**
Several layers of keratinocytes joined
by desmosomes. Cells contain thick
bundles of intermediate filaments
made of pre-keratin.

**Stratum basale**
Deepest epidermal layer; one row
of actively mitotic stem cells; some
newly formed cells become part of
the more superficial layers.

Dermis

**(a)** Dermis

Melanin
granule

Tactile
(Merkel)
cell

Sensory
nerve
ending

Desmosomes    Melanocyte

**(b)**

## Cells of the Epidermis

• **Keratinocytes** (literally, keratin cells): The most abundant epidermal cells, their main function is to produce keratin
fibrils. **Keratin** is a fibrous protein that gives the epidermis
its durability and protective capabilities. Keratinocytes are
tightly connected to each other by desmosomes.

Far less numerous are the following types of epidermal
cells (Figure 2):

• **Melanocytes:** Spidery black cells that produce the brown-
to-black pigment called **melanin.** The skin tans because
melanin production increases when the skin is exposed to
sunlight. The melanin provides a protective pigment umbrella
over the nuclei of the cells in the deeper epidermal layers, thus
shielding their genetic material (DNA) from the damaging
effects of ultraviolet radiation. A concentration of melanin in
one spot is called a *freckle.*

103

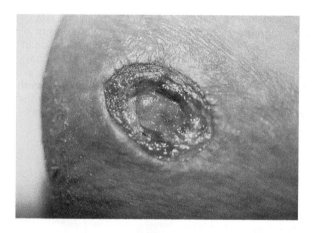

**Figure 3** **Photograph of a deep (stage III) decubitus ulcer.**

• **Dendritic cells:** Also called *Langerhans cells,* these cells play a role in immunity.

• **Tactile (Merkel) cells:** Occasional spiky hemispheres that, in combination with sensory nerve endings, form sensitive touch receptors called *tactile* or *Merkel discs* located at the epidermal-dermal junction.

### Layers of the Epidermis

The epidermis consists of four layers in thin skin, which covers most of the body. Thick skin, found on the palms of the hands and soles of the feet, contains an additional layer, the stratum lucidum. From deep to superficial, the layers of the epidermis are the stratum basale, stratum spinosum, stratum granulosum, stratum lucidum, and stratum corneum (Figure 2).

• **Stratum basale** (basal layer): A single row of cells immediately adjacent to the dermis. Its cells are constantly undergoing mitotic cell division to produce millions of new cells daily, hence its alternate name *stratum germinativum.* From 10% to 25% of the cells in this stratum are melanocytes, which thread their processes through this and the adjacent layers of keratinocytes. Note also the tactile cells of this layer (Figure 2).

• **Stratum spinosum** (spiny layer): A stratum consisting of several cell layers immediately superficial to the basal layer. Its cells contain thick weblike bundles of intermediate filaments made of a pre-keratin protein. The stratum spinosum cells appear spiky (hence their name) because as the skin tissue is prepared for histological examination, they shrink but their desmosomes hold tight. Cells divide fairly rapidly in this layer, but less so than in the stratum basale. Cells in the basal and spiny layers are the only ones to receive adequate nourishment via diffusion of nutrients from the dermis. So as their daughter cells are pushed upward and away from the source of nutrition, they gradually die. Dendritic cells may occur in the spiny layer (Figure 2).

• **Stratum granulosum** (granular layer): A thin layer named for the abundant granules its cells contain. These granules are of two types: (1) *lamellar granules,* which contain a waterproofing glycolipid that is secreted into the extracellular space; and (2) *keratohyaline granules,* which combine with the intermediate filaments in the more superficial layers to

form the keratin fibrils. At the upper border of this layer, the cells are beginning to die.

• **Stratum lucidum** (clear layer): A very thin translucent band of flattened dead keratinocytes with indistinct boundaries. It is not present in regions of thin skin.

• **Stratum corneum** (horny layer): This outermost epidermal layer consists of some 20 to 30 cell layers (fewer layers are present in thin skin), and accounts for the bulk of the epidermal thickness. Cells in this layer, like those in the stratum lucidum (where it exists), are dead, and their flattened scalelike remnants are fully keratinized. They are constantly rubbing off and being replaced by division of the deeper cells.

## Dermis

The dense irregular connective tissue making up the dermis consists of two principal regions—the papillary and reticular areas (Figure 1). Like the epidermis, the dermis varies in thickness. For example, it is particularly thick on the palms of the hands and soles of the feet and is quite thin on the eyelids.

• **Papillary layer:** The more superficial dermal region composed of areolar connective tissue. It is very uneven and has fingerlike projections from its superior surface, the **dermal papillae,** which attach it to the epidermis above. These projections lie on top of the larger dermal ridges. In the palms of the hands and soles of the feet, they produce the *fingerprints,* unique patterns of *epidermal ridges* that remain unchanged throughout life. Abundant capillary networks in the papillary layer furnish nutrients for the epidermal layers and allow heat to radiate to the skin surface. The pain (free nerve endings) and touch receptors (*tactile corpuscles* in hairless skin) are also found here.

• **Reticular layer:** The deepest skin layer. It is composed of dense irregular connective tissue and contains many arteries and veins, sweat and sebaceous glands, and pressure receptors (*lamellar corpuscles*).

Both the papillary and reticular layers are heavily invested with collagenic and elastic fibers. The elastic fibers give skin its exceptional elasticity in youth. In old age, the number of elastic fibers decreases, and the subcutaneous layer loses fat, which leads to wrinkling and inelasticity of the skin. Fibroblasts, adipose cells, various types of macrophages (which are important in the body's defense), and other cell types are found throughout the dermis.

The abundant dermal blood supply allows the skin to play a role in the regulation of body temperature. When body temperature is high, the arterioles serving the skin dilate, and the capillary network of the dermis becomes engorged with the heated blood. Thus body heat is allowed to radiate from the skin surface. If the environment is cool and body heat must be conserved, the arterioles constrict so that blood bypasses the dermal capillary networks temporarily.

Any restriction of the normal blood supply to the skin results in cell death and, if severe enough, skin ulcers (Figure 3). **Bedsores (decubitus ulcers)** occur in bedridden patients who are not turned regularly enough. The weight of the body puts pressure on the skin, especially over bony projections (hips, heels, etc.), which leads to restriction of the blood supply and tissue death. +

The dermis is also richly provided with lymphatic vessels and nerve fibers. Many of the nerve endings bear highly specialized receptor organs that, when stimulated by environmental changes, transmit messages to the central nervous system for interpretation. Some of these receptors—free nerve endings (pain receptors), a lamellar corpuscle, and a hair follicle receptor (also called a *root hair plexus*)—are shown in the diagram of skin structure (Figure 1).

## Skin Color

Skin color is a result of the relative amount of melanin in skin, the relative amount of carotene in skin, and the degree of oxygenation of the blood. People who produce large amounts of melanin have brown-toned skin. In light-skinned people, who have less melanin pigment, the dermal blood supply flushes through the rather transparent cell layers above, giving the skin a rosy glow. *Carotene* is a yellow-orange pigment present primarily in the stratum corneum and in the adipose tissue of the hypodermis. Its presence is most noticeable when large amounts of carotene-rich foods (carrots, for instance) are eaten.

Skin color may be an important diagnostic tool. For example, flushed skin may indicate hypertension, fever, or embarrassment, whereas pale skin is typically seen in anemic individuals. When the blood is inadequately oxygenated, as during asphyxiation and serious lung disease, both the blood and the skin take on a bluish or cyanotic cast. **Jaundice,** in which the tissues become yellowed, is almost always diagnostic for liver disease, whereas a bronzing of the skin hints that a person's adrenal cortex is hypoactive **(Addison's disease).**

## Accessory Organs of the Skin

The accessory organs of the skin—cutaneous glands, hair, and nails—are all derivatives of the epidermis, but they reside in the dermis. They originate from the stratum basale and grow downward into the deeper skin regions.

## Nails

Nails are hornlike derivatives of the epidermis (Figure 4). Their named parts are:

- **Body:** The visible attached portion.

- **Free edge:** The portion of the nail that grows out away from the body.

- **Hyponychium:** The region beneath the free edge of the nail.

- **Root:** The part that is embedded in the skin and adheres to an epithelial nail bed.

- **Nail folds:** Skin folds that overlap the borders of the nail.

- **Eponychium:** The thick proximal nail fold commonly called the cuticle.

- **Nail bed:** Extension of the stratum basale beneath the nail.

- **Nail matrix:** The thickened proximal part of the nail bed containing germinal cells responsible for nail growth. As the matrix produces the nail cells, they become heavily keratinized and die. Thus nails, like hairs, are mostly nonliving material.

- **Lunule:** The proximal region of the thickened nail matrix, which appears as a white crescent. Everywhere else, nails

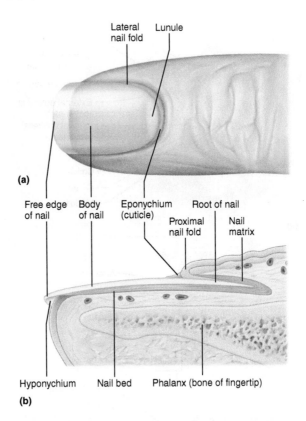

**(a)**

**(b)**

**Figure 4 Structure of a nail. (a)** Surface view of the distal part of a finger showing nail parts. The nail matrix that forms the nail lies beneath the lunule; the epidermis of the nail bed underlies the nail. **(b)** Sagittal section of the fingertip.

are transparent and nearly colorless, but they appear pink because of the blood supply in the underlying dermis. When someone is cyanotic because of a lack of oxygen in the blood, the nail beds take on a blue cast.

### ACTIVITY 2

### Identifying Nail Structures

Identify the parts of a nail (as shown in Figure 4) on yourself or your lab partner. ■

## Hairs and Associated Structures

Hairs, enclosed in hair follicles, are found all over the entire body surface, except for thick-skinned areas (the palms of the hands and the soles of the feet), parts of the external genitalia, the nipples, and the lips.

- **Hair:** Structure consisting of a medulla, a central region surrounded first by the *cortex* and then by a protective *cuticle* (Figure 5). Abrasion of the cuticle results in split ends. Hair color depends on the amount and kind of melanin pigment within the hair cortex. The portion of the hair enclosed within the follicle is called the **root;** that portion projecting from the scalp surface is called the **shaft. The hair bulb** is a collection of well-nourished germinal epithelial cells at the basal end

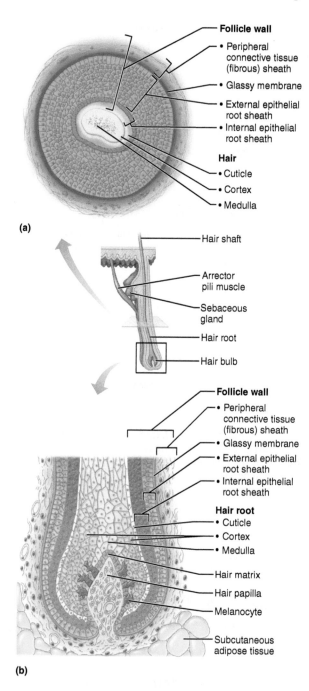

**(a)**

**(b)**

**Figure 5 Structure of a hair and hair follicle. (a)** Diagram of a cross section of a hair within its follicle. **(b)** Diagram of a longitudinal view of the expanded hair bulb of the follicle, which encloses the matrix, the actively dividing epithelial cells that produce the hair.

of the follicle. As the daughter cells are pushed farther away from the growing region, they die and become keratinized; thus the bulk of the hair shaft, like the bulk of the epidermis, is dead material.

- **Follicle:** A structure formed from both epidermal and dermal cells (Figure 5). Its inner epithelial root sheath, with two parts (internal and external), is enclosed by a thickened basement membrane, the glassy membrane, and a peripheral connective tissue (or fibrous) sheath, which is essentially dermal tissue. A small nipple of dermal tissue protrudes into the hair bulb from the peripheral connective tissue sheath and provides nutrition to the growing hair. It is called the **papilla.**

- **Arrector pili muscle:** Small bands of smooth muscle cells connect each hair follicle to the papillary layer of the dermis (Figures 1 and 5). When these muscles contract (during cold or fright), the slanted hair follicle is pulled upright, dimpling the skin surface with goose bumps. This phenomenon is especially dramatic in a scared cat, whose fur actually stands on end to increase its apparent size. The activity of the arrector pili muscles also puts pressure on the sebaceous glands surrounding the follicle, causing a small amount of sebum to be released.

### ACTIVITY 3

## Comparison of Hairy and Relatively Hair-Free Skin Microscopically

While thick skin has no hair follicles or sebaceous (oil) glands, thin skin typical of most of the body has both. The scalp, of course, has the highest density of hair follicles.

1. Obtain a prepared slide of the human scalp, and study it carefully under the microscope. Compare your tissue slide to the photomicrograph **(Figure 6a)**, and identify as many as possible of the diagrammed structures (Figure 1).

How is this stratified squamous epithelium different from that observed in the esophagus?

_____

_____

How do these differences relate to the functions of these two similar epithelia?

_____

_____

_____

2. Obtain a prepared slide of hairless skin of the palm or sole (Figure 6b). Compare the slide to the previous photomicrograph (Figure 6a). In what ways does the thick skin of the palm or sole differ from the thin skin of the scalp?

_____

_____

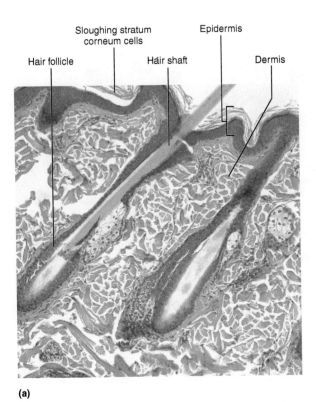

Hair follicle  Sloughing stratum corneum cells  Hair shaft  Epidermis  Dermis

**(a)**

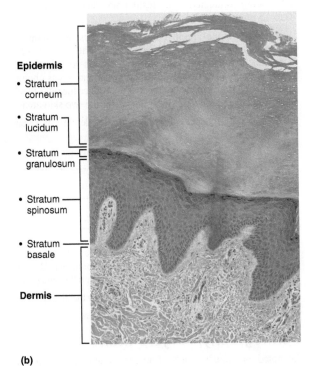

**Epidermis**
• Stratum corneum
• Stratum lucidum
• Stratum granulosum
• Stratum spinosum
• Stratum basale

**Dermis**

**(b)**

**Figure 6 Photomicrographs of skin. (a)** Thin skin with hairs (120×). **(b)** Thick hairless skin (75×).

## Cutaneous Glands

The cutaneous glands fall primarily into two categories: the sebaceous glands and the sweat glands (Figure 1 and Figure 7).

### Sebaceous (Oil) Glands

The sebaceous glands are found nearly all over the skin, except for the palms of the hands and the soles of the feet. Their ducts usually empty into a hair follicle, but some open directly on the skin surface.

**Sebum** is the product of sebaceous glands. It is a mixture of oily substances and fragmented cells that acts as a lubricant to keep the skin soft and moist (a natural skin cream) and keeps the hair from becoming brittle. The sebaceous glands become particularly active during puberty when more male hormones (androgens) begin to be produced; thus the skin tends to become oilier during this period of life.

**Blackheads** are accumulations of dried sebum, bacteria, and melanin from epithelial cells in the oil duct. **Acne** is an active infection of the sebaceous glands. ✚

### Sweat (Sudoriferous) Glands

These exocrine glands are widely distributed all over the skin. Outlets for the glands are epithelial openings called *pores*. Sweat glands are categorized by the composition of their secretions.

• **Eccrine glands:** Also called **merocrine sweat glands,** these glands are distributed all over the body. They produce clear perspiration consisting primarily of water, salts (mostly NaCl), and urea. Eccrine sweat glands, under the control of the nervous system, are an important part of the body's heat-regulating apparatus. They secrete perspiration when the external temperature or body temperature is high. When this water-based substance evaporates, it carries excess body heat with it. Thus evaporation of greater amounts of perspiration provides an efficient means of dissipating body heat when the capillary cooling system is not sufficient or is unable to maintain body temperature homeostasis.

• **Apocrine glands:** Found predominantly in the axillary and genital areas, these glands secrete the basic components of eccrine sweat plus proteins and fat-rich substances. Apocrine sweat is an excellent nutrient medium for the microorganisms typically found on the skin. This sweat is odorless, but when bacteria break down its organic components, it begins to smell unpleasant. The function of apocrine glands is not known, but since their activity increases during sexual foreplay and the glands enlarge and recede with the phases of a woman's menstrual cycle, they may be the human equivalent of the sexual scent glands of other animals.

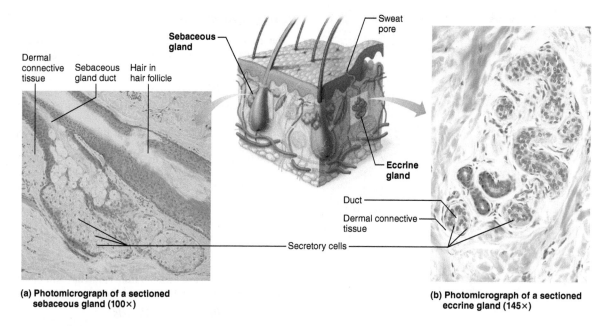

(a) Photomicrograph of a sectioned
sebaceous gland (100×)

(b) Photomicrograph of a sectioned
eccrine gland (145×)

Figure 7 **Cutaneous glands.**

**ACTIVITY 4**

## Differentiating Sebaceous and Sweat Glands Microscopically

Using the slide *thin skin with hairs,* and the photomicrographs of cutaneous glands (Figure 7) as a guide, identify sebaceous and eccrine sweat glands. What characteristics relating to location or gland structure allow you to differentiate these glands?

**ACTIVITY 5**

## Plotting the Distribution of Sweat Glands

1. Form a hypothesis about the relative distribution of sweat glands on the palm and forearm. Justify your hypothesis.

2. The bond paper for this simple experiment has been pre-ruled in cm²—put on disposable gloves and cut along the lines to obtain the required squares. You will need two squares of bond paper (each 1 cm × 1 cm), adhesive tape, and a Betadine (iodine) swab *or* Lugol's iodine and a cotton-tipped swab.

3. Paint an area of the medial aspect of your left palm (avoid the crease lines) and a region of your left forearm with the iodine solution, and allow it to dry thoroughly. The painted area in each case should be slightly larger than the paper squares to be used.

4. Have your lab partner *securely* tape a square of bond paper over each iodine-painted area, and leave them in place for 20 minutes. (If it is very warm in the laboratory while this

test is being conducted, good results may be obtained within 10 to 15 minutes.)

5. After 20 minutes, remove the paper squares, and count the number of blue-black dots on each square. The presence of a blue-black dot on the paper indicates an active sweat gland. The iodine in the pore is dissolved in the sweat and reacts chemically with the starch in the bond paper to produce the blue-black color. You have produced "sweat maps" for the two skin areas.

6. Which skin area tested has the greater density of sweat glands?

7. Tape your results (bond paper squares) to a data collection sheet labeled "palm" and "forearm" at the front of the lab. Be sure to put your paper squares in the correct columns on the data sheet.

8. Once all the data have been collected, review the class results.

9. Prepare a lab report for the experiment. ■

## Dermography: Fingerprinting

As noted previously, each of us has a unique genetically determined set of fingerprints. Because of the usefulness of fingerprinting for identifying and apprehending criminals, most people associate this craft solely with criminal investigations. However, civil fingerprints are invaluable in quickly identifying amnesia victims, missing persons, and unknown deceased such as those killed in major disasters.

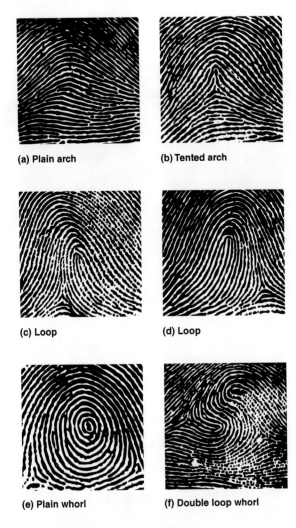

**(a) Plain arch**   **(b) Tented arch**

**(c) Loop**   **(d) Loop**

**(e) Plain whorl**   **(f) Double loop whorl**

**Figure 8 Main types of fingerprint patterns. (a–b)** Arches. **(c–d)** Loops. **(e–f)** Whorls.

The friction ridges responsible for fingerprints appear in several patterns, which are clearest when the fingertips are inked and then pressed against white paper. Impressions are also made when perspiration or any foreign material such as blood, dirt, or grease adheres to the ridges and the fingers are then pressed against a smooth, nonabsorbent surface. The three most common patterns are *arches, loops,* and *whorls* **(Figure 8)**. The *pattern area* in loops and whorls is the only area of the print used in identification, and it is delineated by the *type lines*—specifically the two innermost ridges that start parallel, diverge, and/or surround or tend to surround the pattern area.

### ACTIVITY 6

## Taking and Identifying Inked Fingerprints

For this activity, you will be working as a group with your lab partners. Though the equipment for professional fingerprinting is fairly basic, consisting of a glass or metal inking plate, printer's ink (a heavy black paste), ink roller, and standard

8 in. × 8 in. cards, you will be using supplies that are even easier to handle. Each student will prepare two index cards, each bearing his or her thumbprint and index fingerprint of the right hand.

1. Obtain the following supplies and bring them to your bench: two 4 in. × 6 in. index cards per student, Porelon fingerprint pad or portable inking foils, ink cleaner towelettes, and a magnifying glass.

2. The subject should wash and dry the hands. Open the ink pad or peel back the covering over the ink foil, and position it close to the edge of the laboratory bench. The subject should position himself or herself at arm's length from the bench edge and inking object.

3. A second student, called the *operator,* stands to the left of the subject and with two hands holds and directs movement of the subject's fingertip. During this process, the subject should look away, try to relax, and refrain from trying to help the operator.

4. The thumbprint is to be placed on the left side of the index card, the index fingerprint on the right. The operator should position the subject's right thumb or index finger on the side of the bulb of the finger in such a way that the area to be inked spans the distance from the fingertip to just beyond the first joint, and then roll the finger lightly across the inked surface until its bulb faces in the opposite direction. To prevent smearing, the thumb is rolled away from the body midline (from left to right as the subject sees it; see **Figure 9**) and the index finger is rolled toward the body midline (from right to left). The same ink foil can be reused for all the students at the bench; the ink pad is good for thousands of prints. Repeat the procedure (still using the subject's right hand) on the second index card.

5. If the prints are too light, too dark, or smeary, repeat the procedure.

6. While subsequent members are making clear prints of their thumb and index finger, those who have completed that activity should clean their inked fingers with a towelette and attempt to classify their own prints as arches, loops, or whorls. Use the magnifying glass as necessary to see ridge details.

7. When all members at a bench have completed the above steps, they are to write their names on the backs of their index

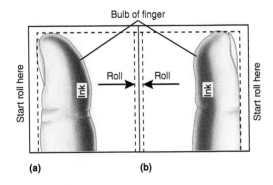

**Figure 9 Fingerprinting.** Method of inking and printing **(a)** the thumb and **(b)** the index finger of the right hand.

cards, then combine their cards and shuffle them before transferring them to the bench opposite for classification of pattern and identification of prints made by the same individuals.

How difficult was it to classify the prints into one of the three categories given?

_____

Why do you think this is so?

_____

Was it easy or difficult to identify the prints made by the same individual?

_____

Why do you think this was so?

_____

# The Integumentary System

R E V I E W   S H E E T

## Basic Structure of the Skin

**1.** Complete the following statements by writing the appropriate word or phrase on the correspondingly numbered blank:

     The two basic tissues of which the skin is composed are dense irregular connective tissue, which makes up the dermis, and __1__, which forms the epidermis. The tough water-repellent protein found in the epidermal cells is called __2__. The pigments melanin and __3__ contribute to skin color. A localized concentration of melanin is referred to as a __4__.

1. _____

2. _____

3. _____

4. _____

**2.** Four protective functions of the skin are

a. _____

b. _____

c. _____

d. _____

**3.** Using the key choices, choose all responses that apply to the following descriptions. Some terms are used more than once.

*Key:*  a.  stratum basale
        b.  stratum corneum
        c.  stratum granulosum

        d.  stratum lucidum
        e.  stratum spinosum
        f.  papillary layer

        g.  reticular layer
        h.  epidermis as a whole
        i.  dermis as a whole

_____ 1. layer of translucent cells in thick skin containing dead keratinocytes

_____ 2. two layers containing dead cells

_____ 3. dermal layer responsible for fingerprints

_____ 4. vascular region of the skin

_____ 5. major skin area as a whole that produces derivatives (nails and hair)

_____ 6. epidermal layer exhibiting the most rapid cell division

_____ 7. layer including scalelike dead cells, full of keratin, that constantly slough off

_____ 8. layer of mitotic cells filled with intermediate filaments

_____ 9. has abundant elastic and collagenic fibers

_____ 10. location of melanocytes and tactile (Merkel) cells

_____ 11. area where weblike pre-keratin filaments first appear

_____ 12. layer of areolar connective tissue

**4.** Label the skin structures and areas indicated in the accompanying diagram of thin skin. Then, complete the statements that follow.

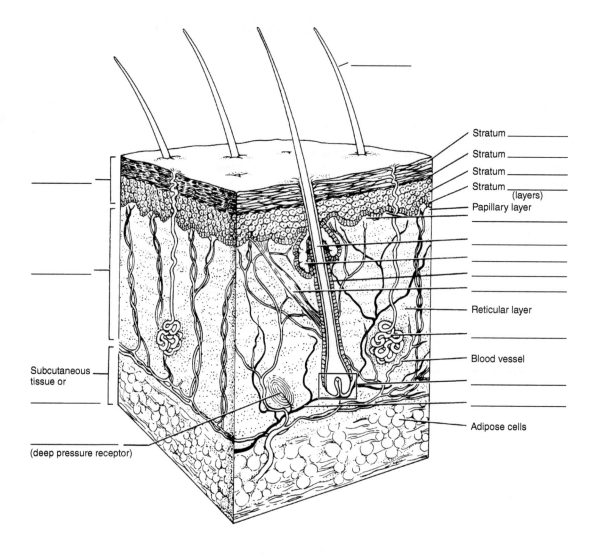

Stratum _____
Stratum _____
Stratum _____
Stratum _____
   (layers)
Papillary layer
_____
_____
_____
Reticular layer
_____
Blood vessel
_____
_____
Adipose cells

Subcutaneous _____
tissue or

_____

_____ _____
(deep pressure receptor)

a.  _____ granules contain glycolipids that prevent water loss from the skin.

b.  Fibers in the dermis are produced by _____.

c.  Glands that respond to rising androgen levels are the _____ glands.

d.  Phagocytic cells that occupy the epidermis are called _____.

e.  A unique touch receptor formed from a stratum basale cell and a nerve fiber is a _____.

f.  What layer is present in thick skin but not in thin skin? _____

g.  What cell-to-cell structures hold the cells of the stratum spinosum tightly together? _____

**5.** What substance is manufactured in the skin and plays a role in calcium absorption elsewhere in the body?

_____

**6.** List the sensory receptors found in the dermis of the skin. _____

_____

_____

**7.** A nurse tells a doctor that a patient is cyanotic. Define *cyanosis*. _____

What does its presence imply? _____

**8.** What is a bedsore (decubitus ulcer)? _____

Why does it occur? _____

_____

# Accessory Organs of the Skin

**9.** Match the key choices with the appropriate descriptions. Some terms are used more than once.

*Key:* a. arrector pili     d. hair follicle    g. sweat gland—apocrine
   b. cutaneous receptors    e. nail    h. sweat gland—eccrine
   c. hair    f. sebaceous glands

_____ 1. produces an accumulation of oily material that is known as a blackhead

_____ 2. tiny muscles, attached to hair follicles, that pull the hair upright during fright or cold

_____ 3. sweat glands with a role in temperature control

_____ 4. sheath formed of both epithelial and connective tissues

_____ 5. less numerous type of sweat-producing gland; found mainly in the pubic and axillary regions

_____ 6. found everywhere on the body except the palms of hands and soles of feet (two from key)

_____ 7. primarily dead/keratinized cells (two from key)

_____ 8. specialized nerve endings that respond to temperature, touch, etc.

_____ 9. secretes a lubricant for hair and skin

_____ 10. "sports" a lunule and a cuticle

**10.** Describe two integumentary system mechanisms that help in regulating body temperature. _____

_____

_____

**11.** Several structures or skin regions are listed below. Identify each by matching its letter with the appropriate area on the figure.

a. adipose cells

b. dermis

c. epidermis

d. hair follicle

e. hair shaft

f. sloughing stratum corneum cells

## Plotting the Distribution of Sweat Glands

**12.** With what substance in the bond paper does the iodine painted on the skin react? _____

**13.** Based on class data, which skin area—the forearm or palm of hand—has more sweat glands? _____

Was this an expected result? _____ Explain. _____

_____

Which other body areas would, if tested, prove to have a high density of sweat glands? _____

_____

**14.** What organ system controls the activity of the eccrine sweat glands? _____

## Dermography: Fingerprinting

**15.** Why can fingerprints be used to identify individuals?

_____

**16.** Name the three common fingerprint patterns.

_____, _____, and _____

## Photo Credits

Credits are listed in order of appearance.

2a, 6b: William Karkow, Pearson Education. 3: Pearson Education. 6a, RS2: Marian Rice. 7a,b: Lisa Lee, Pearson Education.

## Illustration Credits

All illustrations are by Imagineering STA Media Services, except for Review Sheet art and as noted below.

1, 2, 7: Electronic Publishing Services, Inc.

# Overview of the Skeleton: Classification and Structure of Bones and Cartilages

## MATERIALS

- ☐ Long bone sawed longitudinally (beef bone from a slaughterhouse, if possible, or prepared laboratory specimen)
- ☐ Disposable gloves
- ☐ Long bone soaked in 10% hydrochloric acid (HCl) (or vinegar) until flexible
- ☐ Long bone baked at 250°F for more than 2 hours
- ☐ Compound microscope
- ☐ Prepared slide of ground bone (x.s.)
- ☐ Three-dimensional model of microscopic structure of compact bone
- ☐ Prepared slide of a developing long bone undergoing endochondral ossification
- ☐ Articulated skeleton

## OBJECTIVES

1. Name the two tissue types that form the skeleton.
2. List the functions of the skeletal system.
3. Locate and identify the three major types of skeletal cartilages.
4. Name the four main groups of bones based on shape.
5. Identify surface bone markings and list their functions.
6. Identify the major anatomical areas on a longitudinally cut long bone or on an appropriate image.
7. Explain the role of inorganic salts and organic matrix in providing flexibility and hardness to bone.
8. Locate and identify the major parts of an osteon microscopically, or on a histological model or appropriate image of compact bone.

## PRE-LAB QUIZ

1. All the following are functions of the skeleton except:
   a. attachment for muscles
   b. production of melanin
   c. site of red blood cell formation
   d. storage of lipids
2. Circle the correct underlined term. The axial / appendicular skeleton consists of bones that surround the body's center of gravity.
3. The type of cartilage that has the greatest strength and is found in the knee joint and intervertebral discs is
   a. elastic      b. fibrocartilage      c. hyaline
4. Circle the correct underlined term. Compact / Spongy bone looks smooth and homogeneous.
5. _____ bones are generally thin and have a layer of spongy bone between two layers of compact bone.
   a. Flat      b. Irregular      c. Long      d. Short
6. The femur is an example of a(n) _____ bone.
   a. flat      b. irregular      c. long      d. short
7. Circle the correct underlined term. The shaft of a long bone is known as the epiphysis / diaphysis.
8. The structural unit of compact bone is the
   a. osteon      b. canaliculius      c. lacuna
9. Circle True or False. Embryonic skeletons consist primarily of elastic cartilage, which is gradually replaced by bone during development and growth.
10. Circle True or False. Cartilage has a covering made of dense connective tissue called a periosteum.

From Exercise 8 of *Human Anatomy & Physiology Laboratory Manual,* Main Version, Tenth Edition. Elaine N. Marieb, Susan J. Mitchell, Lori A. Smith. Copyright © 2014 by Pearson Education, Inc. All rights reserved.

The **skeleton,** the body's framework, is constructed of two of the most supportive tissues found in the human body—cartilage and bone. In embryos, the skeleton is predominantly made up of hyaline cartilage, but in the adult, most of the cartilage is replaced by more rigid bone. Cartilage persists only in such isolated areas as the external ear, bridge of the nose, larynx, trachea, joints, and parts of the rib cage (see Figure 2).

Besides supporting and protecting the body as an internal framework, the skeleton provides a system of levers with which the skeletal muscles work to move the body. In addition, the bones store lipids and many minerals (most importantly calcium). Finally, the red marrow cavities of bones provide a site for hematopoiesis (blood cell formation).

The skeleton is made up of bones that are connected at *joints,* or *articulations.* The skeleton is subdivided into two

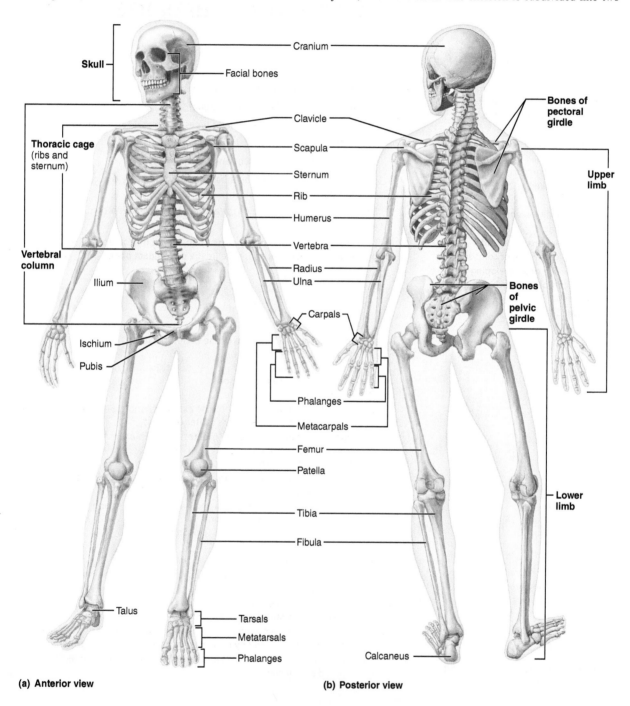

**(a) Anterior view**

**(b) Posterior view**

**Figure 1 The human skeleton.** The bones of the axial skeleton are colored green to distinguish them from the bones of the appendicular skeleton.

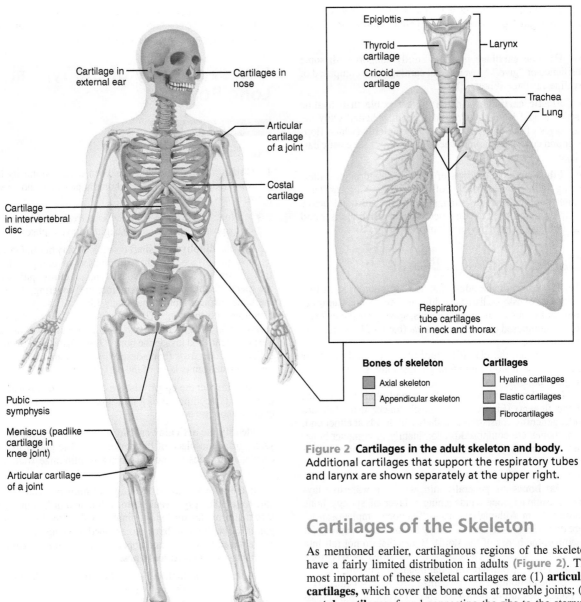

Figure 2 **Cartilages in the adult skeleton and body.**
Additional cartilages that support the respiratory tubes
and larynx are shown separately at the upper right.

## Cartilages of the Skeleton

As mentioned earlier, cartilaginous regions of the skeleton
have a fairly limited distribution in adults **(Figure 2)**. The
most important of these skeletal cartilages are (1) **articular
cartilages,** which cover the bone ends at movable joints; (2)
**costal cartilages,** found connecting the ribs to the sternum
(breastbone); (3) **laryngeal cartilages,** which largely construct the larynx (voice box); (4) **tracheal** and **bronchial
cartilages,** which reinforce other passageways of the respiratory system; (5) **nasal cartilages,** which support the external
nose; (6) **intervertebral discs,** which separate and cushion
bones of the spine (vertebrae); and (7) the cartilage supporting the external ear.

The skeletal cartilages consist of some variety of *cartilage tissue,* which typically consists primarily of water and is
fairly resilient. Cartilage tissues are also distinguished by the
fact that they contain no nerves and very few blood vessels.
Like bones, each cartilage is surrounded by a covering of
dense connective tissue, called a *perichondrium* (rather than
a periosteum), which acts to resist distortion of the cartilage
when it is subjected to pressure, and plays a role in cartilage
growth and repair.

divisions: the **axial skeleton** (those bones that lie around
the body's center of gravity) and the **appendicular skeleton**
(bones of the limbs, or appendages) **(Figure 1)**.

Before beginning your study of the skeleton, imagine for
a moment that your bones have turned to putty. What if you
were running when this change took place? Now imagine
your bones forming a continuous metal framework within
your body, somewhat like a network of plumbing pipes. What
problems could you envision with this arrangement? These
images should help you understand how well the skeletal
system provides support and protection, as well as facilitating
movement.

The skeletal cartilages have representatives from each of the three cartilage tissue types—hyaline, elastic, and fibrocartilage.

• **Hyaline cartilage** provides sturdy support with some resilience or "give." Most skeletal cartilages are composed of hyaline cartilage (Figure 2).

• **Elastic cartilage** is much more flexible than hyaline cartilage, and it tolerates repeated bending better. Only the cartilages of the external ear and the epiglottis (which flops over and covers the larynx when we swallow) are elastic cartilage.

• **Fibrocartilage** consists of rows of chondrocytes alternating with rows of thick collagen fibers. Fibrocartilage, which has great tensile strength and can withstand heavy compression, is used to construct the intervertebral discs and the cartilages within the knee joint (see Figure 2).

## Classification of Bones

The 206 bones of the adult skeleton are composed of two basic kinds of osseous tissue that differ in their texture. **Compact bone** looks smooth and homogeneous; **spongy** (or *cancellous*) **bone** is composed of small *trabeculae* (bars) of bone and lots of open space.

Bones may be classified further on the basis of their relative gross anatomy into four groups: long, short, flat, and irregular bones.

**Long bones,** such as the femur and phalanges (bones of the fingers) (Figure 1), are much longer than they are wide, generally consisting of a shaft with heads at either end. Long bones are composed predominantly of compact bone. **Short bones** are typically cube shaped, and they contain more spongy bone than compact bone. The tarsals and carpals are examples (see Figure 1).

**Flat bones** are generally thin, with two waferlike layers of compact bone sandwiching a layer of spongy bone between them. Although the name "flat bone" implies a structure that is level or horizontal, many flat bones are curved (for example, the bones of the skull). Bones that do not fall into one of the preceding categories are classified as **irregular bones.** The vertebrae are irregular bones (see Figure 1).

Some anatomists also recognize two other subcategories of bones. **Sesamoid bones** are special types of short bones formed in tendons. The patellas (kneecaps) are sesamoid bones. **Sutural bones** are tiny bones between cranial bones. Except for the patellas, the sesamoid and sutural bones are not included in the bone count of 206 because they vary in number and location in different individuals.

## Bone Markings

Even a casual observation of the bones will reveal that bone surfaces are not featureless smooth areas but are scarred with an array of bumps, holes, and ridges. These **bone markings** reveal where bones form joints with other bones, where muscles, tendons, and ligaments were attached, and where blood vessels and nerves passed. Bone markings fall into two categories: projections, or processes that grow out from the bone and serve as sites of muscle attachment or help form joints;

and depressions or cavities, indentations or openings in the bone that often serve as conduits for nerves and blood vessels. (The bone markings are summarized in **Table 1** .)

## Gross Anatomy of the Typical Long Bone

### ACTIVITY 1

### Examining a Long Bone

1. Obtain a long bone that has been sawed along its longitudinal axis. If a cleaned dry bone is provided, no special preparations need be made.

! Note: If the bone supplied is a fresh beef bone, don disposable gloves before beginning your observations.

Identify the **diaphysis** or shaft (**Figure 3** may help). Observe its smooth surface, which is composed of compact bone. If you are using a fresh specimen, carefully pull away the **periosteum,** or fibrous membrane covering, to view the bone surface. Notice that many fibers of the periosteum penetrate into the bone. These fibers are called **perforating (Sharpey's) fibers.** Blood vessels and nerves travel through the periosteum and invade the bone. *Osteoblasts* (bone-forming cells) and *osteoclasts* (bone-destroying cells) are found on the inner, or osteogenic, layer of the periosteum.

2. Now inspect the **epiphysis,** the end of the long bone. Notice that it is composed of a thin layer of compact bone that encloses spongy bone.

3. Identify the **articular cartilage,** which covers the epiphyseal surface in place of the periosteum. The glassy hyaline cartilage provides a smooth surface to minimize friction at joints.

4. If the animal was still young and growing, you will be able to see the **epiphyseal plate,** a thin area of hyaline cartilage that provides for longitudinal growth of the bone during youth. Once the long bone has stopped growing, these areas are replaced with bone and appear as thin, barely discernible remnants—the **epiphyseal lines.**

5. In an adult animal, the central cavity of the shaft *(medullary cavity)* is essentially a storage region for adipose tissue, or **yellow marrow.** In the infant, this area is involved in forming blood cells, and so **red marrow** is found in the marrow cavities. In adult bones, the red marrow is confined to the interior of the epiphyses, where it occupies the spaces between the trabeculae of spongy bone.

6. If you are examining a fresh bone, look carefully to see if you can distinguish the delicate **endosteum** lining the shaft. The endosteum also covers the trabeculae of spongy bone and lines the canals of compact bone. Like the periosteum, the endosteum contains both osteoblasts and osteoclasts. As the bone grows in diameter on its external surface, it is constantly being broken down on its inner surface. Thus the thickness of the compact bone layer composing the shaft remains relatively constant.

! 7. If you have been working with a fresh bone specimen, return it to the appropriate area and properly dispose of your gloves, as designated by your instructor. Wash your hands before continuing to the microscope study. ■

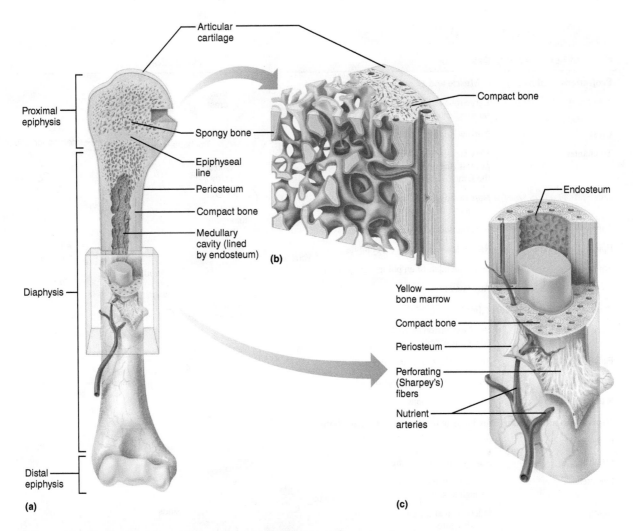

**Figure 3 The structure of a long bone (humerus of the arm). (a)** Anterior view with longitudinal section cut away at the proximal end. **(b)** Pie-shaped, three-dimensional view of spongy bone and compact bone of the epiphysis. **(c)** Cross section of diaphysis (shaft). Note that the external surface of the diaphysis is covered by a periosteum, but the articular surface of the epiphysis is covered with hyaline cartilage.

Longitudinal bone growth at epiphyseal plates (growth plates) follows a predictable sequence and provides a reliable indicator of the age of children exhibiting normal growth. In cases in which problems of long-bone growth are suspected (for example, pituitary dwarfism), X rays are taken to view the width of the growth plates. An abnormally thin epiphyseal plate indicates growth retardation. ✚

## Chemical Composition of Bone

Bone is one of the hardest materials in the body. Although relatively light, bone has a remarkable ability to resist tension and shear forces that continually act on it. An engineer would tell you that a cylinder (like a long bone) is one of the strongest structures for its mass. Thus nature has given us an extremely strong, exceptionally simple and flexible supporting system without sacrificing mobility.

The hardness of bone is due to the inorganic calcium salts deposited in its ground substance. Its flexibility comes from the organic elements of the matrix, particularly the collagen fibers.

### ACTIVITY 2

### Examining the Effects of Heat and Hydrochloric Acid on Bones

Obtain a bone sample that has been soaked in hydrochloric acid (HCl) (or in vinegar) and one that has been baked. Heating removes the organic part of bone, while acid dissolves out the minerals. Do the treated bones retain the structure of untreated specimens?

| Table 1 | Bone Markings | |
|---|---|---|
| **Name of bone marking** | **Description** | **Illustration** |
| **Projections That Are Sites of Muscle and Ligament Attachment** | | |
| Tuberosity | Large rounded projection; may be roughened | |
| Crest | Narrow ridge of bone; usually prominent | |
| Trochanter | Very large, blunt, irregularly shaped process (the only examples are on the femur) | |
| Line | Narrow ridge of bone; less prominent than a crest | |
| Tubercle | Small rounded projection or process | |
| Epicondyle | Raised area on or above a condyle | |
| Spine | Sharp, slender, often pointed projection | |
| Process | Any bony prominence | |
| **Projections That Help Form Joints** | | |
| Head | Bony expansion carried on a narrow neck | |
| Facet | Smooth, nearly flat articular surface | |
| Condyle | Rounded articular projection | |
| Ramus | Armlike bar of bone | |
| **Depressions and Openings for Passage of Blood Vessels and Nerves** | | |
| Groove | Furrow | |
| Fissure | Narrow, slitlike opening | |
| Foramen | Round or oval opening through a bone | |
| Notch | Indentation at the edge of a structure | |
| **Others** | | |
| Meatus | Canal-like passageway | |
| Sinus | Bone cavity, filled with air and lined with mucous membrane | |
| Fossa | Shallow basinlike depression in a bone, often serving as an articular surface | |

Gently apply pressure to each bone sample. What happens to the heated bone?

_____

_____

What happens to the bone treated with acid?

_____

What does the acid appear to remove from the bone?

_____

What does baking appear to do to the bone?

_____

_____

In rickets, the bones are not properly calcified. Which of the demonstration specimens would more closely resemble the bones of a child with rickets?

_____

# Microscopic Structure of Compact Bone

As you have seen, spongy bone has a spiky, open-work appearance, resulting from the arrangement of the **trabeculae** that compose it, whereas compact bone appears to be dense and homogeneous. However, microscopic examination of compact bone reveals that it is riddled with passageways carrying blood vessels, nerves, and lymphatic vessels that provide the living bone cells with needed substances and a way to eliminate wastes. Indeed, bone histology is much easier to

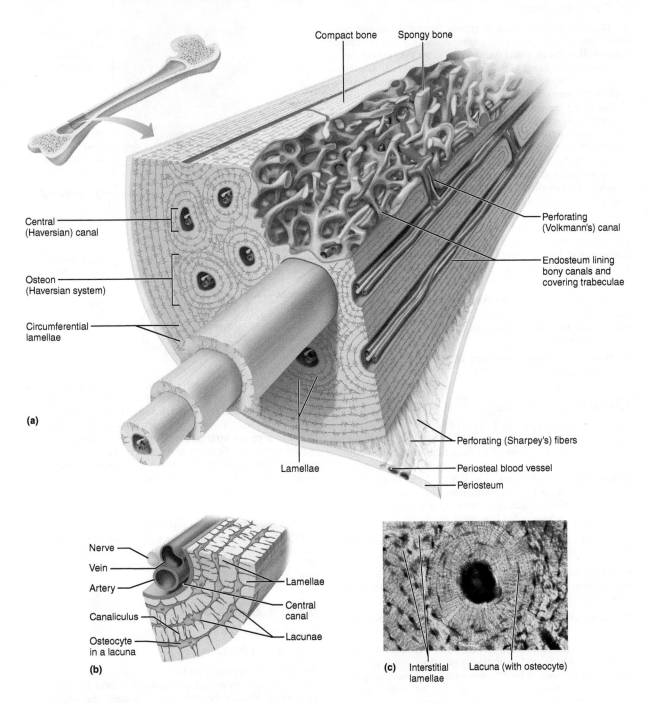

**(a)**

Compact bone    Spongy bone

Central (Haversian) canal

Osteon (Haversian system)

Circumferential lamellae

Perforating (Volkmann's) canal

Endosteum lining bony canals and covering trabeculae

Perforating (Sharpey's) fibers

Periosteal blood vessel

Periosteum

Lamellae

**(b)**

Nerve
Vein
Artery
Canaliculus
Osteocyte in a lacuna

Lamellae
Central canal
Lacunae

**(c)**    Interstitial lamellae    Lacuna (with osteocyte)

**Figure 4 Microscopic structure of compact bone. (a)** Diagrammatic view of a pie-shaped segment of compact bone, illustrating its structural units (osteons). **(b)** Higher-magnification view of a portion of one osteon. Note the position of osteocytes in lacunae. **(c)** Photomicrograph of a cross-sectional view of an osteon (320×).

understand when you recognize that bone tissue is organized around its blood supply.

### Examining the Microscopic Structure of Compact Bone

1. Obtain a prepared slide of ground bone and examine it under low power. Focus on a central canal (Figure 4). The **central (Haversian) canal** runs parallel to the long axis of the bone and carries blood vessels, nerves, and lymphatic vessels through the bony matrix. Identify the **osteocytes** (mature bone cells) in **lacunae** (chambers), which are arranged in concentric circles called **concentric lamellae** around the central canal. Because bone remodeling is going on all the time, you will also see some *interstitial lamellae,* remnants of *circumferential lamellae* that have been broken down (Figure 4c).

A central canal and all the concentric lamellae surrounding it are referred to as an **osteon,** or **Haversian system.** Also identify **canaliculi,** tiny canals radiating outward from a central canal to the lacunae of the first lamella and then from lamella to lamella. The canaliculi form a dense transportation network through the hard bone matrix, connecting all the living cells of the osteon to the nutrient supply. The canaliculi allow each cell to take what it needs for nourishment and to pass along the excess to the next osteocyte. You may need a higher-power magnification to see the fine canaliculi.

2. Also note the **perforating (Volkmann's) canals** (Figure 4). These canals run at right angles to the shaft and complete the communication pathway between the bone interior and its external surface.

3. If a model of bone histology is available, identify the same structures on the model. ▪▪▪

## Ossification: Bone Formation and Growth in Length

Except for the collarbones (clavicles), all bones of the body inferior to the skull form in the embryo by the process of **endochondral ossification,** which uses hyaline cartilage "bones" as patterns for bone formation. The major events of this process, which begins in the (primary ossification) center of the shaft of a developing long bone, are:

• Blood vessels invade the perichondrium covering the hyaline cartilage model and convert it to a periosteum.

• Osteoblasts at the inner surface of the periosteum secrete bone matrix around the hyaline cartilage model, forming a bone collar.

• Cartilage in the shaft center calcifies and then hollows out, forming an internal cavity.

• A *periosteal bud* (blood vessels, nerves, red marrow elements, osteoblasts, and osteoclasts) invades the cavity and forms spongy bone, which is removed by osteoclasts, producing the medullary cavity. This process proceeds in both directions from the *primary ossification center.*

As bones grow longer, the medullary cavity gets larger and larger. Chondroblasts lay down new cartilage matrix on

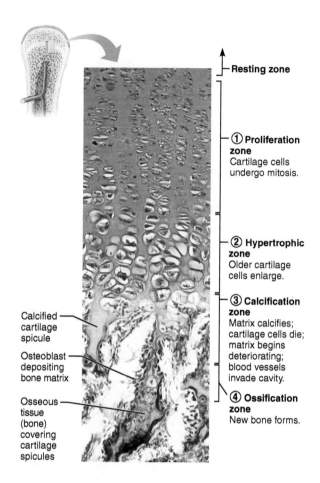

Resting zone

① **Proliferation zone**
Cartilage cells undergo mitosis.

② **Hypertrophic zone**
Older cartilage cells enlarge.

③ **Calcification zone**
Matrix calcifies; cartilage cells die; matrix begins deteriorating; blood vessels invade cavity.

④ **Ossification zone**
New bone forms.

Calcified cartilage spicule

Osteoblast depositing bone matrix

Osseous tissue (bone) covering cartilage spicules

**Figure 5 Growth in length of a long bone occurs at the epiphyseal plate.** The side of the epiphyseal plate facing the epiphysis (distal face) contains resting cartilage cells. The cells of the epiphyseal plate proximal to the resting cartilage area are arranged in four zones—proliferation, hypertrophic, calcification, and ossification—from the region of the earliest stage of growth ① to the region where bone is replacing the cartilage ④ (125×).

the epiphyseal face of the epiphyseal plate, and it is eroded away and replaced by bony spicules on the side facing the medullary cavity (Figure 5). This process continues until late adolescence when the entire epiphyseal plate is replaced by bone.

### Examination of the Osteogenic Epiphyseal Plate

Obtain a slide depicting endochondral ossification (cartilage bone formation) and bring it to your bench to examine under the microscope. Identify the proliferation, hypertrophic, calcification, and ossification zones of the epiphyseal plate (Figure 5). Then, also identify the area of resting cartilage cells distal to the growth zone, some hypertrophied chondrocytes, bony spicules, the periosteal bone collar, and the medullary cavity. ▪▪▪

# Overview of the Skeleton: Classification and Structure of Bones and Cartilages

## Cartilages of the Skeleton

**1.** Using the key choices, identify each type of cartilage described (in terms of its body location or function) below.

*Key:* a.   elastic          b.   fibrocartilage          c.   hyaline

_____ 1. supports the external ear

_____ 2. between the vertebrae

_____ 3. forms the walls of the voice box (larynx)

_____ 4. the epiglottis

_____ 5. articular cartilages

_____ 6. meniscus in a knee joint

_____ 7. connects the ribs to the sternum

_____ 8. most effective at resisting compression

_____ 9. most springy and flexible

_____ 10. most abundant

## Classification of Bones

**2.** The four major anatomical classifications of bones are long, short, flat, and irregular. Which category has the least amount of spongy bone relative to its total volume? _____

**3.** Place the name of each labeled bone in Figure 1 into the appropriate column of the chart here.

| Long | Short | Flat | Irregular |
|------|-------|------|-----------|
|      |       |      |           |
|      |       |      |           |
|      |       |      |           |
|      |       |      |           |
|      |       |      |           |

## Bone Markings

**4.** Match the terms in column B with the appropriate description in column A.

**Column A**

**Column B**

| | |
|---|---|
| _____ 1. sharp, slender process* | a. condyle |
| _____ 2. small rounded projection* | b. crest |
| _____ 3. narrow ridge of bone* | c. epicondyle |
| _____ 4. large rounded projection* | d. facet |
| _____ 5. structure supported on neck† | e. fissure |
| _____ 6. armlike projection† | f. foramen |
| _____ 7. rounded, articular projection† | g. fossa |
| _____ 8. narrow opening‡ | h. head |
| _____ 9. canal-like structure | i. meatus |
| _____ 10. round or oval opening through a bone‡ | j. process |
| _____ 11. shallow depression | k. ramus |
| _____ 12. air-filled cavity | l. sinus |
| _____ 13. large, irregularly shaped projection* | m. spine |
| _____ 14. raised area on or above a condyle* | n. trochanter |
| _____ 15. projection or prominence | o. tubercle |
| _____ 16. smooth, nearly flat articular surface† | p. tuberosity |

*a site of muscle and ligament attachment
† takes part in joint formation
‡ a passageway for nerves or blood vessels

## Gross Anatomy of the Typical Long Bone

**5.** Use the terms below to identify the structures marked by leader lines and braces in the diagrams. (Diagrams appear on the following page; some terms are used more than once.)

*Key:*  a. articular cartilage
   b. compact bone
   c. diaphysis
   d. endosteum

e. epiphyseal line
f. epiphysis
g. medullary cavity
h. nutrient artery

i. periosteum
j. red marrow
k. trabeculae of spongy bone
l. yellow marrow

**6.** Match the terms in question 5 with the information below.

_____ 1. contains spongy bone in adults

_____ 2. made of compact bone

_____ 3. site of blood cell formation

_____ 4. major submembranous sites of osteoclasts

_____ 5. scientific term for bone shaft

_____ 6. contains fat in adult bones

_____ 7. growth plate remnant

_____ 8. major submembranous site of osteoblasts

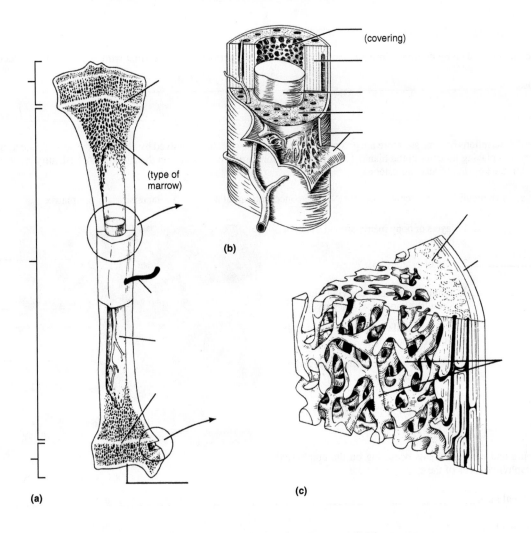

(covering)

(type of marrow)

(b)

(a)

(c)

7. What differences between compact and spongy bone can be seen with the naked eye? _____

_____

8. What is the function of the periosteum? _____

_____

## Chemical Composition of Bone

9. What is the function of the organic matrix in bone? _____

10. Name the important organic bone components. _____

11. Calcium salts form the bulk of the inorganic material in bone. What is the function of the calcium salts?

_____

12. Baking removes _____ from bone. Soaking bone in acid removes _____.

# Microscopic Structure of Compact Bone

**13.** Trace the route taken by nutrients through a bone, starting with the periosteum and ending with an osteocyte in a lacuna.

Periosteum ___→_____ → _____

_____ → _____ → _____ osteocyte

**14.** Several descriptions of bone structure are given below. Identify the structure involved by choosing the appropriate term from the key and placing its letter in the blank. Then, on the photomicrograph of bone on the right (210×), identify all structures named in the key and bracket an osteon.

*Key:* a.  canaliculi     b.  central canal     c.  concentric lamellae     d.  lacunae     e.  matrix

_____ 1. layers of bony matrix around a central canal

_____ 2. site of osteocytes

_____ 3. longitudinal canal carrying blood vessels, lymphatics, and nerves

_____ 4. minute canals connecting osteocytes of an osteon

_____ 5. inorganic salts deposited in organic ground substance

# Ossification: Bone Formation and Growth in Length

**15.** Compare and contrast events occurring on the epiphyseal and diaphyseal faces of the epiphyseal plate.

Epiphyseal face: _____

Diaphyseal face: _____

## Photo Credits

**Credits are listed in order of appearance.**

4c: William Krakow, Pearson Education. 5: Lisa Lee, Pearson Education. RS2: Alan Bell, Pearson Education.

# The Axial Skeleton

## MATERIALS

- ☐ Intact skull and Beauchene skull
- ☐ X rays of individuals with scoliosis, lordosis, and kyphosis (if available)
- ☐ Articulated skeleton, articulated vertebral column, removable intervertebral discs
- ☐ Isolated cervical, thoracic, and lumbar vertebrae, sacrum, and coccyx
- ☐ Isolated fetal skull

## OBJECTIVES

1. Name the three parts of the axial skeleton.
2. Identify the bones of the axial skeleton, either by examining isolated bones or by pointing them out on an articulated skeleton or skull, and name the important bone markings on each.
3. Name and describe the different types of vertebrae.
4. Discuss the importance of intervertebral discs and spinal curvatures.
5. Identify three abnormal spinal curvatures.
6. List the components of the thoracic cage.
7. Identify the bones of the fetal skull by examining an articulated skull or image.
8. Define *fontanelle* and discuss the function and fate of fontanelles in the fetus.
9. Discuss important differences between the fetal and adult skulls.

## PRE-LAB QUIZ

1. The axial skeleton can be divided into the skull, the vertebral column, and the _____.
   - a. thoracic cage
   - b. femur
   - c. hip bones
   - d. humerus
2. Eight bones make up the _____ , which encloses and protects the brain.
   - a. cranium    b. face    c. skull
3. How many bones of the skull are considered facial bones? _____
4. Circle the correct underlined term. The lower jawbone, or <u>maxilla</u> / <u>mandible</u>, articulates with the temporal bones in the only freely movable joints in the skull.
5. Circle the correct underlined term. The <u>body</u> / <u>spinous process</u> of a typical vertebra forms the rounded, central portion that faces anteriorly in the human vertebral column.
6. The seven bones of the neck are called _____ vertebrae.
   - a. cervical    b. lumbar    c. spinal    d. thoracic
7. The _____ vertebrae articulate with the corresponding ribs.
   - a. cervical    b. lumbar    c. spinal    d. thoracic
8. The _____, commonly referred to as the breastbone, is a flat bone formed by the fusion of three bones: the manubrium, the body, and the xiphoid process.
   - a. coccyx    b. sacrum    c. sternum
9. Circle True or False. The first seven pairs of ribs are called floating ribs because they have only indirect cartilage attachments to the sternum.
10. A fontanelle _____ .
    - a. is found only in the fetal skull
    - b. is a fibrous membrane
    - c. allows for compression of the skull during birth
    - d. all of the above

MasteringA&P® For related exercise study tools, go to the Study Area of MasteringA&P. There you will find:
- Practice Anatomy Lab PAL
- PhysioEx PEx
- A&PFlix *A&PFlix*
- Practice quizzes, Histology Atlas, eText, Videos, and more!

The **axial skeleton** can be divided into three parts: the skull, the vertebral column, and the thoracic cage.

## The Skull

The **skull** is composed of two sets of bones. Those of the **cranium** enclose and protect the fragile brain tissue. The **facial bones** support the eyes and position them anteriorly. They also provide attachment sites for facial muscles, which make it possible for us to present our feelings to the world. All but one of the bones of the skull are joined by interlocking joints called *sutures*. The mandible, or lower jawbone, is attached to the rest of the skull by a freely movable joint.

### ACTIVITY 1

### Identifying the Bones of the Skull

The bones of the skull (Figures 1–8) are described below. As you read through this material, identify each bone on an intact and/or Beauchene skull (see Figure 6c).

**Note:** Important bone markings are listed beneath the bones on which they appear, and a color-coded dot before each bone name corresponds to the bone color in the figures. ▄▄

## The Cranium

The cranium may be divided into two major areas for study—the **cranial vault** or **calvaria,** forming the superior, lateral, and posterior walls of the skull, and the **cranial base,** forming the skull bottom. Internally, the cranial base has three distinct depressions: the **anterior, middle,** and **posterior cranial fossae** (see Figure 3). The brain sits in these fossae, completely enclosed by the cranial vault.

Eight bones construct the cranium. *With the exception of two paired bones (the parietals and the temporals), all are single bones.* Sometimes the six ossicles of the middle ear, part of the hearing apparatus, are also considered part of the cranium.

○ **Frontal Bone** (Figures 1, 3, 6, and 8) Anterior portion of cranium; forms the forehead, superior part of the orbit, and floor of anterior cranial fossa.

**Supraorbital foramen (notch):** Opening above each orbit allowing blood vessels and nerves to pass.

**Glabella:** Smooth area between the eyes.

● **Parietal Bone** (Figures 1 and 6) Posterolateral to the frontal bone, forming sides of cranium.

**Sagittal suture:** Midline articulation point of the two parietal bones.

**Coronal suture:** Point of articulation of parietals with frontal bone.

● **Temporal Bone** (Figures 1, 2, 3, and 6) Inferior to parietal bone on lateral skull. The temporals can be divided into three major parts: the **squamous part** borders the parietals; the **tympanic part** surrounds the external ear opening; and the **petrous part** forms the lateral portion of the skull base and contains the mastoid process.

Important markings associated with the flaring squamous part (Figures 1 and 2) include:

**Squamous suture:** Point of articulation of the temporal bone with the parietal bone.

**Zygomatic process:** A bridgelike projection joining the zygomatic bone (cheekbone) anteriorly. Together these two bones form the *zygomatic arch.*

**Mandibular fossa:** Rounded depression on the inferior surface of the zygomatic process (anterior to the ear); forms the socket for the condylar process of the mandible, where the mandible (lower jaw) joins the cranium.

Tympanic part markings (Figures 1 and 2) include:

**External acoustic meatus:** Canal leading to eardrum and middle ear.

**Styloid** (*stylo* = stake, pointed object) **process:** Needlelike projection inferior to external acoustic meatus; attachment point for muscles and ligaments of the neck. This process is often broken off demonstration skulls.

The petrous part (Figures 2 and 3), which helps form the middle and posterior cranial fossae, contains the labyrinth (holding the organs of hearing and balance). It exhibits several obvious foramina with important functions and includes:

**Jugular foramen:** Opening medial to the styloid process through which the internal jugular vein and cranial nerves IX, X, and XI pass.

**Carotid canal:** Opening medial to the styloid process through which the internal carotid artery passes into the cranial cavity.

**Internal acoustic meatus:** Opening on posterior aspect (petrous part) of temporal bone allowing passage of cranial nerves VII and VIII (Figure 3).

**Foramen lacerum:** A jagged opening between the petrous temporal bone and the sphenoid providing passage for a number of small nerves and for the internal carotid artery to enter the middle cranial fossa (after it passes through part of the temporal bone).

**Stylomastoid foramen:** Tiny opening between the mastoid and styloid processes through which cranial nerve VII leaves the cranium.

**Mastoid process:** Rough projection inferior and posterior to external acoustic meatus; attachment site for muscles.

The mastoid process, full of air cavities and so close to the middle ear—a trouble spot for infections—often becomes infected too, a condition referred to as **mastoiditis.** Because the mastoid area is separated from the brain by only a thin layer of bone, an ear infection that has spread to the mastoid process can inflame the brain coverings, or the meninges. The latter condition is known as **meningitis.** ✚

● **Occipital Bone** (Figures 1, 2, 3, and 6). Most posterior bone of cranium—forms floor and back wall. Joins sphenoid bone anteriorly via its narrow basilar part.

**Lambdoid suture:** Site of articulation of occipital bone and parietal bones.

**Foramen magnum:** Large opening in base of occipital, which allows the spinal cord to join with the brain.

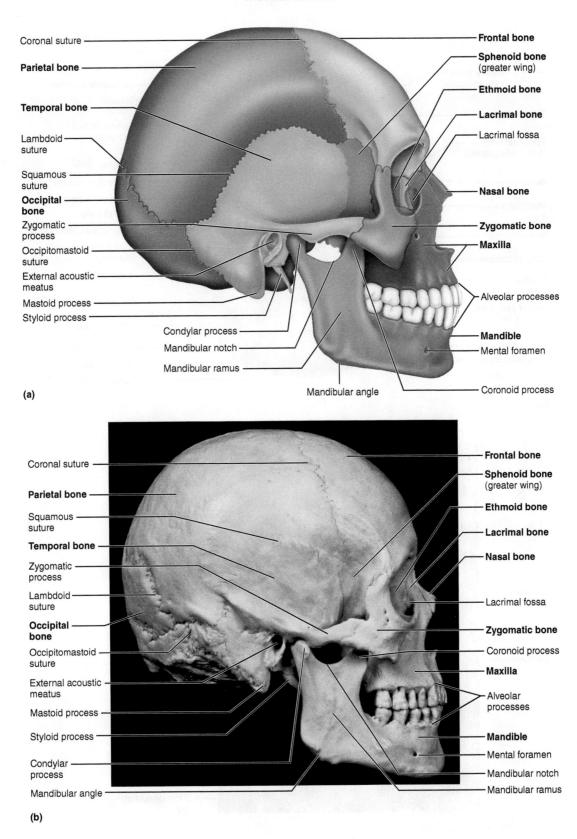

Coronal suture

**Parietal bone**

**Temporal bone**

Lambdoid suture

Squamous suture

**Occipital bone**

Zygomatic process

Occipitomastoid suture

External acoustic meatus

Mastoid process

Styloid process

Condylar process

Mandibular notch

Mandibular ramus

Mandibular angle

**Frontal bone**

**Sphenoid bone** (greater wing)

**Ethmoid bone**

**Lacrimal bone**

Lacrimal fossa

**Nasal bone**

**Zygomatic bone**

**Maxilla**

Alveolar processes

**Mandible**

Mental foramen

Coronoid process

**(a)**

Coronal suture

**Parietal bone**

Squamous suture

**Temporal bone**

Zygomatic process

Lambdoid suture

**Occipital bone**

Occipitomastoid suture

External acoustic meatus

Mastoid process

Styloid process

Condylar process

Mandibular angle

**Frontal bone**

**Sphenoid bone** (greater wing)

**Ethmoid bone**

**Lacrimal bone**

**Nasal bone**

Lacrimal fossa

**Zygomatic bone**

Coronoid process

**Maxilla**

Alveolar processes

**Mandible**

Mental foramen

Mandibular notch

Mandibular ramus

**(b)**

**Figure 1 External anatomy of the right lateral aspect of the skull. (a)** Diagram.
**(b)** Photograph.

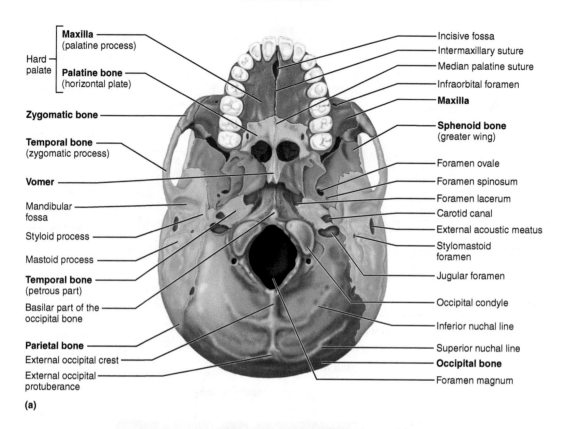

**Maxilla**
(palatine process) ——————— Incisive fossa

Hard palate {

**Palatine bone**
(horizontal plate) ——————— Intermaxillary suture

——————— Median palatine suture

——————— Infraorbital foramen

**Zygomatic bone** ——————— **Maxilla**

**Temporal bone**
(zygomatic process) ——————— **Sphenoid bone**
(greater wing)

**Vomer** ——————— Foramen ovale

Mandibular
fossa ——————— Foramen spinosum

——————— Foramen lacerum

Styloid process ——————— Carotid canal

Mastoid process ——————— External acoustic meatus

**Temporal bone**
(petrous part) ——————— Stylomastoid
foramen

Basilar part of the
occipital bone ——————— Jugular foramen

——————— Occipital condyle

**Parietal bone** ——————— Inferior nuchal line

External occipital crest ——————— Superior nuchal line

External occipital
protuberance ——————— **Occipital bone**

——————— Foramen magnum

**(a)**

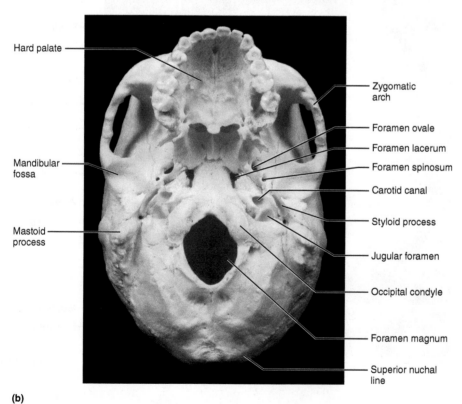

Hard palate ——————— Zygomatic
arch

——————— Foramen ovale

——————— Foramen lacerum

——————— Foramen spinosum

Mandibular
fossa ——————— Carotid canal

——————— Styloid process

Mastoid
process ——————— Jugular foramen

——————— Occipital condyle

——————— Foramen magnum

——————— Superior nuchal
line

**(b)**

**Figure 2  Inferior view of the skull, mandible removed.**

132

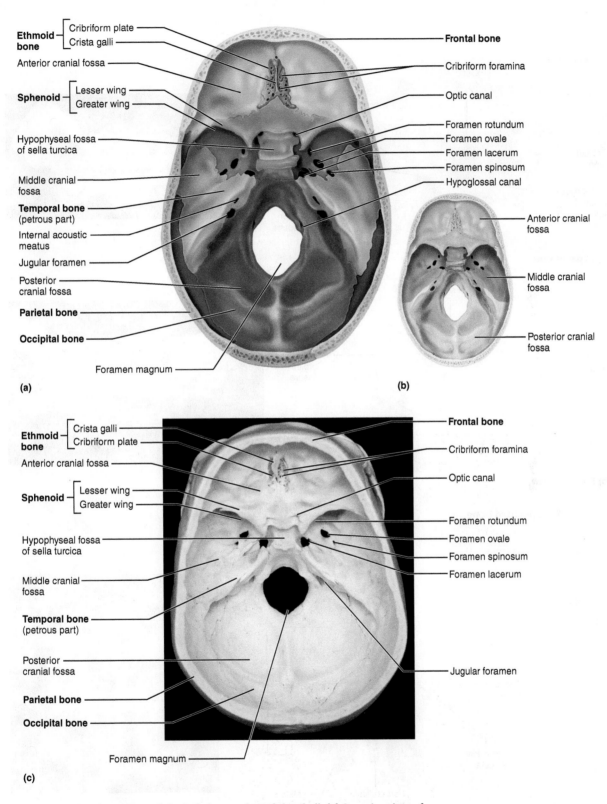

**Figure 3** **Internal anatomy of the inferior portion of the skull.** **(a)** Superior view of the base of the cranial cavity, calvaria removed. **(b)** Schematic view of the cranial base showing the extent of its major fossae. **(c)** Photograph of superior view of the base of the cranial cavity, calvaria removed.

133

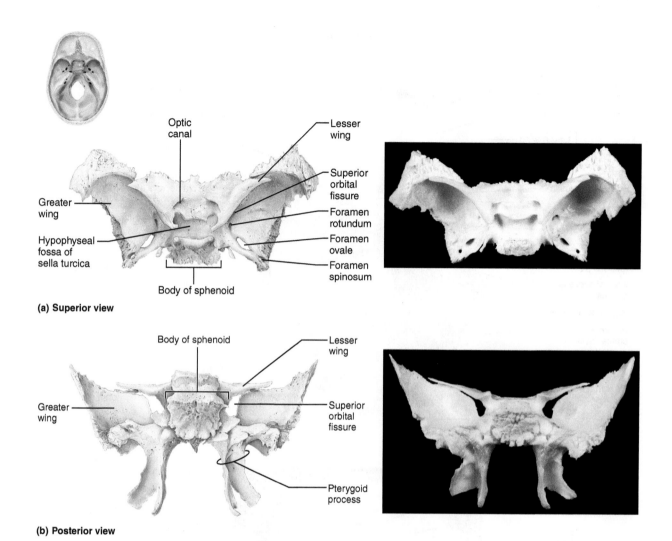

Optic canal

Lesser wing

Superior orbital fissure

Foramen rotundum

Foramen ovale

Foramen spinosum

Greater wing

Hypophyseal fossa of sella turcica

Body of sphenoid

**(a) Superior view**

Body of sphenoid

Lesser wing

Greater wing

Superior orbital fissure

Pterygoid process

**(b) Posterior view**

**Figure 4** **The sphenoid bone.**

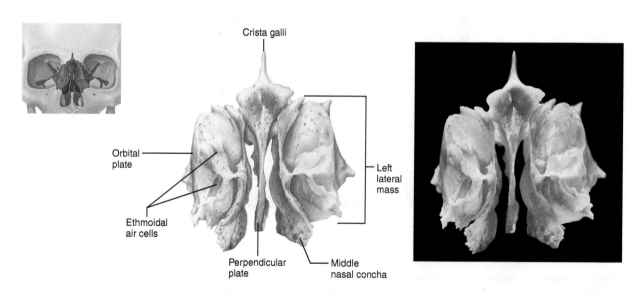

Crista galli

Orbital plate

Ethmoidal air cells

Perpendicular plate

Left lateral mass

Middle nasal concha

**Figure 5** **The ethmoid bone.** Anterior view. The superior nasal conchae are located posteriorly and are therefore not visible in the anterior view.

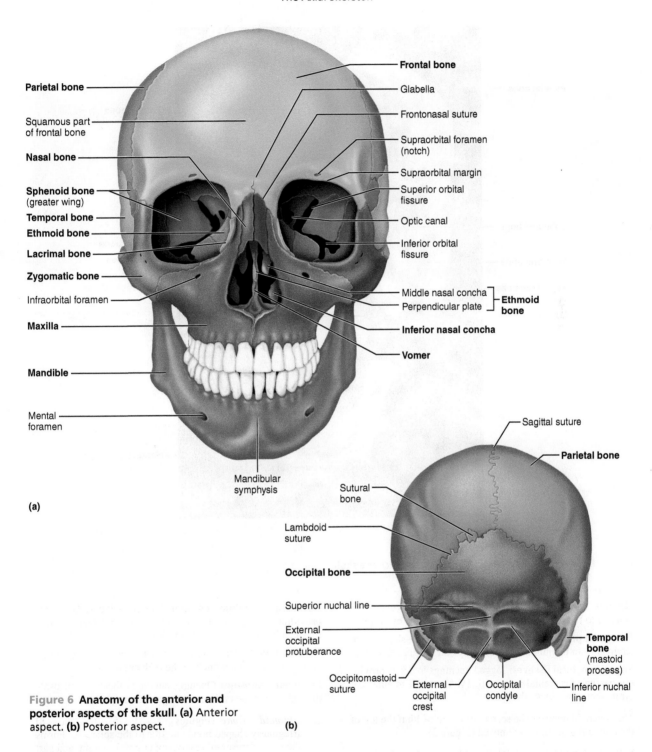

Parietal bone

Squamous part
of frontal bone

Nasal bone

Sphenoid bone
(greater wing)

Temporal bone

Ethmoid bone

Lacrimal bone

Zygomatic bone

Infraorbital foramen

Maxilla

Mandible

Mental
foramen

Frontal bone

Glabella

Frontonasal suture

Supraorbital foramen
(notch)

Supraorbital margin

Superior orbital
fissure

Optic canal

Inferior orbital
fissure

Middle nasal concha ⎤ Ethmoid
Perpendicular plate ⎦ bone

Inferior nasal concha

Vomer

Mandibular
symphysis

(a)

Sagittal suture

Parietal bone

Sutural
bone

Lambdoid
suture

Occipital bone

Superior nuchal line

External
occipital
protuberance

Occipitomastoid
suture

Temporal
bone
(mastoid
process)

External
occipital
crest

Occipital
condyle

Inferior nuchal
line

**Figure 6 Anatomy of the anterior and
posterior aspects of the skull. (a)** Anterior
aspect. **(b)** Posterior aspect.

(b)

**Occipital condyles:** Rounded projections lateral to the foramen magnum that articulate with the first cervical vertebra (atlas).

**Hypoglossal canal:** Opening medial and superior to the occipital condyle through which the hypoglossal nerve (cranial nerve XII) passes.

**External occipital crest and protuberance:** Midline prominences posterior to the foramen magnum.

○ *Sphenoid Bone* (Figures 1–4, 6, and 8) Bat-shaped bone forming the anterior plateau of the middle cranial fossa across the width of the skull. The sphenoid bone is the keystone of the cranium because it articulates with all other cranial bones.

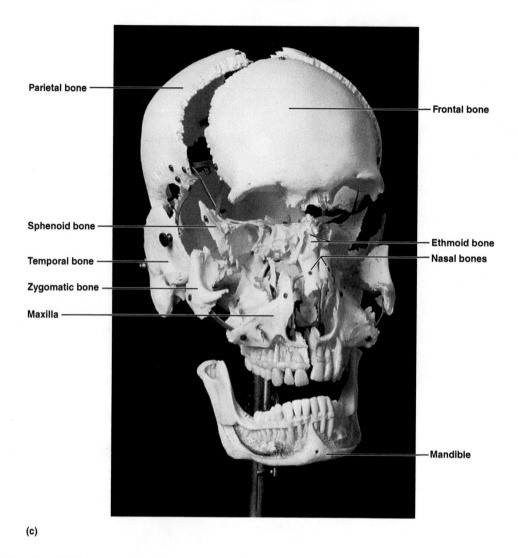

**(c)**

**Figure 6 *(continued)* (c)** Frontal view of the Beauchene skull.

**Greater wings:** Portions of the sphenoid seen exteriorly anterior to the temporal and forming a part of the eye orbits.

**Pterygoid processes:** Inferiorly directed trough-shaped projections from the junction of the body and the greater wings.

**Superior orbital fissures:** Jagged openings in orbits providing passage for cranial nerves III, IV, V, and VI to enter the orbit where they serve the eye.

The sphenoid bone can be seen in its entire width if the top of the cranium (calvaria) is removed (Figure 3).

**Sella turcica** (Turk's saddle): A saddle-shaped region in the sphenoid midline. The seat of this saddle, called the **hypophyseal fossa,** surrounds the pituitary gland (hypophysis).

**Lesser wings:** Bat-shaped portions of the sphenoid anterior to the sella turcica.

**Optic canals:** Openings in the bases of the lesser wings through which the optic nerves (cranial nerve II) enter the orbits to serve the eyes.

**Foramen rotundum:** Opening lateral to the sella turcica providing passage for a branch of the fifth cranial nerve. (This foramen is not visible on an inferior view of the skull.)

**Foramen ovale:** Opening posterior to the sella turcica that allows passage of a branch of the fifth cranial nerve.

**Foramen spinosum:** Opening lateral to the foramen ovale through which the middle meningeal artery passes.

● ***Ethmoid Bone*** (Figures 1, 3, 5, 6, and 8) Irregularly shaped bone anterior to the sphenoid. Forms the roof of the nasal cavity, upper nasal septum, and part of the medial orbit walls.

**Crista galli** (cock's comb): Vertical projection providing a point of attachment for the dura mater, helping to secure the brain within the skull.

**Cribriform plates:** Bony plates lateral to the crista galli through which olfactory fibers (cranial nerve I) pass to the brain from the nasal mucosa through the cribriform foramina.

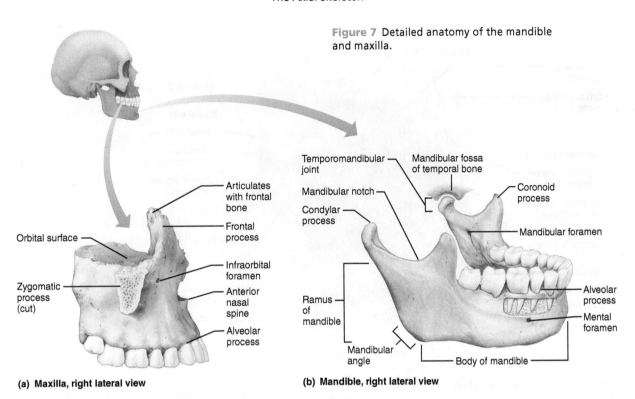

**Figure 7** Detailed anatomy of the mandible and maxilla.

(a) Maxilla, right lateral view

(b) Mandible, right lateral view

Together the cribriform plates and the midline crista galli form the *horizontal plate* of the ethmoid bone.

**Perpendicular plate:** Inferior projection of the ethmoid that forms the superior part of the nasal septum.

**Lateral masses:** Irregularly shaped and thin-walled bony regions flanking the perpendicular plate laterally. Their lateral surfaces *(orbital plates)* shape part of the medial orbit wall.

**Superior and middle nasal conchae** (turbinates): Thin, delicately coiled plates of bone extending medially from the lateral masses of the ethmoid into the nasal cavity. The conchae make air flow through the nasal cavity more efficient and greatly increase the surface area of the mucosa that covers them, thus increasing the mucosa's ability to warm and humidify incoming air.

## Facial Bones

Of the 14 bones composing the face, 12 are paired. *Only the mandible and vomer are single bones.* An additional bone, the hyoid bone, although not a facial bone, is considered here because of its location.

● *Mandible* (Figures 1, 6, and 7) The lower jawbone, which articulates with the temporal bones in the only freely movable joints of the skull.

**Mandibular body:** Horizontal portion; forms the chin.

**Mandibular ramus:** Vertical extension of the body on either side.

**Condylar process:** Articulation point of the mandible with the mandibular fossa of the temporal bone.

**Coronoid process:** Jutting anterior portion of the ramus; site of muscle attachment.

**Mandibular angle:** Posterior point at which ramus meets the body.

**Mental foramen:** Prominent opening on the body (lateral to the midline) that transmits the mental blood vessels and nerve to the lower jaw.

**Mandibular foramen:** Open the lower jaw of the skull to identify this prominent foramen on the medial aspect of the mandibular ramus. This foramen permits passage of the nerve involved with tooth sensation (mandibular branch of cranial nerve V) and is the site where the dentist injects Novocain to prevent pain while working on the lower teeth.

**Alveolar process:** Superior margin of mandible; contains sockets in which the teeth lie.

**Mandibular symphysis:** Anterior median depression indicating point of mandibular fusion.

● *Maxillae* (Figures 1, 2, 6, and 7) Two bones fused in a median suture; form the upper jawbone and part of the orbits. All facial bones, except the mandible, join the maxillae. Thus they are the main, or keystone, bones of the face.

**Alveolar process:** Inferior margin containing sockets in which teeth lie.

**Palatine processes:** Form the anterior hard palate; meet medially in the intermaxillary suture.

**Infraorbital foramen:** Opening under the orbit carrying the infraorbital nerves and blood vessels to the nasal region.

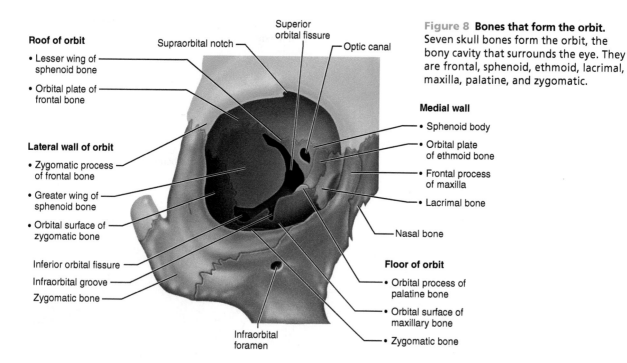

**Figure 8** **Bones that form the orbit.** Seven skull bones form the orbit, the bony cavity that surrounds the eye. They are frontal, sphenoid, ethmoid, lacrimal, maxilla, palatine, and zygomatic.

**Roof of orbit**
• Lesser wing of sphenoid bone
• Orbital plate of frontal bone

Supraorbital notch

Superior orbital fissure

Optic canal

**Lateral wall of orbit**
• Zygomatic process of frontal bone
• Greater wing of sphenoid bone
• Orbital surface of zygomatic bone

Inferior orbital fissure

Infraorbital groove

Zygomatic bone

Infraorbital foramen

**Medial wall**
• Sphenoid body
• Orbital plate of ethmoid bone
• Frontal process of maxilla
• Lacrimal bone

Nasal bone

**Floor of orbit**
• Orbital process of palatine bone
• Orbital surface of maxillary bone
• Zygomatic bone

**Incisive fossa:** Large bilateral opening located posterior to the central incisor tooth of the maxilla and piercing the hard palate; transmits the nasopalatine arteries and blood vessels.

- *Lacrimal Bone* (Figures 1 and 6a) Fingernail-sized bones forming a part of the medial orbit walls between the maxilla and the ethmoid. Each lacrimal bone is pierced by an opening, the **lacrimal fossa,** which serves as a passageway for tears (*lacrima* = tear).

- *Palatine Bone* (Figure 2 and Figure 8) Paired bones posterior to the palatine processes; form posterior hard palate and part of the orbit; meet medially at the median palatine suture.

- *Zygomatic Bone* (Figures 1, 2, 6, and 8) Lateral to the maxilla; forms the portion of the face commonly called the cheekbone, and forms part of the lateral orbit. Its three processes are named for the bones with which they articulate.

- *Nasal Bone* (Figures 1 and 6) Small rectangular bones forming the bridge of the nose.

- *Vomer* (Figures 2 and 6) Blade-shaped bone (*vomer* = plow) in median plane of nasal cavity that forms the posterior and inferior nasal septum.

- *Inferior Nasal Conchae (Turbinates)* (Figure 6a) Thin curved bones protruding medially from the lateral walls of the nasal cavity; serve the same purpose as the turbinate portions of the ethmoid bone.

### GROUP CHALLENGE

## Odd Bone Out

Each of the following sets contains four bones. One of the listed bones does not share a characteristic that the other three do. Circle the bone that doesn't belong with the others and explain why it is singled out. What characteristic

is it missing? Sometimes there may be multiple reasons why the bone doesn't belong with the others. Include as many as you can think of but make sure it does not have the key characteristic. Use an articulated skull, disarticulated skull bones, and the pictures in your lab manual to help you select and justify your answer.

| 1. Which is the "odd bone"? | Why is it the odd one out? |
|---|---|
| Zygomatic bone<br><br>Maxilla<br><br>Vomer<br><br>Nasal bone | |
| **2. Which is the "odd bone"?** | **Why is it the odd one out?** |
| Parietal bone<br><br>Sphenoid bone<br><br>Frontal bone<br><br>Occipital bone | |
| **3. Which is the "odd bone"?** | **Why is it the odd one out?** |
| Lacrimal bone<br><br>Nasal bone<br><br>Zygomatic bone<br><br>Maxilla | |

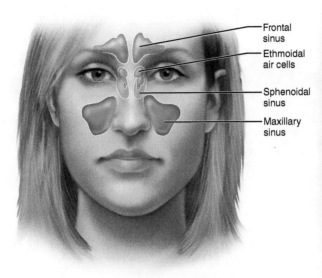

(a)

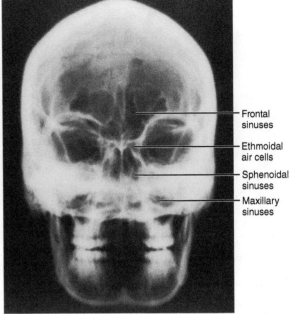

(c)

(b)

Figure 9 **Paranasal sinuses. (a)** Anterior aspect. **(b)** Medial aspect. **(c)** Skull X ray showing the paranasal sinuses, anterior view.

## Paranasal Sinuses

Four skull bones—maxillary, sphenoid, ethmoid, and frontal—contain sinuses (mucosa-lined air cavities) that lead into the nasal passages (see Figure 5 and Figure 9). These paranasal sinuses lighten the facial bones and may act as resonance chambers for speech. The maxillary sinus is the largest of the sinuses found in the skull.

**Sinusitis,** or inflammation of the sinuses, sometimes occurs as a result of an allergy or bacterial invasion of the sinus cavities. In such cases, some of the connecting passageways between the sinuses and nasal passages may become blocked with thick mucus or infectious material. Then, as the air in the sinus cavities is absorbed, a partial vacuum forms. The result is a sinus headache localized over the inflamed sinus area. Severe sinus infections may require surgical drainage to relieve this painful condition. ✚

## Hyoid Bone

Not really considered or counted as a skull bone, the hyoid bone is located in the throat above the larynx. It serves as a point of attachment for many tongue and neck muscles. It does not articulate with any other bone and is thus unique. It is horseshoe shaped with a body and two pairs of **horns,** or **cornua** (Figure 10).

ACTIVITY 2

### Palpating Skull Markings

*Palpate* the following areas on yourself. Place a check mark in the boxes as you locate the skull markings. Seek assistance from your instructor for any markings that you are unable to locate.

☐ Zygomatic bone and arch. (The most prominent part of your cheek is your zygomatic bone. Follow the posterior course of the zygomatic arch to its junction with your temporal bone.)

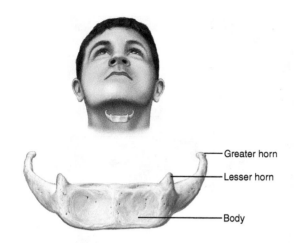

Figure 10 **Hyoid bone.**

☐ Mastoid process (the rough area behind your ear).

☐ Temporomandibular joints. (Open and close your jaws to locate these.)

☐ Greater wing of sphenoid. (Find the indentation posterior to the orbit and superior to the zygomatic arch on your lateral skull.)

☐ Supraorbital foramen. (Apply firm pressure along the superior orbital margin to find the indentation resulting from this foramen.)

☐ Infraorbital foramen. (Apply firm pressure just inferior to the inferomedial border of the orbit to locate this large foramen.)

☐ Mandibular angle (most inferior and posterior aspect of the mandible).

☐ Mandibular symphysis (midline of chin).

☐ Nasal bones. (Run your index finger and thumb along opposite sides of the bridge of your nose until they "slip" medially at the inferior end of the nasal bones.)

☐ External occipital protuberance. (This midline projection is easily felt by running your fingers up the furrow at the back of your neck to the skull.)

☐ Hyoid bone. (Place a thumb and index finger beneath the chin just anterior to the mandibular angles, and squeeze gently. Exert pressure with the thumb, and feel the horn of the hyoid with the index finger.) ▬

## The Vertebral Column

The **vertebral column,** extending from the skull to the pelvis, forms the body's major axial support. Additionally, it surrounds and protects the delicate spinal cord while allowing the spinal nerves to emerge from the cord via openings between adjacent vertebrae. The term *vertebral column* might suggest a rigid supporting rod, but this is far from the truth. The vertebral column consists of 24 single bones called **vertebrae** and two composite, or fused, bones (the sacrum and coccyx) that are connected in such a way as to provide a flexible curved structure **(Figure 11)**. Of the 24 single vertebrae,

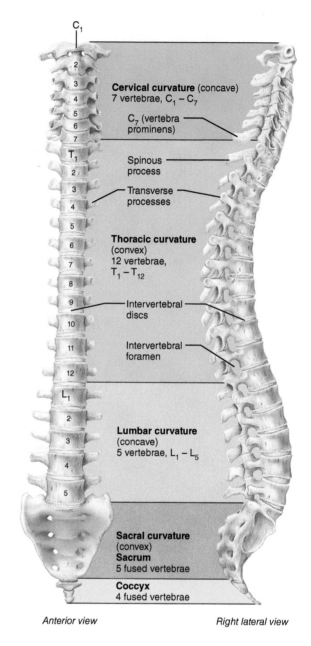

Anterior view          Right lateral view

Figure 11 **The vertebral column.** Notice the curvatures in the lateral view. (The terms *convex* and *concave* refer to the curvature of the posterior aspect of the vertebral column.)

the seven bones of the neck are called *cervical vertebrae;* the next 12 are *thoracic vertebrae;* and the 5 supporting the lower back are *lumbar vertebrae.* Remembering common mealtimes for breakfast, lunch, and dinner (7 A.M., 12 noon, and 5 P.M.) may help you to remember the number of bones in each region.

The vertebrae are separated by pads of fibrocartilage, **intervertebral discs,** that cushion the vertebrae and absorb shocks. Each disc has two major regions, a central gelatinous *nucleus pulposus* that behaves like a fluid, and an outer ring of encircling collagen fibers called the *anulus fibrosus* that stabilizes the disc and contains the pulposus.

As a person ages, the water content of the discs decreases (as it does in other tissues throughout the body), and the discs become thinner and less compressible. This situation, along with other degenerative changes such as weakening of the ligaments and tendons of the vertebral column, predisposes older people to a ruptured disc, called a **herniated disc.** In a herniated disc, the anulus fibrosus commonly ruptures and the nucleus pulposus protrudes (herniates) through it. This event typically compresses adjacent nerves, causing pain. ✚

The presence of the discs and the curvatures create a springlike construction of the vertebral column that prevents shock to the head in walking and running and provides flexibility to the body trunk. The thoracic and sacral curvatures of the spine are referred to as *primary curvatures* because they are present and well developed at birth. Later the *secondary curvatures* are formed. The cervical curvature becomes prominent when the baby begins to hold its head up independently, and the lumbar curvature develops when the baby begins to walk.

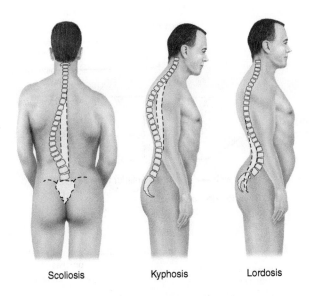

Scoliosis · Kyphosis · Lordosis

**Figure 12 Abnormal spinal curvatures**

---

**ACTIVITY 3**

## Examining Spinal Curvatures

1. Observe the normal curvature of the vertebral column in the articulated vertebral column or laboratory skeleton (compare it to Figure 11). Note the differences between normal curvature and three abnormal spinal curvatures seen in the figure—*scoliosis, kyphosis,* and *lordosis* (Figure 12). These abnormalities may result from disease or poor posture. Also examine X rays, if they are available, showing these same conditions in a living patient.

2. Then, using the articulated vertebral column (or an articulated skeleton), examine the freedom of movement between two lumbar vertebrae separated by an intervertebral disc.

When the fibrous disc is properly positioned, are the spinal cord or peripheral nerves impaired in any way?

_____

Remove the disc and put the two vertebrae back together. What happens to the nerve?

_____

What would happen to the spinal nerves in areas of malpositioned or "slipped" discs?

_____

## Structure of a Typical Vertebra

Although they differ in size and specific features, all vertebrae have some features in common (Figure 13).

**Body (or centrum):** Rounded central portion of the vertebra, which faces anteriorly in the human vertebral column.

**Vertebral arch:** Composed of pedicles, laminae, and a spinous process, it represents the junction of all posterior extensions from the vertebral body.

**Vertebral (spinal) foramen:** Opening enclosed by the body and vertebral arch; a passageway for the spinal cord.

**Transverse processes:** Two lateral projections from the vertebral arch.

**Spinous process:** Single medial and posterior projection from the vertebral arch.

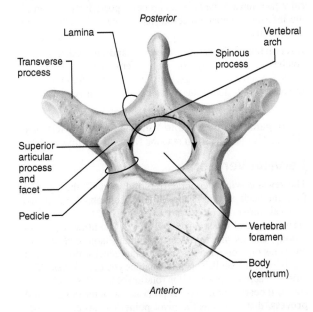

**Figure 13 A typical vertebra, superior view.** Inferior articulating surfaces not shown.

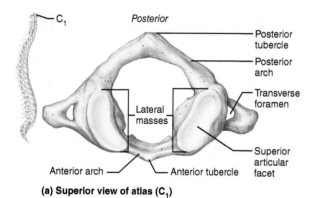

(a) Superior view of atlas (C₁)

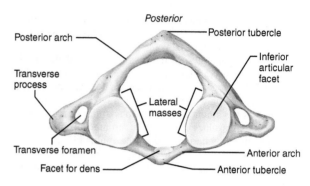

(b) Inferior view of atlas (C₁)

Figure 14 **The first and second cervical vertebrae.**

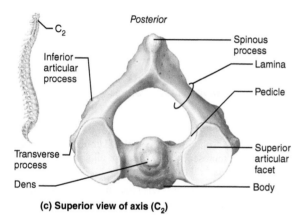

(c) Superior view of axis (C₂)

**Superior and inferior articular processes:** Paired projections lateral to the vertebral foramen that enable articulation with adjacent vertebrae. The superior articular processes typically face toward the spinous process (posteriorly), whereas the inferior articular processes face (anteriorly) away from the spinous process.

**Intervertebral foramina:** The right and left pedicles have notches (see Figure 15) on their inferior and superior surfaces that create openings, the intervertebral foramina, for spinal nerves to leave the spinal cord between adjacent vertebrae.

(Figures 14–16 and Table 1 show how specific vertebrae differ; refer to them as you read the following sections.)

## Cervical Vertebrae

The seven cervical vertebrae (referred to as $C_1$ through $C_7$) form the neck portion of the vertebral column. The first two cervical vertebrae (atlas and axis) are highly modified to perform special functions (Figure 14). The **atlas** ($C_1$) lacks a body, and its lateral processes contain large concave depressions on their superior surfaces that receive the occipital condyles of the skull. This joint enables you to nod "yes." The **axis** ($C_2$) acts as a pivot for the rotation of the atlas (and skull) above. It bears a large vertical process, the **dens,** or **odontoid process,** that serves as the pivot point. The articulation between $C_1$ and $C_2$ allows you to rotate your head from side to side to indicate "no."

The more typical cervical vertebrae ($C_3$ through $C_7$) are distinguished from the thoracic and lumbar vertebrae by several features (see Table 1 and Figure 15). They are the smallest, lightest vertebrae, and the vertebral foramen is triangular. The spinous process is short and often bifurcated (divided into two branches). The spinous process of $C_7$ is not branched, however, and is substantially longer than that of the other cervical vertebrae. Because the spinous process of $C_7$ is visible through the skin, it is called the *vertebra prominens* (Figure 11) and is used as a landmark for counting the vertebrae. Transverse processes of the cervical vertebrae are wide, and they contain foramina through which the vertebral arteries pass superiorly on their way to the brain. Any time you see these foramina in a vertebra, you can be sure that it is a cervical vertebra.

☐ Palpate your vertebra prominens. Place a check mark in the box when you locate the structure.

## Thoracic Vertebrae

The 12 thoracic vertebrae (referred to as $T_1$ through $T_{12}$) may be recognized by the following structural characteristics. They have a larger body than the cervical vertebrae (see Figure 15). The body is somewhat heart shaped, with two small articulating surfaces, or **costal facets,** on each side (one superior, the other inferior) close to the origin of the vertebral arch. Sometimes referred to as *costal demifacets* because of their small size, these facets articulate with the heads of the corresponding ribs. The vertebral foramen is oval or round, and the spinous process is long, with a sharp downward hook. The closer the thoracic vertebra is to the lumbar region, the less sharp and shorter the spinous process. Articular facets on the transverse processes articulate with the tubercles of the ribs. Besides forming the thoracic part of the spine, these vertebrae form the posterior aspect of the bony thorax. Indeed, they are the only vertebrae that articulate with the ribs.

## Lumbar Vertebrae

The five lumbar vertebrae ($L_1$ through $L_5$) have massive block-like bodies and short, thick, hatchet-shaped spinous processes extending directly backward (see Table 1 and Figure 15). The superior articular facets face posteromedially; the inferior ones

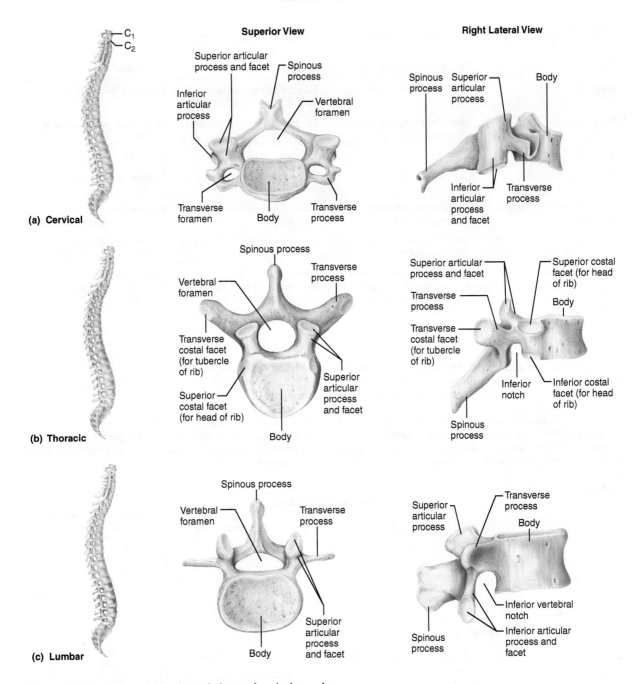

**Superior View**

**Right Lateral View**

(a) Cervical

(b) Thoracic

(c) Lumbar

**Figure 15** **Superior and right lateral views of typical vertebrae.**

are directed anterolaterally. These structural features reduce the mobility of the lumbar region of the spine. Since most stress on the vertebral column occurs in the lumbar region, these are also the sturdiest of the vertebrae.

The spinal cord ends at the superior edge of $L_2$, but the outer covering of the cord, filled with cerebrospinal fluid, extends an appreciable distance beyond. Thus a *lumbar puncture* (for examination of the cerebrospinal fluid) or the administration of "saddle block" anesthesia for childbirth is

normally done between $L_3$ and $L_4$ or $L_4$ and $L_5$, where there is little or no chance of injuring the delicate spinal cord.

## The Sacrum

The **sacrum** (Figure 16) is a composite bone formed from the fusion of five vertebrae. Superiorly it articulates with $L_5$, and inferiorly it connects with the coccyx. The **median sacral crest** is a remnant of the spinous processes of the fused ver-

**Table 1**  **Regional Characteristics of Cervical, Thoracic, and Lumbar Vertebrae**

| Characteristic | (a) Cervical ($C_3$–$C_7$) | (b) Thoracic | (c) Lumbar |
|---|---|---|---|
| Body | Small, wide side to side | Larger than cervical; heart shaped; bears costal facets | Massive; kidney shaped |
| Spinous process | Short; bifid; projects directly posteriorly | Long; sharp; projects inferiorly | Short; blunt; projects directly posteriorly |
| Vertebral foramen | Triangular | Circular | Triangular |
| Transverse processes | Contain foramina | Bear facets for ribs (except $T_{11}$ and $T_{12}$) | Thin and tapered |
| Superior and inferior articulating processes | Superior facets directed superoposteriorly | Superior facets directed posteriorly | Superior facets directed posteromedially (or medially) |
|  | Inferior facets directed inferoanteriorly | Inferior facets directed anteriorly | Inferior facets directed anterolaterally (or laterally) |
| Movements allowed | Flexion and extension; lateral flexion; rotation; the spine region with the greatest range of movement | Rotation; lateral flexion possible but limited by ribs; flexion and extension prevented | Flexion and extension; some lateral flexion; rotation prevented |

tebrae. The winglike **alae,** formed by fusion of the transverse processes, articulate laterally with the hip bones. The sacrum is concave anteriorly and forms the posterior border of the pelvis. Four ridges (lines of fusion) cross the anterior part of the sacrum, and **sacral foramina** are located at either end of these ridges. These foramina allow blood vessels and nerves to pass. The vertebral canal continues inside the sacrum as the **sacral canal** and terminates near the coccyx via an enlarged opening called the **sacral hiatus.** The **sacral promontory** (anterior border of the body of $S_1$) is an important anatomical landmark for obstetricians.

☐ Attempt to palpate the median sacral crest of your sacrum. (This is more easily done by thin people and obviously in privacy.) Place a check mark in the box when you locate the structure.

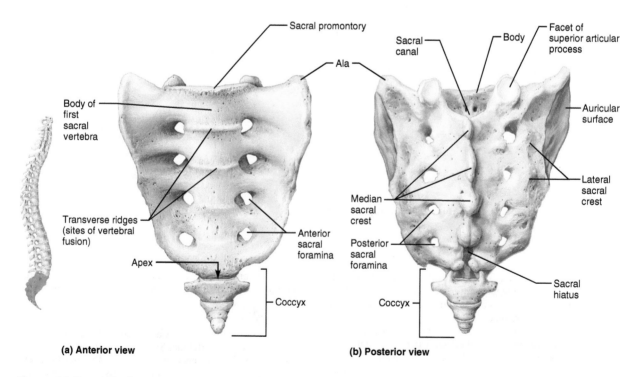

(a) Anterior view

(b) Posterior view

**Figure 16 Sacrum and coccyx.**

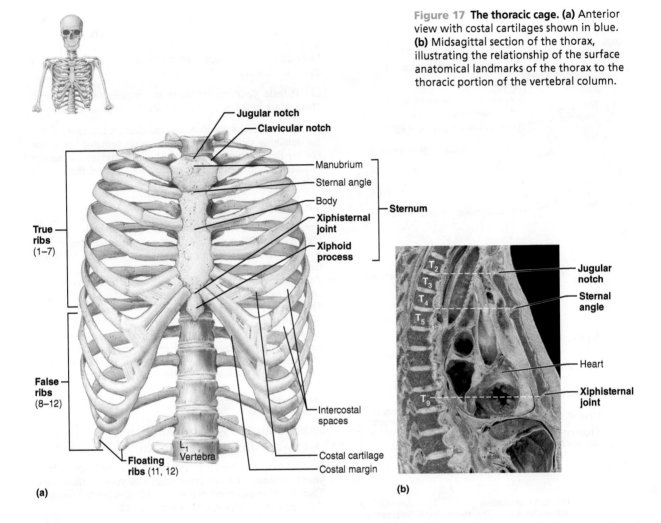

Figure 17 **The thoracic cage. (a)** Anterior view with costal cartilages shown in blue. **(b)** Midsagittal section of the thorax, illustrating the relationship of the surface anatomical landmarks of the thorax to the thoracic portion of the vertebral column.

**Jugular notch**
**Clavicular notch**
Manubrium
Sternal angle
Body
**Xiphisternal joint**
**Xiphoid process**
Sternum
True ribs (1–7)
False ribs (8–12)
Floating ribs (11, 12)
L₁ Vertebra
Intercostal spaces
Costal cartilage
Costal margin

(a)

T₂
T₃
T₄
T₅
T₉

Jugular notch
Sternal angle
Heart
Xiphisternal joint

(b)

# The Coccyx

The **coccyx** (see Figure 16) is formed from the fusion of three to five small irregularly shaped vertebrae. It is literally the human tailbone, a vestige of the tail that other vertebrates have. The coccyx is attached to the sacrum by ligaments.

**ACTIVITY 4**

### Examining Vertebral Structure

Obtain examples of each type of vertebra and examine them carefully, comparing them to the figures and table (Figures 14, 15, 16, and Table 1) and to each other. ■

## The Thoracic Cage

The **thoracic cage** consists of the bony thorax, which is composed of the sternum, ribs, and thoracic vertebrae, plus the costal cartilages **(Figure 17)**. Its cone-shaped cagelike structure protects the organs of the thoracic cavity including the critically important heart and lungs.

### *The Sternum*

The **sternum** (breastbone), a typical flat bone, is a result of the fusion of three bones—the manubrium, body, and xiphoid process. It is attached to the first seven pairs of ribs. The superiormost **manubrium** looks like the knot of a tie; it articulates with the clavicle (collarbone) laterally. The **body** forms the bulk of the sternum. The **xiphoid process** constructs the inferior end of the sternum and lies at the level of the fifth intercostal space. Although it is made of hyaline cartilage in children, it is usually ossified in adults.

In some people, the xiphoid process projects dorsally. This may present a problem because physical trauma to the chest can push such a xiphoid into the underlying heart or liver, causing massive hemorrhage. ✚

The sternum has three important bony landmarks—the jugular notch, the sternal angle, and the xiphisternal joint. The **jugular notch** (concave upper border of the manubrium) can be palpated easily; generally it is at the level of the third thoracic vertebra. The **sternal angle** is a result of the manubrium and body meeting at a slight angle to each other, so that a transverse ridge is formed at the level of the second ribs. It provides a handy reference point for counting ribs to locate

145

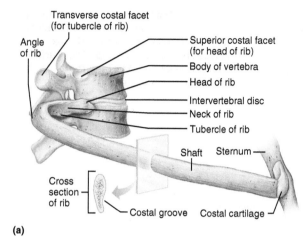

**(a)**

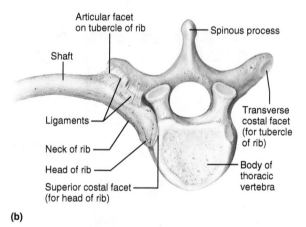

**(b)**

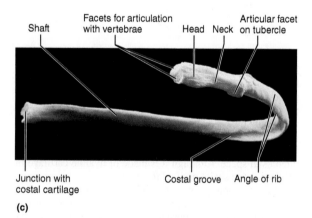

**(c)**

**Figure 18 Structure of a typical true rib and its articulations. (a)** Vertebral and sternal articulations of a typical true rib. **(b)** Superior view of the articulation between a rib and a thoracic vertebra, with costovertebral ligaments. **(c)** Right rib 6, posterior view.

the second intercostal space for listening to certain heart valves, and is an important anatomical landmark for thoracic surgery. The **xiphisternal joint,** the point where the sternal body and xiphoid process fuse, lies at the level of the ninth thoracic vertebra.

☐ Palpate your sternal angle and jugular notch. Place a check mark in the box when you locate the structures.

Because of its accessibility, the sternum is a favored site for obtaining samples of blood-forming (hematopoietic) tissue for the diagnosis of suspected blood diseases. A needle is inserted into the marrow of the sternum and the sample withdrawn (sternal puncture).

## The Ribs

The 12 pairs of **ribs** form the walls of the thoracic cage (see Figure 17 and **Figure 18**). All of the ribs articulate posteriorly with the vertebral column via their heads and tubercles and then curve downward and toward the anterior body surface. The first seven pairs, called the *true,* or *vertebrosternal, ribs,* attach directly to the sternum by their "own" costal cartilages. The next five pairs are called *false ribs;* they attach indirectly to the sternum or entirely lack a sternal attachment. Of these, rib pairs 8–10, which are also called *vertebrochondral ribs,* have indirect cartilage attachments to the sternum via the costal cartilage of rib 7. The last two pairs, called *floating,* or *vertebral, ribs,* have no sternal attachment.

**ACTIVITY 5**

### Examining the Relationship Between Ribs and Vertebrae

First take a deep breath to expand your chest. Notice how your ribs seem to move outward and how your sternum rises. Then examine an articulated skeleton to observe the relationship between the ribs and the vertebrae. ■

## The Fetal Skull

One of the most obvious differences between fetal and adult skeletons is the huge size of the fetal skull relative to the rest of the skeleton. Skull bones are incompletely formed at birth and connected by fibrous membranes called **fontanelles.** The fontanelles allow the fetal skull to be compressed slightly during birth and also allow for brain growth during late fetal life. They ossify (become bone) as the infant ages, completing the process by the time the child is 1½ to 2 years old.

**ACTIVITY 6**

### Examining a Fetal Skull

1. Obtain a fetal skull and study it carefully.
- Does it have the same bones as the adult skull?
- How does the size of the fetal face relate to the cranium?
- How does this compare to what is seen in the adult?

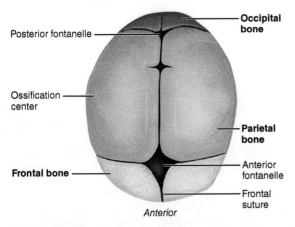

Posterior fontanelle — 

**Occipital bone**

Ossification center — 

Frontal bone — 

**Parietal bone**

Anterior fontanelle

Frontal suture

*Anterior*

**(a) Superior view**

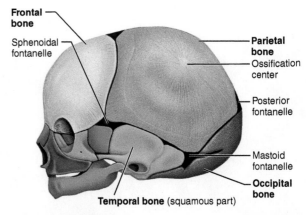

**Frontal bone**

Sphenoidal fontanelle

**Parietal bone**

Ossification center

Posterior fontanelle

Mastoid fontanelle

**Occipital bone**

**Temporal bone** (squamous part)

**(b) Left lateral view**

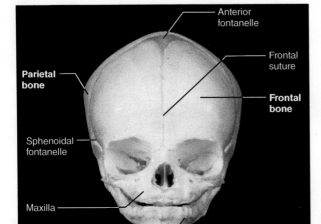

Anterior fontanelle

Frontal suture

**Frontal bone**

**Parietal bone**

Sphenoidal fontanelle

Maxilla

Mandible

**(c) Anterior view**

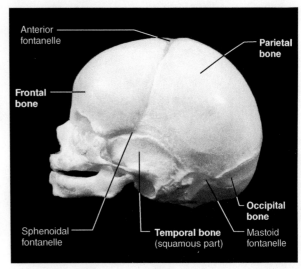

Anterior fontanelle

**Parietal bone**

**Frontal bone**

Sphenoidal fontanelle

**Temporal bone** (squamous part)

**Occipital bone**

Mastoid fontanelle

**(d) Left lateral view**

**Figure 19  Skull of a newborn.**

2. Locate the following fontanelles on the fetal skull (refer to **Figure 19**): *anterior (or frontal) fontanelle, mastoid fontanelle, sphenoidal fontanelle,* and *posterior (or occipital) fontanelle.*

3. Notice that some of the cranial bones have conical protrusions. These are **ossification (growth) centers.** Notice also that the frontal bone is still in two parts, and the temporal bone is incompletely ossified, little more than a ring of bone.

4. Before completing this study, check the questions on the review sheet at the end of this exercise to ensure that you have made all of the necessary observations. ▬

# The Axial Skeleton

## The Skull

**1.** First, match the bone names in column B with the descriptions in column A (the items in column B may be used more than once). <u>Then, circle the bones in column B that are cranial bones.</u>

**Column A**

          **Column B**

_____   1. forehead bone

_____   2. cheekbone

_____   3. lower jaw

_____   4. bridge of nose

_____   5. posterior bones of the hard palate

_____   6. much of the lateral and superior cranium

_____   7. most posterior part of cranium

_____   8. single, irregular, bat-shaped bone forming part of the cranial base

_____   9. tiny bones bearing tear ducts

_____  10. anterior part of hard palate

_____  11. superior and middle nasal conchae formed from its projections

_____  12. site of mastoid process

_____  13. site of sella turcica

_____  14. site of cribriform plate

_____  15. site of mental foramen

_____  16. site of styloid processes

_____, _____, _____

_____  17. four bones containing paranasal sinuses

_____  18. condyles here articulate with the atlas

_____  19. foramen magnum contained here

_____  20. small U-shaped bone in neck, where many tongue muscles attach

_____  21. organ of hearing found here

_____, _____  22. two bones that form the nasal septum

_____  23. bears an upward protrusion, the "cock's comb," or crista galli

_____, _____  24. contain sockets bearing teeth

_____  25. forms the most inferior turbinates

**Column B**

a. ethmoid

b. frontal

c. hyoid

d. inferior nasal concha

e. lacrimal

f. mandible

g. maxilla

h. nasal

i. occipital

j. palatine

k. parietal

l. sphenoid

m. temporal

n. vomer

o. zygomatic

**2.** Using choices from the numbered key to the right, identify all bones (——•), sutures (——►), and bone markings (——) provided with various leader lines in the two diagrams below. Some responses from the key will be used more than once.

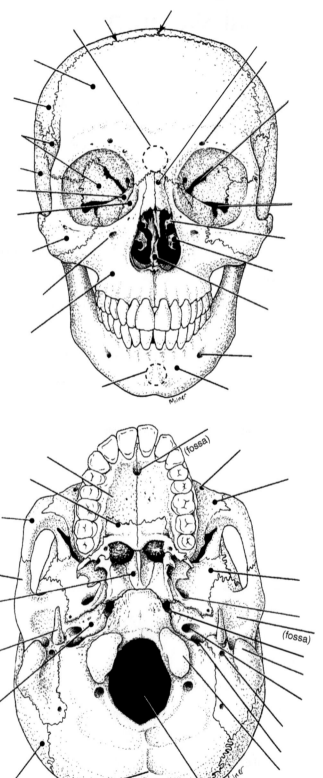

*Key:*
1. carotid canal
2. coronal suture
3. ethmoid bone
4. external occipital protuberance
5. foramen lacerum
6. foramen magnum
7. foramen ovale
8. frontal bone
9. glabella
10. incisive fossa
11. inferior nasal concha
12. inferior orbital fissure
13. infraorbital foramen
14. jugular foramen
15. lacrimal bone
16. mandible
17. mandibular fossa
18. mandibular symphysis
19. mastoid process
20. maxilla
21. mental foramen
22. middle nasal concha of ethmoid
23. nasal bone
24. occipital bone
25. occipital condyle
26. palatine bone
27. palatine process of maxilla
28. parietal bone
29. sagittal suture
30. sphenoid bone
31. styloid process
32. stylomastoid foramen
33. superior orbital fissure
34. supraorbital foramen
35. temporal bone
36. vomer
37. zygomatic bone
38. zygomatic process of temporal bone

(fossa)

(fossa)

**3.** Define *suture.* _____

**4.** With one exception, the skull bones are joined by sutures. Name the exception. _____

_____

**5.** What bones are connected by the lambdoid suture?

_____

What bones are connected by the squamous suture?

_____

**6.** Name the eight bones of the cranium. (Remember to include left and right.)

_____ _____ _____

_____ _____ _____

**7.** Give two possible functions of the sinuses.

_____

_____

**8.** What is the orbit? _____

What bones contribute to the formation of the orbit? _____

_____

**9.** Why can the sphenoid bone be called the keystone of the cranial base? _____

_____

# The Vertebral Column

**10.** The distinguishing characteristics of the vertebrae composing the vertebral column are noted below. Correctly identify each described structure by choosing a response from the key.

*Key:* a.  atlas
     b.  axis
     c.  cervical vertebra—typical

d.  coccyx
e.  lumbar vertebra

f.  sacrum
g.  thoracic vertebra

_____ 1.  vertebral type containing foramina in the transverse processes, through which the vertebral arteries ascend to reach the brain

_____ 2.  dens here provides a pivot for rotation of the first cervical vertebra ($C_1$)

_____ 3.  transverse processes faceted for articulation with ribs; spinous process pointing sharply downward

_____ 4.  composite bone; articulates with the hip bone laterally

_____ 5.  massive vertebrae; weight-sustaining

_____ 6. "tail bone"; vestigial fused vertebrae

_____ 7. supports the head; allows a rocking motion in conjunction with the occipital condyles

**11.** Using the key, correctly identify the vertebral parts/areas described below. (More than one choice may apply in some cases.) Also use the key letters to correctly identify the vertebral areas in the diagram.

*Key:* a. body          d. pedicle          g. transverse process
       b. intervertebral foramina      e. spinous process      h. vertebral arch
       c. lamina          f. superior articular facet      i. vertebral foramen

_____ 1. cavity enclosing the spinal cord

_____ 2. weight-bearing portion of the vertebra

_____, _____ 3. provide levers against which muscles pull

_____, _____ 4. provide an articulation point for the ribs

_____ 5. openings providing for exit of spinal nerves

_____, _____ 6. structures that form an enclosure for the spinal cord

_____, _____, _____ 7. structures that form the vertebral arch

**12.** Describe how a spinal nerve exits from the vertebral column. _____

_____

**13.** Name two factors/structures that permit flexibility of the vertebral column.

_____ and _____

**14.** What kind of tissue makes up the intervertebral discs? _____

**15.** What is a herniated disc? _____

What problems might it cause? _____

_____

**16.** Which two spinal curvatures are obvious at birth? _____ and _____

Under what conditions do the secondary curvatures develop? _____

_____

_____

**17.** On this illustration of an articulated vertebral column, identify each curvature indicated and label it as a primary or a secondary curvature. Also identify the structures provided with leader lines, using the letters of the terms listed in the key below.

*Key:* a.  atlas
  b.  axis
  c.  intervertebral disc
  d.  sacrum
  e.  two thoracic vertebrae
  f.  two lumbar vertebrae
  g.  vertebra prominens

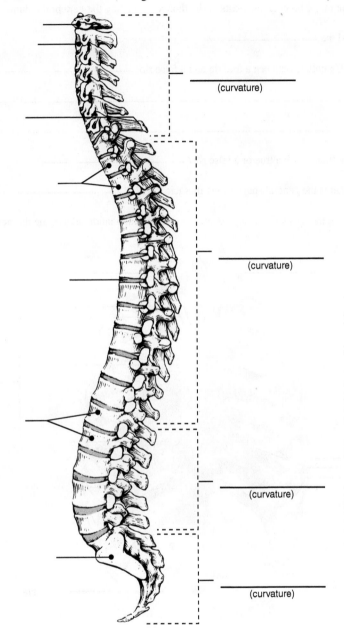

(curvature) _____

(curvature) _____

(curvature) _____

(curvature) _____

# The Thoracic Cage

**18.** The major bony components of the thorax (excluding the vertebral column) are the ——————————————

and the ————————————— .

**19.** Differentiate between a true rib and a false rib. ——————————————————

————————————————————————————————————————

————————————————————————————————————————

Is a floating rib a true or a false rib? ————————————— .

**20.** What is the general shape of the thoracic cage? ——————————————————

**21.** Using the terms in the key, identify the regions and landmarks of the thoracic cage.

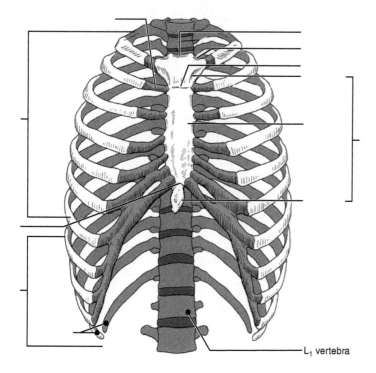

L₁ vertebra

*Key:* a.  body

b.  clavicular notch

c.  costal cartilage

d.  false ribs

e.  floating ribs

f.  jugular notch

g.  manubrium

h.  sternal angle

i.  sternum

j.  true ribs

k.  xiphisternal joint

l.  xiphoid process

## The Fetal Skull

**22.** Are the same skull bones seen in the adult also found in the fetal skull? —————————————

**23.** How does the size of the fetal face compare to its cranium? —————————————————

————————————————————————————————————————————

How does this compare to the adult skull? ————————————————————————

————————————————————————————————————————————

————————————————————————————————————————————

**24.** What are the outward conical projections on some of the fetal cranial bones? ————————————

**25.** What is a fontanelle? ————————————————————————————————————————

What is its fate? —————————————————————————————————————————

What is the function of the fontanelles in the fetal skull? ——————————————————————

————————————————————————————————————————————

**26.** Using the terms listed, identify each of the fontanelles shown on the fetal skull below.

*Key:*

a. anterior fontanelle

b. mastoid fontanelle

c. posterior fontanelle

d. sphenoidal fontanelle

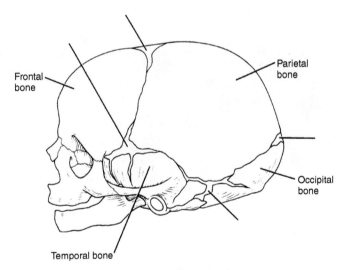

Frontal bone

Parietal bone

Occipital bone

Temporal bone

---

## Photo Credits

**Credits are listed in order of appearance.**

1b, 2b, 4a,b, 19c,d: Larry DeLay, PAL 3.0, Pearson Education. 3c, 5: Michael Wiley, Univ. of Toronto, Imagineering © Pearson Education. 6c: Elena Dorfman, Pearson Education. 9c: From *A Stereoscopic Atlas of Human Anatomy* by David L. Bassett, M.D. 17b: Karen Krabbenhoft, PAL 3.0, Pearson Education. 18c: Pearson Education.

## Illustration Credits

**All illustrations are by Imagineering STA Media Services, except for Review Sheet art and as noted below.**

1–3, 6, 8, 19: Nadine Sokol.

# The Appendicular Skeleton

## MATERIALS

☐ Articulated skeletons
☐ Disarticulated skeletons (complete)
☐ Articulated pelves (male and female for comparative study)
☐ X rays of bones of the appendicular skeleton

## OBJECTIVES

1. Identify the bones of the pectoral and pelvic girdles and their attached limbs by examining isolated bones or an articulated skeleton, and name the important bone markings on each.

2. Describe the differences between a male and a female pelvis and explain the importance of these differences.

3. Compare the features of the human pectoral and pelvic girdles, and discuss how their structures relate to their specialized functions.

4. Arrange unmarked, disarticulated bones in their proper places to form an entire skeleton.

## PRE-LAB QUIZ

1. The _____ skeleton is made up of 126 bones of the limbs and girdles.

2. Circle the correct underlined term. The <u>pectoral</u> / <u>pelvic</u> girdle attaches the upper limb to the axial skeleton.

3. The _____, on the posterior thorax, are roughly triangular in shape. They have no direct attachment to the axial skeleton but are held in place by trunk muscles.

4. The arm consists of one long bone, the _____.
   a. femur
   b. humerus
   c. tibia
   d. ulna

5. The hand consists of three groups of bones. The carpals make up the wrist. The _____ make up the palm, and the phalanges make up the fingers.

6. You are studying a pelvis that is wide and shallow. The acetabula are small and far apart. The pubic arch/angle is rounded and greater than 90°. It appears to be tilted forward, with a wide, short sacrum. Is this a male or a female pelvis? _____

7. The strongest, heaviest bone of the body is in the thigh. It is the
   a. femur
   b. fibula
   c. tibia

8. The _____, or "knee cap," is a sesamoid bone that is found within the quadriceps tendon.

9. Circle True or False. The fingers of the hand and the toes of the foot—with the exception of the great toe and the thumb—each have three phalanges.

10. Each foot has a total of _____ bones.

MasteringA&P® For related exercise study tools, go to the Study Area of MasteringA&P. There you will find:
- Practice Anatomy Lab PAL
- PhysioEx PEx
- A&PFlix A&PFlix
- Practice quizzes, Histology Atlas, eText, Videos, and more!

The **appendicular skeleton** is composed of the 126 bones of the appendages and the pectoral and pelvic girdles, which attach the limbs to the axial skeleton. Although the upper and lower limbs differ in their functions and mobility, they have the same fundamental plan, with each limb made up of three major segments connected together by freely movable joints.

From Exercise 10 of *Human Anatomy & Physiology Laboratory Manual,* Main Version, Tenth Edition. Elaine N. Marieb, Susan J. Mitchell, Lori A. Smith. Copyright © 2014 by Pearson Education, Inc. All rights reserved.

## Examining and Identifying Bones of the Appendicular Skeleton

Carefully examine each of the bones described in this exercise and identify the characteristic bone markings of each. The markings aid in determining whether a bone is the right or left member of its pair; for example, the glenoid cavity is on the lateral aspect of the scapula and the spine is on its posterior aspect. *This is a very important instruction because you will be constructing your own skeleton to finish this laboratory exercise.* Additionally, when corresponding X rays are available, compare the actual bone specimen to its X-ray image. ■

# Bones of the Pectoral Girdle and Upper Limb

## The Pectoral (Shoulder) Girdle

The paired **pectoral**, or **shoulder, girdles (Figure 1)** each consist of two bones—the anterior clavicle and the posterior scapula. The shoulder girdles attach the upper limbs to the axial skeleton and provide attachment points for many trunk and neck muscles.

The **clavicle**, or collarbone, is a slender doubly curved bone—convex forward on its medial two-thirds and concave laterally. Its *sternal* (medial) *end*, which attaches to the sternal manubrium, is rounded or triangular in cross section. The sternal end projects above the manubrium and can be felt and usually seen forming the lateral walls of the *jugular notch*. The *acromial* (lateral) *end* of the clavicle is flattened where it articulates with the scapula to form part of the shoulder joint. On its posteroinferior surface is the prominent **conoid tubercle (Figure 2b)**. This projection anchors a ligament and provides a handy landmark for determining whether a given clavicle is from the right or left side of the body. The clavicle serves as an anterior brace, or strut, to hold the arm away from the top of the thorax.

The **scapulae** (Figure 2c–e), or shoulder blades, are generally triangular and are commonly called the "wings" of humans. Each scapula has a flattened body and two important processes—the **acromion** (the enlarged, roughened end of the spine of the scapula) and the beaklike **coracoid process** (*corac* = crow, raven). The acromion connects with the clavicle. The coracoid process points anteriorly over the tip of the shoulder joint and serves as an attachment point for some of the upper limb muscles. The **suprascapular notch** at the base of the coracoid process allows nerves to pass. The scapula has no direct attachment to the axial skeleton but is loosely held in place by trunk muscles.

The scapula has three angles: superior, inferior, and lateral. The inferior angle provides a landmark for auscultating (listening to) lung sounds. The **glenoid cavity,** a shallow socket that receives the head of the arm bone (humerus), is located in the blunted lateral angle. The scapula also has three named borders: superior, medial (vertebral), and lateral (axillary). Several shallow depressions (fossae) appear on both sides of the scapula and are named according to location; there are the anterior *subscapular fossa* and the posterior *infraspinous* and *supraspinous fossae*.

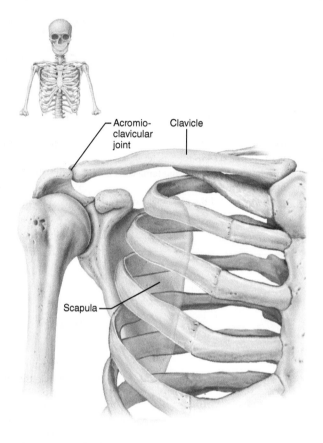

**Figure 1 Articulated bones of the pectoral (shoulder) girdle.** The right pectoral girdle is articulated to show the relationship of the girdle to the bones of the thorax and arm.

The shoulder girdle is exceptionally light and allows the upper limb a degree of mobility not seen anywhere else in the body. This is due to the following factors:

- The sternoclavicular joints are the *only* site of attachment of the shoulder girdles to the axial skeleton.

- The relative looseness of the scapular attachment allows it to slide back and forth against the thorax with muscular activity.

- The glenoid cavity is shallow and does little to stabilize the shoulder joint.

However, this exceptional flexibility exacts a price: the arm bone (humerus) is very susceptible to dislocation, and fracture of the clavicle disables the entire upper limb.

## The Arm

The arm or brachium **(Figure 3)** contains a single bone—the **humerus,** a typical long bone. Proximally its rounded *head* fits into the shallow glenoid cavity of the scapula. The head is separated from the shaft by the *anatomical neck* and the more constricted *surgical neck,* which is a common site of fracture. Opposite the head are two prominences, the **greater** and **lesser tubercles** (from lateral to medial aspect),

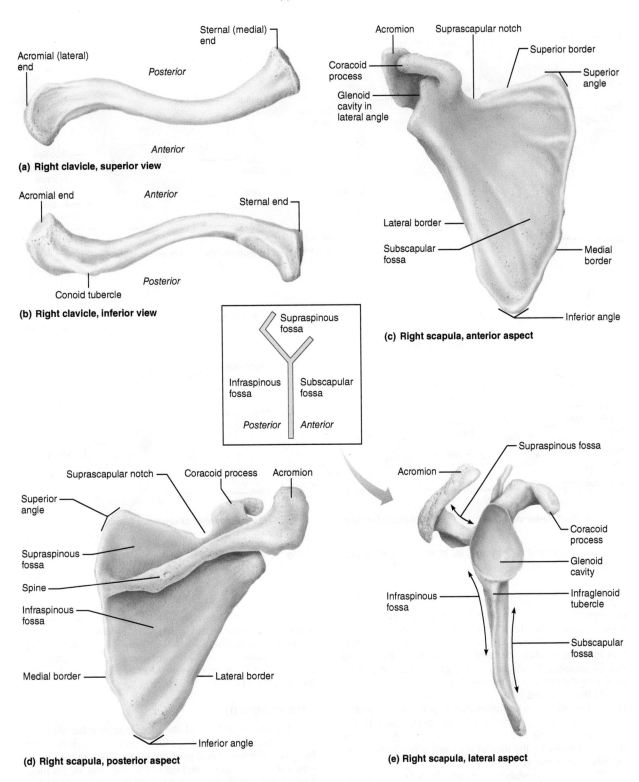

**(a) Right clavicle, superior view**

Acromial (lateral) end

Sternal (medial) end

*Posterior*

*Anterior*

**(b) Right clavicle, inferior view**

Acromial end

*Anterior*

Sternal end

*Posterior*

Conoid tubercle

Supraspinous fossa

Infraspinous fossa

Subscapular fossa

*Posterior*   *Anterior*

**(c) Right scapula, anterior aspect**

Acromion

Suprascapular notch

Coracoid process

Glenoid cavity in lateral angle

Superior border

Superior angle

Lateral border

Subscapular fossa

Medial border

Inferior angle

**(d) Right scapula, posterior aspect**

Suprascapular notch

Coracoid process

Acromion

Superior angle

Supraspinous fossa

Spine

Infraspinous fossa

Medial border

Lateral border

Inferior angle

**(e) Right scapula, lateral aspect**

Acromion

Suprascapular fossa

Coracoid process

Glenoid cavity

Infraglenoid tubercle

Subscapular fossa

Infraspinous fossa

**Figure 2** **Individual bones of the pectoral (shoulder) girdle.** View **(e)** is accompanied by a schematic representation of its orientation.

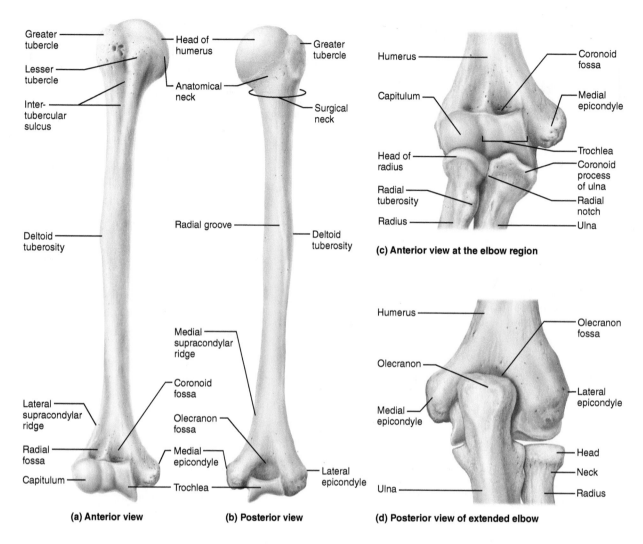

**(a) Anterior view**  **(b) Posterior view**

**(c) Anterior view at the elbow region**

**(d) Posterior view of extended elbow**

**Figure 3** **Bone of the right arm. (a, b)** Humerus. **(c, d)** Detailed views of extended elbow.

separated by a groove (the **intertubercular sulcus,** or **bicipital groove**) that guides the tendon of the biceps muscle to its point of attachment (the superior rim of the glenoid cavity). In the midpoint of the shaft is a roughened area, the **deltoid tuberosity**, where the large fleshy shoulder muscle, the deltoid, attaches. Nearby, the **radial groove** runs obliquely, indicating the pathway of the radial nerve.

At the distal end of the humerus are two condyles—the medial **trochlea** (looking rather like a spool), which articulates with the ulna, and the lateral **capitulum,** which articulates with the radius of the forearm. This condyle pair is flanked medially by the **medial epicondyle** and laterally by the **lateral epicondyle.**

The medial epicondyle is commonly called the "funny bone." The ulnar nerve runs in a groove beneath the medial epicondyle, and when this region is sharply bumped, a temporary, but excruciatingly painful, tingling sensation often occurs. This event is called "hitting the funny bone," a strange expression, because it is certainly *not* funny!

Above the trochlea on the anterior surface is the **coronoid fossa;** on the posterior surface is the **olecranon fossa.** These two depressions allow the corresponding processes of the ulna to move freely when the elbow is flexed (bent) and extended (straightened). The small **radial fossa,** lateral to the coronoid fossa, receives the head of the radius when the elbow is flexed.

## The Forearm

Two bones, the radius and the ulna, compose the skeleton of the forearm, or antebrachium **(Figure 4)**. When the body is in the anatomical position, the **radius** is in the lateral position in the forearm, and the radius and ulna are parallel. Proximally, the disc-shaped head of the radius articulates with the capitulum of the humerus. Just below the head, on the medial aspect of the shaft, is a prominence called the **radial tuberosity,** the point of attachment for the tendon of the biceps muscle of the arm. Distally, the small **ulnar notch** reveals where the radius articulates with the end of the ulna.

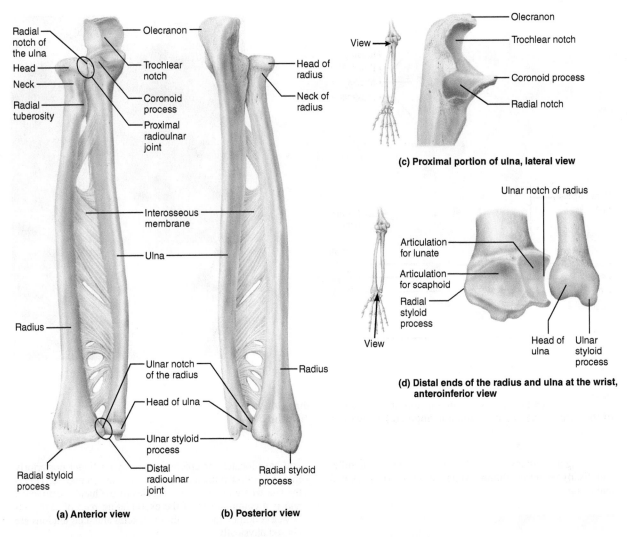

Radial notch of the ulna
Head
Neck
Radial tuberosity
Olecranon
Trochlear notch
Coronoid process
Proximal radioulnar joint
Head of radius
Neck of radius
Interosseous membrane
Ulna
Radius
Ulnar notch of the radius
Head of ulna
Ulnar styloid process
Distal radioulnar joint
Radius
Radial styloid process
Radial styloid process

**(a) Anterior view**

**(b) Posterior view**

View
Olecranon
Trochlear notch
Coronoid process
Radial notch

**(c) Proximal portion of ulna, lateral view**

Ulnar notch of radius
Articulation for lunate
Articulation for scaphoid
Radial styloid process
View
Head of ulna
Ulnar styloid process

**(d) Distal ends of the radius and ulna at the wrist, anteroinferior view**

**Figure 4  Bones of the right forearm. (a, b)** Radius and ulna in anterior and posterior views. **(c, d)** Structural details of the articular surfaces between the radius and ulna, and between the radius and bones of the wrist.

The **ulna** is the medial bone of the forearm. Its proximal end bears the anterior **coronoid process** and the posterior **olecranon,** which are separated by the **trochlear notch.** Together these processes grip the trochlea of the humerus in a plierslike joint. The small **radial notch** on the lateral side of the coronoid process articulates with the head of the radius. The slimmer distal end, the ulnar **head,** bears the small medial **ulnar styloid process,** which serves as a point of attachment for the ligaments of the wrist.

## The Hand

The skeleton of the hand, or manus **(Figure 5)**, includes three groups of bones, those of the carpus (wrist), the metacarpals (bones of the palm), and the phalanges (bones of the fingers).

The wrist is the proximal portion of the hand. It is referred to anatomically as the **carpus;** the eight bones composing it are the **carpals.** (So you actually wear your

wristwatch over the distal part of your forearm.) The carpals are arranged in two irregular rows of four bones each (illustrated in Figure 5). In the proximal row (lateral to medial) are the *scaphoid, lunate, triquetrum,* and *pisiform bones;* the scaphoid and lunate articulate with the distal end of the radius. In the distal row are the *trapezium, trapezoid, capitate,* and *hamate.* The carpals are bound closely together by ligaments, which restrict movements between them.

The **metacarpals,** numbered I to V from the thumb side of the hand toward the little finger, radiate out from the wrist like spokes to form the palm of the hand. The *bases* of the metacarpals articulate with the carpals of the wrist; their more bulbous *heads* articulate with the phalanges of the fingers distally. When the fist is clenched, the heads of the metacarpals become prominent as the knuckles.

Like the bones of the palm, the fingers are numbered from I to V, beginning from the thumb *(pollex)* side of the hand. The 14 bones of the fingers, or digits, are miniature long bones, called **phalanges** (singular: *phalanx*) as noted above.

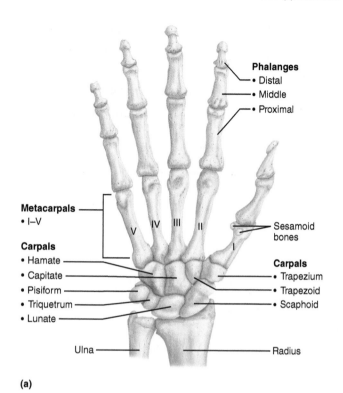

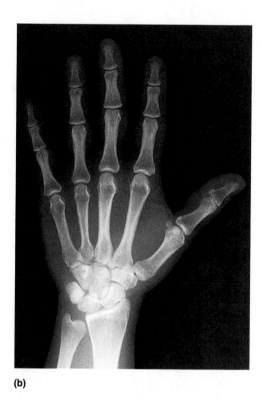

(a)

(b)

**Figure 5 Bones of the right hand. (a)** Anterior view showing the relationships of the carpals, metacarpals, and phalanges. **(b)** X ray of the right hand in the anterior view.

Each finger contains three phalanges (proximal, middle, and distal) except the thumb, which has only two (proximal and distal).

## ACTIVITY 2

### Palpating the Surface Anatomy of the Pectoral Girdle and the Upper Limb

Before continuing on to study the bones of the pelvic girdle, take the time to identify the following bone markings on the skin surface of the upper limb. It is usually preferable to palpate the bone markings on your lab partner since many of these markings can only be seen from the dorsal aspect. Place a check mark in the boxes as you locate the bone markings. Seek assistance from your instructor for any markings that you are unable to locate.

☐ Clavicle: Palpate the clavicle along its entire length from sternum to shoulder.

☐ Acromioclavicular joint: The high point of the shoulder, which represents the junction point between the clavicle and the acromion of the scapular spine.

☐ Spine of the scapula: Extend your arm at the shoulder so that your scapula moves posteriorly. As you do this, your scapular spine will be seen as a winglike protrusion on your dorsal thorax and can be easily palpated by your lab partner.

☐ Lateral epicondyle of the humerus: The inferiormost projection at the lateral aspect of the distal humerus. After you have located the epicondyle, run your finger posteriorly into the hollow immediately dorsal to the epicondyle. This is the site where the extensor muscles of the hand are attached and is a common site of the excruciating pain of tennis elbow, a condition in which those muscles and their tendons are abused physically.

☐ Medial epicondyle of the humerus: Feel this medial projection at the distal end of the humerus.

☐ Olecranon of the ulna: Work your elbow—flexing and extending—as you palpate its dorsal aspect to feel the olecranon of the ulna moving into and out of the olecranon fossa on the dorsal aspect of the humerus.

☐ Ulnar styloid process: With the hand in the anatomical position, feel out this small inferior projection on the medial aspect of the distal end of the ulna.

☐ Radial styloid process: Find this projection at the distal end of the radius (lateral aspect). It is most easily located by moving the hand medially at the wrist. Once you have palpated the radial styloid process, move your fingers just medially onto the anterior wrist. Press firmly and then let up slightly on the pressure. You should be able to feel your pulse at this pressure point, which lies over the radial artery (radial pulse).

☐ Pisiform: Just distal to the ulnar styloid process feel the rounded pealike pisiform bone.

☐ Metacarpophalangeal joints (knuckles): Clench your fist and find the first set of flexed-joint protrusions beyond the wrist—these are your metacarpophalangeal joints. ■

# Bones of the Pelvic Girdle and Lower Limb

## The Pelvic (Hip) Girdle

As with the bones of the pectoral girdle and upper limb, pay particular attention to bone markings needed to identify right and left bones.

The **pelvic girdle,** or **hip girdle** (Figure 6), is formed by the two **coxal** (*coxa* = hip) **bones** (also called the **ossa coxae,** or hip bones) and the sacrum. The deep structure formed by the hip bones, sacrum, and coccyx is called the **pelvis** or *bony pelvis.* In contrast to the bones of the shoulder girdle, those of the pelvic girdle are heavy and massive, and they attach securely to the axial skeleton. The sockets for the heads of the femurs (thigh bones) are deep and heavily reinforced by ligaments to ensure a stable, strong limb attachment. The ability to bear weight is more important here than mobility and flexibility. The combined weight of the upper body rests on the pelvic girdle (specifically, where the hip bones meet the sacrum).

Each coxal bone is a result of the fusion of three bones—the ilium, ischium, and pubis—which are distinguishable in the young child. The **ilium,** a large flaring bone, forms the major portion of the coxal bone. It connects posteriorly, via its **auricular surface,** with the sacrum at the **sacroiliac joint.** The superior margin of the iliac bone, the **iliac crest,** is rough; when you rest your hands on your hips, you are palpating your iliac crests. The iliac crest terminates anteriorly in the **anterior superior spine** and posteriorly in the **posterior superior spine.** Two inferior spines are located below these. The shallow **iliac fossa** marks its internal surface, and a prominent ridge, the **arcuate line,** outlines the pelvic inlet, or pelvic brim.

The **ischium** is the "sit-down" bone, forming the most inferior and posterior portion of the coxal bone. The most outstanding marking on the ischium is the rough **ischial tuberosity,** which receives the weight of the body when sitting. The **ischial spine,** superior to the ischial tuberosity, is an important anatomical landmark of the pelvic cavity. (See Comparison of the Male and Female Pelves, Table 1). The obvious **lesser** and **greater sciatic notches** allow nerves and blood vessels to pass to and from the thigh. The sciatic nerve passes through the latter.

The **pubis** is the most anterior portion of the coxal bone. Fusion of the **rami** of the pubis anteriorly and the ischium posteriorly forms a bar of bone enclosing the **obturator foramen,** through which blood vessels and nerves run from the pelvic cavity into the thigh. The pubis of each hip bone meets anteriorly at the **pubic crest** to form a cartilaginous joint called the **pubic symphysis.** At the lateral end of the pubic crest is the *pubic tubercle* (see Figure 6c) to which the important *inguinal ligament* attaches.

The ilium, ischium, and pubis fuse at the deep hemispherical socket called the **acetabulum** (literally, "wine cup"), which receives the head of the thigh bone.

### ACTIVITY 3

### Observing Pelvic Articulations

Before continuing with the bones of the lower limbs, take the time to examine an articulated pelvis. Notice how each coxal bone articulates with the sacrum posteriorly and how the two coxal bones join at the pubic symphysis. The sacroiliac joint is a common site of lower back problems because of the pressure it must bear. ▪

### *Comparison of the Male and Female Pelves*

Although bones of males are usually larger, heavier, and have more prominent bone markings, the male and female skeletons are very similar. The exception to this generalization is pelvic structure.

The female pelvis reflects modifications for childbearing—it is wider, shallower, lighter, and rounder than that of the male. Not only must her pelvis support the increasing size of a fetus, but it must also be large enough to allow the infant's head (its largest dimension) to descend through the birth canal at birth.

To describe pelvic sex differences, we need to introduce a few more terms. The **false pelvis** is that portion superior to the arcuate line; it is bounded by the alae of the ilia laterally and the sacral promontory and lumbar vertebrae posteriorly. Although the false pelvis supports the abdominal viscera, it does not restrict childbirth in any way. The **true pelvis** is the region inferior to the arcuate line that is almost entirely surrounded by bone. Its posterior boundary is formed by the sacrum. The ilia, ischia, and pubic bones define its limits laterally and anteriorly.

The dimensions of the true pelvis, particularly its inlet and outlet, are critical if delivery of a baby is to be uncomplicated. These dimensions are carefully measured by the obstetrician. The **pelvic inlet,** or **pelvic brim,** is the opening delineated by the sacral promontory posteriorly and the arcuate lines of the ilia anterolaterally. It is the superiormost margin of the true pelvis. Its widest dimension is from left to right, that is, along the frontal plane. The **pelvic outlet** is the inferior margin of the true pelvis. It is bounded anteriorly by the pubic arch, laterally by the ischia, and posteriorly by the sacrum and coccyx. Since both the coccyx and the ischial spines protrude into the outlet opening, a sharply angled coccyx or large, sharp ischial spines can dramatically narrow the outlet. The largest dimension of the outlet is the anterior-posterior diameter.

### ACTIVITY 4

### Comparing Male and Female Pelves

Examine male and female pelves for the following differences:

•    The female inlet is larger and more circular.

•    The female pelvis as a whole is shallower, and the bones are lighter and thinner.

•    The female sacrum is broader and less curved, and the pubic arch is more rounded.

•    The female acetabula are smaller and farther apart, and the ilia flare more laterally.

•    The female ischial spines are shorter, farther apart, and everted, thus enlarging the pelvic outlet. ▪

(The major differences between the male and female pelves are summarized in Table 1).

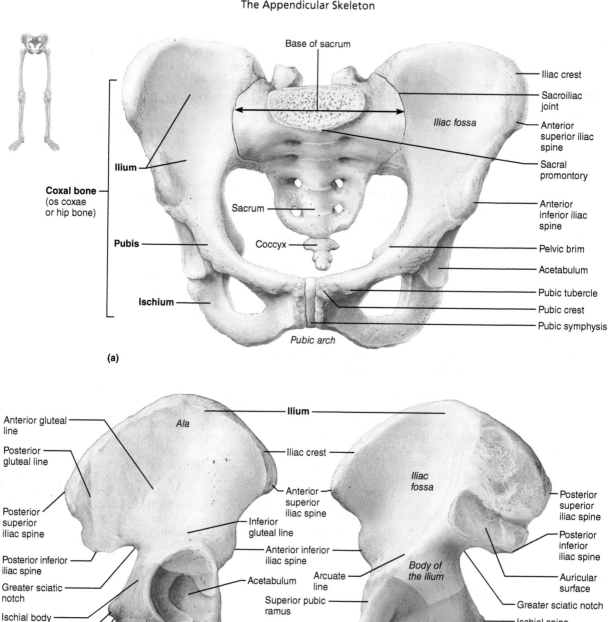

**Coxal bone**
(os coxae
or hip bone)

**Ilium**

**Pubis**

**Ischium**

Base of sacrum

*Iliac fossa*

Sacrum

Coccyx

*Pubic arch*

Iliac crest

Sacroiliac
joint

Anterior
superior iliac
spine

Sacral
promontory

Anterior
inferior iliac
spine

Pelvic brim

Acetabulum

Pubic tubercle

Pubic crest

Pubic symphysis

**(a)**

Anterior gluteal
line

Posterior
gluteal line

Posterior
superior
iliac spine

Posterior inferior
iliac spine

Greater sciatic
notch

Ischial body

Ischial spine

Lesser sciatic
notch

**Ischium**

Ischial
tuberosity

Ischial ramus

*Ala*

**Ilium**

Iliac crest

Anterior
superior
iliac spine

Inferior
gluteal line

Anterior inferior
iliac spine

Acetabulum

Superior pubic
ramus

Pubic tubercle

Pubic body

**Pubis**

Articular surface of
pubis (at pubic
symphysis)

Inferior pubic
ramus

Obturator
foramen

*Iliac
fossa*

Arcuate
line

*Body of
the ilium*

Posterior
superior
iliac spine

Posterior
inferior
iliac spine

Auricular
surface

Greater sciatic notch

Ischial spine

Obturator
foramen

**Ischium**

Ischial ramus

**(b)**

**(c)**

**Figure 6  Bones of the pelvic girdle. (a)** Articulated bony pelvis, showing the two hip
bones (coxal bones), which together with the sacrum comprise the pelvic girdle, and
the coccyx. **(b)** Right hip bone, lateral view, showing the point of fusion of the ilium,
ischium, and pubis. **(c)** Right hip bone, medial view.

| Table 1 | Comparison of the Male and Female Pelves | |
|---|---|---|
| **Characteristic** | **Female** | **Male** |
| General structure and functional modifications | Tilted forward; adapted for childbearing; true pelvis defines the birth canal; cavity of the true pelvis is broad, shallow, and has a greater capacity | Tilted less far forward; adapted for support of a male's heavier build and stronger muscles; cavity of the true pelvis is narrow and deep |
| Bone thickness | Less; bones lighter, thinner, and smoother | Greater; bones heavier and thicker, and markings are more prominent |
| Acetabula | Smaller; farther apart | Larger; closer |
| Pubic angle/arch | Broader angle (80°–90°); more rounded | Angle is more acute (50°–60°) |
| Anterior view | 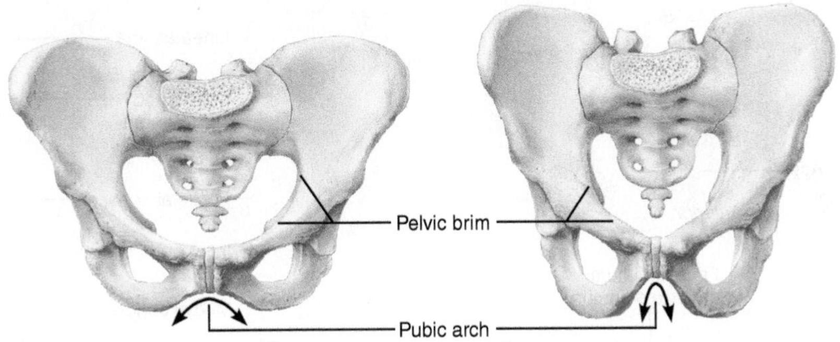 | |

Pelvic brim

Pubic arch

| Sacrum | Wider; shorter; sacrum is less curved | Narrow; longer; sacral promontory more ventral |
|---|---|---|
| Coccyx | More movable; straighter; projects inferiorly | Less movable; curves and projects anteriorly |
| Left lateral view | 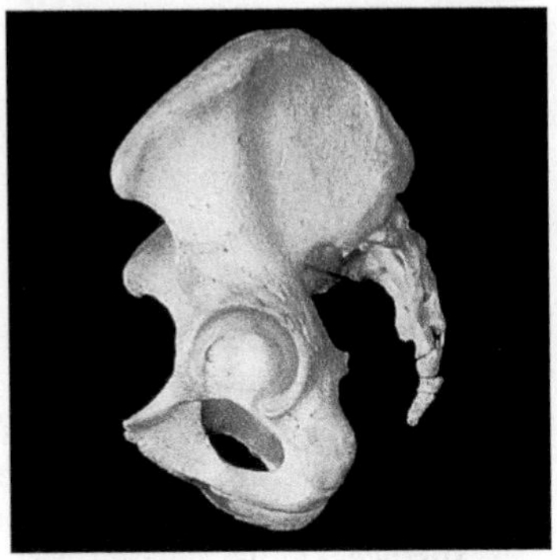 | 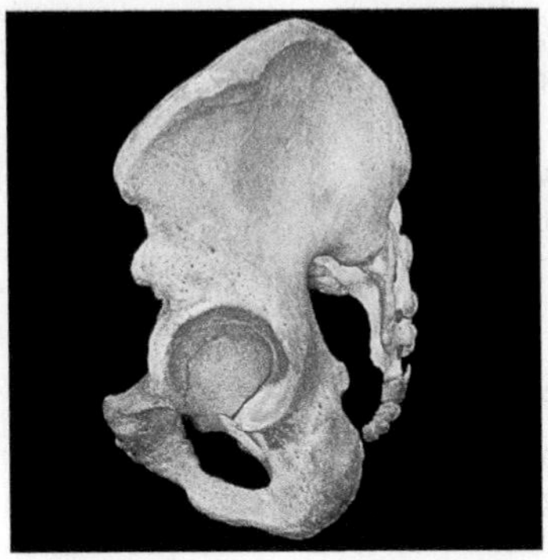 |

| Pelvic inlet (brim) | Wider; oval from side to side | Narrow; basically heart shaped |
|---|---|---|
| Pelvic outlet | Wider; ischial spines shorter, farther apart, and everted | Narrower; ischial spines longer, sharper, and point more medially |
| Posteroinferior view | 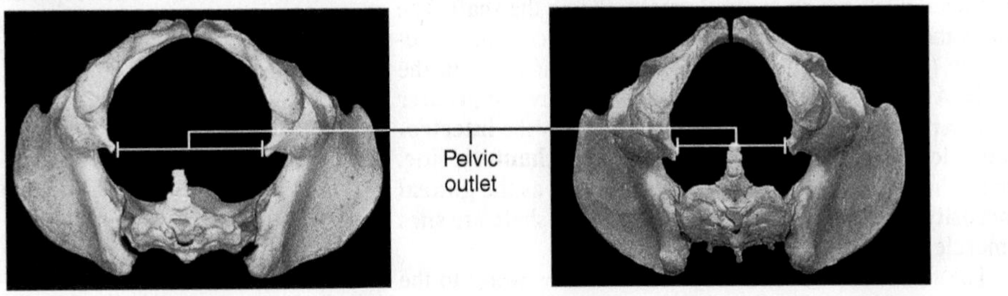 | |

Pelvic outlet

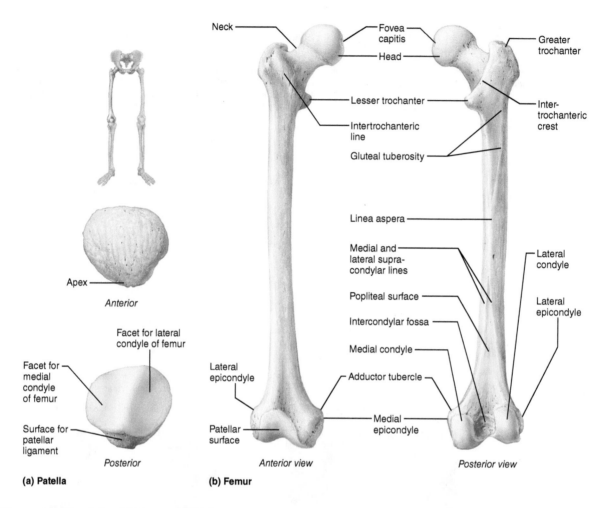

Apex

*Anterior*

Facet for lateral
condyle of femur

Facet for
medial
condyle
of femur

Surface for
patellar
ligament

*Posterior*

**(a) Patella**

Neck

Fovea
capitis

Head

Greater
trochanter

Lesser trochanter

Inter-
trochanteric
crest

Intertrochanteric
line

Gluteal tuberosity

Linea aspera

Medial and
lateral supra-
condylar lines

Lateral
condyle

Popliteal surface

Lateral
epicondyle

Intercondylar fossa

Medial condyle

Lateral
epicondyle

Adductor tubercle

Patellar
surface

Medial
epicondyle

*Anterior view*

*Posterior view*

**(b) Femur**

Figure 7 **Bones of the right knee and thigh.**

## The Thigh

The **femur,** or thigh bone **(Figure 7b),** is the only bone of the thigh. It is the heaviest, strongest bone in the body. The ball-like head of the femur articulates with the hip bone via the deep, secure socket of the acetabulum. Obvious in the femur's head is a small central pit called the **fovea capitis** ("pit of the head"), from which a small ligament runs to the acetabulum. The head of the femur is carried on a short, constricted *neck,* which angles laterally to join the shaft. The neck is the weakest part of the femur and is a common fracture site (an injury called a broken hip), particularly in the elderly. At the junction of the shaft and neck are the **greater** and **lesser trochanters** separated posteriorly by the **intertrochanteric crest** and anteriorly by the **intertrochanteric line.** The trochanters and trochanteric crest, as well as the **gluteal tuberosity** and the **linea aspera** located on the shaft, are sites of muscle attachment.

The femur inclines medially as it runs downward to the leg bones; this brings the knees in line with the body's center of gravity, or maximum weight. The medial course of the femur is more noticeable in females because of the wider female pelvis.

Distally, the femur terminates in the **lateral** and **medial condyles,** which articulate with the tibia below, and the **patellar surface,** which forms a joint with the patella (kneecap) anteriorly. The **lateral** and **medial epicondyles,** just superior to the condyles, are separated by the **intercondylar fossa,** and superior to that on the shaft is the smooth **popliteal surface.** On the superior part of the medial epicondyle is a bump, the **adductor tubercle,** to which the large adductor magnus muscle attaches.

The **patella** (Figure 7a) is a triangular sesamoid bone enclosed in the (quadriceps) tendon that secures the anterior thigh muscles to the tibia. It guards the knee joint anteriorly and improves the leverage of the thigh muscles acting across the knee joint.

## The Leg

Two bones, the tibia and the fibula, form the skeleton of the leg **(Figure 8)**. The **tibia,** or *shinbone,* is the larger and more medial of the two leg bones. At the proximal end, the **medial** and **lateral condyles** (separated by the **intercondylar eminence**) receive the distal end of the femur to form the knee joint. The **tibial tuberosity,** a roughened protrusion on the anterior tibial surface (just below the condyles), is the site of attachment of the patellar (kneecap) ligament. Small facets on the superior and inferior surface of the lateral condyle of the tibia articulate with the fibula. Distally, a process called the

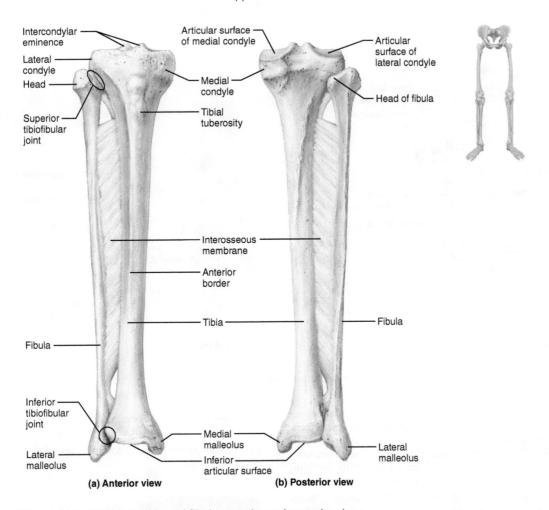

Figure 8 **Bones of the right leg.** Tibia and fibula, anterior and posterior views.

**medial malleolus** forms the inner (medial) bulge of the ankle. Lateral to this process, the inferior articular surface of the tibia articulates with the talus bone of the foot. The anterior surface of the tibia bears a sharpened ridge that is relatively unprotected by muscles. This so-called **anterior border** is easily felt beneath the skin.

The **fibula,** which lies parallel to the tibia, takes no part in forming the knee joint. Its proximal head articulates with the lateral condyle of the tibia. The fibula is thin and sticklike with a sharp anterior crest. It terminates distally in the **lateral malleolus,** which forms the outer part, or lateral bulge, of the ankle.

## The Foot

The bones of the foot include the 7 **tarsal** bones, 5 **metatarsals,** which form the instep, and 14 **phalanges,** which form the toes **(Figure 9)**. Body weight is concentrated on the two largest tarsals, which form the posterior aspect of the foot. These are the *calcaneus* (heel bone) and the *talus,* which lies between the tibia and the calcaneus. (The other tarsals are named and identified in Figure 9). The metatarsals are numbered I through V, medial to lateral. Like the fingers of

the hand, each toe has three phalanges except the great toe, which has two.

The bones in the foot are arranged to produce three strong arches—two longitudinal arches (medial and lateral) and one transverse arch (Figure 9b). Ligaments, binding the foot bones together, and tendons of the foot muscles hold the bones firmly in the arched position but still allow a certain degree of give. Weakened arches are referred to as fallen arches or flat feet.

### ACTIVITY 5

## Palpating the Surface Anatomy of the Pelvic Girdle and Lower Limb

Locate and palpate the following bone markings on yourself and/or your lab partner. Place a check mark in the boxes as you locate the bone markings. Seek assistance from your instructor for any markings that you are unable to locate.

☐ Iliac crest and anterior superior iliac spine: Rest your hands on your hips—they will be overlying the iliac crests. Trace the crest as far posteriorly as you can and then follow it

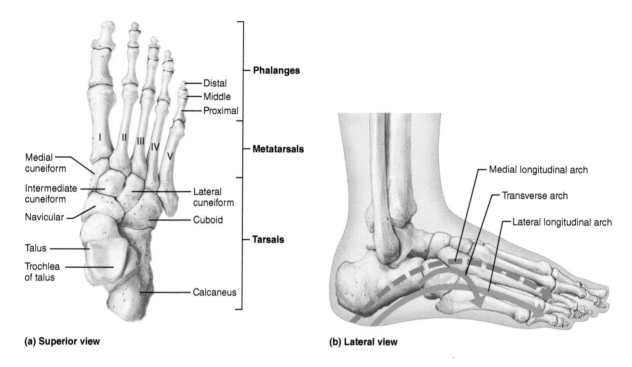

(a) Superior view

(b) Lateral view

Figure 9 **Bones of the right foot.** Arches of the right foot are diagrammed in **(b).**

anteriorly to the anterior superior iliac spine. This latter bone marking is easily felt in almost everyone and is clearly visible through the skin (and perhaps the clothing) of very slim people. (The posterior superior iliac spine is much less obvious and is usually indicated only by a dimple in the overlying skin. Check it out in the mirror tonight.)

☐  Greater trochanter of the femur: This is easier to locate in females than in males because of the wider female pelvis; also it is more likely to be clothed by bulky muscles in males. Try to locate it on yourself as the most lateral point of the proximal femur. It typically lies about 6 to 8 inches below the iliac crest.

☐  Patella and tibial tuberosity: Feel your kneecap and palpate the ligaments attached to its borders. Follow the inferior patellar ligament to the tibial tuberosity.

☐  Medial and lateral condyles of the femur and tibia: As you move from the patella inferiorly on the medial (and then the lateral) knee surface, you will feel first the femoral and then the tibial condyle.

☐  Medial malleolus: Feel the medial protrusion of your ankle, the medial malleolus of the distal tibia.

☐  Lateral malleolus: Feel the bulge of the lateral aspect of your ankle, the lateral malleolus of the fibula.

☐  Calcaneus: Attempt to follow the extent of your calcaneus, or heel bone. ■■■

**ACTIVITY 6**

## Constructing a Skeleton

1.  When you finish examining yourself and the disarticulated bones of the appendicular skeleton, work with your lab partner to arrange the disarticulated bones on the laboratory bench in their proper relative positions to form an entire skeleton. Careful observation of bone markings should help you distinguish between right and left members of bone pairs.

2.  When you believe that you have accomplished this task correctly, ask the instructor to check your arrangement to ensure that it is correct. If it is not, go to the articulated skeleton and check your bone arrangements. Also review the descriptions of the bone markings as necessary to correct your bone arrangement. ■■■

Name _____

Lab Time/Date _____

# The Appendicular Skeleton

R E V I E W   S H E E T

## Bones of the Pectoral Girdle and Upper Limb

**1.** Match the bone names or markings in column B with the descriptions in column A. The items in column B may be used more than once.

**Column A**

_____ 1. raised area on lateral surface of humerus to which deltoid muscle attaches

_____ 2. arm bone

_____, _____, 3. bones of the shoulder girdle

_____, _____, 4. forearm bones

_____ 5. scapular region to which the clavicle connects

_____ 6. shoulder girdle bone that does not attach to the axial skeleton

_____ 7. shoulder girdle bone that articulates with and transmits forces to the bony thorax

_____ 8. depression in the scapula that articulates with the humerus

_____ 9. process above the glenoid cavity that permits muscle attachment

_____ 10. the "collarbone"

_____ 11. distal condyle of the humerus that articulates with the ulna

_____ 12. medial bone of forearm in anatomical position

_____ 13. rounded knob on the humerus; adjoins the radius

_____ 14. anterior depression, superior to the trochlea, that receives part of the ulna when the forearm is flexed

_____ 15. forearm bone involved in formation of the elbow joint

_____ 16. wrist bones

_____ 17. finger bones

_____ 18. heads of these bones form the knuckles

_____, _____, 19. bones that articulate with the clavicle

**Column B**

a. acromion

b. capitulum

c. carpals

d. clavicle

e. coracoid process

f. coronoid fossa

g. deltoid tuberosity

h. glenoid cavity

i. humerus

j. metacarpals

k. olecranon

l. olecranon fossa

m. phalanges

n. radial styloid process

o. radial tuberosity

p. radius

q. scapula

r. sternum

s. trochlea

t. ulna

**2.** How is the arm held clear of the widest dimension of the thoracic cage?

_____

_____

**3.** What is the total number of phalanges in the hand? _____

**4.** What is the total number of carpals in the wrist? _____

Name the carpals (medial to lateral) in the proximal row. _____

In the distal row, they are (medial to lateral) _____

**5.** Using items from the list at the right, identify the anatomical landmarks and regions of the scapula.

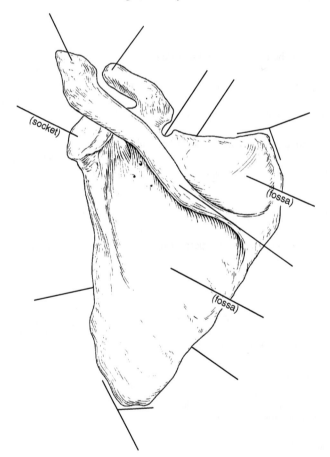

_Key:_

a. acromion

b. coracoid process

c. glenoid cavity

d. inferior angle

e. infraspinous fossa

f. lateral border

g. medial border

h. spine

i. superior angle

j. superior border

k. suprascapular notch

l. supraspinous fossa

**6.** Match the terms in the key with the appropriate leader lines on the drawings of the humerus and the radius and ulna. Also decide whether the bones shown are right or left bones and whether the view shown is an anterior or a posterior view.

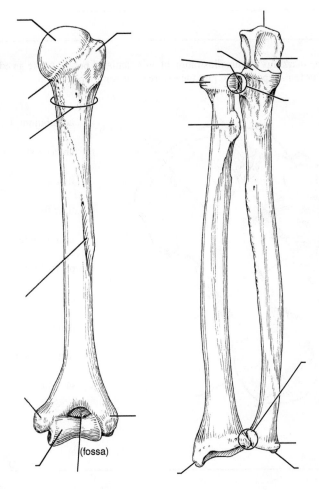

(fossa)

*Key:*

a.   anatomical neck

b.   coronoid process

c.   distal radioulnar joint

d.   greater tubercle

e.   head of humerus

f.   head of radius

g.   head of ulna

h.   lateral epicondyle

i.   medial epicondyle

j.   olecranon

k.   olecranon fossa

l.   proximal radioulnar joint

m.   radial groove

n.   radial notch

o.   radial styloid process

p.   radial tuberosity

q.   surgical neck

r.   trochlea

s.   trochlear notch

t.   ulnar styloid process

Circle the correct term for each pair in parentheses:

The humerus is a (right/left) bone in (an anterior/a posterior) view. The radius and ulna are (right/left) bones in (an anterior/a posterior) view.

# Bones of the Pelvic Girdle and Lower Limb

**7.** Compare the pectoral and pelvic girdles by choosing appropriate descriptive terms from the key.

*Key:*   a.   flexibility most important       d.   insecure axial and limb attachments
        b.   massive       e.   secure axial and limb attachments
        c.   lightweight       f.   weight-bearing most important

Pectoral: _____, _____, _____ Pelvic: _____, _____, _____

**8.** What organs are protected, at least in part, by the pelvic girdle? _____

_____

**9.** Distinguish between the true pelvis and the false pelvis. _____

_____

_____

**10.** Use letters from the key to identify the bone markings on this illustration of an articulated pelvis. Make an educated guess as to whether the illustration shows a male or female pelvis and provide two reasons for your decision.

(fossa)

(socket)

*Key:*

a.   acetabulum

b.   anterior superior iliac spine

c.   iliac crest

d.   iliac fossa

e.   ischial spine

f.   pelvic brim

g.   pubic crest

h.   pubic symphysis

i.   sacroiliac joint

j.   sacrum

This is a _____ (female/male) pelvis because:

_____

_____

**11.** Deduce why the pelvic bones of a four-legged animal such as the cat or pig are much less massive than those of the human.

_____

_____

**12.** A person instinctively curls over his abdominal area in times of danger. Why? _____

_____

**13.** For what anatomical reason do many women appear to be slightly knock-kneed? _____

_____

How might this anatomical arrangement contribute to knee injuries in female athletes?

_____

**14.** What structural changes result in *fallen arches*? _____

_____

**15.** Match the bone names and markings in column B with the descriptions in column A. The items in column B may be used more than once.

**Column A**

**Column B**

_____, _____, _____ and

        a.   acetabulum

_____ 1. fuse to form the coxal bone

        b.   calcaneus

_____ 2. "sit-down" bone of the coxal bone

        c.   femur

_____ 3. point where the coxal bones join anteriorly

        d.   fibula

_____ 4. superiormost margin of the coxal bone

        e.   gluteal tuberosity

_____ 5. deep socket in the coxal bone that receives the head of the thigh bone

        f.   greater and lesser trochanters

_____ 6. joint between axial skeleton and pelvic girdle

        g.   greater sciatic notch

_____ 7. longest, strongest bone in body

        h.   iliac crest

_____ 8. thin lateral leg bone

        i.   ilium

_____ 9. heavy medial leg bone

        j.   ischial tuberosity

_____, _____ 10. bones forming knee joint

        k.   ischium

_____ 11. point where the patellar ligament attaches

        l.   lateral malleolus

_____ 12. kneecap

        m.   lesser sciatic notch

_____ 13. shinbone

        n.   linea aspera

_____ 14. medial ankle projection

        o.   medial malleolus

_____ 15. lateral ankle projection

        p.   metatarsals

_____ 16. largest tarsal bone

        q.   obturator foramen

_____ 17. ankle bones

        r.   patella

_____ 18. bones forming the instep of the foot

        s.   pubic symphysis

_____ 19. opening in hip bone formed by the pubic and ischial rami

        t.   pubis

_____ and _____ 20. sites of muscle attachment on the proximal femur

        u.   sacroiliac joint

        v.   talus

_____ 21. tarsal bone that "sits" on the calcaneus

        w.   tarsals

_____ 22. weight-bearing bone of the leg

        x.   tibia

_____ 23. tarsal bone that articulates with the tibia

        y.   tibial tuberosity

**16.** Match the terms in the key with the appropriate leader lines on the drawings of the femur and the tibia and fibula. Also decide if these bones are right or left bones and whether the view shown is an anterior or a posterior view. Some items may be used more than once.

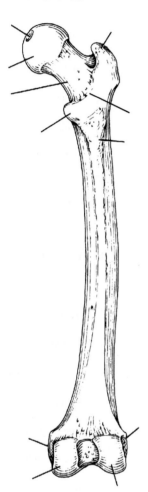

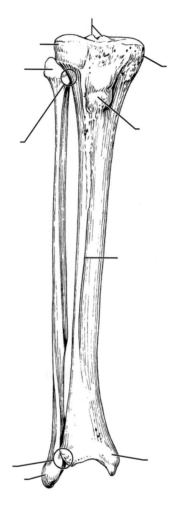

*Key:*

a. fovea capitis

b. gluteal tuberosity

c. greater trochanter

d. head of femur

e. head of fibula

f. inferior tibiofibular joint

g. intercondylar eminence

h. intertrochanteric crest

i. lateral condyle

j. lateral epicondyle

k. lateral malleolus

l. lesser trochanter

m. medial condyle

n. medial epicondyle

o. medial malleolus

p. neck of femur

q. superior tibiofibular joint

r. tibial anterior border

s. tibial tuberosity

Circle the correct term for each pair in parentheses:

The femur is a (right/left) bone in (an anterior/a posterior) view. The tibia and fibula are (right/left) bones in (an anterior/a posterior) view.

# Summary of Skeleton

**17.** Identify all indicated bones (or groups of bones) in the diagram of the articulated skeleton.

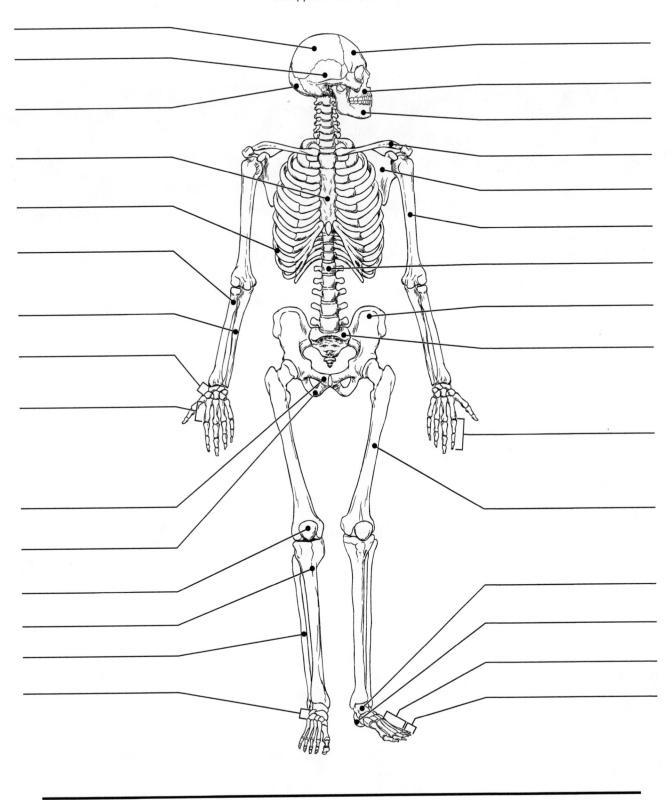

# Articulations and Body Movements

MATERIALS

□ Skull
□ Articulated skeleton
□ X ray of a child's bone showing the cartilaginous growth plate (if available)
□ Anatomical chart of joint types (if available)
□ Diarthrotic joint (fresh or preserved), preferably a beef knee joint sectioned sagittally (Alternatively, pig's feet with phalanges sectioned frontally could be used)
□ Disposable gloves
□ Water balloons and clamps
□ Functional models of hip, knee, and shoulder joints (if available)
□ X rays of normal and arthritic joints (if available)

OBJECTIVES

1. Name and describe the three functional categories of joints.
2. Name and describe the three structural categories of joints, and discuss how their structure is related to mobility.
3. Identify the types of synovial joints; indicate whether they are nonaxial, uniaxial, biaxial, or multiaxial, and describe the movements made by each.
4. Define *origin* and *insertion* of muscles.
5. Demonstrate or describe the various body movements.
6. Compare and contrast the structure and function of the shoulder and hip joints.
7. Describe the structure and function of the knee and temporomandibular joints.

PRE-LAB QUIZ

1. Name one of the two functions of an articulation, or joint. _____ _____
2. The functional classification of joints is based on
   a. a joint cavity
   b. amount of connective tissue
   c. amount of movement allowed by the joint
3. Structural classification of joints includes fibrous, cartilaginous, and _____, which have a fluid-filled cavity between articulating bones.
4. Circle the correct underlined term. Sutures, which have their irregular edges of bone joined by short fibers of connective tissue, are an example of fibrous / cartilaginous joints.
5. Circle True or False. All synovial joints are diarthroses, or freely movable joints.
6. Circle the correct underlined term. Every muscle of the body is attached to a bone or other connective tissue structure at two points. The origin / insertion is the more movable attachment.
7. The hip joint is an example of a _____ synovial joint.
   a. ball-and-socket    c. pivot
   b. hinge              d. plane
8. Movement of a limb *away* from the midline or median plane of the body in the frontal plane is known as
   a. abduction      c. extension
   b. eversion       d. rotation
9. Circle the correct underlined term. This type of movement is common in ball-and-socket joints and can be described as the movement of a bone around its longitudinal axis. It is rotation / flexion.
10. Circle True or False. The knee joint is the most freely movable joint in the body.

MasteringA&P° For related exercise study tools, go to the Study Area of MasteringA&P. There you will find:
• Practice Anatomy Lab PAL
• PhysioEx PEx
• A&PFlix *A&PFlix*
• Practice quizzes, Histology Atlas, eText, Videos, and more!

Articulations and Body Movements

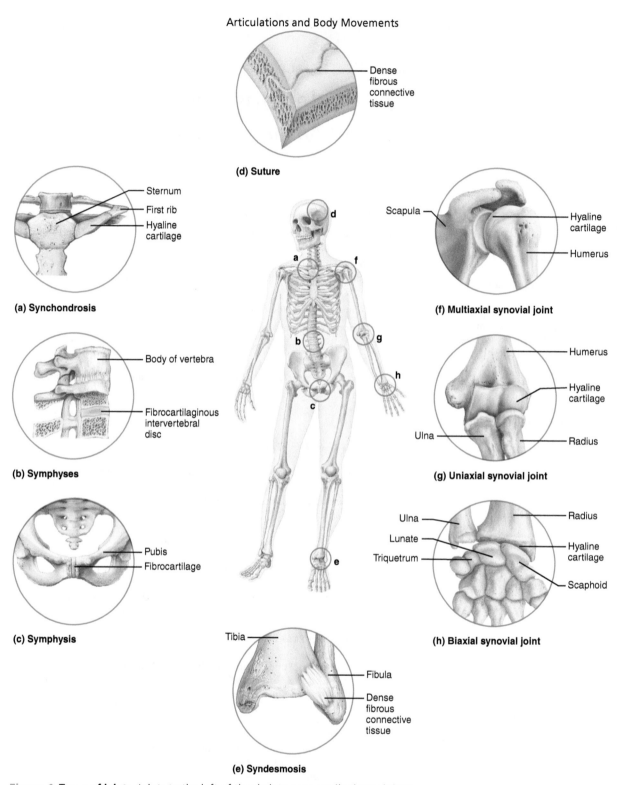

(d) Suture

Dense fibrous connective tissue

Sternum
First rib
Hyaline cartilage

(a) Synchondrosis

Scapula
Hyaline cartilage
Humerus

(f) Multiaxial synovial joint

Body of vertebra

Fibrocartilaginous intervertebral disc

(b) Symphyses

Humerus
Hyaline cartilage
Ulna
Radius

(g) Uniaxial synovial joint

Pubis
Fibrocartilage

(c) Symphysis

Ulna
Lunate
Triquetrum
Radius
Hyaline cartilage
Scaphoid

(h) Biaxial synovial joint

Tibia
Fibula
Dense fibrous connective tissue

(e) Syndesmosis

**Figure 1 Types of joints.** Joints to the left of the skeleton are cartilaginous joints; joints above and below the skeleton are fibrous joints; joints to the right of the skeleton are synovial joints. **(a)** Joint between costal cartilage of rib 1 and the sternum. **(b)** Intervertebral discs of fibrocartilage connecting adjacent vertebrae. **(c)** Fibrocartilaginous pubic symphysis connecting the pubic bones anteriorly. **(d)** Dense fibrous connective tissue connecting interlocking skull bones. **(e)** Ligament of dense fibrous connective tissue connecting the inferior ends of the tibia and fibula. **(f)** Shoulder joint. **(g)** Elbow joint. **(h)** Wrist joint.

With rare exceptions, every bone in the body is connected to, or forms a joint with, at least one other bone. **Articulations,** or joints, perform two functions for the body. They (1) hold the bones together and (2) allow the rigid skeletal system some flexibility so that gross body movements can occur.

Joints may be classified structurally or functionally. The structural classification is based on the presence of connective tissue fiber, cartilage, or a joint cavity between the articulating bones. Structurally, there are *fibrous, cartilaginous,* and *synovial joints.*

The functional classification focuses on the amount of movement allowed at the joint. On this basis, there are **synarthroses,** or immovable joints; **amphiarthroses,** or slightly movable joints; and **diarthroses,** or freely movable joints. Freely movable joints predominate in the limbs, whereas immovable and slightly movable joints are largely restricted to the axial skeleton, where firm bony attachments and protection of enclosed organs are priorities.

As a general rule, fibrous joints are immovable, and synovial joints are freely movable. Cartilaginous joints offer both rigid and slightly movable examples. Since the structural categories are more clear-cut, we will use the structural classification here and indicate functional properties as appropriate.

## Fibrous Joints

In **fibrous joints,** the bones are joined by fibrous tissue. No joint cavity is present. The amount of movement allowed depends on the length of the fibers uniting the bones. Although some fibrous joints are slightly movable, most are synarthrotic and permit virtually no movement.

The two major types of fibrous joints are sutures and syndesmoses. In **sutures** (Figure 1d) the irregular edges of the bones interlock and are united by very short connective tissue fibers, as in most joints of the skull. In **syndesmoses** the articulating bones are connected by short ligaments of dense fibrous tissue; the bones do not interlock. The joint at the inferior end of the tibia and fibula is an example of a syndesmosis (Figure 1e). Although this syndesmosis allows some give, it is classed functionally as a synarthrosis. Not illustrated here is a **gomphosis,** in which a tooth is secured in a bony socket by the periodontal ligament.

**ACTIVITY 1**

### Identifying Fibrous Joints

Examine a human skull. Notice that adjacent bone surfaces do not actually touch but are separated by fibrous connective tissue. Also examine a skeleton and anatomical chart of joint types and the table of joints (**Table 1**) for examples of fibrous joints. ■

## Cartilaginous Joints

In **cartilaginous joints,** the articulating bone ends are connected by a plate or pad of cartilage. No joint cavity is present. The two major types of cartilaginous joints are synchondroses and symphyses. Although there is variation, most cartilaginous joints are *slightly movable* (amphiarthrotic) functionally. In **symphyses** (*symphysis* = a growing together), the bones are connected by a broad, flat disc of fibrocartilage. The intervertebral joints between adjacent vertebral bodies and the pubic symphysis of the pelvis are symphyses (see Figure 1b and c). In **synchondroses** the bony

portions are united by hyaline cartilage. The articulation of the costal cartilage of the first rib with the sternum (Figure 1a) is a synchondrosis, but perhaps the best examples of synchondroses are the epiphyseal plates seen in the long bones of growing children. View an X ray of the cartilaginous growth plate (epiphyseal disc) of a child's bone if one is available. The epiphyseal plates are flexible during childhood, but eventually they are totally ossified.

**ACTIVITY 2**

### Identifying Cartilaginous Joints

Identify the cartilaginous joints on a human skeleton, the table of joints (Table 1), and an anatomical chart of joint types. ■

## Synovial Joints

**Synovial joints** are those in which the articulating bone ends are separated by a joint cavity containing synovial fluid (see Figure 1f–h). All synovial joints are diarthroses, or freely movable joints. Their mobility varies: some synovial joints permit only small gliding movements, and others can move in several planes. Most joints in the body are synovial joints.

All synovial joints have the following structural characteristics (**Figure 2**):

- The joint surfaces are enclosed by a two-layered *articular capsule* (a sleeve of connective tissue), creating a joint cavity.

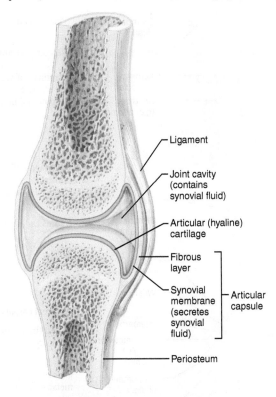

— Ligament

— Joint cavity (contains synovial fluid)

— Articular (hyaline) cartilage

— Fibrous layer

— Synovial membrane (secretes synovial fluid)

} Articular capsule

— Periosteum

**Figure 2 General structure of a synovial joint.** The articulating bone ends are covered with articular cartilage, and enclosed within an articular capsule that is typically reinforced by ligaments externally. Internally the fibrous layer is lined with a smooth synovial membrane that secretes synovial fluid.

| Table 1 | Structural and Functional Characteristics of Body Joints |
|---|---|

| Illustration | Joint | Articulating bones | Structural type* | Functional type; movements allowed |
|---|---|---|---|---|
| | Skull | Cranial and facial bones | Fibrous; suture | Synarthrotic; no movement |
| | Temporo-mandibular | Temporal bone of skull and mandible | Synovial; modified hinge† (contains articular disc) | Diarthrotic; gliding and uniaxial rotation; slight lateral movement, elevation, depression, protraction, and retraction of mandible |
| | Atlanto-occipital | Occipital bone of skull and atlas | Synovial; condylar | Diarthrotic; biaxial; flexion, extension, lateral flexion, circumduction of head on neck |
| | Atlantoaxial | Atlas ($C_1$) and axis ($C_2$) | Synovial; pivot | Diarthrotic; uniaxial; rotation of the head |
| | Intervertebral | Between adjacent vertebral bodies | Cartilaginous; symphysis | Amphiarthrotic; slight movement |
| | Intervertebral | Between articular processes | Synovial; plane | Diarthrotic; gliding |
| | Costovertebral | Vertebrae (transverse processes or bodies) and ribs | Synovial; plane | Diarthrotic; gliding of ribs |
| | Sternoclavicular | Sternum and clavicle | Synovial; shallow saddle (contains articular disc) | Diarthrotic; multiaxial (allows clavicle to move in all axes) |
| | Sternocostal (first) | Sternum and rib 1 | Cartilaginous; synchondrosis | Synarthrotic; no movement |
| | Sternocostal | Sternum and ribs 2–7 | Synovial; double plane | Diarthrotic; gliding |
| | Acromio-clavicular | Acromion of scapula and clavicle | Synovial; plane (contains articular disc) | Diarthrotic; gliding and rotation of scapula on clavicle |
| | Shoulder (glenohumeral) | Scapula and humerus | Synovial; ball and socket | Diarthrotic; multiaxial; flexion, extension, abduction, adduction, circumduction, rotation of humerus |
| | | Ulna (and radius) with humerus | Synovial; hinge | Diarthrotic; uniaxial; flexion, extension of forearm |
| | Elbow | Radius and ulna | Synovial; pivot | Diarthrotic; uniaxial; pivot (head of radius rotates in radial notch of ulna) |
| | Proximal radioulnar | Radius and ulna | Synovial; pivot (contains articular disc) | Diarthrotic; uniaxial; rotation of radius around long axis of forearm to allow pronation and supination |
| | Distal radioulnar | Radius and proximal carpals | Synovial; condylar | Diarthrotic; biaxial; flexion, extension, abduction, adduction, circumduction of hand |
| | Wrist | Adjacent carpals | Synovial; plane | Diarthrotic; gliding |
| | Intercarpal | Carpal (trapezium) and metacarpal I | Synovial; saddle | Diarthrotic; biaxial; flexion, extension, abduction, adduction, circumduction, opposition of metacarpal I |
| | Carpometacarpal of digit 1 (thumb) | Carpal(s) and metacarpal(s) | Synovial; plane | Diarthrotic; gliding of metacarpals |
| | Carpometacarpal of digits 2–5 | Metacarpal and proximal phalanx | Synovial; condylar | Diarthrotic; biaxial; flexion, extension, abduction, adduction, circumduction of fingers |
| | Metacarpo-phalangeal (knuckle) | Adjacent phalanges | Synovial; hinge | Diarthrotic; uniaxial; flexion, extension of fingers |
| | Interphalangeal (finger) | | | |

| Table 1 | (continued) | | | |
|---|---|---|---|---|

| Illustration | Joint | Articulating bones | Structural type* | Functional type; movements allowed |
|---|---|---|---|---|
| | Sacroiliac | Sacrum and coxal bone | Synovial; plane | Diarthrotic; little movement, slight gliding possible (more during pregnancy) |
| | Pubic symphysis | Pubic bones | Cartilaginous; symphysis | Amphiarthrotic; slight movement (enhanced during pregnancy) |
| | Hip (coxal) | Hip bone and femur | Synovial; ball and socket | Diarthrotic; multiaxial; flexion, extension, abduction, adduction, rotation, circumduction of thigh |
| | Knee (tibiofemoral) | Femur and tibia | Synovial; modified hinge† (contains articular discs) | Diarthrotic; biaxial; flexion, extension of leg, some rotation allowed |
| | Knee (femoropatellar) | Femur and patella | Synovial; plane | Diarthrotic; gliding of patella |
| | Superior tibiofibular | Tibia and fibula (proximally) | Synovial; plane | Diarthrotic; gliding of fibula |
| | Inferior tibiofibular | Tibia and fibula (distally) | Fibrous; syndesmosis | Synarthrotic; slight "give" during dorsiflexion |
| | Ankle | Tibia and fibula with talus | Synovial; hinge | Diarthrotic; uniaxial; dorsiflexion, and plantar flexion of foot |
| | Intertarsal | Adjacent tarsals | Synovial; plane | Diarthrotic; gliding; inversion and eversion of foot |
| | Tarsometatarsal | Tarsal(s) and metatarsal(s) | Synovial; plane | Diarthrotic; gliding of metatarsals |
| | Metatarso-phalangeal | Metatarsal and proximal phalanx | Synovial; condylar | Diarthrotic; biaxial; flexion, extension, abduction, adduction, circumduction of great toe |
| | Interphalangeal (toe) | Adjacent phalanges | Synovial; hinge | Diarthrotic; uniaxial; flexion, extension of toes |

*__Fibrous joint__ indicated by orange circles; __cartilaginous joints,__ by blue circles; __synovial joints,__ by purple circles.
†These modified hinge joints are structurally bicondylar.

• The inner layer is a smooth connective tissue membrane, called the *synovial membrane,* which produces a lubricating fluid (synovial fluid) that reduces friction. The outer layer, or *fibrous layer,* is dense irregular connective tissue.

• *Articular* (hyaline) *cartilage* covers the surfaces of the bones forming the joint.

• The articular capsule is typically reinforced with ligaments and may contain *bursae* (fluid-filled sacs that reduce friction where tendons cross bone).

• Fibrocartilage pads *(articular discs)* may be present within the capsule.

## ACTIVITY 3

### Examining Synovial Joint Structure

Examine a beef or pig joint to identify the general structural features of diarthrotic joints as listed above.

⚠ If the joint is freshly obtained from the slaughterhouse and you will be handling it, don disposable gloves before beginning your observations. ▬

## ACTIVITY 4

### Demonstrating the Importance of Friction-Reducing Structures

1. Obtain a small water balloon and clamp. Partially fill the balloon with water (it should still be flaccid), and clamp it closed.

2. Position the balloon atop one of your fists and press down on its top surface with the other fist. Push on the balloon until your two fists touch and move your fists back and forth over one another. Assess the amount of friction generated.

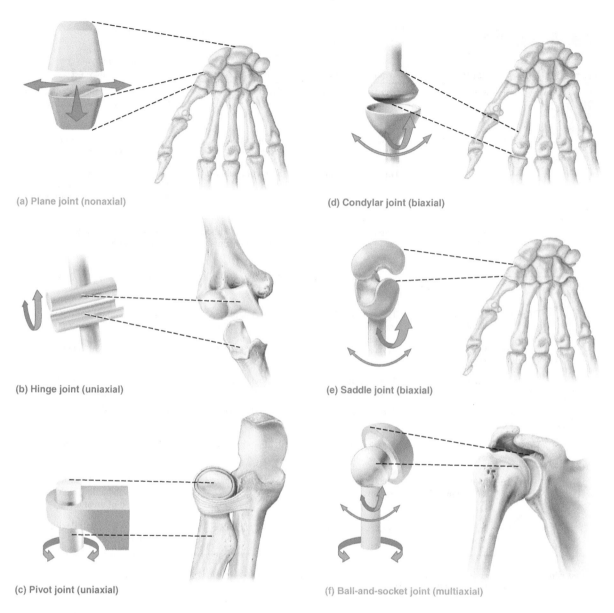

(a) Plane joint (nonaxial)

(d) Condylar joint (biaxial)

(b) Hinge joint (uniaxial)

(e) Saddle joint (biaxial)

(c) Pivot joint (uniaxial)

(f) Ball-and-socket joint (multiaxial)

Figure 3 **Types of synovial joints.** Dashed lines indicate the articulating bones. **(a)** Intercarpal joint. **(b)** Elbow. **(c)** Proximal radioulnar joint. **(d)** Metacarpophalangeal joint. **(e)** Carpometacarpal joint of the thumb. **(f)** Shoulder.

3. Unclamp the balloon and add more water. The goal is to get just enough water in the balloon so that your fists cannot come into contact with one another, but instead remain separated by a thin water layer when pressure is applied to the balloon.

4. Repeat the movements in step 2 to assess the amount of friction generated.

How does the presence of a sac containing fluid influence the amount of friction generated?

_____

What anatomical structure(s) does the water-containing balloon mimic?

_____

What anatomical structures might be represented by your fists?

_____

## Types of Synovial Joints

The many types of synovial joints can be subdivided according to their function and structure. The shapes of the articular surfaces determine the types of movements that can occur at the joint, and they also determine the structural classification of the joints (**Figure 3**):

- Plane (Nonaxial): Articulating surfaces are flat or slightly curved. These surfaces allow only gliding movements as the surfaces slide past one another. Examples include intercarpal joints, intertarsal joints, and joints between vertebral articular surfaces.

- Hinge (Uniaxial): The rounded or cylindrical process of one bone fits into the concave surface of another bone, allowing movement in one plane, usually flexion and extension. Examples include the elbow and interphalangeal joints.

- Pivot (Uniaxial): The rounded surface of one bone articulates with a shallow depression or foramen in another bone, permitting rotational movement in one plane. Examples include the proximal radioulnar joint and the atlantoaxial joint (between atlas and axis—$C_1$ and $C_2$).

- Condylar (Biaxial): The oval condyle of one bone fits into an ellipsoidal depression in another bone to allow movement in two planes, usually flexion/extension and abduction/adduction. Examples include the wrist and metacarpophalangeal (knuckle) joints.

- Saddle (Biaxial): Articulating surfaces are saddle shaped; one surface is convex, and the other is concave. This type of joint permits movement in two planes, flexion/extension and abduction/adduction. Examples include the carpometacarpal joints of the thumbs.

- Ball-and-socket (Multiaxial): The ball-shaped head of one bone fits into a cuplike depression of another bone. These joints permit flexion/extension, abduction/adduction, and rotation, which combine to allow movement in many planes. Examples include the shoulder and hip joints.

## Movements Allowed by Synovial Joints

Every muscle of the body is attached to bone (or other connective tissue structures) at two points—the **origin** (the stationary, immovable, or less movable attachment) and the **insertion** (the movable attachment). Body movement occurs when muscles contract across diarthrotic synovial joints (**Figure 4**). When the muscle contracts and its fibers shorten, the insertion moves toward the origin. The type of movement depends on the construction of the joint and on the placement of the muscle relative to the joint. The most common types of body movements are described below (and illustrated in **Figure 5**).

**ACTIVITY 5**

### Demonstrating Movements of Synovial Joints

Attempt to demonstrate each movement as you read through the following material:

**Flexion** (Figure 5a–c): A movement, generally in the sagittal plane, that decreases the angle of the joint and reduces the distance between the two bones. Flexion is typical of hinge joints (bending the knee or elbow) but is also common at ball-and-socket joints (bending forward at the hip).

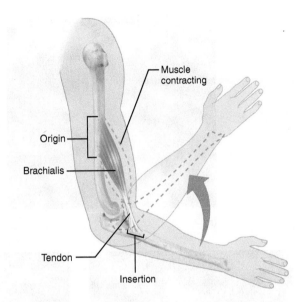

**Figure 4 Muscle attachments (origin and insertion).** When a skeletal muscle contracts, its insertion moves toward its origin.

**Extension** (Figure 5a–c): A movement that increases the angle of a joint and the distance between two bones or parts of the body (straightening the knee or elbow); the opposite of flexion. If extension proceeds beyond anatomical position (bends the trunk backward), it is termed *hyperextension.*

**Abduction** (Figure 5d): Movement of a limb away from the midline or median plane of the body, generally on the frontal plane, or the fanning movement of fingers or toes when they are spread apart.

**Adduction** (Figure 5d): Movement of a limb toward the midline of the body or drawing the fingers or toes together; the opposite of abduction.

**Rotation** (Figure 5e): Movement of a bone around its longitudinal axis without lateral or medial displacement. Rotation, a common movement of ball-and-socket joints, also describes the movement of the atlas around the dens of the axis.

**Circumduction** (Figure 5d): A combination of flexion, extension, abduction, and adduction commonly observed in ball-and-socket joints like the shoulder. The proximal end of the limb remains stationary, and the distal end moves in a circle. The limb as a whole outlines a cone. Condylar and saddle joints also allow circumduction.

**Pronation** (Figure 5f): Movement of the palm of the hand from an anterior or upward-facing position to a posterior or downward-facing position. The distal end of the radius moves across the ulna so that the bones form an X.

**Supination** (Figure 5f): Movement of the palm from a posterior position to an anterior position (the anatomical

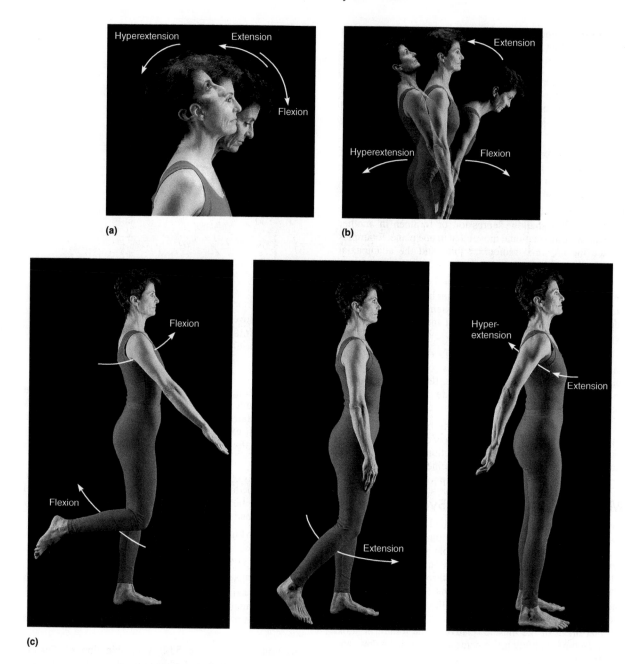

**Figure 5 Movements occurring at synovial joints of the body. (a)** Flexion, extension, and hyperextension of the neck. **(b)** Flexion, extension and hyperextension of the vertebral column. **(c)** Flexion and extension of the knee and shoulder, and hyperextension of the shoulder.

position); the opposite of pronation. During supination, the radius and ulna are parallel.

The last four terms refer to movements of the foot:

**Dorsiflexion** (Figure 5g): A movement of the ankle joint that lifts the foot so that its superior surface approaches the shin.

**Plantar flexion** (Figure 5g): A movement of the ankle joint in which the foot is flexed downward as if standing on one's toes or pointing the toes.

**Inversion** (Figure 5h): A movement that turns the sole of the foot medially.

**Eversion** (Figure 5h): A movement that turns the sole of the foot laterally; the opposite of inversion. ■

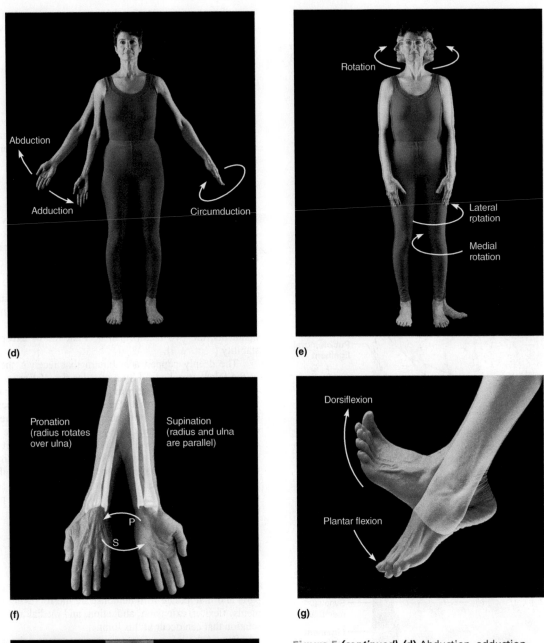

**(d)**

**(e)**

**(f)**

**(g)**

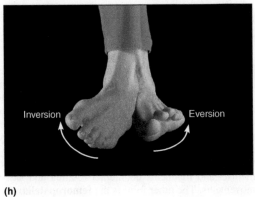

**(h)**

**Figure 5** *(continued)* **(d)** Abduction, adduction, and circumduction of the upper limb. **(e)** Rotation of the head and lower limb. **(f)** Pronation and supination of the forearm. **(g)** Dorsiflexion and plantar flexion of the foot. **(h)** Inversion and eversion of the foot.

185

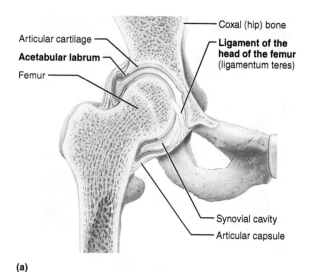

**(a)**

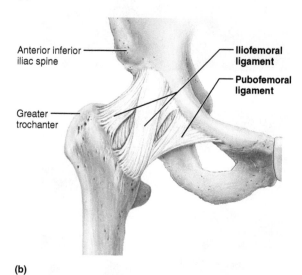

**(b)**

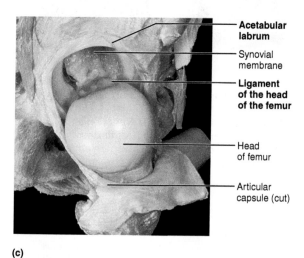

**(c)**

Figure 6 **Hip joint relationships. (a)** Frontal section through the right hip joint. **(b)** Anterior superficial view of the right hip joint. **(c)** Photograph of the interior of the hip joint, lateral view.

# Selected Synovial Joints

Now you will have the opportunity to compare and contrast the structure of the hip and knee joints and to investigate the structure and movements of the temporomandibular joint and shoulder joint.

## The Hip and Knee Joints

Both of these joints are large weight-bearing joints of the lower limb, but they differ substantially in their security. Read through the brief descriptive material below, and look at the questions in the review sheet at the end of this exercise before beginning your comparison.

### The Hip Joint

The hip joint is a ball-and-socket joint, so movements can occur in all possible planes. However, its movements are definitely limited by its deep socket and strong reinforcing ligaments, the two factors that account for its exceptional stability **(Figure 6)**.

The deeply cupped acetabulum that receives the head of the femur is enhanced by a circular rim of fibrocartilage called the **acetabular labrum.** Because the diameter of the labrum is smaller than that of the femur's head, dislocations of the hip are rare. A short ligament, the **ligament of the head of the femur** *(ligamentum teres)* runs from the pitlike **fovea capitis** on the femur head to the acetabulum where it helps to secure the femur. Several strong ligaments, including the **iliofemoral** and **pubofemoral** anteriorly and the **ischiofemoral** that spirals posteriorly (not shown), are arranged so that they "screw" the femur head into the socket when a person stands upright.

### ACTIVITY 6

### Demonstrating Actions at the Hip Joint

If a functional hip joint model is available, identify the joint parts and manipulate it to demonstrate the following movements: flexion, extension, abduction, and medial and lateral rotation that can occur at this joint.

Reread the information on what movements the associated ligaments restrict, and verify that information during your joint manipulations. ■

### The Knee Joint

The knee is the largest and most complex joint in the body. Three joints in one **(Figure 7)**, it allows extension, flexion, and a little rotation. The **tibiofemoral joint,** actually a duplex joint between the femoral condyles above and the **menisci** (semilunar cartilages) of the tibia below, is functionally a hinge joint, a very unstable one made slightly more secure by the menisci (Figure 7b and d). Some rotation occurs when the knee is partly flexed, but during extension, the menisci and ligaments counteract rotation and side-to-side movements. The other joint is the **femoropatellar joint,** the intermediate joint anteriorly (Figure 7a and c).

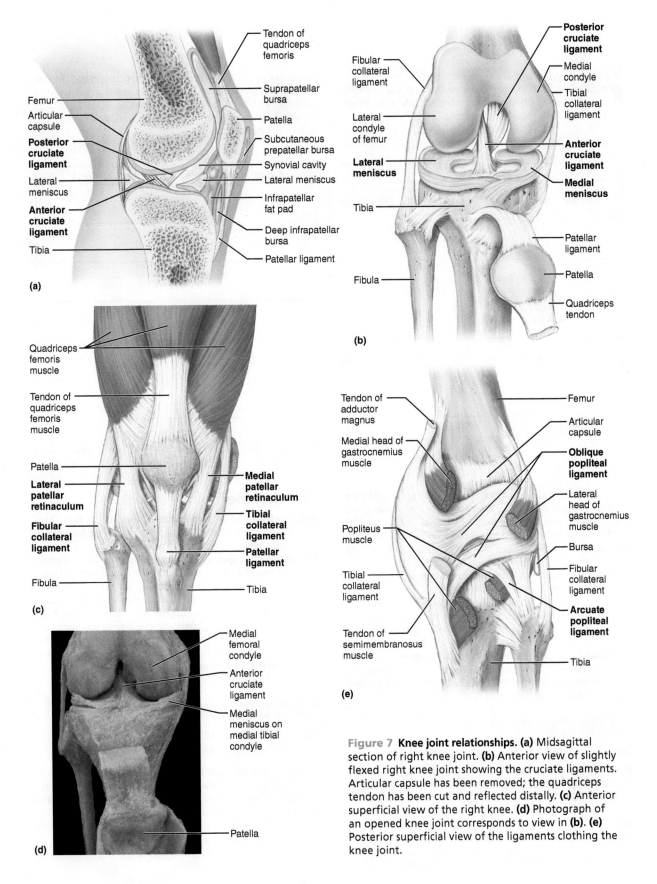

**(a)**

Tendon of quadriceps femoris

Femur

Articular capsule

**Posterior cruciate ligament**

Lateral meniscus

**Anterior cruciate ligament**

Tibia

Suprapatellar bursa

Patella

Subcutaneous prepatellar bursa

Synovial cavity

Lateral meniscus

Infrapatellar fat pad

Deep infrapatellar bursa

Patellar ligament

**(b)**

**Posterior cruciate ligament**

Fibular collateral ligament

Lateral condyle of femur

**Lateral meniscus**

Tibia

Fibula

Medial condyle

Tibial collateral ligament

**Anterior cruciate ligament**

**Medial meniscus**

Patellar ligament

Patella

Quadriceps tendon

**(c)**

Quadriceps femoris muscle

Tendon of quadriceps femoris muscle

Patella

**Lateral patellar retinaculum**

**Fibular collateral ligament**

Fibula

Tibia

**Medial patellar retinaculum**

**Tibial collateral ligament**

**Patellar ligament**

**(d)**

Medial femoral condyle

Anterior cruciate ligament

Medial meniscus on medial tibial condyle

Patella

**(e)**

Tendon of adductor magnus

Medial head of gastrocnemius muscle

Popliteus muscle

Tibial collateral ligament

Tendon of semimembranosus muscle

Femur

Articular capsule

**Oblique popliteal ligament**

Lateral head of gastrocnemius muscle

Bursa

Fibular collateral ligament

**Arcuate popliteal ligament**

Tibia

**Figure 7** **Knee joint relationships. (a)** Midsagittal section of right knee joint. **(b)** Anterior view of slightly flexed right knee joint showing the cruciate ligaments. Articular capsule has been removed; the quadriceps tendon has been cut and reflected distally. **(c)** Anterior superficial view of the right knee. **(d)** Photograph of an opened knee joint corresponds to view in **(b)**. **(e)** Posterior superficial view of the ligaments clothing the knee joint.

187

## Articulations: "Simon Says"

Working in groups of three or four, play a game of "Simon Says" using the movements defined in the exercise. One student will play the role of "Simon" while the others perform the movement. For example, when "Simon" says, "Simon says, perform flexion at the elbow," the remaining students would flex their arm. Take turns playing the role of Simon. As you perform the movements, consider and discuss whether the joint allows for other movements and whether the joint is uniaxial, biaxial, or multiaxial. (Use Table 1 as a guide.) After playing for 15–20 minutes, complete the following tables.

|  | Name of joint | Movements allowed |
|---|---|---|
| 1. List two uniaxial joints and describe the movements at each. |  |  |
|  |  |  |
| 2. List two biaxial joints and describe the movements at each. |  |  |
|  |  |  |
| 3. List two multiaxial joints and describe the movements at each. |  |  |
|  |  |  |

The knee is unique in that it is only partly enclosed by an articular capsule. Anteriorly, where the capsule is absent, are three broad ligaments, the **patellar ligament** and the **medial and lateral patellar retinacula** (retainers), which run from the patella to the tibia below and merge with the capsule on either side.

Capsular ligaments including the **fibular** and **tibial collateral ligaments** (which prevent rotation during extension) and the **oblique popliteal** and **arcuate popliteal ligaments** are crucial in reinforcing the knee. The knees have a built-in locking device that must be "unlocked" by the popliteus muscles (Figure 7e) before the knees can be flexed again. The **cruciate ligaments** are intracapsular ligaments that cross (*cruci* = cross) in the notch between the femoral condyles. They prevent anterior-posterior displacement of the joint and overflexion and hyperextension of the joint.

## Demonstrating Actions at the Knee Joint

If a functional model of a knee joint is available, identify the joint parts and manipulate it to illustrate the following movements: flexion, extension, and medial and lateral rotation.

Reread the information on what movements the various associated ligaments restrict, and verify that information during your joint manipulations. ▬

## The Shoulder Joint

The shoulder joint or **glenohumeral joint** is the most freely moving joint of the body. The rounded head of the humerus fits the shallow glenoid cavity of the scapula (Figure 8). A rim of fibrocartilage, the **glenoid labrum,** deepens the cavity slightly.

The articular capsule enclosing the joint is thin and loose, contributing to ease of movement. Few ligaments reinforce the shoulder, most of them located anteriorly. The **coracohumeral ligament** helps support the weight of the upper limb, and three weak **glenohumeral ligaments** strengthen the front of the capsule. In some people they are absent. Muscle tendons from the biceps brachii and **rotator cuff** muscles (subscapularis, supraspinatus, infraspinatus, and teres minor) contribute most to shoulder stability.

## Demonstrating Actions at the Shoulder Joint

If a functional shoulder joint model is available, identify the joint parts and manipulate the model to demonstrate the following movements: flexion, extension, abduction, adduction, circumduction, and medial and lateral rotation.

Note where the joint is weakest and verify the most common direction of a dislocated humerus. ▬

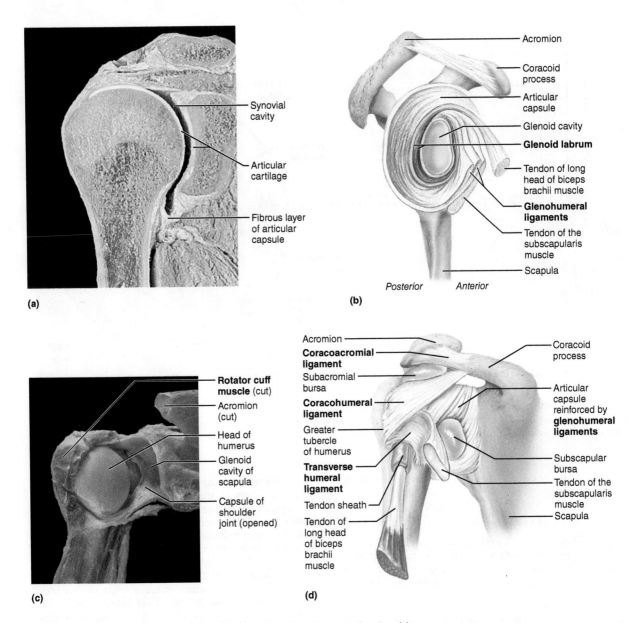

**Figure 8 Shoulder joint relationships. (a)** Frontal section through the shoulder. **(b)** Right shoulder joint, cut open and viewed from the lateral aspect; humerus removed. **(c)** Photograph of the interior of the shoulder joint, anterior view. **(d)** Anterior superficial view of the right shoulder.

## The Temporomandibular Joint

The **temporomandibular joint (TMJ)** lies just anterior to the ear **(Figure 9)**, where the egg-shaped condylar process of the mandible articulates with the inferior surface of the squamous region of the temporal bone. The temporal bone joint surface has a complicated shape: posteriorly is the **mandibular fossa** and anteriorly is a bony knob called the **articular tubercle.** The joint's articular capsule, though strengthened by the **lateral ligament,** is slack; an articular disc divides the joint cavity into superior and inferior compartments. Typically, the condylar process–mandibular fossa connection allows the familiar hingelike movements of elevating and depressing the

mandible to open and close the mouth. However, when the mouth is opened wide, the condylar process glides anteriorly and is braced against the dense bone of the articular tubercle so that the mandible is not forced superiorly when we bite hard foods.

### ACTIVITY 9

### Examining the Action at the TMJ

While placing your fingers over the area just anterior to the ear, open and close your mouth to feel the hinge action at the TMJ. Then, keeping your fingers on the TMJ, yawn to

189

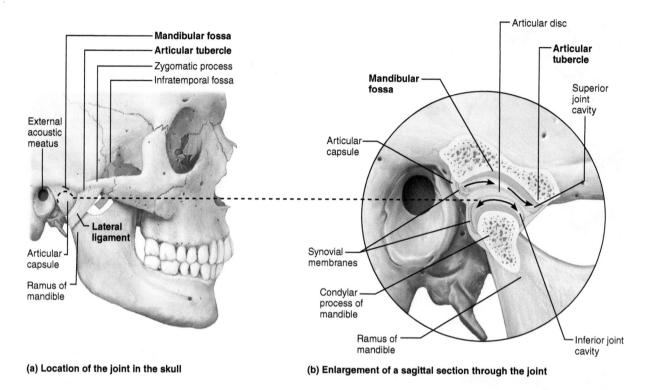

Mandibular fossa
Articular tubercle
Zygomatic process
Infratemporal fossa

External
acoustic
meatus

Lateral
ligament

Articular
capsule

Ramus of
mandible

Articular disc

Articular
tubercle

Mandibular
fossa

Superior
joint
cavity

Articular
capsule

Synovial
membranes

Condylar
process of
mandible

Ramus of
mandible

Inferior joint
cavity

**(a) Location of the joint in the skull**

**(b) Enlargement of a sagittal section through the joint**

**Figure 9** **The temporomandibular (jaw) joint relationships.** Note that the superior and inferior compartments of the joint cavity allow different movements indicated by arrows.

demonstrate the anterior gliding of the condylar process of the mandible. ▄▄

## Joint Disorders

Most of us don't think about our joints until something goes wrong with them. Joint pains and malfunctions are caused by a variety of things. For example, a hard blow to the knee can cause a painful bursitis, known as "water on the knee," due to damage to, or inflammation of, the patellar bursa. Slippage of a fibrocartilage pad or the tearing of a ligament may result in a painful condition that persists over a long period, since these poorly vascularized structures heal so slowly.

Sprains and dislocations are other types of joint problems. In a **sprain,** the ligaments reinforcing a joint are damaged by overstretching or are torn away from the bony attachment. Since both ligaments and tendons are cords of dense connective tissue with a poor blood supply, sprains heal slowly and are quite painful.

**Dislocations** occur when bones are forced out of their normal position in the joint cavity. They are normally accompanied by torn or stressed ligaments and considerable inflammation. The process of returning the bone to its proper position, called reduction, should be done only by a physician. Attempts by the untrained person to "snap the bone back into its socket" are often more harmful than helpful.

Advancing years also take their toll on joints. Weight-bearing joints in particular eventually begin to degenerate. *Adhesions* (fibrous bands) may form between the surfaces where bones join, and extraneous bone tissue *(spurs)* may grow along the joint edges. Such degenerative changes lead to the complaint so often heard from the elderly: "My joints are getting so stiff. . . ."

• If possible, compare an X ray of an arthritic joint to one of a normal joint. ✚

# Articulations and Body Movements

## Fibrous, Cartilaginous, and Synovial Joints

**1.** Use key responses to identify the joint types described below.

*Key:*   a.  cartilaginous          b.  fibrous          c.  synovial

_____ 1.   typically allows a slight degree of movement

_____ 2.   includes joints between the vertebral bodies and the pubic symphysis

_____ 3.   essentially immovable joints

_____ 4.   sutures are the most remembered examples

_____ 5.   characterized by cartilage connecting the bony portions

_____ 6.   all characterized by a fibrous articular capsule lined with a synovial membrane surrounding a joint cavity

_____ 7.   all are freely movable or diarthrotic

_____ 8.   bone regions united by fibrous connective tissue

_____ 9.   include the hip, knee, and elbow joints

**2.** Describe the tissue type and function of the following structures in relation to a synovial joint and label the structures indicated by leader lines in the diagram. Use an appropriate reference if needed.

ligament: _____

_____

tendon: _____

_____

articular cartilage: _____

_____

synovial membrane: _____

_____

_____

bursa: _____

_____

**3.** Match the synovial joint categories in column B with their descriptions in column A.

**Column A**                                                                                   **Column B**

_____ 1. joint between the axis and atlas                                 a.   ball and socket

_____ 2. hip joint                                                        b.   condylar

_____ 3. intervertebral joints (between articular processes)              c.   hinge

_____ 4. joint between forearm bones and wrist                            d.   pivot

_____ 5. elbow                                                            e.   plane

_____ 6. interphalangeal joints                                           f.   saddle

_____ 7. intercarpal joints

_____ 8. joint between talus and tibia/fibula

_____ 9. joint between skull and vertebral column

_____ 10. joint between jaw and skull

_____ 11. joints between proximal phalanges and metacarpal bones

_____ 12. a multiaxial joint

_____ , _____ 13. biaxial joints

_____ , _____ 14. uniaxial joints

**4.** Indicate the number of planes in which each joint can move.

_____ uniaxial joints _____ biaxial joints _____ multiaxial joints

**5.** What characteristics do all joints have in common? _____

_____

# Selected Synovial Joints

**6.** Which joint, the hip or the knee, is more stable?_____

Name two important factors that contribute to the stability of the hip joint.

_____ and _____

Name two important factors that contribute to the stability of the knee.

_____ and _____

**7.** The diagram shows a frontal section of the hip joint. Identify its major structural elements by using the key letters.

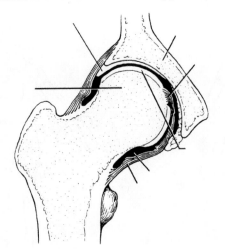

*Key:*

a.   acetabular labrum

b.   articular capsule

c.   articular cartilage

d.   coxal bone

e.   head of femur

f.   ligament of the head of the femur

g.   synovial cavity

**8.** The shoulder joint is built for mobility. List four factors that contribute to the large range of motion at the shoulder:

1.   _____

2.   _____

3.   _____

4.   _____

**9.** In which direction does the shoulder usually dislocate? _____

# Movements Allowed by Synovial Joints

**10.** Which letter of the adjacent diagram marks the origin

of the muscle? _____ Which letter marks the

insertion? _____

Insert the words *origin* and *insertion* into the following sentence:

During muscle contraction, the _____ moves

toward the _____ .

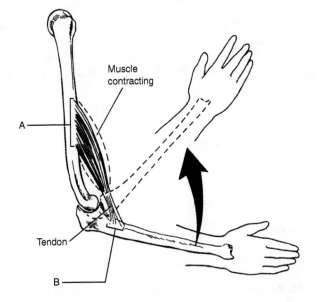

Muscle contracting

A —

Tendon

B —

**11.** Complete the descriptions below the diagrams by inserting the type of movement in each answer blank.

 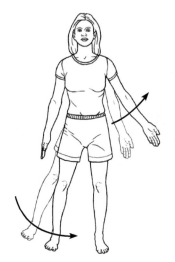 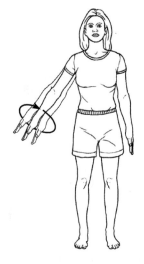

**(a)** _____ of the elbow     **(c)** _____ of the shoulder     **(e)** _____ of the shoulder

**(b)** _____ of the knee      **(d)** _____ of the hip

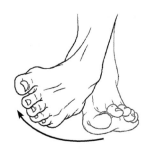 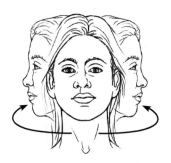 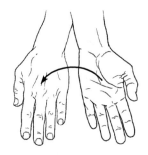

**(f)** _____ of the foot     **(g)** _____ of the head     **(h)** _____ of the hand

## Joint Disorders

**12.** What structural joint changes are common to the elderly? _____

_____

**13.** Define the following terms.

*sprain:* _____

*dislocation:* _____

**14.** What types of tissue damage might you expect to find in a dislocated joint?

_____

—— Illustration Credits _____
All illustrations are by Imagineering STA Media Services, except for Review Sheet art and as noted below.

1: Electronic Publishing Services, Inc. 8, 9: Biopac Systems.

## Photo Credits

**Credits are listed in order of appearance.**

# Microscopic Anatomy and Organization of Skeletal Muscle

## MATERIALS

- ☐ Three-dimensional model of skeletal muscle cells (if available)
- ☐ Forceps
- ☐ Dissecting needles
- ☐ Clean microscope slides and coverslips
- ☐ 0.9% saline solution in dropper bottles
- ☐ Chicken breast or thigh muscle (freshly obtained from the meat market)
- ☐ Compound microscope
- ☐ Prepared slides of skeletal muscle (l.s. and x.s. views) and skeletal muscle showing neuromuscular junctions
- ☐ Three-dimensional model of skeletal muscle showing neuromuscular junction (if available)

MasteringA&P® For related exercise study tools, go to the Study Area of MasteringA&P. There you will find:
- Practice Anatomy Lab PAL
- PhysioEx PEx
- A&PFlix A&PFlix
- Practice quizzes, Histology Atlas, eText, Videos, and more!

## OBJECTIVES

1. Define *fiber, myofibril,* and *myofilament* and describe the structural relationship between them.
2. Describe thick (myosin) and thin (actin) filaments and their relation to the sarcomere.
3. Discuss the structure and location of T tubules and terminal cisterns.
4. Define *endomysium, perimysium,* and *epimysium* and relate them to muscle fibers, fascicles, and entire muscles.
5. Define *tendon* and *aponeurosis* and describe the difference between them.
6. Describe the structure of skeletal muscle from gross to microscopic levels.
7. Explain the connection between motor neurons and skeletal muscle and discuss the structure and function of the neuromuscular junction.

## PRE-LAB QUIZ

1. Which is *not* true of skeletal muscle?
   a. It enables you to manipulate your environment.
   b. It influences the body's contours and shape.
   c. It is one of the major components of hollow organs.
   d. It provides a means of locomotion.
2. Circle the correct underlined term. Because the cells of skeletal muscle are relatively large and cylindrical in shape, they are also known as <u>fibers</u> / <u>tubules</u>.
3. Circle True or False. Skeletal muscle cells have more than one nucleus.
4. The two contractile proteins that make up the myofilaments of skeletal muscle are_____ and _____.
5. Each muscle cell is surrounded by thin connective tissue called the
   a. aponeuroses          c. endomysium
   b. epimysium            d. perimysium
6. A cordlike structure that connects a muscle to another muscle or bone is
   a. a fascicle
   b. a tendon
   c. deep fascia
7. The junction between an axon and a muscle fiber is called a _____.
8. Circle True or False. The neuron and muscle fiber membranes do not actually touch but are separated by a fluid-filled gap.
9. Circle the correct underlined term. The contractile unit of muscle is the <u>sarcolemma</u> / <u>sarcomere</u>.
10. Circle True or False. Larger, more powerful muscles have relatively less connective tissue than smaller muscles.

From Exercise 12 of *Human Anatomy & Physiology Laboratory Manual,* Main Version, Tenth Edition. Elaine N. Marieb, Susan J. Mitchell, Lori A. Smith. Copyright © 2014 by Pearson Education, Inc. All rights reserved.

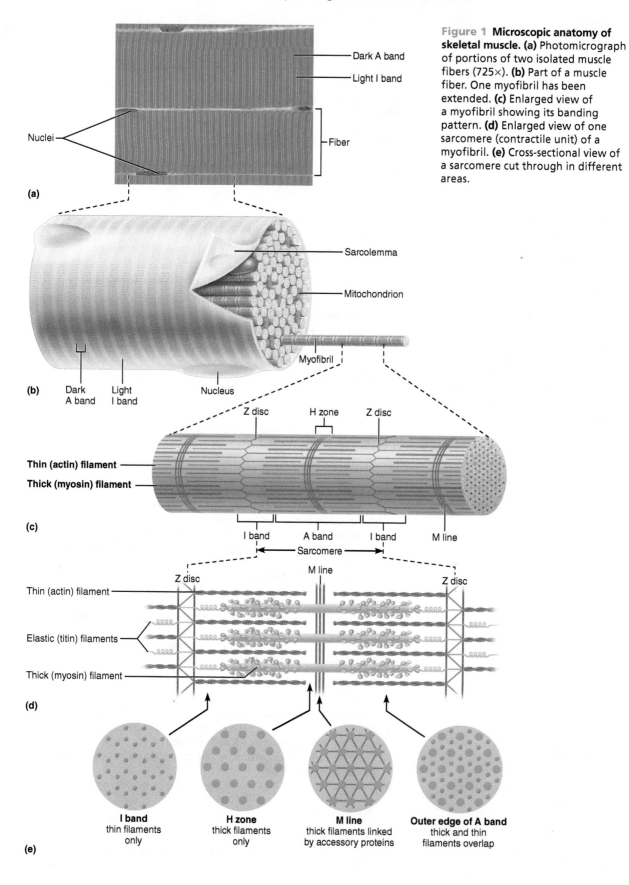

**(a)**

**(b)**

**(c)**

**(d)**

**(e)**

Dark A band
Light I band
Nuclei
Fiber

Sarcolemma
Mitochondrion
Myofibril
Dark A band
Light I band
Nucleus

Z disc    H zone    Z disc
Thin (actin) filament
Thick (myosin) filament
I band    A band    I band    M line
Sarcomere

Z disc    M line    Z disc
Thin (actin) filament
Elastic (titin) filaments
Thick (myosin) filament

**I band**
thin filaments
only

**H zone**
thick filaments
only

**M line**
thick filaments linked
by accessory proteins

**Outer edge of A band**
thick and thin
filaments overlap

**Figure 1 Microscopic anatomy of skeletal muscle. (a)** Photomicrograph of portions of two isolated muscle fibers (725×). **(b)** Part of a muscle fiber. One myofibril has been extended. **(c)** Enlarged view of a myofibril showing its banding pattern. **(d)** Enlarged view of one sarcomere (contractile unit) of a myofibril. **(e)** Cross-sectional view of a sarcomere cut through in different areas.

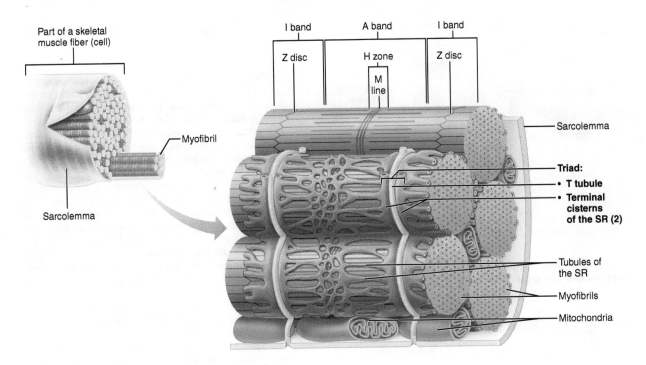

**Figure 2** **Relationship of the sarcoplasmic reticulum and T tubules to the myofibrils of skeletal muscle.**

Most of the muscle tissue in the body is **skeletal muscle,** which attaches to the skeleton or associated connective tissue. Skeletal muscle shapes the body and gives you the ability to move—to walk, run, jump, and dance; to draw, paint, and play a musical instrument; and to smile and frown. The remaining muscle tissue of the body consists of smooth muscle that forms the walls of hollow organs and cardiac muscle that forms the walls of the heart. Smooth and cardiac muscle move materials within the body. For example, smooth muscle moves digesting food through the gastrointestinal system, and urine from the kidneys to the exterior of the body. Cardiac muscle moves blood through the blood vessels.

Each of the three muscle types has a structure and function uniquely suited to its task in the body. Our focus here is to investigate the structure of skeletal muscle.

Skeletal muscle is also known as *voluntary muscle* because it can be consciously controlled, and as striated muscle because it appears to be striped. As you might guess from both of these alternative names, skeletal muscle has some special characteristics. Thus an investigation of skeletal muscle begins at the cellular level.

## The Cells of Skeletal Muscle

Skeletal muscle is made up of relatively large, long cylindrical cells, sometimes called **fibers.** These cells range from 10 to 100 μm in diameter and some are up to 30 cm long.

Since hundreds of embryonic cells fuse to produce each muscle cell, the cells **(Figure 1a and b)** are multinucleate; multiple oval nuclei can be seen just beneath the plasma membrane (called the *sarcolemma* in these cells). The nuclei are pushed peripherally by the longitudinally arranged **myofibrils,** which nearly fill the sarcoplasm. Alternating light (I) and dark (A) bands along the length of the perfectly aligned myofibrils give the muscle fiber as a whole its striped appearance.

Electron microscope studies have revealed that the myofibrils are made up of even smaller threadlike structures called **myofilaments** (Figure 1d). The myofilaments are composed largely of two varieties of contractile proteins—**actin** and **myosin**—which slide past each other during muscle activity to bring about shortening or contraction of the muscle cells. It is the highly specific arrangement of the myofilaments within the myofibrils that is responsible for the banding pattern in skeletal muscle. The actual contractile units of muscle, called **sarcomeres,** extend from the middle of one I band (its Z disc) to the middle of the next along the length of the myofibrils (Figure 1c and d.) Cross sections of the sarcomere in areas where **thick** and **thin filaments** overlap show that each thick filament is surrounded by six thin filaments; each thin filament is enclosed by three thick filaments (Figure 1e).

At each junction of the A and I bands, the sarcolemma indents into the muscle cell, forming a **transverse tubule (T tubule).** These tubules run deep into the muscle cell between cross channels, or **terminal cisterns,** of the elaborate smooth endoplasmic reticulum called the **sarcoplasmic reticulum (SR) (Figure 2).** Regions where the SR terminal cisterns border a T tubule on each side are called **triads.**

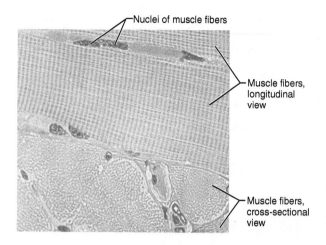

Nuclei of muscle fibers

Muscle fibers, longitudinal view

Muscle fibers, cross-sectional view

**Figure 3** **Photomicrograph of muscle fibers, longitudinal and cross sections (800×).**

## ACTIVITY 1

### Examining Skeletal Muscle Cell Anatomy

1. Look at the three-dimensional model of skeletal muscle cells, noting the relative shape and size of the cells. Identify the nuclei, myofibrils, and light and dark bands.

2. Obtain forceps, two dissecting needles, slide and coverslip, and a dropper bottle of saline solution. With forceps, remove a very small piece of muscle (about 1 mm diameter) from a fresh chicken breast or thigh. Place the tissue on a clean microscope slide, and add a drop of the saline solution.

3. Pull the muscle fibers apart (tease them) with the dissecting needles until you have a fluffy-looking mass of tissue. Cover the teased tissue with a coverslip, and observe under the high-power lens of a compound microscope. Look for the banding pattern by examining muscle fibers isolated at the edge of the tissue mass. Regulate the light carefully to obtain the highest possible contrast.

4. Now compare your observations with the photomicrograph (Figure 3) and with what can be seen in professionally prepared muscle tissue. Obtain a slide of skeletal muscle (longitudinal section), and view it under high power. From your observations, draw a small section of a muscle fiber in the space provided below. Label the nuclei, sarcolemma, and A and I bands.

What structural details become apparent with the prepared slide?

_____

_____

## Organization of Skeletal Muscle Cells into Muscles

Muscle fibers are soft and surprisingly fragile. Thousands of muscle fibers are bundled together with connective tissue to form the organs we refer to as skeletal muscles (Figure 4). Each muscle fiber is enclosed in a delicate, areolar connective tissue sheath called the **endomysium.** Several sheathed muscle fibers are wrapped by a collagenic membrane called the **perimysium,** forming a bundle of fibers called a **fascicle.** A large number of fascicles are bound together by a much coarser "overcoat" of dense connective tissue called the **epimysium,** which sheathes the entire muscle. These epimysia blend into the **deep fascia,** still coarser sheets of dense connective tissue that bind muscles into functional groups, and into strong cordlike **tendons** or sheetlike **aponeuroses,** which attach muscles to each other or indirectly to bones. A muscle's more movable attachment is called its *insertion* whereas its fixed (or immovable) attachment is the *origin.*

Tendons perform several functions, two of the most important being to provide durability and to conserve space. Because tendons are tough collagenic connective tissue, they can span rough bony projections that would destroy the more delicate muscle tissues. Because of their relatively small size, more tendons than fleshy muscles can pass over a joint.

In addition to supporting and binding the muscle fibers, and providing strength to the muscle as a whole, the connective tissue wrappings provide a route for the entry and exit of nerves and blood vessels that serve the muscle fibers. The larger, more powerful muscles have relatively more connective tissue than muscles involved in fine or delicate movements.

As we age, the mass of the muscle fibers decreases, and the amount of connective tissue increases; thus the skeletal muscles gradually become more sinewy, or "stringier."✚

## ACTIVITY 2

### Observing the Histological Structure of a Skeletal Muscle

Identify the muscle fibers, their peripherally located nuclei, and their connective tissue wrappings—the endomysium, perimysium, and epimysium, if visible (use Figure 4 as a reference). ▄▄

## The Neuromuscular Junction

The voluntary skeletal muscle cells must be stimulated by motor neurons via nerve impulses. The junction between an axon of a motor neuron and a muscle cell is called a **neuromuscular,** or **myoneural, junction** (Figure 5).

Each axon of the motor neuron usually divides into many branches called *terminal branches* as it approaches the muscle. Each of these branches ends in an axon terminal that participates in forming a neuromuscular junction with a single muscle cell. Thus a single neuron may stimulate many muscle fibers. Together, a neuron and all the muscle fibers it stimulates make up the functional structure called the

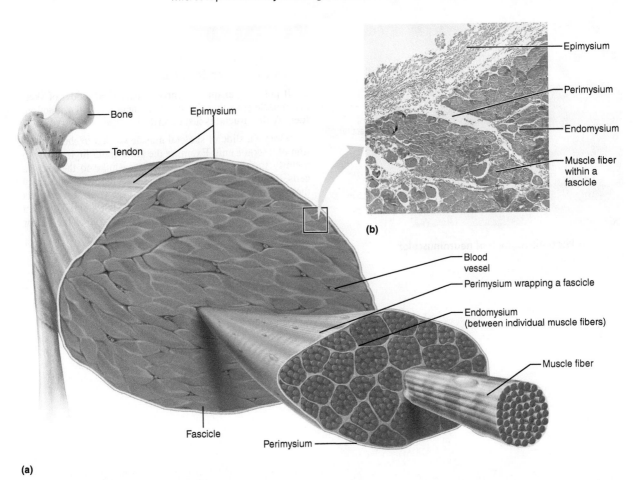

(b)

(a)

**Figure 4 Connective tissue coverings of skeletal muscle. (a)** Diagrammatic view. **(b)** Photomicrograph of a cross section of skeletal muscle (90×).

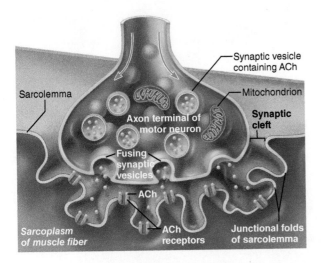

**Figure 5 The neuromuscular junction.** Red arrows indicate arrival of the nerve impulse (action potential), which ultimately causes vesicles to release ACh. The ACh receptor is part of the ion channel that opens briefly, causing depolarization of the sarcolemma.

**motor unit.** (Part of a motor unit, showing two neuromuscular junctions, is shown in **Figure 6.**) The neuron and muscle fiber membranes, close as they are, do not actually touch. They are separated by a small fluid-filled gap called the **synaptic cleft** (see Figure 5).

Within the axon terminals are many mitochondria and vesicles containing a neurotransmitter chemical called acetylcholine (ACh). When a nerve impulse reaches the axon terminal, some of these vesicles release their contents into the synaptic cleft. The ACh rapidly diffuses across the junction and combines with the receptors on the sarcolemma. When receptors bind ACh, a change in the permeability of the sarcolemma occurs. Channels that allow both sodium ($Na^+$) and potassium ($K^+$) ions to pass open briefly. Because more $Na^+$ diffuses into the muscle fiber than $K^+$ diffuses out, depolarization of the sarcolemma and subsequent contraction of the muscle fiber occurs.

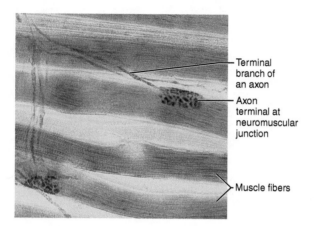

Terminal branch of an axon

Axon terminal at neuromuscular junction

Muscle fibers

**Figure 6 Photomicrograph of neuromuscular junctions (750×).**

## Studying the Structure of a Neuromuscular Junction

1. If possible, examine a three-dimensional model of skeletal muscle cells that illustrates the neuromuscular junction. Identify the structures just described.

2. Obtain a slide of skeletal muscle stained to show a portion of a motor unit. Examine the slide under high power to identify the axon fibers extending leashlike to the muscle cells. Follow one of the axon fibers to its terminus to identify the oval-shaped axon terminal. Compare your observations to the photomicrograph (Figure 6). Sketch a small section in the space provided below. Label the axon of the motor neuron, its terminal branches, and muscle fibers. ▄▄

# Microscopic Anatomy and Organization of Skeletal Muscle

## Skeletal Muscle Cells and Their Organization into Muscles

**1.** Use the items in the key to correctly identify the structures described below.

*Key:*

_____ 1.   connective tissue covering a bundle of muscle cells

a.   endomysium

_____ 2.   bundle of muscle cells

b.   epimysium

_____ 3.   contractile unit of muscle

c.   fascicle

_____ 4.   a muscle cell

d.   fiber

_____ 5.   thin areolar connective tissue surrounding each muscle cell

e.   myofibril

_____ 6.   plasma membrane of the muscle fiber

f.   myofilament

_____ 7.   a long filamentous organelle with a banded appearance found within muscle cells

g.   perimysium

h.   sarcolemma

_____ 8.   actin- or myosin-containing structure

i.   sarcomere

j.   sarcoplasm

_____ 9.   cord of collagen fibers that attaches a muscle to a bone

k.   tendon

**2.** List three reasons why the connective tissue wrappings of skeletal muscle are important.

_____

_____

_____

**3.** Why are there more indirect—that is, tendinous—muscle attachments to bone than there are direct attachments?

_____

_____

_____

**4.** How does an aponeurosis differ from a tendon structurally? _____

_____

How is an aponeurosis functionally similar to a tendon? _____

_____

**5.** The diagram illustrates a small portion of several myofibrils. Using letters from the key, correctly identify each structure indicated by a leader line or a bracket.

*Key:*

    a.  A band         d.  myosin filament     g.  triad
    b.  actin filament     e.  T tubule           h.  sarcomere
    c.  I band            f.  terminal cistern    i.  Z disc

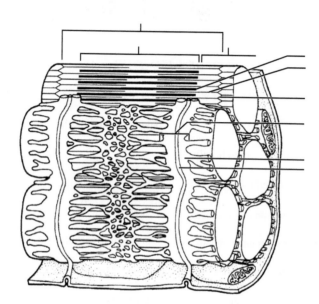

**6.** On the following figure, label a blood vessel, endomysium, epimysium, a fascicle, a muscle cell, perimysium, and the tendon.

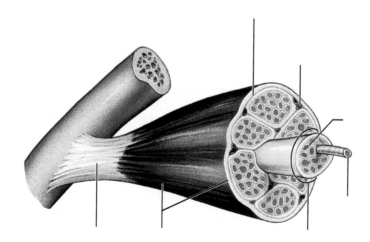

# The Neuromuscular Junction

**7.** Complete the following statements:

The junction between a motor neuron's axon and the muscle cell membrane is called a __1__ junction. A motor neuron and all of the skeletal muscle cells it stimulates is called a __2__. The actual gap between the axon terminal and the muscle cell is called a __3__. Within the axon terminal are many small vesicles containing a neurotransmitter substance called __4__. When the __5__ reaches the ends of the axon, the neurotransmitter is released and diffuses to the muscle cell membrane to combine with receptors there. The combining of the neurotransmitter with the muscle membrane receptors causes the membrane to become permeable to both sodium and potassium. The greater influx of sodium ions results in __6__ of the membrane. Then contraction of the muscle cell occurs.

1. _____

2. _____

3. _____

4. _____

5. _____

6. _____

**8.** The events that occur at a neuromuscular junction are depicted below. Identify by labeling every structure provided with a leader line.

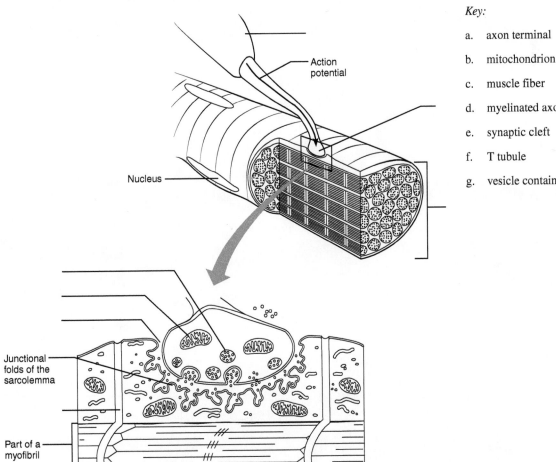

*Key:*

a.  axon terminal

b.  mitochondrion

c.  muscle fiber

d.  myelinated axon

e.  synaptic cleft

f.  T tubule

g.  vesicle containing ACh

Action potential

Nucleus

Junctional folds of the sarcolemma

Part of a myofibril

## Photo Credits

**Credits are listed in order of appearance.**

1a: Marian Rice. 3, 6: Victor P. Eroschenko, Pearson Education. 4b: William Karkow, Pearson Education.

## Illustration Credits

**All illustrations are by Imagineering STA Media Services, except for Review Sheet art and as noted below.**

4: Imagineering STA Media Services/Precision Graphics. 5: Electronic Publishing Services, Inc.

# Gross Anatomy of the Muscular System

## MATERIALS

- ☐ Human torso model or large anatomical chart showing human musculature
- ☐ Human cadaver for demonstration (if available)
- ☐ Disposable gloves
- ☐ *Human Musculature* video
- ☐ Tubes of body (or face) paint
- ☐ 1" wide artist's brushes

## OBJECTIVES

1. Define *prime mover (agonist), antagonist, synergist,* and *fixator.*
2. List the criteria used in naming skeletal muscles.
3. Identify the major muscles of the human body on a torso model, a human cadaver, lab chart, or image, and state the action of each.
4. Name muscle origins and insertions as required by the instructor.
5. Explain how muscle actions are related to their location.
6. List antagonists for the major prime movers.

## PRE-LAB QUIZ

1. A prime mover or _____ produces a particular type of movement.
   a. agonist          c. fixator
   b. antagonist       d. synergist
2. Skeletal muscles are named on the basis of many criteria. Name one.
   _____
3. Circle True or False. Muscles of facial expression differ from most skeletal muscles because they usually do not insert into a bone.
4. The _____ musculature includes muscles that move the vertebral column and muscles that move the ribs.
   a. head and neck     b. lower limb     c. trunk
5. Muscles that act on the _____ cause movement at the hip, knee, and foot joints.
   a. lower limb     b. trunk     c. upper limb
6. This two-headed muscle bulges when the forearm is flexed. It is the most familiar muscle of the anterior humerus. It is the
   a. biceps brachii          c. extensor digitorum
   b. flexor carpi radialis    d. triceps brachii
7. These abdominal muscles are responsible for giving me my "six-pack." They also stabilize my pelvis when walking. They are the _____ muscles.
   a. internal intercostal     c. quadriceps
   b. rectus abdominis         d. triceps femoris
8. Circle the correct underlined term. This lower limb muscle, which attaches to the calcaneus via the calcaneal tendon and plantar flexes the foot when the knee is extended, is the <u>tibialis anterior</u> / <u>gastrocnemius</u>.
9. The _____ is the largest and most superficial of the gluteal muscles.
   a. gluteus internus     c. gluteus maximus
   b. gluteus medius       d. gluteus minimus
10. Circle True or False. The biceps femoris is located in the anterior compartment of the thigh.

MasteringA&P® For related exercise study tools, go to the Study Area of MasteringA&P. There you will find:
- Practice Anatomy Lab PAL
- PhysioEx PEx
- A&PFlix *A&PFlix*
- Practice quizzes, Histology Atlas, eText, Videos, and more!

From Exercise 13 of *Human Anatomy & Physiology Laboratory Manual*, Main Version, Tenth Edition. Elaine N. Marieb, Susan J. Mitchell, Lori A. Smith. Copyright © 2014 by Pearson Education, Inc. All rights reserved.

Skeletal muscles cause movement. Among the movements are smiling, frowning, speaking, singing, breathing, dancing, running, and playing a musical instrument. Most often, purposeful movements require the coordinated action of several skeletal muscles.

## Classification of Skeletal Muscles

### Types of Muscles

Muscles that are most responsible for producing a particular movement are called **prime movers,** or **agonists.** Muscles that oppose or reverse a movement are called **antagonists.** When a prime mover is active, the fibers of the antagonist are stretched and in the relaxed state. The antagonist can also regulate the prime mover by providing some resistance, to prevent overshoot or to stop its action. Antagonists can be prime movers in their own right. For example, the biceps muscle of the arm (a prime mover of elbow flexion) is antagonized by the triceps (a prime mover of elbow extension).

**Synergists** aid the action of agonists either by assisting with the same movement or by reducing undesirable or unnecessary movement. Contraction of a muscle crossing two or more joints would cause movement at all joints spanned if the synergists were not there to stabilize them. For example, you can make a fist without bending your wrist only because synergist muscles stabilize the wrist joint and allow the prime mover to exert its force at the finger joints.

**Fixators,** or fixation muscles, are specialized synergists. They immobilize the origin of a prime mover so that all the tension is exerted at the insertion. Muscles that help maintain posture are fixators; so too are muscles of the back that stabilize or "fix" the scapula during arm movements.

### Naming Skeletal Muscles

Remembering the names of the skeletal muscles is a monumental task, but certain clues help. Muscles are named on the basis of the following criteria:

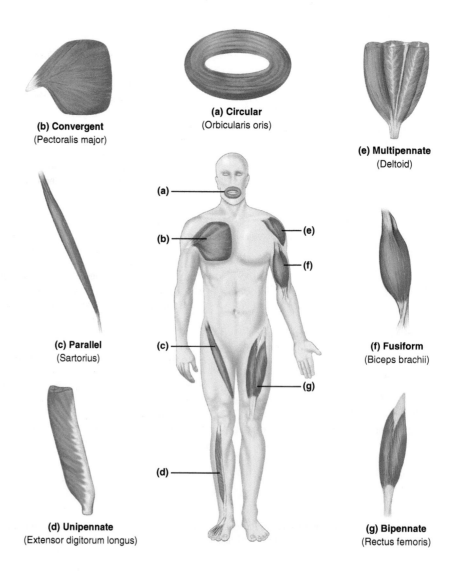

**(b) Convergent**
(Pectoralis major)

**(a) Circular**
(Orbicularis oris)

**(e) Multipennate**
(Deltoid)

**(c) Parallel**
(Sartorius)

**(f) Fusiform**
(Biceps brachii)

**(d) Unipennate**
(Extensor digitorum longus)

**(g) Bipennate**
(Rectus femoris)

**Figure 1 Patterns of fascicle arrangement in muscles.**

- **Direction of muscle fibers:** Some muscles are named in reference to some imaginary line, usually the midline of the body or the longitudinal axis of a limb bone. A muscle with fibers (and fascicles) running parallel to that imaginary line will have the term *rectus* (straight) in its name. For example, the rectus abdominis is the straight muscle of the abdomen. Likewise, the terms *transverse* and *oblique* indicate that the muscle fibers run at right angles and obliquely (respectively) to the imaginary line. Muscle structure is determined by fascicle arrangement (**Figure 1**).

- **Relative size of the muscle:** Terms such as *maximus* (largest), *minimus* (smallest), *longus* (long), and *brevis* (short) are often used in naming muscles—as in gluteus maximus and gluteus minimus.

- **Location of the muscle:** Some muscles are named for the bone with which they are associated. For example, the temporalis muscle overlies the temporal bone.

- **Number of origins:** When the term *biceps, triceps,* or *quadriceps* forms part of a muscle name, you can generally assume that the muscle has two, three, or four origins (respectively). For example, the biceps muscle of the arm has two heads, or origins.

- **Location of the muscle's origin and insertion:** For example, the sternocleidomastoid muscle has its origin on the sternum *(sterno)* and clavicle *(cleido),* and inserts on the mastoid process of the temporal bone.

- **Shape of the muscle:** For example, the deltoid muscle is roughly triangular (*deltoid* = triangle), and the trapezius muscle resembles a trapezoid.

- **Action of the muscle:** For example, all the adductor muscles of the anterior thigh bring about its adduction, and all the extensor muscles of the wrist extend the wrist.

# Identification of Human Muscles

While reading the tables and identifying the various human muscles in the figures, try to visualize what happens when the muscle contracts. Since muscles often have many actions, we have indicated the primary action of each muscle in blue type in the tables. Then, use a torso model or an anatomical chart to again identify as many of these muscles as possible. If a human cadaver is available for observation, your instructor will provide specific instructions for muscle examination. Then carry out the instructions for demonstrating and palpating muscles. (**Figure 2** and **Figure 3** are summary figures illustrating the superficial musculature of the body as a whole.)

## Muscles of the Head and Neck

The muscles of the head serve many specific functions. For instance, the muscles of facial expression differ from most skeletal muscles because they insert into the skin or other muscles rather than into bone. As a result, they move the facial skin, allowing a wide range of emotions to be shown on the face. Other muscles of the head are the muscles of mastication, which move the mandible during chewing, and the six extrinsic eye muscles located within the orbit, which aim the eye. Neck muscles are primarily concerned with the movement of the head and shoulder girdle.

**ACTIVITY 1**

## Identifying Head and Neck Muscles

Read the descriptions of specific head and neck muscles and identify the various muscles in the figures (**Tables 1** and **2** and **Figures 4** and **5**), trying to visualize their action when they contract. Then identify them on a torso model or anatomical chart.

### Demonstrating Operations of Head Muscles

1. Raise your eyebrow to wrinkle your forehead. You are using the *frontal belly* of the *epicranius* muscle.

2. Blink your eyes; wink. You are contracting *orbicularis oculi.*

3. Close your lips and pucker up. This requires contraction of *orbicularis oris.*

4. Smile. You are using *zygomaticus.*

5. To demonstrate the *temporalis,* place your hands on your temples and clench your teeth. The *masseter* can also be palpated now at the angle of the jaw. ■

## Muscles of the Trunk

The trunk musculature includes muscles that move the vertebral column; anterior thorax muscles that act to move ribs, head, and arms; and muscles of the abdominal wall that play a role in the movement of the vertebral column but more importantly form the "natural girdle," or the major portion of the abdominal body wall.

**ACTIVITY 2**

## Identifying Muscles of the Trunk

Read the descriptions of specific trunk muscles and identify them in the figures (**Tables 3** and **4** and **Figures 6–9**), visualizing their action when they contract. Then identify them on a torso model or anatomical chart.

### Demonstrating Operations of Trunk Muscles

Now, work with a partner to demonstrate the operation of the following muscles. One of you can demonstrate the movement; the following steps are addressed to this partner. The other can supply resistance and palpate the muscle being tested.

1. Fully abduct the arm and extend the elbow. Now adduct the arm against resistance. You are using the *latissimus dorsi.*

2. To observe the *deltoid,* try to abduct your arm against resistance. Now attempt to elevate your shoulder against resistance; you are contracting the upper portion of the *trapezius.*

3. The *pectoralis major* is used when you press your hands together at chest level with your elbows widely abducted. ■

## Gross Anatomy of the Muscular System

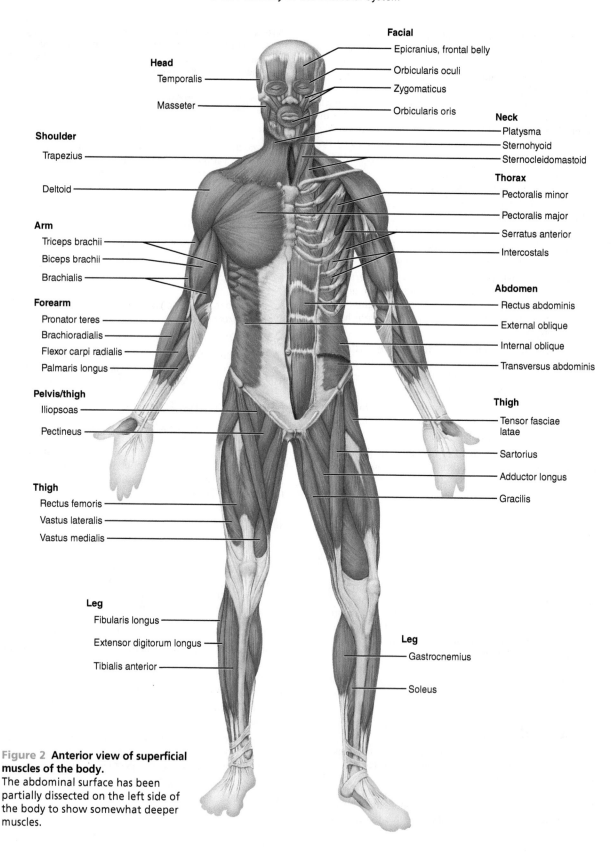

**Facial**
- Epicranius, frontal belly
- Orbicularis oculi
- Zygomaticus
- Orbicularis oris

**Head**
- Temporalis
- Masseter

**Neck**
- Platysma
- Sternohyoid
- Sternocleidomastoid

**Shoulder**
- Trapezius
- Deltoid

**Thorax**
- Pectoralis minor
- Pectoralis major
- Serratus anterior
- Intercostals

**Arm**
- Triceps brachii
- Biceps brachii
- Brachialis

**Forearm**
- Pronator teres
- Brachioradialis
- Flexor carpi radialis
- Palmaris longus

**Abdomen**
- Rectus abdominis
- External oblique
- Internal oblique
- Transversus abdominis

**Pelvis/thigh**
- Iliopsoas
- Pectineus

**Thigh**
- Tensor fasciae latae
- Sartorius
- Adductor longus
- Gracilis

**Thigh**
- Rectus femoris
- Vastus lateralis
- Vastus medialis

**Leg**
- Fibularis longus
- Extensor digitorum longus
- Tibialis anterior

**Leg**
- Gastrocnemius
- Soleus

**Figure 2 Anterior view of superficial muscles of the body.**
The abdominal surface has been partially dissected on the left side of the body to show somewhat deeper muscles.

Gross Anatomy of the Muscular System

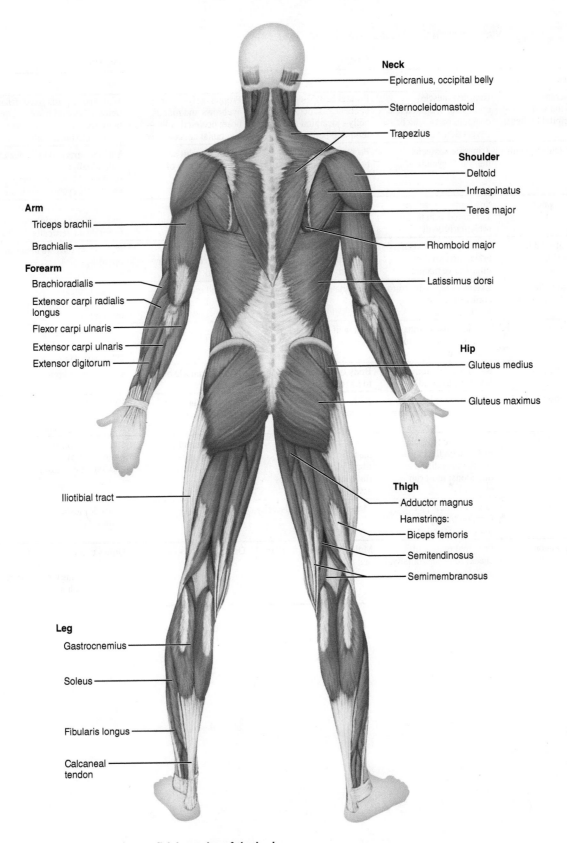

**Neck**
Epicranius, occipital belly
Sternocleidomastoid
Trapezius

**Shoulder**
Deltoid
Infraspinatus
Teres major

Rhomboid major

Latissimus dorsi

**Hip**
Gluteus medius

Gluteus maximus

**Arm**
Triceps brachii
Brachialis

**Forearm**
Brachioradialis
Extensor carpi radialis longus
Flexor carpi ulnaris
Extensor carpi ulnaris
Extensor digitorum

Iliotibial tract

**Thigh**
Adductor magnus
Hamstrings:
Biceps femoris
Semitendinosus
Semimembranosus

**Leg**
Gastrocnemius

Soleus

Fibularis longus

Calcaneal tendon

**Figure 3 Posterior view of superficial muscles of the body.**

| Table 1 | Major Muscles of Human Head (see Figure 4) | | | |
|---|---|---|---|---|
| **Muscle** | **Comments** | **Origin** | **Insertion** | **Action** |

**Facial Expression (Figure 4a)**

| Muscle | Comments | Origin | Insertion | Action |
|---|---|---|---|---|
| Epicranius—frontal and occipital bellies | Bipartite muscle consisting of frontal and occipital parts, which covers dome of skull | Frontal belly—epicranial aponeurosis; occipital belly—occipital and temporal bones | Frontal belly—skin of eyebrows and root of nose; occipital belly—epicranial aponeurosis | With aponeurosis fixed, frontal belly raises eyebrows; occipital belly fixes aponeurosis and pulls scalp posteriorly |
| Orbicularis oculi | Tripartite sphincter muscle of eyelids | Frontal and maxillary bones and ligaments around orbit | Encircles orbit and inserts in tissue of eyelid | Various parts can be activated individually; closes eyes, produces blinking, squinting, and draws eyebrows inferiorly |
| Corrugator supercilii | Small muscle; activity associated with that of orbicularis oculi | Arch of frontal bone above nasal bone | Skin of eyebrow | Draws eyebrows medially and inferiorly; wrinkles skin of forehead vertically |
| Levator labii superioris | Thin muscle between orbicularis oris and inferior eye margin | Zygomatic bone and infraorbital margin of maxilla | Skin and muscle of upper lip and border of nostril | Raises and furrows upper lip; opens lips |
| Zygomaticus—major and minor | Extends diagonally from corner of mouth to cheekbone | Zygomatic bone | Skin and muscle at corner of mouth | Raises lateral corners of mouth upward (smiling muscle) |
| Risorius | Slender muscle; runs inferior and lateral to zygomaticus | Fascia of masseter muscle | Skin at angle of mouth | Draws corner of lip laterally; tenses lip; zygomaticus synergist |
| Depressor labii inferioris | Small muscle from lower lip to mandible | Body of mandible lateral to its midline | Skin and muscle of lower lip | Draws lower lip inferiorly |
| Depressor anguli oris | Small muscle lateral to depressor labii inferioris | Body of mandible below incisors | Skin and muscle at angle of mouth below insertion of zygomaticus | Zygomaticus antagonist; draws corners of mouth downward and laterally |
| Orbicularis oris | Multilayered muscle of lips with fibers that run in many different directions; most run circularly | Arises indirectly from maxilla and mandible; fibers blended with fibers of other muscles associated with lips | Encircles mouth; inserts into muscle and skin at angles of mouth | Closes lips; purses and protrudes lips (kissing and whistling muscle) |
| Mentalis | One of muscle pair forming V-shaped muscle mass on chin | Mandible below incisors | Skin of chin | Protrudes lower lip; wrinkles chin |
| Buccinator | Principal muscle of cheek; runs horizontally, deep to the masseter | Molar region of maxilla and mandible | Orbicularis oris | Draws corner of mouth laterally; compresses cheek (as in whistling); holds food between teeth during chewing |

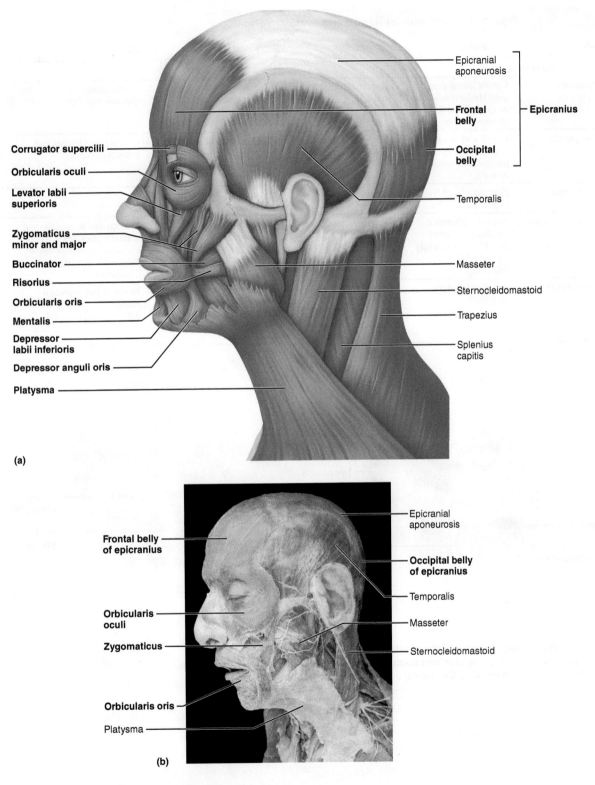

**(a)**

Corrugator supercilii

Orbicularis oculi

Levator labii superioris

Zygomaticus minor and major

Buccinator

Risorius

Orbicularis oris

Mentalis

Depressor labii inferioris

Depressor anguli oris

Platysma

Epicranial aponeurosis

**Frontal belly**

**Occipital belly**

Epicranius

Temporalis

Masseter

Sternocleidomastoid

Trapezius

Splenius capitis

**(b)**

**Frontal belly of epicranius**

**Orbicularis oculi**

**Zygomaticus**

**Orbicularis oris**

Platysma

Epicranial aponeurosis

**Occipital belly of epicranius**

Temporalis

Masseter

Sternocleidomastoid

**Figure 4 Muscles of the head (left lateral view). (a)** Superficial muscles.
**(b)** Photo of superficial structures of head and neck.

213

| Table 1 | Major Muscles of Human Head (continued) | | | |
|---|---|---|---|---|
| **Muscle** | **Comments** | **Origin** | **Insertion** | **Action** |
| **Mastication (Figure 4c, d)** | | | | |
| Masseter | Covers lateral aspect of mandibular ramus; can be palpated on forcible closure of jaws | Zygomatic arch and maxilla | Angle and ramus of mandible | Prime mover of jaw closure; elevates mandible |
| Temporalis | Fan-shaped muscle lying over parts of frontal, parietal, and temporal bones | Temporal fossa | Coronoid process of mandible | Closes jaw; elevates and retracts mandible |
| Buccinator | (See muscles of facial expression.) | | | |
| Medial pterygoid | Runs along internal (medial) surface of mandible (thus largely concealed by that bone) | Sphenoid, palatine, and maxillary bones | Medial surface of mandible, near its angle | Synergist of temporalis and masseter; elevates mandible; in conjunction with lateral pterygoid, aids in grinding movements |
| Lateral pterygoid | Superior to medial pterygoid | Greater wing of sphenoid bone | Condylar process of mandible | Protracts jaw (moves it anteriorly); in conjunction with medial pterygoid, aids in grinding movements of teeth |

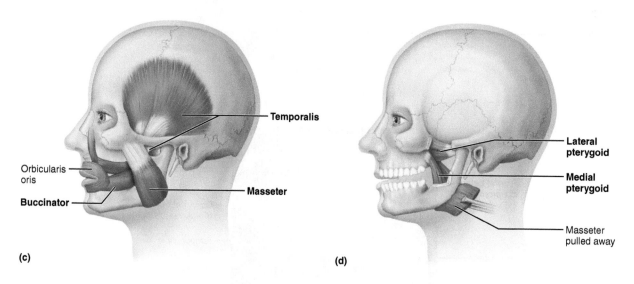

**Figure 4 (continued) Muscles of the head: mastication. (c)** Lateral view of the temporalis, masseter, and buccinator muscles. **(d)** Lateral view of the deep chewing muscles, the medial and lateral pterygoid muscles.

| Table 2 | Anterolateral Muscles of Human Neck (see Figure 5) | | | |
|---------|---------|--------|-----------|--------|
| **Muscle** | **Comments** | **Origin** | **Insertion** | **Action** |
| **Superficial** | | | | |
| Platysma (see Figure 4a) | Unpaired muscle: thin, sheetlike superficial neck muscle, not strictly a head muscle but plays role in facial expression | Fascia of chest (over pectoral muscles) and deltoid | Lower margin of mandible, skin, and muscle at corner of mouth | Tenses skin of neck; depresses mandible; pulls lower lip back and down (i.e., produces downward sag of the mouth) |
| Sternocleidomastoid | Two-headed muscle located deep to platysma on anterolateral surface of neck; fleshy parts on either side indicate limits of anterior and posterior triangles of neck | Manubrium of sternum and medial portion of clavicle | Mastoid process of temporal bone and superior nuchal line of occipital bone | Simultaneous contraction of both muscles of pair causes flexion of neck forward, generally against resistance (as when lying on the back); acting independently, rotate head toward shoulder on opposite side |
| Scalenes—anterior, middle, and posterior (see Figure 5c) | Located more on lateral than anterior neck; deep to platysma and sternocleidomastoid | Transverse processes of cervical vertebrae | Anterolaterally on ribs 1–2 | Flex and slightly rotate neck; elevate ribs 1–2 (aid in inspiration) |

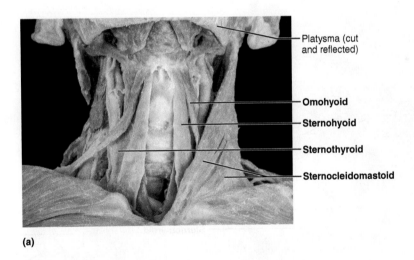

**(a)**

**Figure 5 Muscles of the anterolateral neck and throat. (a)** Photo of the anterior and lateral regions of the neck.

| Table 2 | Anterolateral Muscles of Human Neck *(continued)* | | | |
|---------|---------|--------|-----------|--------|
| **Muscle** | **Comments** | **Origin** | **Insertion** | **Action** |
| **Deep (Figure 5a, b)** | | | | |
| Digastric | Consists of two bellies united by an intermediate tendon; assumes a V-shaped configuration under chin | Lower margin of mandible (anterior belly) and mastoid process (posterior belly) | By a connective tissue loop to hyoid bone | Acting in concert, elevate hyoid bone; open mouth and depress mandible |
| Stylohyoid | Slender muscle parallels posterior border of digastric; below angle of jaw | Styloid process of temporal | Hyoid bone | Elevates and retracts hyoid bone |
| Mylohyoid | Just deep to digastric; forms floor of mouth | Medial surface of mandible | Hyoid bone and median raphe | Elevates hyoid bone and base of tongue during swallowing |
| Sternohyoid | Runs most medially along neck; straplike | Manubrium and medial end of clavicle | Lower margin of body of hyoid bone | Acting with sternothyroid and omohyoid, depresses larynx and hyoid bone if mandible is fixed; may also flex skull |
| Sternothyroid | Lateral and deep to sternohyoid | Posterior surface of manubrium | Thyroid cartilage of larynx | (See Sternohyoid above) |
| Omohyoid | Straplike with two bellies; lateral to sternohyoid | Superior surface of scapula | Hyoid bone; inferior border | (See Sternohyoid above) |
| Thyrohyoid | Appears as a superior continuation of sternothyroid muscle | Thyroid cartilage | Hyoid bone | Depresses hyoid bone; elevates larynx if hyoid is fixed |

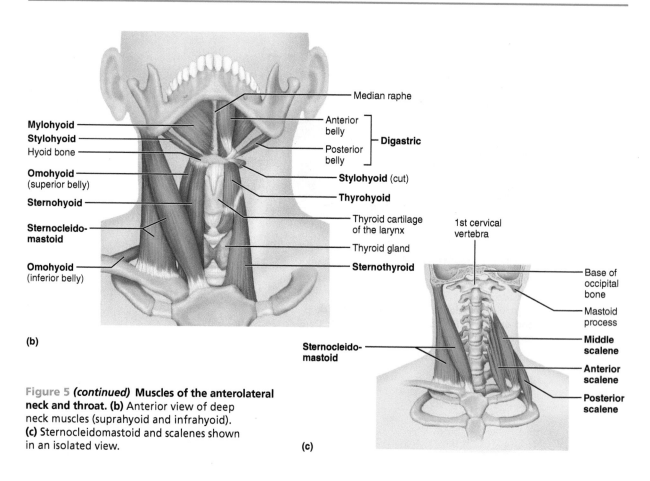

**(b)**

Figure 5 *(continued)* **Muscles of the anterolateral neck and throat. (b)** Anterior view of deep neck muscles (suprahyoid and infrahyoid). **(c)** Sternocleidomastoid and scalenes shown in an isolated view.

**(c)**

| Table 3 | Anterior Muscles of Human Thorax, Shoulder, and Abdominal Wall (see Figures 6, 7, and 8) | | | |
|---|---|---|---|---|
| **Muscle** | **Comments** | **Origin** | **Insertion** | **Action** |
| **Thorax and Shoulder, Superficial (Figure 6)** | | | | |
| Pectoralis major | Large fan-shaped muscle covering upper portion of chest | Clavicle, sternum, cartilage of ribs 1–6 (or 7), and aponeurosis of external oblique muscle | Fibers converge to insert by short tendon into intertubercular sulcus of humerus | Prime mover of arm flexion; adducts, medially rotates arm; with arm fixed, pulls chest upward (thus also acts in forced inspiration) |
| Serratus anterior | Fan-shaped muscle deep to scapula; beneath and inferior to pectoral muscles on lateral rib cage | Lateral aspect of ribs 1–8 (or 9) | Vertebral border of anterior surface of scapula | Prime mover to protract and hold scapula against chest wall; rotates scapula, causing inferior angle to move laterally and upward; essential to raising arm; fixes scapula for arm abduction |
| Deltoid (see also Figure 9) | Fleshy triangular muscle forming shoulder muscle mass; intramuscular injection site | Lateral ⅓ of clavicle; acromion and spine of scapula | Deltoid tuberosity of humerus | Acting as a whole, prime mover of arm abduction; when only specific fibers are active, can aid in flexion, extension, and rotation of humerus |

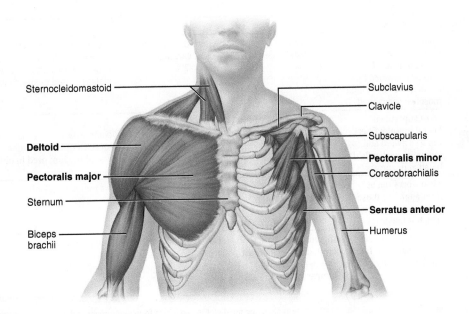

Sternocleidomastoid

**Deltoid**

**Pectoralis major**

Sternum

Biceps brachii

Subclavius

Clavicle

Subscapularis

**Pectoralis minor**

Coracobrachialis

**Serratus anterior**

Humerus

**Figure 6 Muscles of the thorax and shoulder acting on the scapula and arm (anterior view).** The superficial muscles, which effect arm movements, are shown on the left side of the figure. These muscles have been removed on the right side of the figure to show the muscles that stabilize or move the pectoral girdle.

| Table 3 | Anterior Muscles of Human Thorax, Shoulder, and Abdominal Wall (continued) | | | |
|---|---|---|---|---|
| **Muscle** | **Comments** | **Origin** | **Insertion** | **Action** |
| **Thorax and Shoulder, Superficial** (continued) | | | | |
| Pectoralis minor | Flat, thin muscle directly beneath and obscured by pectoralis major | Anterior surface of ribs 3–5, near their costal cartilages | Coracoid process of scapula | With ribs fixed, draws scapula forward and inferiorly; with scapula fixed, draws rib cage superiorly |
| **Thorax, Deep: Muscles of Respiration (Figure 7)** | | | | |
| External intercostals | 11 pairs lie between ribs; fibers run obliquely downward and forward toward sternum | Inferior border of rib above (not shown in figure) | Superior border of rib below | Pull ribs toward one another to elevate rib cage; aid in inspiration |
| Internal intercostals | 11 pairs lie between ribs; fibers run deep and at right angles to those of external intercostals | Superior border of rib below | Inferior border of rib above (not shown in figure) | Draw ribs together to depress rib cage; aid in forced expiration; antagonistic to external intercostals |
| Diaphragm | Broad muscle; forms floor of thoracic cavity; dome-shaped in relaxed state; fibers converge from margins of thoracic cage toward a central tendon | Inferior border of rib and sternum, costal cartilages of last six ribs and lumbar vertebrae | Central tendon | Prime mover of inspiration flattens on contraction, increasing vertical dimensions of thorax; increases intra-abdominal pressure |
| **Abdominal Wall (Figure 8a and b)** | | | | |
| Rectus abdominis | Medial superficial muscle, extends from pubis to rib cage; ensheathed by aponeuroses of oblique muscles; segmented | Pubic crest and symphysis | Xiphoid process and costal cartilages of ribs 5–7 | Flexes and rotates vertebral column; increases abdominal pressure; fixes and depresses ribs; stabilizes pelvis during walking; used in sit-ups and curls |
| External oblique | Most superficial lateral muscle; fibers run downward and medially; ensheathed by an aponeurosis | Anterior surface of last eight ribs | Linea alba,* pubic crest and tubercles, and iliac crest | See rectus abdominis, above; compresses abdominal wall; also aids muscles of back in trunk rotation and lateral flexion; used in oblique curls |
| Internal oblique | Most fibers run at right angles to those of external oblique, which it underlies | Lumbar fascia, iliac crest, and inguinal ligament | Linea alba, pubic crest, and costal cartilages of last three ribs | As for external oblique |
| Transversus abdominis | Deepest muscle of abdominal wall; fibers run horizontally | Inguinal ligament, iliac crest, cartilages of last five or six ribs, and lumbar fascia | Linea alba and pubic crest | Compresses abdominal contents |

*The linea alba (white line) is a narrow, tendinous sheath that runs along the middle of the abdomen from the sternum to the pubic symphysis. It is formed by the fusion of the aponeurosis of the external oblique and transversus muscles.

**Figure 7 Deep muscles of the thorax: muscles of respiration. (a)** The external intercostals (inspiratory muscles) are shown on the left and the internal intercostals (expiratory muscles) are shown on the right. These two muscle layers run obliquely and at right angles to each other. **(b)** Inferior view of the diaphragm, the prime mover of inspiration. Notice that its muscle fibers converge toward a central tendon, an arrangement that causes the diaphragm to flatten and move inferiorly as it contracts. The diaphragm and its tendon are pierced by the great vessels (aorta and inferior vena cava) and the esophagus.

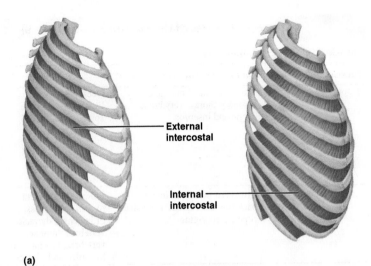

External intercostal

Internal intercostal

**(a)**

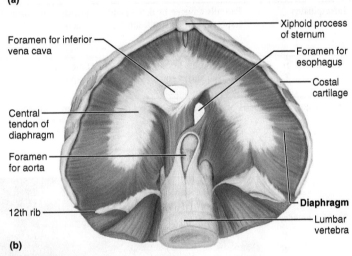

Foramen for inferior vena cava

Xiphoid process of sternum

Foramen for esophagus

Costal cartilage

Central tendon of diaphragm

Foramen for aorta

**Diaphragm**

12th rib

Lumbar vertebra

**(b)**

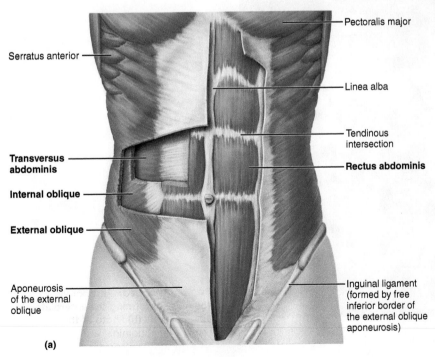

Serratus anterior

Pectoralis major

Linea alba

Tendinous intersection

**Transversus abdominis**

**Internal oblique**

**Rectus abdominis**

**External oblique**

Aponeurosis of the external oblique

Inguinal ligament (formed by free inferior border of the external oblique aponeurosis)

**Figure 8 Anterior view of the muscles forming the anterolateral abdominal wall. (a)** The superficial muscles have been partially cut away on the left side of the diagram to reveal the deeper internal oblique and transversus abdominis muscles.

**(a)**

| Table 4 | Posterior Muscles of Human Trunk (see Figure 9) | | | |
|---------|----------|--------|-----------|--------|
| **Muscle** | **Comments** | **Origin** | **Insertion** | **Action** |
| **Muscles of the Neck, Shoulder, and Thorax (Figure 9a)** | | | | |
| Trapezius | Most superficial muscle of posterior thorax; very broad origin and insertion | Occipital bone; ligamentum nuchae; spines of C₇ and all thoracic vertebrae | Acromion and spinous process of scapula; lateral third of clavicle | Extends head; raises, rotates, and retracts (adducts) scapula and stabilizes it; superior fibers elevate scapula (as in shrugging the shoulders); inferior fibers depress it |
| Latissimus dorsi | Broad flat muscle of lower back (lumbar region); extensive superficial origins | Indirect attachment to spinous processes of lower six thoracic vertebrae, lumbar vertebrae, last three to four ribs, and iliac crest | Floor of intertubercular sulcus of humerus | Prime mover of arm extension; adducts and medially rotates arm; brings arm down in power stroke, as in striking a blow |
| Infraspinatus | Partially covered by deltoid and trapezius; a rotator cuff muscle | Infraspinous fossa of scapula | Greater tubercle of humerus | Lateral rotation of humerus; helps hold head of humerus in glenoid cavity; stabilizes shoulder |
| Teres minor | Small muscle inferior to infraspinatus; a rotator cuff muscle | Lateral margin of scapula | Greater tubercle of humerus | As for infraspinatus |
| Teres major | Located inferiorly to teres minor | Posterior surface at inferior angle of scapula | Intertubercular sulcus of humerus | Extends, medially rotates, and adducts humerus; synergist of latissimus dorsi |

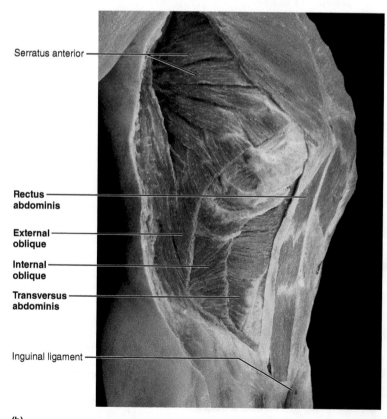

Serratus anterior

Rectus abdominis

External oblique

Internal oblique

Transversus abdominis

Inguinal ligament

**(b)**

**Figure 8 *(continued)* Anterior view of the muscles forming the anterolateral abdominal wall. (b)** Photo of the anterolateral abdominal wall.

| Table 4 | (continued) | | | |
|---|---|---|---|---|
| **Muscle** | **Comments** | **Origin** | **Insertion** | **Action** |
| Supraspinatus | Obscured by trapezius; a rotator cuff muscle | Supraspinous fossa of scapula | Greater tubercle of humerus | Initiates abduction of humerus; stabilizes shoulder joint |
| Levator scapulae | Located at back and side of neck, deep to trapezius | Transverse processes of $C_1$–$C_4$ | Medial border of scapula superior to spine | Elevates and adducts scapula; with fixed scapula, laterally flexes neck to the same side |
| Rhomboids—major and minor | Beneath trapezius and inferior to levator scapulae; rhomboid minor is the more superior muscle | Spinous processes of $C_7$ and $T_1$–$T_5$ | Medial border of scapula | Pull scapula medially (retraction); stabilize scapula; rotate glenoid cavity downward |

**Muscles Associated with the Vertebral Column (Figure 9b)**

| | | | | |
|---|---|---|---|---|
| Semispinalis | Deep composite muscle of the back—thoracis, cervicis, and capitis portions | Transverse processes of $C_7$–$T_{12}$ | Occipital bone and spinous processes of cervical vertebrae and $T_1$–$T_4$ | Acting together, extend head and vertebral column; acting independently (right vs. left) causes rotation toward the opposite side |

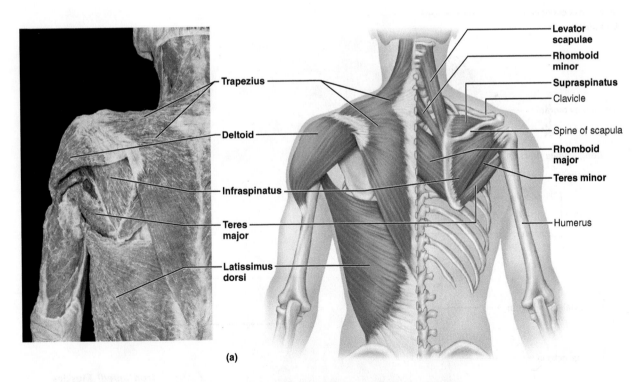

(a)

**Figure 9 Muscles of the neck, shoulder, and thorax (posterior view). (a)** The superficial muscles of the back are shown for the left side of the body, with a corresponding photograph. The superficial muscles are removed on the right side of the illustration to reveal the deeper muscles acting on the scapula and the rotator cuff muscles that help to stabilize the shoulder joint.

| Table 4 | Posterior Muscles of Human Trunk *(continued)* | | | |
|---|---|---|---|---|
| Muscle | Comments | Origin | Insertion | Action |
| **Muscles Associated with the Vertebral Column** *(continued)* | | | | |
| Erector spinae | A long tripartite muscle composed of iliocostalis (lateral), longissimus, and spinalis (medial) muscle columns; superficial to semispinalis muscles; extends from pelvis to head | Iliac crest, transverse processes of lumbar, thoracic, and cervical vertebrae, and/or ribs 3–6 depending on specific part | Ribs and transverse processes of vertebrae about six segments above origin; longissimus also inserts into mastoid process | Extend and bend the vertebral column laterally; fibers of the longissimus also extend head |

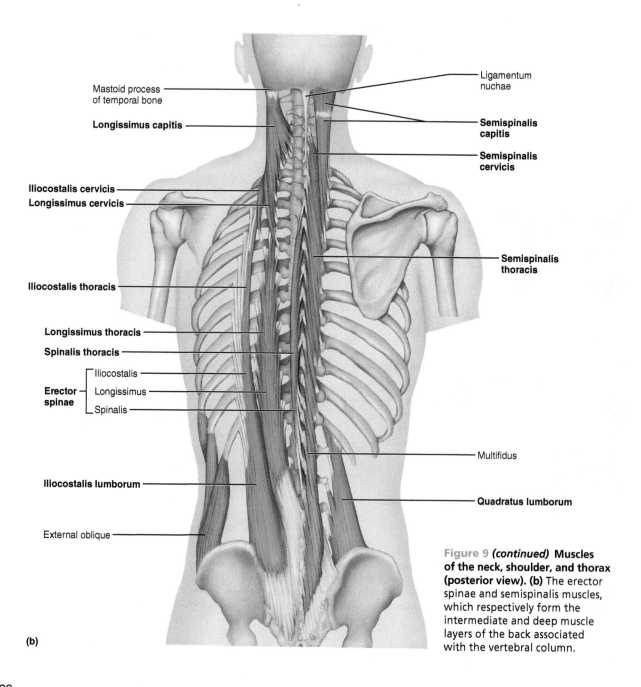

**Figure 9** *(continued)* **Muscles of the neck, shoulder, and thorax (posterior view). (b)** The erector spinae and semispinalis muscles, which respectively form the intermediate and deep muscle layers of the back associated with the vertebral column.

**(b)**

| Table 4 | (continued) | | | |
|---------|-------------|---|---|---|
| **Muscle** | **Comments** | **Origin** | **Insertion** | **Action** |
| Splenius (see Figure 9c) | Superficial muscle (capitis and cervicis parts) extending from upper thoracic region to skull | Ligamentum nuchae and spinous processes of $C_7$–$T_6$ | Mastoid process, occipital bone, and transverse processes of $C_2$–$C_4$ | As a group, extend or hyperextend head; when only one side is active, head is rotated and bent toward the same side |
| Quadratus lumborum | Forms greater portion of posterior abdominal wall | Iliac crest and lumbar fascia | Inferior border of rib 12; transverse processes of lumbar vertebrae | Each flexes vertebral column laterally; together extend the lumbar spine and fix rib 12; maintains upright posture |

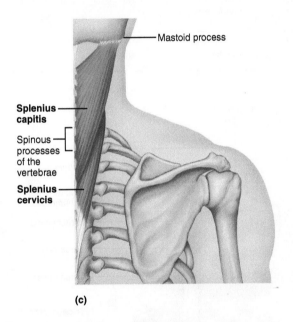

Mastoid process

**Splenius capitis**

Spinous processes of the vertebrae

**Splenius cervicis**

**(c)**

**Figure 9** *(continued)* **Muscles of the neck, shoulder, and thorax (posterior view). (c)** Deep (splenius) muscles of the posterior neck. Superficial muscles have been removed.

## Muscles of the Upper Limb

The muscles that act on the upper limb fall into three groups: those that move the arm, those causing movement at the elbow, and those moving the wrist and hand.

The muscles that cross the shoulder joint to insert on the humerus and move the arm (subscapularis, supraspinatus and infraspinatus, deltoid, and so on) are primarily trunk muscles that originate on the axial skeleton or shoulder girdle. These muscles are included with the trunk muscles.

The second group of muscles, which cross the elbow joint and move the forearm, consists of muscles forming the musculature of the humerus. These muscles arise mainly from the humerus and insert in forearm bones. They are responsible for flexion, extension, pronation, and supination.

The third group forms the musculature of the forearm. For the most part, these muscles insert on the digits and produce movements at the wrist and fingers.

### ACTIVITY 3

### Identifying Muscles of the Upper Limb

Study the origins, insertions, and actions of muscles that move the forearm and identify them in the figure (Table 5 and Figure 10).

Do the same for muscles acting on the wrist and hand (Table 6 and Figure 11). They are more easily identified if their insertion tendons are located first.

Then see if you can identify the upper limb muscles on a torso model, anatomical chart, or cadaver. Complete this portion of the exercise with palpation demonstrations as outlined next.

### Demonstrating Operations of Upper Limb Muscles

1. To observe the *biceps brachii*, attempt to flex your forearm (hand supinated) against resistance. The insertion tendon of this biceps muscle can also be felt in the lateral aspect of the antecubital fossa (where it runs toward the radius to attach).

2. If you acutely flex your elbow and then try to extend it against resistance, you can demonstrate the action of your *triceps brachii*.

3. Strongly flex your wrist and make a fist. Palpate your contracting wrist flexor muscles (which originate from the medial epicondyle of the humerus) and their insertion tendons, which can be easily felt at the anterior aspect of the wrist.

4. Flare your fingers to identify the tendons of the *extensor digitorum* muscle on the dorsum of your hand. ■

223

| Table 5 | Muscles of Human Humerus That Act on the Forearm (see Figure 10) | | | |
|---------|---------|--------|-----------|--------|
| **Muscle** | **Comments** | **Origin** | **Insertion** | **Action** |
| Triceps brachii | Sole, large fleshy muscle of posterior humerus; three-headed origin | Long head—inferior margin of glenoid cavity; lateral head—posterior humerus; medial head—distal radial groove on posterior humerus | Olecranon of ulna | Powerful forearm extensor; antagonist of forearm flexors (brachialis and biceps brachii) |
| Anconeus | Short triangular muscle blended with triceps | Lateral epicondyle of humerus | Lateral aspect of olecranon of ulna | Abducts ulna during forearm pronation; extends elbow |
| Biceps brachii | Most familiar muscle of anterior humerus because this two-headed muscle bulges when forearm is flexed | Short head: coracoid process; long head: supraglenoid tubercle and lip of glenoid cavity; tendon of long head runs in intertubercular sulcus and within capsule of shoulder joint | Radial tuberosity | Flexion (powerful) of elbow and supination of forearm; "it turns the corkscrew and pulls the cork"; weak arm flexor |
| Brachioradialis | Superficial muscle of lateral forearm; forms lateral boundary of antecubital fossa | Lateral ridge at distal end of humerus | Base of radial styloid process | Synergist in forearm flexion |
| Brachialis | Immediately deep to biceps brachii | Distal portion of anterior humerus | Coronoid process of ulna | A major flexor of forearm |

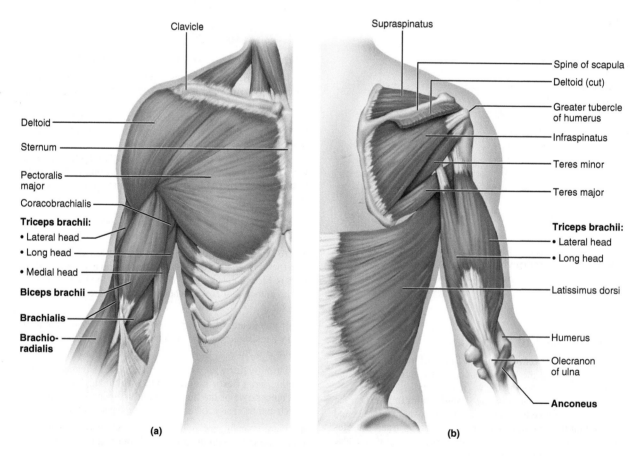

**Figure 10 Muscles causing movements of the arm and forearm. (a)** Superficial muscles of the anterior thorax, shoulder, and arm, anterior view. **(b)** Posterior aspect of the arm showing the lateral and long heads of the triceps brachii muscle.

| Table 6 | Muscles of Human Forearm That Act on Hand and Fingers (see Figure 11) | | | |
|---|---|---|---|---|
| Muscle | Comments | Origin | Insertion | Action |
| **Anterior Compartment, Superficial (Figure 11a, b, c)** | | | | |
| Pronator teres | Seen in a superficial view between proximal margins of brachioradialis and flexor carpi radialis | Medial epicondyle of humerus and coronoid process of ulna | Midshaft of radius | Acts synergistically with pronator quadratus to pronate forearm; weak elbow flexor |
| Flexor carpi radialis | Superficial; runs diagonally across forearm | Medial epicondyle of humerus | Base of metacarpals II and III | Powerful flexor of wrist; abducts hand |
| Palmaris longus | Small fleshy muscle with a long tendon; medial to flexor carpi radialis | Medial epicondyle of humerus | Palmar aponeurosis; skin and fascia of palm | Flexes wrist (weak); tenses skin and fascia of palm |

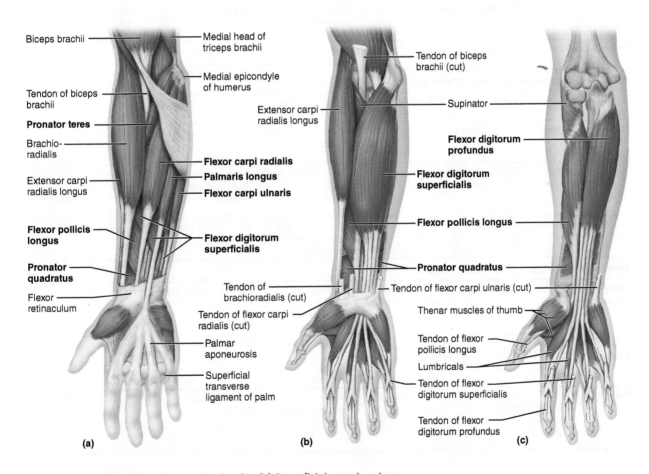

**Figure 11 Muscles of the forearm and wrist. (a)** Superficial anterior view of right forearm and hand. **(b)** The brachioradialis, flexors carpi radialis and ulnaris, and palmaris longus muscles have been removed to reveal the position of the somewhat deeper flexor digitorum superficialis. **(c)** Deep muscles of the anterior compartment. Superficial muscles have been removed. (*Note:* The thenar muscles of the thumb and the lumbricals that help move the fingers are illustrated here but are not described in Table 6.)

| Table 6 | Muscles of Human Forearm That Act on Hand and Fingers *(continued)* | | | |
|---|---|---|---|---|
| **Muscle** | **Comments** | **Origin** | **Insertion** | **Action** |
| **Anterior Compartment, Superficial** *(continued)* | | | | |
| Flexor carpi ulnaris | Superficial; medial to palmaris longus | Medial epicondyle of humerus and olecranon and posterior surface of ulna | Base of metacarpal; pisiform and hamate bones | Powerful flexor of wrist; adducts hand |
| Flexor digitorum superficialis | Deeper muscle (deep to muscles named above); visible at distal end of forearm | Medial epicondyle of humerus, coronoid process of ulna, and shaft of radius | Middle phalanges of fingers 2–5 | Flexes wrist and middle phalanges of fingers 2–5 |
| **Anterior Compartment, Deep (Figure 11a, b, c)** | | | | |
| Flexor pollicis longus | Deep muscle of anterior forearm; distal to and paralleling lower margin of flexor digitorum superficialis | Anterior surface of radius, and interosseous membrane | Distal phalanx of thumb | Flexes thumb (*pollex* is Latin for "thumb") |
| Flexor digitorum profundus | Deep muscle; overlain entirely by flexor digitorum superficialis | Anteromedial surface of ulna, interosseous membrane, and coronoid process | Distal phalanges of fingers 2–5 | Sole muscle that flexes distal phalanges; assists in wrist flexion |
| Pronator quadratus | Deepest muscle of distal forearm | Distal portion of anterior ulnar surface | Anterior surface of radius, distal end | Pronates forearm |
| **Posterior Compartment, Superficial (Figure 11d, e, f)** | | | | |
| Extensor carpi radialis longus | Superficial; parallels brachioradialis on lateral forearm | Lateral supracondylar ridge of humerus | Base of metacarpal II | Extends and abducts wrist |
| Extensor carpi radialis brevis | Deep to extensor carpi radialis longus | Lateral epicondyle of humerus | Base of metacarpal III | Extends and abducts wrist; steadies wrist during finger flexion |
| Extensor digitorum | Superficial; medial to extensor carpi radialis brevis | Lateral epicondyle of humerus | By four tendons into distal phalanges of fingers 2–5 | Prime mover of finger extension; extends wrist; can flare (abduct) fingers |
| Extensor carpi ulnaris | Superficial; medial posterior forearm | Lateral epicondyle of humerus; posterior border of ulna | Base of metacarpal V | Extends and adducts wrist |
| **Posterior Compartment, Deep (Figure 11d, e, f )** | | | | |
| Extensor pollicis longus and brevis | Muscle pair with a common origin and action; deep to extensor carpi ulnaris | Dorsal shaft of ulna and radius, interosseous membrane | Base of distal phalanx of thumb (longus) and proximal phalanx of thumb (brevis) | Extend thumb |
| Abductor pollicis longus | Deep muscle; lateral and parallel to extensor pollicis longus | Posterior surface of radius and ulna; interosseous membrane | Metacarpal I and trapezium | Abducts and extends thumb |
| Supinator | Deep muscle at posterior aspect of elbow | Lateral epicondyle of humerus; proximal ulna | Proximal end of radius | Acts with biceps brachii to supinate forearm; antagonist of pronator muscles |

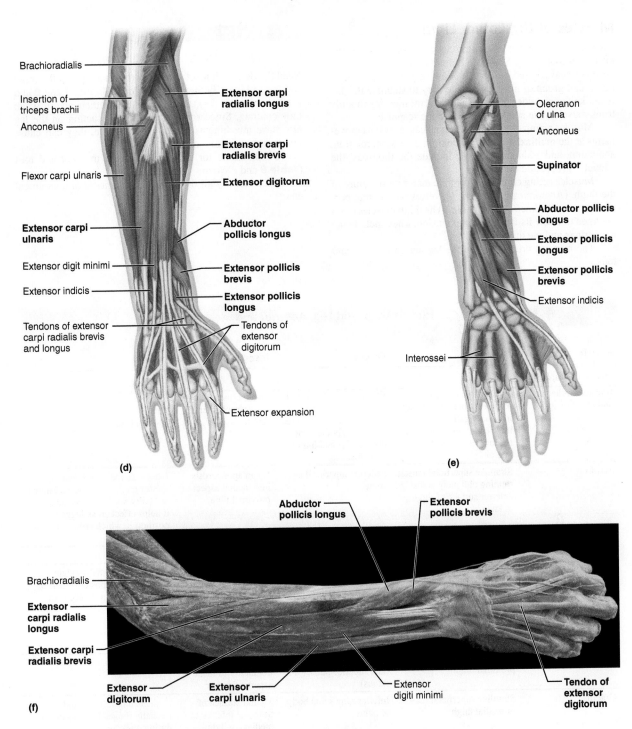

Brachioradialis

Insertion of triceps brachii

Anconeus

Flexor carpi ulnaris

**Extensor carpi ulnaris**

Extensor digit minimi

Extensor indicis

Tendons of extensor carpi radialis brevis and longus

**Extensor carpi radialis longus**

**Extensor carpi radialis brevis**

**Extensor digitorum**

Abductor pollicis longus

**Extensor pollicis brevis**

**Extensor pollicis longus**

Tendons of extensor digitorum

Extensor expansion

**(d)**

Olecranon of ulna

Anconeus

**Supinator**

**Abductor pollicis longus**

**Extensor pollicis longus**

**Extensor pollicis brevis**

Extensor indicis

Interossei

**(e)**

Abductor pollicis longus

Extensor pollicis brevis

Brachioradialis

**Extensor carpi radialis longus**

**Extensor carpi radialis brevis**

**Extensor digitorum**

**Extensor carpi ulnaris**

Extensor digiti minimi

**Tendon of extensor digitorum**

**(f)**

**Figure 11** *(continued)* **Muscles of the forearm and wrist. (d)** Superficial muscles, posterior view. **(e)** Deep posterior muscles; superficial muscles have been removed. The interossei, the deepest layer of instrinsic hand muscles, are also illustrated. **(f)** Photo of posterior muscles of the right forearm.

227

# Muscles of the Lower Limb

Muscles that act on the lower limb cause movement at the hip, knee, and foot joints. Since the human pelvic girdle is composed of heavy, fused bones that allow very little movement, no special group of muscles is necessary to stabilize it. This is unlike the shoulder girdle, where several muscles (mainly trunk muscles) are needed to stabilize the scapulae.

Muscles acting on the thigh (femur) cause various movements at the multiaxial hip joint (flexion, extension, rotation, abduction, and adduction). These include the iliopsoas, the adductor group, and others.

Muscles acting on the leg form the major musculature of the thigh. (Anatomically the term *leg* refers only to that portion between the knee and the ankle.) The thigh muscles cross the knee to allow its flexion and extension. They include the hamstrings and the quadriceps.

The muscles originating on the leg act on the foot and toes.

**ACTIVITY 4**

## Identifying Muscles of the Lower Limb

Read the descriptions of specific muscles acting on the thigh and leg and identify them in the figures (Tables 7 and 8 and Figures 12 and 13), trying to visualize their action when they contract. Since some of the muscles acting on the leg also have attachments on the pelvic girdle, they can cause movement at the hip joint.

Do the same for muscles acting on the foot and toes (Table 9 and Figures 14 and 15).

Then identify all the muscles on a model or anatomical chart.

| Table 7 | Muscles Acting on Human Thigh and Leg, Anterior and Medial Aspects (see Figure 12) | | | |
|---------|-----------|--------|-----------|--------|
| **Muscle** | **Comments** | **Origin** | **Insertion** | **Action** |
| **Origin on the Pelvis** | | | | |
| Iliopsoas—iliacus and psoas major | Two closely related muscles; fibers pass under inguinal ligament to insert into femur via a common tendon; iliacus is more lateral | Iliacus—iliac fossa and crest, lateral sacrum; psoas major—transverse processes, bodies, and discs of $T_{12}$ and lumbar vertebrae | On and just below lesser trochanter of femur | Flex trunk on thigh; flex thigh; lateral flexion of vertebral column (psoas) |
| Sartorius | Straplike superficial muscle running obliquely across anterior surface of thigh to knee | Anterior superior iliac spine | By an aponeurosis into medial aspect of proximal tibia | Flexes, abducts, and laterally rotates thigh; flexes knee; known as "tailor's muscle" because it helps effect cross-legged position in which tailors are often depicted |
| **Medial Compartment** | | | | |
| Adductors—magnus, longus, and brevis | Large muscle mass forming medial aspect of thigh; arise from front of pelvis and insert at various levels on femur | Magnus—ischial and pubic rami and ischial tuberosity; longus—pubis near pubic symphysis; brevis—body and inferior pubic ramus | Magnus—linea aspera and adductor tubercle of femur; longus and brevis—linea aspera | Adduct and medially rotate and flex thigh; posterior part of magnus is also a synergist in thigh extension |
| Pectineus | Overlies adductor brevis on proximal thigh | Pectineal line of pubis (and superior pubic ramus) | Inferior from lesser trochanter to linea aspera of femur | Adducts, flexes, and medially rotates thigh |
| Gracilis | Straplike superficial muscle of medial thigh | Inferior ramus and body of pubis | Medial surface of tibia just inferior to medial condyle | Adducts thigh; flexes and medially rotates leg, especially during walking |

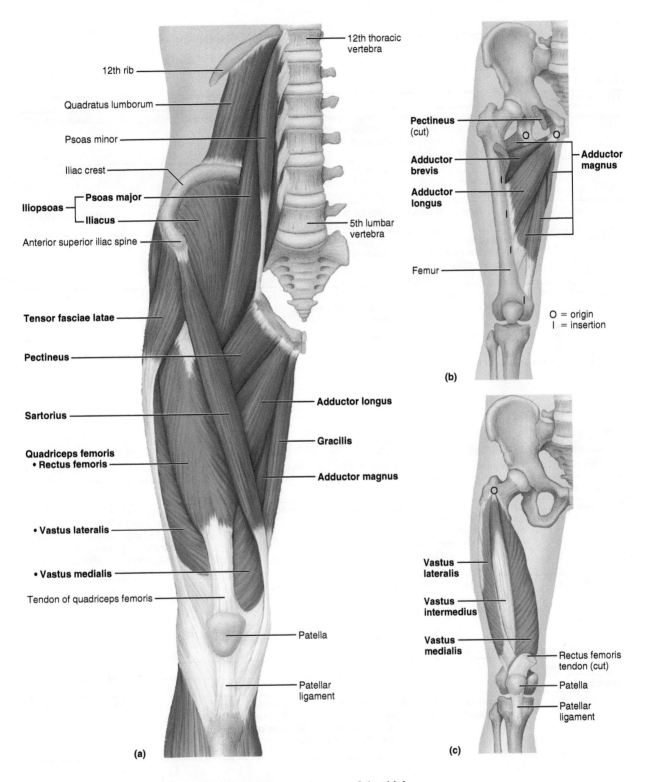

**Figure 12 Anterior and medial muscles promoting movements of the thigh and leg. (a)** Anterior view of the deep muscles of the pelvis and superficial muscles of the right thigh. **(b)** Adductor muscles of the medial compartment of the thigh. **(c)** The vastus muscles (isolated) of the quadriceps group.

229

| Table 7 | Muscles Acting on Human Thigh and Leg, Anterior and Medial Aspects *(continued)* | | | |
|---|---|---|---|---|
| **Muscle** | **Comments** | **Origin** | **Insertion** | **Action** |
| **Anterior Compartment** | | | | |
| Quadriceps femoris* | | | | |
| Rectus femoris | Superficial muscle of thigh; runs straight down thigh; only muscle of group to cross hip joint | Anterior inferior iliac spine and superior margin of acetabulum | Tibial tuberosity and patella | Extends knee and flexes thigh at hip |
| Vastus lateralis | Forms lateral aspect of thigh; intramuscular injection site | Greater trochanter, intertrochanteric line, and linea aspera | Tibial tuberosity and patella | Extends and stabilizes knee |
| Vastus medialis | Forms inferomedial aspect of thigh | Linea aspera and intertrochanteric line | Tibial tuberosity and patella | Extends knee; stabilizes patella |
| Vastus intermedius | Obscured by rectus femoris; lies between vastus lateralis and vastus medialis on anterior thigh | Anterior and lateral surface of femur | Tibial tuberosity and patella | Extends knee |
| Tensor fasciae latae | Enclosed between fascia layers of thigh | Anterior aspect of iliac crest and anterior superior iliac spine | Iliotibial tract (lateral portion of fascia lata) | Flexes, abducts, and medially rotates thigh; steadies trunk |

*The quadriceps form the flesh of the anterior thigh and have a common insertion in the tibial tuberosity via the patellar tendon. They are powerful leg extensors, enabling humans to kick a football, for example.

| Table 8 | Muscles Acting on Human Thigh and Leg, Posterior Aspect (see Figure 13) | | | |
|---|---|---|---|---|
| **Muscle** | **Comments** | **Origin** | **Insertion** | **Action** |
| **Origin on the Pelvis** | | | | |
| Gluteus maximus | Largest and most superficial of gluteal muscles (which form buttock mass); intramuscular injection site | Dorsal ilium, sacrum, and coccyx | Gluteal tuberosity of femur and iliotibial tract* | Complex, powerful thigh extensor (most effective when thigh is flexed, as in climbing stairs—but not as in walking); antagonist of iliopsoas; laterally rotates and abducts thigh |
| Gluteus medius | Partially covered by gluteus maximus; intramuscular injection site | Upper lateral surface of ilium | Greater trochanter of femur | Abducts and medially rotates thigh; steadies pelvis during walking |
| Gluteus minimus (not shown in figure) | Smallest and deepest gluteal muscle | External inferior surface of ilium | Greater trochanter of femur | Abducts and medially rotates thigh; steadies pelvis |
| **Posterior Compartment** | | | | |
| Hamstrings† | | | | |
| Biceps femoris | Most lateral muscle of group; arises from two heads | Ischial tuberosity (long head); linea aspera and distal femur (short head) | Tendon passes laterally to insert into head of fibula and lateral condyle of tibia | Extends thigh; laterally rotates leg; flexes knee |

| Table 8 | (continued) | | | |
|---------|-------------|--------|-----------|--------|
| **Muscle** | **Comments** | **Origin** | **Insertion** | **Action** |
| Semitendinosus | Medial to biceps femoris | Ischial tuberosity | Medial aspect of upper tibial shaft | Extends thigh; flexes knee; medially rotates leg |
| Semimembranosus | Deep to semitendinosus | Ischial tuberosity | Medial condyle of tibia; lateral condyle of femur | Extends thigh; flexes knee; medially rotates leg |

\* The iliotibial tract, a thickened lateral portion of the fascia lata, ensheathes all the muscles of the thigh. It extends as a tendinous band from the iliac crest to the knee.

†The hamstrings are the fleshy muscles of the posterior thigh. The name comes from the butchers' practice of using the tendons of these muscles to hang hams for smoking. As a group, they are strong extensors of the hip; they counteract the powerful quadriceps by stabilizing the knee joint when standing.

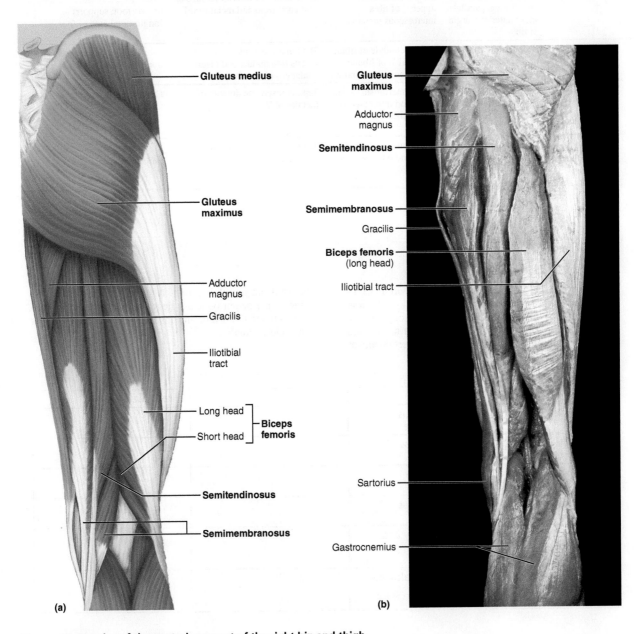

**Figure 13 Muscles of the posterior aspect of the right hip and thigh.**
**(a)** Superficial view showing the gluteus muscles of the buttock and hamstring muscles of the thigh. **(b)** Photo of muscles of the posterior thigh.

| Table 9 | Muscles Acting on Human Foot and Ankle (see Figures 14 and 15) | | | |
|---|---|---|---|---|
| **Muscle** | **Comments** | **Origin** | **Insertion** | **Action** |
| **Lateral Compartment (Figure 14a, b and Figure 15b)** | | | | |
| Fibularis (peroneus) longus | Superficial lateral muscle; overlies fibula | Head and upper portion of fibula | By long tendon under foot to metatarsal I and medial cuneiform | Plantar flexes and everts foot; helps keep foot flat on ground |
| Fibularis (peroneus) brevis | Smaller muscle; deep to fibularis longus | Distal portion of fibula shaft | By tendon running behind lateral malleolus to insert on proximal end of metatarsal V | Plantar flexes and everts foot, as part of fibularis group |
| **Anterior Compartment (Figure 14a, b)** | | | | |
| Tibialis anterior | Superficial muscle of anterior leg; parallels sharp anterior margin of tibia | Lateral condyle and upper ⅔ of tibia; interosseous membrane | By tendon into inferior surface of first cuneiform and metatarsal I | Prime mover of dorsiflexion; inverts foot; supports longitudinal arch of foot |
| Extensor digitorum longus | Anterolateral surface of leg; lateral to tibialis anterior | Lateral condyle of tibia; proximal ¾ of fibula; interosseous membrane | Tendon divides into four parts; inserts into middle and distal phalanges of toes 2–5 | Prime mover of toe extension; dorsiflexes foot |
| Fibularis (peroneus) tertius | Small muscle; often fused to distal part of extensor digitorum longus | Distal anterior surface of fibula and interosseous membrane | Tendon inserts on dorsum of metatarsal V | Dorsiflexes and everts foot |
| Extensor hallucis longus | Deep to extensor digitorum longus and tibialis anterior | Anteromedial shaft of fibula and interosseous membrane | Tendon inserts on distal phalanx of great toe | Extends great toe; dorsiflexes foot |

### GROUP CHALLENGE

## Name That Muscle

Work in groups of three or four to fill out the Group Challenge chart for muscle IDs. Refrain from looking back at the tables. Use the "brain power" of your group and the appropriate muscle models. To assist in this task, recall that when a muscle contracts, the muscle's insertion moves toward the muscle's origin. Also, in the muscles of the limbs, the origin typically lies proximal to the insertion. Sometimes the origin and insertion are even part of the muscle's name!

**Group Challenge: Muscle IDs**

| Origin | Insertion | Muscle | Primary action |
|---|---|---|---|
| Zygomatic arch and maxilla | Angle and ramus of the mandible | | |
| Anterior surface of ribs 3–5 | Coracoid process of the scapula | | |
| Inferior border of rib above | Superior border of rib below | | |
| Distal portion of anterior humerus | Coronoid process of the ulna | | |
| Anterior inferior iliac spine and superior margin of acetabulum | Tibial tuberosity and patella | | |
| By two heads from medial and lateral condyles of femur | Calcaneus via calcaneal tendon | | |

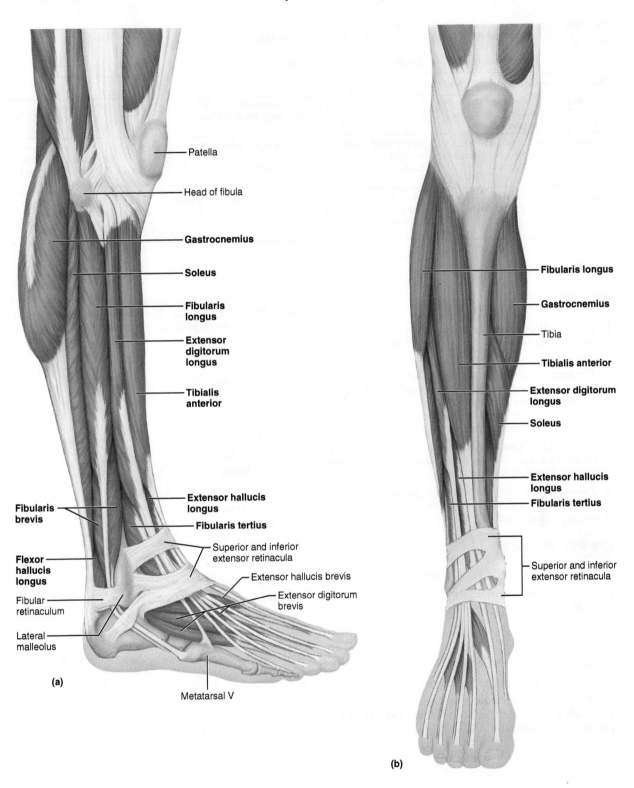

Patella

Head of fibula

**Gastrocnemius**

**Soleus**

**Fibularis longus**

**Extensor digitorum longus**

**Tibialis anterior**

**Extensor hallucis longus**

**Fibularis tertius**

Superior and inferior extensor retinacula

Extensor hallucis brevis

Extensor digitorum brevis

**Fibularis brevis**

**Flexor hallucis longus**

Fibular retinaculum

Lateral malleolus

**(a)**

Metatarsal V

**Fibularis longus**

**Gastrocnemius**

Tibia

**Tibialis anterior**

**Extensor digitorum longus**

**Soleus**

**Extensor hallucis longus**

**Fibularis tertius**

Superior and inferior extensor retinacula

**(b)**

**Figure 14 Muscles of the anterolateral aspect of the right leg.**
**(a)** Superficial view of lateral aspect of the leg, illustrating the positioning of the lateral compartment muscles (fibularis longus and brevis) relative to anterior and posterior leg muscles. **(b)** Superficial view of anterior leg muscles.

| Table 9 | Muscles Acting on Human Foot and Ankle *(continued)* | | | |
|---------|-------------|--------|-----------|--------|
| Muscle | Comments | Origin | Insertion | Action |
| **Posterior Compartment, Superficial (Figure 15a; also Figure 14)** | | | | |
| Triceps surae | Refers to muscle pair below that shapes posterior calf | | Via common tendon (calcaneal) into calcaneus of the heel | Plantar flex foot |
| Gastrocnemius | Superficial muscle of pair; two prominent bellies | By two heads from medial and lateral condyles of femur | Calcaneus via calcaneal tendon | Plantar flexes foot when knee is extended; crosses knee joint; thus can flex knee (when foot is dorsiflexed) |
| Soleus | Deep to gastrocnemius | Proximal portion of tiba and fibula; interosseous membrane | Calcaneus via calcaneal tendon | Plantar flexion; is an important muscle for locomotion |

## Demonstrating Operations of Lower Limb Muscles

1. Go into a deep knee bend and palpate your own *gluteus maximus* muscle as you extend your hip to resume the upright posture.

2. Demonstrate the contraction of the anterior *quadriceps femoris* by trying to extend your knee against resistance. Do this while seated and note how the patellar tendon reacts. The *biceps femoris* of the posterior thigh comes into play when you flex your knee against resistance.

3. Now stand on your toes. Have your partner palpate the lateral and medial heads of the *gastrocnemius* and follow it to its insertion in the calcaneal tendon.

4. Dorsiflex and invert your foot while palpating your *tibialis anterior* muscle (which parallels the sharp anterior crest of the tibia laterally). ■

### ACTIVITY 5

## Review of Human Musculature

Review the muscles by watching the *Human Musculature* video. ■

### ACTIVITY 6

## Making a Muscle Painting

1. Choose a male student to be "muscle painted."

2. Obtain brushes and water-based paints from the supply area while the "volunteer" removes his shirt and rolls up his pant legs (if necessary).

3. Using different colored paints, identify the muscles listed below by painting his skin. If a muscle covers a large body area, you may opt to paint only its borders.

- biceps brachii
- deltoid
- erector spinae
- pectoralis major
- rectus femoris
- tibialis anterior
- triceps brachii
- vastus lateralis
- biceps femoris
- extensor carpi radialis longus
- latissimus dorsi
- rectus abdominis
- sternocleidomastoid
- trapezius
- triceps surae
- vastus medialis

4. Check your "human painting" with your instructor before cleaning your bench and leaving the laboratory. ■

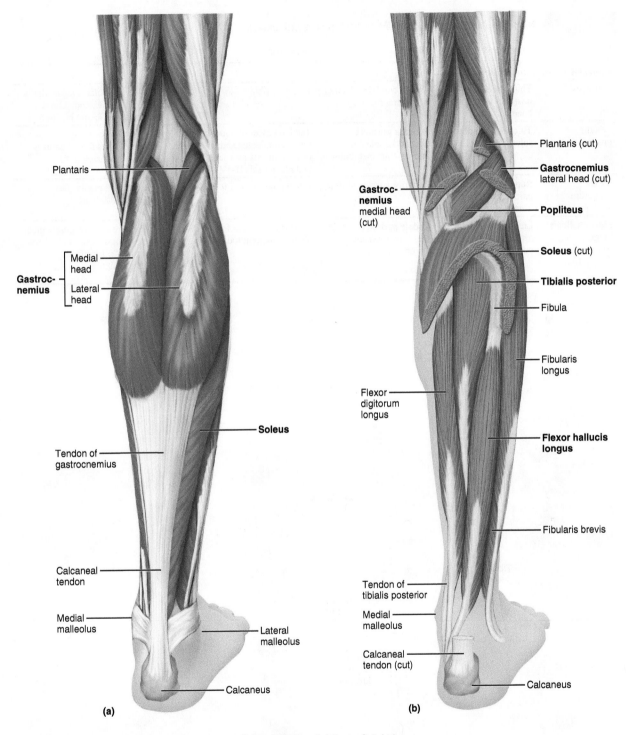

Plantaris

Gastroc-
nemius { Medial
head

Lateral
head

Tendon of
gastrocnemius

Soleus

Calcaneal
tendon

Medial
malleolus

Lateral
malleolus

Calcaneus

**(a)**

Gastroc-
nemius
medial head
(cut)

Plantaris (cut)

**Gastrocnemius**
lateral head (cut)

**Popliteus**

**Soleus** (cut)

**Tibialis posterior**

Fibula

Fibularis
longus

Flexor
digitorum
longus

**Flexor hallucis
longus**

Fibularis brevis

Tendon of
tibialis posterior

Medial
malleolus

Calcaneal
tendon (cut)

Calcaneus

**(b)**

**Figure 15** **Muscles of the posterior aspect of the right leg. (a)** Superficial view
of the posterior leg. **(b)** The triceps surae has been removed to show the deep
muscles of the posterior compartment.

| Table 9 | Muscles Acting on Human Foot and Ankle *(continued)* | | | |
|---|---|---|---|---|
| **Muscle** | **Comments** | **Origin** | **Insertion** | **Action** |
| **Posterior Compartment, Deep (Figure 15b–e)** | | | | |
| Popliteus | Thin muscle at posterior aspect of knee | Lateral condyle of femur and lateral meniscus | Proximal tibia | Flexes and rotates leg medially to "unlock" extended knee when knee flexion begins |
| Tibialis posterior | Thick muscle deep to soleus | Superior portion of tibia and fibula and interosseous membrane | Tendon passes obliquely behind medial malleolus and under arch of foot; inserts into several tarsals and metatarsals II–IV | Prime mover of foot inversion; plantar flexes foot; stabilizes longitudinal arch of foot |
| Flexor digitorum longus | Runs medial to and partially overlies tibialis posterior | Posterior surface of tibia | Distal phalanges of toes 2–5 | Flexes toes; plantar flexes and inverts foot |
| Flexor hallucis longus (see also Figure 14a) | Lies lateral to inferior aspect of tibialis posterior | Middle portion of fibula shaft; interosseous membrane | Tendon runs under foot to distal phalanx of great toe | Flexes great toe (*hallux* = great toe); plantar flexes and inverts foot; the "push-off muscle" during walking |

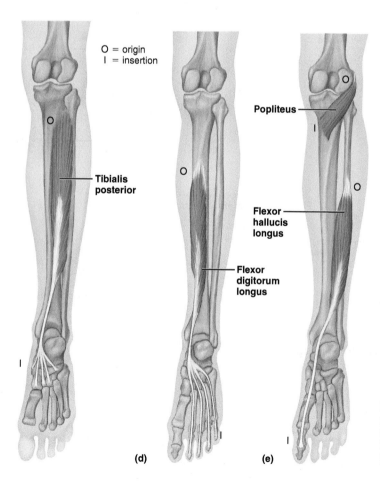

O = origin
I = insertion

**Tibialis posterior**

**Flexor digitorum longus**

**Popliteus**

**Flexor hallucis longus**

**(c)**  **(d)**  **(e)**

**Figure 15 *(continued)* Muscles of the posterior aspect of the right leg.**
**(c–e)** Individual muscles are shown in isolation so that their origins and insertions may be visualized.

# Gross Anatomy of the Muscular System

## Classification of Skeletal Muscles

1. Several criteria were given for the naming of muscles. Match the criteria (column B) to the muscle names (column A). Note that more than one criterion may apply in some cases.

**Column A**

_____ 1. gluteus maximus

_____ 2. adductor magnus

_____ 3. biceps femoris

_____ 4. transversus abdominis

_____ 5. extensor carpi ulnaris

_____ 6. trapezius

_____ 7. rectus femoris

_____ 8. external oblique

**Column B**

a.  action of the muscle

b.  shape of the muscle

c.  location of the origin and/or insertion of the muscle

d.  number of origins

e.  location of the muscle relative to a bone or body region

f.  direction in which the muscle fibers run relative to some imaginary line

g.  relative size of the muscle

2. Match the key terms to the muscles and movements described below.

*Key:*  a.  prime mover (agonist)       b.  antagonist       c.  synergist       d.  fixator

_____ 1. term for the biceps brachii during elbow flexion

_____ 2. term that describes the relation of brachialis to biceps brachii during elbow flexion

_____ 3. term for the triceps brachii during elbow flexion

_____ 4. term for the iliopsoas during hip extension

_____ 5. term for the gluteus maximus during hip extension when walking up stairs

_____ 6. term for the rotator cuff muscles and deltoid when the elbow is flexed and the hand grabs a tabletop to lift the table

# Muscles of the Head and Neck

**3.** Using choices from the key at the right, correctly identify muscles provided with leader lines on the diagram.

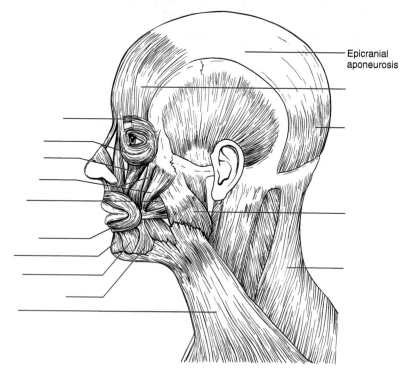

Epicranial
aponeurosis

*Key:*

a. buccinator

b. corrugator supercilii

c. depressor anguli oris

d. depressor labii inferioris

e. epicranius (frontal belly)

f. epicranius (occipital belly)

g. levator labii superioris

h. masseter

i. mentalis

j. orbicularis oculi

k. orbicularis oris

l. platysma

m. trapezius

n. zygomaticus major and minor

**4.** Using the key provided in question 3, identify the muscles described next.

———— 1. used in smiling

———— 2. used to suck in your cheeks

———— 3. used in blinking and squinting

———— 4. used to pout (pulls the corners of the mouth downward)

———— 5. raises your eyebrows for a questioning expression

———— 6. used to form the vertical frown crease on the forehead

———— 7. your "kisser"

———— 8. prime mover to raise the mandible

———— 9. tenses skin of the neck during shaving

# Muscles of the Trunk

**5.** Correctly identify both intact and transected (cut) muscles depicted in the diagram, using the key given at the right. (Not all terms will be used in this identification.)

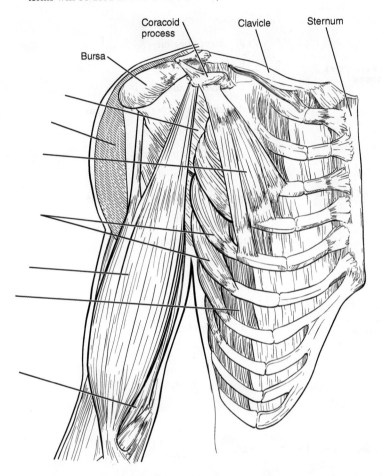

*Key:*

a.  biceps brachii

b.  brachialis

c.  deltoid (cut)

d.  external intercostals

e.  external oblique

f.  internal oblique

g.  latissimus dorsi

h.  pectoralis major

i.  pectoralis minor

j.  rectus abdominis

k.  rhomboids

l.  serratus anterior

m.  subscapularis

n.  transversus abdominis

o.  trapezius

**6.** Using the key provided in question 5 above, identify the major muscles described next.

_____ 1.  a major spine flexor

_____ 2.  prime mover for arm extension

_____ 3.  prime mover for arm flexion

_____ 4.  assume major responsibility for forming the abdominal girdle (three pairs of muscles)

_____ 5.  prime mover of shoulder abduction

_____ 6.  important in shoulder adduction; antagonists of the shoulder abductor (two muscles)

_____ 7.  moves the scapula forward and rotates scapula upward

_____ 8.  small, inspiratory muscles between the ribs; elevate the ribs

_____ 9.  extends the head

_____ 10.  pull the scapulae medially

239

# Muscles of the Upper Limb

**7.** Using terms from the key on the right, correctly identify all muscles provided with leader lines in the diagram. (Not all the listed terms are used in this exercise.)

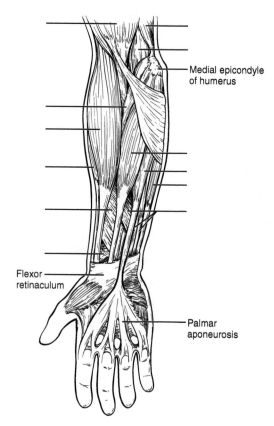

Medial epicondyle
of humerus

Flexor
retinaculum

Palmar
aponeurosis

*Key:*

a. biceps brachii

b. brachialis

c. brachioradialis

d. extensor carpi radialis longus

e. extensor digitorum

f. flexor carpi radialis

g. flexor carpi ulnaris

h. flexor digitorum superficialis

i. flexor pollicis longus

j. palmaris longus

k. pronator quadratus

l. pronator teres

m. supinator

n. triceps brachii

**8.** Use the key provided in question 7 to identify the muscles described next.

_____ 1. flexes the forearm and supinates the hand

_____ 2. synergist for supination of hand

_____ 3. forearm flexors; no role in supination (two muscles)

_____ 4. elbow extensor

_____ 5. power wrist flexor and abductor

_____ 6. flexes wrist and middle phalanges

_____ 7. pronate the hand (two muscles)

_____ 8. flexes the thumb

_____ 9. extends and abducts the wrist

_____ 10. extends the wrist and digits

_____ 11. flat muscle that is a weak wrist flexor; tenses skin of the palm

# Muscles of the Lower Limb

**9.** Using the terms from the key on the right, correctly identify all muscles provided with leader lines in the diagram below. (Not all listed terms are used in this exercise.)

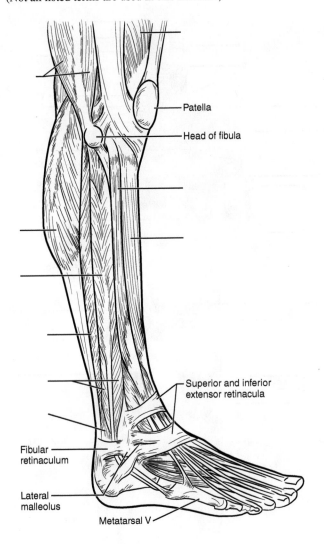

- Patella
- Head of fibula
- Superior and inferior extensor retinacula
- Fibular retinaculum
- Lateral malleolus
- Metatarsal V

*Key:*

a. adductor group

b. biceps femoris

c. extensor digitorum longus

d. fibularis brevis

e. fibularis longus

f. flexor hallucis longus

g. gastrocnemius

h. gluteus maximus

i. gluteus medius

j. rectus femoris

k. semimembranosus

l. semitendinosus

m. soleus

n. tensor fasciae latae

o. tibialis anterior

p. tibialis posterior

q. vastus lateralis

**10.** Use the key terms in question 9 to respond to the descriptions below.

_____ 1. flexes the great toe and inverts the foot

_____ 2. lateral compartment muscles that plantar flex and evert the foot (two muscles)

_____ 3. abduct the thigh to take the "at ease" stance (two muscles)

_____ 4. used to extend the hip when climbing stairs

_____ 5. prime movers of plantar flexion of the foot (two muscles)

_____ 6. prime mover of inversion of the foot

_____ 7. prime mover of dorsiflexion of the foot

_____ 8. adduct the thigh, as when standing at attention

_____ 9. extends the toes

_____ 10. extend thigh and flex knee (three muscles)

_____ 11. extends knee and flexes thigh

# General Review: Muscle Recognition

**11.** Identify each lettered muscle in the diagram of the human anterior superficial musculature by matching its letter with one of the following muscle names:

———— 1. adductor longus

———— 2. biceps brachii

———— 3. brachioradialis

———— 4. deltoid

———— 5. extensor digitorum longus

———— 6. external oblique

———— 7. fibularis longus

———— 8. flexor carpi radialis

———— 9. flexor carpi ulnaris

———— 10. frontal belly of epicranius

———— 11. gastrocnemius

———— 12. gracilis

———— 13. iliopsoas

———— 14. internal oblique

———— 15. latissimus dorsi

———— 16. masseter

———— 17. orbicularis oculi

———— 18. orbicularis oris

———— 19. palmaris longus

———— 20. pectineus

———— 21. pectoralis major

———— 22. platysma

———— 23. pronator teres

———— 24. rectus abdominis

———— 25. rectus femoris

———— 26. sartorius

———— 27. serratus anterior

———— 28. soleus

———— 29. sternocleidomastoid

———— 30. sternohyoid

———— 31. temporalis

———— 32. tensor fasciae latae

———— 33. tibialis anterior

———— 34. transversus abdominis

———— 35. trapezius

———— 36. triceps brachii

———— 37. vastus lateralis

———— 38. vastus medialis

———— 39. zygomaticus

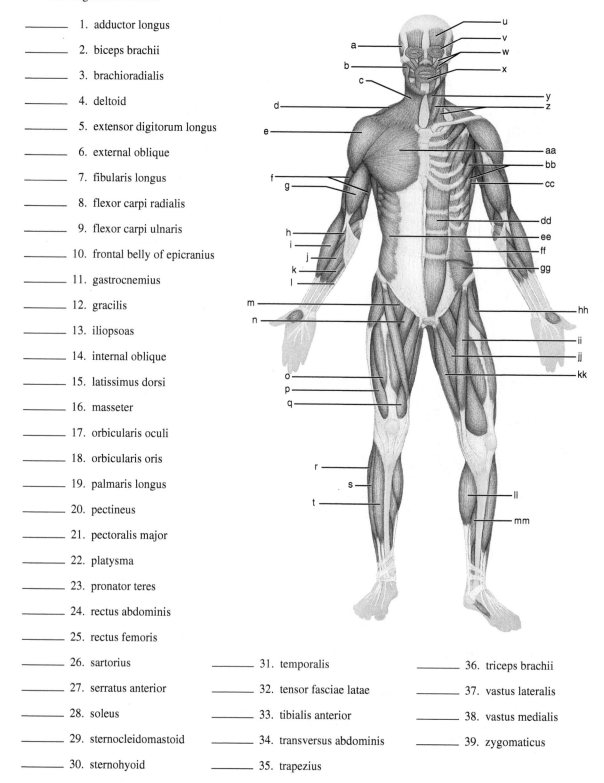

**12.** Identify each lettered muscle in this diagram of the human posterior superficial musculature by matching its letter with one of the following muscle names:

_____ 1. adductor magnus

_____ 2. biceps femoris

_____ 3. brachialis

_____ 4. brachioradialis

_____ 5. deltoid

_____ 6. extensor carpi radialis longus

_____ 7. extensor carpi ulnaris

_____ 8. extensor digitorum

_____ 9. external oblique

_____ 10. flexor carpi ulnaris

_____ 11. gastrocnemius

_____ 12. gluteus maximus

_____ 13. gluteus medius

_____ 14. gracilis

_____ 15. iliotibial tract (tendon)

_____ 16. infraspinatus

_____ 17. latissimus dorsi

_____ 18. occipital belly of epicranius

_____ 19. semimembranosus

_____ 20. semitendinosus

_____ 21. sternocleidomastoid

_____ 22. teres major

_____ 23. trapezius

_____ 24. triceps brachii

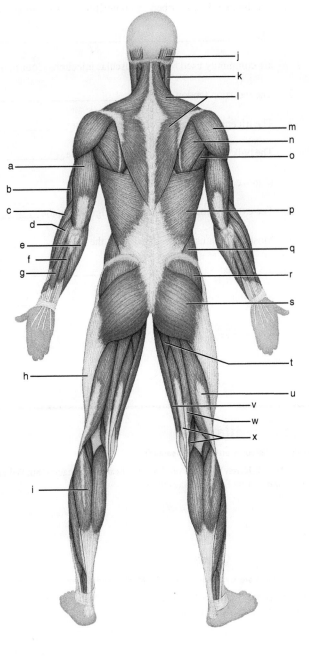

# General Review: Muscle Descriptions

**13.** Identify the muscles described by completing the following statements. Use an appropriate reference as needed.

1. The_____,_____,_____, and_____

   are commonly used for intramuscular injections (four muscles).

2. The insertion tendon of the _____ group contains a large sesamoid bone, the patella.

3. The triceps surae insert in common into the _____ tendon.

4. The bulk of the tissue of a muscle tends to lie _____ to the part of the body it causes

   to move.

5. The extrinsic muscles of the hand originate on the _____.

6. Most flexor muscles are located on the _____ aspect of the body; most extensors

   are located _____. An exception to this generalization is the extensor-flexor

   musculature of the _____.

## Photo Credits

**Credits are listed in order of appearance.**

4b, 5a, 9a, 11f: Karen Krabbenhoft, PAL 3.0, Pearson Education. 8b: William Karkow, Pearson Education. 13b: From *A Stereoscopic Atlas of Human Anatomy* by David L. Bassett, M.D.

## Illustration Credits

**All illustrations are by Imagineering STA Media Services, except for Review Sheet art and as noted below.**

1: Imagineering STA Media Services/Adapted from Martini, *Fundamentals of Anatomy & Physiology,* 4e, F11.1, Upper Saddle River, NJ: Prentice-Hall, © Frederic H. Martini, 1998.

# Histology of Nervous Tissue

## MATERIALS

- Model of a "typical" neuron (if available)
- Compound microscope
- Immersion oil
- Prepared slides of an ox spinal cord smear and teased myelinated nerve fibers
- Prepared slides of Purkinje cells (cerebellum), pyramidal cells (cerebrum), and a dorsal root ganglion
- Prepared slide of a nerve (x.s.)

## OBJECTIVES

1. Discuss the functional differences between neurons and neuroglia.
2. List six types of neuroglia and indicate where each is found in the nervous system.
3. Identify the important anatomical features of a neuron on an appropriate image.
4. List the functions of dendrites, axons, and axon terminals.
5. Explain how a nerve impulse is transmitted from one neuron to another.
6. State the function of myelin sheaths and explain how Schwann cells myelinate axons in the peripheral nervous system.
7. Classify neurons structurally and functionally.
8. Differentiate between a nerve and a tract, and between a ganglion and a CNS nucleus.
9. Define *nerve*.
10. Identify endoneurium, perineurium, and epineurium microscopically or in an appropriate image and cite their functions.

## PRE-LAB QUIZ

1. Circle the correct underlined term. Nervous tissue is made up of <u>two</u> / <u>three</u> main cell types.
2. Neuroglia of the peripheral nervous system include
   a. ependymal cells and satellite cells
   b. oligodendrocytes and astrocytes
   c. satellite cells and Schwann cells
3. _____ are the functional units of nervous tissue.
4. These branching neuron processes serve as receptive regions and transmit electrical signals toward the cell body. They are:
   a. axons          c. dendrites
   b. collaterals     d. neuroglia
5. Circle True or False. Axons are the neuron processes that generate and conduct nerve impulses.
6. Most axons are covered with a fatty material called _____, which insulates the fibers and increases the speed of neurotransmission.
7. Circle the correct underlined term. Neuron fibers (axons) running through the central nervous system form <u>tracts</u> / <u>nerves</u> of white matter.
8. Neurons can be classified according to structure. _____ neurons have many processes that issue from the cell body.
   a. Bipolar     b. Multipolar     c. Unipolar
9. Circle the correct underlined term. Neurons can be classified according to function. <u>Afferent</u> / <u>Efferent</u> or motor neurons carry electrical signals from the central nervous system primarily to muscles or glands.
10. Within a nerve, each axon is surrounded by a covering called the:
    a. endoneurium     b. epineurium     c. perineurium

MasteringA&P® For related exercise study tools, go to the Study Area of MasteringA&P. There you will find:
- Practice Anatomy Lab PAL
- PhysioEx PEx
- A&PFlix *A&PFlix*
- Practice quizzes, Histology Atlas, eText, Videos, and more!

From Exercise 15 of *Human Anatomy & Physiology Laboratory Manual,* Main Version, Tenth Edition. Elaine N. Marieb, Susan J. Mitchell, Lori A. Smith. Copyright © 2014 by Pearson Education, Inc. All rights reserved.

The nervous system is the master integrating and coordinating system, continuously monitoring and processing sensory information both from the external environment and from within the body. Every thought, action, and sensation is a reflection of its activity. Like a computer, it processes and integrates new "inputs" with information previously fed into it to produce an appropriate response. However, no computer can possibly compare in complexity and scope to the human nervous system.

Two primary divisions make up the nervous system: the central nervous system, or CNS, consisting of the brain and spinal cord, and the peripheral nervous system, or PNS, which includes all the nervous elements located outside the central nervous system. PNS structures include nerves, sensory receptors, and some clusters of nerve cells.

Despite its complexity, nervous tissue is made up of just two principal cell types; neurons and neuroglia.

## Neuroglia

The **neuroglia** ("nerve glue") or **glial cells** of the CNS include *astrocytes, oligodendrocytes, microglial cells,* and *ependymal cells* (Figure 1). The neuroglia found in the PNS include *Schwann cells,* also called neurolemmocytes, and *satellite cells.*

Neuroglia serve the needs of the delicate neurons by bracing and protecting them. In addition, they act as phagocytes (microglial cells), myelinate the cytoplasmic extensions of the neurons (oligodendrocytes and Schwann cells), play a role in capillary-neuron exchanges, and control the chemical environment around neurons (astrocytes). Although neuroglia resemble neurons in some ways (they have fibrous cellular extensions), they are not capable of generating and transmitting nerve impulses, a capability that is highly developed in neurons. Our focus in this exercise is the highly excitable neurons.

## Neurons

**Neurons,** or nerve cells, are the basic functional units of nervous tissue. They are highly specialized to transmit messages from one part of the body to another in the form of nerve impulses. Although neurons differ structurally, they have many identifiable features in common (Figure 2a and b). All have a **cell body** from which slender processes extend. The cell body is both the *biosynthetic center* of the neuron and part of its *receptive region.* Neuron cell bodies make up the gray matter of the CNS, and form clusters there that are called **nuclei.** In the PNS, clusters of neuron cell bodies are called **ganglia.**

The neuron cell body contains a large round nucleus surrounded by cytoplasm. Two prominent structures are found in the cytoplasm: One is cytoskeletal elements called **neurofibrils,** which provide support for the cell and a means

**Figure 1 Neuroglia. (a–d)** The four types of neuroglia in the central nervous system. **(e)** Neuroglia of the peripheral nervous system.

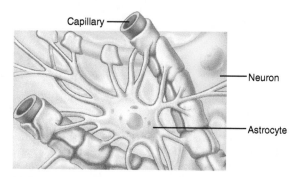

(a) Astrocytes are the most abundant CNS neuroglia.

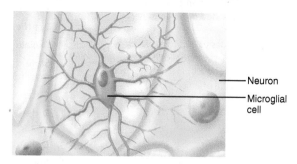

(b) Microglial cells are defensive cells in the CNS.

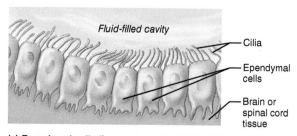

(c) Ependymal cells line cerebrospinal fluid–filled cavities.

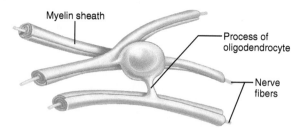

(d) Oligodendrocytes have processes that form myelin sheaths around CNS nerve fibers.

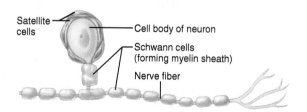

(e) Satellite cells and Schwann cells (which form myelin) surround neurons in the PNS.

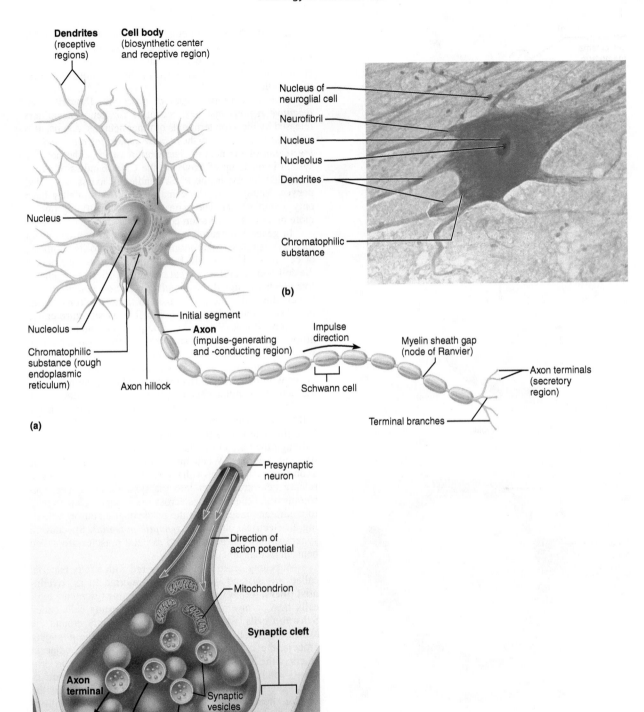

**Figure 2 Structure of a typical motor neuron. (a)** Diagram.
**(b)** Photomicrograph (450×). **(c)** Enlarged diagram of a synapse.

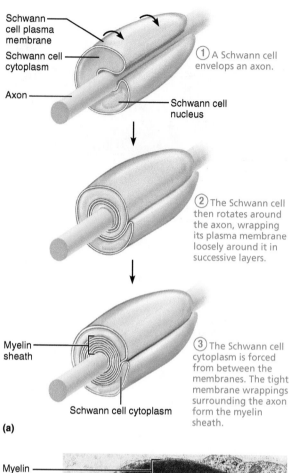

① A Schwann cell envelops an axon.

Schwann cell plasma membrane

Schwann cell cytoplasm

Axon

Schwann cell nucleus

② The Schwann cell then rotates around the axon, wrapping its plasma membrane loosely around it in successive layers.

Myelin sheath

③ The Schwann cell cytoplasm is forced from between the membranes. The tight membrane wrappings surrounding the axon form the myelin sheath.

Schwann cell cytoplasm

**(a)**

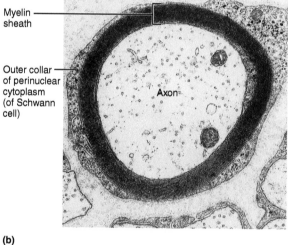

Myelin sheath

Outer collar of perinuclear cytoplasm (of Schwann cell)

Axon

**(b)**

**Figure 3 Myelination of a nerve fiber (axon) by Schwann cells. (a)** Nerve fiber myelination. **(b)** Electron micrograph of cross section through a myelinated axon (7500×).

to transport substances throughout the neuron. The second is darkly staining structures called **chromatophilic substance** (also known as Nissl bodies), an elaborate type of rough endoplasmic reticulum involved in the metabolic activities of the cell.

Neurons have two types of processes. **Dendrites** are *receptive regions* that bear receptors for neurotransmitters released by the axon terminals of other neurons. **Axons**, also called *nerve fibers*, form the *impulse generating and conducting region* of the neuron. The white matter of the nervous system is made up of axons. In the CNS, bundles of axons are called **tracts;** in the PNS, bundles of axons are called **nerves.** Neurons may have many dendrites, but they have only a single axon. The axon may branch, forming one or more processes called **axon collaterals.**

In general, a neuron is excited by other neurons when their axons release neurotransmitters close to its dendrites or cell body. The electrical signal produced travels across the cell body and if it is great enough, it elicits a regenerative electrical signal, an *impulse* or *action potential,* that travels down the axon. The axon in motor neurons begins just distal to a slightly enlarged cell body structure called the **axon hillock** (Figure 2a). The point at which the axon hillock narrows to axon diameter is referred to as the *initial segment.* The axon ends in many small structures called **axon terminals,** or *terminal boutons,* which form **synapses** with neurons or effector cells. These terminals store the neurotransmitter chemical in tiny vesicles. Each axon terminal of the presynaptic neuron is separated from the cell body or dendrites of the next, or postsynaptic, neuron by a tiny gap called the **synaptic cleft** (Figure 2c). Thus, although they are close, there is no actual physical contact between neurons. When an action potential reaches the axon terminals, some of the *synaptic vesicles* rupture and release neurotransmitter into the synaptic cleft. The neurotransmitter then diffuses across the synaptic cleft to bind to membrane receptors on the postsynaptic neuron, initiating an electrical current or *synaptic potential.* Specialized synapses between neurons and skeletal muscles are called neuromuscular junctions.)

Most long nerve fibers are covered with a fatty material called *myelin,* and such fibers are referred to as **myelinated fibers.** Axons in the peripheral nervous system are typically heavily myelinated by special supporting cells called **Schwann cells,** which wrap themselves tightly around the axon in jelly roll fashion **(Figure 3)**. During the wrapping process, the cytoplasm is squeezed from between adjacent layers of the Schwann cell membranes, so that when the process is completed a tight core of plasma membrane (protein-lipid material) encompasses the axon. This wrapping is the **myelin sheath.** The Schwann cell nucleus and the bulk of its cytoplasm end up just beneath the outermost portion of its plasma membrane. This peripheral part of the Schwann cell and its exposed plasma membrane is referred to as the **outer collar of perinuclear cytoplasm** (Figure 3). Since the myelin sheath is formed by many individual Schwann cells, it is a discontinuous sheath. The gaps or indentations in the sheath are called **myelin sheath gaps** or **nodes of Ranvier** (see Figure 2a).

Within the CNS, myelination is accomplished by neuroglia called **oligodendrocytes** (see Figure 1d). Because of its chemical composition, myelin electrically insulates the fibers and greatly increases the transmission speed of nerve impulses.

## ACTIVITY 1

### Identifying Parts of a Neuron

1. Study the illustration of a typical motor neuron (Figure 2), noting the structural details described above, and then identify these structures on a neuron model.

2. Obtain a prepared slide of the ox spinal cord smear, which has large, easily identifiable neurons. Study one representative neuron under oil immersion and identify the cell body; the nucleus; the large, prominent "owl's eye" nucleolus; and the granular chromatophilic substance. If possible, distinguish the axon from the many dendrites.

Sketch the cell in the space provided below, and label the important anatomical details you have observed. (Compare your sketch to Figure 2b.)

3. Obtain a prepared slide of teased myelinated nerve fibers. Identify the following (use **Figure 4** as a guide): myelin sheath gaps, axon, Schwann cell nuclei, and myelin sheath.

Sketch a portion of a myelinated nerve fiber in the space provided below, illustrating a myelin sheath gap. Label the axon, myelin sheath, myelin sheath gap, and the outer collar of perinuclear cytoplasm.

Do the gaps seem to occur at consistent intervals, or are they

irregularly distributed? _____

Explain the functional significance of this finding: _____

_____

_____ ▬

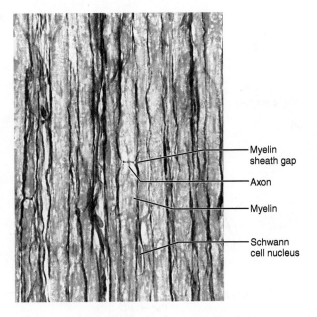

**Figure 4 Photomicrograph of a small portion of a peripheral nerve in longitudinal section (400×).**

## Neuron Classification

Neurons may be classified on the basis of structure or of function.

### Classification by Structure

Structurally, neurons may be differentiated by the number of processes attached to the cell body (**Figure 5a**). In **unipolar neurons,** one very short process, which divides into *peripheral* and *central processes,* extends from the cell body. Functionally, only the most distal parts of the peripheral process act as receptive endings; the rest acts as an axon along with the central process. Unipolar neurons are more accurately called **pseudounipolar neurons** because they are derived from bipolar neurons. Nearly all neurons that conduct impulses toward the CNS are unipolar.

**Bipolar neurons** have two processes attached to the cell body. This neuron type is quite rare, typically found only as part of the receptor apparatus of the eye, ear, and olfactory mucosa.

Many processes issue from the cell body of **multipolar neurons,** all classified as dendrites except for a single axon. Most neurons in the brain and spinal cord and those whose axons carry impulses away from the CNS fall into this last category.

## ACTIVITY 2

### Studying the Microscopic Structure of Selected Neurons

Obtain prepared slides of pyramidal cells of the cerebral cortex, Purkinje cells of the cerebellar cortex, and a dorsal root ganglion. As you observe them under the microscope, try to pick

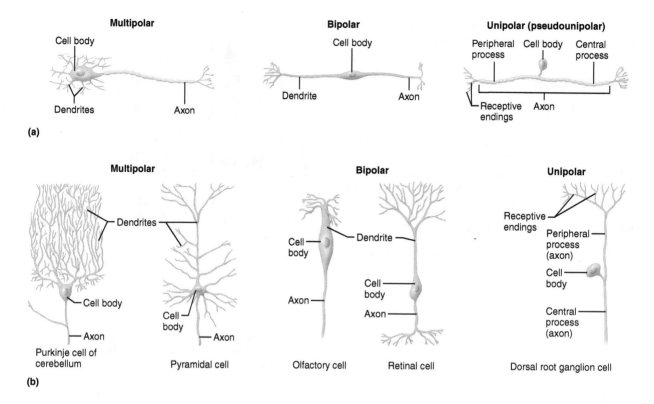

Multipolar

Cell body

Dendrites                  Axon

(a)

Bipolar

Cell body

Dendrite                  Axon

Unipolar (pseudounipolar)

Peripheral    Cell body    Central
process                    process

Receptive   Axon
endings

Multipolar

Dendrites

Cell body

Axon

Purkinje cell of
cerebellum

Cell
body

Axon

Pyramidal cell

Bipolar

Cell
body

Dendrite

Cell
body

Axon

Axon

Olfactory cell      Retinal cell

Unipolar

Receptive
endings
Peripheral
process
(axon)

Cell
body

Central
process
(axon)

Dorsal root ganglion cell

(b)

Figure 5 **Classification of neurons according to structure. (a)** Classification of neurons based on structure (number of processes extending from the cell body). **(b)** Structural variations within the classes.

out the anatomical details (compare the cells to Figure 5b and Figure 6). Notice that the neurons of the cerebral and cerebellar tissues (both brain tissues) are extensively branched; in contrast, the neurons of the dorsal root ganglion are more rounded. The many small nuclei visible surrounding the neurons are those of bordering neuroglia.

Which of these neuron types would be classified as multipolar neurons?

_____

Which as unipolar? _____ ■

## Classification by Function

In general, neurons carrying impulses from sensory receptors in the internal organs (viscera), the skin, skeletal muscles, joints, or special sensory organs are termed **sensory,** or **afferent, neurons** (Figure 7). The receptive endings of sensory neurons are often equipped with specialized receptors that are stimulated by specific changes in their immediate environment. The cell bodies of sensory neurons are always found in a ganglion outside the CNS, and these neurons are typically unipolar.

Neurons carrying impulses from the CNS to the viscera and/or body muscles and glands are termed **motor, or efferent, neurons.** Motor neurons are most often multipolar, and their cell bodies are almost always located in the CNS.

The third functional category of neurons is **interneurons** or *association neurons,* which are situated between and contribute to pathways that connect sensory and motor neurons. Their cell bodies are always located within the CNS, and they are multipolar neurons structurally.

## Structure of a Nerve

A nerve is a bundle of axons found in the PNS. Wrapped in connective tissue coverings, nerves extend to and/or from the CNS and visceral organs or structures of the body periphery such as skeletal muscles, glands, and skin.

Like neurons, nerves are classified according to the direction in which they transmit impulses. **Sensory (afferent) nerves** conduct impulses only toward the CNS. A few of the cranial nerves are pure sensory nerves. **Motor (efferent) nerves** carry impulses only away from the CNS. The ventral roots of the spinal cord are motor nerves. Nerves carrying both sensory (afferent) and motor (efferent) fibers are called **mixed nerves;** most nerves of the body, including all spinal nerves, are mixed nerves.

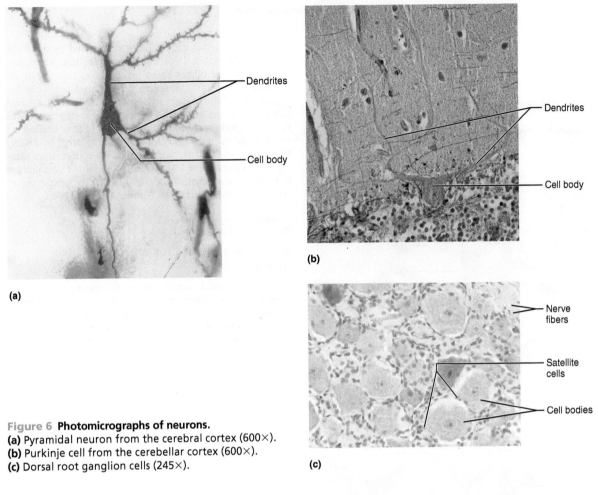

**Figure 6 Photomicrographs of neurons.**
**(a)** Pyramidal neuron from the cerebral cortex (600×).
**(b)** Purkinje cell from the cerebellar cortex (600×).
**(c)** Dorsal root ganglion cells (245×).

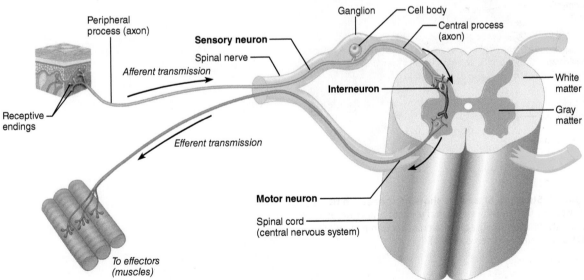

**Figure 7 Classification of neurons on the basis of function.** Sensory (afferent) neurons conduct impulses from the body's sensory receptors to the central nervous system; most are unipolar neurons with their nerve cell bodies in ganglia in the peripheral nervous system (PNS). Motor (efferent) neurons transmit impulses from the CNS to effectors (muscles). Interneurons (association neurons) complete the communication line between sensory and motor neurons. They are typically multipolar, and their cell bodies reside in the CNS.

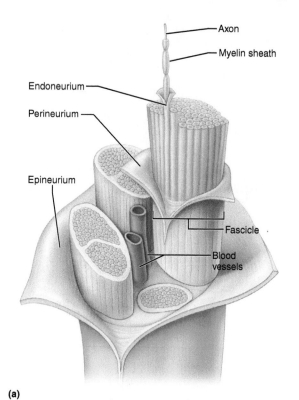

- Axon
- Myelin sheath
- Endoneurium
- Perineurium
- Epineurium
- Fascicle
- Blood vessels

**(a)**

Within a nerve, each axon is surrounded by a delicate connective tissue sheath called an **endoneurium,** which insulates it from the other neuron processes adjacent to it. The endoneurium is often mistaken for the myelin sheath; it is instead an additional sheath that surrounds the myelin sheath. Groups of axons are bound by a coarser connective tissue, called the **perineurium,** to form bundles of fibers called **fascicles.** Finally, all the fascicles are bound together by a white, fibrous connective tissue sheath called the **epineurium,** forming the cordlike nerve (Figure 8). In addition to the connective tissue wrappings, blood vessels and lymphatic vessels serving the fibers also travel within a nerve.

**ACTIVITY 3**

## Examining the Microscopic Structure of a Nerve

Use the compound microscope to examine a prepared cross section of a peripheral nerve. Using the photomicrograph (Figure 8b) as an aid, identify axons, myelin sheaths, fascicles, and endoneurium, perineurium, and epineurium sheaths. If desired, sketch the nerve in the space below. ■

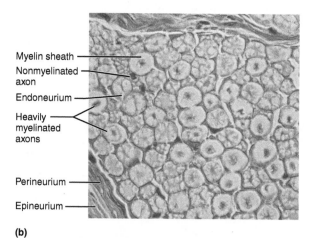

- Myelin sheath
- Nonmyelinated axon
- Endoneurium
- Heavily myelinated axons
- Perineurium
- Epineurium

**(b)**

Figure 8 **Structure of a nerve showing connective tissue wrappings. (a)** Three-dimensional view of a portion of a nerve. **(b)** Photomicrograph of a cross-sectional view of part of a peripheral nerve (510×).

# Histology of Nervous Tissue

**1.** The basic functional unit of the nervous system is the neuron. What is the major function of this cell type?

_____

**2.** Name four types of neuroglia in the CNS, and list a function for each of these cells. (You will need to consult your text for this.)

| **Types** | **Functions** |
|---|---|
| a. _____ | a. _____ |
| | _____ |
| b. _____ | b. _____ |
| | _____ |
| c. _____ | c. _____ |
| | _____ |
| d. _____ | d. _____ |
| | _____ |

Name the PNS neuroglial cell that forms myelin. _____

Name the PNS neuroglial cell that surrounds dorsal root ganglion neurons. _____

**3.** Match each description with a term from the key.

| *Key:* | a. | afferent neuron | e. | interneuron | i. | nuclei |
|---|---|---|---|---|---|---|
| | b. | central nervous system | f. | neuroglia | j. | peripheral nervous system |
| | c. | efferent neuron | g. | neurotransmitters | k. | synapse |
| | d. | ganglion | h. | nerve | l. | tract |

_____ 1. the brain and spinal cord collectively

_____ 2. specialized supporting cells in the CNS

_____ 3. junction or point of close contact between neurons

_____ 4. a bundle of axons inside the CNS

_____ 5. neuron serving as part of the conduction pathway between sensory and motor neurons

_____ 6. ganglia and spinal and cranial nerves

_____ 7. collection of nerve cell bodies found outside the CNS

_____ 8. neuron that conducts impulses away from the CNS to muscles and glands

—————————————— 9. neuron that conducts impulses toward the CNS from the body periphery

—————————————— 10. chemicals released by neurons that stimulate or inhibit other neurons or effectors

## Neuron Anatomy

**4.** Match the following anatomical terms (column B) with the appropriate description or function (column A).

**Column A**

——————— 1. region of the cell body from which the axon originates

——————— 2. secretes neurotransmitters

——————— 3. receptive region of a neuron

——————— 4. insulates the nerve fibers

——————— 5. site of the nucleus and most important metabolic area

——————— 6. involved in the transport of substances within the neuron

——————— 7. essentially rough endoplasmic reticulum, important metabolically

——————— 8. impulse generator and transmitter

**Column B**

a. axon

b. axon terminal

c. axon hillock

d. chromatophilic substance

e. dendrite

f. myelin sheath

g. neurofibril

h. neuronal cell body

**5.** Draw a "typical" multipolar neuron in the space below. Include and label the following structures on your diagram: cell body, nucleus, nucleolus, chromatophilic substance, dendrites, axon, axon collateral branch, myelin sheath, myelin sheath gaps, axon terminals, and neurofibrils.

**6.** What substance is found in synaptic vesicles of the axon terminal? _____

What role does this substance play in neurotransmission? _____

_____

_____

**7.** What anatomical characteristic determines whether a particular neuron is classified as unipolar, bipolar, or multipolar?

_____

Make a simple line drawing of each type here.

**Unipolar neuron**            **Bipolar neuron**            **Multipolar neuron**

**8.** Correctly identify the sensory (afferent) neuron, interneuron (association neuron), and motor (efferent) neuron in the figure below.

Which of these neuron types is/are unipolar? _____

Which is/are most likely multipolar? _____

Receptors (thermal
and pain in the skin)

Effector (biceps
brachii muscle)

**9.** Describe how the Schwann cells form the myelin sheath and the outer collar of perinuclear cytoplasm encasing the nerve fibers.

_____

_____

# Structure of a Nerve

**10.** What is a nerve? _____

**11.** State the location of each of the following connective tissue coverings.

endoneurium: _____

perineurium: _____

epineurium: _____

**12.** What is the function of the connective tissue wrappings found in a nerve? _____

_____

**13.** Define *mixed nerve.* _____

_____

**14.** Identify all indicated parts of the nerve section.

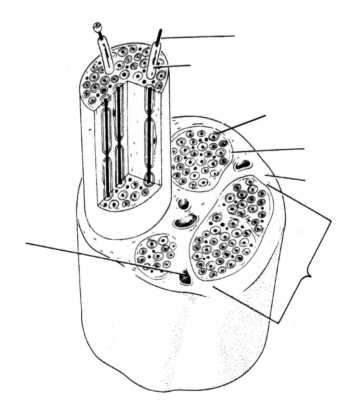

## Photo Credits

**Credits are listed in order of appearance.**

2b, 6b: William Karkow, Pearson Education. 3b: Don W. Fawcett/Photo Researchers. 4: Eroschenko's Interactive Histology. 6a: Sercomi/ Photo Researchers. 6c: Nina Zanetti, Pearson Education. 8b: Victor P. Eroschenko, Pearson Education.

## Illustration Credits

**All illustrations are by Imagineering STA Media Services, except for Review Sheet art and as noted below.**

1: Imagineering STA Media Services/Precision Graphics.

# Gross Anatomy of the Brain and Cranial Nerves

(Text continues on next page.)

## MATERIALS

- ☐ Human brain model (dissectible)
- ☐ Preserved human brain (if available)
- ☐ Three-dimensional model of ventricles
- ☐ Coronally sectioned human brain slice (if available)
- ☐ Materials as needed for cranial nerve testing (see Table 1: aromatic oils (e.g., vanilla and cloves); eye chart; ophthalmoscope; penlight; safety pin; blunt probe (hot and cold); cotton; solutions of sugar, salt, vinegar, and quinine; ammonia; tuning fork; and tongue depressor
- ☐ Preserved sheep brain (meninges and cranial nerves intact)
- ☐ Dissecting instruments and tray
- ☐ Disposable gloves

## OBJECTIVES

1. List the elements of the central and peripheral divisions of the nervous system.
2. Discuss the difference between the sensory and motor portions of the nervous system and name the two divisions of the motor portion.
3. Recognize the terms that describe the development of the human brain and discuss the relationships between the terms.
4. As directed by your instructor, identify the bold terms associated with the cerebral hemispheres, diencephalon, brain stem, and cerebellum on a dissected human brain, brain model, or appropriate image, and state their functions.
5. State the difference between gyri, fissures, and sulci.
6. Describe the composition of gray matter and white matter in the nervous system.
7. Name and describe the three meninges that cover the brain, state their functions, and locate the falx cerebri, falx cerebelli, and tentorium cerebelli.
8. Discuss the formation, circulation, and drainage of cerebrospinal fluid.
9. Identify the cranial nerves by number and name on a model or image, stating the origin and function of each.
10. Identify at least four pertinent anatomical differences between the human and sheep brain.

## PRE-LAB QUIZ

1. Circle the correct underlined term. The <u>central nervous system</u> / <u>peripheral nervous system</u> consists of the brain and spinal cord.
2. Circle the correct underlined term. The most superior portion of the brain is the <u>cerebral hemispheres</u> / <u>brain stem.</u>
3. Circle True or False. Deep grooves within the cerebral hemispheres are known as gyri.
4. On the ventral surface of the brain, you can observe the optic nerves and chiasma, the pituitary gland, and the mammillary bodies. These externally visible structures form the floor of the
   a. brain stem
   b. diencephalon
   c. frontal lobe
   d. occipital lobe
5. Circle the correct underlined term. The inferior region of the brain stem, the <u>medulla oblongata</u> / <u>cerebellum</u> houses many vital autonomic centers involved in the control of heart rate, respiratory rhythm, and blood pressure.
6. Directly under the occipital lobes of the cerebrum is a large cauliflower-like structure known as the _____.
   a. brain stem
   b. cerebellum
   c. diencephalon

MasteringA&P® For related exercise study tools, go to the Study Area of MasteringA&P. There you will find:
- Practice Anatomy Lab PAL
- PhysioEx PEx
- A&PFlix *A&PFlix*
- Practice quizzes, Histology Atlas, eText, Videos, and more!

From Exercise 17 of *Human Anatomy & Physiology Laboratory Manual,* Main Version, Tenth Edition. Elaine N. Marieb, Susan J. Mitchell, Lori A. Smith. Copyright © 2014 by Pearson Education, Inc. All rights reserved.

7. Circle the correct underlined term. The outer cortex of the brain contains the cell bodies of cerebral neurons and is known as <u>white matter</u> / <u>gray matter.</u>

8. The brain and spinal cord are covered and protected by three connective tissue layers called
   a. lobes
   b. meninges
   c. sulci
   d. ventricles

9. Circle True or False. Cerebrospinal fluid is produced by the frontal lobe of the cerebrum and is unlike any other body fluid.

10. How many pairs of cranial nerves are there? _____

When viewed alongside all nature's animals, humans are indeed unique, and the key to their uniqueness is found in the brain. Each of us is a composite reflection of our brain's experience. If all past sensory input could mysteriously and suddenly be "erased," we would be unable to walk, talk, or communicate in any manner. Spontaneous movement would occur, as in a fetus, but no voluntary integrated function of any type would be possible. Clearly we would cease to be the same individuals.

Because of the complexity of the nervous system, its anatomical structures are usually considered in terms of two principal divisions: the central nervous system and the peripheral nervous system. The **central nervous system (CNS)** consists of the brain and spinal cord, which primarily interpret incoming sensory information and issue instructions based on that information and on past experience. The **peripheral nervous system (PNS)** consists of the cranial and spinal nerves, ganglia, and sensory receptors. These structures serve as communication lines as they carry impulses—from the sensory receptors to the CNS and from the CNS to the appropriate glands, muscles, or other effector organs.

The PNS has two major subdivisions: the **sensory portion,** which consists of nerve fibers that conduct impulses toward the CNS, and the **motor portion,** which contains nerve fibers that conduct impulses away from the CNS. The motor portion, in turn, consists of the **somatic division** (sometimes called the *voluntary system*), which controls the skeletal muscles, and the **autonomic nervous system (ANS),** which controls smooth and cardiac muscles and glands. The ANS is often referred to as the *involuntary nervous system.* Its sympathetic and parasympathetic branches play a major role in maintaining homeostasis.

In this exercise the brain (CNS) and cranial nerves (PNS) will be studied because of their close anatomical relationship.

## The Human Brain

During embryonic development of all vertebrates, the CNS first makes its appearance as a simple tubelike structure, the **neural tube,** that extends down the dorsal median plane. By the fourth week, the human brain begins to form as an expansion of the anterior or rostral end of the neural tube (the end toward the head). Shortly thereafter, constrictions appear, dividing the developing brain into three major regions— **forebrain, midbrain,** and **hindbrain** (Figure 1). The remainder of the neural tube becomes the spinal cord.

| (a) Neural tube (contains neural canal) | (b) Primary brain vesicles | (c) Secondary brain vesicles | (d) Adult brain structures | (e) Adult neural canal regions |
|---|---|---|---|---|
| Anterior (rostral) | Prosencephalon (forebrain) | Telencephalon | Cerebrum: cerebral hemispheres (cortex, white matter, basal nuclei) | Lateral ventricles |
| | | Diencephalon | Diencephalon (thalamus, hypothalamus, epithalamus), retina | Third ventricle |
| | Mesencephalon (midbrain) | Mesencephalon | Brain stem: midbrain | Cerebral aqueduct |
| | Rhombencephalon (hindbrain) | Metencephalon | Brain stem: pons | Fourth ventricle |
| | | | Cerebellum | |
| Posterior (caudal) | | Myelencephalon | Brain stem: medulla oblongata | |
| | | | Spinal cord | Central canal |

Figure 1 **Embryonic development of the human brain. (a)** The neural tube subdivides into **(b)** the primary brain vesicles, which subsequently form **(c)** the secondary brain vesicles, which differentiate into **(d)** the adult brain structures. **(e)** The adult structures derived from the neural canal.

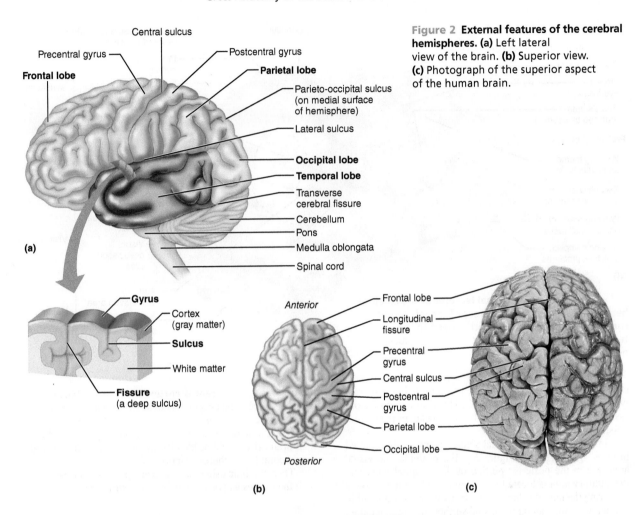

**Figure 2 External features of the cerebral hemispheres. (a)** Left lateral view of the brain. **(b)** Superior view. **(c)** Photograph of the superior aspect of the human brain.

During fetal development, two anterior outpocketings extend from the forebrain and grow rapidly to form the cerebral hemispheres. The skull imposes space restrictions that force the cerebral hemispheres to grow posteriorly and inferiorly, and they finally end up enveloping and obscuring the rest of the forebrain and most midbrain structures. Somewhat later in development, the dorsal hindbrain also enlarges to produce the cerebellum. The central canal of the neural tube, which remains continuous throughout the brain and cord, enlarges in four regions of the brain, forming chambers called **ventricles** (see Figure 8a and b).

### ACTIVITY 1

## Identifying External Brain Structures

Identify external brain structures using the figures cited. Also use a model of the human brain and other learning aids as they are mentioned.

Generally, the brain is studied in terms of four major regions: the cerebral hemispheres, diencephalon, brain stem, and cerebellum. It's useful to be aware of the relationship between these four anatomical regions and the structures of the forebrain, midbrain, and hindbrain (Figure 1).

### Cerebral Hemispheres

The **cerebral hemispheres** are the most superior portion of the brain **(Figure 2)**. Their entire surface is thrown into elevated ridges of tissue called **gyri** that are separated by shallow grooves called **sulci** or deeper grooves called **fissures.** Many of the fissures and gyri are important anatomical landmarks.

The cerebral hemispheres are divided by a single deep fissure, the **longitudinal fissure.** The **central sulcus** divides the **frontal lobe** from the **parietal lobe,** and the **lateral sulcus** separates the **temporal lobe** from the parietal lobe. The **parieto-occipital sulcus** on the medial surface of each hemisphere divides the **occipital lobe** from the parietal lobe. It is not visible externally. A fifth lobe of each cerebral hemisphere, the **insula,** is buried deep within the lateral sulcus, and is covered by portions of the temporal, parietal, and frontal lobes. Notice that most cerebral hemisphere lobes are named for the cranial bones that lie over them.

Some important functional areas of the cerebral hemispheres have also been located (Figure 2d). The **primary somatosensory cortex** is located in the **postcentral gyrus** of the parietal lobe. Impulses traveling from the body's sensory receptors (such as those for pressure, pain, and temperature) are localized in this area of the brain. ("This information is from my big toe.") Immediately posterior to the primary somatosensory area is the **somatosensory association**

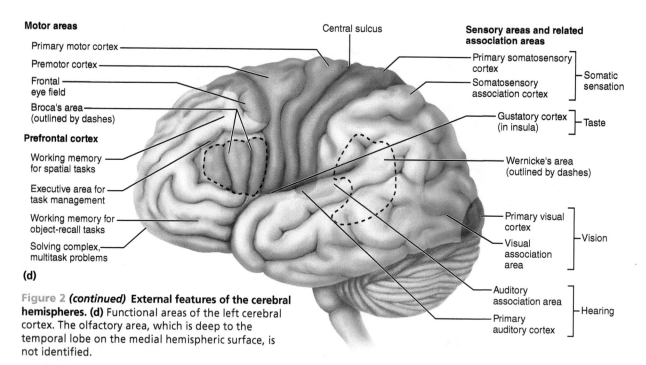

**Motor areas**

Primary motor cortex

Premotor cortex

Frontal eye field

Broca's area (outlined by dashes)

**Prefrontal cortex**

Working memory for spatial tasks

Executive area for task management

Working memory for object-recall tasks

Solving complex, multitask problems

**(d)**

Central sulcus

**Sensory areas and related association areas**

Primary somatosensory cortex

Somatosensory association cortex

Somatic sensation

Gustatory cortex (in insula) — Taste

Wernicke's area (outlined by dashes)

Primary visual cortex

Visual association area

Vision

Auditory association area

Primary auditory cortex

Hearing

**Figure 2** *(continued)* **External features of the cerebral hemispheres. (d)** Functional areas of the left cerebral cortex. The olfactory area, which is deep to the temporal lobe on the medial hemispheric surface, is not identified.

**cortex,** in which the meaning of incoming stimuli is analyzed. ("Ouch! I have a *pain* there.") Thus, the somatosensory association cortex allows you to become aware of pain, coldness, a light touch, and the like.

Impulses from the special sense organs are interpreted in other specific areas (Figure 2d). For example, the visual areas are in the posterior portion of the occipital lobe, and the auditory area is located in the temporal lobe in the gyrus bordering the lateral sulcus. The olfactory area is deep within the temporal lobe along its medial surface, in a region called the **uncus** (see Figure 4a).

The **primary motor cortex,** which is responsible for conscious or voluntary movement of the skeletal muscles, is located in the **precentral gyrus** of the frontal lobe. A specialized motor speech area called **Broca's area** is found at the base of the precentral gyrus just above the lateral sulcus. Damage to this area (which is located in only one cerebral hemisphere, usually the left) reduces or eliminates the ability to articulate words. Many areas involved in intellect, complex reasoning, and personality lie in the anterior portions of the frontal lobes, in a region called the **prefrontal cortex.**

A rather poorly defined region at the junction of the parietal and temporal lobes is **Wernicke's area,** an area in which unfamiliar words are sounded out. Like Broca's area, Wernicke's area is located in one cerebral hemisphere only, typically the left.

Although there are many similar functional areas in both cerebral hemispheres, each hemisphere is also a "specialist" in certain ways. For example, the left hemisphere is the "language brain" in most of us, because it houses centers associated with language skills and speech. The right hemisphere is more concerned with abstract, conceptual, or spatial processes—skills associated with artistic or creative pursuits.

The cell bodies of cerebral neurons involved in these functions are found only in the outermost gray matter of the cerebrum, the **cerebral cortex.** Most of the balance of cerebral tissue—the deeper **cerebral white matter**—is composed of fiber tracts carrying impulses to or from the cortex.

Using a model of the human brain (and a preserved human brain, if available), identify the areas and structures of the cerebral hemispheres described above.

Then continue using the model and preserved brain along with the figures as you read about other structures.

### Diencephalon

The **diencephalon** is embryologically part of the forebrain, along with the cerebral hemispheres.

Turn the brain model so the ventral surface of the brain can be viewed. Starting superiorly (and using **Figure 3** as a guide), identify the externally visible structures that mark the position of the floor of the diencephalon. These are the **olfactory bulbs** (synapse point of cranial nerve I) and **tracts, optic nerves** (cranial nerve II), **optic chiasma** (where the fibers of the optic nerves partially cross over), **optic tracts, pituitary gland,** and **mammillary bodies.**

### Brain Stem

Continue inferiorly to identify the **brain stem** structures—the **cerebral peduncles** (fiber tracts in the **midbrain** connecting the pons below with cerebrum above), the pons, and the medulla oblongata. *Pons* means "bridge," and the **pons** consists primarily of motor and sensory fiber tracts connecting the brain with lower CNS centers. The lowest brain stem region, the **medulla oblongata,** is also composed primarily of fiber tracts. You can see the **decussation of pyramids,** a crossover point for the major motor tracts (pyramidal tracts) descending from the motor areas of the cerebrum to the cord, on the medulla's surface. The medulla also houses many vital autonomic centers involved in the control of heart rate, respiratory rhythm, and blood pressure as well as involuntary centers involved in vomiting, swallowing, and so on.

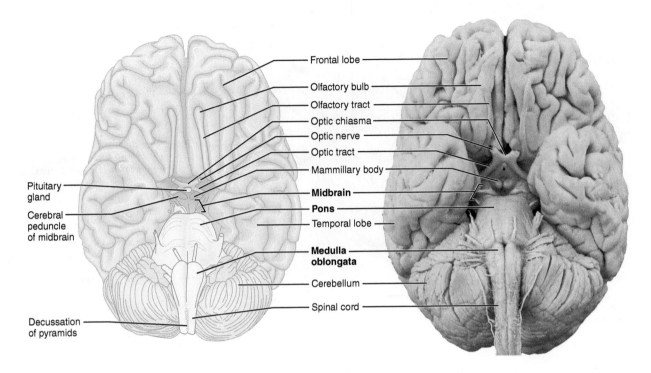

**Figure 3 Ventral (inferior) aspect of the human brain, showing the three regions of the brain stem.** Only a small portion of the midbrain can be seen; the rest is surrounded by other brain regions.

## Cerebellum

1. Turn the brain model so you can see the dorsal aspect. Identify the large cauliflower-like **cerebellum,** which projects dorsally from under the occipital lobes of the cerebrum. Notice that, like the cerebrum, the cerebellum has two major hemispheres and a convoluted surface (see Figure 6). It also has an outer cortex made up of gray matter with an inner region of white matter.

2. Remove the cerebellum to view the **corpora quadrigemina** (Figure 4), located on the posterior aspect of the midbrain, a brain stem structure. The two superior prominences are the **superior colliculi** (visual reflex centers); the two smaller inferior prominences are the **inferior colliculi** (auditory reflex centers). ■

### ACTIVITY 2

## Identifying Internal Brain Structures

The deeper structures of the brain have also been well mapped. Like the external structures, these can be studied in terms of the four major regions. As the internal brain areas are described, identify them on the figures cited. Also, use the brain model as indicated to help you in this study.

## Cerebral Hemispheres

1. Take the brain model apart so you can see a median sagittal view of the internal brain structures (Figure 4). Observe the model closely to see the extent of the outer cortex (gray matter), which contains the cell bodies of cerebral neurons. The pyramidal cells of the cerebral motor cortex

are representative of the neurons seen in the precentral gyrus.

2. Observe the deeper area of white matter, which is composed of fiber tracts. The fiber tracts found in the cerebral hemisphere white matter are called *association tracts* if they connect two portions of the same hemisphere, *projection tracts* if they run between the cerebral cortex and lower brain structures or spinal cord, and *commissures* if they run from one hemisphere to another. Observe the large **corpus callosum,** the major commissure connecting the cerebral hemispheres. The corpus callosum arches above the structures of the diencephalon and roofs over the lateral ventricles. Notice also the **fornix,** a bandlike fiber tract concerned with olfaction as well as limbic system functions, and the membranous **septum pellucidum,** which separates the lateral ventricles of the cerebral hemispheres.

3. In addition to the gray matter of the cerebral cortex, there are several clusters of neuron cell bodies called **nuclei** buried deep within the white matter of the cerebral hemispheres. One important group of cerebral nuclei, called the **basal nuclei** or **basal ganglia,** * flank the lateral and third ventricles. You can see these nuclei if you have a dissectible model or a coronally or cross-sectioned human brain slice. (Otherwise, **Figure 5** will suffice.)

The basal nuclei, part of the *indirect pathway,* are involved in regulating voluntary motor activities. The most important of them are the arching, comma-shaped **caudate**

---

*The historical term for these nuclei, *basal ganglia,* is misleading because ganglia are PNS structures. Although technically not the correct anatomical term, "basal ganglia" is included here because it is widely used in clinical settings.

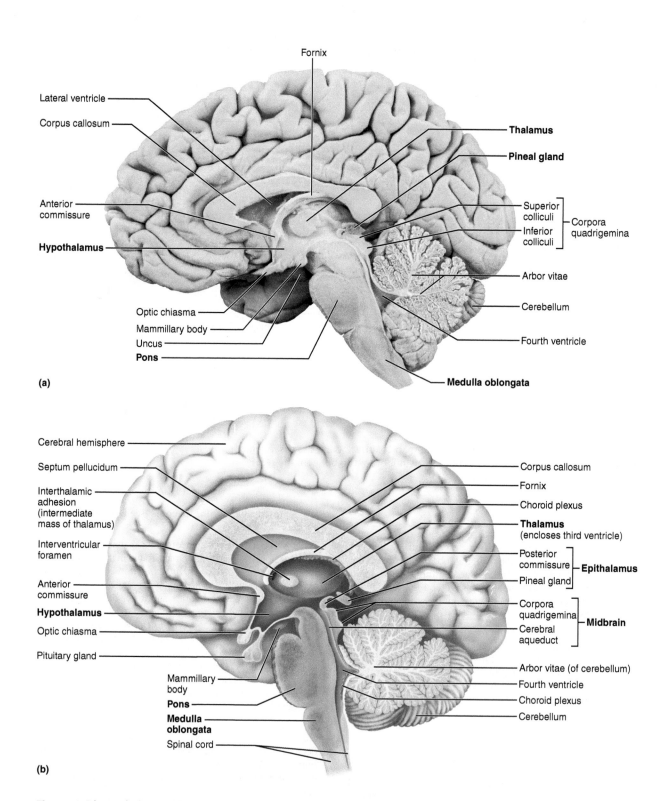

**(a)**

Fornix

Lateral ventricle

Corpus callosum

**Thalamus**

**Pineal gland**

Anterior commissure

Superior colliculi

Inferior colliculi

Corpora quadrigemina

**Hypothalamus**

Arbor vitae

Cerebellum

Optic chiasma

Mammillary body

Uncus

Fourth ventricle

**Pons**

**Medulla oblongata**

**(b)**

Cerebral hemisphere

Corpus callosum

Septum pellucidum

Fornix

Interthalamic adhesion (intermediate mass of thalamus)

Choroid plexus

**Thalamus** (encloses third ventricle)

Interventricular foramen

Posterior commissure

**Epithalamus**

Pineal gland

Anterior commissure

Corpora quadrigemina

**Midbrain**

**Hypothalamus**

Cerebral aqueduct

Optic chiasma

Pituitary gland

Arbor vitae (of cerebellum)

Mammillary body

Fourth ventricle

**Pons**

Choroid plexus

**Medulla oblongata**

Cerebellum

Spinal cord

**Figure 4** **Diencephalon and brain stem structures as seen in a sagittal section of the brain. (a)** Photograph. **(b)** Diagram.

**nucleus,** the **putamen,** and the **globus pallidus.** The closely associated *amygdaloid body* (located at the tip of the caudate nucleus) is part of the *limbic system.*

The **corona radiata,** a spray of projection fibers coursing down from the precentral (motor) gyrus, combines with sensory fibers traveling to the sensory cortex to form a broad band of fibrous material called the **internal capsule.** The internal capsule passes between the diencephalon and the basal nuclei and through parts of the basal nuclei, giving them a striped appearance. This is why the caudate nucleus and the

**6**

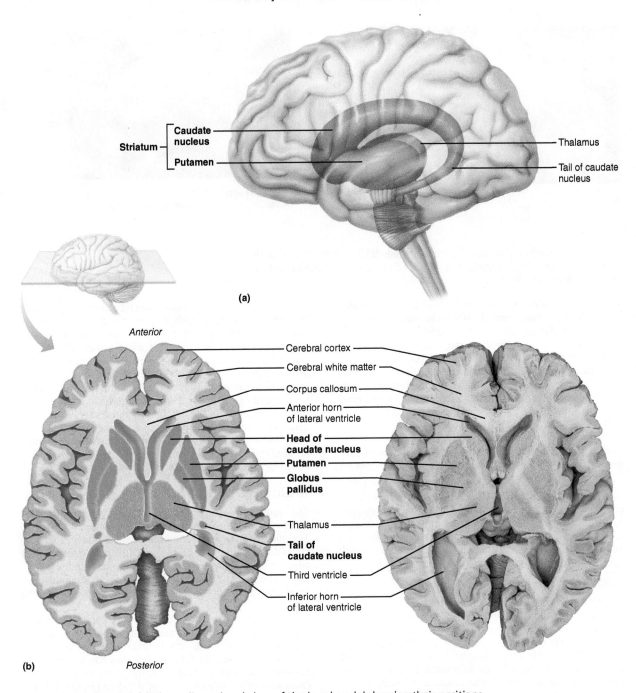

Striatum {
Caudate nucleus
Putamen
}

Thalamus

Tail of caudate nucleus

**(a)**

Anterior

Cerebral cortex

Cerebral white matter

Corpus callosum

Anterior horn of lateral ventricle

**Head of caudate nucleus**

**Putamen**

**Globus pallidus**

Thalamus

**Tail of caudate nucleus**

Third ventricle

Inferior horn of lateral ventricle

**(b)**      Posterior

**Figure 5 Basal nuclei. (a)** Three-dimensional view of the basal nuclei showing their positions within the cerebrum. **(b)** A transverse section of the cerebrum and diencephalon showing the relationship of the basal nuclei to the thalamus and the lateral and third ventricles.

putamen are sometimes referred to collectively as the **striatum,** or "striped body" (Figure 5a).

4. Examine the relationship of the lateral ventricles and corpus callosum to the diencephalon structures; that is, thalamus and third ventricle—from the cross-sectional viewpoint (see Figure 5b).

*Diencephalon*

1. The major internal structures of the diencephalon are the thalamus, hypothalamus, and epithalamus (see Figure 4).

The **thalamus** consists of two large lobes of gray matter that laterally enclose the shallow third ventricle of the brain. A slender stalk of thalamic tissue, the **interthalamic adhesion,** or **intermediate mass,** connects the two thalamic lobes and bridges the ventricle. The thalamus is a major integrating and relay station for sensory impulses passing upward to the cortical sensory areas for localization and interpretation. Locate also the **interventricular foramen,** a tiny opening connecting the third ventricle with the lateral ventricle on the same side.

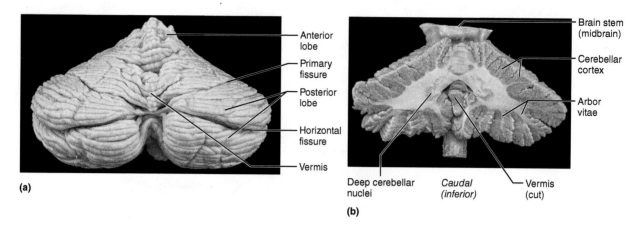

(a)

(b)

**Figure 6** **Cerebellum. (a)** Posterior (dorsal) view. **(b)** Sectioned to reveal the cerebellar cortex. (The cerebellum is sectioned coronally and the brain stem is sectioned transversely in this posterior view.)

2. The **hypothalamus** makes up the floor and the inferolateral walls of the third ventricle. It is an important autonomic center involved in regulation of body temperature, water balance, and fat and carbohydrate metabolism as well as in many other activities and drives (sex, hunger, thirst). Locate again the pituitary gland, which hangs from the anterior floor of the hypothalamus by a slender stalk, the **infundibulum.** The pituitary gland is usually not present in preserved brain specimens. In life, the pituitary rests in the hypophyseal fossa of the sella turcica of the sphenoid bone.

Anterior to the pituitary, identify the optic chiasma portion of the optic pathway to the brain. The **mammillary bodies,** relay stations for olfaction, bulge exteriorly from the floor of the hypothalamus just posterior to the pituitary gland.

3. The **epithalamus** forms the roof of the third ventricle and is the most dorsal portion of the diencephalon. Important structures in the epithalamus are the **pineal gland** (a neuroendocrine structure), and the **choroid plexus** of the third ventricle. The choroid plexuses, knotlike collections of capillaries within each ventricle, form the cerebrospinal fluid.

*Brain Stem*

1. Now trace the short midbrain from the mammillary bodies to the rounded pons below. (Continue to refer to Figure 4). The **cerebral aqueduct** is a slender canal traveling through the midbrain; it connects the third ventricle to the fourth ventricle in the hindbrain below. The cerebral peduncles and the rounded corpora quadrigemina make up the midbrain tissue anterior and posterior (respectively) to the cerebral aqueduct.

2. Locate the hindbrain structures. Trace the rounded pons to the medulla oblongata below, and identify the fourth ventricle posterior to these structures. Attempt to identify the single median aperture and the two lateral apertures, three openings found in the walls of the fourth ventricle. These apertures serve as passageways for cerebrospinal fluid to circulate into the subarachnoid space from the fourth ventricle.

*Cerebellum*

Examine the cerebellum. Notice that it is composed of two lateral hemispheres, each with three lobes (*anterior, pos-*

*terior,* and a deep *flocculonodular*) connected by a midline lobe called the **vermis (Figure 6).** As in the cerebral hemispheres, the cerebellum has an outer cortical area of gray matter and an inner area of white matter. The treelike branching of the cerebellar white matter is referred to as the **arbor vitae,** or "tree of life." The cerebellum is concerned with unconscious coordination of skeletal muscle activity and control of balance and equilibrium. Fibers converge on the cerebellum from the equilibrium apparatus of the inner ear, visual pathways, proprioceptors of tendons and skeletal muscles, and from many other areas. Thus the cerebellum remains constantly aware of the position and state of tension of the various body parts. ■

## Meninges of the Brain

The brain and spinal cord are covered and protected by three connective tissue membranes called **meninges (Figure 7).** The outermost meninx is the leathery **dura mater,** a double-layered membrane. One of its layers (the *periosteal layer*) is attached to the inner surface of the skull, forming the periosteum. The other (the *meningeal layer*) forms the outermost brain covering and is continuous with the dura mater of the spinal cord.

The dural layers are fused together except in three places where the inner membrane extends inward to form a septum that secures the brain to structures inside the cranial cavity. One such extension, the **falx cerebri,** dips into the longitudinal fissure between the cerebral hemispheres to attach to the crista galli of the ethmoid bone of the skull (Figure 7a). The cavity created at this point is the large **superior sagittal sinus,** which collects blood draining from the brain tissue. The **falx cerebelli,** separating the two cerebellar hemispheres, and the **tentorium cerebelli,** separating the cerebrum from the cerebellum below, are two other important inward folds of the inner dural membrane.

The middle meninx, the weblike **arachnoid mater,** underlies the dura mater and is partially separated from it by the **subdural space.** Threadlike projections bridge the **subarachnoid space** to attach the arachnoid to the innermost meninx, the **pia mater.** The delicate pia mater is highly vascular and clings tenaciously to the surface of the brain, following its convolutions.

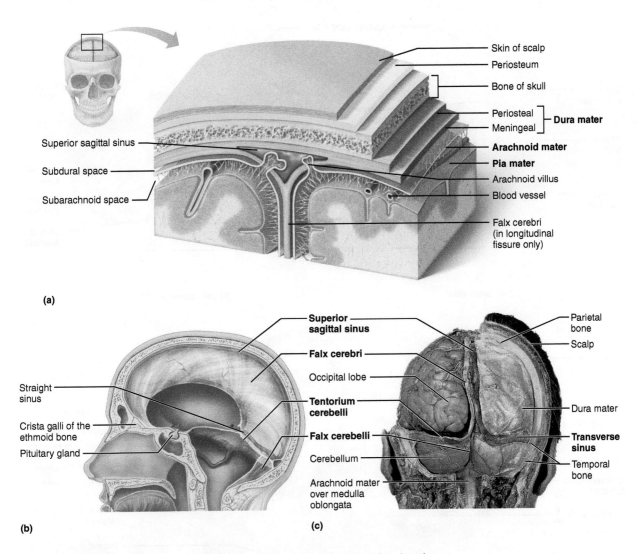

**Figure 7 Meninges of the brain. (a)** Three-dimensional frontal section showing the relationship of the dura mater, arachnoid mater, and pia mater. The meningeal dura forms the falx cerebri fold, which extends into the longitudinal fissure and attaches the brain to the ethmoid bone of the skull. The superior sagittal sinus is enclosed by the dural membranes superiorly. Arachnoid villi, which return cerebrospinal fluid to the dural sinus, are also shown. **(b)** Midsagittal view showing the position of the dural folds: the falx cerebri, tentorium cerebelli, and falx cerebelli. **(c)** Posterior view of the brain in place, surrounded by the dura mater. Sinuses between periosteal and meningeal dura contain venous blood.

In life, the subarachnoid space is filled with cerebrospinal fluid. Specialized projections of the arachnoid tissue called **arachnoid villi** protrude through the dura mater. These villi allow the cerebrospinal fluid to drain back into the venous circulation via the superior sagittal sinus and other dural sinuses.

**Meningitis,** inflammation of the meninges, is a serious threat to the brain because of the intimate association between the brain and meninges. Should infection spread to the neural tissue of the brain itself, life-threatening **encephalitis** may occur. Meningitis is often diagnosed by taking a sample of cerebrospinal fluid from the subarachnoid space. ✚

## Cerebrospinal Fluid

The cerebrospinal fluid (CSF), much like plasma in composition, is continually formed by the **choroid plexuses,** small capillary knots hanging from the roof of the ventricles of the brain. The cerebrospinal fluid in and around the brain forms a watery cushion that protects the delicate brain tissue against blows to the head.

Within the brain, the cerebrospinal fluid circulates from the two lateral ventricles (in the cerebral hemispheres) into the third ventricle via the **interventricular foramina,** and then through the cerebral aqueduct of the midbrain into the fourth ventricle in the hindbrain **(Figure 8)**. CSF enters

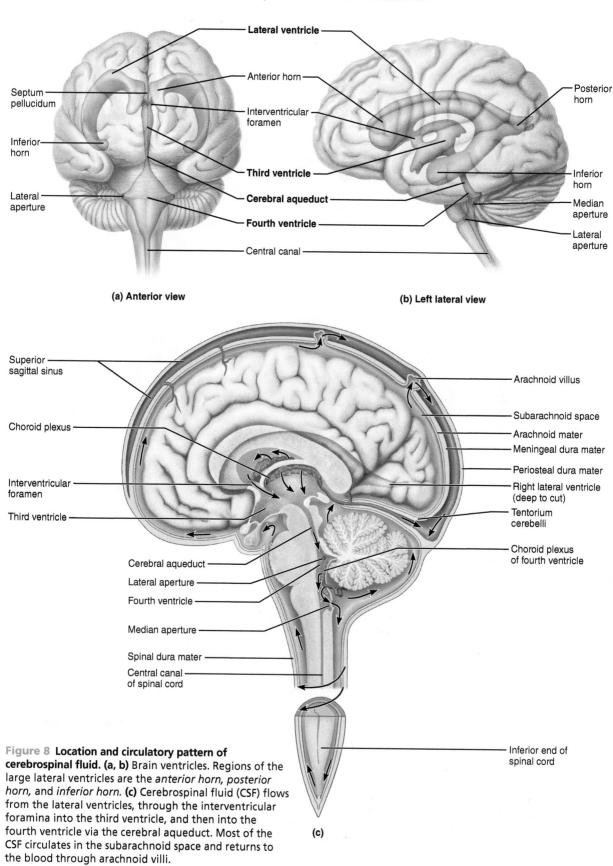

**(a) Anterior view**

**(b) Left lateral view**

**Figure 8 Location and circulatory pattern of cerebrospinal fluid. (a, b)** Brain ventricles. Regions of the large lateral ventricles are the *anterior horn, posterior horn,* and *inferior horn.* **(c)** Cerebrospinal fluid (CSF) flows from the lateral ventricles, through the interventricular foramina into the third ventricle, and then into the fourth ventricle via the cerebral aqueduct. Most of the CSF circulates in the subarachnoid space and returns to the blood through arachnoid villi.

**(c)**

the subarachnoid space through the three foramina in the walls of the fourth ventricle. There it bathes the outer surfaces of the brain and spinal cord. The fluid returns to the blood in the dural sinuses via the arachnoid villi.

Ordinarily, cerebrospinal fluid forms and drains at a constant rate. However, under certain conditions—for example, obstructed drainage or circulation resulting from tumors or anatomical deviations—cerebrospinal fluid accumulates and exerts increasing pressure on the brain which, uncorrected, causes neurological damage in adults. In infants, **hydrocephalus** (literally, "water on the brain") is indicated by a gradually enlarging head. The infant's skull is still flexible and contains fontanelles, so it can expand to accommodate the increasing size of the brain. ✛

# Cranial Nerves

The **cranial nerves** are part of the peripheral nervous system and not part of the brain proper, but they are most appropriately identified while studying brain anatomy. The 12 pairs of cranial nerves primarily serve the head and neck. Only one pair, the vagus nerves, extends into the thoracic and abdominal cavities. All but the first two pairs (olfactory and optic nerves) arise from the brain stem and pass through foramina in the base of the skull to reach their destination.

The cranial nerves are numbered consecutively, and in most cases their names reflect the major structures they control. The cranial nerves are described by name, number (Roman numeral), origin, course, and function in the list (Table 1). This information should be committed to memory. A mnemonic device that might be helpful for remembering the cranial nerves in order is "On occasion, our trusty truck acts funny—very good vehicle anyhow." The first letter of each word and the "a" and "h" of the final word "anyhow" will remind you of the first letter of the cranial nerve name.

Most cranial nerves are mixed nerves (containing both motor and sensory fibers). But close scrutiny of the list (Table 1) will reveal that three pairs of cranial nerves (optic, olfactory, and vestibulocochlear) are purely sensory in function.

Recall that the cell bodies of neurons are always located within the central nervous system (cortex or nuclei) or in specialized collections of cell bodies (ganglia) outside the CNS. Neuron cell bodies of the sensory cranial nerves are located in ganglia; those of the mixed cranial nerves are found both within the brain and in peripheral ganglia.

## ACTIVITY 3

### Identifying and Testing the Cranial Nerves

1. Observe the ventral surface of the brain model to identify the cranial nerves. (**Figure 9** may also aid you in this study.) Notice that the first (olfactory) cranial nerves are not visible on the model because they consist only of short axons that run from the nasal mucosa through the cribriform plate of the ethmoid bone. (However, the synapse points of the first cranial nerves, the *olfactory bulbs,* are visible on the model.)

2. Testing cranial nerves, is an important part of any neurological examination. (See the last column of Table 1 for techniques you can use for such tests.) Conduct tests of cranial nerve function following directions given in the "testing" column of the table. The results may help you understand

cranial nerve function, especially as it pertains to some aspects of brain function.

3. Several cranial nerve ganglia are named in the **Activity 3 chart.** *Using your text or an appropriate reference,* fill in the chart by naming the cranial nerve the ganglion is associated with and stating its location. ■

| Activity 3: Cranial Nerve Ganglia | | |
|---|---|---|
| **Cranial nerve ganglion** | **Cranial nerve** | **Site of ganglion** |
| Trigeminal | | |
| Geniculate | | |
| Inferior | | |
| Superior | | |
| Spiral | | |
| Vestibular | | |

## DISSECTION:
## The Sheep Brain

The sheep brain is enough like the human brain to warrant comparison. Obtain a sheep brain, disposable gloves, dissecting tray, and instruments, and bring them to your laboratory bench.

1. Don disposable gloves. If the dura mater is present, remove it as described here. Place the intact sheep brain ventral surface down on the dissecting pan, and observe the dura mater. Feel its consistency and note its toughness. Cut through the dura mater along the line of the longitudinal fissure (which separates the cerebral hemispheres) to enter the superior sagittal sinus. Gently force the cerebral hemispheres apart laterally to expose the corpus callosum deep to the longitudinal fissure.

2. Carefully remove the dura mater and examine the superior surface of the brain. Notice that its surface, like that of the human brain, is thrown into convolutions (fissures and gyri). Locate the arachnoid mater, which appears on the brain surface as a delicate "cottony" material spanning the fissures. In contrast, the innermost meninx, the pia mater, closely follows the cerebral contours.

3. Before beginning the dissection, turn your sheep brain so that you are viewing its left lateral aspect. Compare the various areas of the sheep brain (cerebrum, brain stem, cerebellum) to the photo of the human brain (**Figure 10**). Relatively speaking, which of these structures is obviously much larger in the human brain?

### Ventral Structures

Turn the brain so that its ventral surface is uppermost. (**Figure 11a** and **b** shows the important features of the ventral surface of the brain.)

1. Look for the clublike olfactory bulbs anteriorly, on the inferior surface of the frontal lobes of the cerebral hemispheres. Axons of olfactory neurons run from the nasal mucosa through

| Table 1 | The Cranial Nerves (see Figure 9) | | |
|---|---|---|---|
| **Number and name** | **Origin and course** | **Function*** | **Testing** |
| I. Olfactory | Fibers arise from olfactory epithelium and run through cribriform plate of ethmoid bone to synapse in olfactory bulbs. | Purely sensory—carries afferent impulses associated with sense of smell. | Person is asked to sniff aromatic substances, such as oil of cloves and vanilla, and to identify each. |
| II. Optic | Fibers arise from retina of eye to form the optic nerve and pass through optic canal of orbit. Fibers partially cross over at the optic chiasma and continue on to the thalamus as the optic tracts. Final fibers of this pathway travel from the thalamus to the visual cortex as the optic radiation. | Purely sensory—carries afferent impulses associated with vision. | Vision and visual field are determined with eye chart and by testing the point at which the person first sees an object (finger) moving into the visual field. Fundus of eye viewed with ophthalmoscope to detect papilledema (swelling of optic disc, or point at which optic nerve leaves the eye) and to observe blood vessels. |
| III. Oculomotor | Fibers emerge from dorsal midbrain and course ventrally to enter the orbit. They exit from skull via superior orbital fissure. | Primarily motor—somatic motor fibers to inferior oblique and superior, inferior, and medial rectus muscles, which direct eyeball, and to levator palpebrae muscles of the superior eyelid; parasympathetic fibers to iris and smooth muscle controlling lens shape (reflex responses to varying light intensity and focusing of eye for near vision). | Pupils are examined for size, shape, and equality. Pupillary reflex is tested with penlight (pupils should constrict when illuminated). Convergence for near vision is tested, as is subject's ability to follow objects with the eyes. |
| IV. Trochlear | Fibers emerge from midbrain and exit from skull via superior orbital fissure. | Primarily motor—provides somatic motor fibers to superior oblique muscle that moves the eyeball. | Tested in common with cranial nerve III. |
| V. Trigeminal | Fibers run from face to pons and form three divisions: mandibular division fibers pass through foramen ovale in sphenoid bone, maxillary division fibers pass via foramen rotundum in sphenoid bone, and ophthalmic division fibers pass through superior orbital fissure of eye socket. | Mixed—major sensory nerve of face; conducts sensory impulses from skin of face and anterior scalp, from mucosae of mouth and nose, and from surface of eyes; mandibular division also contains motor fibers that innervate muscles of mastication and muscles of floor of mouth. | Sensations of pain, touch, and temperature are tested with safety pin and hot and cold objects. Corneal reflex tested with wisp of cotton. Motor branch assessed by asking person to clench the teeth, open mouth against resistance, and move jaw side to side. |
| VI. Abducens | Fibers leave inferior pons and exit from skull via superior orbital fissure to run to eye. | Carries somatic motor fibers to lateral rectus muscle that moves the eyeball. | Tested in common with cranial nerve III. |
| VII. Facial | Fibers leave pons and travel through temporal bone via internal acoustic meatus, exiting via stylomastoid foramen to reach the face. | Mixed—supplies somatic motor fibers to muscles of facial expression and parasympathetic motor fibers to lacrimal and salivary glands; carries sensory fibers from taste receptors of anterior portion of tongue. | Anterior two-thirds of tongue is tested for ability to taste sweet (sugar), salty, sour (vinegar), and bitter (quinine) substances. Symmetry of face is checked. Subject is asked to close eyes, smile, whistle, and so on. Tearing is assessed with ammonia fumes. |

| Number and name | Origin and course | Function* | Testing |
|---|---|---|---|
| **Table 1** (continued) | | | |
| VIII. Vestibulocochlear | Fibers run from inner-ear equilibrium and hearing apparatus, housed in temporal bone, through internal acoustic meatus to enter pons. | Purely sensory—vestibular branch transmits impulses associated with sense of equilibrium from vestibular apparatus and semicircular canals; cochlear branch transmits impulses associated with hearing from cochlea. | Hearing is checked by air and bone conduction using tuning fork. |
| IX. Glossopharyngeal | Fibers emerge from medulla and leave skull via jugular foramen to run to throat. | Mixed—somatic motor fibers serve pharyngeal muscles, and parasympathetic motor fibers serve salivary glands; sensory fibers carry impulses from pharynx, tonsils, posterior tongue (taste buds), and from chemoreceptors and pressure receptors of carotid artery. | A tongue depressor is used to check the position of the uvula. Gag and swallowing reflexes are checked. Subject is asked to speak and cough. Posterior third of tongue may be tested for taste. |
| X. Vagus | Fibers emerge from medulla and pass through jugular foramen and descend through neck region into thorax and abdomen. | Mixed—fibers carry somatic motor impulses to pharynx and larynx and sensory fibers from same structures; very large portion is composed of parasympathetic motor fibers, which supply heart and smooth muscles of abdominal visceral organs; transmits sensory impulses from viscera. | As for cranial nerve IX (IX and X are tested in common, since they both innervate muscles of throat and mouth). |
| XI. Accessory | Fibers arise from the superior aspect of spinal cord, enter the skull, and then travel through jugular foramen to reach muscles of neck and back. | Mixed (but primarily motor in function)—provides somatic motor fibers to sternocleidomastoid and trapezius muscles and to muscles of soft palate, pharynx, and larynx (spinal and medullary fibers respectively). | Sternocleidomastoid and trapezius muscles are checked for strength by asking person to rotate head and shrug shoulders against resistance. |
| XII. Hypoglossal | Fibers arise from medulla and exit from skull via hypoglossal canal to travel to tongue. | Mixed (but primarily motor in function)—carries somatic motor fibers to muscles of tongue. | Person is asked to protrude and retract tongue. Any deviations in position are noted. |

*Does not include sensory impulses from proprioceptors.

the perforated cribriform plate of the ethmoid bone to synapse with the olfactory bulbs.

How does the size of these olfactory bulbs compare with those of humans?

_____

Is the sense of smell more important as a protective and a food-getting sense in sheep or in humans?

_____

2.  The optic nerve (II) carries sensory impulses from the retina of the eye. Thus this cranial nerve is involved in the sense of vision. Identify the optic nerves, optic chiasma, and optic tracts.

3.  Posterior to the optic chiasma, two structures protrude from the ventral aspect of the hypothalamus—the infundibulum (stalk of the pituitary gland) immediately posterior to the optic chiasma and the mammillary body. Notice that the sheep's mammillary body is a single rounded eminence. In humans it is a double structure.

4.  Identify the cerebral peduncles on the ventral aspect of the midbrain, just posterior to the mammillary body of the hypothalamus. The cerebral peduncles are fiber tracts connecting the cerebrum and medulla oblongata. Identify the large oculomotor nerves (III), which arise from the ventral midbrain surface, and the tiny trochlear nerves (IV), which can be seen at the junction of the midbrain and pons. Both of

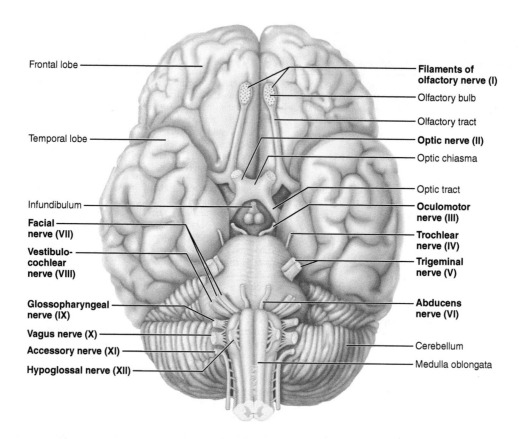

Frontal lobe

**Filaments of olfactory nerve (I)**

Olfactory bulb

Olfactory tract

Temporal lobe

**Optic nerve (II)**

Optic chiasma

Optic tract

Infundibulum

**Oculomotor nerve (III)**

**Facial nerve (VII)**

**Trochlear nerve (IV)**

**Vestibulo-cochlear nerve (VIII)**

**Trigeminal nerve (V)**

**Glossopharyngeal nerve (IX)**

**Abducens nerve (VI)**

**Vagus nerve (X)**

**Accessory nerve (XI)**

Cerebellum

**Hypoglossal nerve (XII)**

Medulla oblongata

**Figure 9** **Ventral aspect of the human brain, showing the cranial nerves.** (See also Figure 3.)

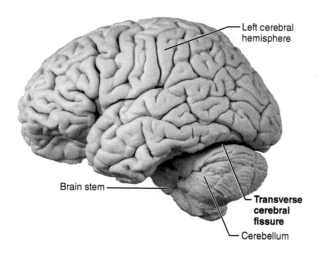

Left cerebral hemisphere

Brain stem

**Transverse cerebral fissure**

Cerebellum

**Figure 10** **Photograph of lateral aspect of the human brain.**

these cranial nerves provide motor fibers to extrinsic muscles of the eyeball.

5. Move posteriorly from the midbrain to identify first the pons and then the medulla oblongata, both hindbrain structures composed primarily of ascending and descending fiber tracts.

6. Return to the junction of the pons and midbrain, and proceed posteriorly to identify the following cranial nerves, all arising from the pons. Check them off as you locate them.

☐ Trigeminal nerves (V), which are involved in chewing and sensations of the head and face.

☐ Abducens nerves (VI), which abduct the eye (and thus work in conjunction with cranial nerves III and IV)

☐ Facial nerves (VII), large nerves involved in taste sensation, gland function (salivary and lacrimal glands), and facial expression.

7. Continue posteriorly to identify and check off:

☐ Vestibulocochlear nerves (VIII), purely sensory nerves that are involved with hearing and equilibrium.

☐ Glossopharyngeal nerves (IX), which contain motor fibers innervating throat structures and sensory fibers transmitting taste stimuli (in conjunction with cranial nerve VII).

☐ Vagus nerves (X), often called "wanderers," which serve many organs of the head, thorax, and abdominal cavity.

☐ Accessory nerves (XI), which serve muscles of the neck, larynx, and shoulder; actually arise from the spinal cord ($C_1$ through $C_5$) and travel superiorly to enter the skull before running to the muscles that they serve.

☐ Hypoglossal nerves (XII), which stimulate tongue and neck muscles.

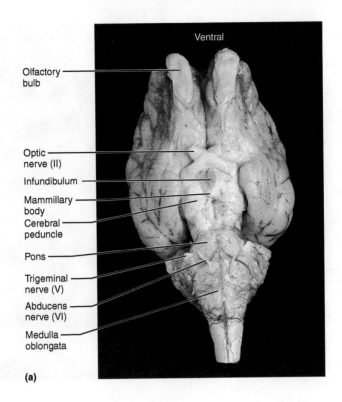

Ventral

Olfactory bulb

Optic nerve (II)

Infundibulum

Mammillary body

Cerebral peduncle

Pons

Trigeminal nerve (V)

Abducens nerve (VI)

Medulla oblongata

**(a)**

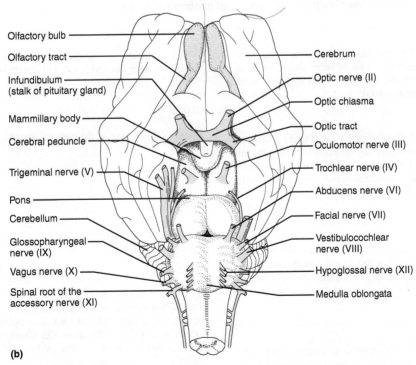

Olfactory bulb

Olfactory tract

Infundibulum (stalk of pituitary gland)

Mammillary body

Cerebral peduncle

Trigeminal nerve (V)

Pons

Cerebellum

Glossopharyngeal nerve (IX)

Vagus nerve (X)

Spinal root of the accessory nerve (XI)

Cerebrum

Optic nerve (II)

Optic chiasma

Optic tract

Oculomotor nerve (III)

Trochlear nerve (IV)

Abducens nerve (VI)

Facial nerve (VII)

Vestibulocochlear nerve (VIII)

Hypoglossal nerve (XII)

Medulla oblongata

**(b)**

**Figure 11 Intact sheep brain. (a)** Photograph of ventral view. **(b)** Diagrammatic ventral view.

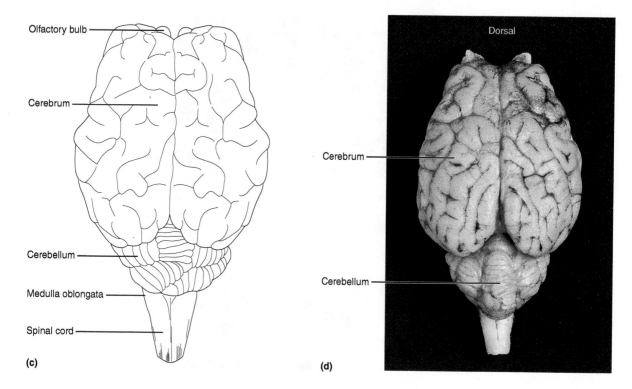

**(c)**

**(d)**

**Figure 11 *(continued)* Intact sheep brain. (c, d)** Diagram and photograph of the dorsal view, respectively.

It is likely that some of the cranial nerves will have been broken off during brain removal. If so, observe sheep brains of other students to identify those missing from your specimen, using your check marks as a guide.

*Dorsal Structures*

1. Refer to the dorsal view illustrations (Figure 11c) as a guide in identifying the following structures. Reidentify the now exposed cerebral hemispheres. How does the depth of the fissures in the sheep's cerebral hemispheres compare to that of the fissures in the human brain?

_____

_____

2. Examine the cerebellum. Notice that, in contrast to the human cerebellum, it is not divided longitudinally, and that its fissures are oriented differently. What dural falx (falx cerebri or falx cerebelli) is missing that is present in humans?

_____

_____

3. Locate the three pairs of cerebellar peduncles, fiber tracts that connect the cerebellum to other brain structures, by lifting the cerebellum dorsally away from the brain stem. The most posterior pair, the inferior cerebellar peduncles, connect the cerebellum to the medulla. The middle cerebellar peduncles attach the cerebellum to the pons, and the superior cerebellar peduncles run from the cerebellum to the midbrain.

4. To expose the dorsal surface of the midbrain, gently separate the cerebrum and cerebellum (as shown in **Figure 12.**) Identify the corpora quadrigemina, which appear as four rounded prominences on the dorsal midbrain surface.

What is the function of the corpora quadrigemina?

_____

_____

Also locate the pineal gland, which appears as a small oval protrusion in the midline just anterior to the corpora quadrigemina.

*Internal Structures*

1. The internal structure of the brain can be examined only after further dissection. Place the brain ventral side down on the dissecting tray and make a cut completely through it in a superior to inferior direction. Cut through the longitudinal fissure, corpus callosum, and midline of the cerebellum. (Refer to **Figure 13** as you work.)

2. A thin nervous tissue membrane immediately ventral to the corpus callosum that separates the lateral ventricles is the septum pellucidum. If it is still intact, pierce this membrane and probe the lateral ventricle cavity. The fiber tract ventral to the septum pellucidum and anterior to the third ventricle is the fornix.

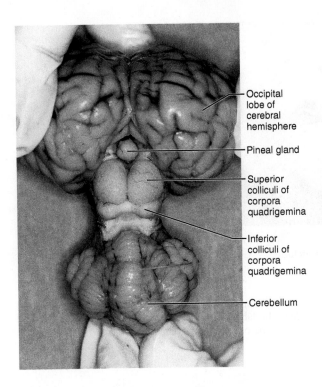

Occipital lobe of cerebral hemisphere

Pineal gland

Superior colliculi of corpora quadrigemina

Inferior colliculi of corpora quadrigemina

Cerebellum

**Figure 12 Means of exposing the dorsal midbrain structures of the sheep brain.**

How does the size of the fornix in this brain compare with the size of the human fornix?

Why do you suppose this is so? (Hint: What is the function of this band of fibers?)

3. Identify the thalamus, which forms the walls of the third ventricle and is located posterior and ventral to the fornix. The intermediate mass spanning the ventricular cavity appears as an oval protrusion of the thalamic wall. Anterior to the intermediate mass, locate the interventricular foramen, a canal connecting the lateral ventricle on the same side with the third ventricle.

4. The hypothalamus forms the floor of the third ventricle. Identify the optic chiasma, infundibulum, and mammillary body on its exterior surface. You can see the pineal gland at the superoposterior end of the third ventricle, just beneath the junction of the corpus callosum and fornix.

5. Locate the midbrain by identifying the corpora quadrigemina that form its dorsal roof. Follow the cerebral aqueduct (the narrow canal connecting the third and fourth ventricles) through the midbrain tissue to the fourth ventricle. Identify the cerebral peduncles, which form its anterior walls.

6. Identify the pons and medulla oblongata, which lie anterior to the fourth ventricle. The medulla continues into the spinal cord without any obvious anatomical change, but the point at which the fourth ventricle narrows to a small canal is generally accepted as the beginning of the spinal cord.

7. Identify the cerebellum posterior to the fourth ventricle. Notice its internal treelike arrangement of white matter, the arbor vitae.

8. If time allows, obtain another sheep brain and section it along the coronal plane so that the cut passes through the infundibulum. Compare your specimen with the photograph of a coronal section **(Figure 14)**, and attempt to identify all the structures shown in the figure.

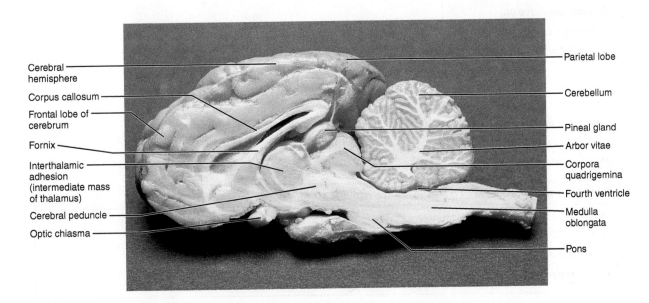

Cerebral hemisphere

Corpus callosum

Frontal lobe of cerebrum

Fornix

Interthalamic adhesion (intermediate mass of thalamus)

Cerebral peduncle

Optic chiasma

Parietal lobe

Cerebellum

Pineal gland

Arbor vitae

Corpora quadrigemina

Fourth ventricle

Medulla oblongata

Pons

**Figure 13 Photograph of sagittal section of the sheep brain showing internal structures.**

275

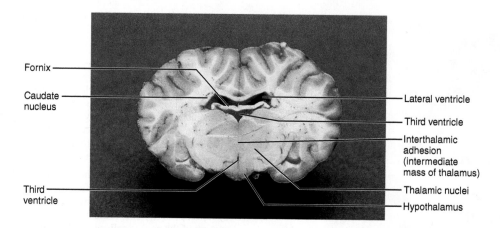

Fornix

Caudate nucleus

Lateral ventricle

Third ventricle

Interthalamic adhesion (intermediate mass of thalamus)

Third ventricle

Thalamic nuclei

Hypothalamus

**Figure 14 Coronal section of a sheep brain.** Major structures include the thalamus, hypothalamus, and lateral and third ventricles.

9. Check with your instructor to determine if a small portion of the spinal cord from your brain specimen should be saved for spinal cord studies Otherwise, dispose of all the organic debris in the appropriate laboratory containers and clean the laboratory bench, the dissection instruments, and the tray before leaving the laboratory. ■

### GROUP CHALLENGE

## Odd (Cranial) Nerve Out

The following boxes each contain four cranial nerves. One of the listed nerves does not share a characteristic with the other three. Circle the cranial nerve that doesn't belong with the others and explain why it is singled out.

What characteristic is it missing? Sometimes there may be multiple reasons why the cranial nerve doesn't belong with the others.

| 1. Which is the "odd" nerve? | Why is it the odd one out? |
|---|---|
| Optic nerve (II) <br> Oculomotor nerve (III) <br> Olfactory nerve (I) <br> Vestibulocochlear nerve (VIII) | |
| **2. Which is the "odd" nerve?** | **Why is it the odd one out?** |
| Oculomotor nerve (III) <br> Trochlear nerve (IV) <br> Abducens nerve (VI) <br> Hypoglossal nerve (XII) | |
| **3. Which is the "odd" nerve?** | **Why is it the odd one out?** |
| Facial nerve (VII) <br> Hypoglossal nerve (XII) <br> Trigeminal nerve (V) <br> Glossopharyngeal nerve (IX) | |

# Gross Anatomy of the Brain and Cranial Nerves

## The Human Brain

**1.** Match the letters on the diagram of the human brain (right lateral view) to the appropriate terms listed at the left.

_____  1. frontal lobe

_____  2. parietal lobe

_____  3. temporal lobe

_____  4. precentral gyrus

_____  5. parieto-occipital sulcus

_____  6. postcentral gyrus

_____  7. lateral sulcus      _____  10. medulla

_____  8. central sulcus      _____  11. occipital lobe

_____  9. cerebellum          _____  12. pons

**2.** In which of the cerebral lobes are the following functional areas found?

auditory cortex: _____

primary motor cortex: _____

primary sensory cortex: _____

olfactory cortex: _____

visual cortex: _____

Broca's area: _____

**3.** Which of the following structures are not part of the brain stem? (Circle the appropriate response or responses.)

cerebral hemispheres    pons    midbrain    cerebellum    medulla    diencephalon

**4.** Complete the following statements by writing the proper word or phrase on the corresponding blanks at the right.

A(n) _1_ is an elevated ridge of cerebral tissue. The convolutions seen in the cerebrum are important because they increase the _2._ Gray matter is composed of _3._ White matter is composed of _4._ A fiber tract that provides for communication between different parts of the same cerebral hemisphere is called a(n) _5._ whereas one that carries impulses from the cerebrum to lower CNS areas is called a(n) _6_ tract. The caudate, putamen, and globus pallidus are collectively called the _7._

1. _____

2. _____

3. _____

4. _____

5. _____

6. _____

7. _____

277

**5.** Identify the structures on the following sagittal view of the human brain stem and diencephalon by matching the numbered areas to the proper terms in the list.

———— a. cerebellum

———— b. cerebral aqueduct

———— c. (small part of) cerebral hemisphere

———— d. cerebral peduncle

———— e. choroid plexus

———— f. corpora quadrigemina

———— g. corpus callosum

———— h. fornix

———— i. fourth ventricle

———— j. hypothalamus

———— k. interthalamic adhesion

———— l. mammillary bodies

———— m. medulla oblongata

———— n. optic chiasma

———— o. pineal gland

———— p. pituitary gland

———— q. pons

———— r. septum pellucidum

———— s. thalamus

**6.** Using the terms from question 5, match the appropriate structures with the descriptions given below.

———— 1. site of regulation of body temperature and water balance; most important autonomic center

———— 2. consciousness depends on the function of this part of the brain

———— 3. located in the midbrain; contains reflex centers for vision and audition

———— 4. responsible for regulation of posture and coordination of complex muscular movements

———— 5. important synapse site for afferent fibers traveling to the sensory cortex

———— 6. contains autonomic centers regulating blood pressure, heart rate, and respiratory rhythm, as well as coughing, sneezing, and swallowing centers

———— 7. large commissure connecting the cerebral hemispheres

———— 8. fiber tract involved with olfaction

———— 9. connects the third and fourth ventricles

———— 10. encloses the third ventricle

7. Embryologically, the brain arises from the rostral end of a tubelike structure that quickly becomes divided into three major regions. Groups of structures that develop from the embryonic brain are listed below. Designate the embryonic origin of each group as the hindbrain, midbrain, or forebrain.

_____ 1. the diencephalon, including the thalamus, optic chiasma, and hypothalamus

_____ 2. the medulla, pons, and cerebellum

_____ 3. the cerebral hemispheres

8. What is the function of the basal nuclei? _____

_____

9. What is the striatum, and how is it related to the fibers of the internal capsule? _____

_____

_____

10. A brain hemorrhage within the region of the right internal capsule results in paralysis of the left side of the body.

Explain why the left side (rather than the right side) is affected. _____

_____

11. Explain why trauma to the base of the brain is often much more dangerous than trauma to the frontal lobes. (Hint: Think about the relative functioning of the cerebral hemispheres and the brain stem structures. Which contain centers more vital to life?)

_____

_____

_____

12. In "split brain" experiments, the main commissure connecting the cerebral hemispheres is cut. First, name this commissure.

_____

Then, describe what results (in terms of behavior) can be anticipated in such experiments. (Use an appropriate reference if you need help with this one!)

_____

_____

_____

_____

_____

# Meninges of the Brain

**13.** Identify the meningeal (or associated) structures described below:

_____ 1. outermost meninx covering the brain; composed of tough fibrous connective tissue

_____ 2. innermost meninx covering the brain; delicate and highly vascular

_____ 3. structures instrumental in returning cerebrospinal fluid to the venous blood in the dural sinuses

_____ 4. structure that forms the cerebrospinal fluid

_____ 5. middle meninx; like a cobweb in structure

_____ 6. its outer layer forms the periosteum of the skull

_____ 7. a dural fold that attaches the cerebrum to the crista galli of the skull

_____ 8. a dural fold separating the cerebrum from the cerebellum

# Cerebrospinal Fluid

**14.** Label the structures involved with circulation of cerebrospinal fluid on the accompanying diagram.

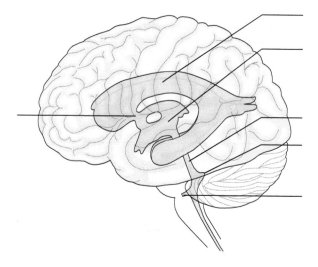

Add arrows to the figure above to indicate the flow of cerebrospinal fluid from its formation in the lateral ventricles to the site of its exit from the fourth ventricle. Then fill in the blanks in the following paragraph.

Cerebrospinal fluid flows from the fourth ventricle into the _1_ space surrounding the brain and spinal cord. From this space it drains through the _2_ into the _3._

1. _____

2. _____

3. _____

# Cranial Nerves

**15.** Using the terms below, correctly identify all structures indicated by leader lines on the diagram.

a.  abducens nerve (VI)

b.  accessory nerve (XI)

c.  cerebellum

d.  cerebral peduncle

e.  decussation of the pyramids

f.  facial nerve (VII)

g.  frontal lobe of cerebral hemisphere

h.  glossopharyngeal nerve (IX)

i.  hypoglossal nerve (XII)

j.  longitudinal fissure

k.  mammillary body

l.  medulla oblongata

m.  oculomotor nerve (III)

n.  olfactory bulb

o.  olfactory tract

p.  optic chiasma

q.  optic nerve (II)

r.  optic tract

s.  pituitary gland

t.  pons

u.  spinal cord

v.  temporal lobe of cerebral hemisphere

w.  trigeminal nerve (V)

x.  trochlear nerve (IV)

y.  vagus nerve (X)

z.  vestibulocochlear nerve (VIII)

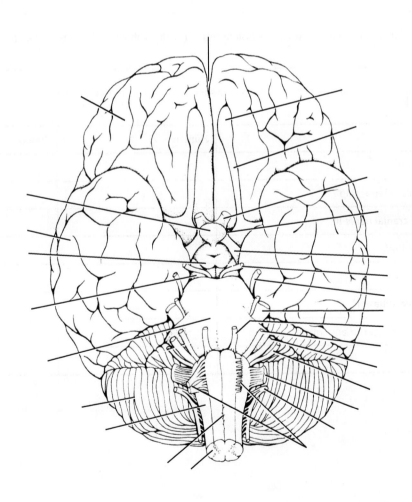

**16.** Provide the name and number of the cranial nerves involved in each of the following activities, sensations, or disorders.

_____ 1. rotating the head

_____ 2. smelling a flower

_____ 3. raising the eyelids; pupillary constriction

_____ 4. slowing the heart; increasing motility of the digestive tract

_____ 5. involved in Bell's palsy (facial paralysis)

_____ 6. chewing food

_____ 7. listening to music; seasickness

_____ 8. secretion of saliva; tasting well-seasoned food

_____ 9. involved in "rolling" the eyes (three nerves—provide numbers only)

_____ 10. feeling a toothache

_____ 11. reading the newspaper

_____ 12. purely sensory in function (three nerves—provide numbers only)

# Dissection of the Sheep Brain

**17.** In your own words, describe the firmness and texture of the sheep brain tissue as observed when cutting into it.

_____

Because formalin hardens all tissue, what conclusions might you draw about the firmness and texture of living brain tissue?

_____

**18.** When comparing human and sheep brains, you observe some profound differences between them. Record your observations in the chart below.

| Structure | Human | Sheep |
|---|---|---|
| Olfactory bulb | | |
| Pons/medulla relationship | | |
| Location of cranial nerve III | | |
| Mammillary body | | |
| Corpus callosum | | |
| Interthalamic adhesion | | |
| Relative size of superior and inferior colliculi | | |
| Pineal gland | | |

## Photo Credits

**Credits are listed in order of appearance.**

2c, 7c: From *A Stereoscopic Atlas of Human Anatomy* by David L. Bassett, M.D. 3, 4a, 5b, 6a,b, 10: Karen Krabbenhoft, PAL 3.0, Pearson Education. 11a,d: Sharon Cummings, Pearson Education. 12–14: Elena Dorfman, Pearson Education.

## Illustration Credits

**All illustrations are by Imagineering STA Media Services, except for Review Sheet art and as noted below.**

1, 5, 7–10: Electronic Publishing Services, Inc. 11: Precision Graphics.

# The Spinal Cord and Spinal Nerves

## MATERIALS

- ☐ Spinal cord model (cross section)
- ☐ Three-dimensional models or laboratory charts of the spinal cord and spinal nerves
- ☐ Red and blue pencils
- ☐ Preserved cow spinal cord sections with meninges and nerve roots intact
- ☐ Dissecting instruments and tray
- ☐ Disposable gloves
- ☐ Stereomicroscope
- ☐ Prepared slide of spinal cord (x.s.)
- ☐ Compound microscope

## OBJECTIVES

1. List two major functions of the spinal cord.
2. Define *conus medullaris, cauda equina,* and *filum terminale*.
3. Name the meningeal coverings of the spinal cord, and state their function.
4. Indicate two major areas where the spinal cord is enlarged, and explain the reasons for the enlargement.
5. Identify important anatomical areas on a model or image of a cross section of the spinal cord, and where applicable name the neuron type found in these areas.
6. Locate on a diagram the fiber tracts in the spinal cord, and state their functions.
7. Note the number of pairs of spinal nerves that arise from the spinal cord, describe their division into groups, and identify the number of pairs in each group.
8. Describe the origin and fiber composition of the spinal nerves, differentiating between roots, the spinal nerve proper, and rami, and discuss the result of transecting these structures.
9. Discuss the distribution of the dorsal and ventral rami of the spinal nerves.
10. Identify the four major nerve plexuses on a model or image, name the major nerves of each plexus, and describe the destination and function of each.

## PRE-LAB QUIZ

1. The spinal cord extends from the foramen magnum of the skull to the first or second lumbar vertebra, where it terminates in the
   a. conus medullaris
   b. denticulate ligament
   c. filum terminale
   d. gray matter
2. How many pairs of spinal nerves do humans have?
   a. 10       c. 31
   b. 12       d. 47
3. Circle the correct underlined term. In cross section, the gray / white matter of the spinal cord looks like a butterfly or the letter H.
4. Circle True or False. The cell bodies of sensory neurons are found in an enlarged area of the dorsal root called the gray commissure.
5. Circle the correct underlined term. Fiber tracts conducting impulses to the brain are called ascending or sensory / motor tracts.
6. Circle True or False. Because the spinal nerves arise from fusion of the ventral and dorsal roots of the spinal cord, and contain motor and sensory fibers, all spinal nerves are considered mixed nerves.

MasteringA&P® For related exercise study tools, go to the Study Area of MasteringA&P. There you will find:
- Practice Anatomy Lab PAL
- PhysioEx PEx
- A&PFlix *A&PFlix*
- Practice quizzes, Histology Atlas, eText, Videos, and more!

*(Text continues on next page.)*

From Exercise 19 of *Human Anatomy & Physiology Laboratory Manual,* Main Version, Tenth Edition. Elaine N. Marieb, Susan J. Mitchell, Lori A. Smith. Copyright © 2014 by Pearson Education, Inc. All rights reserved.

7. The ventral rami of all spinal nerves except $T_2$ through $T_{12}$ form complex networks of nerves known as _____.
   a. fissures
   b. ganglia
   c. plexuses
   d. sulci

8. Severe injuries to the _____ plexus cause weakness or paralysis of the entire upper limb.
   a. brachial
   b. cervical
   c. lumbar
   d. sacral

9. Circle True or False. The femoral nerve is the largest nerve from the sacral plexus.

10. Circle the correct underlined term. The sciatic nerve divides into the tibial and posterior femoral cutaneous / common fibular nerves.

The cylindrical **spinal cord,** a continuation of the brain stem, is an association and communication center. It plays a major role in spinal reflex activity and provides neural pathways to and from higher nervous centers.

# Anatomy of the Spinal Cord

Enclosed within the vertebral canal of the spinal column, the spinal cord extends from the foramen magnum of the skull to the first or second lumbar vertebra, where it terminates in the cone-shaped **conus medullaris (Figure 1).** Like the brain, the cord is cushioned and protected by meninges. The dura mater and arachnoid meningeal coverings extend beyond the conus medullaris, approximately to the level of $S_2$, and the **filum terminale,** a fibrous extension of the pia mater, extends even farther into the coccygeal canal to attach to the posterior coccyx. **Denticulate ligaments,** saw-toothed shelves of pia mater, secure the spinal cord to the bony wall of the vertebral column all along its length (Figure 1c).

The cerebrospinal fluid–filled meninges extend well beyond the end of the spinal cord, providing an excellent site for removing cerebrospinal fluid without endangering the delicate spinal cord. Analysis of the fluid can provide important information about suspected bacterial or viral infections of the spinal cord or meninges. This procedure, called a *lumbar tap,* is usually performed below $L_3$. Additionally, "saddle block," or caudal anesthesia for childbirth, is normally administered (injected) between $L_3$ and $L_5$.

In humans, 31 pairs of spinal nerves arise from the spinal cord and pass through intervertebral foramina to serve the body area at their approximate level of emergence. The cord is about the size of a finger in circumference for most of its length, but there are obvious enlargements in the *cervical* and *lumbar* areas where the nerves serving the upper and lower limbs issue from the cord.

Because the spinal cord does not extend to the end of the vertebral column, the spinal nerves emerging from the inferior end of the cord must travel through the vertebral canal for some distance before exiting at the appropriate intervertebral foramina. This collection of spinal nerves passing through the inferior end of the vertebral canal is called the **cauda equina** (Figure 1a and d) because of its similarity to a horse's tail (the literal translation of *cauda equina).*

## Identifying Structures of the Spinal Cord

Obtain a three-dimensional model or laboratory chart of a cross section of a spinal cord and identify its structures as they are described next. ■

## Gray Matter

In cross section, the **gray matter** of the spinal cord looks like a butterfly or the letter H **(Figure 2).** The two dorsal projections are called the **dorsal (posterior) horns.** The two ventral projections are the **ventral (anterior) horns.** The tips of the ventral horns are broader and less tapered than those of the dorsal horns. In the thoracic and lumbar regions of the cord, there is also a lateral outpocketing of gray matter on each side referred to as the **lateral horn.** The central area of gray matter connecting the two vertical regions is the **gray commissure,** which surrounds the **central canal** of the cord.

Neurons with specific functions can be localized in the gray matter. The dorsal horns contain interneurons and sensory fibers that enter the cord from the body periphery via the **dorsal root.** The cell bodies of these sensory neurons are found in an enlarged area of the dorsal root called the **dorsal root ganglion.** The ventral horns mainly contain cell bodies of motor neurons of the somatic nervous system, which send their axons out via the **ventral root** of the cord to enter the adjacent spinal nerve. Because they are formed by the fusion of the dorsal and ventral roots, the **spinal nerves** are **mixed nerves** containing both sensory and motor fibers. The lateral horns, where present, contain nerve cell bodies of motor neurons of the autonomic nervous system, sympathetic division. Their axons also leave the cord via the ventral roots, along with those of the motor neurons of the ventral horns.

## White Matter

The **white matter** of the spinal cord is nearly bisected by fissures (Figure 2). The more open ventral fissure is the **ventral median fissure,** and the dorsal one is the shallow **dorsal median sulcus.** The white matter is composed of myelinated and nonmyelinated fibers—some running to higher centers, some traveling from the brain to the cord, and some conducting impulses from one side of the cord to the other.

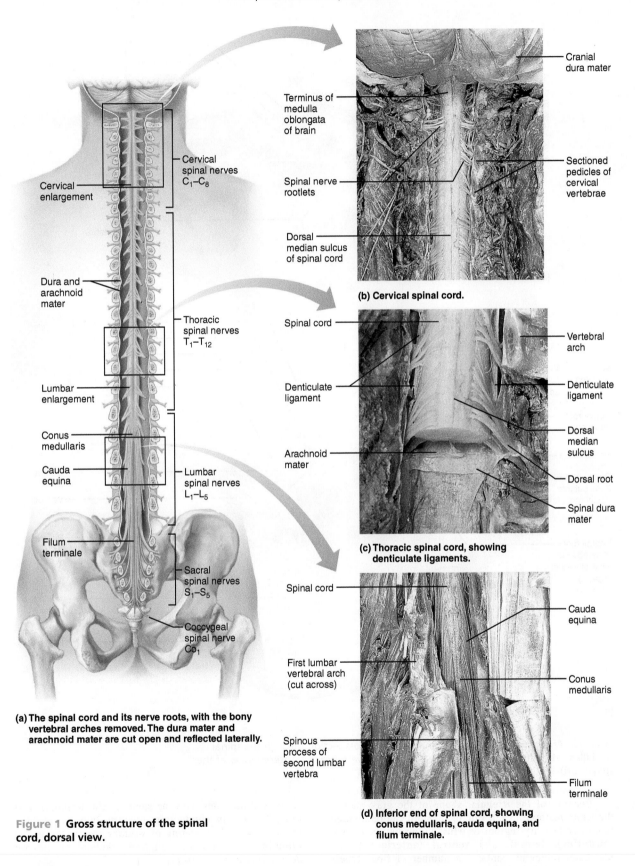

**Cranial dura mater**

**Terminus of medulla oblongata of brain**

**Spinal nerve rootlets**

**Sectioned pedicles of cervical vertebrae**

**Dorsal median sulcus of spinal cord**

**(b) Cervical spinal cord.**

**Cervical spinal nerves C₁–C₈**

**Cervical enlargement**

**Dura and arachnoid mater**

**Thoracic spinal nerves T₁–T₁₂**

**Lumbar enlargement**

**Conus medullaris**

**Cauda equina**

**Lumbar spinal nerves L₁–L₅**

**Filum terminale**

**Sacral spinal nerves S₁–S₅**

**Coccygeal spinal nerve Co₁**

**Spinal cord**

**Denticulate ligament**

**Arachnoid mater**

**Vertebral arch**

**Denticulate ligament**

**Dorsal median sulcus**

**Dorsal root**

**Spinal dura mater**

**(c) Thoracic spinal cord, showing denticulate ligaments.**

**Spinal cord**

**First lumbar vertebral arch (cut across)**

**Spinous process of second lumbar vertebra**

**Cauda equina**

**Conus medullaris**

**Filum terminale**

**(d) Inferior end of spinal cord, showing conus medullaris, cauda equina, and filum terminale.**

**(a)** The spinal cord and its nerve roots, with the bony vertebral arches removed. The dura mater and arachnoid mater are cut open and reflected laterally.

**Figure 1** Gross structure of the spinal cord, dorsal view.

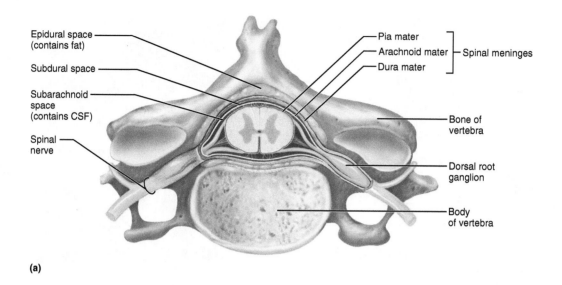

Epidural space (contains fat)

Subdural space

Subarachnoid space (contains CSF)

Spinal nerve

Pia mater
Arachnoid mater — Spinal meninges
Dura mater

Bone of vertebra

Dorsal root ganglion

Body of vertebra

**(a)**

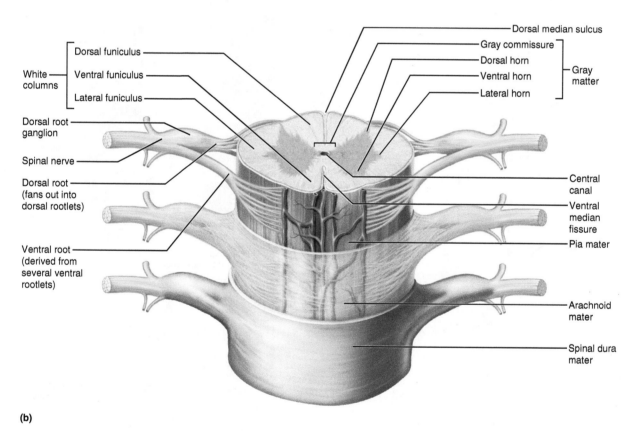

White columns

Dorsal funiculus
Ventral funiculus
Lateral funiculus

Dorsal root ganglion

Spinal nerve

Dorsal root (fans out into dorsal rootlets)

Ventral root (derived from several ventral rootlets)

Dorsal median sulcus
Gray commissure
Dorsal horn — Gray matter
Ventral horn
Lateral horn

Central canal

Ventral median fissure

Pia mater

Arachnoid mater

Spinal dura mater

**(b)**

**Figure 2** **Anatomy of the human spinal cord. (a)** Cross section through the spinal cord illustrating its relationship to the surrounding vertebra. **(b)** Anterior view of the spinal cord and its meningeal coverings.

Because of the irregular shape of the gray matter, the white matter on each side of the cord can be divided into three primary regions or **white columns:** the **dorsal (posterior), lateral,** and **ventral (anterior) funiculi.** Each funiculus contains a number of fiber **tracts** composed of axons with the same origin, terminus, and function. Tracts conducting sensory impulses to the brain are called *ascending* or *sensory tracts;* those carrying impulses from the brain to the skeletal muscles are *descending* or *motor tracts.*

**Ascending tracts**                    **Descending tracts**

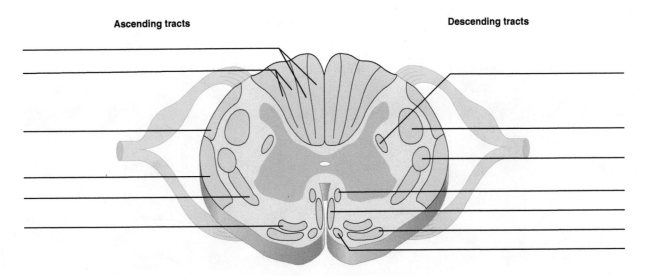

**Figure 3 Cross section of the spinal cord showing the relative positioning of its major tracts.**

Because it serves as the transmission pathway between the brain and the body periphery, the spinal cord is extremely important functionally. Even though it is protected by meninges and cerebrospinal fluid in the vertebral canal, it is highly vulnerable to traumatic injuries, such as might occur in an automobile accident.

When the cord is transected (or severely traumatized), both motor and sensory functions are lost in body areas normally served by that region and lower regions of the spinal cord. Injury to certain spinal cord areas may even result in a permanent flaccid paralysis of both legs, called **paraplegia,** or of all four limbs, called **quadriplegia.** ✚

### ACTIVITY 2

## Identifying Spinal Cord Tracts

With the help of your text, label the spinal cord diagram (Figure 3) with the tract names that follow. Each tract is represented on both sides of the cord, but for clarity, label the motor tracts on the right side of the diagram and the sensory tracts on the left side of the diagram. *Color ascending tracts blue and descending tracts red.* Then fill in the functional importance of each tract beside its name below. As you work, try to be aware of how the naming of the tracts is related to their anatomical distribution.

Dorsal columns

    Fasciculus gracilis _____

    Fasciculus cuneatus _____

Dorsal spinocerebellar _____

Ventral spinocerebellar _____

Lateral spinothalamic _____

Ventral spinothalamic _____

Lateral corticospinal _____

Ventral corticospinal _____

Rubrospinal _____

Tectospinal _____

Vestibulospinal _____

Medial reticulospinal _____

Lateral reticulospinal _____ ■

### ✂ DISSECTION:
## Spinal Cord

1. Obtain a dissecting tray and instruments, disposable gloves, and a segment of preserved spinal cord. Identify the tough outer meninx (dura mater) and the weblike arachnoid mater.

What name is given to the third meninx, and where is it found?

_____

_____

289

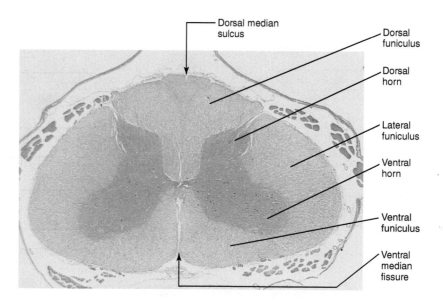

**Figure 4 Cross section of the spinal cord (10×).**

Peel back the dura mater and observe the fibers making up the dorsal and ventral roots. If possible, identify a dorsal root ganglion.

2. Cut a thin cross section of the cord and identify the ventral and dorsal horns of the gray matter with the naked eye or with the aid of a dissecting microscope.

How can you be certain that you are correctly identifying the ventral and dorsal horns?

_____

_____

Also identify the central canal, white matter, ventral median fissure, dorsal median sulcus, and dorsal, ventral, and lateral funiculi.

3. Obtain a prepared slide of the spinal cord (cross section) and a compound microscope. Examine the slide carefully under low power (refer to **Figure 4** to identify spinal cord features). Observe the shape of the central canal.

Is it basically circular or oval? _____

Name the neuroglial cell type that lines this canal. _____

Can any neuron cell bodies be seen? _____

If so, where, and what type of neurons would these most

likely be—motor, sensory, or interneuron? _____

_____ ■

# Spinal Nerves and Nerve Plexuses

The 31 pairs of human spinal nerves arise from the fusions of the ventral and dorsal roots of the spinal cord (see Figure 2a). There are 8 pairs of cervical nerves ($C_1$–$C_8$), 12 pairs of thoracic nerves ($T_1$–$T_{12}$), 5 pairs of lumbar nerves ($L_1$–$L_5$), 5 pairs of sacral nerves ($S_1$–$S_5$), and 1 pair of coccygeal nerves ($Co_1$) **(Figure 5a)**. The first pair of spinal nerves leaves the vertebral canal between the base of the occiput and the atlas, but all the rest exit via the intervertebral foramina. The first through seventh pairs of cervical nerves emerge *above* the vertebra for which they are named; $C_8$ emerges between $C_7$ and $T_1$. (Notice that there are 7 cervical vertebrae, but 8 pairs of cervical nerves.) The remaining spinal nerve pairs emerge from the spinal cord area *below* the same-numbered vertebra.

Almost immediately after emerging, each nerve divides into **dorsal** and **ventral rami.** Thus each spinal nerve is only about 1 or 2 cm long. The rami, like the spinal nerves, contain both motor and sensory fibers. The smaller dorsal rami serve the skin and musculature of the posterior body trunk at their approximate level of emergence. The ventral rami of spinal nerves $T_2$ through $T_{12}$ pass anteriorly as the **intercostal nerves** to supply the muscles of intercostal spaces, and the skin and muscles of the anterior and lateral trunk. The ventral rami of all other spinal nerves form complex networks of nerves called **nerve plexuses.** These plexuses primarily serve the muscles and skin of the limbs. The fibers of the ventral rami unite in the plexuses (with a few rami supplying fibers to more than one plexus). From the plexuses the fibers diverge again to form peripheral nerves, each of which contains fibers from more than one spinal nerve. (The four major nerve plexuses and their chief peripheral nerves are described in Tables 1–4 and illustrated in Figures 6–9. Their names and site of origin should be committed to memory). The tiny

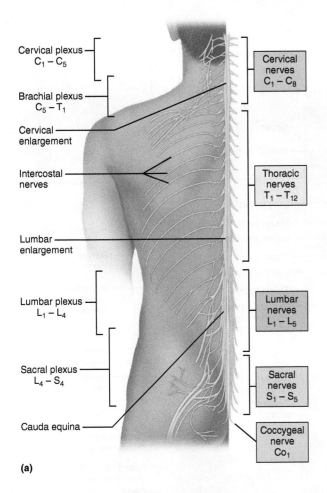

Cervical plexus
$C_1 - C_5$

Brachial plexus
$C_5 - T_1$

Cervical
enlargement

Intercostal
nerves

Lumbar
enlargement

Lumbar plexus
$L_1 - L_4$

Sacral plexus
$L_4 - S_4$

Cauda equina

Cervical
nerves
$C_1 - C_8$

Thoracic
nerves
$T_1 - T_{12}$

Lumbar
nerves
$L_1 - L_5$

Sacral
nerves
$S_1 - S_5$

Coccygeal
nerve
$Co_1$

**(a)**

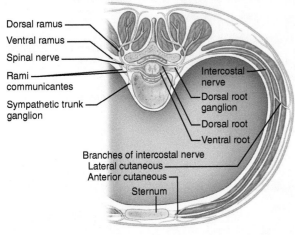

Dorsal ramus

Ventral ramus

Spinal nerve

Rami
communicantes

Sympathetic trunk
ganglion

Intercostal
nerve

Dorsal root
ganglion

Dorsal root

Ventral root

Branches of intercostal nerve

Lateral cutaneous

Anterior cutaneous

Sternum

**(b)**

**Figure 5 Human spinal nerves. (a)** Spinal nerves are shown at right; ventral rami and the major nerve plexuses are shown at left. **(b)** Relative distribution of the ventral and dorsal rami of a spinal nerve (cross section of thorax).

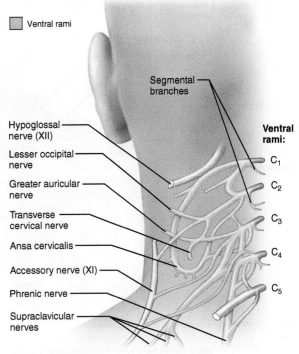

☐ Ventral rami

Segmental
branches

Hypoglossal
nerve (XII)

Lesser occipital
nerve

Greater auricular
nerve

Transverse
cervical nerve

Ansa cervicalis

Accessory nerve (XI)

Phrenic nerve

Supraclavicular
nerves

**Ventral
rami:**

$C_1$

$C_2$

$C_3$

$C_4$

$C_5$

**Figure 6 The cervical plexus.** The nerves colored gray connect to the plexus but do not belong to it. (See Table 1.)

$S_5$ and $Co_1$ spinal nerves contribute to a small plexus that serves part of the pelvic floor.

## Cervical Plexus and the Neck

The **cervical plexus** (**Figure 6** and **Table 1**) arises from the ventral rami of $C_1$ through $C_5$ to supply muscles of the shoulder and neck. The major motor branch of this plexus is the **phrenic nerve,** which arises from $C_3$ through $C_4$ (plus some fibers from $C_5$) and passes into the thoracic cavity in front of the first rib to innervate the diaphragm. The primary danger of a broken neck is that the phrenic nerve may be severed, leading to paralysis of the diaphragm and cessation of breathing. A jingle to help you remember the rami (roots) forming the phrenic nerves is "$C_3$, $C_4$, $C_5$ keep the diaphragm alive."

## Brachial Plexus and the Upper Limb

The **brachial plexus** is large and complex, arising from the ventral rami of $C_5$ through $C_8$ and $T_1$ (**Table 2**). The plexus, after being rearranged consecutively into *trunks, divisions,* and *cords,* finally becomes subdivided into five major *peripheral nerves* (**Figure 7**).

The **axillary nerve,** which serves the muscles and skin of the shoulder, has the most limited distribution. The large **radial nerve** passes down the posterolateral surface of the arm and forearm, supplying all the extensor muscles of the arm, forearm, and hand and the skin along its course.

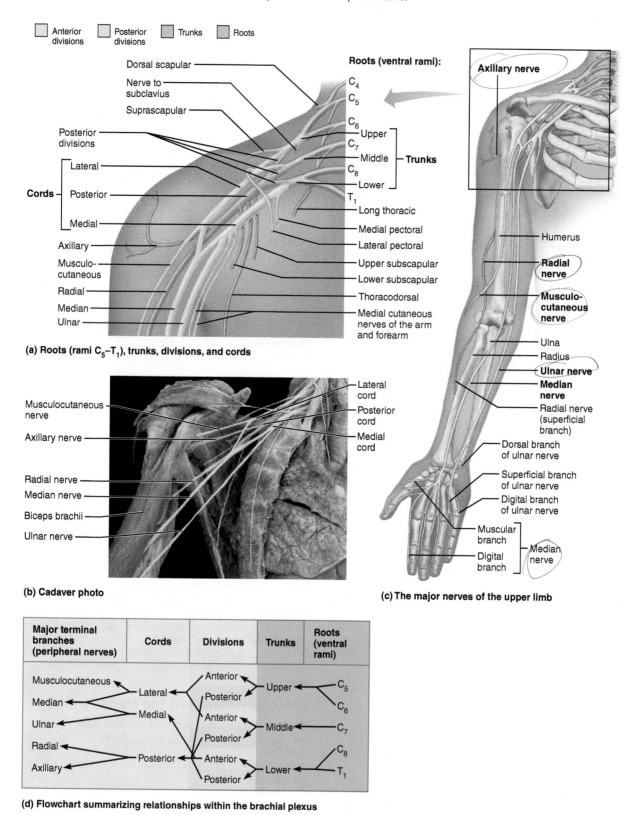

(a) Roots (rami C$_5$–T$_1$), trunks, divisions, and cords

(b) Cadaver photo

(c) The major nerves of the upper limb

(d) Flowchart summarizing relationships within the brachial plexus

Figure 7 The brachial plexus. (See Table 2.)

**Table 1**  **Branches of the Cervical Plexus (See Figure 6)**

| Nerves | Ventral rami | Structures served |
|---|---|---|
| **Cutaneous Branches (Superficial)** | | |
| Lesser occipital | $C_2$ ($C_3$) | Skin on posterolateral aspect of neck |
| Greater auricular | $C_2$, $C_3$ | Skin of ear, skin over parotid gland |
| Transverse cervical | $C_2$, $C_3$ | Skin on anterior and lateral aspect of neck |
| Supraclavicular (medial, intermediate, and lateral) | $C_3$, $C_4$ | Skin of shoulder and clavicular region |
| **Motor Branches (Deep)** | | |
| Ansa cervicalis (superior and inferior roots) | $C_1$–$C_3$ | Infrahyoid muscles of neck (omohyoid, sternohyoid, and sternothyroid) |
| Segmental and other muscular branches | $C_1$–$C_5$ | Deep muscles of neck (geniohyoid and thyrohyoid) and portions of scalenes, levator scapulae, trapezius, and sternocleidomastoid muscles |
| Phrenic | $C_3$–$C_5$ | Diaphragm (sole motor nerve supply) |

**Table 2**  **Branches of the Brachial Plexus (See Figure 7)**

| Nerves | Cord and ventral rami | Structures served |
|---|---|---|
| Axillary | Posterior cord ($C_5$, $C_6$) | Muscular branches: deltoid and teres minor muscles<br>Cutaneous branches: some skin of shoulder region |
| Musculocutaneous | Lateral cord ($C_5$–$C_7$) | Muscular branches: flexor muscles in anterior arm (biceps brachii, brachialis, coracobrachialis)<br>Cutaneous branches: skin on anterolateral forearm (extremely variable) |
| Median | By two branches, one from medial cord ($C_8$, $T_1$) and one from the lateral cord ($C_5$–$C_7$) | Muscular branches to flexor group of anterior forearm (palmaris longus, flexor carpi radialis, flexor digitorum superficialis, flexor pollicis longus, lateral half of flexor digitorum profundus, and pronator muscles); intrinsic muscles of lateral palm and digital branches to the fingers<br>Cutaneous branches: skin of lateral two-thirds of hand on ventral side and dorsum of fingers 2 and 3 |
| Ulnar | Medial cord ($C_8$, $T_1$) | Muscular branches: flexor muscles in anterior forearm (flexor carpi ulnaris and medial half of flexor digitorum profundus); most intrinsic muscles of hand<br>Cutaneous branches: skin of medial third of hand, both anterior and posterior aspects |
| Radial | Posterior cord ($C_5$–$C_8$, $T_1$) | Muscular branches: posterior muscles of arm and forearm (triceps brachii, anconeus, supinator, brachioradialis, extensors carpi radialis longus and brevis, extensor carpi ulnaris, and several muscles that extend the fingers)<br>Cutaneous branches: skin of posterolateral surface of entire limb (except dorsum of fingers 2 and 3) |
| Dorsal scapular | Branches of $C_5$ rami | Rhomboid muscles and levator scapulae |
| Long thoracic | Branches of $C_5$–$C_7$ rami | Serratus anterior muscle |
| Subscapular | Posterior cord; branches of $C_5$ and $C_6$ rami | Teres major and subscapularis muscles |
| Suprascapular | Upper trunk ($C_5$, $C_6$) | Shoulder joint; supraspinatus and infraspinatus muscles |
| Pectoral (lateral and medial) | Branches of lateral and medial cords ($C_5$–$T_1$) | Pectoralis major and minor muscles |

The radial nerve is often injured in the axillary region by the pressure of a crutch or by hanging one's arm over the back of a chair. The **median nerve** passes down the anteromedial surface of the arm to supply most of the flexor muscles in the forearm and several muscles in the hand (plus the skin of the lateral surface of the palm of the hand).

• Hyperextend your wrist to identify the long, obvious tendon of your palmaris longus muscle, which crosses the exact midline of the anterior wrist. Your median nerve lies immediately deep to that tendon, and the radial nerve lies just *lateral* to it.

The **musculocutaneous nerve** supplies the arm muscles that flex the forearm and the skin of the lateral surface of the forearm. The **ulnar nerve** travels down the posteromedial surface of the arm. It courses around the medial epicondyle of the humerus to supply the flexor carpi ulnaris, the ulnar head of the flexor digitorum profundus of the forearm, and all intrinsic muscles of the hand not served by the median nerve. It supplies the skin of the medial third of the hand, both the anterior and posterior surfaces. Trauma to the ulnar nerve, which often occurs when the elbow is hit, produces a smarting sensation commonly referred to as "hitting the funny bone."

Severe injuries to the brachial plexus cause weakness or paralysis of the entire upper limb. Such injuries may occur when the upper limb is pulled hard and the plexus is stretched (as when a football tackler yanks the arm of the halfback), and by blows to the shoulder that force the humerus inferiorly (as when a cyclist is pitched headfirst off his motorcycle and grinds his shoulder into the pavement). ✚

## Lumbosacral Plexus and the Lower Limb

The **lumbosacral plexus,** which serves the pelvic region of the trunk and the lower limbs, is actually a complex of two plexuses, the lumbar plexus and the sacral plexus (Figures 8 and 9). These plexuses interweave considerably and many fibers of the lumbar plexus contribute to the sacral plexus.

### The Lumbar Plexus

The **lumbar plexus** arises from ventral rami of $L_1$ through $L_4$ (and sometimes $T_{12}$). Its nerves serve the lower abdominopelvic region and the anterior thigh (Table 3 and Figure 8). The largest nerve of this plexus is the **femoral nerve,** which passes beneath the inguinal ligament to innervate the anterior thigh muscles. The cutaneous

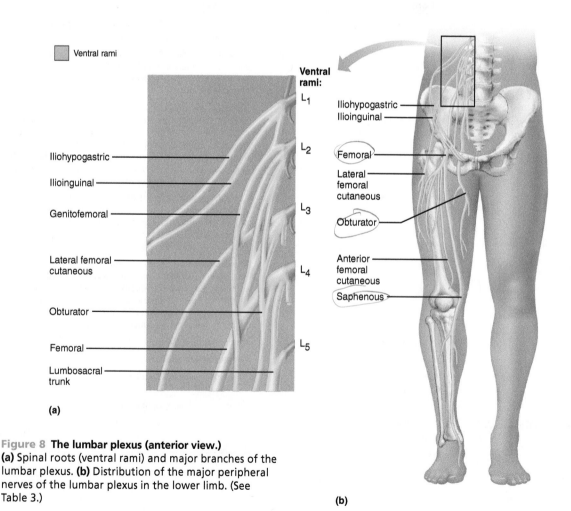

Ventral rami

**Ventral rami:**

$L_1$

$L_2$

$L_3$

$L_4$

$L_5$

Iliohypogastric

Ilioinguinal

Genitofemoral

Lateral femoral cutaneous

Obturator

Femoral

Lumbosacral trunk

**(a)**

Iliohypogastric

Ilioinguinal

Femoral

Lateral femoral cutaneous

Obturator

Anterior femoral cutaneous

Saphenous

**(b)**

**Figure 8 The lumbar plexus (anterior view.)**
**(a)** Spinal roots (ventral rami) and major branches of the lumbar plexus. **(b)** Distribution of the major peripheral nerves of the lumbar plexus in the lower limb. (See Table 3.)

| Table 3 | Branches of the Lumbar Plexus (See Figure 8) | |
|---|---|---|
| **Nerves** | **Ventral rami** | **Structures served** |
| Femoral | $L_2$–$L_4$ | Skin of anterior and medial thigh via *anterior femoral cutaneous* branch; skin of medial leg and foot, hip and knee joints via *saphenous* branch; motor to anterior muscles (quadriceps and sartorius) of thigh and to pectineus, iliacus |
| Obturator | $L_2$–$L_4$ | Motor to adductor magnus (part), longus, and brevis muscles, gracilis muscle of medial thigh, obturator externus; sensory for skin of medial thigh and for hip and knee joints |
| Lateral femoral cutaneous | $L_2$, $L_3$ | Skin of lateral thigh; some sensory branches to peritoneum |
| Iliohypogastric | $L_1$ | Skin of lower abdomen and hip; muscles of anterolateral abdominal wall (obliques and transversus abdominis) |
| Ilioinguinal | $L_1$ | Skin of external genitalia and proximal medial aspect of the thigh; inferior abdominal muscles |
| Genitofemoral | $L_1$, $L_2$ | Skin of scrotum in males, of labia majora in females, and of anterior thigh inferior to middle portion of inguinal region; cremaster muscle in males |

branches of the femoral nerve (median and anterior femoral cutaneous and the saphenous nerves) supply the skin of the anteromedial surface of the entire lower limb.

### The Sacral Plexus

Arising from $L_4$ through $S_4$, the nerves of the **sacral plexus** supply the buttock, the posterior surface of the thigh, and virtually all sensory and motor fibers of the leg and foot (**Table 4** and **Figure 9**). The major peripheral nerve of this plexus is the **sciatic nerve,** the largest nerve in the body. The sciatic nerve leaves the pelvis through the greater sciatic notch and travels down the posterior thigh, serving its flexor muscles and skin. In the popliteal region, the sciatic nerve divides into the **common fibular nerve** and the **tibial nerve,**

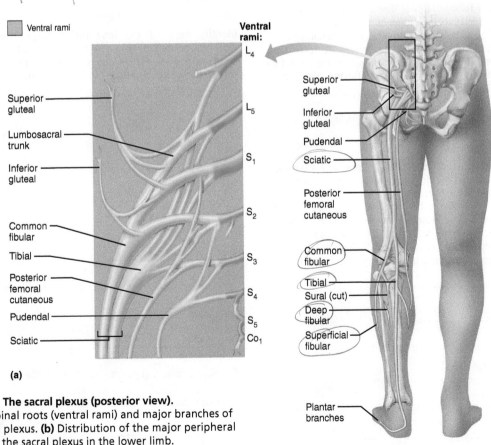

**(a)**

**Figure 9 The sacral plexus (posterior view).**
**(a)** The spinal roots (ventral rami) and major branches of the sacral plexus. **(b)** Distribution of the major peripheral nerves of the sacral plexus in the lower limb.
(See Table 4.)

**(b)**

| Table 4 | Branches of the Sacral Plexus (See Figure 9) | |
|---|---|---|
| **Nerves** | **Ventral rami** | **Structures served** |
| Sciatic nerve | L$_4$–S$_3$ | Composed of two nerves (tibial and common fibular) in a common sheath; they diverge just proximal to the knee |
| • Tibial (including sural, medial and lateral plantar, and medial calcaneal branches) | L$_4$–S$_3$ | Cutaneous branches: to skin of posterior surface of leg and sole of foot<br>Motor branches: to muscles of back of thigh, leg, and foot (hamstrings [except short head of biceps femoris], posterior part of adductor magnus, triceps surae, tibialis posterior, popliteus, flexor digitorum longus, flexor hallucis longus, and intrinsic muscles of foot) |
| • Common fibular (superficial and deep branches) | L$_4$–S$_2$ | Cutaneous branches: to skin of anterior and lateral surface of leg and dorsum of foot<br>Motor branches: to short head of biceps femoris of thigh, fibularis muscles of lateral leg, tibialis anterior, and extensor muscles of toes (extensor hallucis longus, extensors digitorum longus and brevis) |
| Superior gluteal | L$_4$–S$_1$ | Motor branches: to gluteus medius and minimus and tensor fasciae latae |
| Inferior gluteal | L$_5$–S$_2$ | Motor branches: to gluteus maximus |
| Posterior femoral cutaneous | S$_1$–S$_3$ | Skin of buttock, posterior thigh, and popliteal region; length variable; may also innervate part of skin of calf and heel |
| Pudendal | S$_2$–S$_4$ | Supplies most of skin and muscles of perineum (region encompassing external genitalia and anus and including clitoris, labia, and vaginal mucosa in females, and scrotum and penis in males); external anal sphincter |

which together supply the balance of the leg muscles and skin, both directly and via several branches.

Injury to the proximal part of the sciatic nerve, as might follow a fall or disc herniation, results in a number of lower limb impairments. **Sciatica** (si-at′ĭ-kah), characterized by stabbing pain radiating over the course of the sciatic nerve, is common. When the sciatic nerve is completely severed, the leg is nearly useless. The leg cannot be flexed and the foot drops into plantar flexion (dangles), a condition called **footdrop.** ✛

### ACTIVITY 3

## Identifying the Major Nerve Plexuses and Peripheral Nerves

Identify each of the four major nerve plexuses and their major nerves (Figures 6–9) on a large laboratory chart or model. Trace the courses of the nerves and relate those observations to the information provided (Tables 1–4). ▪

### GROUP CHALLENGE

## Fix the Sequence

Listed below are sets of a plexus, a nerve, and a muscle possibly innervated by the listed nerve. Working in small groups, decide if each set is correct for the sequence of a motor signal or needs to be corrected. If correct, simply write "all correct." If incorrect, suggest a corrected flow. Note that there may be more than one way to correct the sequence. Depend only on each other. Refrain from using a figure or other reference to help with your decision.

1. Cervical plexus, phrenic nerve, diaphragm _____

_____

2. Brachial plexus, ulnar nerve, palmaris longus _____

_____

3. Brachial plexus, radial nerve, triceps brachii _____

4. Cervical plexus, axillary nerve, deltoid _____

_____

5. Lumbar plexus, femoral nerve, gracilis _____

_____

6. Lumbar plexus, sciatic nerve, common fibular nerve, tibialis anterior _____

_____

7. Sacral plexus, superior gluteal nerve, gluteus maximus _____

_____

# The Spinal Cord and Spinal Nerves

## Anatomy of the Spinal Cord

**1.** Match each anatomical term in the key to the descriptions given below.

*Key:*   a.   cauda equina      b.   conus medullaris   c.   filum terminale   d.   foramen magnum

_____ 1.   most superior boundary of the spinal cord

_____ 2.   meningeal extension beyond the spinal cord terminus

_____ 3.   spinal cord terminus

_____ 4.   collection of spinal nerves traveling in the vertebral canal below the terminus of the spinal cord

**2.** Match the key letters on the diagram with the following terms.

_____ 1. arachnoid mater

_____ 2. central canal

_____ 3. dorsal horn

_____ 4. dorsal ramus of spinal nerve

_____ 5. dorsal root ganglion

_____ 6. dorsal root of spinal nerve

_____ 7. dura mater

_____ 8. gray commissure

_____ 9. lateral horn

_____ 10. pia mater

_____ 11. spinal nerve

_____ 12. ventral horn

_____ 13. ventral ramus of spinal nerve

_____ 14. ventral root of spinal nerve

_____ 15. white matter

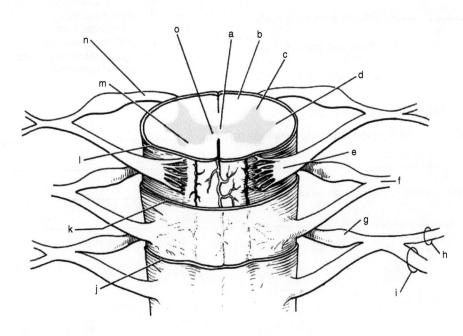

3. Choose the proper answer from the following key to respond to the descriptions relating to spinal cord anatomy. (Some terms are used more than once.)

*Key:*   a.   sensory    b.   motor    c.   both sensory and motor      d.   interneurons

_____ 1.   neuron type found in dorsal horn       _____ 4.   fiber type in ventral root

_____ 2.   neuron type found in ventral horn       _____ 5.   fiber type in dorsal root

_____ 3.   neuron type in dorsal root ganglion       _____ 6.   fiber type in spinal nerve

4. Where in the vertebral column is a lumbar puncture generally done? _____

   Why is this the site of choice? _____

   _____

5. The spinal cord is enlarged in two regions, the _____ and the _____ regions.

   What is the significance of these enlargements? _____

   _____

6. How does the position of the gray and white matter differ in the spinal cord and the cerebral hemispheres?

   _____

   _____

7. From the key, choose the name of the tract that might be damaged when the following conditions are observed. (More than one choice may apply; some terms are used more than once.)

   _____ 1.   uncoordinated movement       *Key:*  a.  dorsal columns (fasciculus cuneatus and fasciculus gracilis)

   _____ 2.   lack of voluntary movement              b.  lateral corticospinal tract

   _____ 3.   tremors, jerky movements               c.  ventral corticospinal tract

   _____ 4.   diminished pain perception               d.  tectospinal tract

   _____ 5.   diminished sense of touch               e.  rubrospinal tract

                                                                   f.  vestibulospinal tract

                                                                    g.  lateral spinothalamic tract

                                                                    h.  ventral spinothalamic tract

# Dissection of the Spinal Cord

8. Compare and contrast the meninges of the spinal cord and the brain. _____

   _____

9. How can you distinguish between the dorsal and ventral horns? _____

   _____

## Spinal Nerves and Nerve Plexuses

**10.** In the human, there are 31 pairs of spinal nerves, named according to the region of the vertebral column from which they issue. The spinal nerves are named below. Indicate how they are numbered.

cervical nerves _____          sacral nerves _____

lumbar nerves _____          thoracic nerves _____

**11.** The ventral rami of spinal nerves $C_1$ through $T_1$ and $T_{12}$ through $S_4$ take part in forming _____ ,

which serve the _____ of the body. The ventral rami of $T_2$ through $T_{12}$ run

between the ribs to serve the _____. The dorsal rami of the spinal nerves

serve _____.

**12.** What would happen if the following structures were damaged or transected? (Use the key choices for responses.)

*Key:*  a.  loss of motor function          b.  loss of sensory function          c.  loss of both motor and sensory function

_____ 1. dorsal root of a spinal nerve          _____ 3. ventral ramus of a spinal nerve

_____ 2. ventral root of a spinal nerve

**13.** Define *plexus.* _____

_____

**14.** Name the major nerves that serve the following body areas.

_____ 1.  head, neck, shoulders (name plexus only)

_____ 2.  diaphragm

_____ 3.  posterior thigh

_____ 4.  leg and foot (name two)

_____ 5.  anterior forearm muscles (name two)

_____ 6.  arm muscles (name two)

_____ 7.  abdominal wall (name plexus only)

_____ 8.  anterior thigh

_____ 9.  medial side of the hand

## Photo Credits

**Credits are listed in order of appearance.**

1b–d: From *A Stereoscopic Atlas of Human Anatomy* by David L. Bassett, M.D. 4: Victor P. Eroschenko, Pearson Education. 7b: Karen Krabbenhoft, PAL 3.0, Pearson Education.

## Illustration Credits

**All illustrations are by Imagineering STA Media Services, except for Review Sheet art and as noted below.**

2b: Electronic Publishing Services, Inc.

# Human Reflex Physiology

- ☐ Reflex hammer
- ☐ Sharp pencils
- ☐ Cot (if available)
- ☐ Absorbent cotton (sterile)
- ☐ Tongue depressor
- ☐ Metric ruler
- ☐ Flashlight
- ☐ 100- or 250-ml beaker
- ☐ 10- or 25-ml graduated cylinder
- ☐ Lemon juice in dropper bottle
- ☐ Wide-range pH paper
- ☐ Large laboratory bucket containing freshly prepared 10% household bleach solution for saliva-soiled glassware
- ☐ Disposable autoclave bag
- ☐ Wash bottle containing 10% bleach solution
- ☐ Reaction time ruler (if available)

**BIOPAC®** BIOPAC® BSL System for Windows with BSL software version 3.7.5 to 3.7.7, or BSL System for Mac OS X with BSL software version 3.7.4 to 3.7.7, MP36/35 data acquisition unit, PC or Mac computer, hand switch, and headphones.

Instructors using the MP36 (or MP35/30) data acquisition unit with BSL software versions earlier than 3.7.5 (for Windows) and 3.7.4 (for Mac OS X) will need slightly different channel settings and collection strategies. Instructions for using the older data acquisition unit can be found on MasteringA&P.

**Note:** Instructions for using PowerLab® equipment can be found on MasteringA&P.

MasteringA&P® For related exercise study tools, go to the Study Area of MasteringA&P. There you will find:
- Practice Anatomy Lab PAL
- PhysioEx PEx
- A&PFlix A&PFlix
- Practice quizzes, Histology Atlas, eText, Videos, and more!

## O B J E C T I V E S

1. Define *reflex* and *reflex arc*.
2. Describe the differences between autonomic and somatic reflexes.
3. Explain why reflex testing is an important part of every physical examination.
4. Name, identify, and describe the function of each element of a reflex arc.
5. Describe and discuss several types of reflex activities as observed in the laboratory; indicate the functional or clinical importance of each; and categorize each as a somatic or autonomic reflex action.
6. Explain why cord-mediated reflexes are generally much faster than those involving input from the higher brain centers.
7. Investigate differences in reaction time between intrinsic and learned reflexes.

## P R E - L A B   Q U I Z

1. Define *reflex.* _____
   _____
2. Circle the correct underlined term. <u>Autonomic</u> / <u>Somatic</u> reflexes include all those reflexes that involve stimulation of skeletal muscles.
3. In a reflex arc, the _____ transmits afferent impulses to the central nervous system.
   a. integration center
   b. motor neuron
   c. receptor
   d. sensory neuron
4. Circle True or False. Most reflexes are simple, two-neuron, monosynaptic reflex arcs.
5. Stretch reflexes are initiated by tapping a _____, which stretches the associated muscle.
   a. bone
   b. muscle
   c. tendon or ligament
6. An example of an autonomic reflex that you will be studying in today's lab is the _____ reflex.
   a. crossed-extensor     c. plantar
   b. gag                  d. salivary
7. Circle True or False. A reflex that occurs on the same side of the body that was stimulated is an ipsilateral response.
8. Name one of the pupillary reflexes you will be examining today. _____
9. Circle the correct underlined term. The effectors of the salivary reflex are <u>muscles</u> / <u>glands.</u>
10. Circle True or False. Learned reflexes involve far fewer neural pathways and fewer types of higher intellectual activities than intrinsic reflexes, which shortens their response time.

Reflexes are rapid, predictable, involuntary motor responses to stimuli; they are mediated over neural pathways called reflex arcs. Many of the body's control systems are reflexes, which can be either inborn or learned. *Inborn* or *intrinsic reflexes* are wired into our nervous system and are unlearned. *Learned* or *acquired reflexes* result from practice or repetition.

Another way to categorize reflexes is into one of two large groups: autonomic reflexes and somatic reflexes. **Autonomic** (or visceral) **reflexes** are mediated through the autonomic nervous system, and we are not usually aware of them. These reflexes activate smooth muscles, cardiac muscle, and the glands of the body, and they regulate body functions such as digestion, elimination, blood pressure, salivation, and sweating. **Somatic reflexes** include all those reflexes that involve stimulation of skeletal muscles by the somatic division of the nervous system. An example of such a reflex is the rapid withdrawal of a hand from a hot object.

Reflex testing is an important diagnostic tool for assessing the condition of the nervous system. Distorted, exaggerated, or absent reflex responses may indicate degeneration or pathology of portions of the nervous system, often before other signs are apparent.

If the spinal cord is damaged, the easily performed reflex tests can help pinpoint the area (level) of spinal cord injury. Motor nerves above the injured area may be unaffected, whereas those at or below the lesion site may be unable to participate in normal reflex activity. ✛

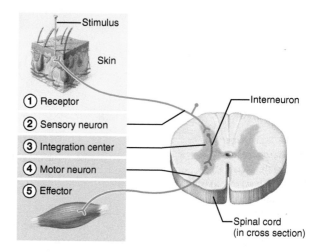

**Figure 1 The five basic components of reflex arcs.** The reflex illustrated is polysynaptic.

## Components of a Reflex Arc

Reflex arcs have five basic components (**Figure 1**):

1. The *receptor* is the site of stimulus action.
2. The *sensory neuron* transmits afferent impulses to the CNS.

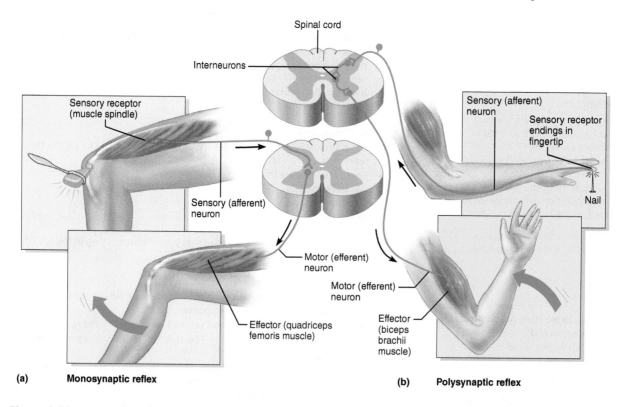

**(a)** **Monosynaptic reflex**

**(b)** **Polysynaptic reflex**

**Figure 2 Monosynaptic and polysynaptic reflex arcs.** The integration center is in the spinal cord, and in each example the receptor and effector are in the same limb. **(a)** The patellar reflex, a two-neuron monosynaptic reflex. **(b)** A flexor reflex, an example of a polysynaptic reflex.

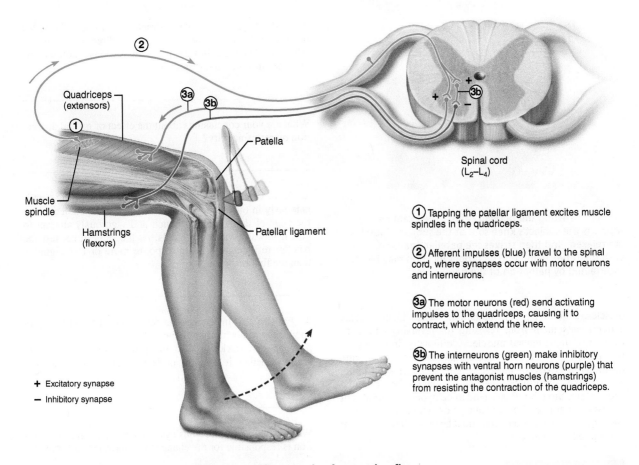

Figure 3 **The patellar (knee-jerk) reflex—a specific example of a stretch reflex.**

Within the figure:

② 

Quadriceps (extensors)

3a 3b

① 

Muscle spindle

Hamstrings (flexors)

Patella

Patellar ligament

Spinal cord (L₂–L₄)

① Tapping the patellar ligament excites muscle spindles in the quadriceps.

② Afferent impulses (blue) travel to the spinal cord, where synapses occur with motor neurons and interneurons.

3a The motor neurons (red) send activating impulses to the quadriceps, causing it to contract, which extend the knee.

3b The interneurons (green) make inhibitory synapses with ventral horn neurons (purple) that prevent the antagonist muscles (hamstrings) from resisting the contraction of the quadriceps.

+ Excitatory synapse
− Inhibitory synapse

---

3. The *integration center* consists of one or more neurons in the CNS.

4. The *motor neuron* conducts efferent impulses from the integration center to an effector organ.

5. The *effector,* a muscle fiber or a gland cell, responds to efferent impulses by contracting or secreting, respectively.

The simple patellar or knee-jerk reflex **(Figure 2a)** is an example of a simple, two-neuron, *monosynaptic* (literally, "one synapse") reflex arc. It will be demonstrated in the laboratory. However, most reflexes are more complex and *polysynaptic,* involving the participation of one or more interneurons in the reflex arc pathway. An example of a polysynaptic reflex is the flexor reflex (Figure 2b). Since delay or inhibition of the reflex may occur at the synapses, the more synapses encountered in a reflex pathway, the more time is required for the response.

Reflexes of many types may be considered programmed into the neural anatomy. Many *spinal reflexes,* reflexes that are initiated and completed at the spinal cord level, occur without the involvement of higher brain centers. Generally these reflexes are present in animals whose brains have been destroyed, as long as the spinal cord is functional. Conversely, other reflexes require the involvement of the brain, since many different inputs must be evaluated before the appropriate reflex is determined. Superficial cord reflexes and

pupillary responses to light are in this category. In addition, although many spinal reflexes do not require the involvement of higher centers, the brain is "advised" of spinal cord reflex activity and may alter it by facilitating or inhibiting the reflexes.

## Somatic Reflexes

There are several types of somatic reflexes, including several that you will be eliciting during this laboratory session—the stretch, crossed-extensor, superficial cord, corneal, and gag reflexes. Some require only spinal cord activity; others require brain involvement as well.

### Spinal Reflexes

#### Stretch Reflexes

**Stretch reflexes** are important postural reflexes, normally acting to maintain posture, balance, and locomotion. Stretch reflexes are initiated by tapping a tendon or ligament, which stretches the muscle to which the tendon is attached **(Figure 3)**. This stimulates the muscle spindles and causes reflex contraction of the stretched muscle or muscles. Branches of the afferent fibers from the muscle spindles also synapse with interneurons controlling the antagonist muscles. The inhibition of those interneurons and the antagonist

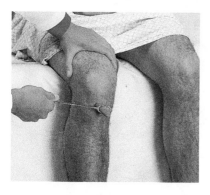

**Figure 4 Testing the patellar reflex.** The examiner supports the subject's knee so that the subject's muscles are relaxed, and then strikes the patellar ligament with the reflex hammer. The proper location may be ascertained by palpation of the patella.

muscles, called *reciprocal inhibition,* causes them to relax and prevents them from resisting (or reversing) the contraction of the stretched muscle. Additionally, impulses are relayed to higher brain centers (largely via the dorsal white columns) to advise of muscle length, speed of shortening, and the like—information needed to maintain muscle tone and posture. Stretch reflexes tend to be hypoactive or absent in cases of peripheral nerve damage or ventral horn disease and hyperactive in corticospinal tract lesions. They are absent in deep sedation and coma.

### ACTIVITY 1

## Initiating Stretch Reflexes

1.  Test the **patellar** or **knee-jerk reflex** by seating a subject on the laboratory bench with legs hanging free (or with knees crossed). Tap the patellar ligament sharply with the reflex hammer just below the knee between the patella and the tibial tuberosity (as shown in **Figure 4**). The knee-jerk response assesses the $L_2$–$L_4$ level of the spinal cord. Test both knees and record your observations. (Sometimes a reflex can be altered by your actions. If you encounter difficulty, consult your instructor for helpful hints.)

_____

_____

Which muscles contracted? _____

_____

What nerve is carrying the afferent and efferent impulses?

_____

2.  Test the effect of mental distraction on the patellar reflex by having the subject add a column of three-digit numbers while you test the reflex again. Is the response more *or* less vigorous than the first response?

_____

What are your conclusions about the effect of mental distraction on reflex activity?

_____

3.  Now test the effect of muscular activity occurring simultaneously in other areas of the body. Have the subject clasp the edge of the laboratory bench and vigorously attempt to pull it upward with both hands. At the same time, test the patellar reflex again. Is the response more or less vigorous than the first response?

_____

4.  Fatigue also influences the reflex response. The subject should jog in position until she or he is very fatigued (*really fatigued*—no slackers). Test the patellar reflex again, and record whether it is more or less vigorous than the first response.

_____

Would you say that nervous system activity *or* muscle function is responsible for the changes you have just observed?

Explain your reasoning. _____

_____

_____

_____

5.  The **calcaneal tendon** or **ankle-jerk reflex** assesses the first two sacral segments of the spinal cord. With your shoe removed and your foot dorsiflexed slightly to increase the tension of the gastrocnemius muscle, have your partner sharply tap your calcaneal tendon with the broad side of the reflex hammer **(Figure 5)**.

What is the result? _____

_____

During walking, what is the action of the gastrocnemius at the ankle?

_____ ■

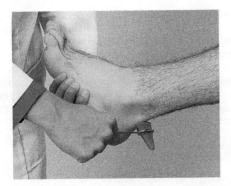

**Figure 5** **Testing the calcaneal tendon reflex.** The examiner slightly dorsiflexes the subject's ankle by supporting the foot lightly in the hand, and then taps the calcaneal tendon just above the ankle.

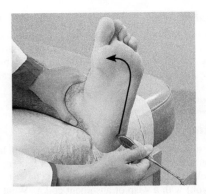

**Figure 6** **Testing the plantar reflex.** Using a moderately sharp object, the examiner strokes the lateral border of the subject's sole, starting at the heel and continuing toward the great toe across the ball of the foot.

### Crossed-Extensor Reflex

The **crossed-extensor reflex** is more complex than the stretch reflex. It consists of a flexor, or withdrawal, reflex followed by extension of the opposite limb.

This reflex is quite obvious when, for example, a stranger suddenly and strongly grips one's arm. The immediate response is to withdraw the clutched arm and push the intruder away with the other arm. The reflex is more difficult to demonstrate in a laboratory because it is anticipated, and under these conditions the extensor part of the reflex may be inhibited.

### ACTIVITY 2

### Initiating the Crossed-Extensor Reflex

The subject should sit with eyes closed and with the dorsum of one hand resting on the laboratory bench. Obtain a sharp pencil, and suddenly prick the subject's index finger. What are the results?

_____

_____

_____

Did the extensor part of this reflex occur simultaneously or more slowly than the other reflexes you have observed?

_____

What are the reasons for this? _____

_____

_____

The reflexes that have been demonstrated so far—the stretch and crossed-extensor reflexes—are examples of reflexes in which the reflex pathway is initiated and completed at the spinal cord level.

### Superficial Cord Reflexes

The **superficial cord reflexes** (abdominal, cremaster, and plantar reflexes) result from pain and temperature changes. They are initiated by stimulation of receptors in the skin and mucosae. The superficial cord reflexes depend *both* on functional upper-motor pathways and on the cord-level reflex arc. Since only the plantar reflex can be tested conveniently in a laboratory setting, we will use this as our example.

The **plantar reflex,** an important neurological test, is elicited by stimulating the cutaneous receptors in the sole of the foot. In adults, stimulation of these receptors causes the toes to flex and move closer together. Damage to the corticospinal tract, however, produces *Babinski's sign,* an abnormal response in which the toes flare and the great toe moves in an upward direction. In newborn infants, it is normal to see Babinski's sign due to incomplete myelination of the nervous system.

### ACTIVITY 3

### Initiating the Plantar Reflex

Have the subject remove a shoe and lie on the cot or laboratory bench with knees slightly bent and thighs rotated so that the posterolateral side of the foot rests on the cot. Alternatively, the subject may sit up and rest the lateral surface of the foot on a chair. Draw the handle of the reflex hammer firmly along the lateral side of the exposed sole from the heel to the base of the great toe (Figure 6).

What is the response? _____

_____

Is this a normal plantar reflex or a Babinski's sign?

_____

## Cranial Nerve Reflex Tests

In these experiments, you will be working with your lab partner to illustrate two somatic reflexes mediated by cranial nerves.

### Corneal Reflex

The **corneal reflex** is mediated through the trigeminal nerve (cranial nerve V). The absence of this reflex is an ominous sign because it often indicates damage to the brain stem resulting from compression of the brain or other trauma.

**ACTIVITY 4**

## Initiating the Corneal Reflex

Stand to one side of the subject; the subject should look away from you toward the opposite wall. Wait a few seconds and then quickly, *but gently,* touch the subject's cornea (on the side toward you) with a wisp of absorbent cotton. What reflexive reaction occurs when something touches the cornea?

_____

What is the function of this reflex?

_____

_____

_____

### Gag Reflex

The **gag reflex** tests the somatic motor responses of cranial nerves IX and X. When the oral mucosa on the side of the uvula is stroked, each side of the mucosa should rise, and the amount of elevation should be equal. The uvula is the fleshy tab hanging from the roof of the mouth just above the root of the tongue.

**ACTIVITY 5**

## Initiating the Gag Reflex

For this experiment, select a subject who does not have a queasy stomach, because regurgitation is a possibility. Gently stroke the oral mucosa on each side of the subject's uvula with a tongue depressor. What happens?

_____

_____

! Discard the used tongue depressor in the disposable autoclave bag before continuing. *Do not* lay it on the laboratory bench at any time.

# Autonomic Reflexes

The autonomic reflexes include the pupillary, ciliospinal, and salivary reflexes, as well as a multitude of other reflexes. Work with your partner to demonstrate the four autonomic reflexes described next.

## Pupillary Reflexes

There are several types of pupillary reflexes. The **pupillary light reflex** and the **consensual reflex** will be examined

here. In both of these pupillary reflexes, the retina of the eye is the receptor, the optic nerve (cranial nerve II) contains the afferent fibers, the oculomotor nerve (cranial nerve III) is responsible for conducting efferent impulses to the eye, and the smooth muscle of the iris is the effector. Many central nervous system centers are involved in the integration of these responses. Absence of normal pupillary reflexes is generally a late indication of severe trauma or deterioration of the vital brain stem tissue due to metabolic imbalance.

**ACTIVITY 6**

## Initiating Pupillary Reflexes

1. Conduct the reflex testing in an area where the lighting is relatively dim. Before beginning, obtain a metric ruler and a flashlight. Measure and record the size of the subject's pupils as best you can.

Right pupil: _____ mm    Left pupil: _____ mm

2. Stand to the left of the subject to conduct the testing. The subject should shield his or her right eye by holding a hand vertically between the eye and the right side of the nose.

3. Shine a flashlight into the subject's left eye. What is the pupillary response?

_____

Measure the size of the left pupil: _____ mm

4. Without moving the flashlight, observe the right pupil. Has the same type of change (called a *consensual response*) occurred in the right eye?

_____

Measure the size of the right pupil: _____ mm

The consensual response, or any reflex observed on one side of the body when the other side has been stimulated, is called a **contralateral response.** The pupillary light response, or any reflex occurring on the same side stimulated, is referred to as an **ipsilateral response.**

What does the occurrence of a contralateral response indicate about the pathways involved?

_____

_____

Was the sympathetic *or* the parasympathetic division of the autonomic nervous system active during the testing of these reflexes?

_____

What is the function of these pupillary responses?

_____

_____

_____ ▄

## Ciliospinal Reflex

The **ciliospinal reflex** is another example of reflex activity in which pupillary responses can be observed. This response may initially seem a little bizarre, especially in view of the consensual reflex just demonstrated.

### ACTIVITY 7

#### Initiating the Ciliospinal Reflex

1. While observing the subject's eyes, gently stroke the skin (or just the hairs) on the left side of the back of the subject's neck, close to the hairline.

What is the reaction of the left pupil? _____

The reaction of the right pupil? _____

2. If you see no reaction, repeat the test using a gentle pinch in the same area.

The response you should have noted—pupillary dilation—is consistent with the pupillary changes occurring when the sympathetic nervous system is stimulated. Such a response may also be elicited in a single pupil when more impulses from the sympathetic nervous system reach it for any reason. For example, when the left side of the subject's neck was stimulated, sympathetic impulses to the left iris increased, resulting in the ipsilateral reaction of the left pupil.

On the basis of your observations, would you say that the sympathetic innervation of the two irises is closely integrated?

_____ Why or why not? _____

_____

_____ ▄

## Salivary Reflex

Unlike the other reflexes, in which the effectors were smooth or skeletal muscles, the effectors of the **salivary reflex** are glands. The salivary glands secrete varying amounts of saliva in response to reflex activation.

### ACTIVITY 8

#### Initiating the Salivary Reflex

1. Obtain a small beaker, a graduated cylinder, lemon juice, and wide-range pH paper. After refraining from swallowing for 2 minutes, the subject is to expectorate (spit) the accumulated saliva into a small beaker. Using the graduated cylinder, measure the volume of the expectorated saliva and determine its pH.

Volume: _____ cc    pH: _____

2. Now place 2 or 3 drops of lemon juice on the subject's tongue. Allow the lemon juice to mix with the saliva for 5 to 10 seconds, and then determine the pH of the subject's saliva by touching a piece of pH paper to the tip of the tongue.

pH: _____

As before, the subject is to refrain from swallowing for 2 minutes. After the 2 minutes is up, again collect and measure the volume of the saliva and determine its pH.

Volume: _____ cc    pH: _____

3. How does the volume of saliva collected after the application of the lemon juice compare with the volume of the first saliva sample?

_____

How does the final saliva pH reading compare to the initial reading?

_____

How does the final saliva pH reading compare to that obtained 10 seconds after the application of lemon juice?

_____

What division of the autonomic nervous system mediates the reflex release of saliva?

_____

⚠ Dispose of the saliva-containing beakers and the graduated cylinders in the laboratory bucket that contains bleach and put the used pH paper into the disposable autoclave bag. Wash the bench down with 10% bleach solution before continuing. ▄

## Reaction Time of Intrinsic and Learned Reflexes

The time required for reaction to a stimulus depends on many factors—sensitivity of the receptors, velocity of nerve conduction, the number of neurons and synapses involved, and the speed of effector activation, to name just a few. There is no clear-cut distinction between intrinsic and learned reflexes, as most reflex actions are subject to modification by learning or conscious effort. In general, however, if the response involves a simple reflex arc, the response time is short. Learned reflexes involve a far larger number of neural pathways and many types of higher intellectual activities, including choice and decision making, which lengthens the response time.

There are various ways of testing reaction time of reflexes. The tests range from simple to ultrasophisticated. The following activities provide an opportunity to demonstrate the major time difference between simple and learned reflexes and to measure response time under various conditions.

### ACTIVITY 9

## Testing Reaction Time for Intrinsic and Learned Reflexes

1. Using a reflex hammer, elicit the patellar reflex in your partner. Note the relative reaction time needed for this intrinsic reflex to occur.

2. Now test the reaction time for learned reflexes. The subject should hold a hand out, with the thumb and index finger extended. Hold a metric ruler so that its end is exactly 3 cm above the subject's outstretched hand. The ruler should be in the vertical position with the numbers reading from the bottom up. When the ruler is dropped, the subject should be able to grasp it between thumb and index finger as it passes, without having to change position. Have the subject catch the ruler five times, varying the time between trials. The relative speed of reaction can be determined by reading the number on the ruler at the point of the subject's fingertips.* (Thus if the number at the fingertips is 15 cm, the subject was unable to catch the ruler until 18 cm of length had passed through his or her fingers; 15 cm of ruler length plus 3 cm to account for the distance of the ruler above the hand.)† Record the number of centimeters that pass through the subject's fingertips (or the number of seconds required for reaction) for each trial:

Trial 1: _____ cm      Trial 4: _____ cm
_____ sec              _____ sec
Trial 2: _____ cm      Trial 5: _____ cm
_____ sec              _____ sec
Trial 3: _____ cm
_____ sec

3. Perform the test again, but this time say a simple word each time you release the ruler. Designate a specific word as a signal for the subject to catch the ruler. On all other words, the subject is to allow the ruler to pass through his fingers. Trials in which the subject erroneously catches the ruler are to be disregarded. Record the distance the ruler travels (or the number of seconds required for reaction) in five *successful* trials:

Trial 1: _____ cm      Trial 2: _____ cm
_____ sec              _____ sec

*Distance (d) can be converted to time (t) using the simple formula:

$$d \text{ (in cm)} = (1/2)(980 \text{ cm/sec}^2)t^2$$
$$t^2 = (d/490 \text{ cm/sec}^2)$$
$$t = \sqrt{(d/490 \text{ cm/sec}^2)}$$

†An alternative would be to use a reaction time ruler, which converts distance to time (seconds).

Trial 3: _____ cm      Trial 5: _____ cm
_____ sec              _____ sec
Trial 4: _____ cm
_____ sec

Did the addition of a specific word to the stimulus increase or decrease the reaction time?

_____

4. Perform the testing once again to investigate the subject's reaction to word association. As you drop the ruler, say a word—for example, *hot.* The subject is to respond with a word he or she associates with the stimulus word—for example, *cold*—catching the ruler while responding. If unable to make a word association, the subject must allow the ruler to pass through his or her fingers. Record the distance the ruler travels (or the number of seconds required for reaction) in five successful trials, as well as the number of times the ruler is not caught by the subject.

Trial 1: _____ cm      Trial 4: _____ cm
_____ sec              _____ sec
Trial 2: _____ cm      Trial 5: _____ cm
_____ sec              _____ sec
Trial 3: _____ cm
_____ sec

Number of times the subject did not catch the ruler:

_____

You should have noticed quite a large variation in reaction time in this series of trials. Why is this so?

_____

_____

_____

_____ ▪

### ACTIVITY 10

## Measuring Reaction Time Using BIOPAC®
### Setting Up the Equipment

1. Connect the BIOPAC® unit to the computer and turn the computer **ON.**

2. Make sure the BIOPAC® unit is **OFF.**

3. Plug in the equipment (as shown in **Figure 7**).

- Hand switch—CH1

- Headphones—back of MP36/35 unit

4. Turn the BIOPAC® unit **ON.**

5. Start the BIOPAC® Student Lab program on the computer by double-clicking the icon on the desktop or by following your instructor's guidance.

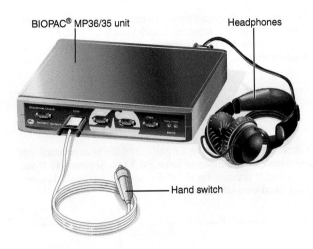

Figure 7 **Setting up the BIOPAC® equipment.** Plug the headphones into the back of the MP36/35 data acquisition unit and the hand switch into Channel 1. Hand switch and headphones are shown connected to the MP36/35 unit.

6. Select lesson **L11-React-1** from the menu and click **OK.**

7. Type in a filename that will save this subject's data on the computer hard drive. You may want to use the subject's last name followed by React-1 (for example, SmithReact-1), then click **OK.**

### Calibrating the Equipment

1. Seat the subject comfortably so that he or she cannot see the computer screen and keyboard.

2. Put the headphones on the subject and give the subject the hand switch to hold.

3. Tell the subject that he or she is to push the hand switch button when a "click" is heard.

4. Click **Calibrate,** and then click **OK** when the subject is ready.

5. Observe the recording of the calibration data, which should look like the waveforms in the calibration example (Figure 8).

- If the data look very different, click **Redo Calibration** and repeat the steps above.
- If the data look similar, proceed to the next section.

### Recording the Data

In this experiment, you will record four different segments of data. In Segments 1 and 2, the subject will respond to random click stimuli. In Segments 3 and 4, the subject will respond to click stimuli at fixed intervals (about 4 seconds). The director will click **Record** to initiate the Segment 1 recording, and **Resume** to initiate Segments 2, 3, and 4. The subject should focus only on responding to the sound.

### Segment 1: Random Trial 1

1. Each time a sound is heard, the subject should respond by pressing the button on the hand switch as quickly as possible.

2. When the subject is ready, the director should click **Record** to begin the stimulus-response sequence. The recording will stop automatically after ten clicks.

- A triangular marker will be inserted above the data each time a "click" stimulus occurs.
- An upward-pointing "pulse" will be inserted each time the subject responds to the stimulus.

3. Observe the recording of the data, which should look similar to the data-recording example (Figure 9).

- If the data look very different, click **Redo** and repeat the steps above.
- If the data look similar, move on to recording the next segment.

### Segment 2: Random Trial 2

1. Each time a sound is heard, the subject should respond by pressing the button on the hand switch as quickly as possible.

2. When the subject is ready, the director should click **Resume** to begin the stimulus-response sequence. The recording will stop automatically after ten clicks.

3. Observe the recording of the data, which should again look similar to the data-recording example (Figure 9).

- If the data look very different, click **Redo** and repeat the steps above.
- If the data look similar, move on to recording the next segment.

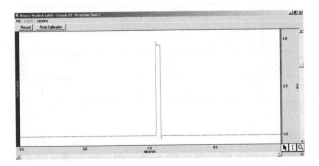

Figure 8 **Example of waveforms during the calibration procedure.**

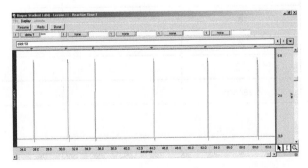

Figure 9 **Example of waveforms during the recording of data.**

### Segment 3: Fixed Interval Trial 3

1. Repeat the steps for Segment 2 above.

### Segment 4: Fixed Interval Trial 4

1. Repeat the steps for Segment 2 above.

2. If the data after this final segment are fine, click **Done.** A pop-up window will appear; to record from another subject select **Record from another subject,** and return to step 7 under Setting Up the Equipment. If continuing to the Data Analysis section, select **Analyze current data file** and proceed to step 2 in the Data Analysis section.

### Data Analysis

1. If just starting the BIOPAC® program to perform data analysis, enter **Review Saved Data** mode and choose the file with the subject's reaction data (for example, SmithReact-1).

2. Observe that all ten reaction times are automatically calculated for each segment and are placed in the journal at the bottom of the computer screen.

3. Write the ten reaction times for each segment in the chart **Reaction Times.**

4. Delete the highest and lowest values of each segment, then calculate and record the average for the remaining eight data points.

5. When finished, exit the program by going to the **File** menu at the top of the page and clicking **Quit.**

Do you observe a significant difference between the average response times of Segment 1 and Segment 2? If so, what might account for the difference, even though they are both random trials?

_____

_____

Likewise, do you observe a significant difference between the average response times of Segment 3 and Segment 4? If so, what might account for the difference, even though they are both fixed interval trials?

_____

_____

### Optional Activity with BIOPAC® Reaction Time Measurement

To expand the experiment, choose another variable to test. Response to visual cues may be tested, or you may have the subject change the hand used when clicking the hand switch button. Design the experiment, conduct the test, then record and analyze the data as described above. ▪

| Reaction Times (seconds) | | | | |
|---|---|---|---|---|
| | Random | | Fixed Interval | |
| Stimulus # | Segment 1 | Segment 2 | Segment 3 | Segment 4 |
| 1 | | | | |
| 2 | | | | |
| 3 | | | | |
| 4 | | | | |
| 5 | | | | |
| 6 | | | | |
| 7 | | | | |
| 8 | | | | |
| 9 | | | | |
| 10 | | | | |
| Average | | | | |

# Human Reflex Physiology

## The Reflex Arc

1. Define *reflex.* _____

   _____

2. Name five essential components of a reflex arc: _____, _____,

   _____, _____, and _____

3. In general, what is the importance of reflex testing in a routine physical examination? _____

   _____

   _____

## Somatic and Autonomic Reflexes

4. Use the key terms to complete the statements given below. (Some terms are used more than once.)

   *Key:*   a. abdominal reflex        d. corneal reflex            g. patellar reflex
            b. calcaneal tendon reflex  e. crossed-extensor reflex   h. plantar reflex
            c. ciliospinal reflex       f. gag reflex                i. pupillary light reflex

   Reflexes classified as somatic reflexes include a _____, _____, _____, _____, _____, _____, and _____.

   Of these, the stretch reflexes are _____ and _____, and the superficial cord reflexes are _____ and _____.

   Reflexes classified as autonomic reflexes include _____ and _____.

5. Name two spinal cord–mediated reflexes. _____ and _____

   _____

   Name two somatic reflexes in which the higher brain centers participate. _____

   and _____

6. Can the stretch reflex be elicited in a pithed animal (that is, an animal in which the brain has been destroyed)? _____

   Explain your answer. _____

   _____

7. Trace the reflex arc, naming efferent and afferent nerves, receptors, effectors, and integration centers, for the two reflexes listed. (Hint: Remember which nerve innervates the anterior thigh, and which nerve innervates the posterior thigh.)

patellar reflex: _____

_____

_____

calcaneal tendon reflex: _____

_____

_____

8. Three factors that influence the speed and effectiveness of reflex arcs were investigated in conjunction with patellar reflex testing—mental distraction, effect of simultaneous muscle activity in another body area, and fatigue.

Which of these factors increases the excitatory level of the spinal cord? _____

Which factor decreases the excitatory level of the muscles? _____

When the subject was concentrating on an arithmetic problem, did the change noted in the patellar reflex indicate that brain

activity is necessary for the patellar reflex or only that it may modify it? _____

_____

9. Name the division of the autonomic nervous system responsible for each of the reflexes listed.

ciliospinal reflex: _____ salivary reflex: _____

pupillary light reflex: _____

10. The pupillary light reflex, the crossed-extensor reflex, and the corneal reflex illustrate the purposeful nature of reflex activity. Describe the protective aspect of each.

pupillary light reflex: _____

corneal reflex: _____

crossed-extensor reflex: _____

_____

_____

_____

11. Was the pupillary consensual response contralateral or ipsilateral? _____

Why would such a response be of significant value in this particular reflex? _____

_____

**12.** Differentiate between the types of activities accomplished by somatic and autonomic reflexes. _____

_____

_____

_____

**13.** Several types of reflex activity were not investigated in this exercise. The most important of these are autonomic reflexes, which are difficult to illustrate in a laboratory situation. To rectify this omission, complete the following chart, using references as necessary.

| Reflex | Organ involved | Receptors stimulated | Action |
|---|---|---|---|
| Micturition (urination) | | | |
| Defecation | | | |
| Carotid sinus | | | |

## Reaction Time of Intrinsic and Learned Reflexes

**14.** How do intrinsic and learned reflexes differ? _____

_____

**15.** Name at least three factors that may modify reaction time to a stimulus. _____

_____

**16.** In general, how did the response time for the learned activity performed in the laboratory compare to that for the simple

patellar reflex? _____

**17.** Did the response time without verbal stimuli decrease with practice? _____ Explain the reason for this.

_____

**18.** Explain, in detail, why response time increased when the subject had to react to a word stimulus.

_____

_____

**19.** When measuring reaction time in the BIOPAC® activity, was there a difference in reaction time when the stimulus was predictable versus unpredictable? Explain your answer.

_____

_____

## Photo Credits

**Credits are listed in order of appearance.**

4–6: Richard Tauber, Pearson Education.

## Illustration Credits

**All illustrations are by Imagineering STA Media Services, except for Review Sheet art and as noted below.**

1: Electronic Publishing Services, Inc. 8, 9: Biopac Systems.

# Special Senses: Anatomy of the Visual System

## MATERIALS

- ☐ Chart of eye anatomy
- ☐ Dissectible eye model
- ☐ Prepared slide of longitudinal section of an eye showing retinal layers
- ☐ Compound microscope
- ☐ Preserved cow or sheep eye
- ☐ Dissecting instruments and tray
- ☐ Disposable gloves

## OBJECTIVES

1. Identify the external, internal, and accessory anatomical structures of the eye on a model or appropriate image and list the function(s) of each; identify the structural components that are present in a preserved sheep or cow eye (if available).
2. Define *conjunctivitis, cataract,* and *glaucoma.*
3. Describe the cellular makeup of the retina.
4. Explain the difference between rods and cones with respect to visual perception and retinal localization.
5. Trace the visual pathway to the primary visual cortex, and indicate the effects of damage to various parts of this pathway.

## PRE-LAB QUIZ

1. Name the mucous membrane that lines the internal surface of the eyelids and continues over the anterior surface of the eyeball.

   _____

2. How many extrinsic eye muscles are attached to the exterior surface of each eyeball?
   a. three               c. five
   b. four               d. six
3. The wall of the eye has three layers. The outermost fibrous layer is made up of the opaque white sclera and the transparent _____.
   a. choroid          c. cornea
   b. ciliary gland     d. lacrima
4. Circle the correct underlined term. The <u>aqueous humor</u> / <u>vitreous humor</u> is a clear, watery fluid that helps to maintain the intraocular pressure of the eye and provides nutrients for the avascular lens and cornea.
5. Circle True or False. At the optic chiasma, the fibers from the medial side of each eye cross over to the opposite side.

## Anatomy of the Eye

### External Anatomy and Accessory Structures

The adult human eye is a sphere measuring about 2.5 cm (1 inch) in diameter. Only about one-sixth of the eye's anterior surface is observable (Figure 1); the remainder is enclosed and protected by a cushion of fat and the walls of the bony orbit.

The **lacrimal apparatus** consists of the lacrimal gland, lacrimal canaliculi, lacrimal sac, and the nasolacrimal duct. The **lacrimal glands** are situated superior

From Exercise 23 of *Human Anatomy & Physiology Laboratory Manual*, Main Version, Tenth Edition. Elaine N. Marieb, Susan J. Mitchell, Lori A. Smith. Copyright © 2014 by Pearson Education, Inc. All rights reserved.

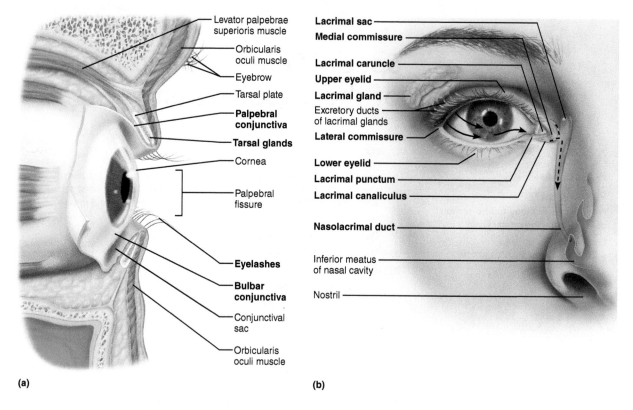

**Figure 1 External anatomy of the eye and accessory structures. (a)** Lateral view; some structures shown in sagittal section. **(b)** Anterior view with lacrimal apparatus.

to the lateral aspect of each eye. They continually release a dilute salt solution (tears) that flows onto the anterior surface of the eyeball through several small ducts. The tears flush across the eyeball and through the **lacrimal puncta,** the tiny openings of the **lacrimal canaliculi** medially, then into the **lacrimal sac,** and finally into the **nasolacrimal duct,** which empties into the nasal cavity. The lacrimal secretion also contains **lysozyme,** an antibacterial enzyme. Because it constantly flushes the eyeball, the lacrimal fluid cleanses and protects the eye surface as it moistens and lubricates it. As we age, our eyes tend to become dry due to decreased lacrimation, and thus are more vulnerable to bacterial invasion and irritation.

The anterior surface of each eye is protected by the **eyelids** or **palpebrae** (Figure 1). The medial and lateral junctions of the upper and lower eyelids are referred to as the **medial** and **lateral commissures** *(canthi),* respectively. The **lacrimal caruncle,** a fleshy raised area at the medial commissure, produces a whitish oily secretion. A mucous membrane, the **conjunctiva,** lines the internal surface of the eyelids (as the *palpebral conjunctiva*) and continues over the anterior surface of the eyeball to its junction with the corneal epithelium (as the *bulbar conjunctiva*). The conjunctiva secretes mucus, which aids in lubricating the eyeball. Inflammation of the conjunctiva, often accompanied by redness of the eye, is called **conjunctivitis.**

Projecting from the border of each eyelid is a row of short hairs, the **eyelashes.** The **ciliary glands,** modified sweat glands, lie between the eyelash hair follicles and help

lubricate the eyeball. Small sebaceous glands associated with the hair follicles and the larger **tarsal glands,** located posterior to the eyelashes, secrete an oily substance. An inflammation of one of the ciliary glands or a small oil gland is called a **sty.**

Six **extrinsic eye muscles** attached to the exterior surface of each eyeball control eye movement and make it possible for the eye to follow a moving object. (The names and positioning of these extrinsic muscles are noted in **Figure 2**). Their actions are given in the chart (Figure 2c).

**ACTIVITY 1**

## Identifying Accessory Eye Structures

Using a chart of eye anatomy or the art of the extrinsic eye muscles (Figure 1), observe the eyes of another student, and identify as many of the accessory structures as possible. Ask the student to look to the left. Which extrinsic eye muscles are responsible for this action?

Right eye: _____

Left eye: _____ ■

## Internal Anatomy of the Eye

Anatomically, the wall of the eye is constructed of three layers **(Figure 3)**. The outermost **fibrous layer** is a protective layer composed of dense avascular connective tissue.

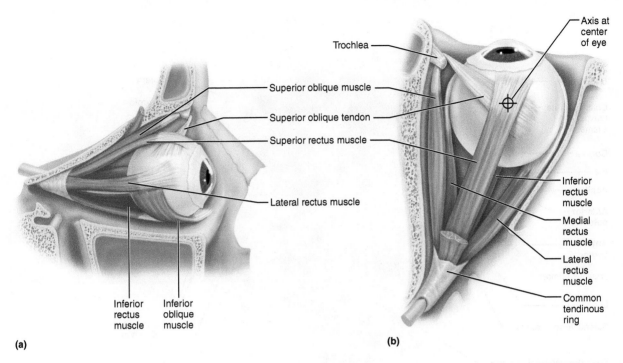

**Figure 2** **Extrinsic muscles of the eye. (a)** Lateral view of the right eye.
**(b)** Superior view of the right eye. **(c)** Summary of actions of the extrinsic eye muscles
and cranial nerves that control them.

It has two obviously different regions: The opaque white **sclera** forms the bulk of the fibrous layer and is observable anteriorly as the "white of the eye." Its anteriormost portion is modified structurally to form the transparent **cornea**, through which light enters the eye.

The middle layer is the **vascular layer**, also called the *uvea*. Its posteriormost part, the **choroid**, is a blood-rich nutritive region containing a dark pigment that prevents light scattering within the eye. Anteriorly, the choroid is modified to form the **ciliary body**, which is chiefly composed of *ciliary muscles*, which are smooth muscles important in controlling lens shape, and *ciliary processes*. The ciliary processes secrete aqueous humor. The most anterior part of the vascular layer is the pigmented **iris**. The iris is incomplete, resulting in a rounded opening, the **pupil**, through which light passes.

The iris is composed of circularly and radially arranged smooth muscle fibers and acts as a reflexively activated diaphragm to regulate the amount of light entering the eye. In close vision and bright light, the sphincter pupillae (circular muscles) of the iris contract, and the pupil constricts. In distant vision and in dim light, the dilator pupillae (radial muscles) contract, enlarging (dilating) the pupil and allowing more light to enter the eye.

Together the sphincter pupillae and dilator pupillae muscles of the iris and the ciliary muscles are the *intrinsic muscles* of the eye, controlled by the autonomic nervous system.

The innermost **sensory layer** of the eye is the delicate, two-layered **retina** (Figure 3 and **Figure 4**). The outer **pigmented layer** abuts the choroid and extends anteriorly to cover the ciliary body and the posterior side of the iris. The pigment cells, like those of the choroid, absorb light and prevent it from scattering in the eye. They also participate in photoreceptor cell renewal by acting as phagocytes, and they store vitamin A needed by the photoreceptor cells. The transparent inner **neural layer** extends anteriorly only to the ciliary body. It contains the photoreceptors, *rods* and *cones*, which begin the chain of electrical events that ultimately result in the

317

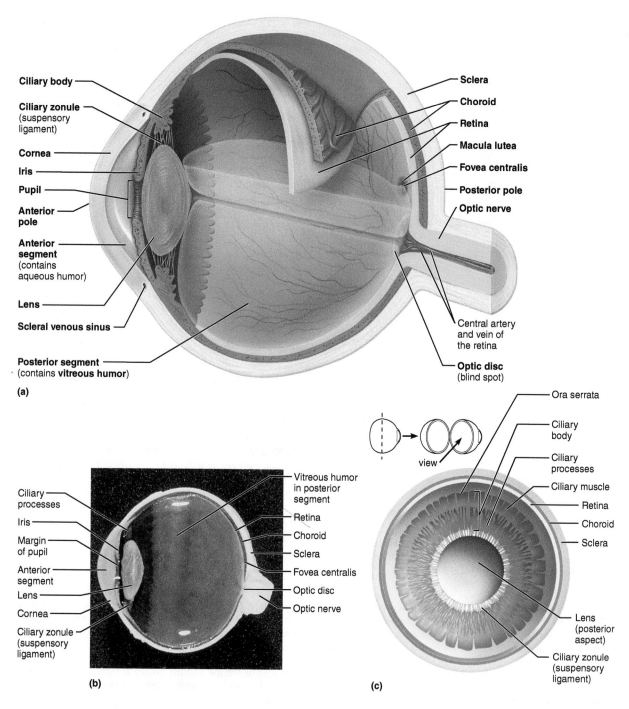

**Ciliary body**

**Ciliary zonule**
(suspensory
ligament)

**Cornea**

**Iris**

**Pupil**

**Anterior pole**

**Anterior segment**
(contains
aqueous humor)

**Lens**

**Scleral venous sinus**

**Posterior segment**
(contains **vitreous humor**)

**(a)**

**Sclera**

**Choroid**

**Retina**

**Macula lutea**

**Fovea centralis**

**Posterior pole**

**Optic nerve**

Central artery
and vein of
the retina

**Optic disc**
(blind spot)

Ciliary
processes

Iris

Margin
of pupil

Anterior
segment

Lens

Cornea

Ciliary zonule
(suspensory
ligament)

**(b)**

Vitreous humor
in posterior
segment

Retina

Choroid

Sclera

Fovea centralis

Optic disc

Optic nerve

view

Ora serrata

Ciliary
body

Ciliary
processes

Ciliary muscle

Retina

Choroid

Sclera

Lens
(posterior
aspect)

Ciliary zonule
(suspensory
ligament)

**(c)**

**Figure 3 Internal anatomy of the eye. (a)** Diagram of sagittal section of the eye. The vitreous humor is illustrated only in the bottom half of the eyeball. **(b)** Photograph of the human eye. **(c)** Posterior view of anterior half of the eye.

transduction of light energy into nerve impulses that are transmitted to the primary visual cortex of the brain. Vision is the result. The photoreceptor cells are distributed over the entire neural retina, except where the optic nerve leaves the eyeball. This site is called the **optic disc,** or *blind spot,* and is located in a weak spot in the **fundus** (posterior wall). Lateral to each blind spot, and directly posterior to the lens, is an area called the **macula lutea** ("yellow spot"), an area of high cone density. In its center is the **fovea centralis,** a tiny pit about 0.4 mm in diameter, which contains only cones and is the area of greatest visual acuity. Focusing for discriminative vision occurs in the fovea centralis.

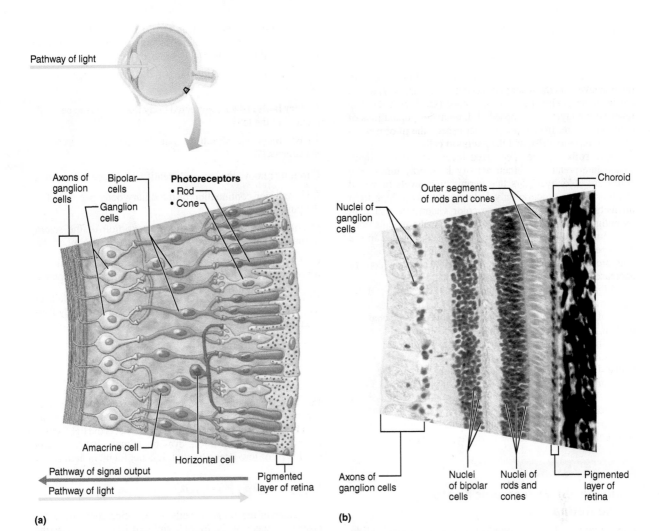

**Figure 4 Microscopic anatomy of the retina. (a)** Diagram of cells of the neural retina. Note the pathway of light through the retina. Neural signals (output of the retina) flow in the opposite direction. **(b)** Photomicrograph of the retina (140×).

Light entering the eye is focused on the retina by the **lens,** a flexible crystalline structure held vertically in the eye's interior by the **ciliary zonule** *(suspensory ligament)* attached to the ciliary body. Activity of the ciliary muscle, which accounts for the bulk of ciliary body tissue, changes lens thickness to allow light to be properly focused on the retina.

In the elderly the lens becomes increasingly hard and opaque. **Cataracts,** which often result from this process, cause vision to become hazy or entirely obstructed. ✛

The lens divides the eye into two segments: the **anterior segment** anterior to the lens, which contains a clear watery fluid called the **aqueous humor,** and the **posterior segment** behind the lens, filled with a gel-like substance, the **vitreous humor,** or **vitreous body.** The anterior segment is further divided into **anterior** and **posterior chambers,** located before and after the iris, respectively. The aqueous humor is continually formed by the capillaries of the **ciliary processes** of the ciliary body. It helps to maintain the intraocular

pressure of the eye and provides nutrients for the avascular lens and cornea. The aqueous humor is reabsorbed into the **scleral venous sinus.** The vitreous humor provides the major internal reinforcement of the posterior part of the eyeball, and helps to keep the retina pressed firmly against the wall of the eyeball. It is formed *only* before birth.

Anything that interferes with drainage of the aqueous fluid increases intraocular pressure. When intraocular pressure reaches dangerously high levels, the retina and optic nerve are compressed, resulting in pain and possible blindness, a condition called **glaucoma.** ✛

### ACTIVITY 2

## Identifying Internal Structures of the Eye

Obtain a dissectible eye model and identify its internal structures described above. (As you work, also refer to Figure 3.) ■

# Microscopic Anatomy of the Retina

Cells of the retina include the pigment cells of the outer pigmented layer and the inner photoreceptors and neurons, which are in contact with the vitreous humor (see Figure 4). The inner neural layer is composed of three major populations of cells. These are, from outer to inner aspect, the **photoreceptors,** the **bipolar cells,** and the **ganglion cells.**

The **rods** are the specialized receptors for dim light. Visual interpretation of their activity is in gray tones. The **cones** are color receptors that permit high levels of visual acuity, but they function only under conditions of high light intensity; thus, for example, no color vision is possible in moonlight. The fovea contains only cones, the macula contains mostly cones, and from the edge of the macula to the retina periphery, cone density declines gradually. By contrast, rods are most numerous in the periphery, and their density decreases as the macula is approached.

Light must pass through the ganglion cell layer and the bipolar cell layer to reach and excite the rods and cones. As a result of a light stimulus, the photoreceptors undergo changes in their membrane potential that influence the bipolar cells. These in turn stimulate the ganglion cells, whose axons leave the retina in the tight bundle of fibers known as the **optic nerve** (Figure 3). The retinal layer is thickest where the optic nerve attaches to the eyeball because an increasing number of ganglion cell axons converge at this point. It thins as it approaches the ciliary body. In addition to these three major cell types, the retina also contains horizontal cells and amacrine cells, which play a role in visual processing.

**ACTIVITY 3**

## Studying the Microscopic Anatomy of the Retina

Use a compound microscope to examine a histologic slide of a longitudinal section of the eye. Identify the retinal layers by comparing your view to the photomicrograph (Figure 4b). ▪

**DISSECTION:**
## The Cow (Sheep) Eye

1. Obtain a preserved cow or sheep eye, dissecting instruments, and a dissecting tray. Don disposable gloves.

2. Examine the external surface of the eye, noting the thick cushion of adipose tissue. Identify the optic nerve (cranial nerve II) as it leaves the eyeball, the remnants of the extrinsic eye muscles, the conjunctiva, the sclera, and the cornea. The normally transparent cornea is opalescent or opaque if the eye has been preserved. (Refer to **Figure 5** as you work.)

3. Trim away most of the fat and connective tissue, but leave the optic nerve intact. Holding the eye with the cornea facing downward, carefully make an incision with a sharp scalpel into the sclera about 6 mm (¼ inch) above the cornea. (The sclera of the preserved eyeball is *very* tough, so you will have to apply substantial pressure to penetrate it.) Using scissors, complete the incision around the circumference of the eyeball paralleling the corneal edge.

4. Carefully lift the anterior part of the eyeball away from the posterior portion. Conditions being proper, the vitreous body should remain with the posterior part of the eyeball.

5. Examine the anterior part of the eye, and identify the following structures:

**Ciliary body:** Black pigmented body that appears to be a halo encircling the lens.

**Lens:** Biconvex structure that is opaque in preserved specimens.

Carefully remove the lens and identify the adjacent structures:

**Iris:** Anterior continuation of the ciliary body penetrated by the pupil.

**Cornea:** More convex anteriormost portion of the sclera; normally transparent but cloudy in preserved specimens.

6. Examine the posterior portion of the eyeball. Carefully remove the vitreous humor, and identify the following structures:

**Retina:** The neural layer of the retina appears as a delicate tan, probably crumpled membrane that separates easily from the pigmented choroid.

Note its point of attachment. What is this point called?

_____

_____

**Pigmented choroid coat:** Appears iridescent in the cow or sheep eye owing to a special reflecting surface called the **tapetum lucidum.** This specialized surface reflects the light within the eye and is found in the eyes of animals that live under conditions of low-intensity light. It is not found in humans. ▪

# Visual Pathways to the Brain

The axons of the ganglion cells of the retina converge at the posterior aspect of the eyeball and exit from the eye as the optic nerve. At the **optic chiasma,** the fibers from the medial side of each eye cross over to the opposite side (**Figure 6**). The fiber tracts thus formed are called the **optic tracts.** Each optic tract contains fibers from the lateral side of the eye on the same side and from the medial side of the opposite eye.

The optic tract fibers synapse with neurons in the **lateral geniculate body** of the thalamus, whose axons form the **optic radiation,** terminating in the **primary visual cortex** in the occipital lobe of the brain. Here they synapse with the cortical neurons, and visual interpretation occurs.

**ACTIVITY 4**

## Predicting the Effects of Visual Pathway Lesions

After examining the visual pathway diagram (Figure 6a), determine what effects lesions in the following areas would have on vision:

In the right optic nerve: _____

_____

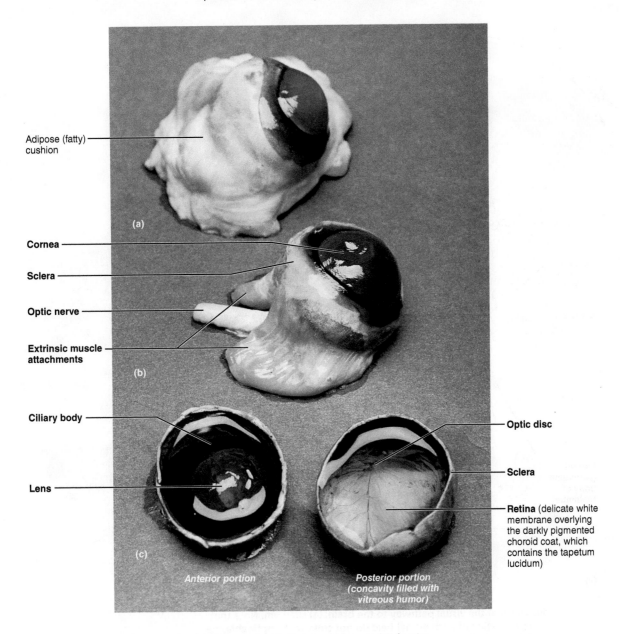

**Figure 5 Anatomy of the cow eye. (a)** Cow eye (entire) removed from orbit (notice the large amount of fat cushioning the eyeball). **(b)** Cow eye (entire) with fat removed to show the extrinsic muscle attachments and optic nerve. **(c)** Cow eye cut along the frontal plane to reveal internal structures.

Through the optic chiasma: _____

_____

In the left optic tract: _____

_____

In the right cerebral cortex (visual area): _____

_____

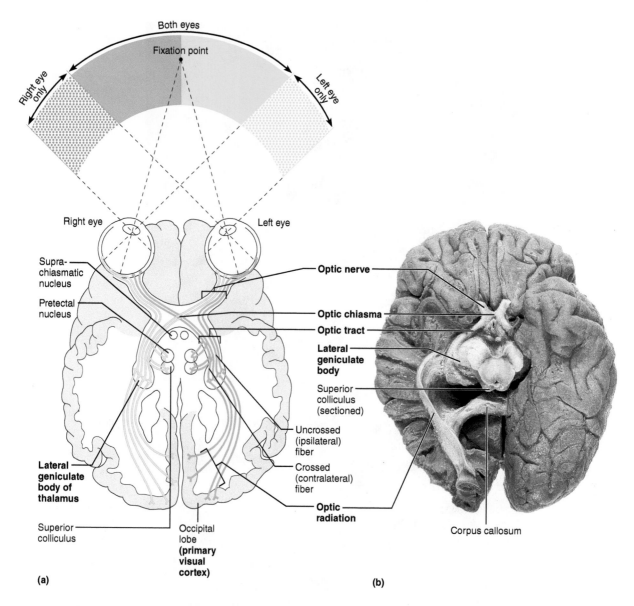

**Figure 6  Inferior views of the visual pathway to the brain. (a)** Diagram. Note that fibers from the lateral portion of each retinal field do not cross at the optic chiasma. **(b)** Photograph. Right side is dissected to reveal internal structures.

# Special Senses: Anatomy of the Visual System

## Anatomy of the Eye

1. Name five accessory eye structures that contribute to the formation of tears and/or aid in lubrication of the eyeball, and then name the major secretory product of each. Indicate which has antibacterial properties by circling the correct secretory product.

| Accessory structures | Product |
|---|---|
|  |  |
|  |  |
|  |  |
|  |  |
|  |  |

2. The eyeball is wrapped in adipose tissue within the orbit. What is the function of the adipose tissue?

_____

3. Why does one often have to blow one's nose after crying? _____

_____

4. Identify the extrinsic eye muscle predominantly responsible for each action described below.

_____ 1. turns the eye laterally

_____ 2. turns the eye medially

_____ 3. turns the eye up and laterally

_____ 4. turns the eye down and medially

_____ 5. turns the eye up and medially

_____ 6. turns the eye down and laterally

5. What is a sty? _____

_____

Conjunctivitis? _____

**6.** Correctly identify each lettered structure in the diagram by writing the letter next to its name in the numbered list. Use an appropriate reference if necessary.

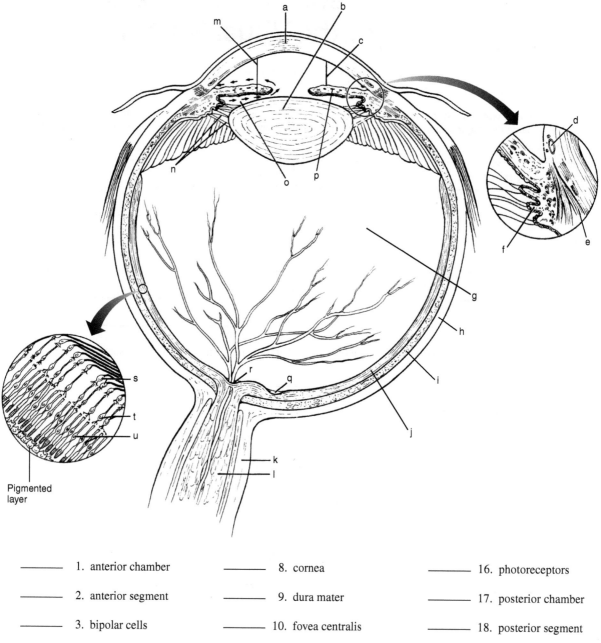

Pigmented
layer

_____ 1. anterior chamber

_____ 2. anterior segment

_____ 3. bipolar cells

_____ 4. choroid

_____ 5. ciliary body and
processes

_____ 6. ciliary muscle

_____ 7. ciliary zonule (suspensory ligament)

_____ 8. cornea

_____ 9. dura mater

_____ 10. fovea centralis

_____ 11. ganglion cells

_____ 12. iris

_____ 13. lens

_____ 14. optic disc

_____ 15. optic nerve

_____ 16. photoreceptors

_____ 17. posterior chamber

_____ 18. posterior segment

_____ 19. retina

_____ 20. sclera

_____ 21. scleral venous sinus

Special Senses: Anatomy of the Visual System

Notice the arrows drawn close to the left side of the iris in the diagram on the previous page. What do they indicate?

_____

**7.** The iris is composed primarily of two smooth muscle layers, one arranged radially and the other circularly.

Which of these dilates the pupil? _____

**8.** You would expect the pupil to be dilated in which of the following circumstances? Circle the correct response(s).

   a.  in bright light     b. in dim light     c. focusing for near vision     d. observing distant objects

**9.** The intrinsic eye muscles are controlled by (circle the correct response):

   autonomic nervous system      somatic nervous system

**10.** Match the key responses with the descriptive statements that follow. (Some choices will be used more than once.)

   *Key:*  a. aqueous humor        e. cornea               j. retina
         b. choroid             f. fovea centralis      k. sclera
         c. ciliary body         g. iris               l. scleral venous sinus
         d. ciliary processes of    h. lens             m. vitreous humor
            the ciliary body        i. optic disc

_____  1. fluid filling the anterior segment of the eye

_____  2. the "white" of the eye

_____  3. part of the retina that lacks photoreceptors

_____  4. modification of the choroid that controls the shape of the crystalline lens and contains the ciliary muscle

_____  5. drains aqueous humor from the eye

_____  6. layer containing the rods and cones

_____  7. substance occupying the posterior segment of the eyeball

_____  8. forms the bulk of the heavily pigmented vascular layer

_____, _____  9. smooth muscle structures (2)

_____  10. area of critical focusing and discriminatory vision

_____  11. form (by filtration) the aqueous humor

_____, _____  12. light-bending media of the eye (4)

_____, _____

_____  13. anterior continuation of the sclera—your "window on the world"

_____  14. composed of tough, white, opaque, fibrous connective tissue

# Microscopic Anatomy of the Retina

**11.** The two major layers of the retina are the pigmented and neural layers. In the neural layer, the neuron populations are arranged as follows from the pigmented layer to the vitreous humor. (Circle the proper response.)

bipolar cells, ganglion cells, photoreceptors        photoreceptors, ganglion cells, bipolar cells

ganglion cells, bipolar cells, photoreceptors        photoreceptors, bipolar cells, ganglion cells

**12.** The axons of the _____ cells form the optic nerve, which exits from the eyeball.

**13.** Complete the following statements by writing either *rods* or *cones* on each blank.

The dim light receptors are the _____. Only _____ are found in the fovea centralis, whereas

mostly _____ are found in the periphery of the retina. _____ are the photoreceptors that operate best

in bright light and allow for color vision.

# Dissection of the Cow (Sheep) Eye

**14.** What modification of the choroid that is not present in humans is found in the cow eye? _____

What is its function? _____

_____

**15.** What does the retina look like? _____

At what point is it attached to the posterior aspect of the eyeball? _____

# Visual Pathways to the Brain

**16.** The visual pathway to the occipital lobe of the brain consists most simply of a chain of five cells. Beginning with the photoreceptor cell of the retina, name them and note their location in the pathway.

1. _____      4. _____

2. _____      5. _____

3. _____

**17.** Visual field tests are done to reveal destruction along the visual pathway from the retina to the optic region of the brain. Note where the lesion is likely to be in the following cases.

Normal vision in left eye visual field; absence of vision in right eye visual field: _____

Normal vision in both eyes for right half of the visual field; absence of vision in both eyes for left half of the visual field:

_____

**18.** How is the right optic *tract* anatomically different from the right optic *nerve*? _____

_____

_____

## Photo Credits

Credits are listed in order of appearance.

3b: From *A Stereoscopic Atlas of Human Anatomy* by David L. Bassett, M.D. 4b: Lisa Lee, Pearson Education. 5a–c: Elena Dorfman, Pearson Education. 6b: Stephen Spector, Pearson Education.

## Illustration Credits

All illustrations are by Imagineering STA Media Services, except for Review Sheet art and as noted below.

1, 3, 4, 6: Electronic Publishing Services, Inc.

# Special Senses: Visual Tests and Experiments

## MATERIALS

- ☐ Metric ruler; meter stick
- ☐ Common straight pins
- ☐ Snellen eye chart, floor marked with chalk or masking tape to indicate 20-ft distance from posted Snellen chart
- ☐ Ishihara's color plates
- ☐ Two pencils
- ☐ Test tubes large enough to accommodate a pencil
- ☐ Laboratory lamp or penlight
- ☐ Ophthalmoscope (if available)

## OBJECTIVES

1. Discuss the mechanism of image formation on the retina.
2. Define the following terms: *accommodation, astigmatism, emmetropic, hyperopia, myopia, refraction,* and *presbyopia,* and describe several simple visual tests to which the terms apply.
3. Discuss the benefits of binocular vision.
4. Define *convergence* and discuss the importance of the pupillary and convergence reflexes.
5. State the importance of an ophthalmoscopic examination.

## PRE-LAB QUIZ

1. Circle the correct underlined term. Photoreceptors are distributed over the entire neural retina, except where the optic nerve leaves the eyeball. This site is called the <u>macula lutea</u> / <u>optic disc</u>.
2. Circle True or False. People with difficulty seeing objects at a distance are said to have myopia.
3. A condition that results in the loss of elasticity of the lens and difficulty focusing on a close object is called
   a. myopia         c. hyperopia
   b. presbyopia     d. astigmatism
4. Photoreceptors of the eye include rods and cones. Which one is responsible for interpreting color; which can function only under conditions of high light intensity?

   _____
5. Circle the correct underlined term. <u>Extrinsic</u> / <u>Intrinsic</u> eye muscles are controlled by the autonomic nervous system.

## The Optic Disc

In this exercise, you will perform several visual tests and experiments focusing on the physiology of vision. The first test involves demonstrating the blind spot (optic disc), the site where the optic nerve exits the eyeball.

### ACTIVITY 1

### Demonstrating the Blind Spot

1. Hold the figure for the blind spot test (**Figure 1**) about 46 cm (18 inches) from your eyes. Close your left eye, and focus your right eye on the X, which should be positioned so that it is directly in line with your right eye. Move the figure slowly toward your face, keeping your right eye focused on the X. When the dot focuses on the blind spot, which lacks photoreceptors, it will disappear.

From Exercise 24 of *Human Anatomy & Physiology Laboratory Manual,* Main Version, Tenth Edition. Elaine N. Marieb, Susan J. Mitchell, Lori A. Smith. Copyright © 2014 by Pearson Education, Inc. All rights reserved.

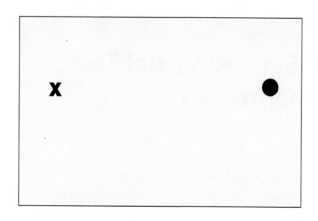

Figure 1 **Blind spot test figure.**

2. Have your laboratory partner record in metric units the distance at which this occurs. The dot will reappear as the figure is moved closer. Distance at which the dot disappears:

Right eye _____

Repeat the test for the left eye, this time closing the right eye and focusing the left eye on the dot. Record the distance at which the X disappears:

Left eye _____ ▬

# Refraction, Visual Acuity, and Astigmatism

When light rays pass from one medium to another, their velocity, or speed of transmission, changes, and the rays are bent, or **refracted.** Thus the light rays in the visual field are refracted as they encounter the cornea, lens, and vitreous humor of the eye.

The refractive index (bending power) of the cornea and vitreous humor are constant. But the lens's refractive index can be varied by changing the lens's shape—that is, by making it more or less convex so that the light is properly converged and focused on the retina. The greater the lens convexity, or bulge, the more the light will be bent and the stronger the lens. Conversely, the less the lens convexity (the flatter it is), the less it bends the light.

In general, light from a distant source (over 6 m, or 20 feet) approaches the eye as parallel rays, and no change in lens convexity is necessary for it to focus properly on the retina. However, light from a close source tends to diverge, and the convexity of the lens must increase to make close vision possible. To achieve this, the ciliary muscle contracts, decreasing the tension on the ciliary zonule attached to the lens and allowing the elastic lens to "round up." Thus, a lens capable of bringing a *close* object into sharp focus is stronger (more convex) than a lens focusing on a more distant object. The ability of the eye to focus differentially for objects of near vision (less than 6 m, or 20 feet) is called **accommodation.** It should be noted that the image formed on the retina as a result of the refractory activity of the lens **(Figure 2)** is a

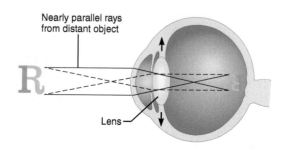

Figure 2 **Refraction and real images.** The refraction of light in the eye produces a real image (reversed, inverted, and reduced) on the retina.

real image (reversed from left to right, inverted, and smaller than the object).

The normal, or **emmetropic, eye** is able to accommodate properly **(Figure 3a)**. However, visual problems may result (1) from lenses that are too strong or too "lazy" (overconverging and underconverging, respectively), (2) from structural problems such as an eyeball that is too long or too short to provide for proper focusing by the lens, or (3) from a cornea or lens with improper curvatures.

Individuals in whom the image normally focuses in front of the retina are said to have **myopia,** or nearsightedness (Figure 3b); they can see close objects without difficulty, but distant objects are blurred or seen indistinctly. Correction requires a concave lens, which causes the light reaching the eye to diverge.

If the image focuses behind the retina, the individual is said to have **hyperopia,** or farsightedness. Such persons have no problems with distant vision but need glasses with convex lenses to augment the converging power of the lens for close vision (Figure 3c).

Irregularities in the curvatures of the lens and/or the cornea lead to a blurred vision problem called **astigmatism.** Cylindrically ground lenses, which compensate for inequalities in the curvatures of the refracting surfaces, are prescribed to correct the condition. ✤

## Near-Point Accommodation

The elasticity of the lens decreases dramatically with age, resulting in difficulty in focusing for near or close vision. This condition is called **presbyopia**—literally, old vision. Lens elasticity can be tested by measuring the **near point of accommodation.** The near point of vision is about 10 cm from the eye in young adults. It is closer in children and farther in old age.

### ACTIVITY 2

### Determining Near Point of Accommodation

To determine your near point of accommodation, hold a common straight pin at arm's length in front of one eye. (If desired, the text in the lab manual can be used rather than a pin.) Slowly move the pin toward that eye until the pin image becomes distorted. Have your lab partner use a metric ruler to measure the distance in centimeters from your eye to the pin at this point, and record the distance below. Repeat the procedure for the other eye.

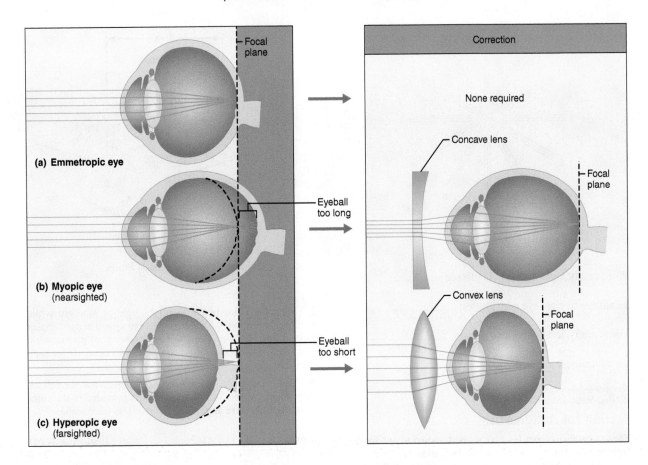

**Figure 3 Problems of refraction. (a)** In the emmetropic (normal) eye, light from both near and far objects is focused properly on the retina. **(b)** In a myopic eye, light from distant objects is brought to a focal point before reaching the retina. It then diverges. Applying a concave lens focuses objects properly on the retina. **(c)** In the hyperopic eye, light from a near object is brought to a focal point behind the retina. Applying a convex lens focuses objects properly on the retina. The refractory effect of the cornea is ignored here.

Near point for right eye: _____

Near point for left eye: _____ ▪

## Visual Acuity

**Visual acuity,** or sharpness of vision, is generally tested with a Snellen eye chart, which consists of letters of various sizes printed on a white card. This test is based on the fact that letters of a certain size can be seen clearly by eyes with normal vision at a specific distance. The distance at which the normal, or emmetropic, eye can read a line of letters is printed at the end of that line.

ACTIVITY 3

### Testing Visual Acuity

1. Have your partner stand 6 m (20 feet) from the posted Snellen eye chart and cover one eye with a card or hand. As your partner reads each consecutive line aloud, check

for accuracy. If this individual wears glasses, give the test twice—first with glasses off and then with glasses on. *Do not remove contact lenses, but note that they were in place during the test.*

2. Record the number of the line with the smallest-sized letters read. If it is 20/20, the person's vision for that eye is normal. If it is 20/40, or any ratio with a value less than one, he or she has less than the normal visual acuity. (Such an individual is myopic.) If the visual acuity is 20/15, vision is better than normal, because this person can stand at 6 m (20 feet) from the chart and read letters that are discernible by the normal eye only at 4.5 m (15 feet). Give your partner the number of the line corresponding to the smallest letters read, to record in step 4.

3. Repeat the process for the other eye.

4. Have your partner test and record your visual acuity. If you wear glasses, the test results *without* glasses should be recorded first.

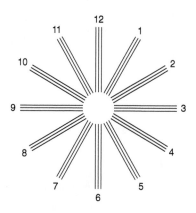

Figure 4 **Astigmatism testing chart.**

Visual acuity, right eye without glasses: _____

Visual acuity, right eye with glasses: _____

Visual acuity, left eye without glasses: _____

Visual acuity, left eye with glasses: _____ ▬

ACTIVITY 4

## Testing for Astigmatism

The astigmatism chart (Figure 4) is designed to test for defects in the refracting surface of the lens and/or cornea.

View the chart first with one eye and then with the other, focusing on the center of the chart. If all the radiating lines appear equally dark and distinct, there is no distortion of your refracting surfaces. If some of the lines are blurred or appear less dark than others, at least some degree of astigmatism is present.

Is astigmatism present in your left eye? _____

Right eye? _____ ▬

# Color Blindness

Ishihara's color plates are designed to test for deficiencies in the cones or color photoreceptor cells. There are three cone types, each containing a different light-absorbing pigment. One type primarily absorbs the red wavelengths of the visible light spectrum, another the blue wavelengths, and a third the green wavelengths. Nerve impulses reaching the brain from these different photoreceptor types are then interpreted (seen) as red, blue, and green, respectively. Interpretation of the intermediate colors of the visible light spectrum is a result of overlapping input from more than one cone type.

ACTIVITY 5

## Testing for Color Blindness

1. Find the interpretation table that accompanies the Ishihara color plates, and prepare a sheet to record data for the test. Note which plates are patterns rather than numbers.

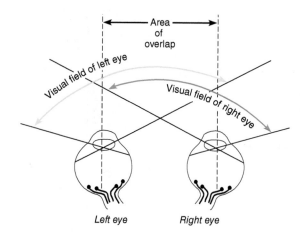

Figure 5 **Overlapping of the visual fields.**

2. View the color plates in bright light or sunlight while holding them about 0.8 m (30 inches) away and at right angles to your line of vision. Report to your laboratory partner what you see in each plate. Take no more than 3 seconds for each decision.

3. Your partner should record your responses and then check their accuracy with the correct answers provided in the color plate book. Is there any indication that you have some

degree of color blindness? _____ If so, what type?

_____

_____

Repeat the procedure to test your partner's color vision. ▬

# Binocular Vision

Humans, cats, predatory birds, and most primates are endowed with *binocular vision*. Their visual fields, each about 170 degrees, overlap to a considerable extent, and each eye sees a slightly different view (Figure 5). The primary visual cortex fuses the slightly different images, providing **depth perception** (or **three-dimensional vision**). This provides an accurate means of locating objects in space.

In contrast, the eyes of rabbits, pigeons, and many other animals are on the sides of their head. Such animals see in two different directions and thus have a panoramic field of view and *panoramic vision*. A mnemonic device to keep these straight is "Eyes in the front—likes to hunt; eyes to the side—likes to hide."

ACTIVITY 6

## Testing for Depth Perception

1. To demonstrate that a slightly different view is seen by each eye, perform the following simple experiment.

Close your left eye. Hold a pencil at arm's length directly in front of your right eye. Position another pencil directly beneath it and then move the lower pencil about half the distance toward you. As you move the lower pencil, make sure it remains in the *same plane* as the stationary pencil, so that the two pencils continually form a straight line. Then, without moving the pencils, close your right eye and open your left eye. Notice that with only the right eye open, the moving pencil stays in the same plane as the fixed pencil, but that when viewed with the left eye, the moving pencil is displaced laterally away from the plane of the fixed pencil.

2. To demonstrate the importance of two-eyed binocular vision for depth perception, perform this second simple experiment.

Have your laboratory partner hold a test tube erect about arm's length in front of you. With both eyes open, quickly insert a pencil into the test tube. Remove the pencil, bring it back close to your body, close one eye, and quickly and without hesitation insert the pencil into the test tube. *(Do not feel for the test tube with the pencil!)* Repeat with the other eye closed.

Was it as easy to dunk the pencil with one eye closed as with both eyes open?

_____ ▬

# Eye Reflexes

Both intrinsic (internal) and extrinsic (external) muscles are necessary for proper eye functioning. The *intrinsic muscles,* controlled by the autonomic nervous system, are those of the ciliary body (which alters the lens curvature in focusing) and the sphincter pupillae and dilator pupillae muscles of the iris (which control pupillary size and thus regulate the amount of light entering the eye). The *extrinsic muscles* are the rectus and oblique muscles, which are attached to the eyeball exterior. These muscles control eye movement and make it possible to keep moving objects focused on the fovea centralis. They are also responsible for **convergence,** or medial eye movements, which is essential for near vision. When convergence occurs, both eyes are directed toward the near object viewed. The extrinsic eye muscles are controlled by the somatic nervous system.

**ACTIVITY 7**

## Demonstrating Reflex Activity of Intrinsic and Extrinsic Eye Muscles

Involuntary activity of both the intrinsic and extrinsic muscle types is brought about by reflex actions that can be observed in the following experiments.

### Photopupillary Reflex

Sudden illumination of the retina by a bright light causes the pupil to constrict reflexively in direct proportion to the light intensity. This protective response prevents damage to the delicate photoreceptor cells.

Obtain a laboratory lamp or penlight. Have your laboratory partner sit with eyes closed and hands over his or her eyes. Turn on the light and position it so that it shines on the subject's right hand. After 1 minute, ask your partner to uncover and open the right eye. Quickly observe the pupil of that eye. What happens to the pupil?

_____

Shut off the light and ask your partner to uncover and open the opposite eye. What are your observations of the pupil?

_____

_____

### Accommodation Pupillary Reflex

Have your partner gaze for approximately 1 minute at a distant object in the lab—*not* toward the windows or another light source. Observe your partner's pupils. Then hold some printed material 15 to 25 cm (6 to 10 inches) from his or her face, and direct him or her to focus on it.

How does pupil size change as your partner focuses on the printed material?

_____

Explain the value of this reflex. _____

_____

_____

_____

### Convergence Reflex

Repeat the previous experiment, this time using a pen or pencil as the close object to be focused on. Note the position of your partner's eyeballs while he or she gazes at the distant object, and then at the close object. Do they change position as the object of focus is changed?

_____ In what way? _____

_____

_____

_____

Explain the importance of the convergence reflex.

_____

_____

_____ ▬

# Ophthalmoscopic Examination of the Eye (Optional)

The ophthalmoscope is an instrument used to examine the *fundus,* or eyeball interior, to determine visually the condition of the retina, optic disc, and internal blood vessels. Certain pathological conditions such as diabetes mellitus, arteriosclerosis, and degenerative changes of the optic nerve and retina can be detected by such an examination. The ophthalmoscope

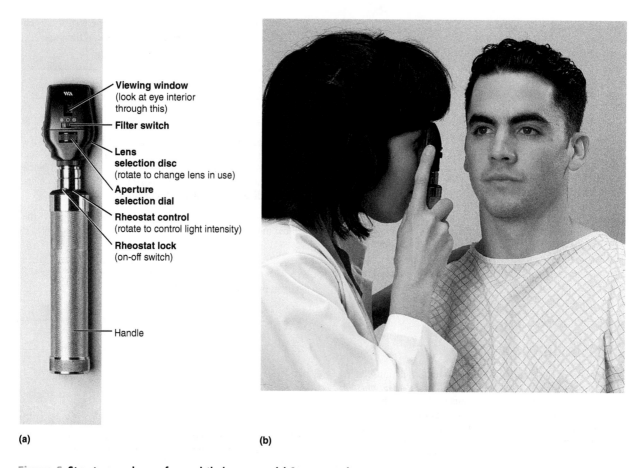

**(a)**

**(b)**

**Figure 6 Structure and use of an ophthalmoscope. (a)** Structure of an ophthalmoscope. **(b)** Proper position for beginning to examine the right eye with an ophthalmoscope.

consists of a set of lenses mounted on a rotating disc (the **lens selection disc**), a light source regulated by a **rheostat control,** and a mirror that reflects the light so that the eye interior can be illuminated **(Figure 6a)**.

The lens selection disc is positioned in a small slit in the mirror, and the examiner views the eye interior through this slit, appropriately called the **viewing window.** The focal length of each lens is indicated in diopters preceded by a plus (+) sign if the lens is convex and by a negative (–) sign if the lens is concave. When the zero (0) is seen in the **diopter window,** on the examiner side of the instrument, there is no lens positioned in the slit. The depth of focus for viewing the eye interior is changed by changing the lens.

The light is turned on by depressing the red **rheostat lock button** and then rotating the rheostat control in the clockwise direction. The **aperture selection dial** on the front of the instrument allows the nature of the light beam to be altered. The **filter switch,** also on the front, allows the choice of a green, unfiltered, or polarized light beam. Generally, green light allows for clearest viewing of the blood vessels in the eye interior and is most comfortable for the subject.

Once you have examined the ophthalmoscope and have become familiar with it, you are ready to conduct an eye examination.

**ACTIVITY 8**

## Conducting an Ophthalmoscopic Examination

1. Conduct the examination in a dimly lit or darkened room with the subject comfortably seated and gazing straight ahead. To examine the right eye, sit face-to-face with the subject, hold the instrument in your right hand, and use your right eye to view the eye interior (Figure 6b). You may want to steady yourself by resting your left hand on the subject's shoulder. To view the left eye, use your left eye, hold the instrument in your left hand, and steady yourself with your right hand.

2. Begin the examination with the 0 (no lens) in position. Grasp the instrument so that the lens disc may be rotated with the index finger. Holding the ophthalmoscope about 15 cm (6 inches) from the subject's eye, direct the light into the pupil at a slight angle—through the pupil edge rather than directly through its center. You will see a red circular area that is the illuminated eye interior.

3. Move in as close as possible to the subject's cornea (to within 5 cm, or 2 inches) as you continue to observe the area.

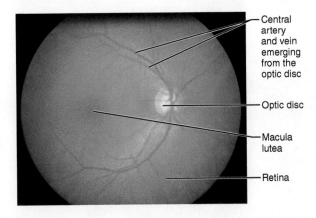

Central
artery
and vein
emerging
from the
optic disc

Optic disc

Macula
lutea

Retina

**Figure 7 Fundus (posterior wall) of right retina.**

Steady your instrument-holding hand on the subject's cheek if necessary. If both your eye and that of the subject are normal, the fundus can be viewed clearly without further adjustment of the ophthalmoscope. If the fundus cannot be focused, slowly rotate the lens disc counterclockwise until the fundus can be clearly seen. When the ophthalmoscope is correctly

set, the fundus of the right eye should appear as in the photograph **(Figure 7)**. (**Note:** If a positive [convex] lens is required and your eyes are normal, the subject has hyperopia. If a negative [concave] lens is necessary to view the fundus and your eyes are normal, the subject is myopic.)

When the examination is proceeding correctly, the subject can often see images of retinal vessels in his own eye that appear rather like cracked glass. If you are unable to achieve a sharp focus or to see the optic disc, move medially or laterally and begin again.

4. Examine the optic disc for color, elevation, and sharpness of outline, and observe the blood vessels radiating from near its center. Locate the macula, lateral to the optic disc. It is a darker area in which blood vessels are absent, and the fovea appears to be a slightly lighter area in its center. The macula is most easily seen when the subject looks directly into the light of the ophthalmoscope.

 Do not examine the macula for longer than 1 second at a time.

5. When you have finished examining your partner's retina, shut off the ophthalmoscope. Change places with your partner (become the subject) and repeat steps 1–4. ∎

# Special Senses: Visual Tests and Experiments

## The Optic Disc, Refraction, Visual Acuity, and Astigmatism

**1.** Explain why vision is lost when light hits the blind spot. _____

**2.** Match the terms in column B with the descriptions in column A.

**Column A**

_____ 1. light bending

_____ 2. ability to focus for close (less than 20 feet) vision

_____ 3. normal vision

_____ 4. inability to focus well on close objects (farsightedness)

_____ 5. nearsightedness

_____ 6. blurred vision due to unequal curvatures of the lens or cornea

_____ 7. medial movement of the eyes during focusing on close objects

**Column B**

a. accommodation

b. astigmatism

c. convergence

d. emmetropia

e. hyperopia

f. myopia

g. refraction

**3.** Complete the following statements:

In farsightedness, the light is focused __1__ the retina. The lens required to treat myopia is a __2__ lens. The "near point" increases with age because the __3__ of the lens decreases as we get older. A convex lens, like that of the eye, produces an image that is upside down and reversed from left to right. Such an image is called a __4__ image.

1. _____

2. _____

3. _____

4. _____

**4.** Use terms from the key to complete the statements concerning near and distance vision. (Some choices will be used more than once.)

*Key:*   a. contracted   b. decreased   c. increased   d. relaxed   e. taut

During distance vision, the ciliary muscle is _____, the ciliary zonule is _____, the convexity of the lens

is _____, and light refraction is _____. During close vision, the ciliary muscle is _____, the ciliary zonule is

_____, lens convexity is _____, and light refraction is _____.

**5.** Using your Snellen eye test results, answer the following questions.

Is your visual acuity normal, less than normal, or better than normal? _____

Explain your answer. _____

_____

Explain why each eye is tested separately when using the Snellen eye chart. _____

_____

Explain 20/40 vision. _____

_____

Explain 20/10 vision. _____

_____

**6.** Define *astigmatism.* _____

_____

How can it be corrected? _____

**7.** Define *presbyopia.* _____

_____

What causes it? _____

## Color Blindness

**8.** To which wavelengths of light do the three cone types of the retina respond maximally?

_____, _____, and _____

**9.** How can you explain the fact that we see a great range of colors even though only three cone types exist?

_____

_____

## Binocular Vision

**10.** Explain the difference between binocular and panoramic vision. _____

_____

_____

What is the advantage of binocular vision? _____

What factor(s) are responsible for binocular vision? _____

_____

## Eye Reflexes

**11.** In the experiment on the convergence reflex, what happened to the position of the eyeballs as the object was moved closer

to the subject's eyes? _____

What extrinsic eye muscles control the movement of the eyes during this reflex? _____

What is the value of this reflex? _____

_____

12. In the experiment on the photopupillary reflex, what happened to the pupil of the eye exposed to light?

_____ What happened to the pupil of the nonilluminated eye? _____

Explanation? _____

_____

## Ophthalmoscopic Examination

13. Why is the ophthalmoscopic examination an important diagnostic tool? _____

_____

14. Many college students struggling through mountainous reading assignments are told that they need glasses for "eyestrain." Why is it more of a strain on the extrinsic and intrinsic eye muscles to look at close objects than at far objects?

_____

_____

## Photo Credits

Credits are listed in order of appearance.

6a,b: Richard Tauber, Pearson Education. 7: Dr. Charles Klettke, Pearson Education.

## Illustration Credits

All illustrations are by Imagineering STA Media Services, except for Review Sheet art and as noted below.

1: Shirley Bortoli. 4: Precision Graphics.

# Special Senses: Olfaction and Taste

## MATERIALS

- [ ] Prepared slides: nasal olfactory epithelium (l.s.); the tongue showing taste buds (x.s.)
- [ ] Compound microscope
- [ ] Small mirror
- [ ] Paper towels
- [ ] Packets of granulated sugar
- [ ] Disposable autoclave bag
- [ ] Paper plates
- [ ] Equal-size food cubes of cheese, apple, raw potato, dried prunes, banana, raw carrot, and hard-cooked egg white (These prepared foods should be in an opaque container; a foil-lined egg carton would work well.)
- [ ] Toothpicks
- [ ] Disposable gloves
- [ ] Cotton-tipped swabs
- [ ] Paper cups
- [ ] Flask of distilled or tap water
- [ ] Prepared vials of oil of cloves, oil of peppermint, and oil of wintergreen or corresponding flavors found in the condiment section of a supermarket
- [ ] Chipped ice
- [ ] Five numbered vials containing common household substances with strong odors (herbs, spices, etc.)
- [ ] Nose clips
- [ ] Absorbent cotton

MasteringA&P° For related exercise study tools, go to the Study Area of MasteringA&P. There you will find:
- Practice Anatomy Lab PAL
- PhysioEx PEx
- A&PFlix A&PFlix
- Practice quizzes, Histology Atlas, eText, Videos, and more!

## OBJECTIVES

1. State the location and cellular composition of the olfactory epithelium.
2. Describe the structure of olfactory sensory neurons and state their function.
3. Discuss the locations and cellular composition of taste buds.
4. Describe the structure of gustatory epithelial cells and state their function.
5. Identify the cranial nerves that carry the sensations of olfaction and taste.
6. Name five basic qualities of taste sensation, and list the chemical substances that elicit them.
7. Explain the interdependence between the senses of smell and taste.
8. Name two factors other than olfaction that influence taste appreciation of foods.
9. Define *olfactory adaptation*.

## PRE-LAB QUIZ

1. Circle True or False. Receptors for olfaction and taste are classified as chemoreceptors because they respond to dissolved chemicals.
2. The organ of smell is the _____, located in the roof of the nasal cavity.
   - a. nares
   - b. nostrils
   - c. olfactory epithelium
   - d. olfactory nerve
3. Circle the correct underlined term. Olfactory receptors are bipolar / unipolar sensory neurons whose olfactory cilia extend outward from the epithelium.
4. Most taste buds are located in _____, peglike projections of the tongue mucosa.
   - a. cilia
   - b. concha
   - c. papillae
   - d. supporting cells
5. Circle the correct underlined term. Vallate papillae are arranged in a V formation on the anterior / posterior surface of the tongue.
6. Circle the correct underlined term. Most taste buds are made of two / three types of modified epithelial cells.
7. There are five basic taste sensations. Name one. _____
8. Circle True or False. Taste buds typically respond optimally to one of the five basic taste sensations.
9. Circle True or False. Texture, temperature, and smell have little or no effect on the sensation of taste.
10. You will use absorbent cotton and oil of wintergreen, peppermint, or cloves to test for olfactory
    - a. accommodation
    - b. adaptation
    - c. identification
    - d. recognition

From Exercise 26 of *Human Anatomy & Physiology Laboratory Manual*, Main Version, Tenth Edition. Elaine N. Marieb, Susan J. Mitchell, Lori A. Smith. Copyright © 2014 by Pearson Education, Inc. All rights reserved.

The receptors for olfaction and taste are classified as **chemoreceptors** because they respond to chemicals in solution. Although five relatively specific types of taste receptors have been identified, the olfactory receptors are considered sensitive to a much wider range of chemical sensations. The sense of smell is the least understood of the special senses.

## Location and Anatomy of the Olfactory Receptors

The **olfactory epithelium** is the organ of smell. It occupies an area of about 5 cm$^2$ in the roof of the nasal cavity **(Figure 1a)**. Since the air entering the human nasal cavity must make a hairpin turn to enter the respiratory passages below, the nasal epithelium is in a rather poor position for performing its function. This is why sniffing, which brings more air into contact with the receptors, increases your ability to detect odors.

The specialized receptor cells in the olfactory epithelium are **olfactory sensory neurons.** They are surrounded by epithelial **supporting cells.** The bipolar neurons have **olfactory cilia** that extend outward from the epithelium. Axons emerging from their basal ends penetrate the cribriform plate of the ethmoid bone and proceed as the *olfactory nerve filaments* (cranial nerve I) to synapse in the olfactory bulbs lying on either side of the crista galli of the ethmoid bone. Impulses from neurons of the olfactory bulbs are then conveyed to the olfactory portion of the cortex without synapsing in the thalamus.

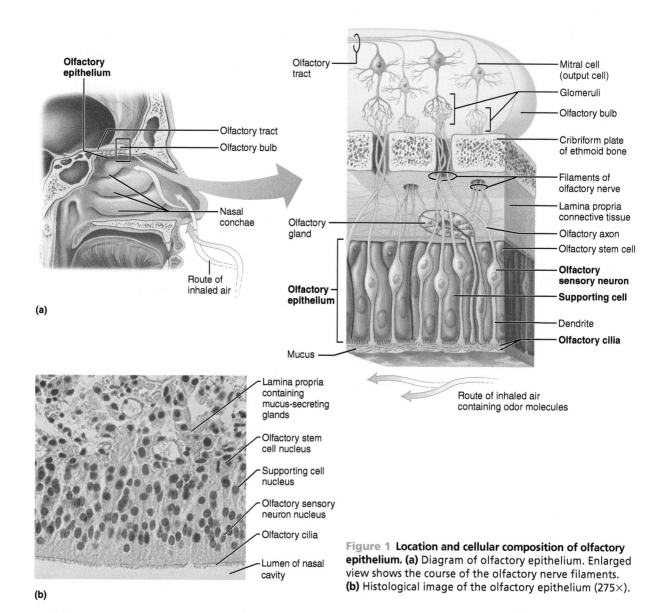

**(a)**

Olfactory epithelium

Olfactory tract
Olfactory bulb

Nasal conchae

Route of inhaled air

Olfactory tract

Olfactory gland

**Olfactory epithelium**

Mucus

Mitral cell (output cell)
Glomeruli
Olfactory bulb
Cribriform plate of ethmoid bone
Filaments of olfactory nerve
Lamina propria connective tissue
Olfactory axon
Olfactory stem cell
**Olfactory sensory neuron**
**Supporting cell**
Dendrite
**Olfactory cilia**

Route of inhaled air containing odor molecules

**(b)**

Lamina propria containing mucus-secreting glands

Olfactory stem cell nucleus

Supporting cell nucleus

Olfactory sensory neuron nucleus

Olfactory cilia

Lumen of nasal cavity

**Figure 1 Location and cellular composition of olfactory epithelium. (a)** Diagram of olfactory epithelium. Enlarged view shows the course of the olfactory nerve filaments. **(b)** Histological image of the olfactory epithelium (275×).

## Microscopic Examination of the Olfactory Epithelium

Obtain a longitudinal section of olfactory epithelium. Examine it closely using a compound microscope, comparing it to the photomicrograph (Figure 1b). ■

# Location and Anatomy of Taste Buds

The **taste buds,** containing specific receptors for the sense of taste, are widely but not uniformly distributed in the oral cavity. Most are located in **papillae,** peglike projections of the mucosa, on the dorsal surface of the tongue (as described next). A few are found on the soft palate, epiglottis, pharynx, and inner surface of the cheeks.

Taste buds are located primarily on the sides of the large **vallate papillae** (arranged in a V formation on the posterior surface of the tongue); in the side walls of the **foliate papillae;** and on the tops of the more numerous, mushroom-shaped **fungiform papillae (Figure 2).**

- Use a mirror to examine your tongue. Which of the various papillae types can you pick out? _____

_____

Each taste bud consists largely of a globular arrangement of two types of modified epithelial cells: the **gustatory epithelial cells,** which are the actual receptor cells for taste, and basal epithelial cells. Several nerve fibers enter each taste bud and supply sensory nerve endings to each of the gustatory epithelial cells. The long microvilli of the receptor cells penetrate the epithelial surface through an opening called the **taste pore.** When these microvilli, called **gustatory hairs,** contact specific chemicals in the solution, the receptor cells depolarize. The afferent fibers from the taste buds to the somatosensory cortex in the postcentral gyrus of the brain are carried in three cranial nerves: the *facial nerve (VII)* serves the anterior two-thirds of the tongue; the *glossopharyngeal nerve (IX)* serves the posterior third of the tongue; and the *vagus nerve (X)* carries a few fibers from the pharyngeal region.

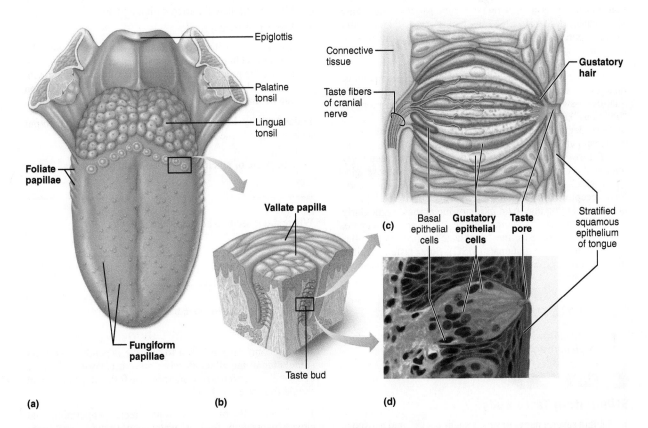

**Figure 2 Location and structure of taste buds. (a)** Taste buds on the tongue are associated with papillae, projections of the tongue mucosa. **(b)** A sectioned vallate papilla shows the position of the taste buds in its lateral walls. **(c)** An enlarged view of a taste bud. **(d)** Photomicrograph of a taste bud (445×).

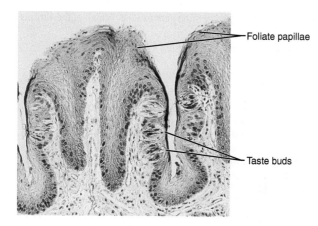

**Figure 3** **Taste buds on the lateral aspects of foliate papillae of the tongue (140×).**

Foliate papillae

Taste buds

## ACTIVITY 2

### Microscopic Examination of Taste Buds

Obtain a microscope and a prepared slide of a tongue cross section. Locate the taste buds on the tongue papillae (use Figure 2b as guide). Make a detailed study of one taste bud. Identify the taste pore and gustatory hairs if observed. Compare your observations to the photomicrograph (Figure 3). ▬

When taste is tested with pure chemical compounds, most taste sensations can be grouped into one of five basic qualities—sweet, sour, bitter, salty, or umami (oo-mom′ ē; "delicious"). Although all taste buds are believed to respond in some degree to all five classes of chemical stimuli, each type responds optimally to only one.

The *sweet* receptors respond to a number of seemingly unrelated compounds such as sugars (fructose, sucrose, glucose), saccharine, some lead salts, and some amino acids. *Sour* receptors are activated by hydrogen ions ($H^+$). *Salty* taste seems to be due to an influx of metal ions, particularly $Na^+$, while *umami* is elicited by the amino acid glutamate, which is responsible for the "meat taste" of beef and the flavor of monosodium glutamate (MSG). *Bitter* taste is elicited by alkaloids (e.g., caffeine and quinine) and other substances such as aspirin.

## Laboratory Experiments

⚠ *Notify instructor of any food or scent allergies before beginning experiments.*

## ACTIVITY 3

### Stimulating Taste Buds

1. Obtain several paper towels, a sugar packet, and a disposable autoclave bag and bring them to your bench.
2. With a paper towel, dry the dorsal surface of your tongue.

⚠ Immediately dispose of the paper towel in the autoclave bag.

3. Tear off a corner of the sugar packet and shake a few sugar crystals on your dried tongue. Do *not* close your mouth.

Time how long it takes to taste the sugar. _____ sec

Why couldn't you taste the sugar immediately?

_____ ▬

## ACTIVITY 4

### Examining the Combined Effects of Smell, Texture, and Temperature on Taste

*Effects of Smell and Texture*

1. Ask the subject to sit with eyes closed and to pinch his or her nostrils shut.

2. Using a paper plate, obtain samples of the food items provided by your laboratory instructor. At no time should the subject be allowed to see the foods being tested. Wear disposable gloves and use toothpicks to handle food.

3. For each test, place a cube of food in the subject's mouth and ask him or her to identify the food by using the following sequence of activities:

• First, manipulate the food with the tongue.

• Second, chew the food.

• Third, if a positive identification is not made with the first two techniques and the taste sense, ask the subject to release the pinched nostrils and to continue chewing with the nostrils open to determine if a positive identification can be made.

In the **Activity 4 chart,** record the type of food, and then put a check mark in the appropriate column for the result.

Was the sense of smell equally important in all cases?

_____

Where did it seem to be important and why?

_____

_____

Discard gloves in autoclave bag.

*Effect of Olfactory Stimulation*

What is commonly referred to as taste depends heavily on stimulation of the olfactory receptors, particularly in the case of strongly odoriferous substances. The following experiment should illustrate this fact.

1. Obtain vials of oil of wintergreen, peppermint, and cloves, paper cup, flask of water, paper towels, and some fresh cotton-tipped swabs. Ask the subject to sit so that he or she cannot see which vial is being used, and to dry the tongue and close the nostrils.

| | | Activity 4: Identification by Texture and Smell | | |
|---|---|---|---|---|
| Food tested | Texture only | Chewing with nostrils pinched | Chewing with nostrils open | Identification not made |
| | | | | |
| | | | | |
| | | | | |
| | | | | |
| | | | | |
| | | | | |
| | | | | |

2. Use a cotton swab to apply a drop of one of the oils to the subject's tongue. Can he or she distinguish the flavor?

_____

 Put the used swab in the autoclave bag. *Do not redip the swab into the oil.*

3. Have the subject open the nostrils, and record the change in sensation he or she reports.

_____

4. Have the subject rinse the mouth well and dry the tongue.

5. Prepare two swabs, each with one of the two remaining oils.

6. Hold one swab under the subject's open nostrils, while touching the second swab to the tongue.

Record the reported sensations. _____

_____

 7. Dispose of the used swabs and paper towels in the autoclave bag before continuing.

Which sense, taste or smell, appears to be more important in the proper identification of a strongly flavored volatile substance?

_____

*Effect of Temperature*

In addition to the effect that olfaction and food texture have in determining our taste sensations, the temperature of foods also helps determine if the food is appreciated or even tasted. To illustrate this, have your partner hold some chipped ice on the tongue for approximately a minute and then close his

or her eyes. Immediately place any of the foods previously identified in his or her mouth and ask for an identification.

Results? _____

_____

_____

### ACTIVITY 5

**Assessing the Importance of Taste and Olfaction in Odor Identification**

1. Go to the designated testing area. Close your nostrils with a nose clip, and breathe through your mouth. Breathing through your mouth only, attempt to identify the odors of common substances in the numbered vials at the testing area. Do not look at the substance in the container. Record your responses on the chart above.

2. Remove the nose clips, and repeat the tests using your nose to sniff the odors. Record your responses in the **Activity 5 chart.**

3. Record any other observations you make as you conduct the tests.

4. Which method gave the best identification results?

_____

What can you conclude about the effectiveness of the senses of taste and olfaction in identifying odors?

_____

### ACTIVITY 6

**Demonstrating Olfactory Adaptation**

Obtain some absorbent cotton and two of the following oils (oil of wintergreen, peppermint, or cloves). Place several drops of oil on the absorbent cotton. Press one nostril shut.

| Vial number | Identification with nose clips | Identification without nose clips | Other observations |
|---|---|---|---|
| **Activity 5: Identification by Mouth and Nasal Inhalation** | | | |
| 1 | | | |
| 2 | | | |
| 3 | | | |
| 4 | | | |
| 5 | | | |

Hold the cotton under the open nostril and exhale through the mouth. Record the time required for the odor to disappear (for olfactory adaptation to occur).

_____ sec

Repeat the procedure with the other nostril.

_____ sec

Immediately test another oil with the nostril that has just experienced olfactory adaptation. What are the results?

_____

What conclusions can you draw? _____

_____

# Special Senses:
# Olfaction and Taste

## Location and Anatomy of the Olfactory Receptors

**1.** Describe the location and cellular composition of the olfactory epithelium. _____

_____

_____

**2.** How and why does sniffing increase your ability to detect an odor? _____

_____

## Location and Anatomy of Taste Buds

**3.** Name five sites where receptors for taste are found, and circle the predominant site.

_____ , _____ , _____ ,

_____ , and _____

**4.** Describe the cellular makeup and arrangement of a taste bud. (Use a diagram, if helpful.) _____

_____

## Laboratory Experiments

**5.** Taste and smell receptors are both classified as _____ , because they both

respond to _____

**6.** Why is it impossible to taste substances with a dry tongue? _____

_____

**7.** The basic taste sensations are mediated by specific chemical substances or groups. Name them for the following taste modalities.

salt: _____     sour: _____     umami: _____

bitter: _____     sweet: _____

**8.** Name three factors that influence our appreciation of foods. Substantiate each choice with an example from the laboratory experience.

1. _____ Substantiation: _____

_____

2. _____ Substantiation: _____

_____

3. _____ Substantiation: _____

_____

Which of the factors chosen is most important? _____ Substantiate your choice with an example from

everyday life. _____

_____

Expand on your explanation and choices by explaining why a cold, greasy hamburger is unappetizing to most people.

_____

_____

**9.** How palatable is food when you have a cold? _____ Explain your answer. _____

_____

**10.** In your opinion, is olfactory adaptation desirable? _____ Explain your answer.

_____

_____

## Photo Credits

**Credits are listed in order of appearance.**

1b, 3: Victor P. Eroschenko, Pearson Education. 2d: Steve Downing, PAL 3.0, Pearson Education.

## Illustration Credits

**All illustrations are by Imagineering STA Media Services, except for Review Sheet art and as noted below.**

1, 2: Electronic Publishing Services, Inc.

# Special Senses: Hearing and Equilibrium

## MATERIALS

☐ Three-dimensional dissectible ear model and/or chart of ear anatomy

☐ Otoscope (if available)

☐ Disposable otoscope tips (if available) and autoclave bag

☐ Alcohol swabs

☐ Compound microscope

☐ Prepared slides of the cochlea of the ear

☐ Absorbent cotton

☐ Pocket watch or clock that ticks

☐ Metric ruler

☐ Tuning forks (range of frequencies)

☐ Rubber mallet

☐ Audiometer and earphones

☐ Red and blue pencils

☐ Demonstration: Microscope focused on a slide of a crista ampullaris receptor of a semicircular canal

☐ Three coins of different sizes

☐ Rotating chair or stool

☐ Blackboard and chalk or whiteboard and markers

MasteringA&P® For related exercise study tools, go to the Study Area of MasteringA&P. There you will find:

• Practice Anatomy Lab PAL

• PhysioEx PEx

• A&PFlix A&PFlix

• Practice quizzes, Histology Atlas, eText, Videos, and more!

## OBJECTIVES

1. Identify the anatomical structures of the external, middle, and internal ear on a model or appropriate diagram, and explain their functions.

2. Describe the anatomy of the organ of hearing (spiral organ in the cochlea), and explain its function in sound reception.

3. Discuss how one is able to localize the source of sounds.

4. Define *sensorineural deafness* and *conduction deafness* and relate these conditions to the Weber and Rinne tests.

5. Describe the anatomy of the organs of equilibrium in the internal ear (cristae ampullares and maculae), and explain their relative function in maintaining equilibrium.

6. State the locations and functions of endolymph and perilymph.

7. Discuss the effects of acceleration on the semicircular canals.

8. Define *nystagmus* and relate this event to the balance and Barany tests.

9. State the purpose of the Romberg test.

10. Explain the role of vision in maintaining equilibrium.

## PRE-LAB QUIZ

1. Circle the correct underlined term. The ear is divided into <u>three</u> / <u>four</u> major areas.

2. The external ear is composed primarily of the _____ and the external acoustic meatus.
   a. auricle           c. eardrum
   b. cochlea           d. stapes

3. Circle the correct underlined term. Sound waves that enter the external acoustic meatus eventually encounter the <u>tympanic membrane</u> / <u>oval window</u>, which then vibrates at the same frequency as the sound waves hitting it.

4. Three small bones found within the middle ear are the malleus, incus, and _____.
   a. auricle           b. cochlea
   c. eardrum           d. stapes

5. The snail-like _____, found in the internal ear, contains sensory receptors for hearing.
   a. cochlea              c. semicircular canals
   b. lobule               d. vestibule

6. Circle the correct underlined term. Today you will use an <u>ophthalmoscope</u> / <u>otoscope</u> to examine the ear.

7. The _____ test is used for comparing bone and air-conduction hearing.
   a. Barany              c. Weber
   b. Rinne

*(Text continues on next page.)*

8. The equilibrium apparatus of the ear, the vestibular apparatus, is found in the
   a. external ear     c. middle ear
   b. internal ear

9. Circle the correct underlined terms. The <u>crista ampullaris</u> / <u>macula</u> located in the semicircular <u>duct</u> / <u>vestibule</u> is essential for detecting static equilibrium.

10. Nystagmus is
    a. ability to hear only high-frequency tones
    b. ability to hear only low-frequency tones
    c. involuntary trailing of eyes in one direction, then rapid movement in the other
    d. sensation of dizziness

The ear is a complex structure containing sensory receptors for hearing and equilibrium. The ear is divided into three major areas: the *external ear*, the *middle ear*, and the *internal ear* (Figure 1). The external and middle ear structures serve the needs of the sense of hearing *only*, whereas internal ear structures function both in equilibrium and hearing reception.

## Anatomy of the Ear

### Gross Anatomy

**ACTIVITY 1**

### Identifying Structures of the Ear

Obtain a dissectible ear model or chart of ear anatomy and identify the structures described below. (Refer to Figure 1 as you work.) ▬

The **external (outer) ear** is composed primarily of the auricle and the external acoustic meatus. The **auricle,** or

**pinna,*** is the skin-covered cartilaginous structure encircling the auditory canal opening. In many animals, it collects and directs sound waves into the external auditory canal. In humans this function of the pinna is largely lost. The portion of the pinna lying inferior to the external auditory canal is the **lobule.**

The **external acoustic meatus,** or **external auditory canal,*** is a short, narrow (about 2.5 cm long by 0.6 cm wide) chamber carved into the temporal bone. In its skin-lined walls are wax-secreting glands called **ceruminous glands.** Sound waves that enter the external auditory meatus eventually encounter the **tympanic membrane,** or **eardrum,** which vibrates at exactly the same frequency as the sound wave(s) hitting it. The membranous eardrum separates the external from the middle ear.

The **middle ear** is essentially a small chamber—the **tympanic cavity**—found within the temporal bone. The

*Although the preferred anatomical terms for *pinna* and *external auditory canal* are *auricle* and *external acoustic meatus*, "pinna" and "external auditory canal" are heard often in clinical situations and will continue to be used here.

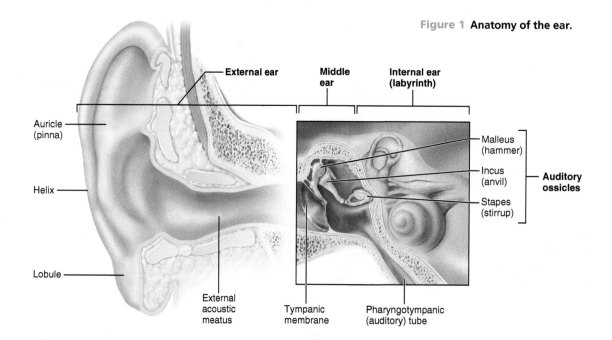

**Figure 1 Anatomy of the ear.**

External ear    Middle ear    Internal ear (labyrinth)

Auricle (pinna)

Helix

Lobule

External acoustic meatus

Tympanic membrane

Pharyngotympanic (auditory) tube

Malleus (hammer)

Incus (anvil)

Stapes (stirrup)

**Auditory ossicles**

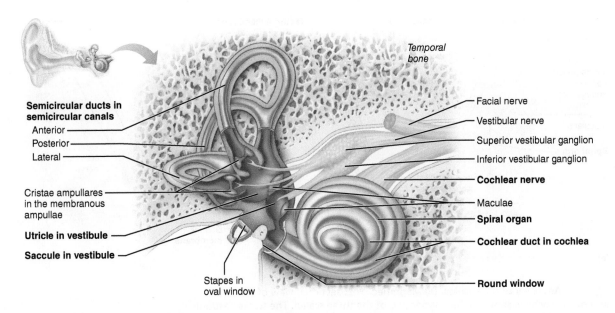

Anterior

Posterior

Lateral

**Semicircular ducts in semicircular canals**

Cristae ampullares in the membranous ampullae

**Utricle in vestibule**

**Saccule in vestibule**

Stapes in oval window

*Temporal bone*

Facial nerve

Vestibular nerve

Superior vestibular ganglion

Inferior vestibular ganglion

**Cochlear nerve**

Maculae

**Spiral organ**

**Cochlear duct in cochlea**

**Round window**

**Figure 2 Internal ear.** Right membranous labyrinth (blue) shown within the bony labyrinth (tan). The locations of sensory organs for hearing and equilibrium are shown in purple.

cavity is spanned by three small bones, collectively called the **auditory ossicles** (**malleus, incus,** and **stapes**), which articulate to form a lever system that amplifies and transmits the vibratory motion of the eardrum to the fluids of the inner ear via the **oval window.** The ossicles are often referred to by their common names: hammer, anvil, and stirrup, respectively.

Connecting the middle ear chamber with the nasopharynx is the **pharyngotympanic (auditory) tube** (formerly known as the eustachian tube). Normally this tube is flattened and closed, but swallowing or yawning can cause it to open temporarily to equalize the pressure of the middle ear cavity with external air pressure. This is an important function. The eardrum does not vibrate properly unless the pressure on both of its surfaces is the same.

Because the mucosal membranes of the middle ear cavity and nasopharynx are continuous through the pharyngotympanic tube, **otitis media,** or inflammation of the middle ear, is a fairly common condition, especially among youngsters prone to sore throats. In cases where large amounts of fluid or pus accumulate in the middle ear cavity, an emergency myringotomy (lancing of the eardrum) may be necessary to relieve the pressure. Frequently, tiny ventilating tubes are put in during the procedure. ✚

The **internal ear** consists of a system of bony and rather tortuous chambers called the **bony labyrinth,** which is filled with an aqueous fluid called **perilymph (Figure 2).** Suspended in the perilymph is the **membranous labyrinth,** a system that mostly follows the contours of the bony labyrinth. The membranous labyrinth is filled with a more viscous fluid called **endolymph.** The three subdivisions of the bony labyrinth are the cochlea, the vestibule, and the semicircular canals, with the vestibule situated between the cochlea and semicircular canals. The **vestibule** and the **semicircular canals** are involved with equilibrium. The snail-like **cochlea** (see Figure 2 and **Figure 3**) contains the sensory receptors for hearing. The membranous

**cochlear duct** is a soft wormlike tube about 3.8 cm long. It winds through the full two and three-quarter turns of the cochlea and separates the perilymph-containing cochlear cavity into upper and lower chambers, the **scala vestibuli** and **scala tympani.** The scala vestibuli terminates at the oval window, which "seats" the foot plate of the stirrup located laterally in the tympanic cavity. The scala tympani is bounded by a membranous area called the **round window.** The cochlear duct is the middle **scala media.** It is filled with endolymph and supports the **spiral organ,** which contains the receptors for hearing—the sensory hair cells and nerve endings of the **cochlear nerve,** a division of the vestibulocochlear nerve (VIII).

### ACTIVITY 2

## Examining the Ear with an Otoscope (Optional)

1. Obtain an otoscope and two alcohol swabs. Inspect your partner's external auditory canal and then select the largest—*diameter* (not length!) speculum that will fit comfortably into his or her ear to permit full visibility. Clean the speculum thoroughly with an alcohol swab, and then attach the speculum to the battery-containing otoscope handle. Before beginning, check that the otoscope light beam is strong. If not, obtain another otoscope or new batteries. Some otoscopes come with disposable tips. Be sure to use a new tip for each ear examined. Dispose of these tips in an autoclave bag after use.

2. When you are ready to begin the examination, hold the lighted otoscope securely between your thumb and forefinger (like a pencil), and rest the little finger of the otoscope-holding hand against your partner's head. This maneuver forms a brace that allows the speculum to move as your partner moves and prevents the speculum from penetrating too deeply into the external auditory canal during unexpected movements.

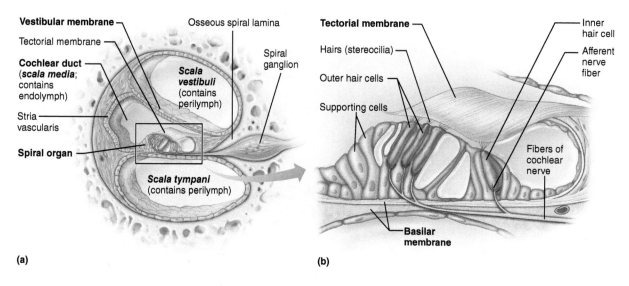

**(a)**

**(b)**

**Figure 3 Anatomy of the cochlea. (a)** Magnified cross-sectional view of one turn of the cochlea, showing the relationship of the three scalae. The scalae vestibuli and tympani contain perilymph; the cochlear duct (scala media) contains endolymph. **(b)** Detailed structure of the spiral organ.

3. Grasp the ear pinna firmly and pull it up, back, and slightly laterally. If your partner experiences pain or discomfort when the pinna is manipulated, an inflammation or infection of the external ear may be present. If this occurs, do not attempt to examine the ear canal.

4. Carefully insert the speculum of the otoscope into the external auditory canal in a downward and forward direction only far enough to permit examination of the tympanic membrane, or eardrum. Note its shape, color, and vascular network. The healthy tympanic membrane is pearly white. During the examination, notice if there is any discharge or redness in the external auditory canal and identify earwax.

5. After the examination, thoroughly clean the speculum with the second alcohol swab before returning the otoscope to the supply area. ■

## Microscopic Anatomy of the Spiral Organ and the Mechanism of Hearing

In the spiral organ, the auditory receptors are hair cells that rest on the **basilar membrane,** which forms the floor of the cochlear duct (Figure 3). Their "hairs" are stereocilia that project into a gelatinous membrane, the **tectorial membrane,** that overlies them. The roof of the cochlear duct is called the **vestibular membrane.**

**ACTIVITY 3**

### Examining the Microscopic Structure of the Cochlea

Obtain a compound microscope and a prepared microscope slide of the cochlea and identify the areas shown in the photomicrograph **(Figure 4).** ■

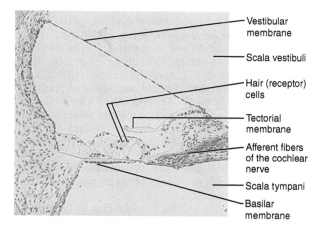

**Figure 4 Histological image of the spiral organ (100×)**

The mechanism of hearing begins as sound waves pass through the external auditory canal and through the middle ear into the internal ear, where the vibration eventually reaches the spiral organ, which contains the receptors for hearing.

Vibration of the stirrup at the oval window initiates traveling pressure waves in the perilymph that cause maximal displacements of the basilar membrane where they peak and stimulate the hair cells of the spiral organ in that region. Since the area at which the traveling waves peak is a high-pressure area, the vestibular membrane is compressed at this point and, in turn, compresses the endolymph and the basilar membrane of the cochlear duct. The resulting pressure on the perilymph in the scala tympani causes the membrane of the round window to bulge outward into the middle ear chamber, thus acting as a relief valve for the compressional wave. High-frequency waves (high-pitch sounds) peak close to the oval window and low-frequency waves (low-pitched sounds)

Special Senses: Hearing and Equilibrium

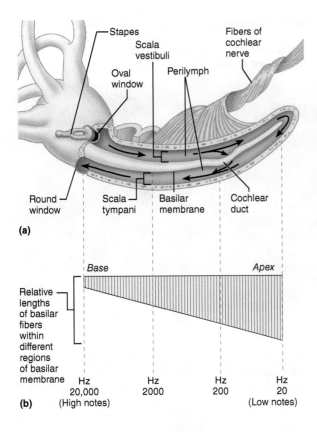

**(a)**

**(b)**

Base                                    Apex

Relative lengths of basilar fibers within different regions of basilar membrane

Hz 20,000 (High notes)  Hz 2000  Hz 200  Hz 20 (Low notes)

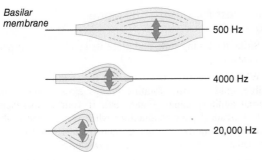

Basilar membrane

— 500 Hz

— 4000 Hz

— 20,000 Hz

**(c)**

**Figure 5 Resonance of the basilar membrane.** The cochlea is depicted as if it has been uncoiled. **(a)** Fluid movement in the cochlea following the stirrup thrust at the oval window. The compressional wave thus created causes the round window to bulge into the middle ear. Pressure waves set up vibrations in the basilar membrane. **(b)** Fibers span the basilar membrane. The length of the fibers "tunes" specific regions to vibrate at specific frequencies. **(c)** Different frequencies of pressure waves in the cochlea stimulate particular hair cells and neurons.

peak farther up the basilar membrane near the apex of the cochlea. The mechanism of sound reception by the spiral organ is complex. Hair cells at any given spot on the basilar membrane are stimulated by sounds of a specific frequency

and amplitude. Once stimulated, they depolarize and begin the chain of nervous impulses that travel along the cochlear nerve to the auditory centers of the temporal lobe cortex. This series of events results in the phenomenon we call hearing (Figure 5).

*Sensorineural deafness* results from damage to neural structures anywhere from the cochlear hair cells through neurons of the auditory cortex. **Presbycusis** is a type of sensorineural deafness that occurs commonly in people by the time they are in their sixties. It results from a gradual deterioration and atrophy of the spiral organ and leads to a loss in the ability to hear high tones and speech sounds. Because many elderly people refuse to accept their hearing loss and resist using hearing aids, they begin to rely more and more on their vision for clues as to what is going on around them and may be accused of ignoring people.

Although presbycusis is considered to be a disability of old age, it is becoming much more common in younger people as our world grows noisier. Prolonged or excessive noise tears the cilia from hair cells, and the damage is progressive and cumulative. Each assault causes a bit more damage. Music played and listened to at deafening levels definitely contributes to the deterioration of hearing receptors. ✚

## ACTIVITY 4

### Conducting Laboratory Tests of Hearing

Perform the following hearing tests in a quiet area. Test both the right and left ears.

#### Acuity Test

Have your lab partner pack one ear with cotton and sit quietly with eyes closed. Obtain a ticking clock or pocket watch and hold it very close to his or her *unpacked* ear. Then slowly move it away from the ear until your partner signals that the ticking is no longer audible. Record the distance in centimeters at which ticking is inaudible and then remove the cotton from the packed ear.

Right ear: _____ Left ear: _____

Is the threshold of audibility sharp or indefinite?

_____

#### Sound Localization

Ask your partner to close both eyes. Hold the pocket watch at an audible distance (about 15 cm) from his or her ear, and move it to various locations (front, back, sides, and above his or her head). Have your partner locate the position by pointing in each instance. Can the sound be localized equally well at all positions?

_____

If not, at what position(s) was the sound less easily located?

_____

_____

353

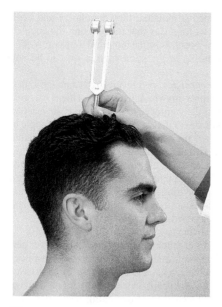

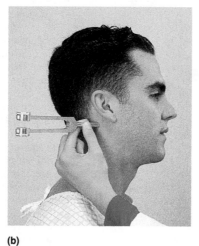

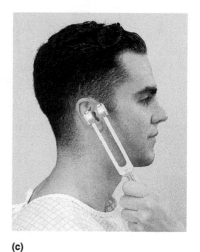

Figure 6 **The Weber and Rinne tuning fork tests. (a)** The Weber test to evaluate whether the sound remains centralized (normal) or lateralizes to one side or the other (indicative of some degree of conduction or sensorineural deafness). **(b, c)** The Rinne test to compare bone conduction and air conduction.

**(a)**　　　　　　　　　　　**(b)**　　　　　　　　　　　**(c)**

The ability to localize the source of a sound depends on two factors—the difference in the loudness of the sound reaching each ear and the time of arrival of the sound at each ear. How does this information help to explain your findings?

_____

_____

### Frequency Range of Hearing

Obtain three tuning forks: one with a low frequency (75 to 100 Hz [cps]), one with a frequency of approximately 1000 Hz, and one with a frequency of 4000 to 5000 Hz. Strike the lowest-frequency fork on the heel of your hand or with a rubber mallet, and hold it close to your partner's ear. Repeat with the other two forks.

Which fork was heard most clearly and comfortably?

_____ Hz

Which was heard least well? _____ Hz

### Weber Test to Determine Conduction and Sensorineural Deafness

Strike a tuning fork and place the handle of the tuning fork medially on your partner's head **(Figure 6a)**. Is the tone equally loud in both ears, or is it louder in one ear?

_____

If it is equally loud in both ears, you have equal hearing or equal loss of hearing in both ears. If sensorineural deafness is present in one ear, the tone will be heard in the unaffected ear but not in the ear with sensorineural deafness.

*Conduction deafness* occurs when something prevents sound waves from reaching the fluids of the internal ear. Compacted earwax, a perforated eardrum, inflammation of

the middle ear (otitis media), and damage to the ossicles are all causes of conduction deafness. If conduction deafness is present, the sound will be heard more strongly in the ear in which there is a hearing loss due to sound conduction by the bone of the skull. Conduction deafness can be simulated by plugging one ear with cotton.

### Rinne Test for Comparing Bone- and Air-Conduction Hearing

1. Strike the tuning fork, and place its handle on your partner's mastoid process (Figure 6b).

2. When your partner indicates that the sound is no longer audible, hold the still-vibrating prongs close to his or her external auditory canal (Figure 6c). If your partner hears the fork again (by air conduction) when it is moved to that position, hearing is not impaired and the test result is to be recorded as positive (+). (Record below step 5.)

3. Repeat the test on the same ear, but this time test air-conduction hearing first.

4. After the tone is no longer heard by air conduction, hold the handle of the tuning fork on the bony mastoid process. If the subject hears the tone again by bone conduction after hearing by air conduction is lost, there is some conduction deafness and the result is recorded as negative (−).

5. Repeat the sequence for the opposite ear.

Right ear: _____ Left ear: _____

Does the subject hear better by bone or by air conduction?

_____ ▪

## Audiometry

When the simple tuning fork tests reveal a problem in hearing, audiometer testing is usually prescribed to determine the precise nature of the hearing deficit. An *audiometer* is

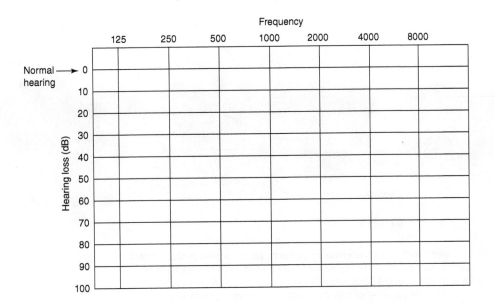

an instrument (specifically, an electronic oscillator with earphones) used to determine hearing acuity by exposing each ear to sound stimuli of differing *frequencies* and *intensities*. The hearing range of human beings during youth is from 20 to 20,000 Hz, but hearing acuity declines with age, with reception for the high-frequency sounds lost first. Though this loss represents a major problem for some people, such as musicians, most of us tend to be fairly unconcerned until we begin to have problems hearing sounds in the range of 125 to 8000 Hz, the normal frequency range of speech.

The basic procedure of audiometry is to initially deliver tones of different frequencies to one ear of the subject at an intensity of 0 decibels (dB). (Zero decibels is not the complete absence of sound, but rather the softest sound intensity that can be heard by a person of normal hearing at each frequency.) If the subject cannot hear a particular frequency stimulus of 0 dB, the hearing threshold level control is adjusted until the subject reports that he or she can hear the tone. The number of decibels of intensity required above 0 dB is recorded as the hearing loss. For example, if the subject cannot hear a particular frequency tone until it is delivered at 30 dB intensity, then he or she has a hearing loss of 30 dB for that frequency.

### ACTIVITY 5

### Audiometry Testing

1. Obtain an audiometer and earphones, and a red and a blue pencil. Before beginning the tests, examine the audiometer to identify the two tone controls: one to regulate frequency and a second to regulate the intensity (loudness) of the sound stimulus. Identify the two output control switches that regulate the delivery of sound to one ear or the other (*red* to the right ear, *blue* to the left ear). Also find the *hearing threshold level control*, which is calibrated to deliver a basal tone of 0 dB to the subject's ears.

2. Place the earphones on the subject's head so that the red cord or ear-cushion is over the right ear and the blue cord or

ear-cushion is over the left ear. Instruct the subject to raise one hand when he or she hears a tone.

3. Set the frequency control at 125 Hz and the intensity control at 0 dB. Press the red output switch to deliver a tone to the subject's right ear. If the subject does not respond, raise the sound intensity slowly by rotating the hearing level control counterclockwise until the subject reports (by raising a hand) that a tone is heard. Repeat this procedure for frequencies of 250, 500, 1000, 2000, 4000, and 8000.

4. Record the results in the grid (above) for frequency versus hearing loss by marking a small red circle on the grid at each frequency-dB junction at which a tone was heard. Then connect the circles with a red line to produce a hearing acuity graph for the right ear.

5. Repeat steps 3 and 4 for the left (blue) ear, and record the results with blue circles and connecting lines on the grid. ▬

## Microscopic Anatomy of the Equilibrium Apparatus and Mechanisms of Equilibrium

The equilibrium receptors of the internal ear are collectively called the **vestibular apparatus,** and are found in the vestibule and semicircular canals of the bony labyrinth. Their chambers are filled with perilymph, in which membranous labyrinth structures are suspended. The vestibule contains the saclike **utricle** and **saccule,** and the semicircular chambers contain **membranous semicircular ducts.** Like the cochlear duct, these membranes are filled with endolymph and contain receptor cells that are activated by the bending of their cilia.

### Semicircular Canals

The semicircular canals monitor angular movements of the head. This process is called **dynamic equilibrium.** The canals are 1.2 cm in circumference and are oriented in three planes—horizontal, frontal, and sagittal. At the base of each semicircular duct is an enlarged region, the **ampulla,** which communicates with the utricle of the vestibule. Within

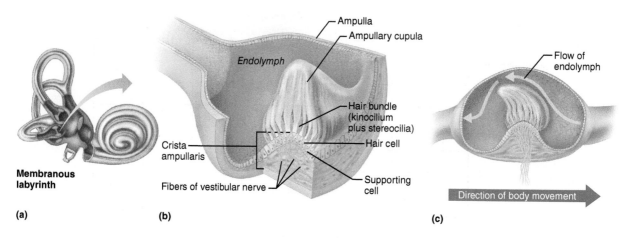

**Figure 7 Structure and function of the crista ampullaris. (a)** Arranged in the three spatial planes, the semicircular ducts in the semicircular canals each have a swelling called an ampulla at their base. **(b)** Each ampulla contains a crista ampullaris, a receptor that is essentially a cluster of hair cells with hairs projecting into a gelatinous cap called the ampullary cupula. **(c)** Movement of the cupula during angular acceleration of the head.

each ampulla is a receptor region called a **crista ampullaris,** which consists of a tuft of hair cells covered with a gelatinous cap, or **ampullary cupula (Figure 7)**.

The cristae respond to changes in the velocity of rotational head movements. During acceleration, as when you begin to twirl around, the endolymph in the canal lags behind the head movement due to inertia pushing the ampullary cupula—like a swinging door—in the opposite direction. The head movement depolarizes the hair cells, and results in enhanced impulse transmission in the vestibular division of the eighth cranial nerve to the brain (Figure 7c). If the body continues to rotate at a constant rate, the endolymph eventually comes to rest and moves at the same speed as the body. The ampullary cupula returns to its upright position, hair cells are no longer stimulated, and you lose the sensation of spinning. When rotational movement stops suddenly, the endolymph keeps on going in the direction of head movement. This pushes the ampullary cupula in the *same* direction as the previous head movement and hyperpolarizes the hair cells, resulting in fewer impulses being transmitted to the brain. This tells the brain that you have stopped moving and accounts for the reversed motion sensation you feel when you stop twirling suddenly.

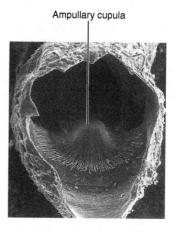

**Figure 8 Scanning electron micrograph of a crista ampullaris (14×).**

Ampullary cupula

---

ACTIVITY 6

## Examining the Microscopic Structure of the Crista Ampullaris

Go to the demonstration area and examine the slide of a crista ampullaris. Identify the areas depicted in the photomicrograph **(Figure 8)** and labeled diagram (Figure 7b). ■

### Maculae

**Maculae** in the vestibule contain another set of **hair cells,** receptors that in this case monitor head position and acceleration in a straight line. This monitoring process is called **static equilibrium.** The maculae respond to gravitational pull, thus providing information on which way is up or down as well as changes in linear speed. They are located on the walls of the saccule and utricle. The hair cells in each macula are embedded in the **otolith membrane,** a gelatinous material containing small grains of calcium carbonate called **otolith.** When the head moves, the otoliths move in response to variations in gravitational pull. As they deflect different hair cells, they trigger hyperpolarization or depolarization of the hair cells and modify the rate of impulse transmission along the vestibular nerve **(Figure 9)**.

Although the receptors of the semicircular canals and the vestibule are responsible for dynamic and static equilibrium respectively, they rarely act independently. Complex interaction of many of the receptors is the rule. Processing is also complex and involves the brain stem and cerebellum as well as input from proprioceptors and the eyes.

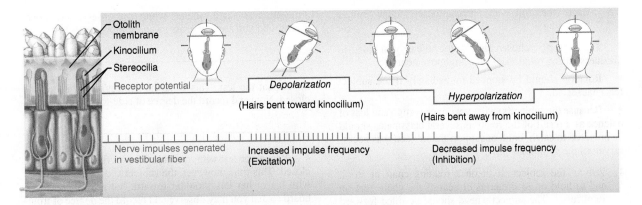

**Figure 9** **The effect of gravitational pull on a macula receptor in the utricle.** When movement of the otolith membrane bends the hair cells in the direction of the kinocilium, the hair cells depolarize, exciting the nerve fibers, which generates action potentials more rapidly. When the hairs are bent in the direction away from the kinocilium, the hair cells become hyperpolarized, inhibiting the nerve fibers and decreasing the action potential rate (i.e., below the resting rate of discharge).

---

**ACTIVITY 7**

## Conducting Laboratory Tests on Equilibrium

The function of the semicircular canals and vestibule are not routinely tested in the laboratory, but the following simple tests illustrate normal equilibrium apparatus function as well as some of the complex processing interactions.

In the first balance test and the Barany test, you will look for **nystagmus,** which is the involuntary rolling of the eyes in any direction or the trailing of the eyes slowly in one direction, followed by their rapid movement in the opposite direction. During rotation, the slow drift of the eyes is related to the backflow of endolymph in the semicircular canals. The rapid movement represents CNS compensation to find a new fixation point. Nystagmus is normal during and after rotation; abnormal otherwise. The direction of nystagmus is that of its quick phase on acceleration.

Nystagmus is often accompanied by **vertigo**—is a sensation of dizziness and rotational movement when such movement is not occurring or has ceased.

### Balance Tests

1. Have your partner walk a straight line, placing one foot directly in front of the other.

Is he or she able to walk without undue wobbling from side to

side? _____

Did he or she experience any dizziness? _____

The ability to walk with balance and without dizziness, unless subject to rotational forces, indicates normal function of the equilibrium apparatus.

Was nystagmus present? _____

2. Place three coins of different sizes on the floor. Ask your lab partner to pick up the coins, and carefully observe his or her muscle activity and coordination.

Did your lab partner have any difficulty locating and picking

up the coins? _____

Describe your observations and your lab partner's observations during the test.

_____

_____

What kinds of interactions involving balance and coordination must occur for a person to move fluidly during this test?

_____

_____

3. If a person has a depressed nervous system, mental concentration may result in a loss of balance. Ask your lab partner to stand up and count backward from ten as rapidly as possible.

Did your lab partner lose balance? _____

### Barany Test (Induction of Nystagmus and Vertigo)

This experiment evaluates the semicircular canals and should be conducted as a group effort to protect the test subject(s) from possible injury.

Read the following precautionary notes before beginning:

• The subject(s) chosen should not be easily inclined to dizziness during rotational or turning movements.

• Rotation should be stopped immediately if the subject feels nauseated.

• Because the subject(s) will experience vertigo and loss of balance as a result of the rotation, several classmates should be prepared to catch, hold, or support the subject(s) as necessary until the symptoms pass.

1. Instruct the subject to sit on a rotating chair or stool, and to hold on to the arms or seat of the chair, feet on stool rungs. The subject's head should be tilted forward approximately 30 degrees (almost touching the chest). The horizontal (lateral) semicircular canal is stimulated when the head is in this position. The subject's eyes are to remain *open* during the test.

2. Four classmates should position themselves so that the subject is surrounded on all sides. The classmate posterior to the subject will rotate the chair.

3. Rotate the chair to the subject's right approximately 10 revolutions in 10 seconds, then suddenly stop the rotation.

4. Immediately note the direction of the subject's resultant nystagmus; and ask him or her to describe the feelings of movement, indicating speed and direction sensation. Record this information below.

_____

_____

_____

If the semicircular canals are operating normally, the subject will experience a sensation that the stool is still rotating immediately after it has stopped and *will* demonstrate nystagmus.

When the subject is rotated to the right, the ampullary cupula will be bent to the left, causing nystagmus during rotation in which the eyes initially move slowly to the left and then quickly to the right. Nystagmus will continue until the ampullary cupula has returned to its initial position. Then, when rotation is stopped abruptly, the ampullary cupula will be bent to the right, producing nystagmus with its slow phase to the right and its rapid phase to the left. In many subjects, this will be accompanied by a feeling of vertigo and a tendency to fall to the right.

### Romberg Test

The Romberg test determines the integrity of the dorsal white column of the spinal cord, which transmits impulses to the brain from the proprioceptors involved with posture.

1. Have your partner stand with his or her back to the blackboard or whiteboard.

2. Draw one line parallel to each side of your partner's body. He or she should stand erect, with eyes open and staring

straight ahead for 2 minutes while you observe any movements. Did you see any gross swaying movements?

_____

3. Repeat the test. This time the subject's eyes should be closed. Note and record the degree of side-to-side movement.

_____

4. Repeat the test with the subject's eyes first open and then closed. This time, however, the subject should be positioned with his or her left shoulder toward, but not touching, the board so that you may observe and record the degree of front-to-back swaying.

_____

Do you think the equilibrium apparatus of the internal ear was operating equally well in all these tests?

_____

The proprioceptors? _____

Why was the observed degree of swaying greater when the eyes were closed?

_____

_____

What conclusions can you draw regarding the factors necessary for maintaining body equilibrium and balance?

_____

_____

### Role of Vision in Maintaining Equilibrium

To further demonstrate the role of vision in maintaining equilibrium, perform the following experiment. (Ask your lab partner to record observations and act as a "spotter.") Stand erect, with your eyes open. Raise your left foot approximately 30 cm off the floor, and hold it there for 1 minute.

Record the observations: _____

_____

_____

Rest for 1 or 2 minutes; and then repeat the experiment with the same foot raised but with your eyes closed. Record the observations:

_____

_____

# Special Senses: Hearing and Equilibrium

## Anatomy of the Ear

**1.** Select the terms from column B that apply to the column A descriptions. (Some terms are used more than once.)

**Column A**

_____, _____, _____, 1. structures composing the external ear

_____, _____, _____, 2. structures composing the internal ear

_____, _____, _____, 3. collectively called the ossicles

_____ 4. involved in equalizing the pressure in the middle ear with atmospheric pressure

_____ 5. vibrates at the same frequency as sound waves hitting it; transmits the vibrations to the ossicles

_____, _____ 6. contain receptors for the sense of balance

_____ 7. transmits the vibratory motion of the stirrup to the fluid in the scala vestibuli of the internal ear

_____ 8. acts as a pressure relief valve for the increased fluid pressure in the scala tympani; bulges into the tympanic cavity

_____ 9. passage between the throat and the tympanic cavity

_____ 10. fluid contained within the membranous labyrinth

_____ 11. fluid contained within the bony labyrinth and bathing the membranous labyrinth

**Column B**

a. auricle (pinna)

b. cochlea

c. endolymph

d. external acoustic meatus

e. incus (anvil)

f. malleus (hammer)

g. oval window

h. perilymph

i. pharyngotympanic (auditory) tube

j. round window

k. semicircular canals

l. stapes (stirrup)

m. tympanic membrane

n. vestibule

**2.** Identify all indicated structures and ear regions in the following diagram.

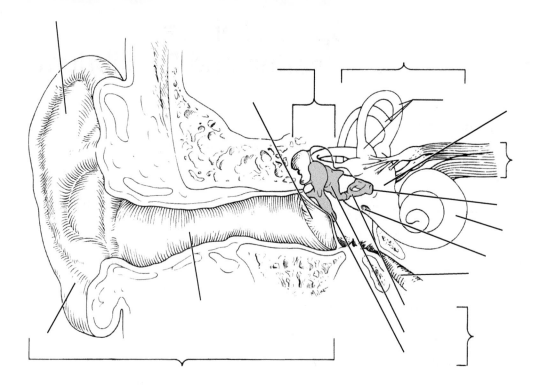

**3.** Match the membranous labyrinth structures listed in column B with the descriptive statements in column A. Some terms are used more than once.

**Column A**

_____, _____ 1. sacs found within the vestibule

_____ 2. contains the spiral organ

_____, _____ 3. sites of the maculae

_____ 4. positioned in all spatial planes

_____ 5. hair cells of spiral organ rest on this membrane

_____ 6. gelatinous membrane overlying the hair cells of the spiral organ

_____ 7. contains the crista ampullaris

_____, _____, _____, _____ 8. function in static equilibrium

_____, _____, _____, _____ 9. function in dynamic equilibrium

_____ 10. carries auditory information to the brain

_____ 11. gelatinous cap overlying hair cells of the crista ampullaris

_____ 12. grains of calcium carbonate in the maculae

**Column B**

a.  ampulla

b.  ampullary cupula

c.  basilar membrane

d.  cochlear duct

e.  cochlear nerve

f.  otoliths

g.  saccule

h.  semicircular ducts

i.  tectorial membrane

j.  utricle

k.  vestibular nerve

**4.** Sound waves hitting the tympanic membrane initiate its vibratory motion. Trace the pathway through which vibrations and fluid currents are transmitted to finally stimulate the hair cells in the spiral organ. (Name the appropriate ear structures in their correct sequence.)

Tympanic membrane → _____

_____

_____

**5.** Describe how sounds of different frequency (pitch) are differentiated in the cochlea. _____

_____

_____

_____

**6.** Explain the role of the endolymph of the semicircular canals in activating the receptors during angular motion.

_____

_____

_____

**7.** Explain the role of the otoliths in perception of static equilibrium (head position). _____

_____

_____

_____

# Laboratory Tests

**8.** Was the auditory acuity measurement made in Activity 4, the same or different for both ears?

_____ What factors might account for a difference in the acuity of the two ears?

_____

_____

**9.** During the sound localization experiment in Activity 4, note the position(s) in which the sound was least easily located.

How can this phenomenon be explained? _____

_____

**10.** In the frequency experiment in Activity 4, note which tuning fork was the most difficult to hear. _____

What conclusion can you draw? _____

_____

**11.** When the tuning fork handle was pressed to your forehead during the Weber test, where did the sound seem to originate?

_____

Where did it seem to originate when one ear was plugged with cotton? _____

How do sound waves reach the cochlea when conduction deafness is present? _____

_____

**12.** Indicate whether the following conditions relate to conduction deafness (C), sensorineural deafness (S), or both (C and S).

_____ 1. can result from the fusion of the ossicles

_____ 2. can result from a lesion on the cochlear nerve

_____ 3. sound heard in one ear but not in the other during bone and air conduction

_____ 4. can result from otitis media

_____ 5. can result from impacted cerumen or a perforated eardrum

_____ 6. can result from a blood clot in the primary auditory cortex

**13.** The Rinne test evaluates an individual's ability to hear sounds conducted by air or bone. Which is more indicative of normal

hearing? _____

**14.** Define _nystagmus._____

_____

Define _vertigo._ _____

_____

**15.** The Barany test investigated the effect that rotatory acceleration had on the semicircular canals. Explain _why_ the subject still

had the sensation of rotation immediately after being stopped. _____

_____

**16.** What is the usual reason for conducting the Romberg test? _____

_____

Was the degree of sway greater with the eyes open or closed? Why? _____

_____

**17.** Normal balance, or equilibrium, depends on input from a number of sensory receptors. Name them.

_____

**18.** What effect does alcohol consumption have on balance and equilibrium? Explain. _____

_____

## Photo Credits

**Credits are listed in order of appearance.**

4: Victor P. Eroschenko, Pearson Education. 6a–c: Richard Tauber, Pearson Education. 8: I. M. Hunter-Duvar, Department of Otolaryngology, The Hospital for Sick Children, Toronto.

## Illustration Credits

**All illustrations are by Imagineering STA Media Services, except for Review Sheet art and as noted below.**

1: Electronic Publishing Services, Inc./Precision Graphics. 2, 3, 7, 9: Electronic Publishing Services, Inc.

# General Sensation

## MATERIALS

- ☐ Compound microscope
- ☐ Immersion oil
- ☐ Prepared slides (longitudinal sections) of lamellar corpuscles, tactile corpuscles, tendon organs, and muscle spindles
- ☐ Calipers or esthesiometer
- ☐ Small metric rulers
- ☐ Fine-point, felt-tipped markers (black, red, and blue)
- ☐ Large beaker of ice water; chipped ice
- ☐ Hot water bath set at 45°C; laboratory thermometer
- ☐ Towel
- ☐ Four coins (nickels or quarters)
- ☐ Three large finger bowls or 1000-ml beakers

## OBJECTIVES

1. List the stimuli that activate general sensory receptors.
2. Define *exteroceptor, interoceptor,* and *proprioceptor.*
3. Recognize and describe the various types of general sensory receptors as studied in the laboratory, and list the function and locations of each.
4. Explain the tactile two-point discrimination test, and state its anatomical basis.
5. Define *tactile localization,* and describe how this ability varies in different areas of the body.
6. Define *adaptation,* and describe how this phenomenon can be demonstrated.
7. Discuss *negative afterimages* as they are related to temperature receptors.
8. Define *referred pain,* give an example for it, and define *projection.*

## PRE-LAB QUIZ

1. Name one of the special senses. _____
2. Sensory receptors can be classified according to their source of stimulus. _____ are found close to the body surface and react to stimuli in the external environment.
   - a. Exteroceptors
   - b. Interoceptors
   - c. Proprioceptors
   - d. Visceroceptors
3. Circle True or False. General sensory receptors are widely distributed throughout the body and respond to, among other things, touch, pain, stretch, and changes in position.
4. Tactile corpuscles respond to light touch. Where would you expect to find tactile corpuscles?
   - a. deep within the dermal layer of hairy skin
   - b. in the dermal papillae of hairless skin
   - c. in the hypodermis of hairless skin
   - d. in the uppermost portion of the epidermis
5. Lamellar corpuscles respond to
   - a. deep pressure and vibrations
   - b. light touch
   - c. pain and temperature
6. Circle True or False. A map of the sensory receptors for touch, heat, cold, and pain shows that they are not evenly distributed throughout the body.
7. Circle the correct underlined term. <u>Two-point threshold</u> / <u>Tactile localization</u> is the ability to determine where on the body the skin has been touched.
8. When a stimulus is applied for a prolonged period, the rate of receptor discharge slows, and conscious awareness of the stimulus declines. This phenomenon is known as
   - a. accommodation
   - b. adaptation
   - c. adjustment
   - d. discernment
9. Circle True or False. Pain is always perceived in the same area of the body that is receiving the stimulus.

*(Text continues on next page.)*

From Exercise 22 of *Human Anatomy & Physiology Laboratory Manual*, Main Version, Tenth Edition. Elaine N. Marieb, Susan J. Mitchell, Lori A. Smith. Copyright © 2014 by Pearson Education, Inc. All rights reserved.

10. You will test referred pain in this activity by immersing the subject's
    a. face in ice water to test the cranial nerve response
    b. elbow in ice water to test the ulnar nerve response
    c. hand in ice water to test the axillary nerve response
    d. leg in ice water to test the sciatic nerve response

People are very responsive to *stimuli,* which are changes within a person's environment. Hold a sizzling steak before them and their mouths water. Flash your high beams in their eyes on the highway and they cuss. Tickle them and they giggle. These and many other stimuli continually assault us.

The body's **sensory receptors** react to stimuli. The tiny sensory receptors of the **general senses** react to touch, pressure, pain, heat, cold, stretch, vibration, and changes in position and are distributed throughout the body. In contrast to these widely distributed *general sensory receptors,* the receptors of the special senses are large, complex *sense organs* or small, localized groups of receptors. The **special senses** include vision, hearing, equilibrium, smell, and taste.

Sensory receptors may be classified by the type of stimulus they detect (for example touch, pain, or temperature), their structure (free nerve endings or complex encapsulated structures), or their body location. **Exteroceptors** react to stimuli in the external environment, and typically they are found close to the body surface. Exteroceptors include the simple cutaneous receptors in the skin and the highly specialized receptor structures of the special senses (the vision apparatus of the eye, and the hearing and equilibrium receptors of the ear, for example). **Interoceptors** or *visceroceptors* respond to stimuli arising within the body. Interoceptors are found in the internal visceral organs and include stretch receptors (in walls of hollow organs), chemoreceptors, and others. **Proprioceptors,** like interoceptors, respond to internal stimuli but are restricted to skeletal muscles, tendons, joints, ligaments, and connective tissue coverings of bones and muscles. They provide information about body movements and position by monitoring the degree of stretch of those structures.

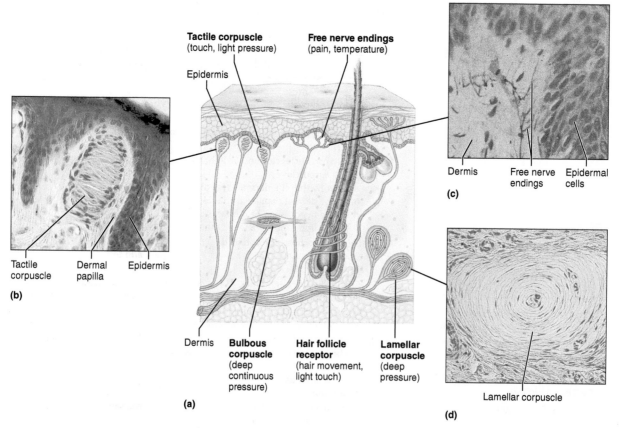

**Figure 1 Examples of cutaneous receptors.** Drawing **(a)** and photomicrographs **(b–d). (a)** Free nerve endings, hair follicle receptor, tactile corpuscles, lamellar corpuscles, and bulbous corpuscle. Tactile (Merkel) discs are not illustrated. **(b)** Tactile corpuscle in a dermal papilla (300×). **(c)** Free nerve endings at dermal-epidermal junction (330×). **(d)** Cross section of a lamellar corpuscle in the dermis (220×).

The receptors of the special sense organs are complex and deserve considerable study. Only the anatomically simpler **general sensory receptors**—cutaneous receptors and proprioceptors—will be studied in this exercise.

# Structure of General Sensory Receptors

You cannot become aware of changes in the environment unless your sensory neurons and their receptors are operating properly. Sensory receptors are either modified dendritic endings or specialized cells associated with the dendrites that are sensitive to specific environmental stimuli. They react to such stimuli by initiating a nerve impulse. Several histologically distinct types of general sensory receptors have been identified in the skin. (Their structures are depicted in **Figure 1**.)

Many references link receptor types to specific stimuli; however, one type of receptor can respond to several kinds of stimuli. Likewise, several different types of receptors can respond to similar stimuli. Certainly, intense stimulation of any of them is always interpreted as pain.

The least specialized of the cutaneous receptors are the **nonencapsulated (free) nerve endings** of sensory neurons (Figure 1c), which respond chiefly to pain and temperature. The pain receptors are widespread in the skin and make up a sizable portion of the visceral interoceptors. Certain free nerve endings associate with specific epidermal cells to form **tactile (Merkel) discs,** or entwine in hair follicles to form **hair follicle receptors.** Both tactile discs and hair follicle receptors function as light touch receptors.

The other cutaneous receptors are a bit more complex, and the nerve endings are **encapsulated** by connective tissue capsules. **Tactile corpuscles** respond to light touch. They are located in the dermal papillae of hairless (glabrous) skin only (Figure 1b). **Bulbous corpuscles** appear to respond to deep pressure and stretch stimuli. **Lamellar corpuscles** are anatomically more distinctive than bulbous corpuscles and lie deepest in the dermis (Figure 1d). Lamellar corpuscles respond only when deep pressure is first applied. They are best suited to monitor high-frequency vibrations.

**ACTIVITY 1**

## Studying the Structure of Selected Sensory Receptors

1. Obtain a compound microscope and histologic slides of lamellar and tactile corpuscles. Locate, under low power, a tactile corpuscle in the dermal layer of the skin. As mentioned above, these are usually found in the dermal papillae. Then switch to the oil immersion lens for a detailed study. Notice that the free nerve fibers within the capsule are aligned parallel to the skin surface. Compare your observations to the photomicrograph of a tactile corpuscle (Figure 1b).

2. Next observe a lamellar corpuscle located much deeper in the dermis. Try to identify the slender naked nerve ending in the center of the receptor and the heavy capsule of connective tissue surrounding it (which looks rather like an onion cut lengthwise). Also, notice how much larger the lamellar corpuscles are than the tactile corpuscles. Compare your observations to the photomicrograph of a lamellar corpuscle (Figure 1d).

3. Obtain slides of muscle spindles and tendon organs, the two major types of proprioceptors (Figure 2). In the slide of **muscle spindles,** note that minute extensions

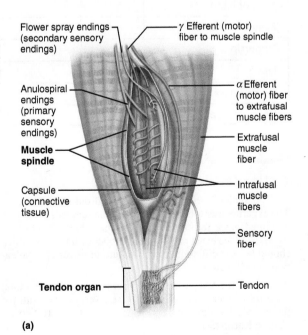

(a)

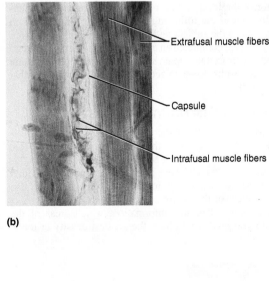

(b)

**Figure 2 Proprioceptors. (a)** Diagram of a muscle spindle and tendon organ. Myelin has been omitted from all nerve fibers for clarity. **(b)** Photomicrograph of a muscle spindle (80×).

of the nerve endings of the sensory neurons coil around specialized slender skeletal muscle cells called **intrafusal fibers.** The **tendon organs** are composed of nerve endings that ramify through the tendon tissue close to the attachment between muscle and tendon. Stretching of muscles or tendons excites these receptors, which then transmit impulses that ultimately reach the cerebellum for interpretation. Compare your observations to the proprioceptor art (Figure 2). ■

# Receptor Physiology

Sensory receptors act as **transducers,** changing environmental *stimuli* into nerve impulses that are relayed to the CNS. *Sensation* (awareness of the stimulus) and *perception* (interpretation of the meaning of the stimulus) occur in the brain. Nerve impulses from cutaneous receptors are relayed to the primary somatosensory cortex, where stimuli from different body regions form a body map. Therefore, each location on the body is represented by a specific cortical area. It is this cortical organization that allows us to know exactly where a sensation comes from. Further interpretation of the sensory information occurs in the somatosensory association cortex.

Four qualities of cutaneous sensations have traditionally been recognized: tactile (touch), heat, cold, and pain. Mapping these sensations on the skin has revealed that the sensory receptors for these qualities are not distributed uniformly. Instead, they have discrete locations and are characterized by clustering at certain points—**punctate distribution.**

The simple pain receptors, extremely important in protecting the body, are the most numerous. Touch receptors cluster where greater sensitivity is desirable, as on the hands and face. It may be surprising to learn that rather large areas of the skin are quite insensitive to touch because of a relative lack of touch receptors.

There are several simple experiments you can conduct to investigate the location and physiology of cutaneous receptors. In each of the following activities, work in pairs with one person as the subject and the other as the experimenter. After you have completed an experiment, switch roles and go through the procedures again so that all class members obtain individual results. Keep an accurate account of each test that you perform.

## Two-Point Discrimination Test

As noted, the density of the touch receptors varies significantly in different areas of the body. In general, areas that have the greatest density of tactile receptors have a heightened ability to "feel." These areas correspond to areas that receive the greatest motor innervation; thus they are also typically areas of fine motor control.

On the basis of this information, which areas of the body do you *predict* will have the greatest density of touch receptors?

### ACTIVITY 2

### Determining the Two-Point Threshold

1. Using calipers or an esthesiometer and a metric ruler, test the ability of the subject to differentiate two distinct sensations when the skin is touched simultaneously at two points. Beginning with the face, start with the caliper arms completely together. Gradually increase the distance between the arms, testing the subject's skin after each adjustment. Continue with this testing procedure until the subject reports that *two points* of contact can be felt. This measurement, the smallest distance at which two points of contact can be felt, is the **two-point threshold.**

2. Repeat this procedure on the back and palm of the hand, fingertips, lips, back of the neck, and ventral forearm. Record your results in the chart **Determining Two-Point Threshold.**

3. Which area has the smallest two-point threshold?

_____ ■

## Tactile Localization

**Tactile localization** is the ability to determine which portion of the skin has been touched. The tactile receptor field of the body periphery has a corresponding "touch" field in the brain's primary somatosensory cortex. Some body areas are well represented with touch receptors, allowing tactile stimuli to be localized with great accuracy, but touch-receptor density in other body areas allows only crude discrimination.

| Determining Two-Point Threshold | |
|---|---|
| **Body area tested** | **Two-point threshold (mm)** |
| Face | |
| Back of hand | |
| Palm of hand | |
| Fingertip | |
| Lips | |
| Back of neck | |
| Ventral forearm | |

### ACTIVITY 3

### Testing Tactile Localization

1. The subject's eyes should be closed during the testing. The experimenter touches the palm of the subject's hand with a pointed black felt-tipped marker. The subject should then try to touch the exact point with his or her own marker, which should be of a different color. Measure the error of localization in millimeters.

2. Repeat the test in the same spot twice more, recording the error of localization for each test. Average the results of the three determinations, and record it in the chart **Testing Tactile Localization.**

| Testing Tactile Localization | |
|---|---|
| Body area tested | Average error (mm) |
| Palm of hand | |
| Fingertip | |
| Ventral forearm | |
| Back of hand | |
| Back of neck | |

Does the ability to localize the stimulus improve the second

time? _____ The third time? _____

Explain. _____

_____

3. Repeat the preceding procedure on a fingertip, the ventral forearm, the back of a hand, and the back of the neck. Record the averaged results in the chart above.

4. Which area has the smallest error of localization?

_____ ▬

# Adaptation of Sensory Receptors

The number of impulses transmitted by sensory receptors often changes both with the intensity of the stimulus and with the length of time the stimulus is applied. In many cases, when a stimulus is applied for a prolonged period, the rate of receptor discharge slows and conscious awareness of the stimulus declines or is lost until some type of stimulus change occurs. This phenomenon is referred to as **adaptation.** The touch receptors adapt particularly rapidly, which is highly desirable. Who, for instance, would want to be continually aware of the pressure of clothing on their skin? The simple experiments to be conducted next allow you to investigate the phenomenon of adaptation.

### ACTIVITY 4

## Demonstrating Adaptation of Touch Receptors

1. The subject's eyes should be closed. Obtain four coins. Place one coin on the anterior surface of the subject's forearm, and determine how long the sensation persists for the subject. Duration of the sensation:

_____ sec

2. Repeat the test, placing the coin at a different forearm location. How long does the sensation persist at the second location?

_____ sec

3. After awareness of the sensation has been lost at the second site, stack three more coins atop the first one.

Does the pressure sensation return? _____

If so, for how long is the subject aware of the pressure in this instance?

_____ sec

Are the same receptors being stimulated when the four coins,

rather than the one coin, are used? _____

Explain. _____

_____

4. To further illustrate the adaptation of touch receptors—in this case, the hair follicle receptors—gently and slowly bend one hair shaft with a pen or pencil until it springs back (away from the pencil) to its original position. Is the tactile sensation greater when the hair is being slowly bent or when it springs back?

_____

Why is the adaptation of the touch receptors in the hair follicles particularly important to a woman who wears her hair in a ponytail? If the answer is not immediately apparent, consider the opposite phenomenon: what would happen, in terms of sensory input from her hair follicles, if these receptors did not exhibit adaptation?

_____

_____ ▬

### ACTIVITY 5

## Demonstrating Adaptation of Temperature Receptors

Adaptation of the temperature receptors can be tested using some very unsophisticated methods.

1. Obtain three large finger bowls or 1000-ml beakers and fill the first with 45°C water. Have the subject immerse her or his left hand in the water and report the sensation. Keep the left hand immersed for 1 minute and then also immerse the right hand in the same bowl.

What is the sensation of the left hand when it is first immersed?

_____

What is the sensation of the left hand after 1 minute as compared to the sensation in the right hand just immersed?

_____

Had adaptation occurred in the left hand? _____

2. Rinse both hands in tap water, dry them, and wait 5 minutes before conducting the next test. Just before beginning the test, refill the finger bowl with fresh 45°C water, fill

a second with ice water, and fill a third with water at room temperature.

3. Place the *left* hand in the ice water and the *right* hand in the 45°C water. What is the sensation in each hand after 2 minutes as compared to the sensation perceived when the hands were first immersed?

_____

_____

Which hand seemed to adapt more quickly?

_____

4. After reporting these observations, the subject should then place both hands simultaneously into the finger bowl containing the water at room temperature. Record the sensa-

tion in the left hand: _____

The right hand:_____

The sensations that the subject experiences when both hands were put into room-temperature water are called **negative afterimages.** They are explained by the fact that sensations of heat and cold depend on the speed of heat loss or gain by the skin and differences in the temperature gradient. ▬

## Referred Pain

Experiments on pain receptor localization and adaptation are commonly conducted in the laboratory. However, there are certain problems with such experiments. Pain receptors are densely distributed in the skin, and they adapt very little, if at all. This lack of adaptability is due to the protective function of the receptors. The sensation of pain often indicates tissue damage or trauma to body structures. Thus no attempt will be made in this exercise to localize the pain receptors or to prove their nonadaptability, since both would cause needless discomfort to those of you acting as subjects and would not add any additional insight.

However, the phenomenon of referred pain is easily demonstrated in the laboratory, and such experiments provide information that may be useful in explaining common examples of this phenomenon. **Referred pain** is a sensory experience in which pain is perceived as arising in one area of the body when in fact another, often quite remote area, is receiving the painful stimulus. Thus the pain is said to be "referred" to a different area. The phenomenon of **projection,** the process by which the brain refers sensations to their *usual* point of stimulation, provides the simplest explanation of such experiences. Many of us have experienced referred pain as a radiating pain in the forehead, sometimes referred to as "brain freeze," after quickly swallowing an ice-cold drink. Referred pain is important in many types of clinical diagnosis because damage to many visceral organs results in this phenomenon. For example, inadequate oxygenation of the heart muscle often results in pain being referred to the chest wall and left shoulder *(angina pectoris)*, and the reflux of gastric juice into the esophagus causes a sensation of intense discomfort in the thorax referred to as *heartburn*.

### ACTIVITY 6

## Demonstrating the Phenomenon of Referred Pain

Immerse the subject's elbow in a finger bowl containing ice water. In the chart **Demonstrating Referred Pain,** record the quality (such as discomfort, tingling, or pain) and the quality progression of the sensations he or she reports for the intervals indicated. The elbow should be removed from ice water after the 2-minute reading. The last recording is to occur 3 minutes after removal of the subject's elbow from the ice water.

Also record the location of the perceived sensations. The ulnar nerve, which serves the medial third of the hand, is involved in the phenomenon of referred pain experienced during this test. How does the localization of this referred pain correspond to the areas served by the ulnar nerve?

_____ ▬

| Demonstrating Referred Pain | | |
|---|---|---|
| **Time of observation** | **Quality of sensation** | **Localization of sensation** |
| On immersion | | |
| After 1 min | | |
| After 2 min | | |
| 3 min after removal | | |

## Odd Receptor Out

Each group below contains four receptors. One of the listed receptors does not share a characteristic with the other three. Circle the receptor that doesn't belong with the others and explain why it is singled out. What characteristic is it missing? Remember to consider both structural and functional similarities. Sometimes there may be multiple reasons why the receptor doesn't belong with the others.

| 1. Which is the "odd receptor"? | Why it is the odd one out? |
|---|---|
| Bulbous corpuscle<br>Lamellar corpuscle<br>Tendon organ<br>Tactile corpuscle | |
| **2. Which is the "odd receptor"?** | **Why it is the odd one out?** |
| Tendon organ<br>Muscle spindle<br>Hair follicle receptor<br>Free nerve endings | |

Name ____________________

Lab Time/Date ____________________

REVIEW SHEET

# General Sensation

## Structure of General Sensory Receptors

**1.** Differentiate between interoceptors and exteroceptors relative to location and stimulus source.

interoceptor: ____________________

exteroceptor: ____________________

**2.** A number of activities and sensations are listed in the chart below. For each, check whether the receptors would be exteroceptors or interoceptors; and then name the specific receptor types. (Because visceral receptors were not described in detail in this exercise, you need only indicate that the receptor is a visceral receptor if it falls into that category.)

| Activity or sensation | Exteroceptor | Interoceptor | Specific receptor type |
|---|---|---|---|
| Backing into a sun-heated iron railing | | | |
| Someone steps on your foot | | | |
| Reading a book | | | |
| Leaning on your elbows | | | |
| Doing sit-ups | | | |
| The "too full" sensation | | | |
| Seasickness | | | |

## Receptor Physiology

**3.** Explain how the sensory receptors act as transducers. ____________________

____________________

**4.** Define *stimulus*. ____________________

**5.** What was demonstrated by the two-point discrimination test? ____________________

____________________

How well did your results correspond to your predictions? ____________________

____________________

What is the relationship between the accuracy of the subject's tactile localization and the results of the two-point discrimination test? ____________________

**6.** Define *punctate distribution.*_____

_____

**7.** Several questions regarding general sensation are posed below. Answer each by placing your response in the appropriately numbered blanks to the right.

    1. Which cutaneous receptors are the most numerous?            1. _____

    2–3. Which two body areas tested were most sensitive to touch?    2-3. _____

    4–5. Which two body areas tested were least sensitive to touch?    4-5. _____

    6–8. Where would referred pain appear if the following organs were receiving painful stimuli: (6) gallbladder, (7) kidneys, and (8) appendix? (Use your text if necessary.)    6. _____

        7. _____

    9. Where was referred pain felt when the elbow was immersed in ice water during the laboratory experiment?    8. _____

        9. _____

    10. What region of the cerebrum interprets the kind and intensity of stimuli that cause cutaneous sensations?    10. _____

**8.** Define *adaptation of sensory receptors.*_____

_____

**9.** Why is it advantageous to have pain receptors that are sensitive to all vigorous stimuli, whether heat, cold, or pressure?

_____

Why is the nonadaptability of pain receptors important?_____

_____

**10.** Imagine yourself without any cutaneous sense organs. Why might this be very dangerous?_____

_____

_____

**11.** Define *referred pain.*_____

_____

What is the probable explanation for referred pain? (Consult your text or an appropriate reference if necessary.)

_____

_____

## Photo Credits

**Credits are listed in order of appearance.**

1b: Lynn McCutchen. 1c,d, 2b: Victor P. Eroschenko, Pearson Education.

# Dissection and Identification of Cat Muscles

## MATERIALS

- ☐ Disposable gloves or protective skin cream
- ☐ Preserved and injected cat (one for every two to four students)
- ☐ Dissecting instruments and tray
- ☐ Name tag and large plastic bag
- ☐ Paper towels
- ☐ Embalming fluid
- ☐ Organic debris container

## OBJECTIVES

1. Name and locate muscles on a dissected cat.
2. Recognize similarities and differences between human and cat musculature.

The skeletal muscles of all mammals are named in a similar fashion. However, some muscles that are separate in lower animals are fused in humans, and some muscles present in lower animals are lacking in humans. This exercise involves dissection of the cat musculature to enhance your knowledge of the human muscular system. Since the aim is to become familiar with the muscles of the human body, you should pay particular attention to the similarities between cat and human muscles. However, pertinent differences will be pointed out as you encounter them. Refer to a discussion of the anatomy of the human muscular system as you work.

Wear a lab coat or apron over your clothes when dissecting to prevent staining your clothes with embalming fluid. Also, read through this entire exercise before coming to the lab.

### ACTIVITY 1

### Preparing the Cat for Dissection

The preserved laboratory animals purchased for dissection have been embalmed with a solution that prevents deterioration of the tissues. The animals are generally delivered in plastic bags that contain a small amount of the embalming fluid. _Do not dispose of this fluid_ when you remove the cat; the fluid prevents the cat from drying out. It is very important to keep the cat's tissues moist because you will probably use the same cat from now until the end of the course. The embalming fluid may cause your eyes to smart and may dry your skin, but these small irritants are preferable to working with a cat that has become hard and odoriferous because of bacterial action.

1. Don disposable gloves and then obtain a cat, dissecting tray, dissecting instruments, and a name tag. Using a pencil, mark the name tag with the names of the members of your group and set it aside. The name tag will be attached to the plastic bag at the end of the dissection so that you may identify your animal in subsequent laboratory sessions.

2. To begin removing the skin, place the cat ventral side down on the dissecting tray. Cutting away from yourself with a newly bladed scalpel, make a short, shallow incision in the midline of the neck, just to penetrate the skin. From this point on, use scissors. Continue to cut the length of the back to the sacrolumbar region, stopping at the tail (Figure 1).

3. From the dorsal surface of the tail region, continue the incision around the tail, encircling the anus and genital organs. The skin will not be removed from this region.

4. Before you begin to remove the skin, check with your instructor. He or she may want you to skin only the right or left side of the cat. Beginning again at the

From Dissection Exercise 1 of _Human Anatomy & Physiology Laboratory Manual,_ Cat Version, Eleventh Edition. Elaine N. Marieb, Susan J. Mitchell, Lori A. Smith. Copyright © 2014 by Pearson Education, Inc. All rights reserved.

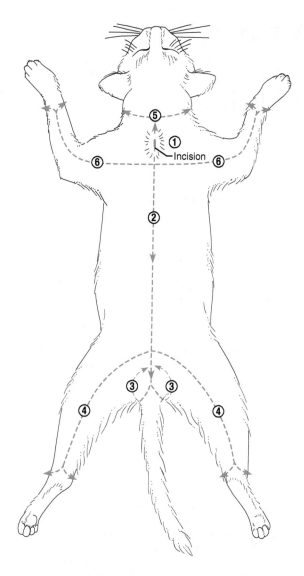

**Figure 1 Incisions to be made in skinning a cat.** Numbers indicate sequence.

These are the cutaneous nerves that serve the skin. You will also see (particularly as you approach the ventral surface) that a thin layer of muscle fibers remains adhered to the skin. This is the **cutaneous maximus** muscle, which enables the cat to move its skin rather like our facial muscles allow us to express emotion. Where the cutaneous maximus fibers cling to those of the deeper muscles, they should be carefully cut free. Along the ventral surface of the trunk, notice the two lines of nipples associated with the mammary glands. These are more prominent in females, especially if they are pregnant or were recently lactating.

8. You will notice as you start to free the skin in the neck that it is more difficult to remove. Take extra care and time in this area. The large flat **platysma** muscle in the ventral neck region (a skin muscle like the cutaneous maximus) will remain attached to the skin. The skin will not be removed from the head since the cat's muscles are not sufficiently similar to human head muscles to merit study.

9. Complete the skinning process by freeing the skin from the forelimbs, the lower torso, and the hindlimbs in the same manner. The skin may be more difficult to remove as you approach the paws so you may need to take additional time in these areas to avoid damaging the underlying muscles and tendons. *Do not discard the skin.*

10. Inspect your skinned cat. Notice that it is difficult to see any cleavage lines between the muscles because of the overlying connective tissue, which is white or yellow. If time allows, carefully remove as much of the fat and fascia from the surface of the muscles as possible, using forceps or your fingers. The muscles, when exposed, look grainy or threadlike and are light brown. If this clearing process is done carefully and thoroughly, you will be ready to begin your identification of the superficial muscles.

11. If the muscle dissection exercises are to be done at a later laboratory session, follow the cleanup instructions noted in the box below. *Prepare your cat for storage in this way every time the cat is used.* ▰

dorsal tail region, make an incision through the skin down each hind leg to be skinned nearly to the ankle. Continue the cut completely around the ankle.

5. Return to the neck. Cut the skin around the circumference of the neck.

6. Cut down each foreleg to be skinned to the wrist. Completely cut through the skin around the wrist (Figure 1).

7. Now free the skin from the loose connective tissue (superficial fascia) that binds it to the underlying structures. With one hand, grasp the skin on one side of the midline dorsal incision. Then, using your fingers or a blunt probe, break through the "cottony" connective tissue fibers to release the skin from the muscle beneath. Work toward the ventral surface and then toward the neck. As you pull the skin from the body, you should see small, white, cordlike structures extending from the skin to the muscles at fairly regular intervals.

---

## Preparing the Dissection Animal for Storage

1. To prevent the internal organs from drying out, dampen a layer of folded paper towels with embalming fluid, and wrap them snugly around the animal's torso. (Do not use *water-soaked* paper towels, which encourages mold growth.) Make sure the dissected areas are completely enveloped.

2. Return the animal's skin flaps to their normal position over the ventral cavity body organs.

3. Place the animal in a plastic storage bag. Add more embalming fluid if necessary, press out excess air, and securely close the bag with a rubber band or twine.

4. Make sure your name tag is securely attached, and place the animal in the designated storage container.

5. Clean all dissecting equipment with soapy water, rinse, and dry it for return to the storage area. Wash down the lab bench and properly dispose of organic debris and your gloves before leaving the laboratory.

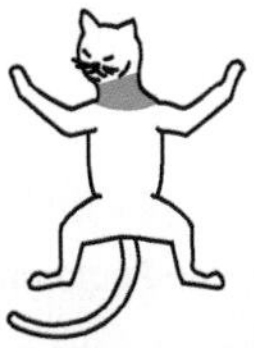

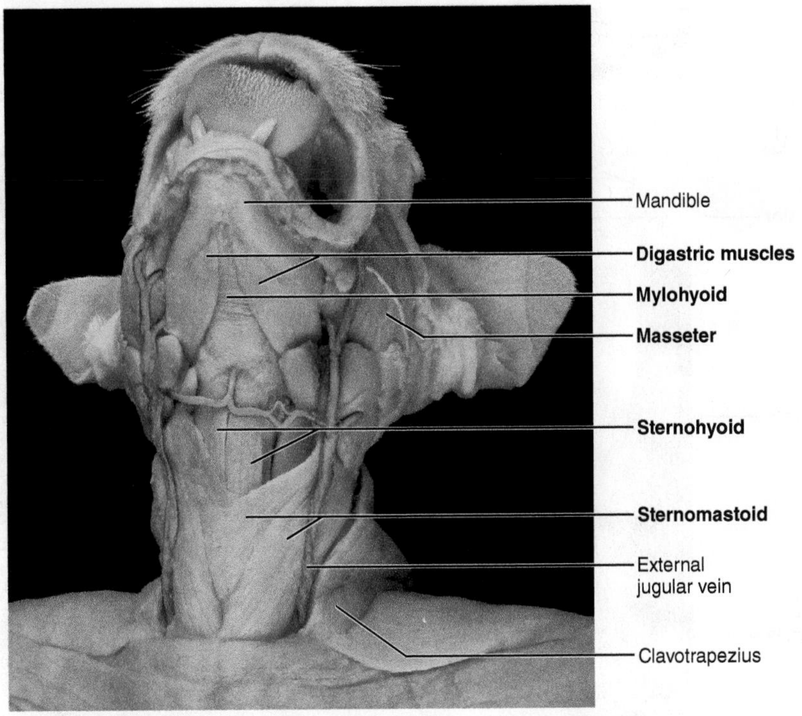
Mandible
Digastric muscles
Mylohyoid
Masseter
Sternohyoid
Sternomastoid
External jugular vein
Clavotrapezius

**Figure 2 Superficial muscles of the anterior neck of the cat.**

ACTIVITY 2

## Dissecting Neck and Trunk Muscles

The proper dissection of muscles involves careful separation of one muscle from another and transection of superficial muscles in order to study those lying deeper. In general, when directions are given to transect a muscle, it first should be completely freed from all adhering connective tissue and *then* cut through the belly (fleshiest part) of the muscle about halfway between its origin and insertion points. *Use caution when working around points of muscle origin or insertion, and do not remove the fascia associated with such attachments.*

As a rule, all the fibers of one muscle are held together by a connective tissue sheath (epimysium) and run in the same general direction. Before you begin dissection, observe your skinned cat. If you look carefully, you can see changes in the direction of the muscle fibers, which will help you to locate the muscle borders. Pulling in slightly different directions on two adjacent muscles will usually expose subtle white lines created by the connective tissue surrounding the muscles and allow you to find the normal cleavage line between them. After you have identified cleavage lines, *use a blunt probe* to break the connective tissue between muscles and to separate them. If the muscles separate as clean, distinct bundles, your procedure is probably correct. If they appear ragged or chewed up, you are probably tearing a muscle apart rather than separating it from adjacent muscles. Only the muscles that are most easily identified and separated out will be identified in this exercise because of time considerations.

### *Anterior Neck Muscles*

1. Examine the anterior neck surface of the cat and identify the following superficial neck muscles. The *platysma* belongs in this group but was probably removed during the skinning process. (Refer to Figure 2 as you work.) The **sternomastoid** muscle and the more lateral and deeper **cleidomastoid** muscle (not visible in Figure 2) are joined in humans to form the sternocleidomastoid. The large external jugular veins, which drain the head, should be obvious crossing the anterior aspect of these muscles. The **mylohyoid** muscle parallels the bottom aspect of the chin, and the **digastric** muscles form a V over the mylohyoid muscle. Although it is not one of the neck muscles, you can now identify the fleshy **masseter** muscle, which flanks the digastric muscle laterally. Finally, the **sternohyoid** is a narrow muscle between the mylohyoid (superiorly) and the inferior sternomastoid.

2. The deeper muscles of the anterior neck of the cat are small and straplike and hardly worth the effort of dissection. However, one of these deeper muscles can be seen with a minimum of extra effort. Transect the sternomastoid and sternohyoid muscles approximately at midbelly. Reflect the cut ends to reveal the bandlike **sternothyroid** muscle (not visible in Figure 2), which runs along the anterior surface of the throat just deep and lateral to the sternohyoid muscle. The cleidomastoid muscle, which lies deep to the sternomastoid, is also more easily identified now.

### *Superficial Chest Muscles*

In the cat, the chest or pectoral muscles adduct the arm, just as they do in humans. However, humans have only two pectoral muscles, and cats have four—the pectoralis major,

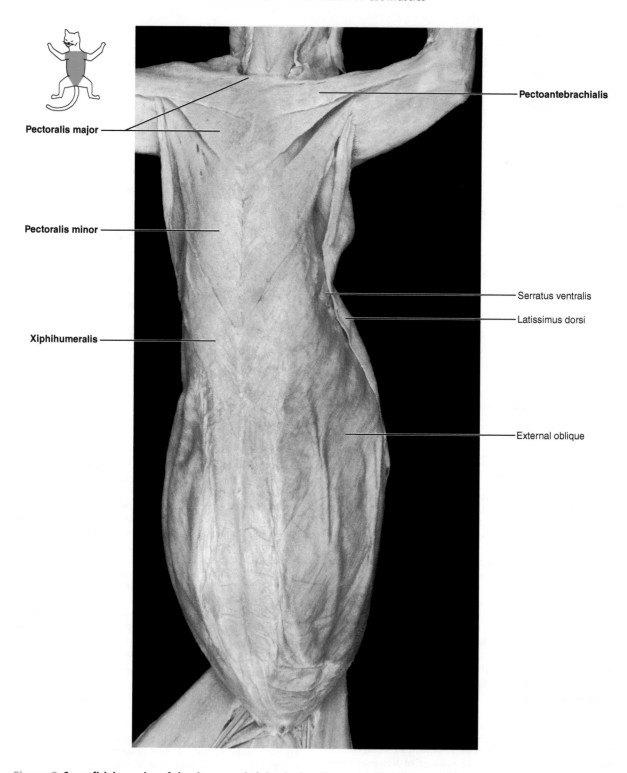

**Pectoantebrachialis**

**Pectoralis major**

**Pectoralis minor**

Serratus ventralis

Latissimus dorsi

**Xiphihumeralis**

External oblique

**Figure 3 Superficial muscles of the thorax and abdominal wall, ventral view.** Note location of the latissimus dorsi.

pectoralis minor, xiphihumeralis, and pectoantebrachialis (**Figure 3**). However, because of their relatively great degree of fusion, the cat's pectoral muscles appear to be a single muscle. The pectoral muscles are rather difficult to dissect and identify, as they do not separate from one another easily.

The **pectoralis major** is 5 to 8 cm (2 to 3 inches) wide and can be seen arising on the manubrium, just inferior to the sternomastoid muscle of the neck, and running to the humerus. Its fibers run at right angles to the longitudinal axis of the cat's body.

The **pectoralis minor** lies beneath the pectoralis major and extends posterior to it on the abdominal surface. It originates on the sternum and inserts on the humerus. Its fibers run obliquely to the long axis of the body, which helps to distinguish it from the pectoralis major. Contrary to what its name implies, the pectoralis minor is a larger and thicker muscle than the pectoralis major.

The **xiphihumeralis** can be distinguished from the posterior edge of the pectoralis minor only by virtue of the fact that its origin is lower—on the xiphoid process of the sternum. Its fibers run parallel to and are fused with those of the pectoralis minor.

The **pectoantebrachialis** is a thin, straplike muscle, about 1.3 cm (½ inch) wide, lying over the pectoralis major. Notice that the pectoralis major is visible both anterior and posterior to the borders of the pectoantebrachialis. It originates from the manubrium, passes laterally over the pectoralis major, and merges with the muscles of the forelimb approximately halfway down the humerus. It has no homologue in humans.

Identify, free, and trace out the origin and insertion of the cat's chest muscles (refer to Figure 3).

## Muscles of the Abdominal Wall

The superficial trunk muscles include those of the abdominal wall (Figure 3 and **Figure 4**). Cat musculature in this area is quite similar in function to that of humans.

1. Complete the dissection of the more superficial anterior trunk muscles of the cat by identifying the origins and insertions of the muscles of the abdominal wall. Work carefully here. These muscles are very thin, and it is easy to miss their boundaries. Begin with the **rectus abdominis,** a long band of muscle approximately 2.5 cm (1 inch) wide running immediately lateral to the midline of the body on the abdominal surface. Humans have four transverse *tendinous intersections* in the rectus abdominis, but they are absent or difficult to identify in the cat. Identify the **linea alba,** the longitudinal band of connective tissue that separates the rectus abdominis muscles. Note the relationship of the rectus abdominis to the other abdominal muscles and their fascia.

2. The **external oblique** is a sheet of muscle immediately beside the rectus abdominis (Figure 4). Carefully free and then transect the external oblique to reveal the anterior attachment of the rectus abdominis. Reflect the external oblique; observe the deeper **internal oblique** muscle. Notice which way the fibers run.

How does the fiber direction of the internal oblique compare to that of the external oblique?

_____

_____

3. Free and then transect the internal oblique muscle to reveal the fibers of the **transversus abdominis,** whose fibers run transversely across the abdomen.

## Superficial Muscles of the Shoulder and the Dorsal Trunk and Neck

Dissect the superficial muscles of the dorsal surface of the trunk (refer to **Figure 5**).

1. Turn your cat on its ventral surface, and start your observations with the **trapezius group.** Humans have a single large *trapezius muscle,* but the cat has three separate muscles—the clavotrapezius, acromiotrapezius, and spinotrapezius—that together perform a similar function. The prefix in each case (clavo-, acromio-, and spino-) reveals the muscle's site of insertion. The **clavotrapezius,** the most anterior muscle of the group, is homologous to that part of the human trapezius that inserts into the clavicle. Slip a probe under this muscle and follow it to its apparent origin.

Where does the clavotrapezius appear to originate?

_____

Is this similar to its origin in humans? _____

The fibers of the clavotrapezius are continuous posteriorly with those of the clavicular part of the cat's deltoid muscle (clavodeltoid), and the two muscles work together to flex the humerus. Release the clavotrapezius muscle from adjoining muscles. The **acromiotrapezius** is a large, thin, nearly square muscle easily identified by its aponeurosis, which passes over the vertebral border of the scapula. It originates from the cervical and $T_1$ vertebrae and inserts into the scapular spine. The triangular **spinotrapezius** runs from the thoracic vertebrae to the scapular spine. This is the most posterior of the trapezius muscles in the cat. Now that you know where they are located, pull on the three trapezius muscles to mimic their action.

Do the trapezius muscles appear to have the same functions in cats as in humans?

_____

2. The **levator scapulae ventralis,** a flat, straplike muscle, can be located in the triangle created by the division of the fibers of the clavotrapezius and acromiotrapezius. Its anterior fibers run underneath the clavotrapezius from its origin at the base of the skull (occipital bone), and it inserts on the vertebral border of the scapula. In the cat it helps to hold the upper edges of the scapulae together and draws them toward the head.

What is the function of the levator scapulae in humans?

_____

_____

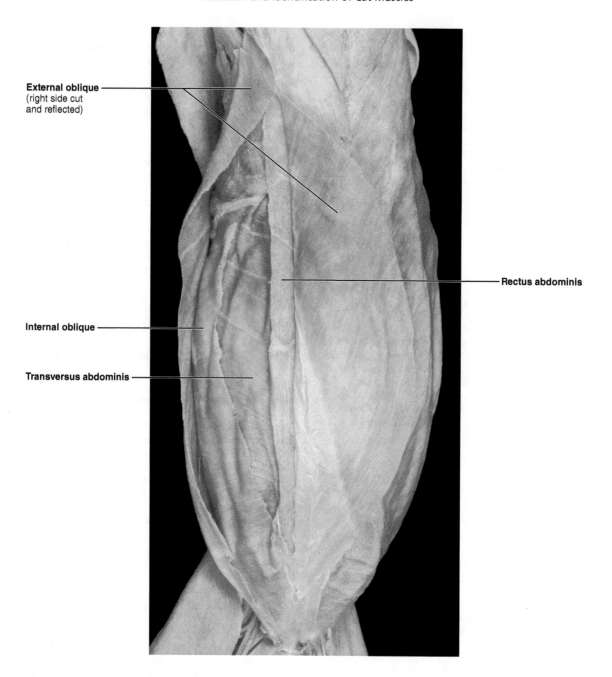

**External oblique**
(right side cut
and reflected)

**Rectus abdominis**

**Internal oblique**

**Transversus abdominis**

**Figure 4 Muscles of the abdominal wall of the cat.**

3. The **deltoid group:** Like the trapezius, the human *deltoid muscle* is represented by three separate muscles in the cat—the clavodeltoid, acromiodeltoid, and spinodeltoid. The **clavodeltoid** (also called the *clavobrachialis*), the most superficial muscle of the shoulder, is a continuation of the clavotrapezius below the clavicle, which is this muscle's point of origin (Figure 5). Follow its course down the forelimb to the point where it merges along a white line with the pectoantebrachialis. Separate it from the pectoantebrachialis, and then transect it and pull it back.

Where does the clavodeltoid insert? _____

What do you think the function of this muscle is?

_____

_____

The **acromiodeltoid** lies posterior to the clavodeltoid and runs over the top of the shoulder. This small triangular muscle originates on the acromion of the scapula. It inserts

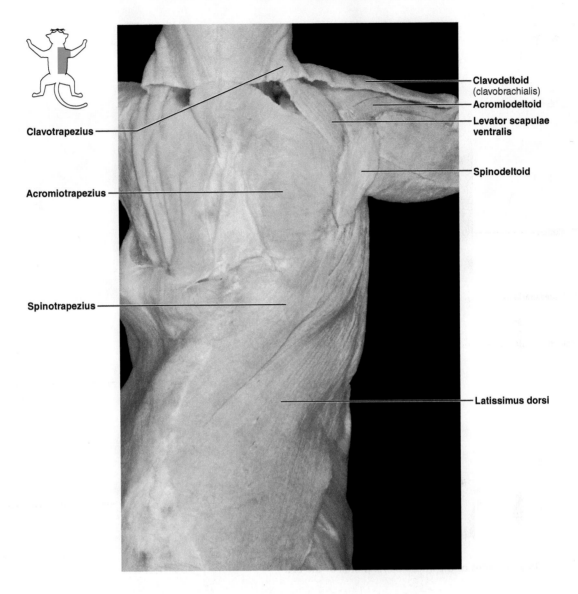

Clavotrapezius

Acromiotrapezius

Spinotrapezius

Clavodeltoid
(clavobrachialis)

Acromiodeltoid

Levator scapulae
ventralis

Spinodeltoid

Latissimus dorsi

**Figure 5 Superficial muscles of the anterodorsal aspect of the shoulder, trunk, and neck of the cat.**

into the spinodeltoid (a muscle of similar size) posterior to it. The **spinodeltoid** is covered with fascia near the anterior end of the scapula. Its tendon extends under the acromiodeltoid muscle and inserts on the humerus. Notice that its fibers run obliquely to those of the acromiodeltoid. Like the human deltoid muscle, the acromiodeltoid and spinodeltoid muscles in the cat abduct and rotate the humerus.

4.   The **latissimus dorsi** is a large, thick, flat muscle covering most of the lateral surface of the posterior trunk; it extends and adducts the arm. Its anterior edge is covered by the spinotrapezius and may appear ragged because it has been cut off from the cutaneous maximus muscle attached to the skin. As in humans, it inserts into the humerus. But before inserting, its fibers merge with the fibers of many other muscles, among them the xiphihumeralis of the pectoralis group.

## Deep Muscles of the Laterodorsal Trunk and Neck

1.   In preparation for identifying deep muscles of the dorsal trunk, transect the latissimus dorsi, the muscles of the pectoralis group, and the spinotrapezius and reflect them back. Be careful not to damage the large brachial nerve plexus, which lies in the axillary space beneath the pectoralis group.

2.   The **serratus ventralis** corresponds to two separate muscles in humans. The posterior portion is homologous to the *serratus anterior* of humans, arising deep to the pectoral muscles and covering the lateral surface of the rib cage. It is easily identified by its fingerlike muscular origins, which arise on the first 9 or 10 ribs. It inserts into the scapula **(Figure 6)**. The anterior portion of the serratus ventralis, which arises from the cervical vertebrae, is homologous to the

383

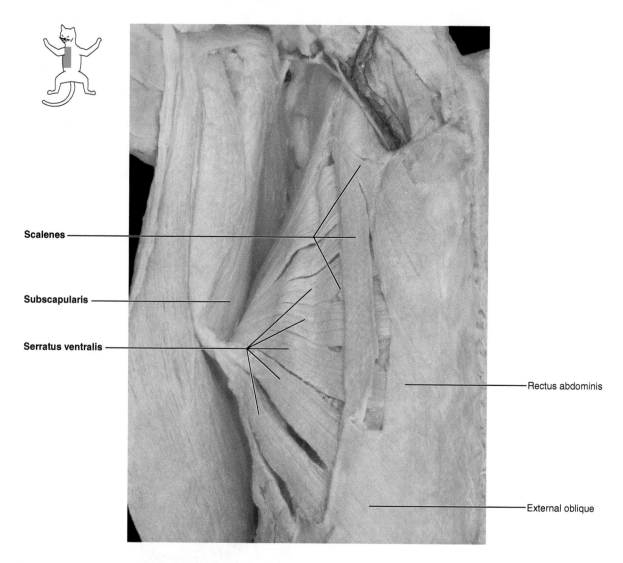

Scalenes

Subscapularis

Serratus ventralis

Rectus abdominis

External oblique

**Figure 6 Deep muscles of the inferolateral thorax of the cat.**

*levator scapulae* in humans; both pull the scapula toward the sternum. Trace this muscle to its insertion. In general, in the cat, this muscle pulls the scapula posteriorly and downward.

3. Reflect the upper limb to reveal the **subscapularis,** which occupies most of the ventral surface of the scapula (Figure 6). Humans have a homologous muscle.

4. Locate the anterior, posterior, and middle **scalene** muscles on the lateral surface of the cat's neck and trunk. The most prominent and longest of these muscles is the middle scalene, which lies between the anterior and posterior members. The scalenes originate on the ribs and run cephalad over the serratus ventralis to insert in common on the cervical vertebrae. These muscles draw the ribs anteriorly and bend the neck downward; thus they are homologous to the human scalene muscles, which elevate the ribs and flex the neck. (Notice that the difference is only one of position. Humans walk erect, but cats are quadrupeds.)

5. Reflect the flaps of the transected latissimus dorsi, spinodeltoid, acromiodeltoid, and levator scapulae ventralis. The

**splenius** is a large flat muscle occupying most of the side of the neck close to the vertebrae (Figure 7). As in humans, it originates on the ligamentum nuchae at the back of the neck and inserts into the occipital bone. It raises the head.

6. To view the rhomboid muscles, lay the cat on its side and hold its forelegs together to spread the scapulae apart. The rhomboid muscles lie between the scapulae and beneath the acromiotrapezius. All the rhomboid muscles originate on the vertebrae and insert on the scapula. They hold the dorsal part of the scapula to the cat's back.

There are three rhomboids in the cat. The ribbonlike **rhomboid capitis,** the most anterolateral muscle of the group, has no counterpart in the human body. The **rhomboid minor,** located posterior to the rhomboid capitis, is much larger. The fibers of the rhomboid minor run transversely to those of the rhomboid capitis. The most posterior muscle of the group, the **rhomboid major,** is so closely fused to the rhomboid minor that many consider them to be one muscle—the **rhomboideus,** which is homologous to human *rhomboid muscles.*

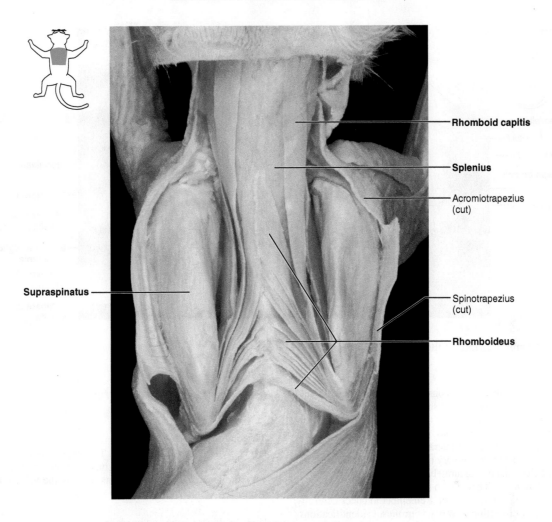

**Figure 7** **Deep muscles of the superior aspect of the dorsal thorax of the cat.**

7. The **supraspinatus** and **infraspinatus** muscles are similar to the same muscles in humans. The supraspinatus can be found under the acromiotrapezius, and the infraspinatus is deep to the spinotrapezius. Both originate on the lateral scapular surface and insert on the humerus. ▬

**ACTIVITY 3**

### Dissecting Forelimb Muscles

Cat forelimb muscles fall into the same three categories as human upper limb muscles, but in this section the muscles of the entire forelimb are considered together (refer to **Figure 8**).

#### *Muscles of the Lateral Surface*

1. The triceps muscle (**triceps brachii**) of the cat is easily identified if the cat is placed on its side. It is a large fleshy muscle covering the posterior aspect and much of the side of the humerus. As in humans, this muscle arises from three heads, which originate from the humerus and scapula and insert jointly into the olecranon of the ulna. Remove the fascia from the superior region of the lateral arm surface to identify the lateral and long heads of the triceps. The long head is approximately twice as long as the lateral head and lies medial to it on the posterior arm surface. The medial head can be exposed by transecting the lateral head and pulling it aside. Now pull on the triceps muscle.

How does the function of the triceps muscle compare in cats and in humans?

_____

_____

Anterior and distal to the medial head of the triceps is the tiny **anconeus** muscle (not visible in Figure 8), sometimes called the fourth head of the triceps muscle. Notice its darker color and the way it wraps the tip of the elbow.

2. The **brachialis** can be located anterior to the lateral head of the triceps muscle. Identify its origin on the humerus, and trace its course as it crosses the elbow and inserts on the ulna. It flexes the cat's foreleg.

Identification of the forearm muscles is difficult because of the tough fascia sheath that encases them, but give it a try.

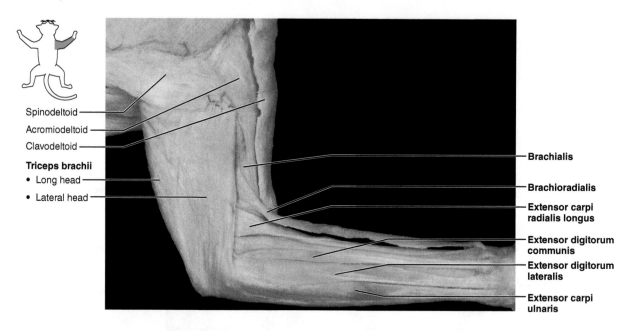

Spinodeltoid
Acromiodeltoid
Clavodeltoid

**Triceps brachii**
• Long head
• Lateral head

**Brachialis**

**Brachioradialis**

**Extensor carpi radialis longus**

**Extensor digitorum communis**

**Extensor digitorum lateralis**

**Extensor carpi ulnaris**

**Figure 8  Lateral surface of the forelimb of the cat.**

3.   Remove as much of the connective tissue as possible and cut through the ligaments that secure the tendons at the wrist (transverse carpal ligaments) so that you will be able to follow the muscles to their insertions. Begin your identification of the forearm muscles at the lateral surface of the forearm. The muscles of this region are very much alike in appearance and are difficult to identify accurately unless a definite order is followed. Thus you will begin with the most anterior muscles and proceed to the posterior aspect. Remember to check carefully the tendons of insertion to verify your muscle identifications.

4.   The ribbonlike muscle on the lateral surface of the humerus is the **brachioradialis.** Observe how it passes down the forearm to insert on the radial styloid process. (If your removal of the fascia was not very careful, this muscle may have been removed.)

5.   The **extensor carpi radialis longus** has a broad origin and is larger than the brachioradialis. It extends down the anterior surface of the radius (Figure 8). Transect this muscle to view the **extensor carpi radialis brevis** (not shown in Figure 8), which is partially covered by and sometimes fused with the extensor carpi radialis longus. Both muscles have origins, insertions, and actions similar to their human counterparts.

6.   You can see the entire **extensor digitorum communis** along the lateral surface of the forearm. Trace it to its four tendons, which insert on the second to fifth digits. This muscle extends these digits. The **extensor digitorum lateralis** (absent in humans) also extends the digits. This muscle lies immediately posterior to the extensor digitorum communis.

7.   Follow the **extensor carpi ulnaris** from the lateral epicondyle of the humerus to the ulnar side of the fifth metacarpal. Often this muscle has a shiny tendon, which helps in its identification.

*Muscles of the Medial Surface*

1.   The **biceps brachii (Figure 9)** is a large spindle-shaped muscle medial to the brachialis on the anterior surface of the humerus. Pull back the cut ends of the pectoral muscles to get a good view of the biceps. This muscle is much more prominent in humans, but its origin, insertion, and action are very similar in cats and in humans. Follow the muscle to its origin.

Does the biceps have two heads in the cat? _____

2.   The broad, flat, exceedingly thin muscle on the postero-medial surface of the arm is the **epitrochlearis.** Its tendon originates from the fascia of the latissimus dorsi, and the muscle inserts into the olecranon of the ulna. This muscle extends the forearm of the cat; it is not found in humans.

3.   The **coracobrachialis** (not illustrated) of the cat is insignificant (approximately 1.3 cm, or ½ inch, long) and can be seen as a very small muscle crossing the ventral aspect of the shoulder joint. It runs beneath the biceps brachii to insert on the humerus and has the same function as the human coracobrachialis.

4.   Turn the cat so that the ventral forearm muscles (mostly flexors and pronators) can be observed (refer to Figure 9). As in humans, most of these muscles arise from the medial epicondyle of the humerus. The **pronator teres** runs from the medial epicondyle of the humerus and declines in size as it approaches its insertion on the radius. Do not bother to trace it to its insertion.

5.   Like its human counterpart, the **flexor carpi radialis** runs from the medial epicondyle of the humerus to insert into the second and third metacarpals.

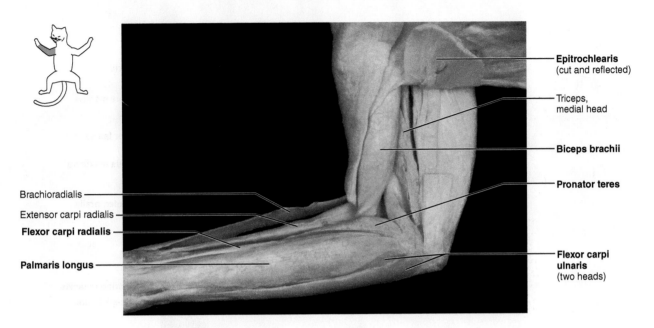

Epitrochlearis
(cut and reflected)

Triceps,
medial head

**Biceps brachii**

**Pronator teres**

Brachioradialis

Extensor carpi radialis

**Flexor carpi radialis**

**Palmaris longus**

Flexor carpi
ulnaris
(two heads)

**Figure 9  Medial surface of the forelimb of the cat.**

6. The large flat muscle in the center of the medial surface is the **palmaris longus.** Its origin on the medial epicondyle of the humerus abuts that of the pronator teres and is shared with the flexor carpi radialis. The palmaris longus extends down the forearm to terminate in four tendons on the digits. This muscle is proportionately larger in cats than in humans.

The **flexor carpi ulnaris** arises from a two-headed origin (medial epicondyle of the humerus and olecranon of the ulna). Its two bellies pass downward to the wrist, where they are united by a single tendon that inserts into the carpals of the wrist. As in humans, this muscle flexes the wrist. ▬

### ACTIVITY 4

## Dissecting Hindlimb Muscles

Remove the fat and fascia from all thigh surfaces, but do not cut through or remove the **fascia lata** (or iliotibial band), which is a tough white aponeurosis covering the anterolateral surface of the thigh from the hip to the leg. If the cat is a male, the cordlike sperm duct will be embedded in the fat near the pubic symphysis. Carefully clear around, but not in, this region.

### Posterolateral Hindlimb Muscles

1. Turn the cat on its ventral surface and identify the following superficial muscles of the hip and thigh (refer to Figure 10). Viewing the lateral aspect of the hindlimb, you will identify these muscles in sequence from the anterior to the posterior aspects of the hip and thigh. Most anterior is the **sartorius,** seen in this view as a thin band (Figure 10a). Approximately 4 cm (1½ inches) wide, it extends around the lateral aspect of the thigh to the anterior surface, where the major portion of it lies (see Figure 12a). Free it from the adjacent muscles and pass a blunt probe under it to trace its origin and insertion. Homologous to the sarto-

rius muscle in humans, it adducts and rotates the thigh, but in addition, the cat sartorius acts as a knee extensor. Transect this muscle.

2. The **tensor fasciae latae** is posterior to the sartorius. It is wide at its superior end, where it originates on the iliac crest, and narrows as it approaches its insertion into the fascia lata, which runs to the proximal tibial region. Transect its superior end and pull it back to expose the **gluteus medius** lying beneath it. This is the largest of the gluteus muscles in the cat. It originates on the ilium and inserts on the greater trochanter of the femur. The gluteus medius overlays and obscures the gluteus minimus, pyriformis, and gemellus muscles, which will not be identified here.

3. The **gluteus maximus** is a small triangular hip muscle posterior to the superior end of the tensor fasciae latae and paralleling it. In humans the gluteus maximus is a large fleshy muscle forming most of the buttock mass. In the cat it is only about 1.3 cm (½ inch) wide and 5 cm (2 inches) long, and is smaller than the gluteus medius. The gluteus maximus covers part of the gluteus medius as it extends from the sacral region to the end of the femur. It abducts the thigh.

4. Posterior to the gluteus maximus, identify the triangular **caudofemoralis,** which originates on the caudal vertebrae and inserts into the patella via an aponeurosis. There is no homologue to this muscle in humans; in cats it abducts the thigh and flexes the vertebral column.

5. The **hamstring muscles** of the hindlimb include the biceps femoris, the semitendinosus, and the semimembranosus muscles. The **biceps femoris** is a large, powerful muscle that covers about three-fourths of the posterolateral surface of the thigh. It is 4 cm (1½ inches) to 5 cm (2 inches) wide throughout its length. Trace it from its origin on the ischial tuberosity to its insertion on the tibia. Part of the **semitendinosus** can be seen beneath the posterior border

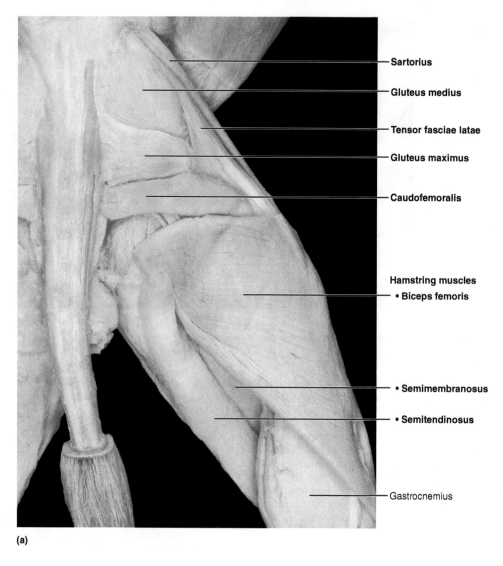

Sartorius

Gluteus medius

Tensor fasciae latae

Gluteus maximus

Caudofemoralis

Hamstring muscles
• Biceps femoris

• Semimembranosus

• Semitendinosus

Gastrocnemius

(a)

**Figure 10 Muscles of the posterolateral thigh in the cat. (a)** Superficial view.

of the biceps femoris. Transect and reflect the biceps muscle to reveal the whole length of the semitendinosus and the large sciatic nerve positioned under the biceps (Figure 10b). Contrary to what its name implies ("half-tendon"), this muscle is muscular and fleshy except at its insertion. It is uniformly about 2 cm (¾ inch) wide as it runs down the thigh from the ischial tuberosity to the medial side of the tibia. It flexes the knee. The **semimembranosus,** a large muscle lying medial to the semitendinosus and largely obscured by it, is best seen in an anterior view of the thigh (Figure 12b). If desired, however, the semitendinosus can be transected to view it from the posterior aspect. The semimembranosus is larger and broader than the semitendinosus. Like the other hamstrings, it originates on the ischial tuberosity and inserts on the medial epicondyle of the femur and the medial tibial surface.

How does the semimembranosus compare with its human homologue?

_____

_____

6. Remove the heavy fascia covering the lateral surface of the shank (leg). Moving from the posterior to the anterior aspect, identify the following muscles on the posterolateral shank **(Figure 11)**. First reflect the lower portion of the biceps femoris to see the origin of the **triceps surae,** the large composite muscle of the calf. Humans also have a triceps surae. The **gastrocnemius,** part of the triceps surae, is the largest muscle on the shank. As in humans, it has two heads and inserts via the calcaneal tendon into the calcaneus. Run a probe beneath this muscle and then transect it to reveal the **soleus,** which is deep to the gastrocnemius.

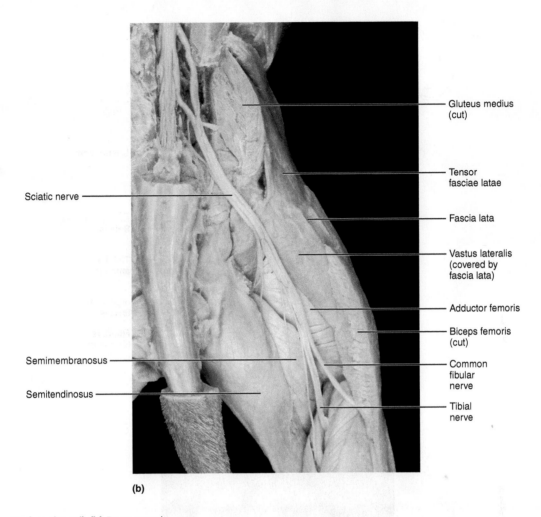

Sciatic nerve

Semimembranosus

Semitendinosus

Gluteus medius
(cut)

Tensor
fasciae latae

Fascia lata

Vastus lateralis
(covered by
fascia lata)

Adductor femoris

Biceps femoris
(cut)

Common
fibular
nerve

Tibial
nerve

**(b)**

**Figure 10** *(continued)* **(b)** Deep muscles.

7. Another important group of muscles in the leg is the **fibularis (peroneus) muscles,** which collectively appear as a slender, evenly shaped superficial muscle lying anterior to the triceps surae. Originating on the fibula and inserting on the digits and metatarsals, the fibularis muscles flex the foot.

8. The **extensor digitorum longus** lies anterior to the fibularis muscles. Its origin, insertion, and action in cats are similar to the homologous human muscle. The **tibialis anterior** is anterior to the extensor digitorum longus. The tibialis anterior is roughly triangular in cross section and heavier at its proximal end. Locate its origin on the proximal fibula and tibia and its insertion on the first metatarsal. You can see the sharp edge of the tibia at the anterior border of this muscle. As in humans, it is a foot flexor.

### Anteromedial Hindlimb Muscles

1. Turn the cat onto its dorsal surface to identify the muscles of the anteromedial hindlimb **(Figure 12)**. Note once again the straplike sartorius at the surface of the thigh, which you have already identified and transected. It originates on the ilium and inserts on the medial region of the tibia.

2. Reflect the cut ends of the sartorius to identify the **quadriceps** muscles. The most medial muscle of this group, the **vastus medialis,** lies just beneath the sartorius. Resting close to the femur, it arises from the ilium and inserts into the patellar ligament. The small spindle-shaped muscle anterior and lateral to the vastus medialis is the **rectus femoris.** In cats this muscle originates entirely from the femur.

What is the origin of the rectus femoris in humans?

_____

Free the rectus femoris from the most lateral muscle of this group, the large, fleshy **vastus lateralis,** which lies deep to the tensor fasciae latae. The vastus lateralis arises from the lateral femoral surface and inserts, along with the other vasti muscles, into the patellar ligament. Transect this muscle to identify the deep **vastus intermedius,** the smallest of the vasti muscles. It lies medial to the vastus lateralis and merges superiorly with the vastus medialis. The vastus intermedius is not shown in the figure.

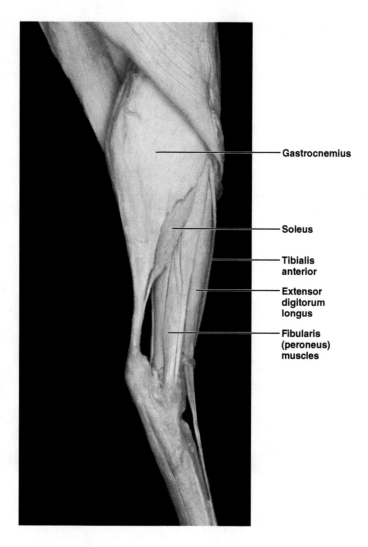

— Gastrocnemius

— Soleus

— Tibialis anterior

— Extensor digitorum longus

— Fibularis (peroneus) muscles

**Figure 11** **Superficial muscles of the posterolateral aspect of the shank (leg).**

3. The **gracilis** is a broad thin muscle that covers the posterior portion of the medial aspect of the thigh (Figure 12a). It originates on the pubic symphysis and inserts on the medial proximal tibial surface. In cats the gracilis adducts the leg and draws it posteriorly.

How does this compare with the human gracilis?

_____

_____

4. Free and transect the gracilis to view the adductor muscles deep to it. The **adductor femoris** is a large muscle that lies beneath the gracilis and abuts the semimembranosus medially. Its origin is the pubic ramus and the ischium, and its fibers pass downward to insert on most of the length of the femoral shaft. The adductor femoris is homologous to the human *adductor magnus*, *brevis*, and *longus*. Its function

is to extend the thigh after it has been drawn forward, and to adduct the thigh. A small muscle about 2.5 cm (1 inch) long—the **adductor longus**—touches the superior margin of the adductor femoris. It originates on the pubis and inserts on the proximal surface of the femur.

5. Before continuing your dissection, locate the **femoral triangle,** an important area bordered by the proximal edge of the sartorius and the adductor muscles. It is usually possible to identify the femoral artery (injected with red latex) and the femoral vein (injected with blue latex), which span the triangle (Figure 12a). If your instructor wishes you to identify the pectineus and iliopsoas, remove these vessels and go on to steps 6 and 7.

6. Examine the superolateral margin of the adductor longus to locate the small **pectineus.** It is sometimes covered by the gracilis (which you have cut and reflected). The pectineus, which originates on the pubis and inserts on the proximal end of the femur, is similar in all ways to its human homologue.

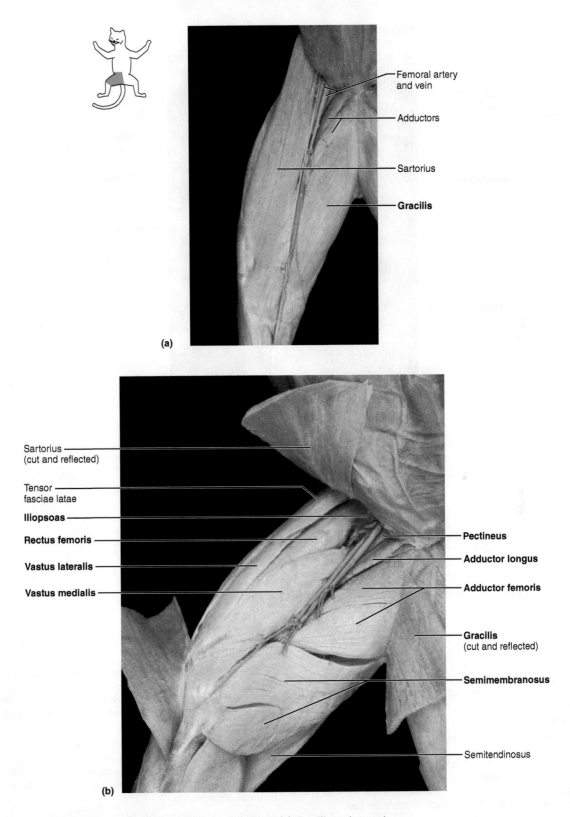

(a)

Femoral artery and vein

Adductors

Sartorius

**Gracilis**

Sartorius
(cut and reflected)

Tensor
fasciae latae

**Iliopsoas**

**Rectus femoris**

**Vastus lateralis**

**Vastus medialis**

**Pectineus**

**Adductor longus**

**Adductor femoris**

**Gracilis**
(cut and reflected)

**Semimembranosus**

Semitendinosus

(b)

**Figure 12 Superficial muscles of the anteromedial thigh. (a)** Gracilis and sartorius are intact in this superficial view of the right thigh. **(b)** The gracilis and sartorius are transected and reflected to show deeper muscles.

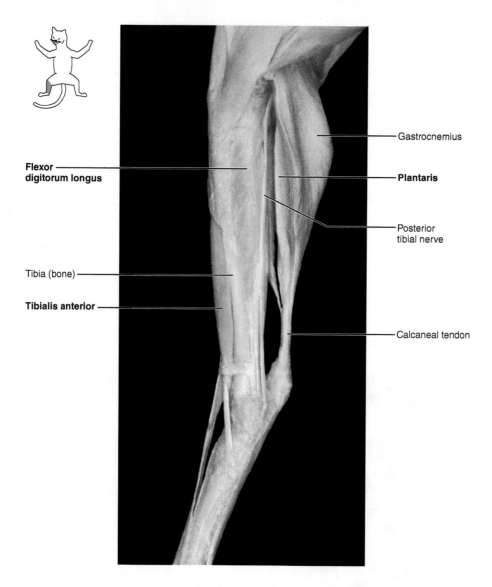

Gastrocnemius

Flexor digitorum longus

**Plantaris**

Posterior tibial nerve

Tibia (bone)

**Tibialis anterior**

Calcaneal tendon

**Figure 13** **Superficial muscles of the anteromedial shank (leg) of the cat.**

7. Just lateral to the pectineus you can see a small portion of the **iliopsoas,** a long and cylindrical muscle. Its origin is on the transverse processes of $T_1$ through $T_{12}$ and the lumbar vertebrae, and it passes posteriorly toward the body wall to insert on the medial aspect of the proximal femur. The iliopsoas flexes and laterally rotates the thigh. It corresponds to the human iliopsoas.

8. Reidentify the gastrocnemius of the shank and then the **plantaris,** which is fused with the lateral head of the gastrocnemius **(Figure 13)**. It originates from the lateral aspect of the femur and patella, and its tendon passes around the calcaneus to insert on the second phalanx. Working with the triceps surae, it flexes the digits and extends the foot.

9. Anterior to the plantaris is the **flexor digitorum longus,** a long, tapering muscle with two heads. It originates on the lateral surfaces of the proximal fibula and tibia and inserts

via four tendons into the terminal phalanges. As in humans, it flexes the toes.

10. The **tibialis posterior** is a long, flat muscle lateral and deep to the flexor digitorum longus (not shown in Figure 13). It originates on the medial surface of the head of the fibula and the ventral tibia. It merges with a flat, shiny tendon to insert into the tarsals.

11. The **flexor hallucis longus** (also not illustrated) is a long muscle that lies lateral to the tibialis posterior. It originates from the posterior tibia and passes downward to the ankle. It is a uniformly broad muscle in the cat. As in humans, it is a flexor of the great toe.

12. Before you leave the laboratory, follow the boxed instructions to prepare your cat for storage and to clean the area. ■

Dissection and Identification of Cat Muscles

Many human muscles are modified from those of the cat (or any quadruped) as a result of the requirements of an upright posture. The following questions refer to these differences.

1. How does the human trapezius muscle differ from the cat's?

_____

2. How does the deltoid differ?

_____

_____

3. How does the biceps brachii differ?

_____

_____

4. How do the size and orientation of the human gluteus maximus muscle differ from that in the cat?

_____

_____

_____

5. Explain these differences between cat and human muscles in terms of differences in function.

_____

_____

6. The human rectus abdominis is definitely divided by four transverse tendons (tendinous intersections). These tendons are absent or difficult to identify in the cat. How do these tendons affect the human upright posture?

_____

_____

_____

7. Match each term in column B to its description in column A.

**Column A**

_____ 1. to separate muscles

_____ 2. to fold back a muscle

_____ 3. to cut through a muscle

_____ 4. to preserve tissue

**Column B**

a. dissect

b. embalm

c. reflect

d. transect

## Photo Credits

Credits are listed in order of appearance.

2–13: Shawn Miller (dissection) and Mark Nielsen (photography), Pearson Education.

## Illustration Credits

All illustrations are by Imagineering STA Media Services, except for Review Sheet art and as noted below.

1: Precision Graphics.

# Index

Page references followed by "f" indicate illustrated figures or photographs; followed by "t" indicates a table.

387-390, 392
  lateral condyle of, 166, 187, 230-232, 236
  medial condyle of, 166, 231
Fetal skull, 129, 146-147, 155
Fetus, 18, 129, 163
  development, 18
Fever, 105
Fiber tracts, 262-263, 271-272, 274, 285, 288, 320
Fibers, 56, 80-89, 95, 104, 111-112, 120-121, 123,
  136, 141, 177, 179, 197-203, 208-209,
  212, 217-220, 222, 228, 237, 245-246,
  248-252, 254-255, 260, 275, 278-279,
  290-291, 367-368, 383-384
  connective tissue, 80-85, 88-89, 95, 104, 111,
    177, 179, 183, 199-201, 250, 252,
    260, 378-379
Fibroblasts, 82, 84-85, 88-89, 104
Fibrocartilage, 73, 86, 88, 95, 120, 125, 140,
  178-179, 181, 186
  in symphyses, 179
  skeletal, 73, 120, 179
Fibrous joints, 178-179
Fibrous layer, 9, 179, 181, 189, 315-317
  of eye, 315-317
Fibula, 118, 157, 166-168, 173-174, 178-179, 181,
  187, 192, 230, 232-236, 241, 389
Fibular collateral ligament, 187
Fibular nerve, 295-296, 389
Fibularis brevis, 233, 235, 241
Fibularis longus, 210-211, 232-233, 235, 241-242
Fibularis (peroneus) longus, 232
Fibularis (peroneus) muscles, 389-390
Fibularis (peroneus) tertius, 232
Fibularis tertius, 233
Filtrate, 66
Filtration, 59-60, 66, 68, 71, 74, 76, 325
Filum terminale, 285-287, 297
Fingerprinting, 108-109, 114
Fingerprints, 104, 108-109, 111, 114
Fingers, 2, 4, 11-12, 109, 140, 157, 161-162, 167,
  183, 189, 223, 225-226, 308
  bones, 120, 140, 157, 161-162, 167, 183, 223,
    226
  muscles, 4, 157, 162, 167, 183, 223, 225-226,
    293, 378
Fissures, 136, 259, 261, 269, 274, 286
  cerebellum, 259, 261, 269, 274
  cerebrum, 259, 269, 274
Fixators, 208
Flagella, 47-48
Flat bones, 120
Flexion, 144, 177, 180-181, 183-186, 188, 208,
  215, 217-218, 223-224, 226, 228, 234,
  236-237, 239, 241
Flexor carpi radialis, 210, 225, 240, 242, 293,
  386-387
Flexor carpi ulnaris, 211, 225-227, 240, 242-243,
  293-294
Flexor digitorum longus, 235-236, 296, 392
Flexor digitorum profundus, 225-226, 293-294
Flexor digitorum superficialis, 225-226, 240, 293
Flexor hallucis longus, 233, 235-236, 241, 296,
  392
Flexor muscles, 223, 244, 293-295
  of thigh, 295
Flexor pollicis longus, 225-226, 240, 293
Flexor retinaculum, 225, 240
Floating ribs, 129, 154
Floor, 130, 138, 218, 220, 259, 262, 266, 275, 291,
  357-358
  of nasal cavity, 138
  of orbit, 138, 270
Fluid mosaic model, 44
Fluid-phase endocytosis, 67
Foliate papillae, 343-344
Fontanelles, 129, 146-147, 155, 269
Food, 20, 27, 48, 81, 199, 271, 282, 341, 344-345,
  348
Foot, 2-3, 11, 157, 167-168, 173, 181, 184-185,
  194, 228, 232, 234, 236, 241, 299,
  304-305, 351, 357-358, 373, 389, 392
  arches, 167-168
  arches of, 168
  bones, 157, 167-168, 173, 181, 228, 351
  bones of, 157, 167-168
  joints, 157, 181, 184, 228, 295
  muscles, 157, 167-168, 228, 232, 234, 236,
    241, 299, 304, 389, 392
  surface anatomy, 2-3, 11

Footdrop, 296
Foramen lacerum, 130, 132-133, 150
Foramen magnum, 130, 132-133, 135, 149-150,
  285-286, 297
Foramen ovale, 132-134, 136, 150, 270
Foramen rotundum, 133-134, 136, 270
Foramen spinosum, 132-134, 136
Forced expiration, 218
Forearm, 2, 108, 114, 160-161, 169, 180, 185,
  192, 207, 223-227, 240, 291-294, 299
  bones of, 161, 169
Forebrain, 260-262, 279
Fornix, 263-264, 274-276, 278
  cerebrum, 263, 274-275
  limbic system, 263-264
Fourth ventricle, 260, 264, 266-269, 275, 278, 280
Fovea, 166, 174, 318, 320, 324-326, 333, 335
  femur, 166, 174
  retina, 318, 320, 324-326, 333, 335
Fovea capitis, 166, 174
Fovea centralis, 318, 324-326, 333
Fracture, 158, 166
  hip, 166
Free edge of nail, 105
Free nerve endings, 104-105, 366-367, 371
Free radicals, 47
Friction ridges, 109
Frontal belly of epicranius, 213, 242
Frontal bone, 130-131, 133, 135-138, 147, 150,
  155, 212
Frontal lobe, 259-263, 272, 275, 277, 281
Frontal plane, 4-6, 163, 177
Frontal sinuses, 139
Frontonasal suture, 135
Fructose, 344
Functional groups, 200
Fundus, 270, 318, 333, 335
  of eye, 270
Fungiform papillae, 343
Funny bone, 160, 294

**G**

Gag reflex, 306, 311
Gallbladder, 9, 77, 374
Gametes, 49
Ganglia, 246, 251, 253, 263, 269
  autonomic, 260
Ganglion cells, 251, 319-320, 324, 326
Gases, 70-71, 87
Gastric juice, 370
Gastrocnemius, 187, 207, 210-211, 231, 233-235,
  241-243, 304, 388, 390, 392
Gastrocnemius muscle, 187, 304
Gemellus muscles, 387
General senses, 366
  chemoreceptors, 366
General sensory receptors, 365-367, 373
Girdles, 157-158, 171
Glabella, 130, 135, 150
Glands, 18, 22-23, 73-79, 88, 94, 101, 104-108,
  112-114, 250, 253, 301-302, 307
  skin, 18, 78, 88, 101, 104-108, 112-114, 270,
    307
  structure, 18, 23, 88, 94, 101, 105-106, 108,
    250, 271
Glandular epithelium, 74
  functions, 74
  structure, 74
Glassy membrane, 106
Glaucoma, 315, 319
Glenohumeral joint, 188
Glenohumeral ligaments, 188-189
Glenoid cavity, 158-160, 169-170, 188-189,
  220-221, 224
Glenoid labrum, 188-189
Glial cells, 246
Globus pallidus, 264-265, 277
Glomeruli, 76, 342
Glossopharyngeal nerve, 272-273, 276, 281, 343
Glucose, 59-64, 69-70, 344
  molecular weight of, 61, 70
Gluteal muscles, 207, 230
Gluteal nerve, 296
Gluteal tuberosity, 166, 173-174, 230
Gluteus maximus, 207, 209, 211, 230-231, 234,
  237, 241, 243, 296, 387-388, 393
Gluteus maximus muscle, 234, 393
Gluteus medius, 207, 211, 230-231, 241, 243, 296,
  387-389

Glycocalyx, 45
Glycogen, 48, 53
Glycolipids, 103, 112
Goblet cells, 77, 80
Golgi apparatus, 46-47
Gomphosis, 179
Goose bumps, 106
Gracilis, 210, 228-229, 231, 242-243, 289,
  295-296, 298, 390-391
Gracilis muscle, 295
Gray commissure, 285-286, 288, 297
Gray matter, 246, 251, 259-263, 265-266, 277,
  285-286, 288, 290
  cerebellum, 259-261, 263, 266, 277
  medulla oblongata, 259-263, 266
  mesencephalon, 260
  of spinal cord, 285
  pons, 260-263, 266, 277
  spinal cord, 246, 251, 259-261, 263, 266,
    285-286, 288, 290
Greater and lesser trochanters, 166, 173
Greater and lesser tubercles, 158
Greater auricular nerve, 291
Greater omentum, 20, 22, 25
Greater sciatic notch, 164, 173, 295
Greater trochanter, 166, 168, 174, 230, 387
Greater tubercle, 160, 171, 189, 220-221
Greater wings, 136
Gross anatomy, 1, 18, 120, 126, 207-244,
  259-263, 265-283
Ground substance, 73, 80-83, 121, 128
Growth, 18, 49-50, 52, 105, 117, 119-121, 124,
  128, 146-147, 179
Gustatory cortex, 262
Gustatory epithelial cells, 341, 343
Gustatory hairs, 343-344
Gyri, 259, 261, 269

**H**

Hair, 101-102, 105-108, 111, 113-114, 343,
  351-353, 356-357, 360-361, 366-367,
  369, 371
  color, 101, 105, 108, 111
  functions, 101-102, 106, 111
  structure, 101-102, 105-106, 108, 111, 343,
    352, 366-367
  types, 102, 367
Hair bulb, 105-106
Hair cells, 351-353, 356-357, 360-361
Hair follicle, 101, 105-108, 113-114, 366-367, 369,
  371
  functions, 101, 106
  structure, 101, 105-106, 108, 366-367
Hair follicle receptors, 367, 369
Hair matrix, 106
Hair papilla, 106
Hair root, 106
Hair shaft, 102, 106, 114, 369
Hallux, 2-3, 10, 236
Hamate, 161-162, 226
Hamstring muscles, 231, 387-388
Hamstrings, 211, 228, 230-231, 296, 303
Hand, 2-4, 32, 109, 114, 157, 161-162, 167, 180,
  183, 194, 223, 225-227, 237, 240, 244,
  293-294, 299, 301-302, 308-310, 331,
  333-335, 354-355, 368-370
  bones, 157, 161-162, 167, 180, 183, 223, 226,
    351, 366
  bones of, 157, 161-162, 167
  intrinsic muscles, 293-294, 333
  joints, 157, 162, 183, 366
  muscles, 4, 157, 162, 167, 183, 223, 225-227,
    237, 240, 244, 293-294, 299,
    301-302, 333, 366
  nerves, 291, 293-294, 299, 302, 305-306
Hard palate, 19, 132, 137-138, 149
Head, 1-4, 8-9, 11-12, 19, 32-33, 122, 126,
  141-143, 146, 152, 158, 160-161, 163,
  166-167, 171, 173-174, 180, 185-189,
  207, 209-210, 212-215, 220-225,
  230-233, 235, 238-239, 241, 267, 269,
  271-272, 296, 353-356, 361, 384-387,
  392
Head of fibula, 167, 174, 230, 233, 241
Head of radius, 160-161, 171, 180
Head of ulna, 161, 171
Headache, 139
Hearing, 8, 14, 130, 149, 262, 271-272, 349-363
  cochlea, 271, 349, 351-353, 359, 361-362

I